CUBA IN TRANSITION

Volume 2

Second Annual Meeting

of the

Association for the Study of the Cuban Economy (ASCE)

Florida International University

Miami, Florida

August 13-15, 1992

Publication of these proceedings in bound form was made possible by the contributions of the Cuban American Research Group, Inc. and José Pepe Fanjul Gómez-Mena, of Okeelanta Corporation.

ISBN 1-879862-04-2

CONTENTS

Cuban American Research Group Inc.

PREFACE

We preface Cuba In Transition, Volume II with a feeling of hope. It is the fruit of professional minds that are using personal time to reflect on the future of the Cuban economy.

We are heartened to see that work of this quality can be produced, as it is living proof that there is a considerable number of highly-trained Cuban economists with a wealth of experience who are able to rise above the purely political discourse. To reflect about the future of the Cuban economy is akin to navigating in uncharted waters. We know about the patient, we see the symptoms but lack sufficient information to issue a definitive diagnosis. All we can do now is to speculate with a greater or lesser degree of accuracy, but this in itself is very important as it prepares the mind and the spirit for the very difficult job that lies ahead in rebuilding the Cuban economy.

The Cuban American Research Group was founded as a non-political not for profit corporation, to foster understanding of Cuban issues. We are happy to co-sponsor the publication of this book by the Association for the Study of the Cuban Economy and congratulate the authors both for their work and their dedication to the Cuban cause.

Alberto Luzarraga
Chairman

Association for the Study of the Cuban Economy

Second Annual Meeting

Florida International University
Miami, Florida
August 13-15, 1992

CONFERENCE PROGRAM

Exiles, Ethics, and Politics

Chair: Joaquín P. Pujol (IMF)

Revolutionary Propensity, Possible Outcomes, and the Political Climate for Cuba's National Reconstruction
Ernesto F. Betancourt (Trade and Economic Development Associates)

Cuban-Owned Enterprises in the United States, 1982 and 1987
Jorge Salazar-Carrillo and Irma Tirado de Alonso (FIU)

El futuro de la ética en el desarrollo integral
Alberto Martínez-Piedra (Catholic University of America)

Discussant: Sergio Díaz-Briquets (Casals and Associates)

Legal Issues

Chair: José Manuel Hernández (Georgetown University)

Legal Issues Raised by the Transition: Cuba From Marxism to Democracy, 199?-200?
Néstor Cruz (Consultant)

El marco jurídico-institucional de un Gobierno Provisional de Unidad Nacional en Cuba
José D. Acosta (Retired, Organization of American States)

En torno al proyecto de ley de viviendas urbanas y rurales
Julio Romañach, Jr. (Louisiana State University)

Discussant: Agustín de Goytisolo (Attorney)

Panel Discussion: Current Political and Economic Developments in Cuba

Moderator: Jorge F. Pérez-López (Department of Labor)

Panelists: José F. Alonso (Radio Martí)
John Paul Rathbone (Sociedad Económica de Amigos del País)
Jaime Suchlicki (University of Miami)

The Sugar Industry

Chair: Armando M. Lago (Ecosometrics, Inc.)

An Integrated Approach to the Cuban Sugar Industry
Nicolás Rivero (Rivero International)

Cuba's Sugar Industry in the 1990s: Potential Exports to the US and World Markets
José Alvarez (University of Florida)

The Sugar Industry (cont.)

Sugar Consumption, Sugar Policy and the Fate of Caribbean Cane Growers
Joseph M. Perry, Louis A. Woods, and Jeffrey W. Steagall (University of North Florida)

Discussant: Jorge F. Pérez-López (Department of Labor)

Agricultural Markets, Informality and the Distribution System

Chair: Francisco Proenza (Food and Agriculture Organization)

The Free Farmers Markets
José F. Alonso (Radio Martí)

The Cuban Second Economy: Methodological and Practical Issues Related to Quantification
Jorge F. Pérez-López (Department of Labor)

The Distribution System in a Centrally Planned Economy
Roger R. Betancourt (University of Maryland)

Discussant: Fernando Alvarez (Babson College)

Macroeconomic Issues I

Chair: Raúl Moncarz (Florida International University)

Una política o un sistema monetario óptimo
Juan Luis Moreno (Development Technologies, Inc.)

Endogenous Political Change
Luis Locay (University of Miami) and Carlos Seiglie (Rutgers University)

Discussant: Lorenzo Pérez (IMF)

Macroeconomic Issues II

Chair: George Plinio Montalván (Consultant)

Reflections on Systemic Economic Policy Reform: Lessons, Evaluation, and Social Costs
Juan J. Buttari (Agency for International Development)

Cuba: Propuesta y fundamentos de un plan para el establecimiento
y desarrollo de una economía social de mercado
Rolando H. Castañeda (Inter-American Development Bank) and José Antonio Herrero (Consultant)

Discussant: Manuel Lasaga (International Management Assistance Corporation)

Constrained Labor Supply, Environmental Deterioration and Agricultural Policy

Chair: Sergio Díaz-Briquets (Casals and Associates)

Non-Walrasian Properties of the Cuban Economy: Rationing, Labor Supply, and Output
Jorge A. Sanguinetty (Development Technologies, Inc.)

Environmental Deterioration and Protection in Socialist Cuba
María Dolores Espino (Florida International University)

Política agrícola cubana a mediano y largo plazo — principales objetivos
Raúl Fernández (Retired, Inter-American Development Bank)

Discussant: Antonio Gayoso (Agency for International Development)

REVOLUTIONARY PROPENSITY, POSSIBLE OUTCOMES AND THE POLITICAL CLIMATE FOR CUBA'S NATIONAL RECONSTRUCTION

Ernesto F. Betancourt

Introductory Note

This paper attempts to offer a basis for combining consideration of two sets of topics that are treated separately in contemporary social science: the political and institutional context in societies, and the formulation of national economic policy. As the Association for the Study of the Cuban Economy (ASCE) progresses in its excellent work, it becomes evident that in the case of Cuba such lack of integration could lead to serious distortions on the feasibility of certain economic approaches, regardless of their intrinsic merits in terms of economic theory and praxis.

This became particularly obvious to me as I heard and read the presentations of Ernesto Hernández Catá, who advocates the shock treatment approach, and Rolando Castañeda, who advocates a gradualist approach. I reached the conclusion that it was perhaps worthwhile to make an effort to sketch, at least in broad terms, the dynamics of the present political situation and the possible outcomes it may lead to. After all, before planning the reconstruction of Cuba, it is necessary for Castro to be out of power and, from all indications so far, he does not seem willing to cooperate. Since Castro's legacy is not limited to the political context, but also includes the institutional context of the most centralized economic management system of any communist country, I felt it was also necessary to extend the sketch to cover the climate for reconstruction offered by the various outcomes. Once one includes both dimensions of the problem in the analysis, the magnitude of the task ahead looms as a very imposing effort and perhaps may help determine which approach is more feasible.

The analysis of the present political situation draws on a comparison between the successful revolutionary effort against Batista in 1959 and the failure of the Tupamaros in 1972, as presented in the final chapter of my book *Revolutionary Strategy: A Handbook for Practitioners*, with an analysis of revolutionary propensity in the current Cuban situation. On the basis of that comparison, some possible outcomes of the present situation are presented with brief comments on the political climates each would offer for the formulation of economic policy.

This paper has been prepared for presentation and discussion at the Second Annual Meeting of the Association for the Study of the Cuban Economy (ASCE), Florida International University, August 13-15, 1992. The approach taken makes explicit the assumptions leading to one policy analyst's conclusions as to why Castro did not fall as was predicted in 1989, 1990, 1991, as well as how it may all end. Other analysts are free to make their own judgments and evaluations of the variables used in the model developed by the author for the analysis of revolutionary propensity and reach different conclusions. It is hoped that making assumptions and observations explicit will lead to a more fruitful basis for discussion than to merely express conclusions or opinions.

In closing, I wish to repeat one of my favorite Chinese sayings: "To forecast is very difficult, particularly about the future."

I. Comparative Analysis of Revolutionary Propensities

In this section of the paper, a comparison will be made of the revolutionary experiences of Cuba in 1958, Uruguay in 1972 and Cuba in 1992. The comparison will be based on selected factors relevant to revolutionary propensity. These factors are the independent variables in the situation, while the outcome of the process is the dependent variable. Each variable will be analyzed in terms of its impact on revolutionary propensity. Afterwards, a synthesis will be made to determine what lessons can be derived from the comparison of the three situations.

There is no one single revolutionary propensity. At times a country may seem to be on the verge of a revolution when we focus only on one factor that increases revolutionary propensity. But in the end there is no outcome of a revolutionary nature. The reason is that the individual factor was offset by other factors that reduced revolutionary propensities. In reading this paper, one must get used to the fact that from the perspective of revolutionary propensity, events or facts we normally consider bad have a positive impact on revolutionary propensity and, conversely, those we normally consider good have negative impacts. Such is the perverse nature of revolutions.

First, a comparison is made of factors drawn from the national context in the three situations that may have a bearing on the final outcome. The comparison starts at the broadest level, including geographic, demographic, historic and international variables relevant to the respective revolutionary situations. It also includes comparing the types of political contexts, that is whether the societies were totalitarian, authoritarian or democratic.

Comparisons are also made of the relative status of development of political organizations, intermediary organizations, mass media and armed forces. A comparison of economic and social indicators relevant to the level of prevailing relative deprivation is the final part of the context section.

Next, a very brief comparison is made of the revolutionary processes of Cuba 1958 and Uruguay 1972 only in terms of operational variables involved. Since there is no ongoing revolutionary effort inside Cuba today, there is no analysis possible of a revolutionary process there. However, a look at the factors involved as commented in those two cases illustrates why it is unlikely that such a process can be started as long as Castro's regime maintains its extremely totalitarian system of repression. Such an approach is consistent with the methodology presented in the *Handbook.* The categories for comparison are: the events, including the trigger event, their time frame, magnitude and nature; the components of revolutionary action, including the ideologies and propaganda; the organizations and their leadership; and, finally, the strategies and policies pursued.

In the final part of this section, summary and conclusions, the profiles of the dynamics of the three situations are compared. The analysis results in a profile for Cuba (1992) which is almost the opposite of Cuba (1958), having more similarity with that for Uruguay (1972) where the revolutionary effort aborted. Since there is no ongoing revolutionary effort in Cuba today, the likelihood of a successful revolutionary process is even less than in Uruguay (1972). However, it is worthwhile to make a comment on this conclusion from the analysis. The regime's repression is creating a mirage. Revolutionary propensity is potentially very high in Cuba (1992), but it is bottled up. That is why the outcome may be an explosion a-la-Hungary, 1956 , rather than a revolutionary process. The longer Castro manages to delay his departure, the bloodier the aftermath is likely to be. And, the bloodier the outcome, the less likely that it will provide a favorable context for the formulation of national reconstruction policy.

A. Comparison of Cuba-Uruguay-Cuba National Contexts

In this section of the paper, the paragraphs in italics are taken from the *Handbook*, while the paragraphs on the comparison with the present situation in Cuba in relation to each variable are shown in regular type.

There is a widely prevalent notion that tries to simplify revolutionary causality by linking it exclusively to economic and social relative deprivation. The comparison of Cuba's and Uruguay's national contexts weakens the explanatory power of that notion and reveals that more complex explanations are necessary.[1]

Geography. The two countries are relatively small, Cuba has 41,000 square miles of territory and Uruguay 72,000. However, Cuba has several mountain ranges suitable for rural guerrilla operations. In particular, the Sierra Maestra range in the eastern end of the island offered an ideal setting for the establishment of a guerrilla redoubt. Castro's revolution was anchored in the vastness of the Sierra Maestra. Therefore, geography was favorable to the revolutionary outcome. Uruguay does not have any region suitable for the establishment of a guerrilla redoubt, a factor that forced the Tupamaros to resort to an urban guerrilla strategy. This was an untested strategy and turned out to be unworkable.

In summary, the geographic variable had a positive impact on revolutionary propensity in the case of Cuba and it had a negative impact in the case of Uruguay.

Geography 1992. The only relevant aspect of this variable that can change is physical integration. There has been a change in the impact of this variable due to two factors: (1) There is no remote inaccessible region in the Sierra Maestra mountains anymore. Castro has established a governmental presence there and opened access roads. (2) Cuba has massive armed forces with modern equipment and the use of helicopters would make a repetition of the Castro enclave there a military impossibility. Therefore, in 1992 this variable moves to negative.

Demography. The population of Cuba was more than twice that of Uruguay at the time of the respective revolutionary conflicts. Cuba had 6.5 million and Uruguay 3.0 million inhabitants. In terms of population location, Uruguay was more urbanized than Cuba. While 81 percent of Uruguayans were estimated to live in urban centers, in Cuba only 55 percent were city dwellers. Montevideo accounted for half the population of Uruguay, while Havana accounted only for about twenty percent of Cuba's population.

Uruguay had a fairly homogeneous racial composition, with 90 percent of the population being white. Cuba's 1953 population census reported 72.8 percent as white, with the rest divided between blacks and mulattoes. However, those proportions have been seriously questioned, with much higher estimates of black and mixed race shares of the population.

Race did not emerge as a relevant issue in the revolutionary struggles in either country, despite the fact that in both cases relative deprivation on the basis of race can be documented. Urbanization was

---

[1]The comparison of national contexts draws on the two case studies developed in chapters 5 and 6 of the *Handbook* and on a study commissioned by the OAS Secretariat in the sixties to two Jesuit priests, Roger Vekemans and J. L. Segundo. The study, entitled *Socioeconomic Typology of the Latin American Countries*, was published by the OAS Secretariat in 1963 as a special issue of the *Inter-American Social Science Review*. For the 1992 situation, the paper draws on the analysis of current events, mostly from press sources, and from "Development Claims and Realities of the Cuban Revolution: a Comparative Analysis," a paper prepared for the U.S. State Department Office of Public Diplomacy in March 1984 by TEDA.

a factor in the case of Uruguay. The Tupamaro urban guerrilla strategy was developed in response to the weight of Montevideo in the Uruguayan population distribution and the geographic constraint to attempt a rural guerrilla strategy. Since the urban guerrilla strategy turned out to be unworkable, the demographic variable had a negative impact on revolutionary propensity in that case. Demography had no impact on revolutionary propensity in the case of Cuba.

Demography 1992. This variable has undergone both a quantitative and a qualitative change. Despite the migration of more than one million citizens, the population of Cuba is now almost 11 million people. The age breakdown has moved towards more young people, which in overall terms may have increased revolutionary propensity. Young people have a very negative attitude towards the regime. They have attained a higher educational level and the regime only offers hardship and a nationalist appeal, while they did not enjoy the victories and increased level of living of the early period of the revolution. However, in view of the overwhelming repressive capacity of the regime, their frustration is expressed more in anomie and passive negative behavior —low productivity, defecting or rafting— than in open defiance. The increased urbanization makes it easier for the regime to control them. But the most important change is qualitative. The emigrants are overwhelmingly from the white middle and upper class. The rapid increase in population in the early period of the revolution has led to a shift in the racial composition. As a result, a majority black population in Cuba faces a majority white population in exile. The aspiration for political leadership from Miami is a threat to all those in Cuba regardless of race. But the better educated Afro-Cubans, perhaps with hopes of a greater leadership role in post-Castro Cuba than they have today, may perceive this possibility as disenfranchising them. Therefore, as long as the prospect of an exile return to power prevails, in 1992 this variable moves to negative.

History. *The two countries share a Spanish colonial tradition. However, their histories are very dissimilar beyond that point. Uruguay became independent in the early part of the 19th Century and, therefore, has had a century and a half to develop its own political institutions. At the beginning of the 20th century, Uruguay attained the pacification of the country and the establishment of the Batllista political system that set the basic rules for peaceful political interaction. At the time of the Tupamaro revolutionary challenge, Uruguay had a strong tradition of nonviolent political action.*

Cuba did not attain independence until 1902, and then only after a long and bloody war against Spain based on guerrilla tactics. Resort to guerrilla warfare was part of a recent enough Cuban historical experience to be transmitted by grandfathers to their grandsons. In 1956, Cuba had had barely a half-century of independence and had experienced a level of political turmoil and violence equivalent to what Uruguay experienced in the 1870s. The revolution against Machado in 1933 had planted the seeds of resorting to terrorism in Cuba. The memory of terrorist tactics was a living experience for many who were involved in the struggle against Batista, himself a product of the revolution against Machado.

The historic variable was favorable to the acceptance of violence as a legitimate political instrument in the case of Cuba. This contributed significantly to raise revolutionary propensities in Cuba. In Uruguay, however, the well established tradition of peaceful political action acted as a powerful deterrent to the acceptance of violence as a legitimate political option. Therefore, the historic variable had a very negative impact on revolutionary propensities.

History 1992. Resort to violence is now an even greater element than before in the national tradition, and most citizens have access to weapons and know how to use them. This would favor the same positive impact on revolutionary propensity it had in 1958. However, the risks involved in resorting to violence due to the ruthless repression prevailing under Castro's Stalinist regime, make resort to violence a suicidal alternative for the disaffected. Each opposition failure, from the Bay of Pigs to the Ochoa case, reinforces the image of the effectiveness of the repressive apparatus. Therefore, recent history has made this variable unfavorable to revolutionary propensity. In fact, in 1992 it is very negative. However, the longer people's frustration is repressed, the more likely that a violent explosion and a collapse of the regime may be the final outcome.

International. The international context for the two struggles was substantially different. In the case of Cuba, there was no international issue or power influencing the revolutionary process. The struggle against Batista was strictly a domestic issue. The United States at the time was concerned with the 1956 Hungarian Revolution and the Suez Canal crisis, both events related to the Cold War. The Hemisphere seemed secure enough from Communism after the overthrow of the Arbenz regime in 1954.

However, the international dimension became a factor due to the pervasive United States influence in Cuba. United States military assistance to the Cuban armed forces became an issue in revolutionary propaganda, even after the March 1958 arms embargo against Batista, leading to Raúl Castro's kidnapping of American servicemen from the Guantánamo Naval Base. On the revolutionary side, Costa Rica and Venezuela provided propaganda and equipment assistance to the 26th of July Movement.

In the case of Uruguay, the international dimension was present since the beginning. First, the Cuban revolution was an issue due to its emotional impact on Uruguayan public opinion and because it provided the rationale for the call to revolution. And, second, because the United States answer to the Cuban challenge, through the Alliance for Progress and the counterinsurgency doctrine, had an impact on Uruguay. Since Cuba never took seriously the chances for a Tupamaro victory, their level of intervention was low profile; and, so was that of the United States. Brazil and Argentina also played a minor role within the international variable. In summary, the international variable was present in both cases. However, it was more relevant in Uruguay than in Cuba. The international variable did not affect revolutionary propensity in Cuba, while increasing it in the case of Uruguay.

International 1992. The last thirty years added a strongly nationalistic component to this variable. Cubans have acquired an exaggerated sense of the international importance of their country. Castro is perceived as an important international leader, even if the collapse of the Soviet Union casts serious doubts on his wisdom in taking their side in the Cold War. An erosion of that image, however, could weaken Castro's charismatic hold over his followers. For example, the recent disastrous visit to Spain shook up Castro's own self-confidence. Further appeals to democratize and criticism of the system by democratic leaders raise questions about legitimacy and increase revolutionary propensity. On the other hand, the right-wing organizations that dominate the exile community convey an image of dependency on U.S. support and a return to the past. The aspirations of right-wing exiles to seize power help coalesce people around Castro and decrease revolutionary propensity. In the end, this exile effort is wasted, because the United States Government seems to have no intention of making a formal military intervention, overtly or covertly in Cuba. In fact, the level of U.S. intervention is limited to ideological actions, broadcasting to Cuba, which expands access to information and economic denial, the U.S. embargo, which increases hardship but is unlikely to lead to a revolt due to the regime's ruthless repression. Nevertheless, the perceived threat of a U.S. invasion, associated with the return of right-wing exiles, helps Castro exploit nationalist feelings —that is why it is a constant theme in Cuban propaganda. Soviet support is now an irrelevant factor. In summary, there is little chance of an overt U.S. intervention, or of covert support to encourage people to rebel against Castro, while the perceived threat of an exile return to power helps him. In 1992, therefore, we are faced with a very negative impact of the international variable on revolutionary propensity. This is changing as Latin democratic leaders press Castro to open up the system.

Political system. At the time the two revolutionary efforts started the political systems were quite different. Uruguay had a democratic situation with a system of representative government that enjoyed widespread national support and offered citizens open channels for redressing grievances both through the various banners of the political parties and the political clubs. The political party system was stable, with two traditional parties dominating the political life of the country, but several smaller parties were also able to participate in the competition for electoral support. There were constitutional reforms and changes in political alignment during the revolutionary period in an effort to make the political system more effective in coping with the economic stagnation affecting the country.

In the case of Cuba, on the other hand, the political system had been severely damaged by the Batista coup d'etat in 1952. As a result of that coup, Cuba had regressed from a democratic political situation into an authoritarian political situation. In fact, restoration of the 1940 Constitution was the essential issue around which the revolutionary effort was waged. The political party system in Cuba was not stable. The traditional parties of the early years of the Republic were no longer relevant and political life centered on the parties that emerged in the thirties as a result of the revolution against Dictator Gerardo Machado. On one side were the democratically oriented parties, the Auténticos and the Ortodoxos, and, on the other, Batista's Unitary Action Party. There were several other personal pocket parties that shifted alliances with the main ones. Only the Communist Party had a distinct ideological, rather than personal basis.

In summary, in Uruguay the political situation variable provided an acceptable democratic framework to find a solution to the national economic problem, making resort to violence unnecessary. In Cuba, on the contrary, the political system became the central issue of the revolutionary struggle and an operational obstacle to finding a peaceful solution to the problem faced by the country. Therefore, this variable had a very positive impact on revolutionary propensity in the Cuba case, while being very negative in the Uruguay case.

Political system 1992. At present, Cuba has a totalitarian political situation, in contrast to the authoritarian political situation under Batista. Both are equally lacking in legitimacy. While Batista tried to regain legitimacy through manipulated elections, Castro rejects them outright. Hopes for an opening towards a more flexible political environment were dashed in October 1991. This was reinforced at the recent meeting of the National Assembly of Popular Power to reform the Constitution. In essence, the Constitutional reforms failed to include the reforms advocated by some elements within the Party who had the illusion Castro was going to tolerate Glasnost and Perestroika in Cuba. The apparent concession of direct elections of delegates to the National Assembly of Popular Power was made moot by the reiteration of the commitment to a one-party system and the introduction of Article 67 and modification of Article 91, now 93, allowing the declaration of a state of emergency during which all powers are vested on the President of the Council of State. That is, in case of emergency, all legal powers have been vested on Castro himself, including the right to declare that an emergency exists. Although there are signals of ideological options being considered within the party, nobody at the Congress dared to challenge Castro's leadership publicly. There is no Solidarity-like movement or even subordinate parties in coalition with the Communists, as was the case in Eastern Europe. Therefore, in 1992 this variable is very negative towards revolutionary propensity.

Professional organizations. Both countries had a highly developed set of intermediary organizations. The professional associations in Cuba were more politicized than in Uruguay and played an active role as mediators during the revolutionary period. Lawyers and doctors were the most politically active professional groups in Cuba, while in Uruguay architects and doctors were very prominent in the Tupamaro organization. This involvement however, was at a personal level. As institutions, professional associations had no significant impact on revolutionary propensity in either country.

Professional organizations 1992. All professional associations are controlled by the party. Therefore, it is highly unlikely that they will reflect the real feelings of the rank and file as they did under Batista. With few exceptions, private practice of professions is not allowed. There have been symptoms of dissatisfaction such as the increased amount of defections among professionals traveling overseas. There have also been manifestations of dissidence. Prize-winning poet María Elena Cruz Varela led a group of members of the writers and artists union (UNEAC) to write to Castro demanding some reforms. She was supported by some members and attacked by others. Eventually, a Government-encouraged mob attacked her at her home and she is at present serving a two-year sentence for subversive activities. There is little likelihood these associations could play any role against Castro. This variable is irrelevant today in terms of revolutionary propensity.

Churches. The Church in both countries was irrelevant to the revolutionary process. Contrary to the generalized impression of the Catholic Church being a dominant institution in all of Latin America, in both countries the Church had a very narrow base of influence, restricted mostly to the upper and middle classes, and therefore was in no position to play a significant role on either side in the respective revolutionary struggles.

Churches 1992. Under Batista, the church was only a moral force with a very limited role in real terms. But today the church is even weaker. There is a very small opening for religious activity as a result of the Fourth Party Congress and the revision of the pertinent article in the Constitution. However, the churches depend so much on the state for everything that they do not dare to challenge the regime. In the Catholic Church, the hierarchy is at odds with the lay members, many of whom consider the hierarchy has been too cooperative with the regime. The hierarchy is very sensitive to this accusation of collaborationism. There are some religious fronts, mostly of protestant denominations, controlled by the regime through the Central Committee official in charge of religious matters. The most defiant church members belong to Jehovah's Witnesses. They have been unyielding in the defense of their beliefs and have suffered harsh repression, but their membership is very small. The most popular religion today is "Santería," a cult lacking a formal hierarchy that can challenge the regime. This variable continues to be irrelevant in terms of revolutionary propensity.

Labor Unions. The labor movement situation was quite different. In Cuba, the national labor federation, the CTC, was a very powerful and solidly established national institution. Batista had vested it with the monopoly of labor representation in the thirties and given its control to the Communist Party, in exchange for Communist Party support for his presidential candidacy. Labor unions had a membership of 1,100,000 out of a total labor force of 2,000,000. At the time of the revolutionary struggle, the unions were controlled by an alliance of Batista and Communist labor leaders, who had displaced the Auténtico labor leaders after Batista's coup. Only once during the revolutionary period, in 1955, did a national sugar workers strike take place on economic issues. It was led by dissident Auténtico labor leaders and supported by the university student federation, but not by Castro's movement. The two calls made by Castro for general strikes failed for lack of adequate penetration in the labor movement. In neither case were the general strikes related to labor issues.

In Uruguay, the labor movement was removed from the influence of the two dominant traditional parties. It was heavily influenced by the Communist Party. The labor movement was also struggling to consolidate itself as a national institution. It was only in 1966 that the National Workers Convention, the CNT, was created. It gathered around 300,000 to 400,000 workers out of a total labor force of more than one million. While during the revolutionary period the CNT fought the existing order with constant strikes related to bread and butter issues, it was reluctant to mobilize the workers in an ideological struggle for revolutionary victory. Therefore, its actions undermined Tupamaro efforts to move workers to resort to violence.

In summary, neither revolutionary movement was able to control the respective labor organizations during their revolutionary struggles. It was the Communist parties allied with Moscow that stood in the way in both countries. Therefore, in both cases the labor variable had a negative impact on revolutionary propensities.

Labor Unions 1992. Unions are controlled by the regime in present-day Cuba to a greater degree than under Batista. They do not represent the demands of the rank and file to those in power. However, since unions are the only institutions in Cuba whose leadership was not totally replaced by the revolution, some leaders still perceive their role in response to the base. Castro has been forced to downplay their role, with frequent replacement of union leaders who reverted to the previous mentality. As living conditions deteriorate with the current economic collapse, labor unions may be a source of anti-regime leadership. But that requires a political opening. For the time being, unions are an effective instrument of control of people at the workplace. As such, they have a very negative impact on revolutionary propensity in present day Cuba.

Students. *Students are another relevant intermediary organization in revolutionary situations. In the Cuba case, university students developed their own revolutionary organization, the Revolutionary Directorate, which fought Batista unsuccessfully through a variety of tactics, including attacking the Presidential Palace in a failed attempt to kill him, their own guerrilla front, demonstrations, strikes, clashes with the police, etc. Although they fought against Batista to the bitter end, student leaders remained rivals of Castro for leadership of the revolution all along.*

In the case of Uruguay, the university students were heavily influenced by the Communist Party. Their activities included demonstrations and protests over international events related to Cuba, the United States or issues closer to home, such as bus fares, government school intervention or killings of students. Secondary school students were heavily involved in these activities. University students provided many of the cadres, along with the labor movement, for the Tupamaros. Their organizations remained under heavy Communist Party influence during the period and the Tupamaros were not able to assume control. The left leaning students were challenged in their own turf by the JUP, a right wing student organization created with police support.

In the case of students, while the Communist Party prevented Tupamaro control of the university federation in Uruguay, it was an eminently anti-Communist and Catholic group that prevented Castro's control of university students in Cuba. Despite the inability to control them, the student variable had a positive impact on revolutionary propensity in both cases.

Students 1992. Aware of the role they played in the overthrow of Batista, Castro moved from the beginning of his regime to neutralize student political activities. Recently, he has started visiting Havana University, an indication that student disaffection is a matter of concern. However, at present this is an irrelevant variable in terms of revolutionary propensity.

Business Groups. Business groups were very influential in both countries. However, neither one had an encroached landowning aristocracy that constituted a ruling oligarchy. In both societies, there was open access to the upper classes and circulation of elites.

In Cuba, sugar industry domination of the country made the trade associations of that industry the most influential. Membership in Cuban business groups changed substantially, with the sugar industry's foreign owners becoming a minority during the period immediately before the revolution. The issue over which the revolution took place was not central to business interests, so business had no vested interest in fighting the revolution, since they were not threatened by Castro during that period. The other political parties were equally responsive to business interests; therefore they had no basic reason for supporting Batista.

In the case of Uruguay, the nature of the social conflict involved the business groups, whose interests were being threatened by the Tupamaros. Faced with a declining economy, there was inter-business group rivalry, particularly between the export-oriented agricultural producers and import substitution-oriented industries. In addition, the interests of all business groups clashed with those of the labor unions. The main basis of the economic reform undertaken during the period was aimed at reducing labor costs, a process that unavoidably led to increasing working class frustration, providing arguments and motivations for Tupamaro revolutionary efforts.

In summary, business groups were not directly threatened by the revolutionary conflict in Cuba, at least until it was too late for them to do anything about it, but they resented Batista's illegitimacy and repression. In Uruguay, there was a definite class conflict directly related to the issues around which the revolutionary struggle was being waged and, therefore, business groups were intensely involved because they had a great stake in the final outcome. The business group variable was very negative to revolutionary propensity in the case of Uruguay and it was mildly positive in the case of Cuba.

Business groups 1992. All industrial, agricultural and commercial activities are undertaken by government enterprises under control from above, either by ministries or the party secretaries. All executives are government officials and in most cases party members. This may change a little under the revised Article 23 of the Constitution to allow mixed enterprises with foreign investors. In fact, the regime is considering extending the mixed enterprise option to exiled businessmen. Perhaps in anticipation of a potential Trojan horse under the guise of mixed enterprises investment, Castro decided to modify Article 32 to make more categoric the inability of those who have renounced their Cuban citizenship to be involved in domestic politics by denying them the right to dual citizenship. However, in real terms, at present there is only one association of private owners left, the ANAP, which gathers small agricultural producers. After the reversal of economic liberalization in 1986, the government has increased measures to control this intermediary organization of private entrepreneurs through various devices, such as the control of inputs, prices and forced-sale of their products to state enterprises. ANAP leadership is government imposed, not freely elected by members. The new president elected at the recent meeting of ANAP was nominated by Castro. Therefore, this variable is irrelevant in terms of revolutionary propensity against the present situation.

Mass media. Electronic media was more developed in Cuba than in Uruguay at the time of the respective revolutionary efforts. Television played a central role in the Cuban case. In 1958, Cuba had 400,000 sets, a larger absolute number of sets than in any other Latin American country at that time. Radio ownership was also widespread, to the point of providing universal access in urban centers. The press had limited circulation nationwide, but a heavy impact in Havana.

Media ownership was widespread, with ample representation for opposition parties and groups. The most prominent weekly and the newspaper with the highest circulation were supporters of the revolutionary cause. A similar situation prevailed in electronic media. In addition, Castro had his own underground paper, <u>Revolución</u>, and a clandestine radio station, <u>Radio Rebelde</u>. Government censorship was imposed frequently during the period, but pro-government media lacked audience and credibility. Press corruption was used by the Batista government to attenuate opposition criticisms, but was not effective in blocking revolutionary propaganda.

In the case of Uruguay, the printed press was the dominant media, with Montevideo newspapers having national circulation. Television was at an incipient stage and ownership of sets was not as widespread as in Cuba, while radio ownership was universal for practical purposes in the capital city. The most influential newspapers were associated with the leading banners of the traditional political parties. The Communists and the Catholics also had newspapers, as did some groups supporting the revolutionaries, though their circulation was very limited. The only prominent publication supporting the revolutionaries was <u>Marcha</u>, a very influential intellectual weekly. SODRE, a government-owned network, had the widest distribution of radio and TV stations nationally. The Tupamaros were never able to develop their own means of mass communication, printed or electronic, to access wide sectors of the population.

Government censorship was imposed from time to time during the revolutionary period, and it was applied on a selective basis to publications sympathetic to the revolutionaries. In the final period the armed forces took direct control of the information to be provided to mass media about events related to the revolutionary conflict. The Tupamaros had their own form of censorship through attacks on radio stations and individual journalists supportive of the existing order.

Mass media is a critical factor in moving people against or towards resorting to violence. The use of mass media had a very positive impact on revolutionary propensity in Cuba and it had a negative impact in Uruguay.

Mass Media 1992. In contrast with the situation under Batista, when censorship of an independent media was on and off, today all media is in the hands of the government. It is controlled through the Department of Ideology or Revolutionary Orientation of the Central Committee, which at present is headed by Carlos Aldana. It is through this Department that radio, TV and the printed media is given guidance as to how to treat stories. There is no local means of communication free of that control. Only Radio Martí and other international broadcasts offer independent information. This is a very negative factor in terms of revolutionary propensity.

Armed forces. As a result of the 1952 Batista coup d'etat, the Cuban armed forces were split between the professional officers, who supported a return to the 1940 Constitution —in other words siding on that issue with the revolutionaries— and the promotion of improvised officers that came to power with Batista in 1933, who supported Batista's dictatorship for the spoils of power it offered them. That split seriously affected the operational capability and competence of the Cuban armed forces during the revolutionary period. Colonel Barquín's conspiracy and the arrest of his followers deprived the Cuban armed forces of the elite of its officers corps, either through imprisonment or dismissal. In addition, there were other conspiracies and an outright rebellion, the Cienfuegos naval uprising.

The lack of legitimacy of the Batista regime was another factor undermining morale of the armed forces. In this respect, the United States arms embargo imposed in March 1958 had a most damaging effect on armed forces morale. The paramilitary groups were significant in Cuba, in particular the so-

called Masferrer Tigers, who played a central role in repressing the April 1958 general strike.

The armed forces were a stable institution within Uruguayan society and were committed to support the existing order without hesitation. There was no significant split among them in their support for the existing order. That is, no conspiracy was uncovered, no command or unit rebelled. Whatever disagreement emerged was limited to the action of individuals who bolted to the revolutionary side or resigned, the most prominent being General Liber Seregni. In fact, the most serious disagreements with the political leadership during the struggle against the Tupamaros came from officers who felt the government was dragging the armed forces into actions not fully consistent with the constitutional role assigned to them. It was after the victory over the Tupamaros that the military went beyond their normal role and eventually took over the government.

The Uruguayan armed forces stayed aloof from the conflict until the last phases of the struggle against the Tupamaros. Their professional competence, enhanced by years of training in counterinsurgency provided by U.S. military assistance programs, was excellent. This competence was evident in the swift and effective implementation of their campaign against the Tupamaros.

The police was the weak link in the repressive capacity of the state in Uruguay. It was seriously affected in its morale by the highly individualized terror campaign the Tupamaros waged against them. The police-supported paramilitary groups were not too relevant in operational terms in the case of Uruguay, except that their actions triggered the Tupamaro reprisals that played a key role in the final actions of the armed forces in the revolutionary struggle.

In summary, the armed forces in Cuba were central to the rationale for a revolutionary struggle, since they were the only basis for the existence of the illegitimate regime that was questioned by the revolutionaries. At the same time, the armed forces loss of morale and the weakening of its professional competence by divisions within them were central factors in facilitating the revolutionary victory. Therefore, in the Cuba case this variable had a very positive impact on revolutionary propensity.

In Uruguay, on the contrary, the armed forces were not in any way responsible for the issue generating the conflict. They acted with firm conviction and high morale. Since their professional competence was up to the needs of the moment, they played the decisive role in defeating the Tupamaro insurrection. Therefore, in the Uruguay case the armed forces variable had a very negative impact on revolutionary propensity.

Armed Forces in 1992. Batista's armed forces cannot even get close enough to present ones to warrant comparison. There are three armies with independent commands under the MINFAR, each of Army Corp size with battle-tested troops, which makes it hard for any general to seize power without having to face other military forces. The MININT has intelligence (DGI), the secret police (State Security), and the regular police, plus elite units called Special Forces, which are equivalent to U.S. Green Berets, for a total force of more than 100,000. There is rivalry between the MINFAR and the MININT. After the Ochoa trial, and the arrest and death in prison of MININT Minister Gral. Abrantes, the MININT became subordinated to MINFAR control through the transfer of Army Gral. Abelardo Colomé. There are the CDRs, neighborhood committees, and the MTT, a territorial militia controlled through the Party Secretariat, with around one million poorly trained and equipped members. Recently, the government established the SUVP, a so-called unified service for vigilance and protection, and goon squads, called Rapid Reaction Battalions, to nip in the bud any protest no matter how small. Resort to violence against such an array is unlikely. Therefore, in 1992 this is a very negative factor for revolutionary propensity, but not for a coup d'etat once there is a consensus among them that Castro offers no future and they perceive a lesser danger from rebelling.

Economic and social conditions. The importance of economic and social conditions as variables in revolutionary propensity is due to the fact that they are associated with the level of relative deprivation in a society. The concept of relative deprivation is not an absolute but changes when expectations increase as a result of factors such as expanded media access —introduction of television and advertising commercials are good examples— or when there is a decrease in the ability to satisfy existing expectations, leading to what is called decremental relative deprivation. Relative deprivation is usually measured by economic and social indicators. A summary table will be used to provide the available indicators to compare the two cases.

Cuba and Uruguay: Selected Social and Economic Indicators

Indicators	Unit	URUGUAY		CUBA	
		Actual	Rank	Actual	Rank
Per capita income	US$1950	440	03	310	05
Energy per capita	Coal eq.	.78	06	.62	07
Cement consumption	kgs.	166	05	125	06
Paper consumption	kgs.	6.5	02	4.8	04
Agric labor force	%	21.	01	41.	03
Industrial occup.	%	55.	02	51.	03
Literacy rate	%	86.	01	78.	02
Prim. Educ. Reg.	%	59.	03	53.	04
Secd. Educ. Reg.	%	13.	05	05.	09
University Reg.	%	45.	05	36.	06
Doctor per 100 000	#	091	04	100	03
Hab/Hospital bed	#	250	01	300	01

Source: Vekemans, Roger and J. L. Segundo, "Tipología Socioecónomica de América Latina," published in *Inter-American Social Science Review*, Special Issue Vol. 2, OAS Secretariat, Washington, D. C., 1963, pp. 5 and 3l.

As can be observed from the table, the comparison of Cuban and Uruguayan economic and social indicators does not reflect such sharp differences to justify attributing to them the revolutionary outcome. The table shows the two countries as being fairly close in most indicators, particularly in the ranking among Latin American countries. The 1952 GNP per capita figure itself is questionable, since studies made at the time report there was a substantial underestimation of GNP in the case of Cuba. In fact, the same OAS study in the economic section reports another source with quite the opposite situation. According to this source, in 1952 Cuba had an estimated GNP per capita of US$406 versus US$271 for Uruguay (Tipología, p. 45).

Cuba had twice the percentage of agricultural labor force of Uruguay, a situation resulting from the more labor-intensive requirements of Cuba's main crop, sugar cane. In education, Cuba was behind Uruguay in secondary and university attendance, but fairly close in the other indicators. In health, Cuba had more doctors per 100,000 inhabitants than Uruguay, and was close enough in hospital beds to share first place in rank. Therefore, in terms of economic and social conditions there is no clear difference between the two countries to explain the different revolutionary outcomes.

As to the dynamics of the economic and social changes in the respective revolutionary times, the *comparison leads to completely opposite results from what conventional wisdom would mandate. During the years of the revolution in Cuba, the economy was expanding after a decline in 1954 and 1955. Batista's government engaged in an active investment effort with state development banks increasing their outstanding loans from US$31 million in 1953 to US$459 million in 1958. Sugar and total exports were at their highest levels during the critical years of 1957 and 1958. There was no inflationary pressure, and the Cuban peso maintained its parity with the U.S. dollar for many years. Therefore, there was no decremental relative deprivation resulting from economic decline to generate frustration leading to violence. Even though Cuba was a poor country and there were many social injustices, economic and social conditions had no impact on revolutionary propensity in Cuba.*

In the case of Uruguay, however, the years of the Tupamaro revolutionary effort coincided with a period of economic decline. In fact, the deterioration in the population's standard of living, the decline in real salaries, the runaway inflation, along with the inability of the political system to produce a turnaround, were the factors that in the eyes of the Tupamaros justified resorting to violence. Therefore, this variable had a very positive impact on revolutionary propensity in Uruguay.

Socio-Economic Conditions 1992. This final contextual variable is very positive in terms of encouraging revolutionary propensity in 1992, while under Batista economic conditions were improving in what amounted to a real boom. The *World Development Report 1983* published by the World Bank reveals that, despite the claims of the Castro regime, the progress made by Cuba has not been as significant in social indicators and abysmal in economic indicators.

In GNP per capita, by 1982 Cuba's ranking fell from third to sixteenth during the revolution in comparison with the ranking quoted above for 1953. In other words, moving from the level of Argentina and Uruguay to the level of Central America. In increase of energy consumption per capita during the period, Cuba's rank was eighteenth compared to 1960. In percentage share of exports of manufactures, Cuba had made no progress at all between 1960 and 1980, according to the World Bank report, retaining a modest 5 percent proportion. This compares with an increase from 5 to 53 percent for Jamaica, of 6 to 39 per cent for El Salvador and from 5 to 34 percent for Costa Rica for the same period.

As to social indicators, Cuba started from a high ranking in the region; therefore, in terms of progress made it ranked eleventh in percentage increase between 1960 and 1980 in population per physician, fourteenth in improvement in life expectancy, from 63 to 73; twelfth in improved infant mortality rate per 1000 births, from 32 to 19; in expansion of secondary education enrollment it ranked first and in higher education enrollment it ranked fourth. These figures reveal that, although it cannot be denied that significant progress was made up to the early eighties in social indicators, the mere comparison of absolute data is misleading since Cuba had a high standing at the beginning of the period.

The collapse of the Soviet Union and Communism affects Cuba at three levels: psychological-ideological, social and economic. The failure of ideology has led to confusion and disorientation among those who accepted the myths of Marxist dogma. Perhaps the most important setback to Castro is the weakening of his charismatic appeal as a result of the end of internationalism due to the loss of the Soviet strategic umbrella. Cubans feel proud of their acquired international importance and this helps Castro maintain the aura of a world leader. In terms of human rights violations and denial of basic freedoms, Cuba has the most negative conditions in the Hemisphere. The relative deprivation faced by Cubans in terms of human rights and basic freedoms has been heightened by events in the former Soviet Bloc and by the United Nations resolutions condemning the regime. In terms of social services, progress in health and education still evokes favorable comments, although one can question some qualitative aspects, as well as their long term feasibility under a declining economic capability.

In economic terms, the collapse of energy supplies in particular, has caused a massive decline in living standards. Cuba is heading for 19th Century living conditions. Recently, there has been a small improvement in food supplies as a result of mobilizing urban residents to grow their own food. But there is little hope of any economic growth for the foreseeable future. The reason is the change in the relationship between oil consumption and sugar production and the relative prices of the two products. Under the Revolution, Cuba expanded oil consumption, while the expansion of sugar output has lagged in proportion and as shown above Cuba has failed to diversify its exports significantly. The main export product Castro developed, surrogate troops for Soviet imperial expansion, has no market anymore. In terms of prices, oil prices increased dramatically in 1973 and 1980, while sugar prices have been depressed in relative terms due to competition from artificial sweeteners and subsidized production, particularly in Europe.

As long as the oil-sugar output-price relation continues to be negative to Cuba, the country would have to use all its sugar output merely to pay its oil bill. In other words, as a result of the loss of Soviet subsidies, Cuba is doomed to a no-growth future for lack of ability to generate revenue to maintain its present energy consumption and much less to expand it. That is, unless ongoing and proposed oil exploration is successful or the Uruguay Round at GATT is finally agreed upon and subsidies for sugar in Europe and the United States are phased out, expanding the demand for Cuba's sugar. But, both are long-term propositions. Therefore, the economic situation could erode regime support. This erosion has not been manifested more openly due to ruthless resort to repression.

As to revolutionary propensity, the impact of the socio-economic variable is relevant in terms of relative deprivation, whether incremental or decremental. It can be argued that this variable has been favorable to the regime up to the events of the late eighties, in other words it was negative to revolutionary propensity. However, when the Soviet Bloc collapsed and Cuba was set adrift in the world to fend for itself strategically and economically, the resulting massive economic decline has made this variable very positive to revolutionary propensity.

B. Cuba-Uruguay Revolutionary Dynamics

The categories for comparison of operational variables impacting revolutionary dynamics include the events, the revolutionary actions and the strategies and policies. There is no data on which to base a comparison with Cuba (1992) because the totalitarian nature of the regime does not allow space for a revolutionary process to manifest itself. However, drawing on relevant parallels from the two previous cases will help highlight the difficulty for such a process to develop in Cuba (1992).

Events. In discussing the events, we will consider the trigger event and its relevance, the time frame, the nature of events and their magnitude to the extent that they had an impact on the revolutionary outcome.

The attack on the Moncada Barracks on July 26, 1953 is the trigger event for the Cuban Revolution. It became the symbol of the revolutionary effort against Batista and was important in Castro's propaganda. The march of the Artigas sugar cane workers is the trigger event in the case of Uruguay. The trigger event was irrelevant to the revolutionary cause in Uruguay (1972). No such event has occurred in Cuba (1992) to start the chain of events leading to a revolutionary process, although the collapse of Communism could have been such an event, if the political system had been similar to those in Eastern Europe.

The time frame of the Cuban revolution spans over five years. This variable was favorable to the revolutionaries in the case of Cuba (1958) and had a positive impact on revolutionary propensity. In Uruguay, the time span extended over a decade. The longer time frame for events is a variable unfavorable to the revolutionaries in the case of Uruguay (1972). As to Cuba (1992), the two time frames indicate that were a revolutionary process to start, it could take years before a revolutionary leadership becomes known and asserts itself, articulates an ideology and mobilizes the opposition forces and is successful in defeating the regime, should other factors be favorable to such an outcome.

The nature of events generated by the revolutionaries in Cuba was consistent with the strategy and the need to appeal to the population to resort to violence. Businessmen, politicians and military officers, not to mention soldiers, were reassured in subtle ways by the events selected and in their execution, that the target was Batista and his henchmen, but that all others were safe and did not have to fear for their interests. Consequently the nature of the events had a very positive impact on revolutionary propensity in Cuba (1958). In the case of Uruguay, the nature of the events produced by the revolutionaries was clearly threatening to the whole upper class, the politicians and the armed forces. They themselves were the targets, not anybody else. Such events pushed these sectors toward supporting use of violence against the revolutionaries. Therefore, in Uruguay (1972) this variable had a very negative impact on revolutionary propensity.

In Cuba (1992), the nature of events is limited to the international variable discussed above under national context. The potential revolutionaries who are trying to start a revolutionary process are in exile in the U.S. So far, they are perceived as a threat by those inside the regime similar to the threat implicit in the events generated by the Tupamaros in Uruguay (1972), without having been able to generate any internal events to mobilize a following among the disaffected inside Cuba. Therefore, the impact is equally negative to revolutionary propensity.

The magnitude of the operations in Cuba (1958) was much less than the international image created by Castro's propaganda. The battles on the guerrilla side of the insurrection were mostly small skirmishes, until the last few months of the conflict. The civic resistance underground had around 30,000 individuals contributing regularly through the purchase of M-26 bonds. The underground action groups had some 5,000 to 6,000 members and the guerrilla columns at most around 3,000 and quite likely less. Batista's army had been expanded by the end of the conflict to a force of around 60,000 soldiers. Therefore, the magnitude of effort variable had attained an adequate level to bring victory to the revolutionaries. The success in Cuba (1958), however, was due to a great extent to the inadequate performance of Batista's army, which was split and beset by problems of incompetence, lack of morale, and outright corruption.

In the case of Uruguay, the magnitude of the effort was considerable, involving many small urban actions. The Uruguayan army estimated there were 4,200 Tupamaros in 1972. Total police and army strength in Uruguay at the time was estimated to be around 30,000. The number of police operations undertaken in Montevideo over the last three years of conflict went into the tens of thousands. In August 1970 alone, the police undertook more than 20,000 house searches in Montevideo. Therefore, the magnitude of effort variable was favorable to the Uruguayan revolutionaries. It was not for lack of trying that they were defeated.

The magnitude of these events in comparison with the meager resources and very limited space for actions available to internal dissidents explains more than any other factor how difficult it will be to start a revolutionary process in Cuba (1992).

Revolutionary action components. The categories for this variable include ideology and propaganda, organization, and leadership of the revolutionary movements.

The ideology and propaganda factor was essential to the success of the 26th of July Movement in Cuba. The main thrust of the ideology was based on a simple combination of themes: the goal, restoration of the 1940 Constitution; the strategy, resort to violence mainly through guerrilla warfare. The third basic theme of the ideology emerged from the struggle: rejection of repression and torture. Economic and social reform was not an issue over which the revolutionaries appealed to the people. That came after victory. As to propaganda, the slogans were again very consistent with the goals, strategy and ideology: "Fatherland or death; we shall win!" Words were reinforced by events and vice-versa. As to means of dissemination, Castro was masterful in managing the press, both national and international —as he has up to this day— and received excellent coverage.

In the case of the Tupamaros, the ideology was too heavily influenced by the Cuban revolution and Marxist dogma. As a result, there was dissonance in the message sent to the people. Furthermore, the economic and social analysis and prognosis in the Tupamaro documents were based on an ideology that not even the working class in Uruguay considered acceptable. The call to violence was completely inconsistent with the historical tradition and cultural values of the Uruguayan people. In essence, the Tupamaros advanced an ideology with little appeal to the majority of Uruguayans. To compound the inadequacy of the message, the Tupamaros failed to develop an effective domestic media capability, despite the fact that there were many journalists and writers sympathetic to their cause. For this reason, at the critical moment they lacked access to mass media to inform, much less mobilize the population.

The present situation in Cuba (1992) is worse than it was for the Tupamaros. The dominant message sent from exile reflects an ideology of restoration of the past and revenge most threatening to those inside the regime and not appealing enough to those opposing it to move them into action. The internal dissidence is clearly distancing itself from a revolutionary appeal. There are no events on which to base a revolutionary propaganda. As to media, Radio Martí, the most effective means of reaching the Cuban people, cannot play the role of a revolutionary radio station since it is an official station of the U.S. Government. Miami radio broadcasts are addressed to the exile audience. Only the CID shortwave radio broadcasts seem to have built an audience inside Cuba which could mobilize people into opposition action when other factors are favorable.

In summary, while ideology and propaganda had a very positive impact on revolutionary propensity in Cuba (1958), they had a very negative impact in Uruguay (1972) and are not relevant in Cuba (1992).

The revolutionary organization in Cuba developed along with the revolutionary process. The various columns in the guerrilla forces were created in response to military needs. The civic resistance underground in the cities provided money, supplies, people, and intelligence. The revolutionary organization of the Tupamaros took years to build and managed to attain an effective capability for urban guerrilla operations. However, the Tupamaros created an excessively centralized and elaborate reporting system of their activities that was disastrous for their survival when compromised by the betrayal of key leaders. The organizations inside Cuba today have a very limited membership, are unable to make propaganda, proselytize, organize and mobilize their potential followers due to constant harassment by the repressive apparatus of the regime. In summary, the organizational variable had a very positive impact on revolutionary propensity in Cuba (1958), while it had a very negative impact in the case of Uruguay (1972) and is practically non-existent in Cuba (1992).

Leadership is the most important variable in determining the effectiveness of the revolutionary response. On this variable the results were very positive for the Cuban revolutionaries, who benefitted from the charismatic personality of Castro and his unquestionable ability as a leader. This was not the case with the Tupamaros. Raúl Sendic lacked the personality and leadership conditions required to symbolize and articulate the urban guerrilla struggle in Uruguay. In this case, the leadership variable had a very negative impact on revolutionary propensity.

Since no internal leadership has emerged in Cuba to lead a revolution —all dissidents inside Cuba wisely refuse to endorse any recourse to violence which could provide the regime with an excuse to crush them and close even the limited space they enjoy today— the only possible source of leadership has to be abroad. So far, no leader of the dominant forces abroad has emerged to offer to those inside the ideology, particularly in terms of nationalism and reassurance of no return to pre-revolutionary Cuba, required to mobilize them into action.

Strategy and policies. In the case of Cuba (1958), Batista followed the classical hesitant repression strategy of authoritarian rulers who lack legitimacy. He could not make the one concession that would have restored legitimacy to the regime —turning power over to an opposition leader in a fair election— because his goal was to stay in power by any means. His strategy, therefore, was saddled with an impossible goal to start with. In trying to attain that goal, he never developed a decisive strategy based on a clear understanding of the challenge Castro represented to his rule.

On the revolutionary side, Castro's strategy and policies were most adequate to the situation. By taking from the outset a long-range strategy of resorting to violence, and locating himself in a redoubt from which he could out-wait both the other opposition group's unsuccessful efforts against Batista, as well as Batista's own fumbling efforts against him, Castro ensured that time was on his side. By the time Batista fled, Castro had persuaded all political groups in the opposition, peaceful or violent, as well as the business community and the rank and file of the population, to accept his rule.

In Uruguay (1972), the status quo leadership initially ignored the existence of a revolutionary challenge. The strategy of hesitant repression used at first helped push some segments of the population toward resorting to violence, particularly among young labor leaders and student activists. As to the armed forces, once they joined the battle, their strategy was superbly conceived and executed.

As to the Tupamaros, their strategy, like their ideological constructs, was too influenced by mimicry of what was happening in other countries. The central flaw of their strategy was that it ignored the historical, geographic and political realities of Uruguay and the strength, competence and commitment of its military opponent.

In Cuba (1992), the Castro government is very aware of the threat implicit in any loosening of control or allowing any space for an opposition to emerge. The totalitarian nature of the regime and its repressive tactics, resembling those of the Nazis and the Stalinists, are a decisive factor in making a revolutionary process highly unlikely. The strategy and policies of the opposition are not related thus far to a revolutionary process. Most of those who have emerged inside take the position of dissidents, that is, a peaceful opposition seeking marginal changes without challenging the regime through resort to violence, at least as a beginning.

The only significant opposition that has emerged is abroad. The strategy of the groups that dominate the exile community seems to be predicated on hopes for an eventual U.S. intervention, with lobbying in Washington, and more recently in Moscow, taking precedence over serious efforts to understand and mobilize the aspirations of the disaffected inside contemporary Cuba. Those who have a different perspective constitute a small minority, which so far has been unable to gain any significant influence in exile politics. Under such conditions, it is unlikely that any internal action may be encouraged from outside the island.

In summary, the government strategy and policies variable had a very negative impact for the interests of status quo forces in the case of Cuba (1958), therefore being very helpful to the revolutionary cause and reinforcing the extremely positive impact on revolutionary propensity of Castro's effective strategy and policies. On the other hand, in Uruguay (1972) the opposite is the case but with a caveat. Although the policies of the political leaders were inadequate, the actual strategy and policies of the military against the Tupamaros were very effective. On balance, the variable had a negative impact on revolutionary propensity. This was reinforced by a Tupamaro strategy that was faulty and had a very negative impact on revolutionary propensity. Their inadequate strategy was a key factor in determining their defeat. In Cuba (1992), there is no strategy at present for a revolutionary process because there is none underway.

C. Summary and Conclusions

The summary comparison of revolutionary dynamics will be made on the basis of a synthesis of the impact that the contextual and operational variables analyzed in the previous section had on revolutionary propensity. This is presented in the form of a Kurt Lewin force-field analysis diagram in the chart "Comparative Profiles of Revolutionary Propensity," which is taken from a training aid for a workshop on revolutionary propensity. The chart shows for each variable whether the impact was very negative, negative, irrelevant, positive, or very positive.

In reading the chart, it is necessary to keep in mind that a very positive ranking indicates the variable increased revolutionary propensities substantially, while a very negative ranking indicates that it caused a substantial decrease in revolutionary propensities. As can be observed, the two outcomes of closed revolutionary processes, revolutionary victory in the case of Cuba (1958) and revolutionary defeat in the case of Uruguay (1972), result in almost opposite profiles. As to Cuba (1992), the profile is the opposite of what it was in 1958 and has great similarity with that of Uruguay in 1972. No profile is given for Cuba (1992) operational variables because, as is explained above, there is no ongoing revolutionary process at present in Cuba.

In the case of Cuba (1958), the impact of the contextual variables was overwhelmingly favorable to revolutionary propensities. Geography and history of the country were positive factors for revolutionary propensity, as were the attitudes of students and business groups. The political system, the armed forces and the mass media were also very positive factors in determining Castro's victory. Socio-economic conditions were irrelevant, as were demographic and international factors.

The labor movement was the only contextual variable with a negative impact on the revolutionary propensity of Cuba at that time: unions remained under Batista's control until the end of the regime. Only after Batista fled was it possible for Castro to call a successful general strike. Quite an irony for a revolution that, after coming to power, embraced the cause of the proletariat.

In the case of Uruguay (1972), however, the behavior of the contextual variables is almost the opposite. The only positive factors in terms of revolutionary propensity were the international situation, due to the demonstration effect of the Cuban Revolution, and the students, who in turn were heavily influenced by those events. The very positive factor in generating revolutionary propensity in Uruguay was the economic crisis, which caused severe decremental relative deprivation for the Uruguayan people.

By focusing excessively on the socio-economic contextual variable, however, the Uruguayan revolutionaries ignored the extremely negative impact on revolutionary propensity of the other contextual variables. Neither the geography nor the demography of the country offered favorable conditions for imitating the Cuban revolution. The labor unions and the mass media were not favorable either. The historical tradition of non-violent solution of problems was reinforced by the existence of an effective democratic system, and both had a very negative impact on revolutionary propensity, making revolution a remote possibility. Finally, the armed forces and business groups reactions also had very negative impact on the feasibility of a revolutionary victory. In view of such a negative array of contextual variables, it was foolhardy for the Tupamaros to attempt a revolutionary effort. Both the Cubans and the Uruguayan Communist Party were more realistic than them in their assessment of the feasibility of revolutionary success in Uruguay.

The profile of Cuba (1992) reveals a situation more similar to that of Uruguay in 1972 than with the Cuba of 1958. This provides an explanation for the failure of the predictions made in 1989, 1990 and 1991 in terms that Cuba was about to follow the dramatic events of Eastern Europe and the Soviet Union. Unfortunately, many of those predictions were predicated on wishful thinking, more than on solid analysis of relevant factors. In other cases they were based on simplistic extrapolations from one society into another.

If a systematic analysis is made of those events, it will reveal that instead of a revolution, what took place was the abdication of Soviet power by Gorbachev, first in Eastern Europe and afterwards in the Soviet Union itself. At no time did Gorbachev make use of the overwhelming repressive capacity of the Soviet Union; either the Red Army, the KGB or KGB controlled secret police agencies in Eastern Europe. Honnecker openly accused Gorbachev of undermining his regime and in Rumania it was revealed that the military group that overthrew Ceaucescu had Soviet links and encouragement. In other words, the Soviet leader reassured the oppressed that no resort to violence was to take place in response to their actions. Apparently, he really believed people liked socialism and with a little tinkering it would work. Gorbachev's passivity turned upside down the equilibrium between the Soviet regime's repressive capacity and the bottled-up resentment of Communist rule.

The forces of nationalism were much stronger than Gorbachev anticipated, both in Eastern Europe and inside the Soviet Union. Initially, the frustrated in those societies made modest reform demands. Afterwards, emboldened by the lack of risk they faced due to the hesitation of the doomed communist leaders, they raised the ante until the whole system collapsed. But revolutions, involving resort to violence to change the system, they were not.

If one contrasts the behavior of Soviet Bloc leaders with Castro's behavior, it is clear why there was no domino effect. Due to the tremendous repressive capacity at the disposition of Castro and the ruthlessness with which he uses it, there is little likelihood that a revolutionary process can take place in Cuba in 1992. The cruel reality is evident in the fact that one cannot analyze the operational variables of a revolutionary situation in Cuba (1992) to compare them with operational variables in Cuba (1958) or Uruguay (1972). If anything, the analysis of those variables made above reveals how far the situation in Cuba today is from the beginnings of a revolutionary process. Under these conditions, for the U.S. to suspend enforcement of the Neutrality Act, as was requested recently from President Bush, is likely to accomplish nothing more than produce unnecessary loss of life and another wave of embarrassing incidents for the Cuban-American community, as well as for the U.S. Government.

II. Possible Outcomes and Political Climate for Reconstruction

The analysis in the previous chapter reveals that the possibility of a revolutionary process leading to a change of government is a most unlikely outcome under present conditions. We must now consider other possible outcomes that have been discussed and review them in terms of their feasibility and the political climate they may create for the formulation of economic policy for the reconstruction period. They are:

a) A change of policy by Castro allowing an opening and starting a process of transition towards democracy and a market-based economy.

b) The action of one individual or "Mother Nature" removing Castro without any conspiracy.

c) A coup d'etat by elements within the regime's armed forces.

d) A popular explosion leading to the disintegration of the regime.

e) A U.S. intervention in response to a deliberate Castro provocation.

The feasibility of each option will be considered first. Then, for purposes of the evaluation of the impact of each outcome on the political climate for reconstruction, criteria will include:

1) legitimacy of the resulting regime, both in terms of acceptance by the Cuban people and the exile community;

2) international acceptance by the United States, Western Europe and Latin America;

3) adequate control of the repressive capacity of the state to be able to maintain order and enforce the law; and,

4) political cohesion within the government to be able to make difficult decisions and follow a coherent economic policy.

REVOLUTIONARY PROPENSITY WORKSHOP
Comparative Profiles of Revolutionary Propensity

Training Aid No. 7   *Page No. 1*

The comparison of profiles of revolutionary propensity between Cuba (1958), Uruguay (1972) and Cuba (1992) only reflects one analyst's judgments. Perhaps other analysts may differ. With this caveat, the analysis results in a profile for Cuba (1992) which is almost the opposite of Cuba (1958), having more similarity with that for Uruguay (1972) where the revolutionary effort aborted. There is no Cuba (1992) evaluation of operational variables. There is no ongoing revolutionary effort in Cuba to provide data for analysis. The regime's repression is creating a mirage. Revolutionary propensity exists but is bottled up. That is why the outcome may be an explosion, rather than a revolutionary process. The longer Castro manages to delay his departure, the bloodier the aftermath is likely to be.

```
                           CUBA (1958)            URUGUAY (1972)           CUBA (1992)

VARIABLE IMPACT:     VN--N---I---P--VP       VN--N---I---P--VP       VN--N---I---P--VP

CONTEXTUAL

Geography                I--->                   <---I                   <---I
Demography               I                       <---I                   <---I
History                  I--->                   <------I            <------I
International             I                           I--->           <------I
Political System         I------>             <------I                <------I
Intermediary Org.:
  -Labor unions      <---I                       <---I                <------I
  -Students             I--->                        I--->                I
  -Business groups       I--->             <------I                       I
  -Professionals         I                       I                        I
  -Church                I                       I                        I
Mass Media               I------>                <---I                <------I
Armed Forces             I------>            <------I                 <------I
Socio-Econ.cond.         I                           I----->              I------>

OPERATIONAL

Events:
  -Trigger               I--->                       I                -- ---I--- --
  -Time Frame            I--->                   <---I                -- ---I--- --
  -Nature                I--->                   <---I                -- ---I--- --
  -Magnitude             I                           I--->            -- ---I--- --
Action components:
  -Ideology-propaganda   I----->             <------I                 -- ---I--- --
  -Organization          I----->                 <---I                -- ---I--- --
  -Leadership            I----->             <------I                 -- ---I--- --
Strategy and policies:
  -Status quo            I------>                 <---I                -- ---I--- --
  -Revolutionaries       I------>            <------I                 -- ---I--- --
```

LEGEND: (VN) Very Negative (N) Negative (I) Irrelevant (P) Positive (VP) Very Positive

A. Policy Change by Castro

This option is the one advocated by several Latin American presidents and the Government of Spain as the most desirable outcome to avoid a bloodbath in Cuba. It would require Castro to allow the process of elections to be started, restore human rights such as freedom of expression, organization, movement, etc., free political prisoners and open domestic markets to private enterprise, for example, restoring the banished "Free Farmers Markets."

Feasibility. Castro has rejected this option which was initially advocated by some leaders inside the Party, such as Carlos Aldana and Roberto Robaina, during the preparatory stage for the Fourth Party Congress that took place in October 1991. The idea was not approved at the Party Congress. Aldana has publicly regretted his initiative and praised the wisdom of Castro in rejecting Glasnost and Perestroika. Castro's argument was that such a weakening of socialism would be the beginning of the end of the system. Cuban propaganda hammers on what is happening in the former Soviet Bloc as examples of how disastrous the change would be: unemployment, inflation, collapse of law and order, etc. There is very little chance that such a policy change would take place. Therefore its feasibility is very low.

Political Climate. Needless to say, this change is unacceptable to the Cuban opposition in exile and many inside Cuba who have endured Castro's despotism, although it has been encouraged by several prominent dissidents. Therefore, it is unlikely such an option will obtain legitimacy. For that reason, it is also unlikely it could lead to the normalization of relations with the United States, although the pressure to do so would increase very significantly, since the last obstacle for the U.S. ending the isolation of Cuba would have disappeared. Latin America and Western Europe would certainly welcome it. Under such circumstances, obtaining international acceptance is doubtful.

This outcome could create an orderly climate for the transition, such as has been the case in Chile and some of the Eastern European countries, and was the great accomplishment of Franco in Spain. Unpleasant as it is in terms of one's personal feelings, it could be the less bloody of the transition outcomes, would enjoy the support of the repressive apparatus of the state and provide a coherent political leadership for the necessary economic decisionmaking, although it is doubtful Castro would accept the dissipation of central authority unavoidable in a move towards political liberalization and a market-based economy.

B. Castro's Removal Without a Conspiracy

This outcome could occur as the result of the actions of a lone assassin escaping Castro's extraordinary security or due to natural death.

Feasibility. This is one of the most difficult outcomes to analyze, since nobody can predict when or how they may occur, depending as they do on the will of an individual to risk his life or on "Mother Nature." But indeed it is a feasible outcome no matter its unpredictability.

Political climate. Such an event would lead initially to a transition long planned by Castro himself, since for quite some time Raúl Castro has been the designated heir. The change in the Constitution allowing Castro to declare a state of emergency and assume even more powers than he has at present addresses such a situation. However, Raúl lacks Fidel's charisma and would be forced to rule in some collegiate form. Once the opening starts, he will be less likely than Fidel to have enough control to provide a stable climate for the transition, although he is known to have been an advocate of liberalization and not totally antagonistic to Glasnost and Perestroika. Challenges to the new order would come from dissidents, labor unions, displaced party leaders and the many officers within MINFAR, and particularly MININT, who have contempt for Raúl. The possibility of attaining legitimacy will be very low.

Externally, the Cuban opposition in exile will be as opposed to normalization of U.S. relations as if Fidel stays in power. However, U.S. domestic public opinion and economic interests are likely to be unwilling to accompany the exile community on this position. For Latin America and Western Europe the change will be acceptable, subject perhaps to conditions on restoration of democracy and respect for human rights. In other words, obtaining international acceptance is doubtful.

Regardless of what the U.S. and the foreign community do, turbulence is a certainty under this outcome and civil war or a coup d'etat could be a possibility. The control of the repressive capacity of the state is likely to be challenged. Under such conditions, the government is likely to be unstable and therefore, the climate for economic policy formulation could be doubtful.

C. A Coup d'Etat

Despite the measures taken by Castro to make this outcome very difficult, such as rotation of commanders, severe intelligence monitoring within the armed forces, limited distribution of ammunition to units and even separate armies leading to a dispersion of control of troops, the overall deterioration of the internal situation does not permit this outcome to be ruled out completely.

Feasibility. For this to occur, it would be necessary for a consensus to develop among military commanders, and perhaps some political leaders, that Castro's continuation in power is a bigger threat to the interests of the armed forces than his removal from power. Perhaps an event that gets out of control and forces the army to make a hard choice, such as having to repress a popular demonstration because of increased police abuses under the SUVP or a protest by farmers who are now being threatened with having their land taken away if they don't sell their products to Government "acopio" agencies, may be the trigger event for the coup.

At present, the high profile of exile leaders projecting themselves as "protagonists" in a post-Castro government, with their image within Cuba of being intent on a policy of restoration of the past and revenge, is the greatest asset Castro has to discourage this outcome. Castro is openly playing this theme in his domestic propaganda along with the threat of a U.S. invasion. Unfortunately, that is the biggest flaw in the present U.S policy towards Cuba. The Administration has issued low-profile statements to reassure those potential plotters inside the regime that, if they move, we will accept and support them. At the same time, the Bush Administration provides a high-profile support for right-wing elements in the exile community which undermine the credibility of the low profile statements and convey the image of an intention to try to impose on Cuba a leadership to the liking of the U.S. This is an area in which the outcome of the U.S. elections could change the situation radically. However, that will require that a Clinton Administration include among its promised changes that of freeing U.S. foreign policy towards Cuba from the present PAC-financed right-wing stranglehold.

Political climate. Such an option could involve so many variations that it is hard to anticipate what climate will result. If the consensus is broad within the armed forces and the commanders of the three armies are in, it would lead to a transition similar to the ones that have taken place all over the Eastern Bloc in which the armed forces provided a factor of stability as the communist regimes were dismantled. Legitimacy would be reinforced if the National Assembly of Popular Power has been elected by direct vote as is proposed and somehow emerges during the transition as a forum for the required institutional changes. If previous experiences are an indication, once the dominant figure of Castro is out of the scene, a collegiate body such as the Assembly is likely to attempt to assert its constitutional powers. More so if it is vested with the legitimacy of being elected by direct vote.

Once the coup occurs, however, it will immediately take a life of its own. The desire of the exile community rank and file to help their relatives in Cuba is likely to override the political ambitions of their more conservative leaders and support for an opening towards Cuba is likely to prevail, vesting the regime with a semblance of legitimacy. Pressure on the U.S. from all sources, in particular Latin America and Western Europe, will be such that it is hard to visualize a long delay in lifting the embargo, although normalization of relations may take a little longer. In other words, the possibility of obtaining international acceptance is high.

Control of repressive capacity would depend on how broad is popular acceptance of the emerging leadership. By definition, if they are capable of taking power, it must be assumed they will have control of substantial forces. If that situation obtains, it would be the most favorable climate for reconstruction and the formulation of economic policy. However, if there is a split between a significant number of diehard Castro loyalists and the plotters, then there could be a civil war and the conditions of turbulence and instability would make control of repressive capacity doubtful. As a consequence, the formulation of sound economic policy for reconstruction would be equally doubtful. Has anyone heard of any investments, foreign or domestic, in Yugoslavia or Armenia?

D. A Popular Explosion

This would be the most violent of the outcomes, since it would mean that the revolutionary propensity bottled-up by Castro's repression reached a point that it exceeded the repressive capacity of the state, with the likely outcome being a disintegration of the regime and the armed forces, as well as a total breakdown of law and order.

Feasibility. The more Castro delays his departure or setting the machinery for an orderly transfer of power, the more likely that the armed forces will become discredited as happened to the army under Batista in Cuba 1958 or the *Guardia Nacional* under Somoza in Nicaragua, particularly if they become associated with repression.

The Cuban armed forces are the most prestigious institution of the revolutionary regime. Millions of Cubans have served in the military and the success of "internationalism" has been a source of national self-importance and pride. The professionalization of the armed forces and their external projection spared them the repressive role that has so discredited the armed forces in Latin America. However, after the trial of General Ochoa they are being dragged into internal repression. First, with the takeover of the MININT by Raúl Castro's protege General Abelardo Colomé and them with the appointment of General Sixto Batista to oversee the Committees for the Defense of the Revolution.

The increased disaffection of the population has led to the creation of the SUVP and the rapid response battalions. It is not impossible to visualize a situation of significant disturbances sometime in the future. Government measures are a clear indication that the regime anticipates this. If that happens, there are two choices for the armed forces, to repress brutally in a bloodbath or to refuse to do so and rebel instead. The future options for Cuba will be decided at that crucial moment. That is why it is so important and urgent for those who may face such a dilemma to have a clear alternative reassuring them that they will be accepted by the exile community and the U.S.

Political climate. Popular explosions usually lead to fragmentation of authority and chaos. The divisions of the exile community and the dissident movement within the island is a good indication of what will be the situation under this outcome. The more violent the transition, the less likely that there will be a central authority having legitimacy, international recognition, control of repressive capacity and enough political cohesion to take the decisions required to bring about an orderly transition and create a climate conducive to whatever economic policy is more attractive for the reconstruction. It does not matter if it is the shock treatment or the gradualist approach. Either one requires a government in charge capable of discharging its functions. Under mob rule that is not possible. On the other hand, this option could trigger either a coup d'etat or a U.S. intervention.

E. A U.S. Intervention

This outcome could result either from chaos inside Cuba or from a deliberate provocation by Castro. It would be a historical disaster for both countries. At the time of the Bay of Pigs, the wisest decision made by President Kennedy, after making the great mistake of buying the plan presented to him for the operation, was to refuse to be dragged into an intervention. There are many who do not share this viewpoint and argue that merely an air strike would have been enough. However, the death and destruction an intervention would have brought to Cuba would have been very high, since resistance would have been intense even from revolutionaries critical of Castro. And by crushing the high Cuban nationalist expectations prevailing at the time, it would have generated a wave of resentment that would still be haunting us.

Feasibility. Fortunately, there is only a remote possibility this could happen. There are some elements within the U.S. military who believe this option should be considered, particularly now that there is no threat of a Soviet reaction escalating to a nuclear conflict. This is reinforced by influential groups in the exile community who downplay the nationalist feelings aroused by Castro as a temporary thing that is being discredited by the failure of the regime. So far, this position has failed to elicit support, but could gain acceptance if there is chaos and bloodshed in Cuba or Castro decides to end his regime, once he becomes convinced there is no hope for him, with a final provocation against his hated enemy the U.S.

Political climate. The legitimacy of the resulting regime would be highly questionable, although there is no doubt that there will a percentage of people who, out of disillusionment with the experience of self-rule in Cuba with Machado, Batista and now Castro, or out of sheer opportunism, would support it. This is a small minority, probably with more advocates among those in exile than among those inside Cuba. As to international acceptance, Latin America cannot and will not do anything, and much less Western Europe, except for a few lofty "deplore" and "encourage" resolutions at the OAS and the UN. But the resulting regime will have more difficulty in gaining international acceptance than the post-invasion government in Panama which, after all, had won an election.

Control of repressive forces would be ensured by the American presence, but a constant resistance is highly likely to be faced. Cuba has crossed thresholds in its historical evolution as an independent nation that many people, in particular among the young, are unlikely to abandon in exchange for material well being. Nationalism is the most powerful force today in the world. Current events show clearly that people are more likely to die for the right to be of their nation, region, race or culture than for the right to consume material goods, even if they like to have them. The experience of the Soviet Bloc is a dramatic reminder of the pervasiveness and intensity of nationalism. To ignore it in Cuba would be foolish and tragic.

The burden of reconstruction would be on the U.S. under this outcome and, therefore, the policy will be formulated outside Cuba as happened under the American occupation at the beginning of the century. Under those conditions, what the Cuban government will decide or how coherent its policy is would be irrelevant.

F. Summary Evaluation of Political Climates

The above brief review of the various alternative outcomes to the Cuban dilemma can be summarized for purposes of comparison in a table showing for each outcome considered how it would meet the criteria set for facilitating reconstruction and economic policymaking. For each criterion, the various alternatives are rated in terms of whether their chances of meeting them is very low, low, doubtful or high. Keep in mind that this table does not address the issue of feasibility of each outcome. However, it is revealing that none of the outcomes is totally favorable in the resulting comparison. This reflects the unfortunate reality facing us and may explain in some way why Castro is able to continue in power: no clear alternative has emerged yet capable of reconciling the diverse forces involved in the Cuban situation.

EVALUATION OF ALTERNATIVE OUTCOMES

Alternative Outcomes	Political Legitimacy	International Acceptance	Control and Law Enforcement	Economic Policies
Castro Policy change	Very Low	Doubtful	High	High
Castro out - Raúl in	Very Low	Doubtful	Doubtful	Doubtful
A Coup d' Etat	High-doubtful	High	High-doubtful	High-doubtful
A popular explosion	Very low	Very low	Very low	Very low
A U.S. intervention	Very low	Doubtful	High-Doubtful	High

As far as economic policymaking, the one outcome offering the best mix of evaluations is the coup d'etat. It seems to offer the optimum combination of decisionmaking, control of repressive capacity, potential legitimacy for the transition and international acceptance. At the other end of the spectrum, a popular explosion leading to chaos and anarchy would provide the worst climate for everything. The continuation of Castro in power would create a favorable climate for decisionmaking, since Castro would control the decisions himself, were he to decide to change policy. This is unlikely to happen, however, because Castro himself has ruled it out in no uncertain terms. Besides, this outcome is unlikely to generate legitimacy or international acceptance. Raúl Castro replacing his brother would be an unworkable outcome because his lack of charisma would drift into a doubtful control of repressive capacity and decisionmaking, with a very low possibility of attaining legitimacy and doubtful international acceptance. Finally, under the U.S. intervention outcome, economic decisionmaking is likely to have a high degree of cohesiveness, although its direction may depend on the Administration in power at the time. The evaluation of this outcome is mixed on the other factors. But legitimacy would be very low and international acceptance will be doubtful, particularly in Latin America. An apocalyptic ending seems to appeal to Castro and should not be ruled out. Were he to succeed, it would be the last sacrifice of the Cuban people for the sake of Castro's personal ambition for glory and a place in history.

CUBAN-OWNED ENTERPRISES IN THE UNITED STATES, 1982 and 1987

Irma T. de Alonso
Jorge Salazar-Carrillo

Introduction

Just 30 years ago only a small minority of Cubans owned and operated their own businesses in the United States. In spite of widespread obstacles and risks, since that time an increasing number of Cubans decided to start their own businesses, thus taking advantage of the background as entrepreneurs they had acquired in Cuba. As well, in the more recent past significant social, political, and economic changes have created more opportunities for Cubans, thus giving them greater acceptance in the business world. By 1982, 4.1 percent of all Cuban-Americans were entrepreneurs. By 1987, their relative share had increased to 6.1 percent, which exceeded the share of all Americans, and was slightly less than that of Japanese-Americans, which was 6.6 percent.

Using statistics furnished by the Bureau of the Census it is possible to outline the progress of Cuban-Americans in the business sector in the U.S. These statistics correspond to the Economic Censuses, Surveys of Minority-Owned Business Enterprises, which have been conducted every five years, on a regular basis, since 1972. It is the purpose of this paper to undertake comparisons for Cuban-owned businesses, among those Hispanic-owned, utilizing data from the last two surveys, conducted in 1982 and 1987.

I.   General Characteristics

The relevant census data are divided into two main classifications: (1) data for all firms, which includes the total number of firms, and the value of total sales and receipts, and (2) data for firms with paid employees, which in addition to the number of firms and value of sales and receipts, include data for number of employees and annual payroll.

A.   Data for all firms

From 1982 to 1987, the growth of Hispanic-owned firms has been spectacular. The total number of firms increased from 248,141 to 422,373, representing a 70 percent expansion, or an average annual growth rate of 11.2 percent. For the same time period, total sales and receipts were equally impressive increasing from $15.0 billion to $24.7 billion, depicting a 65.1 percent change, or an average annual growth rate of 10.6 percent.

Table I provides information for all firms of the most important minority owned businesses in the U.S., for both 1982 and 1987. The number of Cuban-owned firms increased from 36,631 in 1982 to 61,470 in 1987, which represents a 67.8 percent change, or an average growth rate of 10.9 percent per year. At the same time, their sales and gross receipts increased from $2.15 billion to $5.48 billion, thus representing a 155 percentage change. These figures are more revealing when Cubans are compared to other Hispanic groups who have been in the U.S. for a much longer period than 30 years, as is the case of Mexicans and Puerto Ricans. This is even more impressive, when the population of these groups are taken into consideration. The census data for the U.S. in 1990 confirm a Hispanic population of 21.9 million. Among this total, the Mexican group was the most important, given that 61.2 percent of the Hispanic population belonged to this group, while Puerto Ricans were 12.1 percent, and Cubans were only 4.8 percent of this group. This information gives a ratio of number of firms per person of 0.035 for Cubans, while it is 0.011 for Mexicans, and 0.006 for Puerto Ricans. In terms of sales and receipts, the difference in the figures per capita are even more noticeable: sales per person are equal to $2,040 for Cubans, $536 for Mexicans, and $250 for Puerto Ricans.

Hispanic-owned enterprises had a slight growth in gross revenues during this period (Table II). In 1982, 80.9 percent of all Hispanic-owned firms grossed less than $50,000, while only 10.4 percent grossed over $100,000. Five years later, 80.7 percent had revenues under $50,000 while 10.7 percent had revenues over $100,000. Even though the mode of the distribution of receipts was in the "less than $5,000" bracket for both years, the median of the distribution had grown from $10,830 in 1982 to $12,560 in 1987, reflecting an increase of 16 percent in the five years, or an average growth rate of about 3.0 percent per year.

The number of Hispanic-owned businesses varies from state to state. They are more prevalent in California (31.3%) and Texas (22.4%), in Florida (15.2%), and in New York (6.6%).

Cuban-owned firms are more predominant in the state of Florida where close to 70 percent of them are located. It is startling to find that Cuban-owned firms are also significant, either in terms of number of firms and/or value of sales and receipts in the states of Connecticut, Georgia, Massachusetts, New Hampshire, New Jersey, and North Carolina (Table III).

The number of Hispanic-owned firms in the state of Florida increased from 32,404 in 1982 to 64,413 in 1987, which is almost a two-fold increase. As percent of total Hispanic-owned firms in the United States, Florida's share increased from 13.8 percent in 1982 to 15.2 percent in 1987. Sales and receipts of them increased from $1.7 billion to $4.9 billion, which represented a 186 percent change in the five year period. In terms of all Hispanic-owned firms in the United States, Florida's share of total sales and receipts increased from 14.7 percent to 20.0 percent. These changes were accompanied by corresponding impressive growth in employment and payroll.

In Florida, Cuban-owned firms increased from 24,570 in 1982 to 42,162 in 1987, which is a 72 percentage change. In 1982, 74 percent of all Hispanic-owned firms were located in the Miami-Hialeah SMSA, and 85 percent of all Cuban-owned firms were located in this area as well. By 1987, the Miami-Hialeah Primary Metropolitan Statistical Area (PMSA) retained 74 of all Hispanic-owned firms but only 73 percent of all Cuban-owned firms. However, in 1982 Cuban-owned firms generated 52 percent of all sales and receipts, and by 1987, despite their lower share, they managed to accomplish 76 percent of all sales and receipts.

It is also revealing to find out that Cuban-owned businesses are of notable importance in other Metropolitan Statistical Areas (MSA) with 100 or more Hispanic-owned firms. The data for 1987 is presented in Table IV. Some of the most noticeable are the MSA of Fort Lauderdale, Jacksonville, Jersey City, Melbourne, Naples, Tampa, and West Palm Beach, where close to half of the Hispanic-owned businesses belong to Cubans.

B.   Firms with paid employees

From 1982 to 1987, Hispanic-owned firms with paid employees increased from 39,272 to 82,908, which is a 107.7 percent increment, while their sales and receipts expanded from $10.6 billion to $17.7 billion, revealing a 66.4 percent change (Table V). Employment in these firms increased from 189,636 to 264,846 employees, which was a 40 percent change. The annual payroll of these firms increased from $1,750 million to $3,243 million, representing an 85.3 percent change, or an average annual growth rate of 13.1 percent.

The total number of Cuban-owned firms with paid employees more than doubled increasing from 5,215 to 10,768, while their sales tripled, increasing from $1.4 billion to $4.2 billion (Table V). Likewise, the number of employees more than doubled, increasing from 22,639 to 47,266, while the annual payroll more than tripled escalating from $200.5 million to $638.5 million. Cuban-owned firms lead the other Hispanic-owned firms in terms of their growth in total sales and receipts and in the creation of employment.

In 1982, Cuban-owned firms created 59 percent of all employment in Hispanic-owned firms in the state of Florida, and by 1987 this share had increased to 72 percent. Annual payroll followed a similar path, increasing from $136.1 million in 1982 to $417.9 million in 1987, corresponding to 52 percent and 74 percent, of total annual payroll of Hispanic-owned firms in the State of Florida, respectively.

The size of employment in Hispanic-owned firms decreased from 1982 to 1987 (Table VI). The typical business employed 4.75 employees in 1982 and the size was reduced to 3.19 employees in 1987. Cuban-owned firms, on the other hand, had a slight increase, expanding the size of the firm from 4.34 employees in 1982 to 4.39 employees in 1987.

II.   Type of Businesses

Another important feature of Hispanic-owned businesses is the nature of the business endeavor (Table VII). In 1982, 39.6 percent of all Hispanic-owned firms were in the service sector, and 23.5 percent were in retail trade. By 1987, the relative share of the service sector had increased to 43.6 percent, while the relative share of retail trade had decreased to 16.6 percent. In the meantime, the relative importance of firms in construction increased from 10.8 percent to 13.1 percent. These three sectors were also the most vital in generating employment and income, as represented by the level of their annual payroll.

In both 1982 and 1987, 44 percent of all Cuban-owned firms were in the service sector. The relative importance of retail trade decreased from 18.4 percent in 1982 to 14.5 percent in 1987, while that of construction increased from 8.7 percent to 11.9 percent, thus following the same pattern of all Hispanic-owned firms in the United States.

Corresponding to national trends, Florida's Hispanic-owned firms (Table VIII) have been predominantly in the service sector (44.7 % in 1982 and 43.9% in 1987), followed distantly by retail trade (15.8% in 1982 and 12.5% in 1987) and construction (9.5% in 1982 and 12.8% in 1987).

In the Miami-Hialeah SMSA, the service sector predominated as well, with 45 percent of the firms in 1982 and 43 percent in 1987. The relative importance of retail trade decreased from 15 percent to 12 percent, while that of construction increased from 10 percent to 13 percent, for the same period.

Within the service sector some transformations have taken place during the period of analysis. In 1982, most of the Hispanic-owned businesses were in the personal services area, which includes beauty shops, barber shops, and laundry services. At that time most of Cuban-owned businesses were in the health services area, which includes offices of physicians, dentists, and other health practitioners. By 1987, Hispanic businesses in general, and Cuban businesses in particular, have started to provide services to the business sector in a predominant way, while the importance of personal and health services has diminished. The services to business sector include, among others, data processing and computer related services, where high growth opportunities exist.

III.   The Future

If it is assumed that the 11.2 percent annual growth rate of Hispanic-owned businesses continued for the subsequent five years, it could be expected that by 1992 the estimated number of these firms have grown from 422,323 in 1987 to nearly 718,000. If the annual growth rate of 10.9 percent of Cuban-owned businesses was maintained for the succeeding five years, it could be approximated that by 1992 the estimated number of these enterprises have expanded from 61,470 in 1987 to around 103,000. From a business perspective this will have significant impact. Cuban entrepreneurs, among Hispanics, will no longer be a negligible minority. Their contribution is not measured only by the number of firms, but by their significant growth in sales, employment, and income.

Table 1. United States: Total Number of Hispanic-Owned Firms and Total Sales and Receipts, by Principal Minority Groups, 1982 and 1987

Concept	Total	Cuban	Mexican	Puerto Rican
1982				
Number of Firms	248,141	36,631	143,177	14,690
Sales & Receipts ($mill)	14,976	2,149	7,177	663
1987				
Number of Firms	422,373	61,470	229,706	27,697
Sales & Receipts ($mill)	24,732	5,482	11,837	1,448
Percent Change 1982-1987				
Number of Firms	70.2	67.8	60.4	88.5
Sales & Receipts ($mill)	65.1	155.1	64.9	118.4

Source: U.S. Department of Commerce, Bureau of the Census, *1982 Survey of Minority-Owned Business Enterprises, Minority-Owned Businesses, Hispanics* and *1987, Economic Censuses, Survey of Minority-Owned Business Enterprises, Hispanics.*

Table 2. United States: Size of Hispanic-Owned Firms by Receipts, 1982 and 1987

Size	1982	1987
Less than $5,000	83,694	120,717
$5,000 to $9,999	37,638	74,711
$10,000 to $24,999	49,359	92,386
$25,000 to $49,000	30,042	52,737
$50,000 to $99,999	21,776	36,589
$100,000 to $199,999	13,847	23,711
$200,000 to $249,999	3,015	5,105
$250,000 to $499,999	5,173	9,581
$500,000 to $999,999	2,161	4,292
$1,000,000 or more	1,435	2,544
Total	248,141	422,373

Source: *Ibid*.

Table 3. United States: Cuban-Owned Firms in Selected States, 1987

State	Firms	% of total Hispanic firms	Sales & Receipts ($mill)	% of Total Sales & Receipts
Connecticut	335	15.0	58.7	33.4
Florida	42,162	65.4	3,760.8	76.0
Georgia	414	21.4	51.7	35.6
Massachussetts	382	14.5	44.8	25.8
New Hampshire	38	15.6	4.0	30.8
New Jersey	4,188	34.6	410.8	45.5
North Carolina	148	16.1	42.7	46.0

Source: *Ibid*.

Table 4. U.S.: Cuban-Owned Firms in Selected Metropolitan Statistical Areas (MSA), 1987

MSA	Number of Cuban-owned firms	% of Cuban-owned firms as % of Hispanic firms
Atlanta, GA	322	22.6
Ft.Lauderdale-Hollywood-Pompano Beach, FL	1,704	47.7
Ft. Myers-Cape Coral, FL	67	28.2
Ft. Pierre, FL	40	26.0
Gainesville, FL	61	35.5
Jacksonville, FL	176	39.6
Jersey City, NJ	1,998	50.6
Lakeland-Winter Haven, FL	133	32.6
Melbourne-Titusville-Palm Bay, FL	155	32.6
Miami-Hialeah, FL	34,771	72.9
Middlesex-Somerset-Hunterdon, NJ	256	24.6
Naples, FL	287	47.6
Newark, NJ	932	32.4
Ocala, FL	64	33.9
Orlando, FL	733	37.7
Pensacola, FL	51	33.8
Sarasota, FL	82	31.7
Tampa-St.Petersburg-Clearwater, FL	1,986	44.0
West Palm Beach-Boca Raton-Delray Beach, FL	1,012	54.1

Source: *Ibid.*

**Table 5. U.S.: Hispanic-Owned Firms with Paid Employees,
1982 and 1987**

Category	Total	Cuban	Mexican	Puerto-Rican
1982:				
Number of Firms	39,917	5,215	24,110	1,700
Sales & Receipts ($mill)	10,653	1,396	4,847	332
Employees	189,636	22,639	106,712	5,528
Payroll ($mill)	1,750	201	871	50
1987:				
Number of Firms	82,908	10,768	49,078	4,629
Sales & Receipts ($mill)	17,729	4,227	8,404	904
Employees	264,846	47,266	148,008	13,231
Payroll ($mill)	3,243	638	1,687	179
Percent Change 1982-1987				
Number of Firms	107.7	106.5	103.6	172.3
Sales & Receipts	66.4	202.8	73.4	172.3
Employess	39.7	108.8	38.7	139.3
Payroll	85.3	217.4	93.7	258.0

Source: *Ibid*.

Table 6. U.S.: Employment Size of Hispanic-Owned Firms,
1982 and 1987

Size	1982	1987
Number of firms with		
no paid employees	208,223	339,465
paid employess	39,917	82,908
Percentage distribution of firms with paid employees:		
less than 4	76.5	83.2
5 - 9	13.6	9.9
10 - 19	6.3	4.4
20 - 49	2.8	1.9
50 - 99	0.5	0.4
over 100	0.2	0.2

Source: *Ibid.*

Table 7. U.S.: Number of Hispanic-Owned and Cuban-Owned Firms,
by Industrial Origin, 1982 and 1987

Sectors	1982		1987	
	Hispanic	Cuban	Hispanic	Cuban
Agriculture	2.8	2.0	3.9	2.5
Construction	10.8	8.7	13.1	11.9
Manufacturing	1.8	1.6	2.6	2.5
Transportation & Public Utilities	5.3	5.5	6.4	7.4
Wholesale Trade	1.5	2.8	2.4	3.9
Retail Trade	23.5	18.4	16.6	14.5
Finance, Insurance & Real Estate	4.5	5.8	5.2	6.6
Services	39.6	44.1	43.6	44.0
Not classified	10.0	10.8	5.9	6.6

Source: *Ibid.*

**Table 8. Florida: Hispanic-Owned Firms and Sales and Receipts,
by Industry, 1982 and 1987**
(percentage distribution)

	1982		1987	
Sector	Firms	Sales	Firms	Sales
Agriculture	2.7	0.8	3.4	1.9
Construction	9.5	5.6	12.8	13.0
Manufacturing	1.3	14.7	2.3	5.4
Transportation & Public Utilities	6.0	3.6	7.6	5.4
Wholesale Trade	3.2	27.9	4.0	17.4
Retail Trade	15.8	21.3	12.5	27.1
Finance, Insurance & Real Estate	6.9	3.5	6.6	5.6
Services	44.8	19.1	43.9	21.7
Not classified	9.8	3.3	7.0	2.6
Total, All Industries	33,516	$2,757,332	64,413	$4,949,151

Source: *Ibid.*

ÉTICA EMPRESARIAL Y EL DESARROLLO INTEGRAL DE CUBA

Alberto Martínez Piedra

Mucho se oye hablar acerca del sistema económico que ha de prevalecer en Cuba después de la caída del régimen marxista-leninista impuesto por Castro en el fatídico año de 1959. Con el fracaso económico del socialismo y las transformaciones políticas que están ocurriendo en la que fue la Unión Soviética y los países de Europa del Este, la caída del marxismo "a lo Castro" parece hacerse inevitable. El pueblo cubano, después de más de treinta años de dictadura castrista y sometido a los rigores de un desprestigiado sistema marxista-leninista, al fin vislumbra y espera con ansiedad la posibilidad de un cambio que le traiga la tan merecida libertad. Es de esperar que estos vaticinios se cumplan y Cuba pueda de nuevo formar parte del concierto de naciones libres del mundo.

Con toda probabilidad, la caída del régimen marxista-leninista en Cuba traerá consigo cambios sustanciales en el país que conducirán no solo al restablecimiento de un régimen constitucional democrático sino también al establecimiento de un sistema económico de libre empresa.[1] La transformación de un sistema totalitario marxista en uno de libertades políticas y económicas va a necesitar cambios drásticos de difícil implementación y de aun más difícil aceptación, al menos por aquellos sectores del país que se vieran adversamente afectados por dichos cambios.

Todo cambio económico de por sí implica riesgo e incertidumbre y, más aun, si se lleva a efecto dentro de un sistema de libertades democráticas que, a diferencia de los regímenes que imponen su voluntad por la fuerza, rechaza el uso de medidas represivas y coacción estatal y quiere conservar un mínimo de respetabilidad ante la opinión publica mundial. En el caso de Cuba los cambios económicos que será necesario introducir se tendrán que hacer dentro de un régimen de libertades ciudadanas desconocidas por el pueblo cubano durante más de tres décadas. Paradójicamente, este hecho, en sí favorable, pudiera prolongar y aun torpedear el período de transición y retrasar la recuperación política y económica del país. Tal parecería como si la necesidad del cambio unida a la euforia de la libertad nuevamente adquirida serían suficientes para rápidamente llevar a efecto las transformaciones estructurales pertinentes y garantizar un futuro de paz y prosperidad para el pueblo cubano. Sin embargo, esto no necesariamente tiene que ser cierto a menos que el pueblo cubano utilice su nueva libertad en forma responsable y con miras al bien común.

Damos por sentado que a la caída del régimen castrista se establecerá en lo político una democracia constitucional y en lo económico un sistema de libre empresa que reconozca el papel positivo que desempeñan la propiedad privada de los bienes de la producción, la libre concurrencia, los precios como reguladores de la oferta y la demanda y la iniciativa personal.

Creemos que muy pocos de los que han sufrido o presenciado los efectos negativos de la revolución castrista estén en desacuerdo con estos objetivos. Sin embargo, dentro de un marco de libertad económica puede haber diversas variantes y es precisamente en esta area "gris" donde pueden surgir serios y graves conflictos que puedan poner en crisis no solo el período de transición sino todo el proceso de recuperación económica y, a la larga, la misma libertad que tantas lágrimas está costando al pueblo de Cuba.

---

[1]Para los efectos de este trabajo usaremos indistintamente los términos sistema de libre empresa, liberalismo económico y capitalismo.

Este trabajo se limitará a señalar la importancia del período de transición para el futuro político y económico de Cuba y a identificar las dos variables que, en nuestra opinión, van a ser cruciales para que dicho período conduzca no solo a la recuperación económica del país sino que también se produzca al menor costo social posible. La primera se refiere al desarrollo de una clase empresarial capacitada y responsable y la segunda a la necesidad de reconocer que la empresa económica consiste de una comunidad de personas dentro de la cual el factor laboral desempeña un papel preponderante.

El hecho de que en este trabajo no examinemos más a fondo otros factores económicos —el capital, la tecnología, los recursos naturales, etc.— así como otras variables relacionadas con el sistema legal y el ambiente cultural, no quiere decir que no sean también necesarios para un desarrollo económico equilibrado e integral de la isla. La razón por la cual se han escogido las variables señaladas se debe sencillamente al hecho de que ambas están íntimamente ligadas a la persona humana —ya sea empresario o trabajador— que está dotada de libertad y que, por consiguiente, no puede desconectarse de la ética. Es precisamente en esta area de decisiones libres donde la economía, a pesar de ser una ciencia autónoma, no puede desligarse de la ética. Ambas se complementan.

I. El período de transición

El período de transición en Cuba va a ser decisivo para el futuro político y económico del país. Después de décadas de un totalitarismo marxista no van a ser fáciles los cambios que será necesario implantar y que indudablemente no van a agradar a todos los sectores de la sociedad.[2]

La implantación de un sistema de libre empresa supone la existencia de un sistema legal y contractual que permita su funcionamiento efectivo. También supone el respeto a la propiedad privada y la aceptación de un sistema fiscal y monetario que no entorpezca el libre juego de la oferta y la demanda dentro de un régimen de competencia legal. Pero, ante todo, como muy bien dijo hace muchos años el ya fallecido economista alemán Wilhelm Roepke, es necesario que nos que nos percatemos de que si el sistema de libre empresa ha de perdurar necesita de una sólida base moral en que apoyarse.[3] En Cuba, como en otros países que también han sufrido las consecuencias del marxismo, la transformación del colectivismo centralizado de Castro en un sistema de libre empresa tiene que ir acompañado de un alto grado de responsabilidad y de comprensión por parte del gobierno, de la clase empresarial y del pueblo cubano en general si los cambios se han de realizar con un mínimo de conflicto y las nuevas libertades han de perdurar.[4]

Mucho se podría especular acerca de cual debería ser la política económica de un futuro gobierno democrático que acepte los principios básicos sobre los cuales descansa un sistema libre de empresa, pero ello nos alejaría demasiado del tema de esta presentación. Sin embargo, sí haremos unos breves comentarios que consideramos pertinentes.

---

[2]Esto se ha comprobado en Europa del Este donde el proceso de privatización y la liberalización de los precios esta ocasionando serios problemas. Ver "Key Russian Economic Figures Plunge, Overall Production Falls in First Half of Year: Grain Estimates Cut". *Washington Post*, July 21,1992.

[3]Roepke, Wilhelm, *A Humane Economy*, Chicago: Henry Regnery Company, 1960. p. 124.

[4]Los cubanos deben poner mucha atención a los múltiples problemas que están surgiendo en Europa del Este después de la cabida del marxismo y así hacer todo lo posible para que no se vuelvan a repetir los errores que posiblemente se hayan cometido en el período de transición de un colectivismo centralizado a un sistema de mayores libertades económicas.

Las autoridades encargadas de la nueva política económica tendrán que enfrentarse con múltiples y serios problemas y tomar decisiones muchas de las cuales no estarán exentas de contenido moral. Por ejemplo, es muy probable que el reto más grave que se le va a presentar al nuevo gobierno será el de como alimentar a la población cubana después del ineficiente sistema alimenticio castrista, basado en el sistema de "acopio" soviético cuya aplicación fue y sigue siendo en gran medida responsable de las escaseces que actualmente esta sufriendo el pueblo de Cuba.[5]

Es innegable que la aceptación de un sistema de libre empresa conlleva necesariamente la liberación de los precios. Este es un principio elemental de la economía de mercado. El nuevo gobierno podría optar por una total liberación de los precios y aplicar un *shock treatment* que pusiera fin al sistema de control de precios y subsidios.[6] Desde el punto de vista estrictamente económico es posible que ésta sea la medida más apropiada, pero aquí es precisamente donde pudiera surgir un conflicto entre la economía y la ética. La actuación más acertada desde el punto de vista de una pura teoría económica puede en ciertas ocasiones entrar en conflicto con ciertos principios éticos de más alta prioridad ante los cuales las decisiones económicas tienen que subordinarse.

Lo más probable es que durante la fase inicial del período de transición las autoridades cubanas tendrán que liberar los precios gradualmente y con gran cautela debido, entre otras cosas, a la gran diferencia que se producirá entre los precios de los productos alimenticios (precios subsidiados) y los que resultaran como consecuencia de una total liberación de los mismos (precios de equilibrio). Debido a la subida de los precios que **inevitablemente** tendrá que ocurrir se hará necesario establecer ciertos ajustes o algún tipo de *safety net* que proteja al trabajador pues, de lo contrario, su salario real se vera reducido sustancialmente y su poder adquisitivo se reducirá de tal forma que no podrá adquirir los productos necesarios para el sustento familiar. Una liberación total e indiscriminada de los precios, no acompañada de un sustancial incremento de la productividad que permita una correspondiente subida de salarios, desataría un proceso inflacionario de nefastas consecuencias, cuyas repercusiones políticas y sociales no son difíciles de predecir.[7] Esto no quiere decir que se abandone el objetivo de liberar los precios, algo absolutamente indispensable para el funcionamiento del sistema de libre empresa, sino sencillamente que durante el período de transición, en particular durante su fase inicial, se debe actuar con prudencia, en forma gradual y con un gran sentido de responsabilidad, tanto por parte del gobierno como por parte de los sectores empresarial y laboral.

La liberación de los precios es solo uno de los innumerables problemas que se le van a presentar al nuevo gobierno en la era post castrista. Por ejemplo, las políticas fiscales y monetarias que se necesitara llevar a cabo para reconstruir la economía cubana también serán objeto de serios debates entre los economistas y políticos responsables de los destinos de Cuba. Para aminorar la incertidumbre y los riesgos característicos de todo proceso de cambio, convendrá que el pueblo de Cuba este bien informado sobre la necesidad de dichos cambios y así evitar sorpresas y posibles

---

[5]La desastrosa política agrícola practicada por las autoridades soviéticas durante muchos años está siendo finalmente reconocida por la prensa occidental. Ver "Collective Farming Facing Collapse", *Washington Post*, May 25, 1992.

[6]Mucho se ha discutido acerca de los pros y los contras de la aplicación de un *shock treatment* para acelerar el proceso de recuperación económica en los países que han sufrido las consecuencias del marxismo. En el caso de Cuba hay que evitar que la recuperación se produzca a un costo social elevado y que sean las clases menos privilegiadas las que tengan que absorber la mayor parte del costo. Ver "In Russian Heartland, Post-Reform Life is Bleak", *The Washingon Post*, August 9, 1992.

[7]El gobierno polaco ha tenido que hacerle frente a un descontento general debido a la política de reforma y de austeridad que ha tratado de implantar en el país. Hay una reacción violenta contra las medidas gubernamentales y ya se oye decir que el país lo que necesita es un tercer camino ni capitalismo, ni marxismo. Ver "Stability Eludes Post-Soviet Eastern Europe", *Washington Post*, May 23, 1992.

conflictos en el futuro, pero, quizá sea la clase empresarial, con la cooperación del sector laboral, la que más pueda contribuir al éxito del período de transición y al mismo tiempo sentar las bases de una economía más humana que redunde en beneficio de todos los sectores de la sociedad cubana.

II.   El desarrollo de una clase empresarial capacitada y responsable

No cabe duda que el empresario desempeña un papel clave en proceso de desarrollo económico.   Resultaría redundante enumerar la contribución del empresario al crecimiento económico del mundo occidental durante los últimos doscientos años. Son muchos los economistas que lo han hecho resaltar pero fue el economista Joseph Schumpeter, de la Universidad de Harvard, quien en su libro *Capitalism, Socialism and Democracy* hizo hincapié en lo que él llamó *the entrepreneurial function* como factor decisivo en todo proceso de desarrollo económico.[8] El capitalismo, gracias a la función empresarial (*entrepreneurial function*) y su contribución a la innovación, no solo ha sido el responsable de las altas tasas de crecimiento económico sino que también le ha proporcionado al pueblo en general el más alto nivel de vida que jamás se ha visto en el mundo occidental.

Algunos economistas han puesto como pretexto para una mayor intervención gubernamental y la creación de empresas estatales en los países en vías de desarrollo, el hecho de que los mismos carecen de una clase empresarial competente que sea capaz de contribuir eficazmente al crecimiento económico. Según ellos, el sector privado, carente de una clase empresarial eficiente, no esta capacitado para ser el motor principal del desarrollo.[9] Este argumento, por regla general, carece de validez, pues las estadísticas tienden a demostrar que la mayoría de las empresas industriales establecidas bajo el control estatal en los países en vías de desarrollo han operado a bajos niveles de productividad y a costos de producción extremadamente altos.[10] Creemos que América Latina ofrece suficientes ejemplos de un sector publico ineficiente que en gran parte es responsable de no pocos de los males que hoy en día aquejan a nuestros países hermanos.

El error de los socialistas utópicos y de los socialistas en general es el haber confiado demasiado en ministerios y agencias de planificación centralizada desconociendo el espíritu de innovación de los empresarios individuales. Se olvidan que, como principal organizador y director de la empresa, el *entrepreneur* constituye la fuerza dinámica por excelencia en todo proceso de cambio económico.[11]

Es innegable que el interés personal y la obtención de un beneficio son los dos factores que más influyen en la función creadora —usando una expresión utilizada por el economista Albert Hirshman en su libro *The Strategy of Economic Development*[12]— el hombre de empresa. Si la posibilidad de obtener un beneficio desapareciera o se coartara en forma significativa, cesarían las innovaciones y desaparecería la subjetividad creativa del hombre. Por consiguiente, se estancaría la economía y no habría desarrollo. Juan Pablo II en su encíclica *Sollicitudo Rei Socialis* ha sido muy

---

[8]Schumpeter,Joseph, *Capitalism, Socialism and Democracy*, George Allen & Unwin Ltd., London 1952, p, 83 and 132. Ver también del mismo autor, *The Theory of Economic Development*, Harvard University Press, 1951.

[9]Gunnar Myrdal, *Asian Drama: An Inquiry into the Poverty of Nations*, London, l968.

[10]Bauer P.T., *Dissent on Development*, Harvard University Press, 1972, pp.226-227.

[11]Ver Leibenstein, Harvey, "Allocative Efficiency versus X-Efficiency," *American Economic Review*, June 1966; y del mismo autor "Entrepreneurship and Development," *American Economic Review*, May 1968.

[12]Hirschman, Albert O., *The Strategy of Economic Development*, Yale University Press, 1956, p. l7.

claro en esto al decir que el derecho a la iniciativa económica tan característica del hombre de empresa es un derecho que no solo es importante para el individuo sino también para el bien común. La experiencia nos ha demostrado que la negación de dicho derecho o su limitación en nombre de una supuesta igualdad disminuye o en la practica destruye en forma absoluta el espíritu de iniciativa, es decir la subjetividad *creativa del ciudadano*.[13]

La función primordial de la empresa es producir bienes y servicios en la forma más eficiente posible y en el proceso obtener un beneficio. Al ejercer dicha función, el empresario esta contribuyendo en forma directa al bienestar material de todos los participantes en la producción e indirectamente al bien común de la sociedad; al bienestar material del publico en general. Este es el objetivo formal de todo hombre de empresa. Pero, el empresario, como cualquier otro profesional que quiere tener éxito en su profesión, sería muy tonto si dijera que él solo estaba interesado en obtener un beneficio. Qué pensaríamos de un médico que proclamara abiertamente que a él lo único que le interesa es tener muchos clientes para así ganar mucho dinero. El empresario, como cualquier otro profesional, tiene que ir más allá del aspecto puramente económico de su ocupación si de veras quiere ser un buen profesional. Se da por supuesto que quiera obtener un beneficio así como el médico espera verse remunerado por sus servicios. Pero, el interés personal y la adquisición de un beneficio material no debe ser su única motivación. Si el empresario solo piensa en el beneficio, podría muy bien destruir su capacidad para hacer bien eso mismo que él tiene que hacer de todas formas para obtener una ganancia.

Nadie pone en duda que una adecuada remuneración de los factores de la producción es necesaria para la realización de un buen trabajo. El empresario, por ejemplo, no tiene por qué avergonzarse por obtener un beneficio. Todo lo contrario, es su justa recompensa por su contribución al bienestar de la sociedad. Pero al mismo tiempo, el empresario no puede despreocuparse del bienestar de sus colaboradores en el proceso de la producción. Su motivación no debe limitarse a la producción de bienes y servicios sino que debe ir más allá de la conveniencia, aunque no la excluya.

Una empresa será exitosa cuando existe un buen entendimiento entre los obreros y la administración de la misma. Sin entrar en una polémica sobre los pros y los y los contras de las empresas japonesas, creo es provechoso citar a Aldo Morita, Presidente de la Sony Corporation. Según él: "Ninguna teoría, ni plan, ni política gubernamental hace que una empresa triunfe: eso solo lo puede conseguir la gente. La misión más importante de un gerente japonés es desarrollar una sana relación con sus empleados, crear dentro de la sociedad comercial un sentimiento de familia, la sensación de que sus empleados y directivos comparten el mismo destino". También dijo Morita que "la gente necesita dinero, pero también quiere estar feliz en su trabajo, y orgullosa de él. Por eso, si a un hombre jóven le damos mucha responsabilidad, ese hombre, aún cuando no tenga un cargo jerárquico, creerá que tiene un buen futuro y estará feliz al trabajar con intensidad".[14] Este estado de ánimo, como diría el economista español Rafael Gómez Pérez, es una cuestión ética. Si existe un fundamento ético —independientemente de los otros factores que obviamente son indispensables para la producción— "habrá mejor trabajo, mejor organización, mejor negocio y mayores beneficios. He aquí, por un camino aparentemente insólito, como la ética entra en la

---

[13]Juan Pablo II, <u>Sollicitudo Rei Socialis</u> #15.

[14]Gómez Pérez, Rafael, *Ética Empresarial*, Ediciones Rialp, Madrid, 1990, p. 63.

cuestión de resultados".[15]

La preocupación por mantener buenas relaciones humanas dentro de la empresa para así mejorar el nivel de eficiencia e incrementar los volúmenes de producción es digno de alabanza y constituye un paso de avance significativo sobre el capitalismo *a outrance* del siglo pasado y principios de este siglo.[16] Pero este paso de avance no es suficiente. Hay que llegar a la convicción que la empresa es una comunidad de personas con derechos humanos muy específicos; derechos que van más allá de un simple adelanto material.

III.   La empresa como una comunidad de personas

La empresa debe considerarse como una comunidad de personas en la cual tanto el empresario como el obrero cooperan en un esfuerzo común para producir los bienes y servicios que han de satisfacer las necesidades materiales de la sociedad. En 1983, Juan Pablo II en un discurso dado en Milán al sector empresarial, definió la figura dinámica del hombre de negocios como el organizador del trabajo humano y de los medios de producción para así poder producir los bienes y servicios necesarios para garantizar el bienestar y la prosperidad de la sociedad. Su responsabilidad consiste, continuo el Papa, en crear un espíritu de convivencia entre todos los participantes en el proceso de la producción y al mismo tiempo contribuir al bien común de la sociedad. El Romano Pontífice insistió en que la empresa es una comunidad de personas en la cual todos los participantes contribuyen a la producción.[17]

Hay que rechazar de una vez para siempre la inevitabilidad de la lucha de clases entre el capitalista y el proletariado, tal como insistió Marx. Este concepto de lucha es totalmente falso, ya que negaría la posibilidad de toda coexistencia pacífica entre el capital y el trabajo. La verdad es exactamente la opuesta, ya que debe existir armonía entre los dos, aunque solo sea porque ambos se necesitan mutuamente. Sin un acuerdo mutuo, el buen orden no puede prevalecer en la sociedad y esto no ocurrirá hasta que ambas partes actúen con sentido común y buena voluntad, lo que implica que cada uno de los participantes en la producción rechace la tentación de fomentar exclusivamente su propio interés personal a expensas de los demás y del bien común.

Quizá, uno de los conceptos que más hace falta "humanizar" es la llamada función de la producción. Es bien sabido por todos que la producción de bienes y servicios esta en función de los diversos factores que contribuyen al proceso de la producción.[18] La empresa, como entidad productora por excelencia, puede caracterizarse como una función de la producción en la cual los diversos insumos suelen reducirse a meras entidades cuantificables que son valorizadas de acuerdo con la ley de la productividad marginal. Según este concepto, la remuneración del factor trabajo se determina en forma similar a la de cualquier otro factor de la producción. Por ejemplo, el salario

---

[15]Ibid., p. 63.

[16]Esto no implica una crítica de la importante aportación de los economistas clásicos al éxito del capitalismo. Según ha dicho con gran acierto el economista español Miguel Alfonso Martínez Echevarría: "No se trata de negar la valiosísima aportación que los economistas clásicos hicieron a la ciencia económica en los dos últimos siglos, también en los métodos de cálculo y econometría, sino de descubrir su verdadera potencialidad y sentido". Ver, Miguel Alfonso Martínez Echevarría, "Individualismo Metodológico y Solidaridad", en *Estudios sobre la Encíclica "Sollicitudo Rei Socialis"*, Asociación para el Estudio de la Doctrina Social de la Iglesia, AEDOS, Madrid, 1990, p.236.

[17]Juan Pablo II, *L'Osservatore Romano*, June 20, 1983.

[18]Ver Baumol, William J., *Economic Theory and Operation Analysis*, Prentice Hall, 1965. p. 251-252.

viene determinado por el valor de la productividad física marginal del trabajador.[19]

No pretendemos ni por un momento negar la validez ni la importancia de la función de la producción en el campo de la teoría económica. Ni tampoco la que tiene y seguirá teniendo la ley de la productividad marginal. Todo lo contrario, reconocemos el gran valor de las mismas y el mérito de los economistas clásicos, en particular el de los de la escuela austríaca, al desarrollar el concepto marginal.[20] Pero, por otro lado, también creemos que la ciencia económica no puede llegar a un grado tal de abstracción que se divorcie completamente de otras ciencias sociales y en particular de la ética. Por ejemplo, tratar en el mercado al trabajo humano de la misma manera que se trata al factor capital puede prestarse a serias injusticias ya que "hay una serie de concausas inaccesibles al mecanismo del mercado, pero de gran importancia para los intereses humanos".[21] Habrá ocasiones en que no se podrá subordinar al mecanismo del mercado —al libre juego de la oferta y la demanda— los intereses personales de los que se encuentran, por las razones que sean, en posición de inferioridad.

Es importante tener en cuenta que detrás de las fuerzas impersonales del mercado existen personas; de una parte están los que trabajan sin ser los dueños de los bienes de la producción y de la otra los que actúan como empresarios y que generalmente son los dueños de la producción. Al ser personas humanas y no fuerzas impersonales las que operan en el mercado, todo proceso de producción debe tener en cuenta la verdadera dignidad de la persona humana y darle el lugar que le corresponda a los valores éticos. La economía, no lo olvidemos, está al servicio del hombre y no el hombre al servicio de la economía.

El empresario, por lo tanto, no debe limitarse a ejercer su *entrepreneurial function* o función creadora, sino que también debe ejercer una función social. Esta función social, que por regla general va encaminada hacia el mejoramiento del nivel de vida del obrero, no debe ni puede ser ignorada por el empresario si de veras quiere beneficiarse de relaciones más cordiales con sus empleados y con el sector laboral en general: función que fluye directamente del concepto de la empresa como comunidad de personas unidas por los lazos de una genuina solidaridad.[22]

IV. Las dimensiones técnica y humana del mercado libre

Desgraciadamente muchas de las críticas encaminadas al capitalismo se han dirigido también al mercado libre. A la vista del gran público, los dos conceptos se han hecho sinónimos y como consecuencia de ello los abusos del capitalismo liberal se han atribuido también al mecanismo del mercado libre. Esta apreciación constituye un grave error por lo siguiente: hay que considerar al mercado desde dos puntos de vista diferentes, por una parte tiene una dimensión técnica y por otra una humana. En su dimensión técnica, el mercado es neutro desde el punto de vista de valoración ética. Por ejemplo, explica el profesor español de análisis económico, Antonio Argandoña: "Decir que un aumento de la demanda de un producto eleva su precio es una descripción fenomenológica,

[19]Ibid, p. 393-396.

[20]Ver Schumpeter, Joseph, *History of Economic Analysis*, Oxford University Press, New York, 1963, p. 844-849.

[21]Joseph Hoffner, *Manual de Doctrina Social Cristiana*, Ediciones Rialp, S.A., Madrid, 1974, p. 204.

[22]La responsabilidad del empresario no puede limitarse a una función social que solo se dedica al adelanto material del hombre. El empresario no puede ni debe ignorar la existencia de valores que van más allá de una simple utilidad económica o material. Es más, el bienestar material del hombre está condicionado por el nivel moral existente.

no valorativa, como lo es que los cuerpos se atraen de acuerdo con la ley de la gravedad".[23]

Esta dimensión técnica del mercado libre ha servido muy bien al sistema capitalista que premia a los que aportan sus recursos a la producción de bienes y servicios de acuerdo con las leyes de la oferta y la demanda. El problema, por lo tanto, no radica en la dimensión técnica del mercado libre que, históricamente, se ha demostrado fomenta la eficiencia y la producción, sino en los hombres que son los que están detrás de los mecanismos económicos y son los que confieren un contenido ético a la actuación del mercado. Las deficiencias y abusos del capitalismo o sistema de libre empresa hay que buscarlos más bien en la dimensión humana del mercado libre y no en su dimensión técnica.

Una sociedad materialista, cuyas estructuras e instituciones se prestan a actividades económicas inmorales, generará también actuaciones que ignoren toda valorización ética; actuaciones que también se manifiestan en el mercado. Por eso resulta del todo necesario que se creen estructuras e instituciones que favorezcan conductas morales.[24]

La libertad es una de las características más salientes del sistema de libre empresa. El mercado está compuesto de hombres libres y responsables que no pueden escudarse ante la acción de un mercado calificado como impersonal, reclamando su imposibilidad de ejercer influencia sobre el mismo. Tal postura le daría al mercado la categoría de valor absoluto y sometería al hombre en forma ineludible a las fuerzas del mercado, lo que negaría su capacidad para escoger entre varias alternativas y destruiría su propia libertad. Esto atentaría contra la misma esencia del sistema de libre empresa que se fundamenta en el principio de la libertad.

Por lo tanto, el empresario, al actuar en el mercado dentro de un sistema de libre empresa y ejercer su libertad de opción, no está exento de responsabilidad moral. Todas sus actuaciones están sujetas a una valorización moral. Entre sus responsabilidades cae la de humanizar el mercado y, en la medida de lo posible, contribuir al establecimiento de reformas que fomenten estructuras, instituciones y legislaciones que respeten la moral y la ética. Con ello le estará dando un contenido ético a la dimensión humana del mercado y contribuyendo al bien común de la sociedad.

Le corresponde al empresario, como *leader* de la sociedad, dar ejemplo de creatividad y solidaridad dentro de su propia empresa. El empresario debe convertirse en el alma de un nuevo espíritu de confianza y cooperación que redunde en beneficio propio y de todos sus empleados, tanto a nivel profesional como a nivel de trabajador manual. Pero, aun más, este nuevo espíritu de solidaridad tendrá un efecto multiplicador que se esparcirá a todos los niveles de la sociedad. En esta forma, la sociedad y la empresa en particular estarán en condiciones de disfrutar de un ambiente más cordial y productivo y, como consecuencia, los niveles de eficiencia y producción mejorarán. Una vez más se demostraría la falsedad de la doctrina que proclama la inevitabilidad de la lucha de clases propiciada por Marx y sus seguidores.

Pero para que el empresario cumpla con su dimensión creadora, tan indispensable para el desarrollo económico, como con su dimensión social, es indispensable que se percate de su responsabilidad moral ante Dios y la sociedad. Y, para ello, necesita convencerse de la relación que existe entre la economía y la ética.

---

[23]Argandoña, Antonio, "Razones y formas de la solidaridad", en *Estudios sobre la encíclica "Sollicitudo Rei Socialis"*, Asociación para el Estudio de la Doctrina Social de la Iglesia, AEDOS, Unión Editorial, S.A., Madrid, 1990, p. 351.

[24]Ver Juan Pablo II, *De Sollicitudo Rei Socialis*, #36 y 43, y Juan Pablo II, *Centesimus Anno* #36.

En última instancia, el comportamiento moral de la persona humana dependerá de las virtudes que posea. En el caso del empresario su virtud principal consiste en hacer las cosas bien pero esto implica no solo la obtención de un rendimiento al menor costo posible (beneficio) sino también una actuación honrada que siempre tenga presente el bien común de la sociedad (solidaridad).

V.   Conclusiones

En este trabajo hemos tratado de hacer hincapié en la importancia de la clase empresarial y del sector privado dentro del sistema capitalista o de libre empresa. Estamos convencidos que el mercado dentro de un sistema de libertad económica, tal como lo expusieron Adam Smith y muchos de sus seguidores de la escuela clásica inglesa de los siglos XVIII y XIX, ha sido uno de los factores que más han contribuido al logro de un óptimo en la producción y por consiguiente a altos niveles de crecimiento económico. Con gran acierto la experiencia histórica ha demostrado que la iniciativa privada y el interés personal han sido los motores principales del desarrollo económico y que el intervencionismo estatal, ya desde la época mercantilista, ha coartado la creatividad del hombre e impedido su crecimiento.

Pero una cosa es reconocer la importancia de la función creadora de la clase empresarial y del sector privado dentro de un sistema de libertades económicas, y otra muy distinta es darle *carte blanche* a los mismos para que actúen sin restricciones de tipo alguno y se guíen exclusivamente por un afán de lucro que desconozca la función social que les corresponde. Como muy bien dijo Juan Pablo II en su última encíclica *Centesimus Anno*, un capitalismo que reconoce "el papel fundamental y positivo de la empresa, del mercado, de la propiedad privada y de la consiguiente responsabilidad para con los medios de producción, así como la libre creatividad humana en el sector de la economía, no puede dejar de ser un sistema digno de alabanza". Pero, continúa el Papa, si el mismo no está encuadrado "en un sólido contexto jurídico que lo ponga al servicio de la libertad humana integral y la considere como una particular dimensión de la misma, cuyo centro es ético y religioso" entonces el capitalismo deja mucho por desear.[25]

Este es precisamente el peligro que hay que evitar en Cuba. Una vez fracasada la experiencia marxista existe la tentación de caer en una ideología radical de tipo capitalista que solo confíe en las fuerzas del mercado para la solución de los problemas económicos y no se preocupe de establecer una sólida base ética y legal sobre la cual descanse el sistema. Dejarse llevar por esta tentación seria un error garrafal de consecuencias incalculables para el futuro político, económico y social de Cuba.

Una filosofía "libertina" que habla de libertad pero no de responsabilidad puede conducir fácilmente a una sociedad de consumo en la que el hombre solo busca la satisfacción de sus instintos o deseos materiales. El disfrute casi exclusivo de bienes materiales, facilitado por un sistema económico eficiente tal como es el capitalismo *a outrance*, hace de la virtud algo superfluo. La solidaridad y aun la creatividad pasan a segundo plano. La producción y la ética del trabajo, piedras fundamentales del éxito del capitalismo, son remplazadas por un consumismo malsano que necesariamente tiene que afectar en forma adversa el ahorro y la inversión, las fuentes del crecimiento.

La nueva clase empresarial que se desarrolle en Cuba a la caída del marxismo-leninismo de

---

[25]Juan Pablo II, *Centesimus Anno*, #42.

Castro no debe caer en los errores antes mencionados. Sería también una gran equivocación si los empresarios que regresaran a Cuba, volvieran con un espíritu de superioridad debido a los éxitos bien merecidos en el exilio, y con el fin de introducir un sistema capitalista que fomentará la creación de nuevos mercados para la venta de productos de consumo, no muy necesarios para el pueblo en general y que a veces pudieran ser poco recomendables. Esto podría destruir lo poco de la herencia cultural que todavía perdurará en Cuba después de la pesadilla castrista. Hacemos hincapié en la palabra destruir porque, como dijo el profesor Thomas Molnar refiriéndose al caso de Hungría, la influencia de este tipo de capitalismo no haría distinción entre valores y posiblemente destruirla el mismo concepto de nación en aras de una libre concurrencia desprovista de una base moral. Con ello se disolvería el concepto de familia en nombre de unas mal entendidas libertades, tanto políticas como económicas. De acuerdo con Molnar, la introducción de un sistema de libre empresa, a pesar de todas sus ventajas desde el punto de vista económico, no necesariamente satisfacería las aspiraciones del pueblo húngaro.[26]

En el caso de Cuba, estamos seguros que el pueblo en general y la juventud en particular también están deseosas de un cambio y en particular de mejorar su nivel de vida pero no a expensas de una mayor corrupción. La mayoría de dicha juventud se sentiría defraudada si viera que la producción y el comercio se encaminaran hacia la venta de artículos y servicios de lujo que solo tuvieran por objeto la satisfacción de las nuevas élites —compuestas en gran parte por ex miembros del partido comunista de la era castrista— y atraer al turismo extranjero.

En la nueva era que se aproxima, la contribución del *entrepreneur* o empresario al desarrollo económico de Cuba y por consiguiente al desarrollo integral del hombre se hará más indispensable que nunca. Ahí descansa su fuerza y al mismo tiempo su gran responsabilidad. Pero, el fracaso del colectivismo castrista no debe significar un retorno a lo que Hirshman llama "*an ego-focused image of change*". El afán de lucro y la mera acumulación de riqueza no debe ser la motivación de la nueva clase empresarial cubana, la cual debe tener siempre presente que una desmedida adquisición de bienes temporales puede conducir a la avaricia, al deseo insaciable de poseer bienes materiales y al afán de poder. Esto sería nefasto para el futuro de Cuba. Por su parte, también el sector obrero y en particular los sindicatos obreros deben evitar los peligros de un consumismo materialista y en vez cooperar con el empresario en un genuino espíritu de solidaridad que permita el desarrollo integral de todos los cubanos.

Desde la fase inicial del período de transición, el empresario cubano, a través de sus funciones creadora y solidaria, debe darle un nuevo significado al concepto del desarrollo; un sentido más humano. Si el desarrollo clama por una mayor dedicación a la investigación y nuevas técnicas de producción, también necesita un enfoque más humano que aminore las tendencias egoístas del hombre y evite el peligro de recias oposiciones y antagonismos que solo conducen a la desunión y a la lucha de clases. Pero esto solo puede ocurrir si se reconoce la existencia de unos valores morales superiores a los económicos y se fomenta al mismo tiempo el cultivo de las virtudes humanas. ¿Quién mejor que el empresario para llevar a efecto estos objetivos en su propia empresa y con su ejemplo influir favorablemente en todo el proceso de la producción y contribuir con ello al desarrollo integral del hombre? Es conveniente recordar que, en última instancia, la ciencia que se preocupa por el bien del hombre como persona humana es la ética y no la economía. Aristóteles parece reafirmar este postulado al subordinar su economía pura, todavía en forma embriónica, a la

---

[26]Molnar, Thomas, "Don't Go West Young Man", *Crisis*, June, 1992.

política y, en especial, a la ética. Su interés primordial era el *Summum Bonum*.[27]

Afortunadamente, Cuba no carece de una clase empresarial capacitada y de gran eficiencia. ¡Qué mejor prueba que el ejemplo del empresario cubano en Miami y en otras partes de Estados Unidos! Lo que Schumpeter llama la *entrepreneurial function*, y que nosotros hemos denominado la función creadora del empresario, nunca dejo de existir en Cuba y estamos convencidos que seguirá desempeñando el papel que le corresponde en el futura económico del país. No nos cabe la menor duda que el empresario cubano de la era post-marxista —tanto el que potencialmente se encuentra en Cuba en la actualidad como el del exilio— no se dejará llevar exclusivamente por un desenfrenado espíritu de lucro y ejercerá su función solidaria con la misma eficiencia que sabe desempeñar su función creadora.

---

[27]Ver Schumpeter Joseph, *History of Economic Analysis*, op.cit., p. 57-65.

Comments

Sergio Díaz-Briquets

I must begin my comments by stating that I may not do justice to the presenters' papers. As often happens in this type of meeting, I just received copies of two of the papers a few minutes ago. I barely had the opportunity to glance at them. My reaction to the third paper is based solely on what I heard during the oral presentation.

The paper by Ernesto Betancourt on revolutionary propensities reflects the author's ability to bridge the gap between politics —in this case revolutionary politics— and economics. Betancourt offers some rather perceptive interpretations regarding the likely future course of political events in Cuba, and what they might mean for the country's economic future. Like Betancourt, I do not have a crystal ball, but I do share many of his conclusions. The similarity of our conclusions, however, does not follow from the same reasoning.

Questions can be raised regarding Ernesto's paradigm, since when he compares pre-revolutionary propensities in pre-Castro Cuba and Uruguay, with present-day Cuba, he is comparing apples and oranges. It is unrealistic to contrast traditional military dictatorships in capitalist societies and Castro,s totalitarian state, as it is to ignore the vast global context of change with which Cuban communism must contend. There is also clear evidence that the Havana regime is facing enormous pent-up political, ideological, and economic pressures. Some of these pressures manifest themselves overtly. The discontent among the youth is reflected in the *jineteras*, the complaints about tourism *apartheid*, and the growing number of rafters, to name but a few of the symptoms. We can also infer the discontent in many other sectors of Cuban society if for no other reason than that the economy is virtually paralyzed. Almost, but not completely hidden, is the more ominous discontent among at least some members of the armed forces. The Ochoa affair and the ensuing purge in the Interior Ministry were merely the most glaring indications that all is not well with Castro's strongest power pillar. Is the situation in Cuba very different from that of Romania in 1990? Time will tell.

It is difficult to comment on the presentation by Irma T. de Alonso and Jorge Salazar-Carrillo. In reality, Jorge's remarks had very little to do with the paper. The paper's goal was rather limited: all it does is present some simple descriptive statistics derived from the 1982 and 1987 Bureau of the Census' surveys of minority-owned businesses. His comments, possibly because of time constraints, were hurried and somewhat careless. Many of the assertions made during the oral presentation are unsupported by existing data, and in fact betray a disregard for the literature.

When discussing Cuban entrepreneurship in the United States, Salazar-Carrillo could certainly profit from the growing literature on this topic, and especially the landmark contributions of Alejandro Portes and his associates. Jorge should also take into consideration the rich tradition of academic studies of ethnic enterprise in America associated with the likes of Ivan Light and Edna Bonacich. The paper's idealization of a complex and dynamic economic and social reality was somewhat disconcerting. Salazar-Carrillo offers no answers to the many questions that can be raised regarding Cuban-American entrepreneurship, and what it may mean to Cuba's future.

I enjoyed Martínez-Piedra's presentation and look forward to reading what I am certain is a thought-provoking paper. Cuba's future, politically and economically, is intimately tied to the delicate balance that the labor and entrepreneurial sectors must forge. That many members of the Cuban-American community are aware of this issue must be urgently communicated to the people of Cuba. Castro portrays a future non-communist Cuba as one dominated by heartless capitalists. Martínez-Piedra's exposition reflects the deep ethical and social concerns arising from the ideological debates of the last two centuries, and the more recent struggle between the now-discredited communist ideology and the proponents of Western-style, market-oriented liberal democracies. The Catholic Church and many other religious groups also were active participants in the debate. While the confrontation with totalitarian communism is now history, the concerns that gave rise to so many struggles remain with us. Participatory schemes (*cogestión*, ESOPs, etc.) that under some circumstances can facilitate social peace and prosperity offer promising alternatives that deserve close study.

LEGAL ISSUES RAISED BY THE TRANSITION: CUBA FROM MARXISM TO DEMOCRACY, 199?-200?

Néstor Cruz

I. Introduction

The transition of Cuba from Marxism to democracy raises a number of important constitutional and legal issues. In this short paper all I can hope to do is make the reader aware of some of these questions and suggest solutions for some of them. However, as almost always in law, especially when dealing with policy issues, the answers are charged with political and economic considerations, and one man's prescription is another man's poison. Each of the issues discussed can be isolated for purposes of research and further discussion in separate papers. The eleven topics discussed herein are the Constitution, eminent domain, privatization, labor legislation, antitrust, safety nets, taxes, higher education, economists as policymakers, privatization of the administration of justice, and government crimes.

A. Constitutional and Organizational Issues

The first question after the fall of the regime is who will govern and under what kind of governmental organization. It appears to me that the provisional government that will be inevitably established should be short-lived and have only two objectives: keeping the peace and calling for immediate elections under the Constitution of 1940 with a very brief campaign period as in the United Kingdom. There are, of course, problems with this scheme. The provisional government will have few powers to deal decisively with a mountain of problems, political parties which are not well organized will be handicapped, and a government which will soon self destruct will lack credibility.

On the other hand, there are advantages: one of Cuba's long-standing problems has been the legitimacy or lack thereof, of government. Cuba, as other countries, cannot have economic stability without constitutional[1] rule and without the consent of the people. It seems to me that post-1958 organic laws are flawed in this respect, unless an interpretation is given to them, such that the government will be periodically accountable to the people. Moreover, purely from a legal standpoint, post-1958 laws were passed by a government which is illegitimate.

Another advantage of the scheme suggested is that it will prevent the perpetuation in power of a provisional government. Always and everywhere there has been a marked tendency for temporary governments to become permanent. One should remember that after promising quick elections, the Cuban revolutionary government ended up by asking the people the rhetorical question: "Why elections?" Indeed, why? To have an executive power to take charge of government quickly and legitimately, a legislative power which can change the Constitution and laws whenever pre-1959 legislation is deemed obsolete, and last, but certainly not least, to establish an independent judiciary to decide the myriad disputes which will inevitably arise in the transition and post-transition periods, not only between person and person, but even more pressing, between persons and government. Clearly, a new elected government can amend the Constitution, and change or revoke old laws and pass new ones in a comparatively short period of time.

---

[1]Barro, "Economic Growth in a Cross-Section of Countries," 106 *Quarterly Journal of Economics* 407 (1991).

To understand the prima facie legal and economic absurdities resulting from illegitimate government, one need not look beyond February 7, 1959, around five weeks after the revolutionary government was established. On that date, the government "reformed" the Constitution of 1940 without benefit of constitutional processes. Some of the provisions: ex post facto criminal laws applicable to the prior regime's supporters (Art. 21 and 22; Title IV, Order No. 4); Death penalty [in the form of a Bill of Attainder] for members of the prior regime plus death penalty for "treason" against the new regime and "subversives" [not defined] (Art. 25). Under this clause many honest people who had nothing to do with the prior regime were shot; Exclusion from public life of citizens who, because of their "public acts" and participation in the prior regime's "electoral processes", "aided" the prior regime to "stay in power" (Title IV, Order No. 5). None of the prior terms were defined; minimum wages for **all** workers, according to each worker's occupation or profession, and standing as head of family (Art. 61). The Executive and Legislative Branches were merged and neither the President, nor the Ministers were subject to election (Art. 119, 120, 121, and 125). Judicial tenure was suspended (Title XII, Sec. 2 Order; Added Transitional Order No. 5). Prosecutorial tenure **and** independence was suspended (Title XII, Sec. 5 Order; Order No. 5). Laws and Regulations of the High Command of the Rebel Army remained in force (Added Transitional Order No. 1). Habeas Corpus and the jurisdiction of ordinary courts were suspended for all members of the prior regime, as well as for persons subject to the jurisdiction of Revolutionary Tribunals, as established by the criminal laws issued by the High Command of the Rebel Army (Order No. 3). Again, many honest people were prosecuted before Revolutionary Tribunals and shot under Order No. 3. The right of persons "defined" in Order No. 3, supra, to file appeals based on the unconstitutionality of the government's laws and inferior court judicial opinions, before the Supreme Court and the Tribunal of Constitutional and Social Guarantees, was suspended (Order No. 4). Public Defender tenure was suspended (Order No. 5). No pensions were payable to judicial officers removed by the government, until such time as the government completed the "reorganization" of the Judicial Power (Order No. 5). Public employee tenure was suspended (Title VII, Sec. 2, Order No. 3). Thus did the revolutionary government "pack" the courts and the ministries with its adherents, eliminate the jurisdiction of ordinary courts over its presumed enemies, and abolish appeals to the highest courts when defendants complained about government violations of its own "reformed" constitution.

The constitutional "reform" was a big mistake, even just on its face, let alone in its use. It is human to make a big mistake once. Quaere whether a similar mistake will be made during the transition.

After the elected government is in place, the laws and the Constitution itself can be changed swiftly. Some will say such a scheme is a luxury and what is needed for some time is a period of "*mano dura*" without the distractions of parliamentary maneuvers and interfering courts. Certainly such worked in post-civil war Spain and post-popular front Chile. The Adenauer-Erhard scenario, however, is also a valid alternative model. What actually transpires, however, will be a function of the degree of entropy during the transition. If it is very high, there will be a strong temptation to imitate the Spanish and Chilean model. On the other hand, if the majority of the people are sufficiently fed up with the quiescent chaos of the revolution, they may have the self-discipline for self-rule, without ukases from above, which are, after all, the distinctive marks of the revolutionary government.

B. Compensation for Nationalizations

The Neanderthal exile in Miami with the title to his house in Guanabacoa firmly in the coat pocket of his *Drill 100* suit waiting to jump on a plane to *Rancho Boyeros* in order to summarily evict the occupants of his confiscated property is an amusing caricature, but not a very helpful one analytically. Nowhere is it written that compensation must be in kind. In fact, eminent domain is almost by definition a matter of payment in money, not kind.

Cuba will confront two questions: whether there will be compensation for nationalizations and what form it will take. From a strictly legal point of view, under the Constitution of 1940 *and/or* some post-1958 laws, property taken by the State must be compensated. The revolutionary government even took legal steps to issue bonds. The question of whether the post-revolutionary government **ought** to compensate will inevitably become a political and economic question decided by the popular branches. However, the possibility exists that if an independent judiciary is established and the government denies compensation, the Supreme Tribunal may overrule the government and hold compensation is required constitutionally.

The form of compensation, including valuation schemes and sources of funds, will present a number of legal issues. As to valuation: will it be at market, present value of future earning streams of businesses, or earnings times a reasonable multiple such as 15? Will compensation be reduced by the net amount recovered from deductions from U.S. income? Will payment be in cash or bonds? If in bonds, at what interest rate? Will interest be paid from the time of nationalization? If so, at what rate? Three percent real plus the rate of inflation in the United States? Will those bonds issued by the revolutionary government be honored? Another problem will be: if compensation is to be paid at all, from where will the funds come--taxation, borrowing, privatization?

C. Privatization

Privatization raises some of the same issues as compensation, especially with respect to valuation. I assume that, analytically, property nationalized will be compensated and only property created post-1958 by the revolutionary government will be privatized. In reality, such division will be difficult because some property, say a sugar mill, will have some plant and equipment from the original owner and some added by the revolutionary government. A careful accounting must be made to separate out the components, allocate them to total value, and compensate or privatize, as the case may be, in proportion to the accounting results. Since compensation in money is administratively simpler, the government may give the former owner the choice of receiving the value of the property offset by the part of the value that would have been privatized. Alternatively, an investor may pay the government the value of the property to be privatized, if the investor pays over to the former owner that portion of value which is former ownership to be compensated.

With respect to the ascertainment of price for purposes of privatization the bottom line may be who will pay the most for a particular property although other factors are being taken into consideration in Eastern Europe.[2] But another question will arise, especially at the beginning. Will the bids be so low that it might behoove the government to retain properties to be privatized and operate them until sufficient investor confidence and interest builds up or should there be a conclusive presumption that no matter how low the bids, the properties should be privatized post-haste in order to let investors propel the economy forward without delay?

---

[2]Collier, "On the First Year of German Monetary, Economic, and Social Union," 5 *Journal of Economic Perspectives* 179, 184 (1991).

D.   Labor Laws

Any discussion of post-revolutionary legal issues will inevitably involve the "advanced" labor laws of the Republic, especially with respect to unions, discharge only for cause (Decree No. 798 of 1938), women's equality and benefits, and others.   Many have argued persuasively that such legislation burdened the Cuban economy while others have argued, equally persuasively, that a secure worker is a productive worker. The debate boils down to the age old equity vs. efficiency conundrum in a subtropical setting. The post-revolutionary government will face the following issues: are such laws desirable? From whose point of view? Economically? Socially? Equitably? Morally? The assumptions, analyses, and answers are frequently value-laden. Are economic values paramount? Are they necessarily at odds with other human values? Are they necessarily mutually exclusive? Are they complementary? Can they be harmonized?

When I suggest for pragmatic reasons that the post-revolutionary government be quickly elected under the Constitution of 1940, I do not mean to imply that the Constitution and prior labor laws ought to be immutable. To the contrary, such an elected government would give the people, through its representatives in Congress assembled, the opportunity to revise what was before under rules of procedure established for that purpose. Whenever the Cuban people (or any people for that matter) have circumvented established processes in the name of some type of expediency ("straightening" the economy, "eliminating" corruption, establishing "true" democracy) the results have not been pleasant as all manner of passion has been unleashed.

An alternative is to use the Constitution of 1940 only for three purposes: electing officials, appointing the judiciary, and securing elementary civil liberties of speech, habeas corpus, and due process. All other laws would be deemed revoked and the new government would write on a tabula rasa.   The Congress may delegate to the President authority to legislate, reserving to itself a legislative veto.   That would quicken the pace of legislative reform, and the people would be protected from Executive excesses by the Congress and the courts.

Another topic on this subject arises, i.e., the validity of government acts post-March 9, 1952 and pre-1959. It would appear that they are prima facie invalid as the Constitutional process was not followed. However, to the extent that such acts were consistent with the Constitution and its laws, I would argue for their validity, especially as the government made an attempt, albeit hypocritical, to maintain the form of government. On the other hand, the post-1958 government repudiated the Constitution and its laws, openly, in substance, in form, and in process. One would reason that that is a completely different species.

In any event, whatever labor laws Cuba adopts will have an economic impact. The debate leading up to such adoption should consider experiences in Eastern European countries undergoing liberalization, and in other developing countries, especially successful Asian NICs. The experience of European nations with "advanced" labor laws (e.g., Germany, Scandinavia, Benelux, and others), although not completely relevant because of the two very different levels of development, is partially relevant for "costing purposes"; i.e., can Cuba "afford" such laws?[3]

E.   Antitrust

In "Long-Term Objectives and Transitional Policies - A Reflection on Pazos' 'Economic

---

[3]Cf. S. Houseman, *Industrial Restructuring With Job Security: The Case of European Steel* (1991).

Problems of Cuba'" [p. 13] (August 13, 1991), E. Hernández-Catá[4] makes the excellent suggestion that post-revolutionary Cuba adopt "at a very early stage, comprehensive antitrust legislation". This is a point worth elaborating. First, it should be emphasized that due to the unmanageable nature of antitrust litigation[5] (a case can take more than ten years just in the discovery phase) trustbusting has not been as effective as free trade in fostering competition.[6] Nevertheless, the most egregious acts of price fixing, market division, and cartelization (so prevalent in pre-WWII Europe and even in Latin America today) can be prevented with proper enforcement.

Another neglected aspect of antitrust enforcement in the United States, due in no small part to the lobbying of professional and occupational associations, is the encouragement by government of the proliferation of licensed "professions" whose main objective is to keep outsiders from the ranks of the "profession" under the guise of quality control. This can be considered rent-seeking. The antitrust laws may serve to promote maximum competition by allowing freer entry, prohibiting minimum fee schedules, allowing price advertising, and, in general, doing away with unreasonable restrictive practices. For example, professional associations may be required to accredit all schools which meet minimum admission standards of intellectual ability for entrants into particular professions and minimum standards of instruction quality. Moreover, associations may be prohibited from dictating to schools the maximum number of students they may graduate each year (again, as long as such students are qualified for the profession in question). Furthermore, all post-graduation exams administered by the government or by associations with government sanction may be eliminated. Entry into a profession may be made automatic upon graduation from an accredited school. Finally, some professions, such as law or accounting, may be opened to persons who "read law" or "do numbers" for a number of years under another professional, thus permitting entry into the profession by persons who cannot afford college training.

An aspect of partial failure of antitrust in the United States has been the neglect to specify violations, other than the obvious ones of price fixing and market division. Some commentators have proposed (and this may be worth looking into in drafting Cuban legislation) that possible antitrust violations (such as "shared" monopolies or conscious parallelism) be defined statutorily, rather than left to protracted case-by-case adjudication.[7] This would presumably let firms know precisely what the law is and would save judicial time. There are three aspects of U.S. antitrust legislation and enforcement that should be avoided. First, price discrimination and resale price maintenance, which were designed not to protect competition but to protect inefficient competitors. Another one is to penalize successful firms which achieve economic profits through efficient and superior management rather than market power. Although theoretically economic profit should disappear in the long run, the fact is that there are firms,[8] or at least individual entrepreneurs,[9] who year in, year out produce outstanding results through ability not predation. Antitrust authorities should be mindful that one of the principal raisons d'etre for such legislation is to provide fertile soil for entrepreneurial activity, which, after all, is the only source of wealth.[10] A third aspect, related somewhat to personal

---

[4]Available from the Association for the Study of the Cuban Economy.

[5]McAllister, "The Big Case: Procedural Problems in Antitrust Litigation," 64 *Harvard Law Review* 27 (1950).

[6]W. Adams, *Restructuring the French Economy: Government and the Rise of Market Competition Since World War II* (1989).

[7]Adams, "The 'Rule of Reason': Workable Competition or Workable Monopoly?" 63 *Yale Law Journal* 348 (1954).

[8]T. Peters and R. Waterman, *In Search of Excellence*, 200-24 (1982).

[9]P. Drucker, *Innovation and Entrepreneurship* 188, 191-194, 202 (1985).

[10]Z. Acs and D. Audretsch, *Innovation and Small Firms* (1990).

occupational restrictions, is business licensing restrictions. There appears to be no reason why a person should not have free entry into any business. Capital, competence, licensing, and other restrictions for purely money-making enterprises such as real estate brokerage, contracting, pest control, and many others may be viewed as an attempt to restrict competition, again under the guise of public safety and other abstract concepts that have little to do with delivering a service.

F.   Safety Nets

In the aforementioned paper, Hernández-Catá also makes a second excellent suggestion, i.e. full price decontrol and elimination of price subsidies coupled with safety net payments, is the liberalization option "most compatible with the concept of a free-market economy where poverty issues are tackled through a system of direct government transfers rather than through subsidies and price-distorting measures" [p. 16]. This is another point worth elaborating. "Welfare" legislation in the United States is an abject failure.[11] In an attempt to devise an impossibly perfect system which leaves nothing to chance or to wrong decision-making by clients, legislatures have produced the opposite of what was desired. As Justice Antonin Scalia would put it, this is a good example of the operation of the Law of Unintended Consequences. There are no incentives to work because after-tax and after-childcare expense income from work is less than from "welfare." There is no curb on irresponsible childbearing. Clients may lose health insurance if they leave the system to work for employers who have no health plan, another lessening of the incentive to work. Housing is sometimes provided in kind, with resulting overcrowding, lack of pride of ownership, no incentive for working on maintenance or an aesthetic environment, crime, drug-dealing, and prostitution.

It appears that these problems can be avoided in at least one of two ways: a negative income tax which gives people some incentive to work or a requirement for work for the government in exchange for "welfare" payments. Predictably, public employee labor unions fight the latter proposal tooth and nail because they have a good thing going and do not want competition. This is an illustration of the necessity of integrating legislation with an economic effect so it works to the advantage of society and not of entrenched groups. Under either alternative, public housing may be undesirable and clients may be better off seeking housing in the private market. Even a "bad" slum may be better than a "good" housing project.

G.   Tax Legislation

A third excellent suggestion by Hernández-Catá is that the tax system in post-revolutionary Cuba ought to be "administratively simple and transparent" [p. 12]. This point also merits brief discussion from a comparative law point of view. Whether taxes are on consumption (as Hernández-Catá correctly suggests) or on income (as others argue), complexity and obscurity should not be part of a tax system. First, some of the best minds are drawn to a redistributive activity like the interpretation and administration of the tax system, rather than to productive endeavors. In may own experience, the first man in our law school class, who scored at the 99th percentile in the LSAT and had an undergraduate cum of 3.9, went on to become a tax consultant and professor. To waste such talent on taxation instead of using it on something productive is a serious misallocation of resources. Moreover, the sheer number of people in the tax field is staggering: lawyers, CPAs, CFPs, ChFCs, CLUs, tax preparers, estate planners, internal revenue agents, forms analysts, drafters of legislation and regulations, judges, and economists. It is not without some truth that the Internal Revenue Code of 1986 is referred to as the "Lawyers and Accountants Welfare Act."

---

[11]Friedman, "Why the Welfare Mess Gets Messier," 111 *U.S. News and World Report* NO. 22 30 (1991).

The products of this enormous amount of pointless ingenuity are a thick, incomprehensible tax code which reminds one of "certain passages of Hegel: they were no doubt written with a passion for rationality; but one cannot help wonder whether to the reader they have any significance save that the words are strung together with syntactical correctness." [Hand, "Thomas Walter Swan," 57 *Yale Law Journal* 167, 169 (1947); tax treaties; voluminous IRS regulations, revenue rulings, revenue procedures, letter rulings, and technical advice memoranda; and decisions by the Tax Court, the Claims Court, the district courts, the courts of appeal, and the Supreme Court.] There are at least five major tax services running into the dozens of volumes, which are expensive, but also indispensable to good tax research. There are also at least 16 major tax journals. If Cuba cannot afford "advanced" labor laws, it can afford a similar tax system even less.

H.   Legislation Subsidizing Higher Education

All higher education is not created equal. For example, the social return on engineering, science, and management (ESM) is higher than that on law. Probably most reasonable men would agree on that point. In Cuba, higher education of **all** types was heavily subsidized. Consequently, there was a great outpouring of rent-seeking lawyers and physicians. If a person wishes to self-finance a nonsocially productive career, that is fine, but I question whether such an education should be subsidized in whole or in part by the government. On the other hand, careers in ESM should be prime candidates for subsidies, especially in a developing country needing above all technical, rather than forensic, skills. Dare one speculate that if in pre-1959 Cuba careers in law had been priced at full cost, perhaps the country might have had fewer revolutionaries and more engineers?

There are other studies, especially in the liberal arts and the social sciences that are not only desirable in themselves as consumption items, but also socially desirable, if only so that ESM students and practitioners understand the context of their activities. It is hard to consider an engineer educated who ignores literature and economics, and just as hard to consider a writer or sociologist cultivated who ignores the physical sciences and business. It is important to give incentives to technical education, and indeed it is through the high standard of living which results from applied science, that the arts are available to the average man. Conversely, the direction of technological and economic change must be guided, at least in part, by the humanities and their long tradition of thinking about problems that seem to appear always and everywhere.

I.   The Role of Economists in Policymaking

Something may be wrong when economic policy is administered **exclusively** by politicians. Even partially granting the popular view that all economists laid end to end around the globe could never reach a conclusion, it is incredible to watch the enormous number of laws pouring out of legislatures every year without any input[12] from economists or, at most, with token participation. The same can be said of courts, with the possible exception of trailblazers like Federal Appellate Judges Richard Posner and Frank Easterbrook. There is, in fact, deep in the bowels of agencies such as EEOC and NLRB, that have economic impact, at best an arrogant fear, at worst a petulant ignorance, of anything remotely connected with the operation of markets or quantitative methods.

I would suggest that in a restored republic, some function be given to economists in legislation, execution, and adjudication beyond merely advising. I do not know the precise contours, but, for example, in the area of litigation with economic repercussions, it can be required that apart

---

[12]D. Bromley, *Economic Interests and Institutions: The Conceptual Foundations of Public Policy* (1989).

from expert witnesses presented by the parties, tribunals have at least one third of their membership composed of economists. In cases of one person courts, it can be required that an economist master be appointed to make findings of fact on all economic issues.

In legislation and execution it would perhaps be difficult to have unelected economists hold actual power, but it can be required that a Council of Economists, one in each branch, be appointed for long terms (14 years?) with almost absolute job security, like Federal judges, and instructed to comment critically and publicly on all executive policy, legislation, and landmark judicial opinions with economic impact. Perhaps, the fear of being exposed as frauds might nudge presidents, congressmen, senators, and judges to act less irresponsibly. The annual cost in salaries and xerox copying may be minimal compared to the intangible gains of letting the people know that public economists who are not under the thumb of the politicians may speak truths worth listening to. At present, there are numerous private economists who speak publicly on important issues (e.g., shadow FOMC, shadow SEC). However, their reach is limited because they speak in hypertechnical terms **and** some members of the public believe they have an ax to grind. An independent Council of Economists that, because of its members' long terms would straddle administrations, could have credibility, especially if it speaks clearly, allowing, of course, for dissenting opinions from a minority of the body.

J. The Privatization of the Administration of Justice in Civil and Administrative Matters

I assume that after the revolution, the Cuban Government will return to the civil law system,[13] with its simplicity and efficiency,[14] rather than convert to the common law system, with its complexity[15] and inefficiency.[16] In fact, some American lawyers believe that the United States is suffering from "terminal jurisprudence."[17] It would be well worth it for an econometrician to test the hypothesis that the increasing complexity of our legal system is a partial cause of the post-1973 growth slowdown. (See statistical appendix). Even U.S. Supreme Court Justice Antonin Scalia, a pure product of the Common Law, is increasingly having grave doubts about the viability and predictability of our present system. ["The Rule of Law as a Law of Rules," 56 *University of Chicago Law Review* 1175, 1178-79 (1989).]

In any event, even under an efficient civil law system, Cuba can still reach both higher efficiency **and** more just results by partial privatization of the administration of justice. Ironically, such experiments have been conducted in the United States after WWII and with increasing speed recently. First, it should be kept in mind that ultimately the courts have the final say by deciding the most difficult cases and setting the few important precedents allowed in a civil law system. However, parties to almost any type of dispute can enter into agreements to resolve their differences extrajudicially. As long as such agreements meet certain predetermined standards of due process, they are virtually uncontestable, with little recourse to the courts. In effect, the parties gain speedy

---

[13]Cf. Valle v. AII Co., 79 *JTS de Puerto Rico* 50 (1979).

[14]Murray, "A Survey of Civil Procedure in Spain and Some Comparisons with Civil Procedure in the United States," 37 *Tulane Law Review* 399 (1963).

[15]Younger, "In Praise of Simplicity," 62 *American Bar Association Journal* 632 (1976).

[16]R. Schlesinger, *Comparative Law* 269-441 (1970).

[17]Kieve, "Discovery Reform" 77 *American Bar Association Journal* 78 (1991); Cruz, "The Jurisprudence of Simplicity: Civil Law v. Common Law," 27 *Comparative Juridical Review* 111 (1990).

justice (justice delayed is justice denied) and the services of a reputable arbitrator/mediator in exchange for giving up protracted litigation and interminable appeals, not a very tasty prospect anyhow. Some of these alternative dispute resolution (ADR) mechanisms even operate in the absence of lawyers, a consummation devoutly to be wished in many cases.

ADR, moreover, is not an untested, theoretical, abstract concept. Ever since the U.S. Supreme Court Steelworkers Trilogy[18] in 1960, and its progeny, literally hundreds of thousands of purely legal disputes arising under the National Labor Relations Act have been decided by *private* arbitrators *without* direct court supervision. Currently, construction, stock brokerage, insurance, contract and other claims are resolved under the rubric of "commercial" arbitration. Domestic relations matters, so sensitive from a human standpoint, are also arbitrated as a matter of course. Thus, the privatization of justice works. It economizes on judicial, attorney, and litigant time, and, because of the simplified rules of civil procedure and evidence obtaining in such ADR schemes, the parties can focus on the substantive issues indispensable to a fair result, rather than on the procedural and evidentiary sideshows which make contemporary litigation so frustrating for parties and so burdensome for the courts.

K.   Government Crimes

The crimes committed by the revolutionary government against the life, liberty, and bodily integrity of citizens are so well established as to require no further documentation.[19] Such acts were crimes under the Constitution of 1940 and its laws (not even necessarily political crimes, but common crimes) and, therefore, the suspects should be investigated and prosecuted if cause found. Those found guilty should be sentenced, the only question left being the severity of the punishment. Note there is no Nuremberg or ex post facto issue. No punishment should exceed that permitted by prior law. The precise sentence that can be imposed on a particular criminal can only be determined by the court at the time of the trial and there is enough jurisprudence and legislation to make legally justifiable decisions.

Some will be tempted to go outside the law to punish crimes committed during the revolution. Such temptation should be resisted as one ought only remember that the revolutionary government established extra-constitutional military courts and passed ex post facto laws to try "war crimes" and "crimes against the people." Many of the accused were innocent, yet they suffered the death penalty or life imprisonment. These trials were evidence enough that the revolutionary government had a program totally unconnected to constitutional means and processes, and that it was prepared to deal harshly with those who would not follow the program. A post-revolutionary government showing similar disregard for the law should at least raise suspicion.

II. Conclusion

The reconstruction of Cuba will be impossible in the absence of a solid, legitimate, legal foundation. Much as a new government may try to rush events, cut corners, or jump steps, if the foundation is not sound, the superstructure will suffer. Moreover, the superstructure of the most libertarian economy is itself built upon beams and columns of contract and property rights, which can ultimately be vindicated only in court, even in the presence of good alternative dispute resolution

---

[18]1 C. Morris, *The Developing Labor Law* 917 (2d. Ed. 1983).

[19]Charles J. Brown and Armando M. Lago, *The Politics of Psychiatry in Revolutionary Cuba*, passim (1991).

mechanisms. Hence, the emphasis on procedure and availability of *independent* courts with a decided tilt towards speedy justice, no matter what the substantive rules of law. Simplicity in civil procedure, and substantive civil and administrative law is essential to prevent the arteries of industry and commerce from getting sclerotic from "hyperlexis". The siren song of the richness of complex law should be appealing only to those who earn their living by obfuscating rather than clarifying. Nature is difficult and complex enough. Law is man-made for the service of man not vice-versa. Ergo, law should be simple. Man is not made for the care and feeding of lawyers.[20]

Statistical Appendix
(Refer to Section 10 of text)

[From Cruz, Can We Afford Our Legal System? (in preparation)]

A simple linear regression of the following form was estimated:

$$Y = a + b\,(\ln X)$$

where: Y = percentage point changes in output per hour from 1961 to 1989.
          X = U.S. Courts of Appeals cases terminated per capita per year from 1961 to 1989.

RSQRD = 0.2755

F test = 10.27 (significant at the 1% level).

          n = 29
          k = 2
          b = -1.38
          a = 7.67

---

[20]R. Townsend, *Up the Organization* 97 (1970).

EL MARCO JURÍDICO-INSTITUCIONAL DE UN GOBIERNO PROVISIONAL DE UNIDAD NACIONAL EN CUBA[1] [2]

José D. Acosta[3]

I.   Introducción

A.   Temática

Este papel constituye un intento preliminar de determinar, utilizando la técnica jurídica, cuál sería el marco institucional que estaría vigente en el caso en que un Gobierno Provisional de Unidad Nacional (GPUN), cuya necesidad histórica explicaré más adelante, tome el poder en Cuba.

Con ese propósito, primeramente se examinarán, a partir de los compromisos internacionales vigentes del país y la restauración en 1955 de la Constitución de 1940, los actos de gobierno de carácter normativo que han tenido lugar en Cuba.

Será preciso distinguir entre aquellos actos normativos que constituyen el ejercicio del Poder Constituyente, de los que reflejan el ejercicio del Poder Legislativo, pues considero jurídicamente inaceptable, como sustanciaré más adelante, que un gobierno provisional asuma, **motu proprio**, el Poder Constituyente, como, siguiendo la tradición de los Machado y los Batista, ha ocurrido abiertamente en Cuba a partir del 10 de enero de 1959, fecha del primer intento de reforma de la Constitución de 1940.

Se   presentarán, primero, en cada una de las dos categorías mencionadas, los varios instrumentos en secuencia histórica, para intentar a continuación el análisis que permita formular opinión jurídica sobre su vigencia.

Finalmente, se harán algunas recomendaciones encaminadas a optimizar la legitimidad del GPUN, a fin de **asegurar la máxima juridicidad del Gobierno Constitucional** que resulte de su gestión.   Esa máxima juridicidad es un elemento esencial para asegurar la naturaleza indiscutiblemente democrática, la autoridad política y el apoyo popular para las difíciles y traumáticas decisiones estratégicas de reorganización de la presente economía estatista y su sustitución por una de empresa privada y mercados libres, dentro del marco de la justicia social.[4]

---

[1]Este papel fue leído en la Segunda Reunión Anual de la Association for the Study of the Cuban Economy (ASCE) que tuvo lugar en la Florida International University en agosto de 1992. Esta versión tiene el carácter de definitiva pues a mi juicio refleja los comentarios, cuestionamientos y observaciones formulados después de su presentación.

[2]En las citas textuales, el énfasis, caracterizado por letras negritas, es mío.

[3]Agradezco a Frank Calzón haber puesto a mi disposición la Biblioteca Jurídica de OF HUMAN RIGHTS y los valiosos comentarios de George P. Montalván antes y de Agustín de Goytisolo después, de la presentación de este papel en las Segundas Reuniones Anuales de ASCE. Cualesquiera errores u omisiones son de mi exclusiva responsabilidad.

[4]Este esfuerzo no es nuevo, pues se han publicado otros programas o proyectos sobre los aspectos jurídicos del proceso de transición, lo que es un valioso aporte de los profesionales del derecho a quienes resulten electos para la Convención Constituyente que deberá convocarse por el GPUN, y en las Elecciones Generales pluripartidistas que deberá presidir; pero ninguno ha enfocado el entorno institucional del "escenario" previo que, como he anticipado, considero ineludible: el establecimiento de ese Gobierno Provisional de Unidad Nacional y el marco jurídico fundamental que habrá de regirlo. Véanse la Agenda de Trabajo para un Congreso sobre Descomunización de Cuba, Miami, 1990, del Colegio de Abogados de la Habana en exilio y el documento "A National Reconciliation Program for Cuba: Preparing the Transition to Democratic Government, Broader Individual Freedom and Comprehensive Economic Growth" elaborado conjuntamente en 1991 por el Research Institute for Cuban Studies, North-South Center, University of Miami, Coral

B.   Antecedentes

1.   **El Imperio de la Ley en Cuba**[5]. La publicación en 1962 de este valioso ensayo que, como se verá más adelante, 30 años después de publicado sigue siendo de la mayor utilidad para el estudio del proceso de "desinstitucinalización" que ha tenido lugar en Cuba a partir de 1959, fue un valioso espaldarazo para los abogados cubanos que, como yo, optamos por emigrar a este país (Estados Unidos) para no sancionar, con nuestra presencia en Cuba, las aberraciones jurídicas del régimen.

Sin embargo, no obstante su profesionalismo, entereza moral y precisión técnica, fue un consuelo efímero para quienes, siendo además economistas, entramos en ese año al servicio de la Alianza para el Progreso en la Secretaría General de la OEA, para asistir a los Estados miembros de esa Organización en el profundo movimiento de reforma tributaria que se inició en América Latina a impulsos del Programa Conjunto de Tributación OEA/BID/CEPAL.   Constituye responsabilidad básica del personal de la OEA no expresarse públicamente respecto a cuestiones que sean de interés para la Organización o sus Estados miembros; y, como expondré a continuación, Cuba no ha perdido ese carácter.   Ello me impuso un silencio de treinta años.

2.   **Resolución VI de la Octava Reunión de Consulta de Ministros de Relaciones Exteriores**.   Cuando se produjo mi traslado del área económico-social para el área de asuntos jurídicos en 1980 y cambié mi birrete de economista por el de abogado, al menos tuve nuevamente el consuelo de emitir opinión jurídica, en más de una ocasión, en reuniones oficiales de órganos principales de la Organización, en el sentido de que conforme a esta resolución, que se acompaña como Apéndice I, si bien la República de Cuba era Estado miembro de la OEA, debido a que "la adhesión de cualquier miembro de la Organización de los Estados Americanos al marxismo-leninismo es incompatible con el Sistema Interamericano y el alineamiento de tal gobierno con el bloque comunista quebranta la unidad y la solidaridad del Hemisferio",... "el actual Gobierno de Cuba, que oficialmente se ha identificado como un gobierno marxista-leninista, es incompatible con los principios y propósitos del Sistema Interamericano". Por consiguiente, "esta incompatibilidad excluye al actual Gobierno de Cuba de su participación en el Sistema Interamericano", y al respecto se encarga al "Consejo de la Organización de los Estados Americanos y a los órganos y organismos del Sistema Interamericano [que] adopten sin demora las providencias necesarias para cumplir esta resolución".   Para bien o para mal, ésta es la única medida, de las adoptadas por la OEA contra el actual Gobierno de Cuba en 1962, que se mantiene aún en vigor y, por consiguiente, la opinión jurídica vertida producía la paralización de cualquier gestión para admitir la acreditación de una representación oficial del régimen ante el respectivo órgano principal de la OEA[6].

Quiere eso decir que en el marco internacional, si bien el régimen mantiene relaciones con la mayoría de los gobiernos iberoamericanos, el régimen está aislado a nivel multinacional regional, sin perjuicio de que la República de Cuba, mantenga la calidad de Estado Miembro de la OEA.   Sin

---

Gables, Miami, FL y el Center for National Security Law, University of Virginia School of Law, Charlottesville, VA. Posteriormente, este proyecto ha circulado bajo el patrocinio exclusivo del segundo de los centros mencionados, pero parece no estar en operación.   También hay un proyecto del American Bar Association.

[5]Comisión Internacional de Juristas, *El Imperio de la Ley en Cuba*, Ginebra, 1962.

[6]Sirva de ejemplo la Conferencia Especializada de Estadística (CIE), celebrada en Buenos Aires en 1983, en la cual actuó como Secretario y Representante Oficial del Secretario General, George P. Montalván, y a mí me correspondió la función de Asesor Jurídico.   La propuesta de admitir una representación del régimen en la CIE la hizo la Delegación del Gobierno de Nicaragua, la que, vertida la opinión jurídica, fue rechazada por la asamblea.

embargo, desde el interior del organismo interamericano y ante la actitud del exilio en general, las perspectivas eran, desde mi punto de vista, casi totalmente negativas en lo que concierne a las posibilidades de que Cuba regresase a un sistema democrático, al menos desde el punto de vista jurídico-institucional; y esa actitud mía continuó después de mi jubilación en diciembre de 1989.

3. **Descomposición del Marxismo-Leninismo en Europa del Este.** Este proceso, que culminó en diciembre de 1991 con la desmembración de la URSS, abrió en mi mente una nueva esperanza de que las posibilidades de retorno a la democracia para nuestro país de origen seguían vigentes y de que no era estéril dedicarles tiempo y atención. Ese cambio de actitud de mi parte coincidió con una serie de experiencias que fueron teniendo un impacto, no solo positivo, sino hasta creador, en mi modo de ver las cosas de Cuba.

La primera fue la lectura del libro de mi compañero de clase, en el Colegio de Dolores en Santiago de Cuba, Luis Aguilar León, titulado *Reflexiones sobre Cuba y su futuro*[7], que contemplando un regreso a lugares de inolvidables recuerdos de mi vida juvenil, me tocó profundamente. Allí se plantea, de modo convincente, el cese del "revanchismo" que ha caracterizado la actitud del exilio cubano respecto a la liberación del país, lo que considero constituye un ingrediente ineludible para el inicio del proceso de retorno a la democracia en Cuba.

La segunda fue el excelente resultado de la First Annual Meeting of the Association for the Study of the Cuban Economy, en la que un impresionante grupo de jóvenes profesionales cubano-americanos del más alto nivel, muy bien situados en los sectores profesional, internacional, federal y académico, demostraron su disposición a dedicar tiempo y esfuerzo a agotar la problemática de la transición, en Cuba, de una economía centralmente planificada a una de mercado, ante el reto recibido del maestro común, Felipe Pazos.

Cuando me disponía a editar la grabación videográfica que tomé en aquella reunión memorable, se produjo la tercera: Frank Calzón, Director Ejecutivo de *Of Human Rights*, me pidió ayuda en varias publicaciones, que no pude negarle. Entre ellas estaba lo que después salió, en versión provisional en español, bajo el título de "Mensaje de la disidencia a la diáspora", del conjunto de entrevistas efectuadas en La Habana, en octubre pasado, por Christopher Kean, de Freedom House, a los dirigentes de la disidencia cubana. La reorganización de mis pensamientos sobre Cuba que tuvo lugar con motivo de la lectura y edición de esa publicación, que traté de reflejar en el breve prólogo que escribí al efecto, constituye el antecedente próximo de este trabajo.[8]

C. Presupuesto: Gobierno Provisional de Unidad Nacional

1. **Caracteres del GPUN.** Como ni la ciencia jurídica ni la económica operan en el vacío sino en una realidad concreta, el presente trabajo de análisis jurídico-formal parte de ciertos presupuestos de carácter político, que surgen de mis lecturas de Aguilar León, del Mensaje de la disidencia y del reciente libro de Ernesto Betancourt titulado *Revolutionary Strategy: A Handbook for Practitioners*[9]. No es esencial que esos presupuestos se conviertan en realidad, aunque estoy convencido de que no sólo son posibles sino, quizás, hasta en alguna medida, probables. Lo

---

[7]Luis Aguilar León, *Reflexiones sobre Cuba y su futuro*, Ediciones Universal, Miami, 1991.

[8]La versión definitiva de la edición en español fue distribuida a los participantes de la Segunda Reunión Anual de ASCE: "Diez Días en la Habana, Mensaje de la Disidencia a la Diáspora", Freedom House, New York y Of Human Rights, Washington D.C.,1992.

[9]Ernesto Betancourt, *Revolutionary Strategy, A Manual for Practitioners*, Transaction Publishers, New Brunswick (U.S.A.) and London (U.K.), 1992.

importante es que proveen escenario concreto para llevar a cabo mi ejercicio.[10]

Ya sea como resultado de un conjunto de hechos políticos o de una explosión violenta, y por consiguiente cruenta, que cada vez pierde más popularidad, o como desenlace de una serie de regímenes militares, el comienzo del retorno de Cuba a la libertad habrá de partir necesariamente del establecimiento de un GPUN, en el que estén democráticamente representadas todas las tendencias y grupos de dentro y de fuera de Cuba, el que deberá actuar dentro de un marco institucional determinado, cuyos componentes constitucionales y legales me propongo, con carácter preliminar, comenzar a precisar en este trabajo.

2. Marco Jurídico-Institucional: Principios Fundamentales del Derecho Constitucional. Toda constitución es esencialmente un instrumento jurídico-político que se origina en el pueblo y su objetivo es dejar establecidas las condiciones bajo las cuales el pueblo, en forma soberana, decide someterse, voluntariamente y sin resistencia, renunciando en esa medida a su libertad irrestricta, a la autoridad de un gobierno determinado. Por ello, siempre se ha considerado como un "pacto social" del cual surge el Estado de Derecho, que comprende dos sectores diferenciados de la sociedad: los gobernados y los gobernantes. Estos principios son "doctrina recibida" en esta materia, y semejante marco institucional constituye un requisito previo al establecimiento del GPUN. Citemos, como ejemplo dos fuentes:

a. Félix Varela, Primer Constitucionalista Cubano. El primero "que nos enseñó a pensar" también fue el primer constitucionalista cubano. Veamos qué nos dice recientemente respecto a las ideas de Varela en materia constitucional otro filósofo cubano, pero contemporáneo:[11]

Qué enseñaba Varela como maestro de ciencia política

En 1821, cuando el Obispo Espada le pidió que ofreciera en el Seminario un curso de derecho constitucional, Varela escribió, para uso de sus alumnos, un manual que tituló **Observaciones sobre la constitución política de la monarquía española.** Una gran parte de esta obra está dedicada a explicar los principales preceptos contenidos en dicha Constitución, y no tiene otro valor que el puramente didáctico. Lo más notable de todo el pensamiento de Varela son, en cambio, las consideraciones sobre filosofía de la sociedad y el estado que aparecieron en dicho libro y que complementan las doctrinas por él esbozadas en las **Lecciones de Filosofía.**
Varela supone que la sociedad civil surge cuando los hombres primitivos, que vivían organizados en grupos familiares, comprendieron la necesidad de establecer una autoridad que coordinara los esfuerzos de todos los grupos y así protegiera los derechos de los ciudadanos y las familias. 25/
Los derechos humanos (como hoy decimos) o derechos del hombre (como Varela prefería

[10]La concepción de estos presupuestos no es exclusivamente mía, ni responde sólo a las lecturas que he identificado como antecedentes. En ella hay el impacto de largas discusiones con George P. Montalván y con José Alonso. Ambos se han interesado en temas estrechamente vinculados con esta concepción. De materializarse, considero que los estudios respectivos sobre un fondo de ayuda de emergencia y sobre los mercados libres campesinos serán una importante contribución para atraer la atención de los miembros de ASCE hacia la problemática de inmediato plazo de la transición política hacia la democracia y un valiosísimo aporte a los esfuerzos que tendrá que encarar lo que he dado en llamar GPUN.

[11]José I. Lasaga, "Varela, El Maestro" en *El Padre Varela, Pensador, Sacerdote, Patriota,* Simposio celebrado el 4 de noviembre de 1988, bajo los auspicios de la División Hispánica, Biblioteca del Congreso, y del Departamento de Español, Escuela de Lenguas y Lingüística, Georgetown University, Roberto Esquenazi Mayo, Editor, Georgetown University Press, Washington, D.C., 1990, pág. 18.

llamarlos) van a constituir, por tanto, un punto central de su teoría política. Al surgir la autoridad civil, los individuos y familias tienen que entregarle a ésta algunos de sus derechos. Pero esta entrega se hace precisamente para asegurar otros derechos todavía más básicos.

b.   **Black's Law Dictionary.** En igual sentido, esta fuente de referencia fundamental de derecho norteamericano e inglés, bajo el término *Constitution*, dice:

Constitution. The organic and fundamental law of a nation or state, which may be written or unwritten, establishing the character and conception of its government, laying the basic principles to which its internal life is to be conformed, organizing the government, and regulating, distributing, and limiting the functions of its different departments, and prescribing the extent and manner of the exercise of sovereign powers. **A charter of government deriving its whole authority from the governed.** The written instrument agreed upon by the people of the Union (e.g, United States Constitution) or of a particular state, as the absolute rule of action and decision for all departments (i.e. branches) and officers of the government in respect to all the points covered by it, **which must control until it shall be changed by the authority which established it (i.e. by amendment), and in opposition to which any act or ordinance of any such department or officer is null and void.** The full text of the U.S. Constitution appears at the end of this dictionary. In a more general sense, any fundamental or important law or edict; as the Novel Constitutions of Justinian; the Constitutions of Clarendon.[12]

En conclusión: todo instrumento constitucional se origina en el pueblo; se dicta en ejercicio del Poder Constituyente, que es esencialmente diferente del Poder Legislativo; constituye el marco jurídico que sustenta la legitimidad de un gobierno y su reforma sólo puede hacerse mediante el procedimiento que la misma constitución establezca, o mediante la convocatoria a una Asamblea Constituyente formada por delegados electos en voto universal y secreto de todo el pueblo.

3.   **Único Objetivo: Democracia Política.** El Gobierno de Unidad Nacional, gobierno *de facto* al fin, no podrá ofrecer, durante su breve período, el marco adecuado para que el pueblo de Cuba adopte decisiones concretas de política económica; sólo cabrán aquéllas que sean imprescindibles para asegurar la producción a un nivel superior a la subsistencia, y el orden público. Su objetivo será, principalmente, abrir paso a una genuina democracia política dentro de un ambiente de plena libertad y respeto a la opinión ajena, aunque sea contraria a la propia, en el que, en un marco de legitimidad institucional, puedan adoptarse, con el imprescindible apoyo del pueblo, las difíciles decisiones y medidas de política económica de carácter estratégico que lleven a un proceso de transición hacia la libertad económica, lo que supone el desmantelamiento del sistema de control absoluto de la economía por el gobierno y su remplazo por un sistema de empresa privada y economía de mercado, dentro del mayor respeto a la dignidad plena del hombre, es decir, con el menor impacto negativo posible en las condiciones de vida del pueblo. Estoy convencido, tal como interpreto las experiencias en Europa del Este, que ese objetivo sólo puede lograrse mediante dos ejercicios básicos ineludibles:

a.   **Convención Constituyente.** Su convocatoria y celebración deberán implicar un reexamen a fondo del fundamento institucional del país, pero cuidándose de no caer en detalles que hagan de la Constitución resultante en una minuciosa plataforma política, que se convierta en camisa

---

[12]Black's Law Dictionary, Fifth Edition, West Publishing Co., St. Paul, MN, 1979, pág. 282.

de fuerza para el Gobierno Constitucional que surja dentro de ese marco. Los principios de la Constitución de 1940 bien pueden actualizarse y ajustarse a la muy especial situación histórica presente, aprovechando así la experiencia de estos últimos cincuenta años.

b. **Elecciones Generales Pluripartidistas.** Su convocatoria y celebración, dentro del marco de la renovada Constitución, deberán resultar en un Gobierno Constitucional del más amplio apoyo popular posible, que se desenvuelva en un entorno institucional conducente a la adopción e implementación de las políticas económicas más adecuadas para el retorno a la economía de empresa privada y libertad de mercados.

Todavía quedarían otras funciones imprescindibles a cargo del GPUN:

c. **Normalización del Suministro de Alimentos, Servicios Médicos y otros.** Con este propósito, el GPUN deberá maximizar el esfuerzo interno y la ayuda externa para asegurar el logro de este difícil objetivo. Para ello habrá de valerse de las posibilidades de producción de la agricultura de subsistencia y de los mercados libres campesinos[13], como mecanismos productivos de reacción rápida y probada eficacia, junto con un ambicioso programa de ayuda externa pública y privada, multilateral y bilateral, en la que el liderazgo corresponda a los cubanos de la diáspora, genuinamente comprometidos a que este esfuerzo no falle.

d. **Pacificación/Desarme y Reempleo del Actual Sector Represivo[14].** Ésta es una de las tareas más delicadas que tendrá que encarar el GPUN. Dentro de la organización económica vigente, resultaría imposible la simple disolución de la gigantesca *nomenklatura* represiva que comprende varios centenares de miles de cubanos y su lanzamiento al hambre, pues ello impediría una genuina reconciliación nacional. Será imprescindible, en consecuencia, reemplear personal excedente en actividades de restablecimiento de la infraestructura nacional en total estado de deterioro, a fin de facilitar la creación y distribución de la producción agrícola de subsistencia.

e. **Mantenimiento del Orden Público.** Para organizar, a la mayor brevedad posible, una nueva fuerza de policía profesional y para cubrir el vacío que habrá de producirse, en muy corto plazo, el GPUN deberá gestionar y obtener ayuda externa multinacional, de una organización internacional experimentada en esta materia, por ejemplo, las Naciones Unidas.

f. **Promover, pero no Participar en la Reorganización del Poder Judicial.** El GPUN deberá, con urgencia, promover la reorganización del Poder Judicial, de acuerdo con los principios generalmente aceptados de separación de poderes. Para preservar la necesaria autonomía, esa tarea deberá encomendarse a una Comisión de ex miembros del Poder Judicial, antes del 10 de marzo de 1952. Reconozco que encontrar integrantes para esta comisión, después de 40 años, no es tarea fácil, pero deberá intentarse. Los abogados de dentro y de fuera deberán colaborar. Para aspectos simplemente operativos como computerización de la actividad judicial se han producido grandes adelantos, y hay asistencia técnica y financiera disponible tanto a nivel multilateral como bilateral.

g. **Comisiones de Estudio y Sistematización del Material Acumulado sobre la Transición.** Constituye esta tarea un ejercicio que sería de gran utilidad para el Gobierno Constitucional, pues pondría a su disposición, ya sistematizado e integrado, todo el material que en

---

[13]Este constituye uno de los temas incluidos en la agenda de estas Reuniones, a cargo de mi estimado colega José Alonso.

[14]Este es un tema que ha planteado originalmente George P. Montalván, y sobre el cual ha mostrado interés y reunido valioso material.

los dos últimos años ha comenzado a producirse en Cuba y fuera de Cuba sobre el proceso de transición económica. Ello aceleraría la toma de decisiones de política económica sin necesidad de que ese Gobierno Constitucional tenga que acometer esta tarea desde el principio, y como en el material hay aportes tanto cubanos como ajenos, se reducirá en significativa medida la necesidad de asistencia técnica externa en esta materia.

Finalmente, es obvio que el GPUN deberá abstenerse de crear problemas de hecho o de derecho que agraven las dificultades que habrá de encarar el Gobierno Constitucional que lo sustituya, en el más breve plazo posible, por ejemplo, alterando la tenencia de los bienes de producción.

II. El Marco Constitucional y Legal

A. El Marco Constitucional de Cuba en el Derecho Internacional

Al iniciarse el GPUN, se encontrará con que la República de Cuba está insertada en un sistema de Derecho Internacional, del cual el Estado cubano nunca se ha separado, que resulta en ciertas ventajas y determinados compromisos, que dicho gobierno deberá tomar muy en cuenta para preservar su legitimidad en el campo internacional. Se explicarán a continuación los más relevantes:

1.   A Nivel Mundial. Durante la vigencia de la Constitución de 1940, la Asamblea General de las Naciones Unidas adoptó, con la participación y el voto favorable del Gobierno Constitucional de la República de Cuba, la Resolución 217 A (III) de 10 de diciembre de 1948, por la que aprobó una Carta (Charter) Internacional de Derechos Humanos. Este instrumento no tiene la jerarquía jurídica de una constitución, pero mediante su voto favorable la República de Cuba aceptó la obligación, en derecho internacional, de preservar dentro del régimen constitucional del país esta "concepción común de los derechos y libertades", como dice uno de sus considerandos, entre todos los Estados miembros de esa organización mundial suprema.

No quiere ello decir que la República de Cuba, o los demás Estados miembros de las Naciones Unidas que han aprobado esta Carta o se han adherido a ella con posterioridad, hayan renunciado a su soberanía para darse el instrumento constitucional que consideren más adecuado, pero sí implica, sin embargo, que para no reconocer constitucionalmente alguno de los derechos y libertades enunciados en la Carta deberán, conforme al derecho internacional, denunciar y separarse, total o parcialmente, de este compromiso internacional, cosa que, al menos en el caso de Cuba, no se ha producido.

2.   A Nivel Interamericano. Unos meses antes de la adopción de esta Carta, en la Novena Conferencia Internacional Americana celebrada en Bogotá, del 30 de marzo al 2 de mayo de 1948, con la participación y adhesión de la representación del Gobierno Constitucional de Cuba, y no obstante el intento del famoso "bogotazo" en el que participó activamente el líder del régimen actual, "se reorganizó, consolidó y fortaleció el Sistema Interamericano, dentro del marco de la Resolución IX, aprobada en la Conferencia Interamericana sobre Problemas de la Guerra y de la Paz, que tuvo lugar en México en 1945"[15], y se adoptó una serie de compromisos de gran significación, también a nivel internacional, pero dentro del marco regional interamericano que, por ello, hacen al tema de este trabajo:

---

[15]*Conferencias Internacionales Americanas*, Segundo Suplemento: 1945-1954, Unión Panamericana, Washington, D.C. 1956.

a. **Declaración Americana de los Derechos y Deberes del Hombre**. El más importante es la Resolución XXX titulada Declaración Americana de los Derechos y Deberes del Hombre, cuyo texto, muy similar y en algunos casos de más alcance que el de la Carta de las Naciones Unidas antes mencionada, constituye el Apéndice II, y que es, sin duda, un compromiso internacional de la República de Cuba.

b. **Otras Resoluciones**. Otras resoluciones de interés respecto al tema de este trabajo, emanadas del mismo foro interamericano son: (a) la Resolución XXXII, denominada Preservación y Defensa de la Democracia en América (cuyo texto constituye el Apéndice III), instrumento que constituye fundamento de la Resolución VI de la Octava Reunión de Consulta de Ministros de Relaciones Exteriores de 1962, que, como hemos visto, excluyó al régimen actual de Cuba de intervenir en el Sistema Interamericano, por su orientación marxista-leninista, y (b) la Resolución XXXI, denominada Corte Interamericana para Proteger los Derechos del Hombre (que constituye el Apéndice IV), que es el mandato inicial para la formulación de un estatuto de la actual Corte Interamericana de Derechos Humanos, ya creada y en operación, con sede en Costa Rica.

Respecto a estos instrumentos interamericanos, debe dejarse constancia de que constituyen, en los mismos términos y condiciones que el de las Naciones Unidas, obligaciones internacionales de la República de Cuba, como Estado miembro de la Organización de los Estados Americanos, máximo organismo regional interamericano y el más antiguo organismo internacional, pues es ya más que centenario. Ello, sin perjuicio del prestigio que quiera reconocerse al organismo regional, que no constituye otra cosa que el reflejo de los ministerios de relaciones exteriores de sus Estados miembros.

B. Legitimidad y Juridicidad de la Constitución de 1940

Tanto desde el punto de vista político, como desde el jurídico formal, la Constitución de 1940 ha sido siempre considerada como un instrumento legítimo y válido. Nunca se ha puesto en duda la convocatoria a la respectiva Asamblea, ni el resultado electoral de los que fueron electos para integrarla. Representaban todos los intereses y aspiraciones del pueblo cubano —después de la alteración del orden institucional de 1929, cuando la dictadura de Machado intentó modificar la constitución vigente entonces para la famosa "prórroga de poderes"— a tal extremo que, si ha de anotársele algún defecto, es el de haber sido demasiado extensa, porque con ella se intentó dar solución a todos los problemas contemporáneos que propiamente eran materia de legislación complementaria u ordinaria, aunque para ello haya resultado en un instrumento excesivamente detallista y "reglamentario". Constituyó la superación de la Enmienda Platt que había ensombrecido, junto con las restricciones en su convocatoria emanadas del gobernador norteamericano General Woods, la legitimidad de la Constitución de 1902. El pueblo cubano pudo sentirse fundadamente orgulloso de contar con un instrumento fundamental de los más progresistas de América, donde se incorporaban las conquistas laborales y sociales de la Revolución de 1933. Produjo un período de estabilidad institucional de sucesivos gobiernos democráticos, a tal extremo que uno de los crímenes fundamentales que se atribuyen a la dictadura batistiana es el de haber roto el ritmo institucional del país, sin justificación política aceptable y a pocos meses de unas elecciones generales convocadas en completa adherencia a los preceptos constitucionales. Tan es ello así que, en un intento de alcanzar una legitimidad que nunca pudo lograr, la dictadura batistiana tomó las medidas necesarias para la restauración de la Constitución de 1940, en el plano jurídico-formal, en 1955, cuando Batista tomó posesión como presidente electo cuando se presentó como candidato único en las elecciones celebradas entonces, a las que Grau, con indudable perspicacia, se negó a comparecer, haciendo así más difícil el logro de la legitimidad a que se aspiraba. Finalmente, nunca en los doce años de su vigencia se produjo ningún intento hacia su modificación total o parcial, sino que al contrario, la aspiración a su restauración resultó ser el factor aglutinante de la oposición a aquella dictadura.

C.   Historia Constitucional de Cuba, 1952-1992

1.   Restauración formal de la Constitución de 1940 en 1955. "La ley constitucional de 1952[16] disponía en su Art. 256, de acuerdo con la modificación que se le hiciera por Decreto Ley No. 1133, de 30 de octubre de 1953 (Gaceta Oficial de 6 de noviembre de 1953, Edic. Extr. No. 90) que la Constitución de 1940 sería restablecida a partir de la fecha en que tomara posesión el presidente electo. Las elecciones presidenciales se celebraron el día 3 de noviembre de 1954, resultando electo Fulgencio Batista. El día 24 de febrero de 1955, Fulgencio Batista, único candidato presentado para la elección presidencial prestó juramento y tomó posesión del mando como Presidente de la República. Automáticamente, en virtud de la citada cláusula de tránsito constitucional, comenzó a regir nuevamente la Constitución de 1940"[17].

Quiere ello decir que cuando los pasajeros del GRANMA desembarcaron en la costa oeste de Oriente el 2 de diciembre de 1956, la Constitución de 1940 era la ley fundamental de la República de Cuba; y uno de los primeros postulados básicos de ese grupo, compartidos con la resistencia urbana y prácticamente con la totalidad de la oposición del país, era precisamente, la restauración, no sólo formal, sino sustantiva, de la Constitución de 1940.

2.   Actitud del Ejército Rebelde. Antes de detentar el poder, se dictaron por el Alto Mando del "Ejército Rebelde" —no alcanzo a descubrir el fundamento de su poder para hacerlo[18]— varias disposiciones normativas que se reseñan brevemente a continuación:

a.   "Reglamento" No. 1 de 21 de febrero de 1958 (Boletín Oficial del Ejército Rebelde, Régimen Penal del Ejército Rebelde). Por este instrumento se atribuye a "**la jurisdicción de guerra del Ejército Revolucionario (sic)** el conocimiento de los delitos cometidos por militares **o civiles, al servicio de la tiranía**". Este instrumento aparece suscrito por Fidel Castro, Comandante en Jefe, y por Humberto Sorí Marín, Auditor General[19].

b.   "Ley" No. 2 de 10 de octubre de 1958 (Inhabilitación Política de Candidatos). Se tipifican los delitos de (i) "**tomar parte en la farsa electoral** del día 3 de noviembre de 1958" al que se fija una pena "**de treinta años,** que le inhabilitará durante ese tiempo para ejercer el derecho de sufragio, desempeñar cargo público electivo o por designación y percibir jubilaciones y pensiones del Estado, la Provincia y el Municipio, sin perjuicio de la responsabilidad penal en que hubiere incurrido"; (ii) **dedicarse "al corrompido sistema de recoger cédulas para la farsa electoral** [el que] será **juzgado en Consejo Sumarísimo de Guerra y condenado a la pena de muerte**", y (iii) el de "el candidato que **haciendo labor política relacionada con la farsa electoral sea capturado en zona de operaciones del Ejército Rebelde** [el que] será condenado a **pena que puede fluctuar entre diez años**

---

[16]Otro intento de Constitución jurídicamente espuria.

[17]Comisión Internacional de Juristas, *El Imperio de la Ley en Cuba*, Ginebra, 1962, pág. 92.

[18]En efecto, en aquel momento, el Alto Mando del Ejército Rebelde controlaba una fracción pequeña del territorio nacional, y obviamente, no detentaba el poder público. Por consiguiente, carecía de poder para legislar respecto a la responsabilidad penal de la población civil, y menos en contradicción con lo establecido en la Constitución de 1940.

[19]*Folletos de Divulgación Legislativa*, I. 1o. a 31 de enero de 1959, Editorial Lex, La Habana, 1959, pág. 101.

de prisión y la pena de muerte". También está suscrita por las mismas autoridades.[20]

c. **"Ley" No. 3 de 10 de octubre de 1958** (Reforma Agraria). Se da en propiedad "la tierra que cultiven a los poseedores de tierras del Estado, así como a los arrendatarios, sub-arrendatarios, aparceros, colonos, sub-colonos y precaristas que ocupen lotes de cinco o menos caballerías de tierra particular". Suscrita por las mismas autoridades[21].

3. **Resolución del Tribunal Supremo Constitucional.** En las primeras horas del 1o. de enero de 1959, ante el vacío institucional que representaba el abandono del Poder Ejecutivo y Legislativo por quienes lo detentaban, de conformidad con el Artículo 149 de la Constitución de 1940, el Magistrado más antiguo del Tribunal Supremo se dirigió a ese cuerpo para que, conforme al Artículo 141 de la misma Constitución, le tomara el juramento como Presidente Provisional de la República. Por Resolución de la misma fecha, tomada es sesión plenaria, bajo la presidencia del titular, Magistrado Santiago Rosell y Leyte Vidal, y ponencia del Magistrado Julio Garcerán, se declaró sin lugar "el pedimento del Dr. Carlos M. Piedra, en su carácter de magistrado más antiguo de este Alto Tribunal, para ocupar, por sustitución constitucional, la Presidencia de la República; y sí, en cambio, **reconocer el derecho del Dr. Manuel Urrutia Lleó, para ocupar la Presidencia de la República, con carácter interino...**" Esta resolución se adoptó ante la solicitud del Magistrado Piedra y se fundó en tres consideraciones: (a) el triunfo de la Revolución era un hecho consumado; (b) la revolución es fuente de derecho y (c) el Frente Cívico Revolucionario, "integrado por diversos sectores" había designado al Magistrado Urrutia, desde julio de 1958, y ratificado posteriormente, para ocupar la Presidencia de la República[22]. Obsérvese que salvo concluir que no había lugar a la aplicación del Artículo 149, la Resolución no pone en duda la vigencia de la Constitución de 1940, y al caracterizar al Presidente Urrutia de Presidente **provisional**, lo deja obligado a cumplir el resto de ese Artículo respecto a convocar a elecciones generales dentro de los noventa días siguientes, o continuar en el poder hasta la celebración de las elecciones si el plazo restante era inferior a un año.

4. **Primer Mes del Régimen.** Entre el 1o. de enero y el 7 de febrero de 1959, el régimen, ejercitando por sí y ante sí el Poder Constituyente, aprobó modificaciones a la Constitución de 1940 en cinco ocasiones, que se describen sucintamente a continuación:

a. **Reforma Constitucional I, de 10 de enero de 1959.** Se **suspende la vigencia** de: (i) "los preceptos constitucionales que establecen requisitos de edad mínima y de tiempo mínimo de ejercicio profesional para el desempeño de cargos públicos **hasta que se promulgue la Ley Fundamental de la República**"[23] y (ii) la inamovilidad de los miembros del Tribunal de Cuentas **hasta tanto el mismo quede reorganizado.**"

b. **Reforma Constitucional II, de 10 de enero de 1959.** Se suspenden: "Por... 30 días la **inamovilidad** judicial establecida en el Artículo 200"; la del Ministerio Fiscal, establecida por los Artículos 180 y 208; la electoral establecida en el Artículo 187, y el ingreso en la carrera fiscal por oposición establecido en el Artículo 189, todos de la Constitución de 1940. Es decir, que se elimina

---

[20]*Folletos de Divulgación Legislativa*, II (Cuaderno Extraordinario).

[21]Ibíd, pág. 127.

[22]Ramón A. Barquín, *El Día que Fidel Castro se Apoderó de Cuba*, Editorial Rambar, San Juan, Puerto Rico, 1978, Anexo 23A.

[23]Obsérvese que ya el gobierno ha concebido la idea de sustituir la Constitución de 1940 con una ley fundamental dictada por el mismo gobierno.

la independencia del Poder Judicial.

  c. **Reforma Constitucional III, de 10 de enero de 1959.** Se modifican, introduciendo **excepciones** a lo en ellos dispuesto en sentido general, los Artículos (i) 21, sobre **retroactividad de las leyes penales** favorables al delincuente; (ii) 24, sobre prohibición de la **confiscación de bienes,** y (iii) 25, sobre la **prohibición de la pena de muerte,** todas las cuales constituyen garantías constitucionales básicas de la Constitución de 1940.

  e. **Reforma Constitucional IV, de 20 de enero de 1959.** Se suspenden las disposiciones constitucionales sobre los **regímenes provincial y municipal,** y las funciones de los Gobernadores, Consejos de Alcaldes, Alcaldes y Ayuntamientos se asignan a las autoridades que designe el Consejo de Ministros.

  f. **Reforma Constitucional V, de 30 de enero de 1959.** Se suspenden por 90 días: (i) los Artículos 27, 29, 196 y 197 sobre el procedimiento de *Habeas Corpus* "respecto a aquellas personas sometidas a la jurisdicción de los Tribunales Revolucionarios", y (ii) los incisos d) del Artículo 174 y a) del Artículo 182 sobre **la competencia del Tribunal Supremo para conocer recursos de inconstitucionalidad,** es decir, que se elimina la posibilidad de accionar para obtener la declaratoria de inconstitucionalidad de los actos del gobierno.

  El régimen intentó fundamentar todas estas reformas en "la necesidad inaplazable de **usar el Poder Constituyente para viabilizar los hechos que impone la Revolución,** haciendo uso de los plenos poderes de que está investido"; y todas están firmadas por el Presidente de la República y los miembros del Consejo de Ministros[24].

  5. **La Ley Fundamental de 1959, Apéndices y Reformas.** Esta "constitución" adoptada por el Presidente, asistido del Consejo de Ministros, el 7 de febrero de 1959, incluye un buen número de artículos de la Constitución de 1940, pero modifica o sustituye un número similar, para adaptar ese instrumento a las necesidades del régimen, que es exactamente lo inverso del objetivo esencial de toda constitución.

  a. **Principales Disposiciones.** Por este instrumento, además de incorporarse todas las reformas individuales antes mencionadas, se introducen otras:

  (1) **Poder Constituyente.** La reforma más significativa, sin duda, está constituida por el nuevo Artículo 232, que **atribuye el Poder Constituyente al Consejo de Ministros,** ya se trate de reforma específica, parcial o total.

  (2) **"Legislación" del Ejército Rebelde.** Curiosamente, además, por las Disposiciones Transitorias Adicionales Primera y Segunda, se declaran vigentes "todas las disposiciones legales y reglamentarias penales, civiles y administrativas promulgadas por el Alto Mando del Ejército Rebelde durante el desarrollo de la lucha armada contra la tiranía derrocada el día 31 de diciembre de 1958... **hasta que se instaure el Gobierno de elección popular**[25], salvo modificación o derogación posterior".

---

[24]*Folletos de Divulgación Legislativa*, I, 1o. a 31 de enero de 1959, Editorial Lex, La Habana, 1959.

[25]Entonces, ¿quiere ello decir que la Ley Fundamental considera que la toma del poder por el régimen surgen retroactivamente, desde el 21 de febrero de 1958, fecha del Reglamento No. 1?, y ¿debe entenderse que estos Apéndices continúan aún en vigor hoy, a falta de derogación expresa, a pesar de la "vigencia" de la denominada Constitución de la República de Cuba de 1976?

Con estas dos medidas quedó desvirtuada la naturaleza constitucional del instrumento que el régimen dio en llamar Ley Fundamental.

b.   **Reformas Posteriores.**   Examinada una de las compilaciones más completas[26] disponibles, sólo he podido encontrar una reforma específica, de 26 de junio de 1959, publicada en la G.O. de 6 de julio, por la que se modificó el Artículo 25 de la Ley Fundamental de 1959. Mediante esta reforma, la pena de muerte, ya ampliada a casos no contemplados por la Constitución de 1940, se extiende a los "delitos contrarrevolucionarios", que aparecen tipificados en la Ley No. 425 de 7 de julio de 1959 que aprobó importantes modificaciones del Código de Defensa Social de 1936[27]. Sin embargo, en una búsqueda directa en la Gaceta Oficial he encontrado otra reforma, del Artículo 24, sobre confiscación de bienes, en la que ésta se extiende a quienes abandonen el país para eludir la acción de los Tribunales Revolucionarios, o que después de abandonar el país, se dediquen en el extranjero a actividades conspirativas, de 22 de diciembre de 1959 (G. O. Ext. de la misma fecha).

6.   **La "Constitución" de la República de Cuba, como estado socialista, de 1976.**   Esta "constitución", que es la que el régimen considera "vigente", promulgada el 24 de febrero de 1976 y que acaba de ser profusamente modificada por reforma aprobada el 13 de julio corriente,[28] tuvo un elaborado proceso de gestación que duró dieciséis años.   Un distinguido y benevolente exégeta de este instrumento[29] distingue tres etapas en su preparación[30]:

a.   **Acuerdo de 22 de octubre de 1974.**   Contiene las "pautas" para la elaboración del nuevo instrumento, y es el resultado de la colaboración entre el Consejo de Ministros y el Buró Político del Partido Comunista de Cuba. Confieso no haber tenido a la vista este interesante documento que aparentemente no fue publicado oficialmente.

b.   **Comisión Mixta del Partido y del Gobierno.**   Formada por veinte "camaradas" procedentes del Partido y del Gobierno, presidida por Blas Roca, miembro de la Secretaría del Comité Central del Partido Comunista de Cuba y veterano de la Asamblea Constituyente de 1940, con un vicepresidente, el Ministro de Justicia, Armando Torres Santrayll.   Esta Comisión, que sesionó en privado, cumplió su cometido en el plazo estipulado y elevó su "Anteproyecto" el 24 de febrero de 1975.

c.   **Estudio por el Politburó y el Consejo de Ministros.**   Esta etapa duró del 24 de febrero al 10 de abril de 1975.   Se desconoce en qué medida el "Anteproyecto" sufrió modificaciones como resultado de este estudio y cuáles pueden haber sido las modificaciones, pues el estudio no fue público. De aquí salió el "Proyecto" que se hizo público.

d.   **Discusión Pública Popular.**   Esta etapa duró entre el 10 de abril y el 16 de septiembre y sobre ella el autor citado comenta lo siguiente:

---

[26]Bruce Zagaris y Jay Rosenthal, "A Selected Bibliography of the Cuban Legal System, 1959-1983", *Lawyer of the Americas,* Vol. 15:3, pág. 546-577, University of Miami, 1984.

[27]*Folletos de Divulgación Legislativa,* X, 1o. a 31 de julio de 1959, Editorial Lex, La Habana, 1959, pág. 7-25.

[28]La información disponible en este momento no incluye textos modificados, pero se sabe que el Artículo 5, no ha sido modificado.

[29]L. B. Klein, "The Socialist Constitution of Cuba (1976)", *Columbia Journal of Transnational Law,* Vol. 17, No. 3, 1978, pág. 451-515.

[30]No obstante, el autor parece identificar después seis etapas en ese complicado proceso, y no sólo tres, como menciona en su ensayo.

The Committees for the Defense of the Revolution (CDRs) and other mass organizations were charged with "a task of propaganda of great intensity" in guiding the much emphasized discussions of the draft. A prime purpose of this stage was to educate the nation about the intended meaning of each provision. However, since the Anteproyecto had been written by appointed officials, a more important function of the mass discussions, which are common in the drafting of socialist constitutions, was to lend the process the appearance of an exercise in direct democracy: the discussions were the answer to those who, remembering the Constitution of 1940, might have expected a national convention of popularly elected delegates...[31]

Contrasta esta percepción con en discurso de Raúl Castro en el acto de proclamación de esta "constitución" el 24 de febrero de 1976:

En todo este proceso y como una exigencia para el mejor desarrollo de las tareas de construcción del socialismo, es necesario asegurar la participación, cada vez más creciente y cada vez más regular y sistemática del pueblo en todos los asuntos de la administración estatal y en las decisiones relativas a las cuestiones de gobierno. Y condición determinante para ello es que las masas conozcan y dominen todo lo relativo a las estructuras y mecanismos del Estado. Que dominen el contenido de la Constitución y de las leyes... Éstos deben ser documentos... que se incorporen a los correspondientes programas de estudio del Sistema Nacional de Educación[32].

De la misma fuente, pero de mi antiguo compañero de estudios de Derecho Emilio Marill, que es quien cita el anterior discurso, tomo otra cita interesante, esta vez del autor mismo:

Sin embargo, por incomprensible que parezca, no hemos sido capaces de llevar adelante estas orientaciones. Veamos lo que dijo recientemente, a los 12 años de proclamada la Constitución, el presidente de la Unión Nacional de Juristas de Cuba:

"Se trata esencialmente de un problema de educación. Durante el proceso revolucionario, se suprimió en Cuba una asignatura de los planes de estudio de la enseñanza media que se denominó primero Moral y Cívica y más tarde Cívica de la Comunidad. En ella se explicaban algunos aspectos del Derecho y del Estado, cuestiones elementales cuyo conocimiento es imprescindible para la vida social... por lo que es frecuente encontrar en nuestros egresados universitarios y técnicos medios —con excepción, desde luego del minúsculo número de graduados en Derecho o en determinadas técnicas relacionadas con el Derecho— una ignorancia jurídica absoluta. La mayoría de los graduados de la enseñanza media y universitaria no conoce la diferencia entre el Consejo de Estado y el Consejo de Ministros, ni las atribuciones de la Asamblea del Poder Popular, y tampoco tiene claro el papel del Partido como fuerza dirigente de la sociedad y del Estado.

Este analfabetismo jurídico afecta también a gran parte de los dirigentes estatales, que no distingue entre una ley y una resolución administrativa, ni entre un tribunal de justicia y un órgano de arbitraje estatal, ni domina, en lo fundamental, la legislación laboral[33].

---

[31]Ibíd., pág. 462.

[32]Citado por Emilio Marill, *Constitución de la República de Cuba, Temática/Legislación complementaria*, Editorial de Ciencias Sociales, La Habana, 1989, pág. 3.

[33]Ibíd., pág. 4.

Las citas precedentes ponen de manifiesto la risible "profundidad" que puede haber tenido la participación popular, democrática y directa, en el ejercicio del Poder Constituyente en 1976.

e. **Estudio por el Primer Congreso del Partido.** Este Congreso se efectuó en 1975 y la revisión misma del "Proyecto" constitucional se llevó a efecto del 17 al 22 de diciembre.

f. **Referéndum Popular.** Este ejercicio, aparentemente, cubrió todo el país, pero no me ha sido posible encontrar su convocatoria ni la descripción de cómo se llevó a cabo. Sólo dispongo de esta cita del informe del presidente al Consejo de Ministros:

I myself estimated that 90% in favor of the constitution... would have been... a very high percentage. Nevertheless, 97.7% of the electors have voted in favor of the Constitution... And the percentage obtained is so high that at times I have wondered whether, when they see these figures abroad, they will really believe that we have held very honest elections, because the figures are so surprising that they could induce any skeptic to doubt.[34]

g. **Promulgación y vigencia.** Finalmente, la "constitución" fue promulgada el 17 de febrero, y entró en vigor el 24 de febrero de 1976, precisamente dos años después de haberse iniciado el proceso. Para no omitir siquiera alguna cita de este interesante instrumento, resultado de tan cuidadoso estudio, veamos los Artículos 5 y 141:

Artículo 5. El Partido Comunista de Cuba, vanguardia organizada marxista-leninista de la clase obrera, es la fuente dirigente superior de la sociedad y del Estado, que organiza y orienta los esfuerzos comunes hacia los altos fines de la construcción del socialismo y el avance hacia la sociedad comunista.

Artículo 141. Esta Constitución sólo puede ser reformada, total o parcialmente, por la Asamblea Nacional del Poder Popular mediante acuerdo adoptado, en votación nominal, por una mayoría no inferior a las dos terceras partes del número total de sus integrantes.
Si la reforma es total o se refiere a la integración y facultades de la Asamblea Nacional del Poder Popular o de su Consejo de Estado o a derechos y deberes consagrados en la Constitución, requiere, además, la ratificación por el voto favorable de la mayoría de los ciudadanos con derecho electoral, en referendo convocado al efecto por la propia Asamblea.

7. **La Reforma Constitucional de 1992.** Para cumplir acuerdos adoptados durante el Cuarto Congreso del Partido Comunista de Cuba, que tuvo lugar en Santiago de Cuba, en octubre de 1991, la Asamblea Nacional del Poder Popular sesionó en La Habana, los días 10, 11 y 12 de julio de 1992 y produjo una reforma que un comentarista oficial resume así:

Se adicionaron a la Constitución... tres nuevos capítulos, de modo que ahora cuenta con quince. El total de los artículos se redujo de 141 a 137, de ellos fueron revisados, parcial o totalmente, 77.[35]

La Asamblea Nacional del Poder Popular, sospecho que con el propósito de agilizar la

---

[34]Citado en traducción libre al inglés en el estudio de L. B. Klein, *op. cit.* Este informe, rendido por Fidel Castro al discutirse el resultado del misterioso "referendo", también refleja un agudo contraste con el discurso de Raúl Castro, pocos días después, en el acto de proclamación de esa "constitución".

[35]Hugo Azcuy, "Aspectos de la Ley de Reforma Constitucional Cubana de julio de 1992", mimeografiado, La Habana, 17 de julio de 1992.

discusión del "proyecto de ley", publicó un Proyecto de Modificaciones a la Constitución de la República, en el cual, como es usual en los cuerpos deliberativos, se incluyen tres columnas denominadas Texto actual, Propuesta, y Fundamentación, en las que se presenta el respectivo articulado, en su orden, comenzando por el Preámbulo.[36] Posiblemente por las dudas que pueden existir de si esta reforma es integral o total, y, por consiguiente, si es necesario un referendo,[37] el texto "constitucional de 1976", tal como quedó modificado por la Asamblea Nacional del Poder Popular el 12 de julio se ha publicado por primera vez en la edición de *Granma* del 22 de septiembre de 1992.

En ese texto subsiste, en el preámbulo, la referencia a las "ideas político-sociales de Marx, Engels y Lenín", y el Artículo 5, antes citado en su versión original, clara evidencia del grado de "apertura" de la reforma, quedó así:

> *Artículo 5. El Partido Comunista de Cuba, martiano y marxista-leninista, vanguardia organizada de la nación cubana, es la fuerza dirigente superior de la sociedad y del estado que organiza y orienta los esfuerzos comunes hacia los altos fines de la construcción del socialismo y el avance hacia la sociedad comunista.*

D. Legislación Socialista

1. **Legislación del Poder Judicial.** Debe recordarse aquí que una de las primeras reformas de la Constitución de 1940 fue la "suspensión" de la inamovilidad del Poder Judicial. Con ello, de entrada, se erosionó profundamente uno de los fundamentos importantes del principio constitucional de total independencia del Poder Judicial, pues se confirió al Presidente de la República (calificado como "Provisional" por el Tribunal Supremo en su Resolución de 1o. de enero de 1959), asistido del Consejo de Ministros, la facultad de llenar libremente las vacantes producidas por la suspensión de la inamovilidad, en los cargos de Presidente, Presidente de Sala, Magistrados, Fiscales y Tenientes Fiscales del Tribunal Supremo. Desde entonces (10 de enero de 1959) el Poder Judicial dejó de ser independiente del Poder Ejecutivo.

En la actualidad, "rige" al Poder Judicial, en lugar de la Ley Orgánica del Poder Judicial, un instrumento denominado Ley de Organización del Sistema Judicial, Ley No. 4 de 10 de agosto de 1977 (G. O. del 25) cuyo título pone de manifiesto que la función judicial ha dejado de ser un Poder independiente para convertirse en un sistema al servicio del gobierno y del Partido Comunista de Cuba, en fiel obediencia de lo dispuesto en términos generales en el Artículo 5 de la "constitución" de 1976, ya citado, y concretamente en el Artículo 122 de dicho instrumento, que dice:

> *Artículo 122. Los tribunales constituyen un sistema de órganos estatales, estructurados con independencia funcional de cualquier otro, y sólo subordinados, jerárquicamente, a la Asamblea Nacional del Poder Popular y al Consejo de Estado[38].*

---

[36]República de Cuba, Asamblea Nacional del Poder Popular, Proyecto de Reformas a la Constitución de la República, mimeografiado, sin fecha. Sin embargo, el título no deja dudas de que es anterior a la reforma.

[37]En efecto, Andrés Oppenheimer, en su ya famoso libro *Castro's Final Hour: The Secret Story Behind the Coming Downfall of Communist Cuba* (New York: Simon & Schuster, 1992), atribuye a Juan Escalona, ex-Ministro de Justicia, designado Presidente de la Asamblea del Poder Popular antes de que ésta se abocara al estudio de la reforma constitucional, presidió este ejercicio, señaló que lo inoportuno de un referendo en 1992 influyó en el proceso y alcance de la reforma adoptada.

[38]Conforme a los Artículos 67 y 68 del mismo instrumento, la Asamblea Nacional del Poder Popular es "el órgano supremo del poder del Estado" y el único "con potestad constituyente y legislativa".

2.   **Legislación Civil**. El viejo Código Civil español de 1889, que siguió vigente en Cuba después de la independencia, fue sustituido por Ley No. 59 de 16 de julio de 1987 (G. O. del 15) por un nuevo Código Civil "en vigor" desde el 12 de abril de 1988. Aunque los Títulos I al IX, Artículos 1-126, constituyen un interesante intento de formular una teoría general de la relación jurídica que me parece plausible. Sin embargo, ya el Artículo 2 dice:

Artículo 2. Las disposiciones del presente Código se interpretan y aplican de conformidad con los fundamentos políticos, sociales y económicos del Estado cubano expresados en la Constitución de la República.

Semejante disposición, claramente tendenciosa, convierte al código en un instrumento político en lugar de un instrumento jurídico. Por otro lado, hay varios aspectos de interés que conviene destacar:

a.   **Código de Familia**. El derecho de familia no está regulado en el Código, sino en otro instrumento, adoptado por Ley No. 1289 de 14 de febrero de 1975 (G. O. del 15) por consiguiente, anterior a la Constitución de 1976, a la que este Código, consecuentemente, no hace alusión.

b.   **Usucapión**. Como este Código entró en vigor el 12 de abril de 1988, impidió el cumplimiento del plazo de 30 años desde el 1o. de enero de 1959 para que llegara a operar la prescripción adquisitiva sobre bienes inmuebles (usucapión) que regulaba el viejo Código Civil[39], respecto a los bienes "abandonados" en Cuba por los exilados. Sin embargo, la nueva institución, regulada en los Artículos 184 a 190, muestra algunos aspectos que es bueno destacar: (i) La usucapión no procede respecto a bienes propiedad del Estado ni a los bienes inmuebles rústicos (Artículos 185.1 y 186.2) y (ii) El plazo de la usucapión sobre bienes inmuebles urbanos es de sólo 5 años, pero la posesión deberá ser de buena fe, no siendo eficaz la posesión "meramente tolerada por el dueño u obtenida clandestinamente o sin conocimiento del poseedor legítimo o con violencia".

3.   **Legislación Penal**.   A pesar de que los "delitos contrarrevolucionarios" se incorporaron desde 1959 mediante extensas reformas al Código de Defensa Social de 1936 de las que ya nos hicimos eco, por Ley No. 21 de 15 de febrero de 1979 (G. O. de 1o. de marzo) se adoptó un nuevo Código Penal que comenzó a regir ocho meses después de dicha publicación; es decir, desde el 1o. de noviembre de 1979.

Una de las disposiciones más "peligrosas" de este Código, es la del Artículo 8 que "considera delito toda acción u omisión **socialmente peligrosa** prohibida por la ley", concepto este último que el Código no define. Similar situación se plantea en los Artículos 76 y 77 f) que dicen:

*Artículo 76. Se considera **estado peligroso** la especial proclividad en que se halla una persona para cometer delitos, demostrada por la **conducta** que observa **en contradicción manifiesta con las normas de la moral socialista**.*

Artículo 77. El estado peligroso se aprecia cuando en el sujeto concurre alguno de los índices de peligrosidad siguientes:...

---

[39] En relación con la usucapión o prescripción adquisitiva, el Artículo 1959 del viejo Código Civil dice que "se prescriben también el dominio y demás derechos reales sobre los bienes inmuebles por su posesión no interrumpida durante treinta años, sin necesidad de título ni de buena fe, y sin distinción entre presentes y ausentes, salvo la excepción determinada en el artículo 539." Este Artículo 539 se refiere a las servidumbres y, por consiguiente, no se aplica al dominio que pudiera llamarse "integral" para destacar la plenitud del derecho de propiedad sobre bienes inmuebles.

*f) La conducta antisocial. Se considera en estado peligroso por conducta antisocial al que habitualmente mediante actos de violencia, o frases o gestos o por otros medios provocadores o amenazantes o por su **comportamiento en general quebranta o pone en peligro las reglas de la convivencia socialista**, o burla derechos de los demás o perturba con frecuencia el orden de la comunidad.*

Como las "reglas de convivencia socialista" tampoco se definen, con gran frecuencia estas disposiciones se utilizan como medio de represión política, lo que no ocurre si los actos los realizan los integrantes de "brigadas de acción rápida" y los participantes en los "actos de repudio".

Este Código se complementa por la Ley de Procedimiento Penal aprobada por la Ley No. 6 de 13 de agosto de 1977 que es concordante con la Ley de Organización del Sistema Judicial antes mencionada.

4.   Legislación Laboral. El derecho laboral "vigente" está contenido en el Código de Trabajo, aprobado por la Ley No. 49 de 28 de diciembre de 1984, que rige desde el 26 de julio de 1985. Este instrumento está referido a un sistema productivo de corte estatal o cooperativo. No obstante, entre las "entidades laborales" (empleadores) se incluyen "las empresas y propietarios del sector privado, con respecto a los trabajadores asalariados" (Artículo 7 d)).

Entre sus disposiciones está la relativa al denominado "expediente laboral" definido como "el documento que contiene los datos y antecedentes de la historia laboral del trabajador, estando la entidad laboral en la obligación de confeccionar, actualizar y custodiar el de cada uno de sus trabajadores" (Artículo 61) el que, si bien puede ser examinado por el trabajador, en la práctica parece haberse constituido en formidable arma de control y represión en manos de la entidad laboral, con plena indefensión del trabajador.

También es de interés destacar que conforme al Artículo 48 b) el contrato de trabajo termina, entre otras causas, por iniciativa de alguna de las partes; y según el Artículo 53 son causas de terminación a iniciativa de la administración de la entidad laboral, entre otras, (a) la ineptitud debidamente demostrada; (b) la falta de idoneidad del trabajador; (c) la declaración de disponibilidad del trabajador (**despido por economía**), y (d) la separación del trabajador por violar la disciplina laboral.

5.   Legislación Tributaria. En su texto original, aprobado por Ley No. 447 de 14 de julio de 1959 (G.O. del 16) modificada por la Ley 863 de 17 de agosto de 1960 (G. O. del 27) la Ley de Reforma Tributaria fue redactada por un conjunto de compañeros de estudio de economía nuestros, algunos de los cuales son miembros de ASCE[40]. Constituye el primer Código Tributario que haya regido en Cuba; refleja un racional esfuerzo de consolidar el vasto número de impuestos regulados separadamente por la legislación anterior, y establece procedimientos tributarios comunes a todos los impuestos internos. Incluye, además, un nuevo Impuesto sobre la Compraventa, cuya base es el "valor agregado", infortunadamente, sólo en la primera etapa, sea producción o importación[41]. Aunque este código no rige actualmente, porque el sistema que establece está concebido para ser

---

[40]Éste no es el fundamento de su conveniencia y mérito. No me animo a concebir al GPUN tratando de aplicar los 200 y pico de impuestos sustituidos por esta Ley que aparecían disgregados en un conjunto, punto menos que inmanejable, de leyes y reglamentos distintos, con procedimientos diferentes para cada impuesto.

[41]Esta es materia importante, porque la ventaja administrativa del autocontrol del cumplimiento por los contribuyentes tiene lugar cuando se da la "cascada tributaria" en las sucesivas etapas de cobro del impuesto.

aplicado en un ámbito de economía mixta, constituye un instrumento que será preciso considerar aun desde el inicio de un GPUN.

El texto original del Reglamento de este Código fue aprobado por Decreto No. 2038 de 23 de septiembre de 1959 (G. O. del 28).

6.   Otros códigos y legislaciones especializadas. En mi proyección original aspiraba a examinar en alguna medida la Ley de Reforma Agraria de 17 de mayo de 1959 (G.O. del 10 de junio), para destacar al menos que no conozco ningún caso en que un propietario que cumpliera con las disposiciones de esta ley haya podido conservar las treinta caballerías que la ley autoriza (Artículo 1) y menos percibir la indemnización resultante de la expropiación forzosa del exceso del límite mencionado a que también se refiere la ley (Artículo 29). Sin embargo, debo abstenerme porque en mis investigaciones he determinado que se dictó nueva legislación en 1963 que no he tenido oportunidad de examinar en el corto tiempo disponible para preparar este trabajo. El tema, además, tiene tal trascendencia a los efectos del proceso de transición a la economía de mercado y, presumiblemente, tal impacto distorsionante sobre la producción agrícola de productos alimenticios de primera e inmediata necesidad, que opinar sobre ella requeriría un estudio especial de carácter multidisciplinario[42].

Lo mismo cabe decir de la Ley de Reforma Urbana, de 14 de octubre de 1960 (G.O. del mismo 14), pues se han dictado leyes en 1984 y 1988[43], cuyo contenido habría que estudiar con similar profundidad y la misma cautela, por el impacto distorsionante que cualquier acción al respecto puede tener sobre la totalidad del sector habitacional.

III. Opiniones Jurídicas y Recomendaciones Prácticas

A.   Vigencia de la Constitución de 1940

Situado en un estricto punto de vista jurídico, opino que la Constitución de 1940 se encuentra vigente aún, sin que para ello un GPUN tenga que tomar medida alguna. Fundamento esta opinión jurídica en los siguientes argumentos:

1.   La Constitución de 1940 Nunca Ha Sido Válidamente Derogada ni Modificada. En su Artículo 285, esta Constitución dispone:

Artículo 285.— La Constitución sólo podrá reformarse:
a) Por iniciativa del pueblo, mediante presentación al Congreso de la correspondiente proposición, suscrita, ante los organismos electorales, por no menos de cien mil electores que sepan leer y escribir y de acuerdo con lo que la Ley establezca. Hecho lo anterior, el Congreso se reunirá en un solo Cuerpo y dentro de los treinta días subsiguientes votará sin discusión la ley procedente para convocar a elecciones de Delegados o a un referendo.
b) Por iniciativa del Congreso, mediante la proposición correspondiente, suscrita por no menos de la cuarta parte de los miembros del Cuerpo Colegislador a que pertenezcan los proponentes.

---

[42] Importa tener presente que la Disposición Adicional Final de la ley citada dice que "en uso del Poder Constituyente que compete al Consejo de Ministros, se declara la presente Ley parte integrante de la Ley Fundamental de la República la que así queda adicionada". De esa manera, esta ley ha quedado sometida, respecto a su vigencia, a las vicisitudes de la Ley Fundamental de 1959.

[43] Visto el Programa, parece que estas leyes se examinarán en otro de los estudios que se presentarán en esta sesión.

En el Artículo 286, además de por el origen popular o congresional de la iniciativa de reforma, la Constitución de 1940 distingue entre reforma específica o parcial y reforma integral. En especial, para el caso de una reforma integral de la Constitución, como el intento que resultó en la Ley Fundamental de la República de 1959, ese Artículo dispone en su párrafo cuarto:

Artículo 286.— ...
En el caso de que la reforma sea integral o se contraiga a la soberanía nacional o a los artículos veintidós, veintitrés, veinticuatro y ochenta y siete de esta Constitución, o a la forma de Gobierno, después de cumplirse los requisitos anteriormente señalados, según que la iniciativa proceda del pueblo o del congreso se convocará a elecciones para Delegados a una Asamblea Plebiscitaria, que tendrá lugar seis meses después de acordada, la que se limitará exclusivamente a aprobar o rechazar las reformas propuestas.

El primer punto que caracteriza una reforma integral está regulado por los Artículos 1 al 3; el 22 se refiere a la retroactividad de la ley; el 23 a la libertad de contratación; el 24 a la prohibición de la confiscación de bienes, y el 87 al reconocimiento de la propiedad privada. Ello nos permite concluir que las cinco reformas iniciales de enero de 1959 fueron todas integrales.

No es necesario ser abogado, ni siquiera profesional, para concluir que en ningún momento a partir del 1o. de enero de 1959 se ha producido ninguno de los actos jurídicos que la Constitución establece para su reforma integral. No ha habido ninguna iniciativa popular ni ninguna del Congreso, pues, en realidad, desde el 10 de marzo de 1952 no ha existido un Congreso en Cuba y el pueblo cubano no ha prestado su iniciativa a ninguno de los casos examinados precedentemente de reforma parcial o total, pero siempre integral, de la Constitución de 1940.

No se intente argumentar que la Constitución dejó de estar en vigor en virtud de la Resolución del Tribunal Supremo de 1o. de enero de 1959. Ese cuerpo no tiene competencia, conforme a la misma Constitución, para derogarla, y la Resolución se limitó a declarar que, en virtud de la doctrina del hecho consumado, era necesario concluir que el gobierno anterior había abandonado el poder y el sector revolucionario lo detentaba, con el beneplácito de la mayoría del pueblo y que, por consiguiente, la Revolución, constituida en gobierno provisional, había devenido en fuente de derecho.

Además, el texto mismo de la Resolución da a la Constitución de 1940 por vigente, no obstante considerar inaplicable el Artículo 149 sobre sucesión presidencial por el Magistrado más antiguo del Tribunal Supremo, porque dicho precepto se refiere a casos de sustitución "normal" y no de detentación del poder público, como hecho consumado, en las condiciones entonces existentes. Es más, como se ha explicado precedentemente, el régimen dio por vigente a la Constitución de 1940 e intentó modificarla en cinco ocasiones durante el primer mes de detentar el poder, hasta que decidió modificarla integralmente por la Ley Fundamental de la República, de 7 de febrero de 1959.

2.   El Régimen Nunca ha Detentado Legítimamente el Poder Constituyente. Uno de los principios básicos generales de Derecho Constitucional postula que el Poder Constituyente en una democracia sólo radica en el pueblo, o en sus representantes especialmente electos para ese propósito. Quiere ello decir que el Poder Constituyente es de carácter excepcional y extraordinario y esencialmente sólo corresponde al pueblo o a sus delegados especialmente electos, y nunca se atribuye al gobierno.

El régimen, al afirmar que está investido de "plenos poderes", alude a los Poderes Ejecutivo y Legislativo, etc. pero no al Poder Constituyente. Es más, en sentido estricto, en virtud del principio de separación de poderes, al gobierno nunca corresponde el Poder Judicial. De ahí que el régimen se tomara 16 años para institucionalizar la conversión del Poder Judicial en el "sistema judicial" y, por consiguiente, en mera dependencia del Poder Central.

En esa situación, uno de los principales postulados de la Revolución que tomó el poder el 1o. de enero de 1959 era el restablecimiento, no sólo en la letra sino en el espíritu, y sobre todo en la práctica, de la Constitución de 1940, mediante su fiel cumplimiento y la rápida generación de la legislación complementaria. El 1º de enero de 1959, al tomar el poder, la Revolución constató que la Constitución de 1940 estaba plenamente restablecida, al menos desde el punto de vista jurídico-formal. Por eso, resulta inconcebible que el régimen, presidido por el Magistrado Urrutia, que la misma Resolución del Tribunal Supremo había calificado de **interino**, pudiese entender que dentro del poder inherente al gobierno *de facto* estuviera incluido el Poder Constituyente.

Por ello, es completamente irrazonable e infundado el argumento, que se esgrime en las cinco reformas parciales iniciales, todas integrales, de que existe "la necesidad inaplazable de usar el poder constituyente para viabilizar la legislación que haga posible la realización de los hechos que le impone la Revolución". Tal argumento, expresado de otro modo, significa que ya el 10 de enero de 1959, el régimen había llegado a la conclusión que la Constitución, lejos de ser un objetivo, era un obstáculo para que la Revolución realizara una serie de hechos precisa y expresamente prohibidos por la misma Constitución.

Es más, si se comparan los artículos objeto de las reformas parciales iniciales del régimen (21, 24, 25, 27, 29 y 196) con los mencionados en el párrafo cuarto del Artículo 286 de la Constitución de 1940 sobre reforma integral de la constitución (1 al 3, 22, 23, 24, 87), se observan muy interesantes coincidencias: en uno y otro caso se trata de materias como la forma de gobierno, la retroactividad de la ley, la libertad contractual, la confiscación de bienes y el derecho de propiedad, respecto de las cuales resulta ahora claro que el régimen tenía especiales intenciones. De lo contrario, el régimen hubiera cumplido desde el principio con la Constitución, no hubiera intentado reformarla parcialmente cinco veces, ni tenido, desde el 10 de enero de 1959, el proyecto de, irrogándose a plenitud el Poder Constituyente, por sí y ante sí y sin intervención del pueblo mediante el procedimiento establecido en la misma Constitución, remplazarla por una Ley Fundamental que le abrió la posibilidad legislativa de establecer un régimen marxista-leninista que no se atrevió a "institucionalizar" constitucionalmente hasta 1976.

3. **El Procedimiento de Reforma Constitucional Es Elemento Esencial.** Si el poder constituyente pudiera ejercerse por un gobierno *de facto*, serían innecesarias o inanes las disposiciones sobre Reforma Constitucional que existen en toda constitución. Bastaría que el gobierno "interino" acordase una nueva constitución. Precisamente, para que ello no pueda jurídicamente tener lugar, existen las disposiciones constitucionales sobre reformas y las alternativas jurídicamente aceptables sólo son dos: ajustarse al **procedimiento establecido** en la constitución vigente, o **convocar** a una Asamblea Constituyente, lo que no constituye ejercicio del Poder Constituyente, sino del legislativo, que es a lo que se refería la Resolución del Tribunal Supremo de 1º de enero de 1959. En definitiva, en ambos casos, es el pueblo directamente, o a través de delegados especialmente electos para ese propósito, quien ejercita el Poder Constituyente, nunca el gobierno, y, menos, un gobierno *de facto*.

4. **El Pueblo Apoyó la Revolución para Mantener la Constitución, No para Remplazarla.** Si bien este argumento es de carácter político y no jurídico, no vacilo en esgrimirlo, porque el 1º de

enero de 1959, como percibió claramente el Tribunal Supremo, estábamos frente a un **hecho consumado** y no ante un acto jurídico como una elección o sustitución presidencial. Es decir, que el gobierno "interino", en vez de cumplir con el mandato político de mantener la Constitución de 1940[44], se aprovechó del apoyo popular irrogándose un Poder Constituyente que nunca se le delegó, para hacer, precisamente, lo contrario de lo que aquel "mandato" implicaba, lo que en definitiva no es otra cosa que un simple abuso de poder.

5.   **La Modificación Integral de la Constitución Tuvo un Objetivo Concreto.** Ese objetivo es el de modificar la normas sobre reforma constitucional, y ello se consiguió con el Artículo 232 de esa ley fundamental de 1959, que dice:

> *Artículo 232.— Esta Ley Fundamental podrá reformarse por el Consejo de Ministros, en votación nominal, con la conformidad de las dos terceras partes de sus componentes, ratificada por igual votación en tres sesiones sucesivas y con la aprobación del Presidente de la República.*

En este punto cabe preguntarse: si desde el 10 de enero de 1959 el régimen afirmó como fundamento de las cinco reformas parciales de la Constitución de 1940 que aprobó, que tenía necesidad inaplazable de usar el Poder Constituyente, y así lo hizo válidamente, ¿porqué consideró necesario hacerlo constar de nuevo en el artículo 232 del instrumento de 7 de febrero de 1959?, ¿acaso tenía dudas de la validez del fundamento de tales reformas parciales? Tampoco este Artículo debe haber parecido satisfactorio al régimen, cuando dieciséis años después, al modificar totalmente esta "ley fundamental" **se inventó un nuevo procedimiento ad hoc** para hacerlo.

6.   **El Procedimiento de Reforma Integral de 1976 Es "Inconstitucional".** El régimen, que en enero de 1959 afirmó estar investido del Poder Constituyente, se sintió inclinado a conferírselo nuevamente en febrero de 1959. Sin embargo, como se ha comprobado más arriba, en 1975 no se ajustó al proceso de reforma del artículo 232 de la ley fundamental, sino que inventó uno nuevo en el que el Poder Constituyente fue compartido por el Consejo de Ministros con el Buró Político del Partido Comunista de Cuba, a nivel de "Anteproyecto", y con una inusitada innovación, consultado directamente con el pueblo a través de un proceso de **consulta-indoctrinación.** Y ello, con un pueblo que, doce años después, se califica por altos personeros del régimen, como víctima de "analfabetismo jurídico". Es decir, que la consulta-indoctrinación, no obstante haber durado cinco meses, parece no haber logrado imbuir de los más elementales conceptos constitucionales al pueblo cubano. Pero todavía hay más: esa consulta fue examinada después en el primer Congreso del Partido Comunista de Cuba, con lo que se elevó al mayor rango posible, el de los terceros ajenos que, sin autorización preestablecida jurídicamente, intervinieron en el proceso de reforma constitucional sin estar llamados a ello por la ley fundamental que entonces se consideraba en vigor. Y más: el "Proyecto" fue sometido a un "referéndum popular", cuya convocatoria y términos se desconocen por no haber estado prescritos ni en la ley fundamental ni en una convocatoria formal y la votación fue del 97.7% a favor. ¿Se habrá logrado alguna vez en algún país democrático y progresista semejante porcentaje de **participación total** en un proceso electoral? Si ello es cierto, entonces ¿qué porcentaje votó en contra, y cuál fue el porcentaje de participación total en el referéndum de 1976?

---

[44]Éste, como se ha dicho, constituía el principal factor de aglutinación de los sectores de oposición en la lucha contra la dictadura batistiana.

B.   Normas Constitucionales Inaplicables: Acto Institucional

Si la Constitución de 1940 entrase en vigor en determinado momento, es obvio que un cierto número de artículos serían inaplicables en el caso de un GPUN, sólo compuesto inicialmente por el Poder Ejecutivo, integrado por el Presidente Provisional, el Primer Ministro y el Consejo de Ministros.   Por ejemplo, una de sus tareas iniciales de gran urgencia será la de organizar una comisión, integrada por ex miembros del Poder Judicial, que se encargue de reorganizar, con total independencia, al Poder Judicial conforme a las disposiciones del Título Décimocuarto de la Constitución; en cambio, no sería ese el caso del Título Noveno, relativo al Poder Legislativo, que no existirá hasta que se celebren elecciones generales. Por ese motivo, sería recomendable que como paso previo a la instalación del GPUN, se dicte, por todos los grupos y tendencias de dentro y fuera de Cuba, un Acto Institucional que al designar el GPUN determine, además, las normas de la Constitución que entrarán de inmediato en vigor y las que serían inaplicables durante ese período.

Prima facie, a guisa de ejemplo, y sin que ello signifique prejuzgar, parecería que claramente entrarían en vigor la gran mayoría de los artículos de la Constitución, mientras que unos pocos serían inaplicables. Pongamos un ejemplo: ¿por qué no podría entrar en vigor el Artículo 15 del Título Segundo? Porque su párrafo a) excluiría de participar en el proceso político cubano a los exilados que hayan optado por la ciudadanía del país de su residencia. Dice ese Artículo 15:

Artículo 15.— Pierden la ciudadanía cubana:

a)los que adquieran una ciudadanía extranjera.

b)los que, sin permiso del Senado, entren al servicio militar de otra nación, o al desempeño de funciones que lleven aparejada autoridad o jurisdicción propia.

c)los cubanos por naturalización que residan tres años consecutivos en el país de su nacimiento, a no ser que expresen cada tres años, ante la autoridad consular correspondiente, su voluntad de conservar la ciudadanía cubana.

La ley podrá determinar delitos y causas de indignidad que produzcan la pérdida de la ciudadanía por naturalización, mediante sentencia firme de los tribunales competentes.

d)los naturalizados que aceptaren una doble ciudadanía.

Es difícil, ante estas disposiciones, que los cubanos de fuera de Cuba puedan participar en la vida pública del país, si en el Acto Institucional no se incluye una aclaración de que ese Artículo no es aplicable a los cubanos que abandonaron el país a partir del 1o. de enero de 1959, por tratarse de una situación que la Asamblea Constituyente no pudo haber anticipado. Bastaría con esta advertencia, referida al Artículo 15, para considerar aplicable el resto de este título, pues la cuestión de si a tales personas se les aceptará mantener una doble nacionalidad será materia de la competencia de la Asamblea Constituyente que el GPUN deberá convocar dentro del plazo que se le fije en el mismo Acto Institucional. Es decir, que este instrumento operaría como determinante del tránsito constitucional. Parecidas situaciones ocurren con otros Artículos de la Constitución.[45]

---

[45]El reconocimiento de la vigencia de la Constitución de 1940 conlleva la declaración de que todo propietario privado de sus bienes por un acto de gobierno tiene el derecho a la devolución o a una indemnización "fijada judicialmente", como dice el Artículo 24 de esa Constitución. Corresponderá al Gobierno Constitucional que se elija en las Elecciones Generales multipartidistas, en un acto de gobierno

Sin embargo, el examen de cada uno de esos casos concretos no sería posible cubrirlo en este trabajo, sino más bien en una etapa siguiente.[46]

C. Posibilidad de un Consejo Supremo de Unidad Nacional (CSUN)[47]

En principio, concibo al GPUN como investido solamente de los poderes que contemplan los Títulos respectivos de la Constitución y, por consiguiente, carente de Poder Legislativo. No parecería necesario, para las tareas concretas que serán de su incumbencia, que el GPUN lo requiera. Así, por ejemplo, no necesita ese poder para convocar a Asamblea Constituyente ni a Elecciones Generales; bastará que utilice las disposiciones constitucionales al respecto, la ley empleada para convocar a la Asamblea Constituyente de 1940 y la empleada para convocar a las Elecciones Generales que no tuvieron lugar por el golpe de Estado del 10 de marzo de 1952, complementadas con las disposiciones reglamentarias que la Constitución de 1940 autoriza al Poder Ejecutivo a dictar. No obstante, el foro democrático integrado por los grupos y tendencias que convengan en el Acto Institucional podría asumir la función de órgano de consulta legislativa para los casos en que el GPUN así lo requiera. Obsérvese que en ningún caso he contemplado que el GPUN o el CSUN asuman poderes legislativos.

D. Declaración de Ineficacia y Nulidad de la Legislación Anómala

Otra de las materias que podrían incluirse en el Acto Institucional sería la declaración de ineficacia y nulidad, por responder al marco institucional de una constitución apócrifa, de la las leyes que he analizado previamente y el reconocimiento de la vigencia de la legislación que se pretendió derogar, con el texto que tenía el día anterior al 10 de marzo de 1952. Hago, sin embargo una excepción: considero que la Ley de Reforma Tributaria se adoptó válidamente por el régimen, al que he reconocido estar investido del poder legislativo, siempre que ese poder se haya ejercitado dentro del marco de las disposiciones de la Constitución de 1940. Si bien la Ley de Reforma Tributaria se aprobó por el Consejo de Ministros estando ya en vigor la denominada Ley Fundamental de la República de 1959, ninguna de sus disposiciones parece estar en conflicto con la Constitución de 1940. Se trata realmente de una codificación y racionalización del conjunto de impuestos internos en vigor en la fecha en que se aprobó, e incluye un procedimiento común para la tributación interna, concebido sobre la base de los procedimientos existentes y el conjunto, que constituye más bien el primer Código Tributario que haya regido en Cuba, responde a la concepción de una economía mixta, que será seguramente dentro de la cual habrá de gobernar el GPUN.

Este aparente retroceso jurídico no debe, como primera aproximación, levantar preocupaciones. Por ejemplo, en materia de derecho civil, la reinstauración de la usucapión no debe preocupar excesivamente a los privados de sus bienes ilegítimamente por un acto de gobierno.

---

de política económica, o al tribunal competente, una vez reorganizado el Poder Judicial, la determinación de lo que proceda ante la acción que, a ese efecto, pueda ejercitar al propietario.

[46]Mis compañeros Agustín de Goytisolo y José M. Hernández Puente, que actuaron respectivamente como Comentarista y Moderador en la sesión en la que leí este papel, se han ofrecido para que preparemos un trabajo conjunto sobre esta materia que presentaríamos en la próxima Reunión Anual.

[47]Este Consejo sólo tiene de común el nombre con el Consejo Consultivo de los primeros meses de la dictadura de Batista, responsable de haberle reconocido a ese régimen alguna legitimidad, pues en vez de ser designado por el gobierno, estaría integrado por los líderes de los distintos grupos y facciones políticas que participen en la concertación de la unidad nacional, de la que resultaría el Gobierno Provisional.

Examinar las razones en detalle no es materia de este trabajo, pero la cuestión dista de ser insoluble.[48]

Lo mismo cabe decir, por citar otro caso, de la legislación laboral que regía el dia anterior al 10 de marzo de 1952. Aunque como hemos visto, el código laboral socialista contempla como causa de extinción del contrato de trabajo, la "declaración de disponibilidad del trabajador" que interpreto como un eufemismo para describir un simple despido por economía, no creo que el retorno al histórico Decreto 798 de 13 de abril de 1938 que estableció, en la práctica, la inamovilidad laboral al no contemplar el despido por economía y hacer tremendamente costoso y engorroso el procedimiento de despido laboral. Considero que por tratarse de un Decreto Presidencial este texto normativo no es "inamovible".[49]

No obstante, debo enfatizar que estas salvedades, que incluyo como mera especulación profesional, deberán ser objeto de un estudio especial, posterior al estudio conjunto a que se refiere la Nota al Pie No. 46.[50]

---

[48]En lo referente al derecho civil, esta declaratoria significaría el restablecimiento de la vigencia, sin solución de continuidad, de la usucapión o prescripción adquisitiva del viejo Código Civil, cuyo Artículo 1959 se ha transcrito en la Nota al Pie No. 35. Sin embargo, opino que el legislador civil lo que intenta por medio de esta disposición es definir la *prescripción extintiva*, para el titular del dominio en el Registro de la Propiedad, como consecuencia de una actitud ante su derecho que por negligencia, desidia o cualquier otro motivo incompatible con la diligencia de un buen "padre de familia", refleja una intención implícita de abandono de ese derecho del que es titular. Me resisto a creer que un tribunal de justicia pueda aplicar esta institución a quien abandonó el país para preservar su vida o su libertad personal, o que fue desposeído del inmueble por un acto de gobierno.

[49]En efecto, la reforma y derogación de Decretos Presidenciales, como es el Decreto 798, es competencia propia, según la Constitución de 1940, del Poder Ejecutivo y, por consiguiente, estaría al alcance del Gobierno Provisional. Espero que esta explicación, junto con mis seguridades de que las causales de extinción del contrato de trabajo no están específicamente establecidas en la Constitución de 1940, aplacarán la preocupación, exteriorizada por mi compañero economista el Dr. Armando Lago, como comentario a mis conclusiones por el obstáculo que representarían para el proceso de privatización de las empresas estatales.

[50]Me atrevo a anticipar, aunque no he hecho las consultas respectivas, que Agustín de Goytisolo y José M. Hernández Puente, "exigirán" participar en este tercer estudio sobre estos temas, en el que no podrá faltar el examen de la situación jurídica de la propiedad agraria estatal y de la propiedad residencial urbana.

Apéndice **I**

OCTAVA REUNIÓN DE CONSULTA de
MINISTROS de RELACIONES EXTERIORES
Para Servir de Órgano de Consulta en Aplicación del
TRATADO INTERAMERICANO DE ASISTENCIA RECÍPROCA

Punta del Este, Uruguay, 22 a 31 de enero de 1962

ACTA FINAL

VI

EXCLUSIÓN DEL ACTUAL GOBIERNO DE CUBA
DE SU PARTICIPACIÓN EN EL SISTEMA INTERAMERICANO

La Octava Reunión de Consulta de Ministros de Relaciones Exteriores para Servir de Órgano de Consulta en Aplicación del Tratado Interamericano de Asistencia Recíproca,

CONSIDERANDO:

Que el Sistema Interamericano está basado en la constante adhesión de los Estados que de él forman parte a determinados propósitos y principios de solidaridad, fijados en los instrumentos que lo rigen;

Que entre esos propósitos y principios están los del respeto a la libertad de la persona humana, la preservación de sus derechos y el pleno ejercicio de la democracia representativa; la no intervención de un Estado en los asuntos internos o externos de otro y el rechazo de las alianzas o entendimientos que motiven la intervención de potencias extracontinentales en América;

Que la Séptima Reunión de Consulta de Ministros de Relaciones Exteriores efectuada en San José, Costa Rica, condenó la intervención o amenaza de intervención de las potencias comunistas extracontinentales en el Hemisferio y reiteró la obligación de los Estados Americanos de observar fielmente los principios del sistema regional;

Que el actual Gobierno de Cuba se ha identificado con los principios de la ideología marxista-leninista, ha establecido un régimen político, económico y social fundado en esta doctrina y acepta la militar de las potencias comunistas extracontinentales e inclusive la amenaza de intervención armada de la Unión Soviética en América

Que el Informe de la Comisión Interamericana de Paz a la Octava Reunión de Consulta de Ministros de Relaciones Exteriores establece que:

> "Las actuales vinculaciones del Gobierno de Cuba con los países del bloque chino-soviético son ostensiblemente incompatibles con los principios y normas que rigen el sistema regional y, en especial, el de seguridad colectiva establecido por la Carta de la Organización de los Estados Americanos y el Tratado Interamericano de Asistencia Recíproca", (pág. 48);

Que el mencionado Informe de la Comisión Interamericana de Paz igualmente conceptúa que:

> "Es evidente que las vinculaciones del Gobierno cubano con el bloque chino-soviético inhabilitan a dicho gobierno para cumplir las obligaciones estipuladas en la Carta de la Organización y en el Tratado Interamericano de Asistencia Recíproca", (pág. 49);

Que una situación semejante de un Estado Americano es violatoria de los deberes inherentes a la calidad de miembro del sistema regional e incompatible con éste;

Que la actitud asumida por el actual Gobierno de Cuba y su aceptación de la ayuda militar proporcionada por las potencias comunistas extracontinentales destruyen la eficacia defensiva del Sistema Interamericano; y

Que ningún Estado miembro del Sistema Interamericano puede reclamar los derechos y privilegios del mismo si niega o desconoce las obligaciones correlativas,

DECLARA:

1. Que el actual Gobierno de Cuba, como consecuencia de sus actos reiterados, se ha colocado voluntariamente fuera del Sistema Interamericano;

2. Que esta situación requiere la más continua vigilancia de parte de los países miembros de la Organización de los Estados Americanos, los que deben informar al Consejo de todo hecho o situación capaz de poner en peligro la paz y seguridad del Continente;

3. Que existe un interés colectivo de los Estados Americanos para reforzar al Sistema Interamericano y reconstituir su unidad, sobre la base del respeto a los derechos humanos y a los principios y propósitos que señala para el ejercicio de la democracia la Carta de la Organización; y

Por tanto,

RESUELVE:

1. Que la adhesión de cualquier miembro de la Organización de los Estados Americanos al marxismo-leninismo es incompatible con el Sistema Interamericano y el alineamiento de tal gobierno con el bloque comunista quebranta la unidad y la solidaridad del Hemisferio.

2. Que el actual Gobierno de Cuba, que oficialmente se ha identificado como un gobierno marxista-leninista, es incompatible con los principios y propósitos del Sistema Interamericano.

3. Que esta incompatibilidad excluye al actual Gobierno de Cuba de su participación en el Sistema Interamericano.

4. Que el Consejo de la Organización de los Estados Americanos y los otros órganos y organismos del Sistema Interamericano adopten sin demora las providencias necesarias para cumplir esta resolución.

Apéndice II

NOVENA CONFERENCIA INTERNACIONAL AMERICANA
Bogotá, 30 de marzo a 2 de mayo de 1948

RESOLUCIÓN XXX

DECLARACIÓN AMERICANA DE LOS DERECHOS Y DEBERES DEL HOMBRE

La IX Conferencia Internacional Americana,

CONSIDERANDO

Que los pueblos americanos han dignificado la persona humana y que sus constituciones nacionales reconocen que las instituciones jurídicas y políticas, rectoras de la vida en sociedad, tienen como fin principal la protección de los derechos esenciales del hombre y la creación de circunstancias que le permitan progresar espiritual y materialmente y alcanzar la felicidad;

Que, en repetidas ocasiones, los Estados Americanos han reconocido que los derechos esenciales del hombre no nacen del hecho de ser nacional de determinado Estado sino que tienen como fundamento los atributos de la persona humana;

Que la protección internacional de los derechos del hombre debe ser guía principalísima del derecho americano en evolución;

Que la consagración americana de los derechos esenciales del hombre unida a las garantías ofrecidas por el régimen interno de los Estados, establece el sistema inicial de protección que los Estados Americanos consideran adecuado a las actuales circunstancias sociales y jurídicas, no sin reconocer que deberán fortalecerlo cada vez más en el campo internacional, a medida que esas circunstancias vayan siendo más propicias,

ACUERDA: Adoptar la siguiente

DECLARACIÓN AMERICANA DE LOS DERECHOS Y DEBERES DEL HOMBRE

PREÁMBULO

Todos los hombres nacen libres e iguales en dignidad y derechos y, dotados como están por naturaleza de razón y conciencia, deben conducirse fraternalmente los unos con los otros.

El cumplimiento del deber de cada uno es exigencia del derecho de todos.

Derechos y deberes se integran correlativamente en toda actividad social y política del hombre. Si los derechos exaltan la libertad individual, los deberes expresan la dignidad de esa libertad.

Los deberes de orden jurídico presuponen otros, de orden moral, que los apoyan conceptualmente y los fundamentan.

Es deber del hombre servir al espíritu con todas sus potencias y recursos porque el espíritu es la finalidad suprema de la existencia humana y su máxima categoría.

Es deber del hombre ejercer, mantener y estimular por todos los medios a su alcance la cultura, porque la cultura es la máxima expresión social e histórica del espíritu.

Y puesto que la moral y buenas maneras constituyen la floración más noble de la cultura, es deber de todo hombre acatarlas siempre.

CAPÍTULO PRIMERO
DERECHOS

ARTÍCULO I. Todo ser humano tiene derecho a la vida, a la libertad y a la seguridad de su persona.

Derecho a la vida, a la libertad, la seguridad de integridad de la persona.

ARTÍCULO II. Todas las personas son iguales ante la Ley y tienen los derechos y deberes consagrados en esta declaración sin distinción de raza, sexo, idioma, credo ni otra alguna.

Derecho de igualdad ante la Ley.

ARTÍCULO III. Toda persona tiene el derecho de profesar libremente una creencia religiosa y de manifestarla y practicarla en público y en privado.

Derecho a la libertad religiosa y de culto.

ARTÍCULO IV. Toda persona tiene derecho a la libertad de investigación, de opinión y de expresión y difusión del pensamiento por cualquier medio.

Derecho de libertad de investigación, opinión, expresión y difusión.

ARTÍCULO V. Toda persona tiene derecho a la protección de la Ley contra los ataques abusivos a su honra, a su reputación y a su vida privada y familiar.

Derecho a la protección a la honra, la reputación personal y la vida privada y familiar.

ARTÍCULO VI. Toda persona tiene derecho a constituir familia, elemento fundamental de la sociedad, y a recibir protección para ella.

Derecho a la constitución y a la protección de la familia.

ARTÍCULO VII. Toda mujer en estado de gravidez o en época de lactancia, así como todo niño, tienen derecho a protección, cuidados y ayuda especiales.

Derecho de protección a la maternidad y a la infancia.

ARTÍCULO VIII. Toda persona tiene el derecho de fijar su residencia en el territorio del Estado de que es nacional, de transitar por él libremente y no abandonarlo sino por su voluntad.

Derechos de residencia y tránsito.

ARTÍCULO IX. Toda persona tiene el derecho a la inviolabilidad de su domicilio.

Derecho a la inviolabilidad del domicilio.

ARTÍCULO X. Toda persona tiene derecho a la inviolabilidad y circulación de su correspondencia.

Derecho a la inviolabilidad y circulación de la correspondencia.

ARTÍCULO XI. Toda persona tiene derecho a que su salud sea preservada por medidas sanitarias y sociales, relativas a la alimentación, el vestido, la vivienda y la asistencia médica, correspondientes, al nivel que permitan los recursos públicos y los de la comunidad.

Derecho a la preservación de la salud y al bienestar.

ARTÍCULO XII. Toda persona tiene derecho a la educación, la que debe estar inspirada en los principios de libertad, moralidad y solidaridad humanas.

Derecho a la educación.

Asimismo tiene el derecho de que, mediante esa educación, se le capacite para lograr una digna subsistencia, en mejoramiento de nivel de vida y para ser útil a la sociedad.

El derecho de educación comprende el de igualdad de oportunidades en todos los casos, de acuerdo con las dotes naturales,]os méritos y el deseo de aprovechar los recursos que puedan proporcionar la comunidad y el Estado.

Toda persona tiene derecho a recibir gratuitamente la educación primaria, por lo menos.

ARTÍCULO XIII. Toda persona tiene el derecho de participar en la vida cultural de la comunidad, gozar de las artes y disfrutar de los beneficios que resulten de los progresos intelectuales y especialmente de los descubrimientos científicos.

Derecho a los beneficios de la cultura.

Tiene asimismo derecho a la protección de los intereses morales y materiales que le correspondan por razón de los inventos, obras literarias, científicas o artísticas de que sea autor.

ARTÍCULO XIV. Toda persona tiene derecho al trabajo en condiciones dignas y a seguir libremente su vocación, en cuanto lo permitan las oportunidades existentes de empleo.

Derecho al trabajo y una justa retribución.

Toda persona que trabaja tiene derecho de recibir una remuneración que, en relación con su capacidad y destreza le asegure un nivel de vida conveniente para sí misma y su familia.

ARTÍCULO XV. Toda persona tiene derecho descanso, a honesta recreación y a la oportunidad de emplear útilmente el tiempo libre en beneficio de su mejoramiento espiritual, cultural y físico.

Derecho al descanso y a su aprovechamiento.

ARTÍCULO XVI. Toda persona tiene derecho a la seguridad social que le proteja contra las consecuencias de la desocupación, de la vejez y de la incapacidad que, proveniente de cualquier otra causa ajena a su voluntad, la imposibilite física o mentalmente para obtener los medios de subsistencia.

Derecho a la seguridad social.

ARTÍCULO XVII. Toda persona tiene derecho a que se le reconozca en cualquier parte como sujeto de derechos y obligaciones, y a gozar de los derechos civiles fundamentales.

Derecho de reconocimiento de la personalidad jurídica y de los derechos civiles.

ARTÍCULO XVIII. Toda persona puede ocurrir a los tribunales para hacer valer sus derechos. Asimismo debe disponer de un procedimiento sencillo y breve por el cual la justicia lo ampare contra actos de la autoridad que violen, en perjuicio suyo, alguno de los derechos fundamentales consagrados constitucionalmente.

Derecho de justicia.

ARTÍCULO XIX. Toda persona tiene derecho a la nacionalidad que legalmente le corresponda y el de cambiarla, si así lo desea, por la de cualquier otro país que esté dispuesto a otorgársela.

Derecho de nacionalidad.

ARTÍCULO XX. Toda persona, legalmente capacitada, tiene el derecho de tomar parte en el gobierno de su país, directamente o por medio de sus representantes, y de participar en las elecciones populares, que serán de voto secreto, genuinas, periódicas y libres.

Derecho de sufragio y de participación en el gobierno.

ARTÍCULO XXI. Toda persona tiene el derecho de reunirse pacíficamente con otras, en manifestación pública o en asamblea transitoria, en relación con sus intereses comunes de cualquier índole.

Derecho de reunión.

ARTÍCULO XXII. Toda persona tiene el derecho de asociarse con otras para promover, ejercer y proteger sus intereses legítimos de orden político, económico, religioso, social, cultural, profesional, sindical o de cualquier otro orden.

Derecho de asociación.

ARTÍCULO XXIII. Toda persona tiene derecho a la propiedad privada correspondiente a las necesidades esenciales de una vida decorosa, que contribuya a mantener la dignidad de la persona y del hogar.

Derecho a la propiedad.

ARTÍCULO XXIV. Toda persona tiene derecho de presentar peticiones respetuosas a cualquiera autoridad competente, ya sea por motivo de interés general, ya de interés particular, y el de obtener pronta resolución.

Derecho de petición.

- 90 -

ARTÍCULO XXV. Nadie puede ser privado de su libertad sino en los casos y según las formas establecidas por leyes preexistentes.

Derecho de protección contra la detención arbitraria.

Nadie puede ser detenido por incumplimiento de obligaciones de carácter netamente civil.

Todo individuo que haya sido privado de su libertad tiene derecho a que el juez verifique sin demora la legalidad de la medida y a ser juzgado sin dilación injustificada, o, de lo contrario, a ser puesto en libertad. Tiene derecho también a un tratamiento humano durante la privación de su libertad.

ARTÍCULO XXVI. Se presume que todo acusado es inocente, hasta que se pruebe que es culpable.

Derecho a proceso regular.

Toda persona acusada de delito tiene derecho a ser oída en forma imparcial y pública, a ser juzgada por tribunales anteriormente establecidos de acuerdo con leyes preexistentes y a que no se le imponga penas crueles, infamantes o inusitadas.

ARTÍCULO XXVII. Toda persona tiene el derecho de buscar y recibir asilo en territorio extranjero, en caso de persecución que no sea motivada por delitos de derecho común y de acuerdo con la legislación de cada país y con los convenios internacionales.

Derecho de asilo.

ARTÍCULO XXVIII. Los derechos de cada hombre están limitados por los derechos de los demás, por la seguridad de todos y por las justas exigencias del bienestar general y del desenvolvimiento democrático.

Alcance de los derechos del hombre.

CAPÍTULO SEGUNDO
DEBERES

ARTÍCULO XXIX. Toda persona tiene el deber de convivir con las demás de manera que todas y cada una puedan formar y desenvolver integralmente su personalidad.

Deberes ante la sociedad.

ARTÍCULO XXX. Toda persona tiene el deber de asistir, alimentar, educar y amparar a sus hijos menores de edad, y los hijos tienen el deber de honrar siempre a sus padres y el de asistirlos, alimentarlos y ampararlos cuando éstos lo necesiten.

Deberes para con los hijos y los padres.

ARTÍCULO XXXI. Toda persona tiene el deber de adquirir a lo menos la instrucción primaria.

Deberes de instrucción.

ARTÍCULO XXXII. Toda persona tiene el deber de votar en las elecciones populares del país de que sea nacional, cuando esté legalmente capacitada para ello.

Deber de sufragio.

ARTÍCULO XXXIII. Toda persona tiene el deber de obedecer a la Ley y demás mandamientos legítimos de las autoridades de su país y de aquél en que se encuentre.

Deber de obediencia a la Ley.

ARTÍCULO XXXIV. Toda persona hábil tiene el deber de prestar los servicios civiles y militares que la Patria requiera para su defensa y conservación, y en caso de calamidad pública, los servicios de que sea capaz.

Deber de servir a la comunidad y a la nación.

Asimismo tiene el deber de desempeñar los cargos de elección popular que le correspondan en el Estado de que sea nacional.

ARTÍCULO XXXV. Toda persona tiene el deber de cooperar con el Estado y con la comunidad en la asistencia y seguridad sociales de acuerdo con sus posibilidades y con las circunstancias.

Deberes de asistencia y seguridad sociales.

ARTÍCULO XXXVI. Toda persona tiene el deber de pagar los impuestos establecidos por la Ley para el sostenimiento de los servicios públicos.

Deber de pagar impuestos.

ARTÍCULO XXXVII. Toda persona tiene el deber de trabajar, dentro de su capacidad y posibilidades, a fin de obtener los recursos para su subsistencia o en beneficio de la comunidad.

Deber de trabajo.

ARTÍCULO XXXVIII. Toda persona tiene el deber de no intervenir en las actividades políticas que, de conformidad con la Ley, sean privativas de los ciudadanos del Estado en que sea extranjero.

Deber de abstenerse de actividades políticas en país extranjero.

Apéndice III

RESOLUCIÓN XXXII

PRESERVACIÓN Y DEFENSA DE LA DEMOCRACIA EN AMÉRICA

Las Repúblicas representadas en la IX Conferencia Internacional Americana,

CONSIDERANDO:

Que para salvaguardar la paz y mantener el mutuo respeto entre los Estados, la situación actual del mundo exige que se tomen medidas urgentes que proscriban las tácticas de hegemonía totalitaria, inconciliables con la tradición de los países de América, y que eviten que agentes al servicio del comunismo internacional o de cualquier totalitarismo pretendan desvirtuar la auténtica y libre voluntad de los pueblos de este Continente,

DECLARAN:

Que por su naturaleza antidemocrática y por su tendencia intervencionista, la acción política del comunismo internacional o de cualquier totalitarismo es incompatible con la concepción de la libertad americana, la cual descansa en dos postulados incontestables: la dignidad del hombre como persona y la soberanía de la nación como Estado.

REITERAN,

La fe que los pueblos del Nuevo Mundo han depositado en el ideal y en la realidad de la democracia, al amparo de cuyo régimen ha de alcanzarse la justicia social ofreciendo a todos oportunidades cada día más amplias para gozar de los bienes espirituales y materiales que constituyen la garantía de la civilización y el patrimonio de la humanidad.

CONDENAN,

En nombre del Derecho de Gentes, la injerencia en la vida pública de las naciones del continente americano de cualquier potencia extranjera o de cualquier organización política que sirva intereses de una potencia extranjera; y

RESUELVEN:

1. Reafirmar su decisión de mantener y estimular una efectiva política social y económica, destinada a elevar el nivel de vida de sus pueblos, así como su convicción de que sólo en un régimen fundado en la garantía de las libertades y derechos esenciales de la persona humana, es posible alcanzar este propósito.

2. Condenar los métodos de todo sistema que tienda a suprimir los derechos y libertades políticos y civiles, especialmente la acción del comunismo internacional o de cualquier totalitarismo.

3. Adoptar, dentro de sus territorios respectivos y de acuerdo con los preceptos constitucionales de cada Estado, las medidas necesarias para desarraigar e impedir actividades dirigidas, asistidas o instigadas por gobiernos, organizaciones o individuos extranjeros, que tiendan a subvertir, por la violencia, las instituciones de dichas Repúblicas, a fomentar el desorden en su vida política interna, o a perturbar por presión, propaganda subversiva, amenazas o en cualquier otra forma, el derecho libre y soberano de sus pueblos a gobernarse por sí mismos de acuerdo con las aspiraciones democráticas.

4. Proceder a un amplio intercambio de informaciones acerca de las mencionadas actividades que se desarrollen en sus jurisdicciones respectivas.

Apéndice IV

RESOLUCIÓN XXXI

CORTE INTERAMERICANA PARA PROTEGER LOS DERECHOS DEL HOMBRE

La IX Conferencia Internacional Americana,

CONSIDERANDO:

Que los derechos del hombre, internacionalmente reconocidos, deben tener protección adecuada;

Que esa protección debe ser garantizada por un órgano jurídico, como quiera que no hay derecho propiamente asegurado sin el amparo de un tribunal competente;

Que, tratándose de derechos internacionalmente reconocidos, la protección jurídica para ser eficaz debe emanar de un órgano internacional,

RECOMIENDA:

Que el Comité Jurídico Interamericano elabore un proyecto de estatuto para la creación y funcionamiento de una Corte Interamericana destinada a garantizar los derechos del hombre. Ese proyecto, después de ser sometido al examen y a las observaciones de los Gobiernos de todos los Estados Americanos, deberá ser remitido a la X Conferencia Interamericana para que ésta lo estudie si considera que ha llegado el momento para una decisión sobre la materia.

EN TORNO AL PROYECTO DE LEY DE VIVIENDAS URBANAS Y RURALES

Julio Romañach, Jr.

Introducción

Conviene comenzar este trabajo exponiendo las metas que persigue el Proyecto de Ley que comentamos. El orden en que se han de exponer y discutir dichas metas no es un orden de prelación, ya que todas ellas son de fundamental importancia.

Las metas que persigue el Proyecto son las siguientes: 1) Evitar el desalojo de personas que en la actualidad ocupan viviendas en Cuba; 2) Establecer un sistema de prelación de títulos de propiedad y de compensación para los dueños desposeídos; y 3) Establecer un sistema factible de derecho de tanteo del Estado respecto a la propiedad de la vivienda actual en Cuba.

El Proyecto que comentamos da por sentado que a la caída del gobierno de Fidel Castro se establecerá en Cuba un régimen democrático que habrá de seguir una política económica más o menos liberal. Pero también se asume que las conquistas legislativas de tipo socio-económico plasmadas en la Constitución de 1940 se mantendrán en pleno vigor. Una de dichas conquistas legislativas es la aseveración tajante del artículo 87 de nuestra Carta Magna de 1940 al declarar la función social que debe desempeñar la propiedad privada. Reza el artículo 87 constitucional: "El Estado cubano reconoce la existencia y legitimidad de la propiedad privada en su más amplio concepto de función social y sin más limitaciones que aquellas que por motivos de necesidad pública o interés social establezca la Ley."

Dada la escasez de viviendas en Cuba, dado el estado de bancarrota total de la economía cubana, y dada la indigencia y penuria en que viven nuestros hermanos en Cuba, yo entiendo que sobran motivos de necesidad pública e interés social para confirmar la constitucionalidad del Proyecto al amparo del artículo 87 de la Constitución de 1940.

I. Prohibición de Desahucios y Desalojos

Disposiciones Generales

El artículo primero del Proyecto que comentamos declara una moratoria por término indefinido en los desahucios y desalojos. Los beneficiarios de esta moratoria son aquellas personas que al terminar el gobierno de Castro sean "ocupantes legítimos" de viviendas. Según el segundo párrafo del artículo, ocupante legítimo es "todo aquel que se encuentre en posesión pacífica de una vivienda, ya sea por dominio, arrendamiento, usufructo u otro derecho real, permiso de la autoridad pública o de la persona con derecho a ocupar, u ocupación precaria." Luego para ser ocupante legítimo y, consecuentemente, beneficiario de la moratoria, es necesario hallarse en posesión pacífica de una vivienda.

Según el artículo 2, el ocupante legítimo será considerado, de derecho, poseedor de buena fe con derecho de permanencia. En Derecho civil, la posesión de buena fe otorga importantes derechos a su titular.[1] El derecho de permanencia es el derecho del arrendatario a permanecer en la vivienda arrendada siempre que se cumplan ciertos requisitos legales y convencionales, tales como el pago del alquiler o renta.[2] El Proyecto que comentamos concede al ocupante legítimo de una vivienda el derecho de permanencia, sin importar el hecho de que la ocupación de que se trata se deba a un contrato de arrendamiento o no.

Como el fin que persigue la moratoria de desahucios es amparar a las personas que ocupan viviendas al terminar el gobierno de Castro, parece lógico que la extensión patrimonial de dicho derecho sea acorde con la función que desempeña: o sea, evitar que el ocupante pierda su habitación. Consecuente con esta proposición el artículo tres declara la intransferabilidad de los derechos del ocupante legítimo como tal. Reza el artículo: "Los derechos del ocupante legítimo bajo los artículos 1 y 2 de esta Ley son intransferibles e inembargables, debiendo considerarse derechos personalísimos del beneficiario."

Los artículos 4 y 5 de esta Ley protegen la ocupación del ocupante legítimo al prohibir a los miembros de la autoridad pública el amparo de solicitudes de desahucio o desalojo contrarias al Proyecto que comentamos y al proveer medidas punitivas contra los que violen los derechos del ocupante legítimo.[3]

El artículo 6 dispone que cualquier ocupante legítimo que haya sido desalojado o desahuciado de manera contraria a las disposiciones de esta Ley tendrá derecho a ser reintegrado en la posesión de la vivienda de que se trata mediante una breve instancia ante el Ministerio de Vivienda y Urbanismo.[4] En dicho proceso, el ocupante legítimo sólo tendrá que demostrar su condición de tal respecto a la vivienda de que se trata.

Pago de Alquileres

La moratoria no es una piñata jurídica; el hecho de ser ocupante legítimo no conlleva la propiedad de la vivienda para su titular, ni siquiera da derecho a una rebaja en el alquiler de que se trata. Según el artículo 8, todo aquel que pagaba alquiler por el derecho a ocupar una vivienda

---

[1]Véanse, p. ej., los artículos 1955 y 1957, del Código Civil de la República de Cuba (1902) respecto a los derechos de prescripción del poseedor de buena fe.

[2]Véase, p. ej., artículo 9 del Decreto No. 804 de 28 de Marzo de 1944. Véase también el Decreto 2105 de 4 de Julio de 1949 sobre el Derecho de Permanencia Comercial e industrial. Véase, finalmente, la Sentencia del t.s. No. 46 de 5 de Marzo de 1951 amparando al inquilino en el caso de nuevo adquirente.

[3]El artículo 4 dispone: "Se prohibe terminantemente todo intento de desahucio o desalojo que contravenga alguna disposición de esta Ley. Ningún miembro de la autoridad pública amparará solicitud de desahucio o desalojo alguna contraria a las disposiciones de esta Ley." El artículo 5 reza: "Toda persona que, mediante fuerza o intimidación, desaloje a un ocupante legítimo de la vivienda que habitaba, será penado con una multa de 1,000 a 5,000 pesos. Será penado de igual manera el que por medio de artificios fraudulentos o dolosos logre que la autoridad pública efectúe un desahucio o desalojo contrario a las disposiciones de esta Ley.

El importe de las multas impuestas bajo este artículo se le entregará al ocupante legítimo injustamente desahuciado o desalojado.

La multa que dispone este artículo se impondrá en adición a cualquier otra pena aplicable bajo las leyes penales."

[4]Reza el artículo 6: "Todo ocupante legítimo desahuciado o desalojado en contra de las disposiciones de esta Ley tendrá derecho a ser restaurado en la posesión de la vivienda que habitaba mediante un sumarísimo proceso, ventilado ante el Ministerio de Vivienda y Urbanismo, en el que deberá acreditar su condición de ocupante legítimo de la vivienda al terminar el gobierno de Castro y el desahucio o desalojo de que se trata."

deberá seguir haciéndolo.[5] De hecho, bajo el artículo 8 hasta el precarista deberá pagar un alquiler que será fijado por el Ministerio de Vivienda y Urbanismo a petición de parte.[6]

Excepciones

El Proyecto contiene ciertas excepciones a la moratoria de desahucios y desalojos. Quedan exceptuados de la moratoria los miembros de las fuerzas armadas y otros ciudadanos de países no democráticos estacionados en Cuba.[7] La Ley concede un plazo de 72 horas a los militares y de diez días a los demás extranjeros exceptuados de la moratoria para desocupar las viviendas que ocupan.[8] El Ministerio de Vivienda y Urbanismo podrá aplazar el desahucio de personas exceptuadas de la moratoria por causa justificada.[9]

II. Titularidad de Viviendas; Reglas de Prelación; Compensación

El Proyecto que comentamos reconoce tres títulos de propiedad respecto a las viviendas existentes en Cuba a la caída del gobierno de Fidel Castro.[10] Los títulos que se reconocen son los siguientes:

"a) Títulos expedidos por el Gobierno de Reconstrucción Nacional.

b) Títulos, o su equivalente, expedidos por el gobierno de Fidel Castro.

c) Títulos, o adquisiciones por usucapión, de acuerdo al derecho imperante antes del primero de enero de 1959."

Según el artículo 10, toda persona que, ostentando uno de los títulos enumerados en el artículo 9, ocupe una vivienda de su propiedad, tendrá derecho a permanecer en ella sin necesidad de pagar alquiler. Sin embargo, si el poseedor u ocupante de la vivienda debe parte del precio de la misma, no parece equitativo que se le permita continuar viviendo en ella sin efectuar el pago del saldo de lo que se comprometió a pagar. Es por este motivo que el artículo 10 dispone que en tales casos el titular de la vivienda "deberá continuar efectuando el pago del saldo bajo las condiciones y términos en que el título o derecho de permanencia fue adquirido."

Uno de los artículos de la Ley que comentamos que, sin lugar a dudas, no ha de estar exento de controversia es el artículo 11. Dicho artículo provee las reglas de prelación respecto a los títulos

---

[5]El primer párrafo del artículo 8 dispone: "Toda persona que al terminar el gobierno de Fidel Castro pagaba una cantidad periódica, en calidad de alquiler o su equivalente, por el derecho de habitar una vivienda, deberá seguir haciéndolo. El acreedor de dicho alquiler o su equivalente será el Estado o la persona física o jurídica que ostente la propiedad de la vivienda de acuerdo con esta Ley. El importe del aquiler o su equivalente se calculará de la misma forma que se hacía al terminar el gobierno de Fidel Castro."

[6]El segundo párrafo del artículo 8 dispone: "En los casos en que más de una persona tenga título de propiedad sobre la misma vivienda, la persona con derecho a recibir el pago del alquiler o su equivalente será aquella cuyo título tenga prelación de acuerdo a las reglas que establece el artículo 11 de esta Ley. Mientras no se determine la persona con derecho a recibir el alquiler o su equivalente, el ocupante cumplirá su obligación de pago entregando el importe del alquiler o su equivalente a la colecturía del Ministerio de Vivienda y Urbanismo."

[7]Véase el artículo 7 del Proyecto.

[8]Véase el artículo 7, incisos "a" y "b".

[9]Véase el artículo 7, inciso "b".

[10]Véase el artículo 9 del Proyecto.

de propiedad reconocidos en la Ley. Reza el artículo:

"Se establece el siguiente orden de prelación de títulos de propiedad sobre viviendas:

a)   Títulos expedidos por el Gobierno de Reconstrucción Nacional.

b)   Títulos expedidos por el Gobierno de Fidel Castro cuyos beneficiarios o sucesores en derecho ocupaban la vivienda al momento de terminar el gobierno de Fidel Castro y que continúen siendo ocupantes legítimos de la misma.

c)   Títulos, o derecho de propiedad obtenido por usucapión, obtenidos de acuerdo al derecho imperante antes del primero de enero de 1959.

d)   Títulos expedidos por el gobierno de Fidel Castro cuyos beneficiarios o sucesores no ocupaban la vivienda al momento de terminar el gobierno de Fidel Castro o no continúan siendo ocupantes legítimos de la misma."

El artículo 12 añade que la prelación de títulos respecto a solares sin edificación se decidirá de forma consecuente con las disposiciones del artículo 11.[11]

Según el artículo 11, los títulos expedidos por el gobierno de Reconstrucción Nacional han de gozar de la más alta preferencia. Esto es lógico. Sería un absurdo jurídico que el nuevo gobierno otorgara títulos de valor inferior a otros en colisión con ellos.

El segundo rango preferencial se le concede a los títulos expedidos par el gobierno de Fidel Castro, siempre y cuando el titular de la vivienda sea, a la vez, ocupante legítimo de la misma. Según un estudio reciente, se calcula que entre el 80 y 90 por ciento de las viviendas en Cuba son de propiedad privada _ entiéndase de propietarios que residen en Cuba o cuya titularidad reconoce el gobierno de Fidel Castro.[12] El derecho no puede desconocer esta realidad fáctica.

La Ley que comentamos concede la tercera preferencia a los propietarios que adquirieron sus títulos, o el dominio por usucapión, "de acuerdo al derecho imperante antes del primero de enero de 1959."[13]

Finalmente, la cuarta preferencia bajo la Ley corresponde a aquellos dueños con "títulos expedidos por el gobierno de Fidel Castro cuyos beneficiarios o sucesores no ocupaban la vivienda

---

[11]El artículo 12 reza así: "La prelación de títulos respecto a solares sin edificación o yermos se decidirá de forma consecuente con las disposiciones del artículo precedente.

En aquellos casos en que haya habido edificación de vivienda en solares de propiedad ajena, el dueño de la vivienda edificada en el solar tendrá prelación con respecto a la propiedad de la vivienda y del solar sobre el dueño del solar. Lo mismo procederá en casos en que la edificación tenga lugar en solares donde antiguamente existieron otras viviendas, derrumbadas para efectuar la edificación existente, o destruidas por cualquier motivo con anterioridad a la edificación actual."

[12]Véase el Boletín no. 15 de la Sociedad Económica (1992).

[13]El artículo 1957 del Código civil de la República de Cuba (de 1902) dispone: "El dominio y demás derechos reales sobre bienes inmuebles se prescriben por la posesión durante diez años entre presentes y veinte entre ausentes, con buena fe y justo título". El artículo 1950 del mismo Código reza: "Se prescriben también el dominio y demás derechos reales sobre los bienes inmuebles por su posesión no interrumpida durante treinta años, sin necesidad de título ni de buena fe, y sin distinción entre presentes y ausentes, salvo la excepción determinada en el art. 539."

al momento de terminar el gobierno de Fidel Castro o no continúan siendo ocupantes legítimos de la misma."[14]

Compensación

Puesto que bajo la normativa de prelación de títulos ordenado por la Ley habrá casos en que personas con títulos reconocidos por la misma no tengan el derecho de ocupar la vivienda de su propiedad, surge el problema del derecho a compensación de los desposeídos. Puede pensarse, por una parte, que el sistema de prelación de títulos utilizado por esta Ley, al provocar la pérdida efectiva de un título que se reconoce merced a la preferencia dada a otro título, equivale a una expropiación del titular desposeído. Dicha expropiación sería ilegal bajo el artículo 24 de la Constitución de 1940 de no mediar el pago de la correspondiente indemnización en efectivo fijada judicialmente.[15]

Por otra parte, no es menos cierto que el compensar integramente a todo el que la presente Ley priva del goce de la vivienda a que su título le acredita sería incosteable para la República, ya que el total a pagar podría ascender a varios miles de millones de dólares. Supongamos, por ejemplo, que el total de viviendas que resultan "expropiadas" bajo esta Ley asciende a 100,000, cifra que tal vez sea conservadora. Tomando como fecha de avalúo el momento del triunfo de la Revolución de Castro, si el valor promedio de una vivienda en 1959 era de 20,000 pesos, y en ese momento el peso equivalía al dólar, la compensación total a pagar por el Estado por concepto de viviendas expropiadas ascendería a dos mil millones de dólares.[16] Parece claro que el Estado cubano, que es sabido se encuentra en un estado de bancarrota total, no puede de ninguna manera hacerle frente a una deuda de tal índole.

El Proyecto que comentamos toma una posición intermedia entre los posibles extremos de compensación íntegra y no ofrecer compensación alguna. El Proyecto limita el monto de la compensación obtenible a 20,000 pesos —no dólares— no importa el valor de la vivienda expropiada.[17] También se limita el derecho de compensación a razón de una vivienda por persona "sin importar el número de viviendas de que la persona fuese propietaria."[18]

El artículo 13 del Proyecto condiciona el derecho a compensación a la pérdida del uso de la vivienda por su dueño por alguna de las siguientes razones:

"a)   La vivienda se encuentra ocupada por una persona con título de propiedad,

---

[14]Véase el artículo 11, inciso "d" del Proyecto.

[15]El artículo 24 de la Constitución de 1940 reza: "Se prohibe la confiscación de bienes. Nadie podrá ser privado de su propiedad sino por autoridad judicial competente y por causa justificada de utilidad pública o interés social y siempre previo el pago de la correspondiente indemnización en efectivo, fijada judicialmente. La falta de cumplimiento de estos requisitos determinará el derecho del expropiado a ser amparado por los Tribunales de Justicia y, en su caso, reintegrado en su propiedad.

La certeza de la causa de utilidad pública o interés social y la necesidad de la expropiación, corresponderá decidirla a los Tribunales de Justicia en caso de impugnación."

[16]Sería de sobremanera difícil establecer un precio de mercado, a raíz de la caída del gobierno de Castro, respecto a las viviendas existentes en Cuba, dada la ausencia de datos fehacientes, a menos que se subastaran las viviendas en cuestión. Es por esta razón que en el ejemplo ofrecido en el texto se emplean cifras de avalúo de 1959.

[17]Véase el artículo 14 del Proyecto.

[18]Véase el artículo 13 del Proyecto, segundo párrafo.

o derecho de habitar sin pagar compensación, expedido por el gobierno de Fidel Castro.

b)   La vivienda se encuentra ocupada por ocupante legítimo que realiza una declaración de intención de comprar el inmueble al Ministerio de Vivienda y Urbanismo.

c)   El ocupante legítimo que habitaba la vivienda al terminar el gobierno de Fidel Castro continúa ocupando la misma por un período de no menos de seis meses después de terminar el gobierno de Fidel Castro."

El Proyecto concede al propietario con derecho a compensación la selección de la clase de compensación a recibir de entre tres posibles métodos. Según el artículo 14, la persona con derecho a compensación podrá elegir entre los siguientes métodos de compensación:

"a)   Obtención de una nueva vivienda de entre las que el Estado habrá de construir, de un valor equivalente a la cantidad de compensación que se le debe.

b)   Obtención de una vivienda en posesión del Estado de valor equivalente a la que fundamenta su derecho a compensación.

c)   Recibir bonos del Estado por la cantidad que se le adeuda, pagaderos en veinte años, con interés al cinco por ciento anual."

III. Derecho de Tanteo del Estado

Introducción

El derecho de tanteo da a su titular la oportunidad de obtener un derecho—generalmente el dominio— sobre una cosa mueble o inmueble, preferencialmente a otros posibles adquirentes, cuando el propietario de la cosa decide enajenarla o conceder un derecho sobre la misma. En la Constitución cubana de 1940 se reconoce al Estado el derecho de tanteo respecto a bienes inmuebles en adjudicación o venta forzosa.[19] El Proyecto que comentamos, con el fin de evitar la especulación respecto a las viviendas existentes en Cuba a la caída del gobierno de Castro, concede al Estado el derecho de tanteo sobre cualquier venta o traspaso de posesión de dichas viviendas.[20]

Antes de entrar a discutir en detalle el articulado de esta parte del Proyecto, conviene hacer ciertas acotaciones sobre el fin que persigue, o sea, impedir la especulación respecto a las viviendas que actualmente existen en Cuba.

De nada o muy poco serviría el proteger al ocupante legítimo de una vivienda contra el desahucio o desalojo si se permite a ese mismo ocupante, siendo propietario de la vivienda que ocupa, vender la vivienda a un comprador cuyo único interés sea el de revenderla al mejor postor. Este resultado es nocivo al bienestar socio-económico de Cuba por las siguientes razones:

---

[19]El artículo 89 de la Constitución de 1940 dispone: "El Estado tendrá el derecho de tanteo en toda adjudicación o venta forzosa de propiedades inmuebles y de valores representativos de propiedades inmobiliarias."

[20]Véase artículos 19 y 20 del Proyecto.

Primero. Dada la enorme escasez de viviendas en la Isla, es probable que el dueño de vivienda que vende su casa no tenga habitación donde vivir, lo que lo pondría en un estado de desamparo que desvirtúa el propósito de las normas que amparan al inquilino contra el desahucio: o sea, evitar que una familia se halle sin habitación. Al dársele al Estado el derecho de tanteo, el Estado puede evitar el desalojo del vendedor ofreciéndole la casa en alquiler.

Segundo. Dada la desesperación de la población cubana por la obtención de bienes de consumo, es muy probable que un gran número de propietarios estén más que dispuestos a vender la vivienda de su propiedad por cantidades irrisorias. Por ejemplo, bien puede producirse el caso de que, dado el ínfimo valor del peso cubano en comparación con el dólar, una persona pueda adquir una vivienda promedio en Cuba por el equivalente en pesos de $1,000 (mil dólares). O sea, que una entidad dotada de cierto capital _ digamos un banco o una compañía de seguros _ podría por una cantidad irrisoria comprar buena parte de La Habana. Como estos capitales provendrían de entidades foráneas, se daría entonces una situación que en Cuba se luchó largo tiempo por corregir: La propiedad de la tierra estaría en manos extranjeras.[21] El éxodo de divisas que provocaría tal situacción sería un pesado fardo para la economía cubana.

Tercero. Puede darse por sentado que el inversionista, nacional o extranjero, deseará obtener los mayores dividendos posibles que su inversión le pueda rendir. No es difícil imaginarse que el mayor rédito para el capital invertido en La Habana Vieja, o el Vedado, por ejemplo, no provendría, precisamente, de la construcción de edificios de apartamento de bajo costo para familias de bajos ingresos. Aunque la construcción de hoteles, edificios de oficina, y grandes almacenes en lugares donde actualmente hay casas de vivienda propendrá _ no hay duda _ en gran beneficio para la colectividad cubana a largo y mediano plazo, no es menos cierto que a corto plazo crearía un problema de desplazamiento habitacional de enormes proporciones que propendría a la inestabilidad social.

Para poder atender a los fines para los cuales existe, es imprescindible darle al Estado las herramientas para planificar. El derecho de tanteo permite al Estado evitar las ventas de vivienda a precios irrisorios y de esta manera propender a que la propiedad inmueble permanezca en manos cubanas, preferiblemente las mismas que habitan las viviendas.

Viviendas Afectadas

El Proyecto no da al Estado el derecho de tanteo sobre todas las viviendas que puedan construirse en Cuba, sino únicamente sobre las viviendas actuales": o sea, aquellas viviendas construídas, o en proceso de construcción, a la caída del gobierno de Fidel Castro. Luego el Estado carece de derecho de tanteo respecto a cualquier vivienda que se construya después de la caída de Castro.[22]

La razón para distinguir entre viviendas construídas antes y después de la caída del gobierno de Castro en lo que concierne al derecho de tanteo del Estado es que, con respecto a las viviendas

---

[21]El artículo 90 de la Constitución de 1940, en su segundo párrafo, dispone: "La Ley limitará restrictivamente la adquisición y posesión de la tierra por personas y compañías extranjeras y adoptará medidas que tiendan a revertir la tierra al cubano."

[22]El artículo 16 de esta Ley dispone: "Para los efectos de esta Ley, "vivienda actual" es toda vivienda construída, o en proceso de construcción, en el momento de la caída del gobierno de Fidel Castro. Para los efectos de este Capítulo no importará el que la vivienda de que se trate se encuentre ocupada o no." El artículo 17 reza: "Se establece el derecho de tanteo del Estado respecto a toda transferencia de posesión de propiedad inmueble que contenga una vivienda actual."

construídas después de la caída de Castro no se darán, en la generalidad de los casos, los mismos peligros vislumbrados respecto a la venta de viviendas existentes. Un propietario que adquiere una nueva vivienda, posiblemente a un costo relativamente más alto que el precio de adquisición de la mayoría de las viviendas que actualmente existen, difícilmente vendería dicha vivienda a un precio irrisorio quedándose sin habitación. Además, el hecho de que la casa de vivienda es nueva la hace más deseable a su propietario. Luego parece más adecuado el permitir que el mercado sea el elemento determinante en la transferencia de viviendas de nueva construcción.

Mecanismo de Tanteo

Los artículos 19 y 20 del Proyecto establecen el mecanismo fundamental del tanteo. Según el artículo 19, toda persona que desee transferir la posesión de una vivienda actual "deberá primero ofrecerla al Estado por el mismo precio y bajo las mismas condiciones."[23] La oferta de que trata el artículo 19 debe hacerse en un espacio de tiempo no mayor de cinco días después de la conclusión del contrato u otro acto jurídico que contempla la transferencia de posesión de la vivienda de que se trata.[24]

El artículo 20 dispone que, una vez recibida la notificación del traspaso de posesión, el Estado tendrá 60 días para decidir si acepta o rechaza el tanteo. Si lo acepta, "deberá pagar el importe ofrecido por el comprador o beneficiario del contrato o acto jurídico de que se trate."[25] Si el precio a pagar es 20,000 pesos o menos, el Estado deberá pagar el precio al contado. Si el precio excede los 20,000 pesos el artículo 20 concede al Estado un plazo de 12 meses para efectuar el pago.

El artículo 21 concede al Estado el derecho de tanteo respecto a solares en áreas urbanas en los mismos casos y condiciones aplicables a las viviendas.

Rechazos de tanteo

En muchos casos es probable que al Estado no le interese ejercer el derecho de tanteo a que lo hace acreedor esta Ley. En tales casos, el Estado, a través del Ministerio de Vivienda y Urbanismo, deberá expedir un "certificado de desinterés" al interesado.[26] El interesado procurará obtener el certificado de desinterés lo antes posible, ya que sin el mismo no le será posible inscribir el traspaso de que se trata en el Registro de la Propiedad.[27] Según el primer párrafo del artículo 24:

"Se prohibe terminantemente a los registradores la inscripción en el Registro de la Propiedad de una compraventa u otro acto registrable respecto a un inmueble que contenga una vivienda actual en el que no conste el certificado de desinterés del Ministerio de Vivienda y Urbanismo de que trata el artículo precedente."

---

[23]El texto íntegro del artículo 19 reza: "Cualquier persona que desee vender, arrendar, permutar, otorgar opción, donar, o transferir de alguna otra forma la posesión actual o futura de una vivienda actual, deberá primero ofrecerla al Estado por el mismo precio y bajo las mismas condiciones."

[24]Véase el artículo 20 de la Ley.

[25]Véase el tercer párrafo del artículo 20.

[26]Véase el artículo 23 del Proyecto.

[27]Véase el artículo 24 del Proyecto.

Prohibición de Especulación

Para complementar el derecho de tanteo del Estado respecto a todo traspaso de posesión de una vivienda actual, el artículo 25 prohibe expresamente la especulación respecto a viviendas actuales. Partiendo de la premisa de que sólo en muy raros casos —quizá nunca— habrá real necesidad de poseer más de una vivienda actual en un término municipal, el artículo 25 prohibe el que alguien sea dueño de más de una vivienda actual en cada término municipal.[28]

En los casos en que una persona sea dueña de más de una vivienda actual dentro de un mismo término municipal, el Estado tendrá derecho a expropiar las viviendas excedentes, pudiendo el propietario elegir la vivienda que desee conservar.[29] El precio que el Estado deberá pagar al propietario expropiado es el justiprecio de la vivienda de que se trata, cuyo importe no podrá exceder a la cantidad pagada por el inmueble por el propietario expropiado.[30]

APÉNDICE

LEY DE VIVIENDAS URBANAS Y RURALES

Capítulo Primero:
Disposiciones Generales; Prohibición de Desahucios y Desalojos

ART. 1   Se declara una moratoria por término indefinido en los desahucios y desalojos. A dicho efecto, no se podrá desahuciar o desalojar a ninguna persona que al terminar el gobierno de Fidel Castro sea ocupante legítimo de una vivienda urbana o rural.

Para los efectos de esta Ley, ocupante legítimo será todo aquel que se encuentre en posesión pacífica de una vivienda, ya sea por dominio, arrendamiento, usufructo u otro derecho real, permiso de la autoridad pública o de la persona con derecho a ocupar, u ocupación precaria.

ART. 2   Todo ocupante legítimo de una vivienda al terminar el gobierno de Fidel Castro se considerará poseedor de buena fe con derecho de permanencia.

ART. 3   Los derechos del ocupante legítimo bajo los artículos 1 y 2 de esta Ley son intransferibles e inembargables, debiendo considerarse derechos personalísimos del beneficiario.

ART. 4   Se prohibe terminantemente todo intento de desahucio o desalojo que contravenga alguna disposición de esta Ley. Ningún miembro de la autoridad pública amparará

---

[28]El artículo 25 del Proyecto reza: "Se prohibe terminantemente la especulación respecto a viviendas actuales. A dicho efecto, nadie podrá ser propietario de más de una vivienda actual en un término municipal.

El Estado tendrá el derecho de expropiar, sin que sea menester probar necesidad o utilidad pública, aquellas viviendas pertenecientes a un mismo propietario que excedan el límite fijado por este artículo. El propietario expropiado podrá seleccionar la vivienda actual de la cual desea continuar siendo dueño dentro de cada término municipal."

[29]Véase el segundo párrafo del artículo 25.

[30]Véase el artículo 26 del Proyecto.

solicitud de desahucio o desalojo alguna contraria a las disposiciones de esta Ley.

ART. 5   Toda persona que, mediante fuerza o intimidación, desaloje a un ocupante legítimo de la vivienda que habitaba, será penado con una multa de 1,000 a 5,000 pesos. Será penado de igual manera el que por medio de artificios fraudulentos o dolosos logre que la autoridad pública efectúe un desahucio o desalojo contrario a las disposiciones de esta Ley.

El importe de las multas impuestas bajo este artículo se le entregará al ocupante legítimo injustamente desahuciado o desalojado.

La multa que dispone este artículo se impondrá en adición a cualquier otra pena aplicable bajo las leyes penales.

ART. 6   Todo ocupante legítimo desahuciado o desalojado en contra de las disposiciones de esta Ley tendrá derecho a ser restaurado en la posesión de la vivienda que habitaba mediante un sumarísimo proceso, ventilado ante el Ministerio de Vivienda y Urbanismo, en el que deberá acreditar su condición de ocupante legítimo de la vivienda al terminar el gobierno de Castro y el desahucio o desalojo de que se trata.

ART. 7   Quedan exceptuadas de la moratoria de desahucio las siguientes personas:

a) Los miembros de las fuerzas armadas de la antigua Unión Soviética, de los países de Europa que formaron parte del Pacto de Varsovia o que tengan gobiernos comunistas, de China, de Vietnam, de Corea del Norte, de Nicaragua, de Etiopía, de Angola, y de otros países comunistas así como también los provinientes de países con gobiernos no democráticos, sean o no comunistas, estacionados en Cuba. Los miembros de las fuerzas armadas de estos países deberán desalojar las viviendas que ocupen dentro de las 72 horas de la promulgación de esta Ley. Los miembros de "movimientos de liberación", tales como los miembros del Movimiento de Liberación de Palestina, provengan o no de países o Estados reconocidos como tales por Cuba, serán equiparados a los miembros de las fuerzas armadas de los países referidos en este artículo para todos los efectos que del mismo se desprendan.

b) Los técnicos, burócratas, asesores, y otros ciudadanos de cualquiera de los países incluídos en el inciso "a" de este artículo. Dichas personas deberán desalojar las viviendas que ocupen dentro de los diez días siguientes a la promulgación de esta Ley.

El Ministerio de Vivienda y Urbanismo podrá aplazar el desahucio de las personas incluídas en los incisos "a" y "b" de este artículo por causa justificada.

Las personas incluídas en los incisos "a" y "b" de este artículo no tendrán derecho a compensación de parte del Estado por motivo de desahucio o desalojo o por algún otro concepto amparado por esta Ley.

ART. 8   Toda persona que al terminar el gobierno de Fidel Castro pagaba una cantidad periódica, en calidad de alquiler o su equivalente, por el derecho de habitar una vivienda, deberá seguir haciéndolo. El acreedor de dicho alquiler o su equivalente será el Estado o la persona física o jurídica que ostente la propiedad de la vivienda de acuerdo con esta Ley. El importe del aquiler o su equivalente se calculará de la misma forma que se hacía al terminar el gobierno de Fidel Castro.

En los casos en que más de una persona tenga título de propiedad sobre la misma vivienda, la persona con derecho a recibir el pago del alquiler o su equivalente será aquella cuyo título tenga prelación de acuerdo a las reglas que establece el artículo 11 de esta Ley. Mientras no se determine la persona con derecho a recibir el alquiler o su equivalente, el ocupante cumplirá su obligación de pago entregando el importe del alquiler o su equivalente a la colecturía del Ministerio de Vivienda y Urbanismo.

El precarista deberá pagar la mensualidad que el Ministerio de Vivienda y Urbanismo, a petición de parte interesada, asigne como justo precio del alquiler de la vivienda de que se trate.

Capítulo Segundo:
Titularidad de Viviendas; Reglas de Prelación; Compensación

ART. 9 Se reconocen los siguientes títulos de propiedd sobre viviendas:

a) Títulos expedidos por el Gobierno de Reconstrucción Nacional.

b) Títulos, o su equivalente, expedidos por el gobierno de Fidel Castro.

c) Títulos, o adquisiciones por usucapión, de acuerdo al derecho imperante antes del primero de enero de 1959.

ART. 10 Toda persona aque ocupe una vivienda urbana o rural bajo cualquiera de los títulos enumerados en el artículo anterior tendrá derecho a permanecer en posesión de la misma sin pagar alquiler. Si el ocupante con título debe parte del precio de compraventa o adquisición permanente de la vivienda deberá continuar efectuando el pago del saldo bajo las condiciones y términos en que el título o derecho de permanencia fue adquirido.

ART. 11 Se establece el siguiente orden de prelación de títulos de propiedad sobre viviendas:

a) Títulos expedidos por el Gobierno de Reconstrucción Nacional.

b) Títulos expedidos por el Gobierno de Fidel Castro cuyos beneficiarios o sucesores en derecho ocupaban la vivienda al momento de terminar el gobierno de Fidel Castro y que continúen siendo ocupantes legítimos de la misma.

c) Títulos, o derecho de propiedad obtenido por usucapión, obtenidos de acuerdo al derecho imperante antes del primero de enero de 1959.

d) Títulos expedidos por el gobierno de Fidel Castro cuyos beneficiarios o sucesores no ocupaban la vivienda al momento de terminar el gobierno de Fidel Castro o no continúan siendo ocupantes legítimos de la misma.

ART. 12   La prelación de títulos respecto a solares sin edificación o yermos se decidirá de forma consecuente con las disposiciones del artículo precedente.

En aquellos casos en que haya habido edificación de vivienda en solares de propiedad ajena, el dueño de la vivienda edificada en el solar tendrá prelación con respecto a la propiedad de la vivienda y del solar sobre el dueño del solar. Lo mismo procederá en casos en que la edificación tenga lugar en solares donde antiguamente existieron otras viviendas, derrumbadas para efectuar la edificación existente, o destruídas por cualquier motivo con anterioridad a la edificación actual.

ART. 13   Toda persona física que tuviere un título de propiedad, o que hubiere adquirido el dominio por usucapión, de acuerdo al derecho imperante antes del primero de enero de 1959 o de acuerdo al derecho en vigor durante el gobierno de Fidel Castro, tendrá derecho a ser compensado por el Estado si no puede ocupar la vivienda de su propiedad por alguna de las siguientes razones:

a)   La vivienda se encuentra ocupada por una persona con título de propiedad, o derecho de habitar sin pagar compensación, expedido por el gobierno de Fidel Castro.

b)   La vivienda se encuentra ocupada por ocupante legítimo que realiza una declaración de intención de comprar el inmueble al Ministerio de Vivienda y Urbanismo.

c)   El ocupante legítimo que habitaba la vivienda al terminar el gobierno de Fidel Castro continúa ocupando la misma por un período de no menos de seis meses después de terminar el gobierno de Fidel Castro.

La persona que reclame compensación al amparo de este artículo no tendrá derecho a élla cuando otra persona tenga derecho a compensación, con respecto a la vivienda de que se trata, por virtud de título, o usucapión, adquirido con anterioridad al reclamante. Tampoco habrá derecho a compensación por más de una vivienda por persona, sin importar el número de viviendas de que la persona fuese propietaria.

ART. 14   Las personas con derecho a compensación con arreglo al artículo anterior tendrán derecho a ser compensadas por el valor que el Estado reconozca a la vivienda de que se trata hasta la cantidad de 20,000 (viente mil) pesos. El acreedor de compensación podrá elegir entre los siguientes modos de compensación:

a)   Obtención de una nueva vivienda de entre las que el Estado habrá de construir, de un valor equivalente a la cantidad de compensación que se le debe.

b)   Obtención de una vivienda en posesión del Estado de valor equivalente a la que fundamenta su derecho a compensación.

c)   Recibir bonos del Estado por la cantidad que se le adeuda, pagaderos en veinte años, con interés al cinco por ciento anual.

ART. 15   Los propietarios de solares que hallan perdido la titularidad de los mismos por virtud de lo dispuesto en el segundo párrafo del artículo 12 serán compensados de forma consecuente con las disposiciones de los artículos 13 y 14 de esta Ley.

Capítulo Tercero:
Enajenación de Viviendas Actuales; Derecho de Tanteo del Estado; Especulaciones Prohibidas

ART. 16   Para los efectos de esta Ley, "vivienda actual" es toda vivienda construída, o en proceso de construcción, en el momento de la caída del gobierno de Fidel Castro. Para los efectos de este Capítulo no importará el que la vivienda de que se trate se encuentre ocupada o no.

ART. 17   Se establece el derecho de tanteo del Estado respecto a toda transferencia de posesión de propiedad inmueble que contenga una vivienda actual.

ART. 18   En la escritura u otro acto de traspaso de propiedad inmueble deberá constar claramente la existencia o no de una vivienda en la misma. El notario que autorice una escritura o acto de traspaso sobre un inmueble en que no haya constancia respecto a la existencia de vivienda en el mismo será separado de su cargo notarial.

ART. 19   Cualquier persona que desee vender, arrendar, permutar, otorgar opción, donar, o transferir de alguna otra forma la posesión actual o futura de una vivienda actual, deberá primero ofrecerla al Estado por el mismo precio y bajo las mismas condiciones.

ART. 20   La oferta al Estado de que trata el artículo precedente deberá hacerse no más tarde de cinco (5) días después de concluído el contrato o acto jurídico mediante el cual se pretende transferir la posesión de la vivienda. Dicha oferta se hará mediante presentación de copia fiel del original del contrato o acto jurídico unilateral de que se trate al Ministerio de Vivienda y Urbanismo.

El Estado, a través del Ministerio de Vivienda y Urbanismo, tendrá 60 días contados a partir del día siguiente al que recibe la presentación del contrato o acto jurídico unilateral para ejercitar el derecho de tanteo.

Si el Estado, a través del Ministerio de Vivienda y Urbanismo, decide ejercer el derecho a que lo hace acreedor el tanteo deberá pagar el importe ofrecido por el comprador o beneficiario del contrato o acto jurídico de que se trate. Si el precio excede la cantidad de 20,000 pesos el Estado tendrá un plazo de 12 meses para efectuar el pago. En caso de cesiones a título gratuito, el Estado pagará el justiprecio de la cesión de que se trata.

ART. 21   El Estado tendrá derecho de tanteo respecto a solares sin edificación o yermos ubicados en las áreas urbanas del país en los mismos casos, y bajo las mismas condiciones, aplicables en casos de vivienda actual.

ART. 22   En los casos en que el Estado no recibe la notificación de que tratan los artículos 19 y 20 el Estado tendrá 3 años después de la inscripción en el Registro de la Propiedad del contrato o acto jurídico de que se trata para ejercer el derecho de tanteo.

ART. 23   Si el Estado, actuando a través del Ministerio de Vivienda y Urbanismo, decide no ejercer el derecho a que lo hace acreedor el tanteo deberá otorgar un certificado de desinterés al interesado en el contrato u otro acto jurídico en el que habrá de constar el rechazo de que se trata.

ART. 24   Se prohibe terminantemente a los registradores la inscripción en el Registro de la Propiedad de una compraventa u otro acto registrable respecto a un inmueble que contenga una vivienda actual en el que no conste el certificado de desinterés del Ministerio de Vivienda y Urbanismo de que trata el artículo precedente.

Cualquier persona que intencionalmente viole la prohibición de este artículo será penado con una multa de 100 o 500 pesos en adición a cualquier otra pena aplicable bajo las leyes penales.

ART. 25   Se prohibe terminantemente la especulación respecto a viviendas actuales. A dicho efecto, nadie podrá ser propietario de más de una vivienda actual en un término municipal.

El Estado tendrá el derecho de expropiar, sin que sea menester probar necesidad o utilidad pública, aquellas viviendas pertenecientes a un mismo propietario que excedan el límite fijado por este artículo. El propietario expropiado podrá seleccionar la vivienda actual de la cual desea continuar siendo dueño dentro de cada término municipal.

ART. 26   En los casos de expropiación de viviendas actuales bajo el artículo precedente, el Estado deberá pagar el justiprecio de la vivienda expropiada. En ningún caso podrá el justiprecio exceder el importe de lo que el propietario pagó, o se comprometió a pagar, por la vivienda actual. Si el precio que deberá pagar el Estado excediera la cantidad de 20,000 pesos, el Estado tendrá 12 meses para efectuar el pago de la vivienda expropiada.

ART. 27   En los casos de expropiación por exceso en la titularidad permisible de viviendas bajo este Capítulo, el Estado, a través del Ministerio de Vivienda y Urbanismo, deberá notificar al propietario de su decisión de expropiar las viviendas actuales que posee en violación de esta Ley.

El propietario expropiado tendrá 10 días para acceder a, o contestar, la expropiación. Si contesta la expropiación, el Ministerio de Vivienda y Urbanismo citará el caso para una vista contencioso administrativa que tendrá lugar dentro de los 30 días siguientes a la contestación. El tribunal contencioso administrativo dictará una sentencia en la cual expondrá la procedencia o improcedencia de la expropiación. De proceder la expropiación, el tribunal dictaminará el precio que deberá pagarse al propietario.

Capítulo Cuarto:
Viviendas Nuevas

ART. 28 Para los efectos de este Capítulo, "vivienda nueva" será toda vivienda cuya construcción comience después de la caída del gobierno de Fidel Castro. Una vivienda en proceso de construcción al momento de la caída del gobierno de Fidel Castro no es una vivienda nueva bajo este Capítulo.

ART. 29 El Estado promoverá por todos los medios a su alcance la construcción de viviendas nuevas. A dicho efecto, el Gobierno de Reconstrucción Nacional facilitará la adquisición de terrenos o solares sin edificación o yermos de propiedad del Estado a personas físicas y jurídicas que deseen edificar nuevas viviendas mediante la expedición de títulos de propiedad y la extensión de crédito.

El Ministerio de Vivienda y Urbanismo será la entidad del Gobierno de Reconstrucción Nacional que expedirá nuevos títulos de propiedad. El Banco Nacional de Cuba dictará el reglamento normativo regulando las condiciones, plazos, y tasas de interés aplicables a la concesión del crédito.

Comments

Agustín de Goytisolo

(A)   Néstor Cruz's "Legal Issues Raised by the Transition: Cuba from Marxism to Democracy, 199?-200?"

Néstor Cruz's paper raises ten legal issues which he correctly labels "sticky" during the transition that will follow the demise of the Castro regime. These are my brief comments thereon:

(1)   Constitutional and Organizational Issues: Taking into account a hopefully short-lived provisional government that will call for immediate elections, Mr. Cruz introduces the intriguing and novel idea of restoring immediately the 1940 Constitution solely for the following important purposes:

(i)   To elect officials;
(ii)   To appoint the judiciary;
(iii) To secure civil liberties of speech, habeas corpus and due process.

A careful revision during a recent vacation where I read several times the 90-page text of the 1940 Constitution (hereinafter, the "Constitution"), including its 287 Articles, and 17 pages of Transitory Provisions, has led me to conclude that we can be much more aggressive, since it appears that **eighty-eight percent (88%) of it can be restored**. The 33 Articles that require suspension for its gradual re-enactment or revision by a constitutional convention to be called by the provisional government (the Constitution calls it an "*Asamblea Plebiscitaria*") are highlighted in an Appendix to these comments.

(2)   Compensation for Nationalizations: Mr. Cruz, a strong supporter of the Constitution, taking into account the realities following the demise of post-Castro, leaving a legacy of economic disaster, a government and a nation not only poor but broke, makes interesting suggestions regarding compensations, which the undersigned defers to economists and more competent experts.

(3)   Privatizations: A most difficult but indispensable issue for the economic revival of the Cuban economy. In this respect, La Sociedad Económica, a London-based "think tank" should be commended for competently gathering information regarding the privatizations that have occurred during the last ten years which run the gamut from Chile to Czechoslovakia. Again, regarding this issue, I suggest comments by economists with ample experience in this area, recognizing that the privatizations of most of the industry held by the Cuban government is a most important task to be undertaken immediately by a post-Castro democratic government.

(4)   Labor Laws: Mr. Cruz refers to the pre-1959 very advanced laws existing in a pre-Castro Cuba and insists on the need to revise them considering the disastrous economic condition that Cuba will face after the demise of the Castro regime. In this respect, the Constitution's provisions of Title VI need to be suspended or updated as suggested in the attached memorandum.

(5)   Anti-Trust: Although an important issue which Mr. Cruz raises, and an area in which we attorneys become deeply involved, being an area in which I have no major professional experience, I defer comments to specialists in a more developed post-Castro Cuba. I do not believe that it will be an initial priority of the post-Castro provisional government.

(6)   Safety Nets: My comments are similar to those regarding Anti-Trust.

(7)   Tax Legislation: Agreeing with Mr. Cruz that simplification of the tax system is required, a careful review should be made of the 1959 Tax Reform Law sponsored by Rufo López Fresquet, which needs to be updated.

(8)   Legislation Subsidizing Higher Education: Although an important area, it is not necessarily a domain for attorneys, except if we are asked to draft the laws required by educators.

(9)   The Role of Economists in Policymaking: I respectfully disagree with Mr. Cruz's suggestion that economists should be empowered in a Council of Economists (recognizing the invaluable worth of the ASCE economists and the much weight that they shall have in a nascent post-Castro provisional government), appointed for long terms with much to say and comment "critically and publicly on all executive policies, legislation and landmark judicial decisions with economic impact."

(10)   Privatization of Administration of Justice: I agree that the use of arbitration to resolve controversies should be encouraged and that other alternatives be considered for the more appropriate administration of justice. In this respect, I strongly believe that Cuba should follow the Civil Law with which it has lived since its discovery 500 years ago. In particular, in a poor developing country, it is indispensable that the very expensive and foreign (to Cuba) judicial system and process of the Common Law countries be avoided in its entirety.

(B)   José D. Acosta's "El marco jurídico-institucional de un Gobierno Provisional de Unidad Nacional en Cuba" ("El GPUN")

I found Dr. Acosta's paper most exhaustive, full of competent research, sometimes sprinkled with "*palabrotas*" like "*desinstitucionalización*" (which I can hardly even try to pronounce notwithstanding my Cuban background and training).

(1)   Regarding Dr. Acosta's GPUN, where all tendencies and groups in-out of Cuba will be democratically represented, I believe that the paper misses insight into the classical quote which we learned when in the "middle ages" they tried to teach us Literatura Preceptiva: "¿por qúe?" "¿dónde?" "¿cuándo?" "¿cómo?" I concur with Dr. Acosta that it would be very important to have a "short-lived provisional government," like that also suggested by Dr. Cruz, to achieve political stability, call a constitutional convention, supervise elections, facilitate supplies and be sector representative". The achieving of the latter, however, is difficult to foresee because again: "¿por qúe?" "¿dónde?" "¿cuándo?" "¿cómo?".

Regarding Dr. Acosta's suggestions that Cuba adopt the International Charter of Human Rights, although a well-thought idea taking into account the values of this Charter, I believe that such novelties should be avoided considering that similar results will be available upon the restoration of Title IV of the Constitution dealing with "Basic Rights."

Dr. Acosta artfully espouses the present continued life of our famous Constitution and makes an exhaustive and complete chronology of this important Cuban Constitution, its cannibalization following the Castro regime, its replacement by the 1976 Castro Constitution, recently amended without acceptable consultation of the people.

(2)   The undersigned respectfully disagrees with Dr. Acosta's conclusion that the 1940 Constitution "*is in force.*" Much has been written as to whether a revolution or similar lasting social commotion can be a source of law. Just consider how at the end of the 18th Century France abruptly changed from the autocratic "Roi Soleil" to a republican democratic system, and in Cuba while on May 19, 1902 the King of Spain was the sovereign, the following day, May 20, 1902, the 1901 Constitution enthroned a tri-body democratic government to govern the Cuban people. Nonetheless, I find Dr. Acosta's review of certain titles of the Constitution to be immediately implemented to be somewhat timid since, as I indicated above, a more daring (88%) restoration thereof appears possible.

Regarding the GPUN without legislative powers capable of calling it a constitutional convention (more appropriately, an "*Asamblea Plebiscitaria*" and the possibility of ASCE becoming a "Batista" type of "Consejo Consultivo", again I query: "¿por qúe?" "¿dónde?" "¿cuándo?" "¿cómo?"

In general, Dr. Acosta's serious research of the Constitution and its cannibalization should be congratulated, and I encourage him to lead a group of scholars like him in a more extensive effort and research for a more daring possible restoration of eighty-eight percent (88%) of the Cuban Constitution. This would pave the way for future efforts by the Cuban government to sort out and suggest alternatives for the adaptation or phased reenactment of the remaining thirty-three (33) Articles in a fair and viable manner, hopefully by a future "*Asamblea Plebiscitaria.*"

(C)   **Julio Romañach, Jr.'s "En torno al proyecto de ley de viviendas urbanas y rurales"**

(1)   This thorough paper recognizes and seeks solutions to a harsh reality, the fact that most existing usable Cuban urban properties are occupied and have been so for more than 30 years by persons who may not be their original owners. Therefore, Mr. Romañach's paper, based on Article 87 of the 1940 Constitution (which while recognizing the existence and legitimacy of private property, suggests that it can be limited as required by reasons of public necessity or social interest established in the law) supports the recognition of permanent residency rights to "long-time occupiers".

Mr. Romañach limits substantially such "long-time occupier" rights by granting the sole right to acquire such properties to the Government in the event of demise or desire to transfer the property by the "long-time occupiers". I have serious doubts about the economic and social advisability of such a prohibition, as it may freeze and cause unhealthy delays in the required revitalization of the Cuban real estate market and create a monstrous bureaucratic institution for the exercise of the Government's preemptive rights to all urban properties that its "long-time" occupiers seek to transfer. It may be much better to authorize the outright sales by "long-time occupiers," only granting a right of first refusal to the prior dispossessed owner, to be exercised within a short period with appropriate notice.

(2)   Mr. Romañach's paper also includes interesting priorities for the recognition of rights to "long-time occupiers" which will need much consideration and evaluation by a future government.

(3)   Regarding compensation to prior owners, considering the economic impossibility to compensate fully the prior owners, Mr. Romañach suggests a sole lump sum payment of 20,000 Pesos following appropriate release by prior owners, only available for one house per owner (irrespective of the number of urban properties owned before).

In general, Mr. Romañach's paper contains interesting and well-thought-out suggestions. However, I believe that all such legislation could prove futile, for only those in control of a provisional government will give the necessary guidelines for attorneys to prepare appropriate legislation to implement their suggestions and, moreover, that legislating in a "vacuum" may provide grounds for the Castro regime to seek its perpetuation.

In general, all three papers were prepared with great detail and much work, and Messrs. Cruz, Acosta and Romañach should be highly commended.

Appendix[1]

The last Cuban democratic Constitution[2] is comprised of 286 articles spread over more than 90 small-print pages, including 19 pages with Transitory Provisions.[3] I am convinced that it is possible to reenact our Constitution notwithstanding its vintage, extension and changed circumstances affecting Cuba. To support this contention, hereinafter follows a recitation of its Titles indicating the few articles that may need updating:

Title Number:	Titled:	Articles Needing Possible Updating:	Other Comments:
First	On the Nation, Its Territory, and Form of Government (Articles 1 to 7)	2nd Paragraph of Article 4 naming its 6 Provinces	Otherwise OK
Second	On Nationality (Articles 8 to 18)	Article 15 regarding the loss of citizenship	Otherwise OK
Third	On Foreigners (Article 19)	None	

---

[1]In the past, prior to this detailed and restive examination of the Constitution, I had unduly taken for granted its impossible re-enactment, considering its vintage (more than **fifty-two years old**), its incredible detailed extension which may have reflected a legal, social and economic "panorama" which has suffered much cruel adjustment under the Castro regime, and bearing in mind that the Constitution was adopted under much political stress and civil unrest, as indicated in the excellent work by Dr. Nestor Carbonell Cortina.

[2]Cuba had 6 democratic constitutions: 4 promulgated during the War of Liberation, the 1901 Constitution, its Machado amendment seeking re-election, and the 1940 Constitution, signed in Guáimaro on July 1, 1940 promulgated the following 15th, and effective as of October 10th of that year.

[3]These Transitory Provisions ("TP") primarily sought to facilitate the prompt but gradual enactment of many of its novel provisions, considering its respective particulars. The majority of the TP need not be part of the "re-enacted" 1940 Constitution. However, some TP's need to be reviewed for the prompt restoration of Banco Nacional, Tribunal de Cuentas and other valuable organizations of the 1940 Constitution. New TP's have been included for the fair, gradual and feasible re-evaluation of the legislation enacted between 1 January 1959 and at a future re-enactment of the Constitution by a future "*Asamblea Plesbicitaria*" following its Title 19.

Title Number:	Titled:	Articles Needing Possible Updating:	Other Comments:
Fourth	Basic Rights (Articles 20 to 42)	Consideration must be given to the feasibility of re-enacting these Arts: — Regarding: 21 — retroactivity of the law 22 — prohibiting the death sentence	Otherwise OK
Fifth	On the Family and Culture (Articles 43 to 59)	Consideration must be given to the feasibility of re-enacting these Arts: — Regarding: 52 — educational budget 56 — citizenship required to hold certain teaching posts 59 — regarding an Institution that did not ¿exist?	Otherwise OK
Sixth	On Labor[4] and Property (Art. 60 to 96)	Consideration must be given to the feasibility of re-enacting these Arts: — Regarding: 66 — day & weekly journeys, etc. 67 — vacations 77 — firing proceedings 88 — may need relief regarding citizenship requirement (as Art. 15) 90 — limiting property ownership by foreigners 91 — Homestead[5]	Otherwise OK

---

[4]In general, the Labor provisions are too detailed, a product of the "compromise" that gave birth to the Constitution, and may have been better included in Complementary Laws to the Constitution capable of changing, as now may be advisable, when circumstances require.

[5]Due to its extremely detailed nature, belonging better in a Complementary Law, it is outdated and requires up-dating at least.

Title Number:	Titled:	Articles Needing Possible Updating:	Other Comments:
Seventh	On Voting and Public Offices (Art. 97 to 117)	Consideration must be given to the feasibility of re-enacting these Arts: Regarding: 106 Firing of governmental employees 107 Post of trust 108 Competitions 110/111 Replacements 112 Dual employment 113 Retirements 114 Notary Publics 115 (regarding an institution that did not ¿exist?)	Otherwise OK
Eighth	Governmental Bodies (Article 118)	None	
Ninth	The Legislative Power (Article 119 to 137)	Consideration must be given to the feasibility of re-enacting these Arts: Regarding: 120 9 senators for Province[6] 123 1 representative for each 35,000	Otherwise OK
Tenth	The Executive Power (Articles 138 to 146)	None	
Eleventh	The Vice President (Articles 147 to 150)	None	
Twelfth	The Council of Ministers (Articles 151 to 163)	None	
Thirteenth	Inter-Governmental Relations (Articles 164 to 169)	None	

---

[6]Taking into account the current provinces of Cuba, this Legislative Body would be a "crowd", to say nothing of the House of Representatives referred in Article 123, that would have over 315 members considering the current insular population of Cuba and that of the "diaspora."

Title Number:	Titled:	Articles Needing Possible Updating:	Other Comments:
Fourteenth	The Judicial Power (Articles 170 to 208)	None	
Fifteenth	The Municipalities (Articles 209 to 232)	None	
Sixteenth	The Provinces (Articles 233 to 250)	None	
Seventeenth	The National Treasury (Articles 251 to 280)	Consideration must be given to the feasibility of re-enacting these	Otherwise OK

Seventeenth — continued:

Arts:	Regarding:
253	Borrowing "cap"
259	The Budget
266-270	Accounts Tribunal
274	Farm leases, etc.
275	Sugarmill owned properties
276	Antitrust

Title Number:	Titled:	Articles Needing Possible Updating:	Other Comments:
Eighteenth	State of Emergency (Articles 281 to 284)	None	
Nineteenth	Constitutional Reform (Articles 285 and 286)	None	

Not being an expert on Constitutional Law and removed from our Constitution and private practice in Cuba for more than thirty-three (33) years, there may be other provisions which may need updating.

PANEL DISCUSSION

CURRENT POLITICAL AND ECONOMIC TRENDS IN CUBA

José F. Alonso[1]

1. Sugar

The 1991-1992 Sugar Campaign (Zafra)

The sugar campaign (*zafra*) officially ended in Cienfuegos with a ceremony on August 1st. We have not yet received news or confirmation on the amount of sugar produced. Estimates range from less than 6 million tons to 7 million tons. The guessing game goes on until the leadership announces the results.[2]

The Forthcoming 1992-1993 Sugar Campaign

Preparations are already underway for the 1992-93 campaign and it is clear that the sector will have less resources than anticipated. Sugarcane planting is not at the same levels of a year ago. Spring planting decreased by 4,700 *caballerías*, or 63,700 hectares (1 Ha. = 2.5 acres). It can be expected that there will be less sugarcane available for the forthcoming crop. Minister Herrera announced that the country is presently engaged in planting 11,000 *caballerías*, or 147,620 Ha., through the month of August for the 1993-94 sugar campaign. Soybeans will be planted as an alternative crop to sugarcane this year (*Rebelde*, 3 August 1992).

Affecting the Next Sugar Campaign

Spare parts are critical for the harvesting and industrial processing of the sugarcane. Critical parts for the sugar mills and the refineries were previously obtained from the former Eastern bloc countries —Czechoslovakia and East Germany— and many of those installations are equipped with old vintage machinery supplied by those countries. Very little foreign trade is currently taking place because the former socialist countries now demand convertible currency. During this past sugar campaign the supply of spare parts became very critical. The forthcoming campaign will have less.

The quantity of oil products and lubricants needed to operate the mills becomes critical at the start of the sugar campaign. Sugar Minister Herrera Machado predicted less energy resources available.

A return to hand cutting instead of using harvesters/combines was announced by Herrera Machado. He indicated that "cane cutting brigades are being organized nationwide." He declared that "there will be even fewer mechanized resources for the next harvest in comparison with the last harvest." Sugarcane burning has been banned nationwide." (*Rebelde*, 3 August 1992)

---

[1]The comments by Mr. José F. Alonso may not be attributed in any way to any U.S. Government agencies, including the U.S. Information Agency, the Voice of America, Bureau of Broadcasting, Radio Martí Program. Any part of this discussion is only his own interpretation and thoughts on the subject matter.

[2]Fidel Castro announced in Cienfuegos, during the postponed 26th of July speech, that the 1991-92 sugarcane crop amounted to 7.0 million metric tons of sugar.

Minister Herrera announced on August 4th, in an interview with *Radio Rebelde*, that "Cuba will build by the end of the year an additional 15 distilleries, which will triple alcohol production." In 1989, alcohol production of various graduations was 4.1 million hl. Thus, within a two-year period, production will increase to 10 million hl. of alcohol.

Sugar marketing

F. O. Licht reported in the latest bulletin —July 20, 1992— that sugar exports were at about the same level of a year ago March.

2. Energy

Oil Supplies

Carlos Lage (in charge of the economy) announced that Cuba will have to cope with less than 6 million tons of oil overall for this year. That represents 50 percent less than last year.

Domestic oil production during 1992 is below last year's level of 700,000 tons.

Electricity

In Havana, the population is currently receiving 48 less hours of electricity per week, or nearly 7 less hours per day. The rest of the country is operating with 52-55 less hours of electricity per week.

Transportation & Industrial Sectors

The transportation sector is greatly affected by the energy shortage. The number of bus trips have been reduced by at least half of the normal trips in Ciudad Habana. This reduction in transportation is affecting an already besieged industrial sector due to energy shortages. The industrial sector is currently operating at no more than 46 percent capacity utilization, as discussed by Carlos Lage. Meanwhile, Jorge Lezcano announced in Havana that during July and August several work centers will stop temporarily. Workers in the affected factories will be relocated to agriculture, other chores, or will go on vacation.

Nuclear Plants

Russia appears temporarily committed to finish installation of 2-VVER reactors each of 440 MW under construction in Juraguá, Cienfuegos. Work is proceeding and the government announced that the plant will begin to operate sometime in 1993.[3]

Consumers

Consumers are paying dearly for the lack of electrical power, and power outages are frequent.

---

[3]Fidel Castro announced the suspension of the Juraguá Nuclear Power Plant project in Cienfuegos during the delayed speech commemorating the 26th of July anniversary. The September 6, 1992 edition of the *New York Times* reported the cause of the project's postponement as follows: "He bitterly attributed the suspension to Russia's insistence that the plant's skyrocketing costs be paid in hard currency, rather than through the subsidized barter arrangements of the past. Mr. Castro said the Russian terms were 'totally impossible.'"

They are experiencing loss of food, appliances burn out and other major inconveniences for lack of energy supplies, including mobility and transportation.

Oil Industry Prospects-Exploration

As is known, Cuba has looked all over the world for oil on concessionaire terms. Thus far, no Latin American government has provided oil in exchange for other products. Oil arriving in Cuba is purchased at world market prices. No deals for the future with Russia —that is, barter of sugar for oil. In the meantime, Cuba's National Bank president, Hector Rodríguez Llompart, is visiting Iran in an attempt to set up a sugar for oil deal. There have been some banking-related difficulties between both governments. The government of Iran indicated that it will deal only through a letter of credit.

CUPET (*Unión Cuba Petróleo*) continues to make deals with foreign oil companies towards the government goal of finding hydrocarbon deposits. CGG (Geophysics General Co.) French company will offer services to foreign companies with oil exploration agreements with Cuba. Companies with exploration agreements so far are: Canada NW Energy Ltd., Taurus of Sweden, and Petrobras of Brazil. The Canada NW contract is for in-shore exploration in central Cuba. These are all standard commercial risk contracts.[4]

3. Tourism

Tourism appears to have been a bright spot during this period. Rafael Sed Pérez, head of the tourist industry (INTUR), released a report that during the first six months of 1992, 420,000 tourists arrived in Cuba. Net income associated with these tourists was estimated at US$ 210 million for the industry. Cuba expects one million tourists in 1995.

4. Nickel

Production of various types of nickel amounted to 42,000 tons for 1991, of which 36,000 tons were produced by Moa and Nicaro. The Soviet-built Punta Gorda plant, programmed to produce 30,000 tons of nickel ore, had an output in 1990 of only 6,000 tons (*Cuadernos del Este*, May 1992). Meanwhile, CAME1, a plant under construction, is not yet near being operational. Cuba is seeking partners to finish the plant because CMEA no longer exists. In the meantime, Sherrit Gordon, a Canadian company, signed a US$ 1.2 billion joint venture agreement with the nickel industry enterprise CUBANICKEL. Canada is buying nickel, and sales in 1991 amounted to a little over 5,000 tons. Apparently there were other sales in exchange for equipment and other needed inputs.

5. Development Assistance

UNDR recently provided funds in the amount of US$695,000 to finance consultants and technical assistance in the construction of a mineral research pilot plant. The plant when operational will research on an under pressure acid lixiviation process which will attempt to improve the rate of nickel extraction per ton.

---

[4] *Platt's Oilgram News* announced on June 25, 1992 that in October CUPET will begin a new round of oil exploration licensing in London to attract foreign investment. A minimum of eight blocs will be auctioned and their sizes are approximately 2,000 to 6,000 square kilometers.

6. Foreign Debt

In an interview with *Komsomolskaya Pravda* on 28 July 1992, Russia's Minister for Foreign Economic Relations, Pyotr Aven, revealed that Cuba's debt to Russia amounted to US$ 75 billion. This is equivalent to almost half of the total outstanding Russian debt by Third World countries of US$ 140 billion. This debt, as he indicated, does not include military hardware and assistance. Previously, in November 1990, the debt was reported to be US$ 22 billion in a communiqué issued by the Central Committee of the Communist Part of the former Soviet Union.[5]

Combining this debt with the Paris Club (US$ 7 billion) and Eastern European countries (US$ 4 billion) the total debt amounts to approximately US$ 86 billion.[6] A per capita debt of over US$ 7,800. If the debt reported is correct, then Cuba's debt represents 3.2 times its GSP (Gross Social Product). We can expect a very difficult round of negotiations between both countries. Aven informed that this debt cannot be sold without the consent of Cuba, as stipulated on their agreements.

7. Food Supplies

Once the potato harvest ended, we did not hear anything else about any other crop or the "Food Program." Nowadays plantains and other tubers are being programmed for late summer harvest. These are mostly produced by the private agricultural sector. Why is the leadership so silent about this critical small sector?

8. General Consumption and Consumer Issues

General conditions seems to deteriorate in the countryside. Life becomes more difficult as reflected by the severe austerity facing consumers. Consumer complaints continue about shortages and longer lines. The word nowadays is *No Hay Nada*. Everything is under strict rationing and the government prosecutes those caught stealing or diverting resources from government warehouses. The government is under pressure to curtail black market operations and it has undertaken a serious effort. Meanwhile, the leadership is aware that serious accumulation of money occurs (liquidity) as a result of supply shortages and inflationary trends continue unabated.

John Paul Rathbone

The current situation and short-term prospects for the Cuban economy are gloomy indeed. My objective here is to examine why, focusing, in turn, on three main threads of thought:

---

[5]A new announcement on Cuba's debt was reported by Russia's Foreign Economic Minister Petr O. Aven on 24 September 1992, while attending the IMF meeting. Aven stated: "Fidel Castro is refusing to pay Russia some US$ 28 billion Cuba was loaned over the years as one of the Soviet Union's closest allies. Not only will Castro not repay it, he will not even discuss it" (*The Houston Chronicle*, September 25, 1992, p.24). The debt in question was originally negotiated in rubles and its value, due to foreign exchange considerations, is very difficult to assess. Prior to this announcement, the debt was postponed several times between Cuba and the ex-USSR (see Mesa-Lago, *The Economy of Socialist Cuba: A Two Decade Appraisal*, p.104-107). There is scant information on the nature, terms and composition of this debt.

[6]As a new figure on Cuba's debt to Russia was reported, the total amount of external debt has been considerably reduced to US$39 billion. This represents a per capita debt of over US$ 3,900. The newly recalculated debt represents 1.6 times Cuba's Gross Social Product (GSP) reported for 1989.

1. The known economic effects of the collapse of the former Soviet bloc on Cuba.

2. The strategies —other than cut-backs— that Cuba has adopted to face the crisis.

3. The likelihood that these strategies will succeed.

1. The Effect on Cuba of the Collapse of the Socialist Bloc

(a) Drastic: the traditional five/one year planning process has virtually collapsed and the centralized control of the past has been replaced by perpetual crisis management.

(b) Shortages of food are dramatic and inconvenience has been transformed into hardship. While there may not be starvation, there is hunger, and the dividing line between the two is thin. According to one newspaper report, Cubans are now eating cats (LV: 13/8/92).[7]

(c) One month's rations now includes: 4 eggs, 2½ lbs. of rice, ½ lb. of beans, 2½ lbs. of sugar, 30 bread rolls, and 1 roll of toilet paper (LAT: 30/6/92).

(d) The black market is used by those that can to supplement lack of supplies. But black market exchange rates and prices are inflating rapidly making it increasingly difficult for people with lower incomes to supplement their rations. Eggs now cost $5 each on the black market, compared to the official price of 15 cents (LAT: 30/6/92), and black market prices for the starchy *malanga* has risen to $40, from $10 a year ago (MH: 29/5/92).

Black market exchange rates have also risen since October of last year, from 15 to 33 Cuban pesos to the dollar, compared with the official dollar exchange rate of 1:1 (FT: 14/7/92). Average monthly wages remain at around 135 pesos (MH: 29/5/92).

(e) Imports from the former Socialist bloc are down by 60% since 1989,[8] and from the West —using UK figures as a marker— by 55%.[9] All told, there has been a drop from US $8.1 billion of imports in 1989, to around US$3.5 billion in 1991.

(f) Furthermore, as most of these imports are raw materials, or intermediate goods, their absence has had a further negative effect on production. For example, shortages have reduced tobacco production by 10-15% this year (Reuters: 2/7/92).

(g) Potential revenues from Cuban exports have also been severely curtailed. With trade subsidies now a feature of the past, sugar price reductions alone have cost —according to Fidel Castro— US $2.5 billion this year (Castro: 4/4/92).

(h) Also important has been the loss of niche markets in the former Soviet bloc: now at lest 1 million tons less of sugar can be sold there than in 1990.

---

[7]Codes for newspaper references are as follows: LV - *La Vanguardia*; FT - *Financial Times*; LAT - *Los Angeles Times*; MH - *The Miami Herald*; JC - *Journal of Commerce*; CB - *Cuba Business*.

[8]Carlos Lage in "UK Embassy's Quarterly Economic Report" (30/6/92).

[9]UK Department of Trade and Industry, bilateral trade figures, 1989-92.

(i) In addition, the loss of markets in the former socialist bloc has affected plans for the expansion of sales of important nontraditional exports, such as biotechnology and citrus fruit. These products have much in common with many East European products, namely they were only sellable at CMEA rates of exchange to CMEA consumers who tend to be less fastidious than others. For example:

CITRUS: Cuban citrus is of poor quality by world standards. Cuban oranges's skins are green. But Europeans —now pegged to become one of Cuba's main citrus markets— prefer their oranges to be orange. Cuban grapefruit suffers from similar problems. True, Cuban grapefruit can undercut European prices somewhat to compensate, and has recently been doing so (JC: 17/6/92). But selling at a discount merely represents another cost and, even so, Cuba is still awash with unsold surplus citrus fruit (Fidel Castro: Speech to National Assembly 12/7/92).

BIOTECH: Cuba's medicines have no published test results. In 1991, according to one study, none of Cuba's medicines met US or European licensing standards. Cuba also lacks any kind of international marketing or distribution network and, according to one Havana-based representative of a multi-national pharmaceutical firm, "cannot afford to open sales offices abroad as it only has one or two products to sell."[10] Finally, many of Cuba's medicines are non-original and are not based on new genetic research, i.e. they do not respect international patents. Of course, Cuba is not the only country that does not respect international patents. But there is no doubt that the sanctioning power of multinational pharmaceutical companies should not be underestimated.[11] (In 1989, Cuba had planned sales of US $700 million to the USSR. But these are probably largely lost now).

(j) Lost markets and lower prices: what then can Cuba's exports bring in hard currency for 1992/3? The Cubans have said that they believe that the economy can function on a minimum of US$4 billion of exports per annum (CB: 6/92). But this begs two questions: First, is this an adequate, minimal strategy? (Barely.) Second —and more to the point perhaps— can $4 billion in export revenues even be realized? (Probably not.)

1992/3 Estimated Export Revenues

Sugar exports..	US$1.10 - 1.40 billion

Non-sugar exports

- Fish products...	US$150 million
- Tobacco...	US$100 million
- Nickel..	US$450 - 550 million
- Citrus & other agricultural goods.............	US$200 - 250 million
- Biotechnology..	US$100 - 200 million
Total non-sugar exports................................	US$1.00 - 1.25 billion

TOTAL: US$2.10 - 2.65 billion

---

[10]See Andrés Oppenheimer, *Castro's Final Hour* (New York: Simon & Shuster, 1992), p. 297.

[11]See A. Maingot in CARICOM's "Perspectives," Summer issue 1992.

Even the high end of the range —which gives the benefit of the doubt wherever possible— nowhere meets the hoped-for US$4 billion figure, and is around 50% less than 1989 levels[12].

(k) It is well-nigh impossible to gauge the effect of the above on the internal economy. But according to Pedro Monreal, Senior Researcher at the Center for the Study of the Americas and Adjunct Professor at the Institute for International Relations in Havana (CB: June, 1992), the Cuban economy contracted by 25% during 1991, will have contracted by another 10% in 1992, and will stabilize (or more realistically, stagnate) during 1993. This, however, must be considered a very optimistic viewpoint.

2. Strategies to Meet the Crisis

There are two essential components to the Cuban government's current economic strategy:

i) Increase domestic food production in the state-run INTERNAL SECTOR's agricultural program.

ii) Increase, or at least maintain, hard currency earnings from an increasingly market-oriented EXTERNAL SECTOR.

i) The Agricultural Program

The agricultural program is Cuba's big hope. But targets are very optimistic. There are expected increases of 15% - 100% in selected goods. But production of all these has actually declined since the mid-80s.

There are three main elements to the food program:

a) Increase irrigation.

Problem: the number of hectares under irrigation has only grown by 15% since 1980. Is a more dramatic increase possible now, in such straightened circumstances[13]?

b) Replant land with agricultural food crops by removing cane. Some 64% of land is now in crops other than cane (CB: June 1992) and replanting has been especially heavy near the capital, in Havana province, for obvious reasons.

Problem: this approach frames agricultural production in terms of area, not in output; land is not the scarcest resource. To boost output, Cuba's agricultural program needs fertilizers, as well as other imported goods such as seed, herbicides and equipment, all of which are in very short supply. It also needs labor —labor that is simultaneously needed for the sugar harvests. True, surplus labor can be diverted from the cities. But this is unpopular.

Problem: who will farm the land? Answer: the State sector. Yet international experience has shown time and time again that, after services, agriculture is the sector least productive

---

[12]For more on Cuba's short term export potential, see Andrew Zimbalist, *Journal of Latin American Studies*, May 1992.

[13]Carmelo Mesa-Lago, Americas Society Conference, "Cuba at the Turning Point," New York, May 1992.

under state control. In 1989, the non-state sector —accounting for under 17% of cultivated land— provided 65% of Cuba's tomatoes and other market vegetables, 28% of root crops, and 35% of plantains.[14] Clearly, it would be an expanded non-state sector that could feed Cuba.

c) Encourage self-reliance and appeal to individual resourcefulness. Two examples illustrate this drive: i) baby chicks have been distributed to be reared at home; and ii) energy-efficient charcoal stoves have been also distributed for domestic use.[15]

Problem with the first example: where can one find enough feed to rear the chicks? Problem with the second: where can Cubans get the 14 sacks of charcoal needed per annum, to run the stoves? In both cases: the black market. Yet the government has recently increased its attempts to prosecute anyone found trading on the black market.

Herein lies the program's fundamental contradiction: a matching of state-controlled production and distribution, against appeals to individual initiative. The program could well unravel over it.

ii) Increase Hard Currency Earnings

(a) Through diversified trade partners. But China, although increasingly important, cannot substitute for the loss of the USSR and East European markets; Latin America is not a natural market for Cuba as it produces much the same export goods; the USA market, of course, is closed; and it is hard for Cuba to expand its trade into the EEC as Cuba is in default of previous EEC loans and has received no European trade credits since 1986.

(b) Promote non-traditional exports and other sources of hard currency. Tourism and biotechnology are usually cited as the two main hopes here.

However, although biotechnology might show some promise over the long run, for the reasons outlined above, it promises little significant relief over the short term. Time is a problem.

Nor is tourism the savior it is often heralded as being. Despite the publicity, potential revenues from tourism —even taking into account the most optimistic Cuban projections— are quite small. Half a million visitors are planned for 1992, grossing US$600 million. But due to tourism's high import component and Cuba's profit-sharing with its foreign partners, only one third of this, some US $200 - 250 million will stick to Cuba. The best estimate for 1993/4 is US $300 million in tourist revenues for Cuba.[16]

In addition, tourism carries its own fair share of problems; the domestic political fallout from tourism should not be underestimated.

(c) Through foreign investment that brings technology, management skills, inputs and, most

---

[14]*Anuario Estadístico 1989.*

[15]*Caribbean Insight*, July 1992, page 7.

[16]The main incentive for European tourists (reckoned to supply 80% of Cuba's tourism by 1995) is low-cost. For example, a two-week holiday in Havana and Varadero, with flight and accommodation in a three-star hotel included, is currently on offer in London for only £400. By comparison, a commercial return flight to Miami from London costs at least £400. Indeed, Cuba's stated strategy is to increase levels of Cuban tourism through low-cost package tours (address by Vice Foreign Minister Raúl Roa, Canning House, London, 3/9/92).

especially, marketing know-how.

Considering its relatively small amount, foreign investment in Cuba has received a disproportionate amount of publicity.[17] Some US$400 - 500 million has been invested so far (José Luis Rodríguez, in CB: June 1992). These monies are distributed through about 50 joint ventures, mostly in the tourist sector, but also in oil and nickel. The Cuban government has said that it hopes foreign investment will reach US$400 - 500 million a year (FT: 14/7/92).

Cuba's drive to attract foreign investment begs two questions: how attractive is Cuba to a foreign investor? And would the hoped-for annual amount of US$400 - 500 million in investment bridge the gap?

Aside from nickel, tourism and oil (Cuba's only possible ace-in-the-hole) Cuba is not a very attractive destination for investors, because:

i) Prior to the changes in Eastern Europe in 1989, Eastern Europe had very similar foreign investment laws to Cuba's despite Cuba's recent constitutional changes - and very few traded. Foreign investors lacked confidence in the system and its government. Cuba probably faces similar circumstances;

ii) The general world economic climate is not encouraging, and;

iii) It is probably a truism that there are a number of other more attractive destinations for foreign investors around the world, with less risk.

There are three consequences to the above:

i) First, although foreign investors are probably keen to position themselves in Cuba, in anticipation of lasting economic and political changes and an opening in the US market, their exposure —tourism, nickel and oil aside— will be quite small.[18]

ii) Cuba, as a high-risk investment, demands a high return. For instance, foreign partners in tourist joint ventures are currently offered the fire-sale rate of a guaranteed three year return on their money.

iii) To offset the above, Cuba is today taking its most attractive assets —the *filet mignons* as it were— and selling them at a considerable discount. The tragedy here is that the minimal economic returns to Cuba derived from these sales are not re-invested to create tomorrow's opportunities for Cubans; they are used to fund today's survival. (Also, there is only a limited

---

[17]Exact figures on levels of foreign investment in Cuba are extremely scarce. However, the largest single investment in Cuba's tourist sector has so far been the Spanish Grupo Sol's joint venture in Varadero, valued at US $60 million (*Business International Special Report*: 3/92, page 62). Italcable's joint venture to improve international telecommunications is valued at US $41 million (CB: 2/92). Oil exploration contracts with Canada North West Energy Limited, Taurus of Sweden and Brazil's Petrobras are all commercial risk contracts. And Sherrit Gordon's much-touted US $1.2 billion investment in Cuban nickel now looks instead to be a 20-year supply contract based on 1991 trade worth US $54 million. Apparently, however, discussions are underway between Sherrit Gordon and Cuba over the possibility of a US $70 million investment in Cuban nickel refining (*Business Week*: 3/8/92).

[18] For example, the joint venture between the Chilean company New World Fruit, based in Rotterdam, and Cubafrutas, was mostly at the marketing end and was used to boost quality, and therefore competitiveness, by managing fruit acquisition, packing, palletization and shipping. This required no great investment, however (JC: 17/6/92).

number of *filet mignon*.)

In short, levels of foreign investment are at a minimum to what they could be under different circumstances, and look unlikely to grow significantly under current conditions. In spite of the fact that Cuba is currently offering its most attractive assets, investor interest has been relatively low. US$400 million a year in foreign investment looks unlikely and, even if this level were to be reached, it would not be sufficient to close the gap.[19]

d) Increased autonomy for Cuban state enterprises in the external sector. Cuba's external sector is increasingly characterized by autonomous enterprises that are being encouraged and created to act in almost any way that is commercially viable and that earns hard currency. Currency earnings are then retained in an autonomous branch of the national banking system.[20]

This process first began in the 1980s, to circumvent the US embargo, and is still most true only for the tourist sector. But it does seem to be gaining momentum. In January 1991, only 30 autonomous enterprises were registered with the Cuban Chamber of Commerce; by December of the same year, the known number (which does not include military-run enterprises, such as Gaviota) had risen to 72.[21]

This is one of the most interesting of recent developments and its central contradiction is hard to miss: market-run enclaves are to rescue Cuba's socialist economy from its own shortcomings.

It is necessary but risky strategy for the regime. First, because the possibilities for corruption are huge.[22] Second, because not all of these market-orientated enterprises can be contained within enclaves. The biotechnology and nickel industries can be run behind closed doors, perhaps, but certainly not tourism. Negotiating those points where an increasingly capitalist external sector meets the tightly-controlled state-run internal sector will be extremely tricky.

For example, a "worker's aristocracy" could emerge and agricultural and other workers in the internal sector could well come to resent their counterparts's higher earnings.[23]

Also, freeing some sectors of the economy, while leaving others controlled, could lead to an uncontrollable shift of resources and workers into free markets, leaving the official sector to fall apart. This tension is already illustrated by the fact that private farmers now face the threat of having their land confiscated if they sell their produce on the black market (FT: 14/7/92).

---

[19]For more on business perspectives on investing in Cuba, please seem comments by James D. Whisenand, Euromoney conference, Cancún, Mexico, 9/6/92.

[20]"Cuba: New Opportunities for British Business," Caribbean Trade Advisory Group, January 1992.

[21]Corporación Cimex —the first, and now the largest, of these autonomous enterprises— was set up in 1979. Registered in Panama, Cimex acts as a holding company for 40 subsidiary companies, including Havanatur, Cubapack, and Tropicala. In 1991, a report of independent auditors put Cimex's total assets at US$296.44 million, and annual net income at US$41.64 million.

[22]Most recently, Everto López —Sony's representative in Cuba— and Rolando de Armas —an executive at the Cuban trading enterprise CUBALSE— were arrested on corruption charges, according to a recent Cuban defector (MH: 18/8/92).

[23]On 29th April, 1992, the Mexican periodical *Novedades*, reported Pedro Ross Leal, Secretary of the Cuban Worker's Central, as saying that the number of new jobs generated by tourism joint venture's was projected to grow to 70,000 by 1992.

3. What is the Possibility that the Strategies Will Succeed?

To re-cap: the Cuban economy is no longer monolithic. Changes, limited but significant, are underway.

On the one hand, the internal sector will remain strictly controlled. On the other hand, in the external sector, selected enterprises are being encouraged to act in any way that is commercially viable and that earns hard currency. Foreign investment and know-how are also being actively courted.

The vanishing point of these changes seems to be an attempt to turn the economy inside out, rather than let it unravel at the edges, as happened in Eastern Europe prior to 1989. The approach suggests a half-hearted compromise between reformers and conservatives within the Cuban Communist Party.

But turning economies inside out is a technique hard to succeed. Figures alone suggest that it is not viable. Time is also a constraint. In the meantime, the regime runs the risk of the whole process blowing-up in its face.

What do these observations lead one to conclude? Even if one imagines, by hook or by crook, that Cuba —somehow— can make more than US$2.5 billion in exports, this is still barely enough to keep 10½ million Cubans alive. It certainly does not provide for economic development or growth OF ANY KIND.

In other words, and the one closing point that should be made here: if the strategy fails, it fails (and there is every indication that it will); whereas if it succeeds (by which I merely mean that it will continue, a process that will almost certainly require increased levels of repression) it is not going to be able to maintain the current system, i.e: it will fail anyway.

As Spanish Prime Minister Felipe González recently said during the Hispano-American summit in Madrid, the problem with the Cuban economy is not the US embargo, but that its economic system is inherently unproductive.

THOUGHTS ON THE CUBAN SUGAR INDUSTRY

Nicolás Rivero

I.   Introduction

Remember the classic Cuban axiom "Sin azúcar no hay país"? The question should now be asked: is this principle still valid in the last decade of the Twentieth Century, after approximately 200 years of dominating all aspects of the island's psychological and economic existence? This question has to be raised regardless of whether the country has a controlled economy under a communist dictatorship or a free market economy under a democratic government.

A central issue in formulating any economic strategy for Cuba is directly related to the sugar cane agroindustry; its impact and contribution to the future growth of the economy. Will it be a dynamic source of progress or will it be a constraint?

I believe there is a future for the Cuban sugar agroindustry, but it has to be based on sound agribusiness principles and not on a state-owned or controlled monopoly or oligopoly as it was in the past.

A re-evaluation of the role of sugar within the Cuban economy can set off a very lively debate —which I strongly believe should take place— but we shall limit this discussion to an overview of the current situation and to comment on some of the changes that appear to be taking place in Cuba at this time.

II.   Current Situation

Information available on Cuba reflects an intense preoccupation on the future of the island's sugar industry. The sugar problem has come about as a direct result of the break-up of the Soviet Union and the end of its 30 years of considerable economic aid. This assistance basically was made up of purchases of large quantities of Cuban raw sugar paid at prices substantially above those of the world market, coupled with shipments of oil priced below international prices.

Fidel Castro is in the process of adjusting to the new political and economic realities of a post-Soviet world. He hopes to compensate for the loss of the Soviet sugar subsidy with a strategy based on attracting foreign investment and joint ventures from Western and Far Eastern countries. Actually, he began this scheme on a limited scale a few years ago with tourism. Now, according to Carlos Lage, Politburo member in charge of economic matters, necessity has forced an opening of other sectors of the economy, including sugar.[1]

This aperture to foreign investors must not be confused or construed as a signal that Fidel Castro has, or is willing to, initiate a transition to a free market economy or is willing to build a democracy like the countries of Eastern Europe and the former Soviet Union are doing. This is clearly capitalism *a la* neo—Castro.

---

[1]Carlos Lage, a Politburo member in charge of economic matters, stated in an interview that was published in *Juventud Rebelde* of 26 January, 1992 that the 1991/92 sugar harvest was going to be lower as a result of poor maintenance and repairs due to shortages of spare parts, lack of adequate fertilization as well as fuels and lubricants needed for field operations and mill boilers. This made it necessary to explore other economic activities.

III.   The Consequences of the Loss of Soviet Aid

Sugar is still the backbone of the economy. In dealing with sugar under present conditions, I believe, the first step is to restructure this key economic sector. The classical Cuban sugar economy model —based on guaranteed markets and premium prices— abruptly died on 27 December 1991 when the Soviet Union ceased to exist.

Since the country is bankrupt, ways and means are being sought by the government to implement a restructuring policy hopefully with the participation of international sugar businesses. As a result, several questions arise.

Can the government make conditions sufficiently attractive and persuade foreign investors to come in?

How competitive can Cuban sugar production become in the absence of all external subsidies? and,

From a political viewpoint, will these measures help sustain Fidel Castro in power and for how much longer?

The backdrop of a new sugar strategy revolves around four basic points.

Cuba's sugar milling complex is old. Upwards of 90 percent of the factories were built before 1925. Most of the sugar is manufactured as raws to be further refined by importers. Capacity to make refined sugar is limited to less than 900,000 tons. The island is not an efficient sugar producer and production costs are surely way above today's world market price of around US$0.10 per pound.

The Cuban sugar industry for most of the 20th century has been subsidized by a foreign country. First, by the United States until 1960 under the old Sugar Act and then by the ex-Soviet Union till the end of 1991. Considering sugar alone, the loss of Soviet economic aid and trade is staggering. Cuba's sugar exports to that region of the world in 1992, in terms of volume, will be about 2 million tons or 1.8 million tons less than in 1991. Fidel Castro has stated that this projected loss will be equivalent to about US$2.5 billion.[2] Soviet prices in 1991 were reported at US$0.36 per pound and those for this year are estimated at about US$0.09.

Cuba's primary source of energy is imported oil. Until the end of 1991 one ton of Cuban sugar used to buy 7 tons of Soviet oil. The ratio now is 1 ton of sugar to 1.7 tons of oil. This means that Cuba was able to buy 13 million tons of oil —its annual consumption— with 1.9 million tons of sugar, but now needs to sell 7.2 million tons of sugar to import the same amount. As a result Fidel Castro and Carlos Lage were saying that oil imports this year will be around 6 million tons. In reality even this figure might turn out to be too high.

Cuba now needs to develop new markets and marketing techniques for its sugar. Sugar authorities are more accustomed to government-to-government centralized trade negotiations than free market operations.

---

[2]Fidel Castro's closing speech to the Congress of the Unión de Juventud Comunista, 4 May 1992.

IV.   The Crisis Year, 1992

The gravity of the looming 1992 sugar disaster on the economy can be measured in terms of the foreign exchange that sugar sales can generate this year. Sugar accounts for more than 75 percent of the total value of Cuba's exports. I estimated that sugar sales this year (1992) will amount to approximately US$978 million compared to US$3.6 billion in 1991, a walloping drop of 73 percent in just one year's time.

With regards to the 1991/92 sugar harvest, Cuban officials have kept all production figures in secret, but do admit that it will below the 7.6mmt produced the year before. My estimate for this year's zafra is 5.8mmt. This is based on those statements made indicating the multitude of problems both of resources and logistical support that are being encountered as well the fact that operations were delayed by two months.

If the 1992 sugar situation is bleak in comparison to 1991 and previous years, it appears to me that there will be no noticeable improvement in 1993. In fact, the USDA's first estimate for sugar crop year 1992/93 (June 1992) places the Cuban harvest at 6.0mmt or at the same level as the 1991/92 estimate.

The bottom line is that the government of Cuba lacks the financial and material resources to prepare for next year's (1993) crop. In the medium and longer term —if the Castro regime does not fall— the situation could improve only to the extent foreign investors come in with needed capital and technology. In a post-Castro era the two key requirement are capital and management that will not only bring in processing technology but also an agribusiness concept to the whole industry.

V.   The Three Faces of the Sugar Problem

Faced with a three-fold sugar problem, serious difficulties in production, loss of traditional preferential market and lack of capital for repairs and maintenance, the government has to embark on a new approach. Based on the information available, it looks as if Cuba is adopting a strategy that includes aligning output to market demand, promoting foreign investment, and vertical integration.

A.   Aligning output to market demand

The first part of the restructuring program could well be to rationalize the size of the industry by reducing planted area and milling capacity to realistic market demand. This could be done by the dismantling of the smaller and more inefficient mills. Out of a total of 156 sugar factories the majority —82 have a crushing capacity of 3,500 tons a day or less— are considered small and inefficient by today's world industry standards. The taking apart of small mills will not only reduce production costs but also make available cannibalized parts and machinery for other mills. There is no evidence that all 156 mills operated in the 1991/92 harvest.

Since Cuba no longer receives preferential prices for its raw sugar, and world sugar demand is shifting from raws to refined, or whites, it must adapt production to world market conditions. Under these realities diversification away from raw sugar and molasses into higher value added is needed. Products basically can be grouped into three categories: sugar, alcohol and by-products.

In the case of sugar the government wants to increase production and sales of refined sugar and high polarization sugar (99.2º), and also produce for export a high sucrose syrup using a Cuban biotechnological process.[3] This product is said to be suitable for use in soft drinks. An other export product line is the pre—packaged sugar ready for direct distribution specially for the Middle East markets.

B.   Investments in communist Cuba

In order to achieve the above Cuba has to modernize and most of all install additional refining capacity and is looking for foreign investors such as multinational sugar companies —not trade or commission houses— who have the required capital and technology. Some of these companies are already entering into ventures in the former communist countries of Central and Eastern Europe that produce beet sugar and have been exploring opportunities in the Commonwealth of Independent States (CIS) republics that produce beet sugar.

Cuba could present an interesting opening for European-based multinationals to position themselves in this hemisphere. Mexico and especially Canada could be important markets for refined sugar and could present interesting possibilities under a North American Free Trade Agreement (NAFTA) for non-U.S. sugar refiners.

At this time it is appropriate to bring up a related key issue concerning possible new foreign investments in Cuba made under the present regime. This point is directly connected with the complicated and highly politically sensitive question of the expropriations of sugarcane farms "*colonias*" and mills made by the revolutionary government in the early 1960s, but never compensated, of properties belonging to Cuban citizens and corporations as well as those of the United States. Under a post—Castro democratic government, the legal question of prior ownership could become an object of a very complex and lengthy litigation process.

C.   Vertical integration

Over the last two decades research has gone into a more efficient use of the sugarcane industry by-products. Beside the traditional use of bagasse as boiler fuel for the mills it can be used to make paper pulp, compress boards for construction and as an ingredient in animal feeds. Sugarcane is a renewable source of energy that can be processed —directly from cane juice or from molasses— into fuel alcohol or ethanol.

As in the case of sugar refineries Cuba —a country with a very large sugar sector— has a very small alcohol distillation industry with limited production capacity. This in part is due to Cuba's role as a supplier of raw sugar within the central planning scheme of the Soviet Union. Cuban raw sugar was refined by the Soviet, specially the Ukrainian, sugar beet factories in their off season. Fuel alcohol would of given Cuba some margin of domestic fuel independence.

There is speculation of a possible alcohol strategy that could involve a triangular venture whereby: Brazil would supply Cuba the technology and the distilleries; Cuba would produces fuel ethanol from sugarcane for shipment to Mexico and the latter would pay for the ethanol directly to Brazil with oil and thus pay off Cuba's debt.

---

[3]A Reuter's news-cable datelined Havana 20 April 1992 stated that the *Instituto Cubano de Investigaciones Azucareras* had developed a biotechnological process to make syrups from raw or refined sugar that was to be produced in a pilot plant. The product was of excellent quality and purity and could be used in soft drinks.

A domestic renewable fuel like ethanol could become a very important asset for an oil starved country like Cuba. Oil is principal source of primary energy and almost the totality of these requirements are imported —up till 1991 from the ex-Soviet Union.

D.   Sugar and energy

In Cuba sugar and energy have a very close relationship. First, as a means of payment for imported oil, and second, bagasse is the country's second energy source.

In 1989 Cuba's energy requirements totalled over 116 million barrels of oil equivalent, or 15.8mmt. On a per capita basis oil consumption at that time was about 8 barrels a day and rated as the highest among the developing countries of the world.

From the supply side, the major portion of Cuba's primary energy requirements are provided by petroleum (73 percent) and sugarcane bagasse (24 percent). The balance is made up of firewood (2 percent) and coal and others (1 percent).

Consumption of oil products in 1989 reached 228,448 barrel/day (83.4 million barrels a year or 11.3 million MT) and was broken down by products: residual (47 percent), diesel (23 percent), kerosene (6 percent), gasoline (12 percent) and other (12 percent).[4]

In order to have an approximation of the quantity of ethanol that could be used domestically the following calculations are indicative. Assuming that motor gasoline demand in 1989 reached 10 million barrel/year (1.4 million MT) or about 484.2 million gallons of gasoline. For example, if Cuba adopted —as Brazil has— a national gasoline/ethanol blend of 88 percent gasoline and 22 percent ethanol, then ethanol demand would be 106.5 million gallons. In order to produce this amount of fuel alcohol 746,000 tons of raw sugar are required.

As the economy recuperates, the demand for gasoline will increase and if ethanol is used or exported, then also will the sugar inputs. It is important to point out that the U.S. is the world's largest consumer of reformulated gasolines that are blended by federal law with oxygenated fuels such as ethanol. As a result of the Clean Air Act of 1990, U.S. requirements of oxygenated fuels will have a strong incremental demand.

With an expanded alcohol production Cuba could also further increase its rum output as well as its pharmaceutical and biotechnological product lines, especially those for export.

The sugar-ethanol issue has to be carefully analyzed as part of a national sugar strategy. It could be an important option within an integrated industry strategy.

E.   Foreign markets

Regarding the substantial loss of the former Soviet —at least the preferential treatment— and Eastern European markets it appears that Cuban sugar authorities are trying to develop new markets such as Iran and South Korea and are interested in negotiating long term arrangements with refiners. They hope to secure market stability by means of long term contracts with refiners in industrialized countries who control distribution. Refiners can offer better conditions than trade houses and have

---

[4]East-West Center, Energy Advisory Nº 87, 1 February 1992.

greater financial resources. Also, to negotiate, wherever possible, government-to-government contracts as in the case of Iran and South Korea.

As Cuba begins to adjust its sugar strategy to the post—Soviet era, the process of restructuring and its eventual results could have important political and trade implications for many interested parties both inside as well as outside the country.

VI.   A New Home for Cuban Sugar

Where does this leave us? I believe that low key strategic planning should be made in order to find, first, internal solutions for Cuba within a diversified sugar sector. Second on the export side, for example, explore the possibilities of an expanded North American sweetener market resulting from a NAFTA agreement and maintain the CIS market.

The question being asked not only in Havana but in many cities in other countries is: Does there exist a home for the Cuban sugar that was traded to the Soviets and Eastern Europe? Will Cuban sugar displace domestic producers or foreign suppliers in any of the importing markets, particularly in the United States? These are very relevant questions.

Since sugar was first planted in the New World almost 500 years ago this commodity has been the most politically sensitive and highly emotional of all those products traded international or for that matter even domestically.

It is important to point out that on the day that a significant political change takes place in Cuba the sugar issue will certainly be the most volatile items in any future Cuban-American agenda.

The time is right —now in mid 1992— to start looking for possible avenues of solutions to Cuba's sugar dilemma.

It is obvious one cannot go back to pre-Castro times when there was a Sugar Act in the United States and Cuba had a preferential market of over 3mmt. Also, it is evident that Cuba's sugar industry cannot continue to be a state-owned monopoly or operate as an oligopoly as it did under the "Ley de Coordinación Azucarera" from 1937 to 1958.[5] Moreover, Cuba without a preferential market has to prove that it can be internationally competitive in the world or "free" market.   The economic viability of an export industry is directly dependent on foreign markets. Cuba's domestic market justifies an industry of not more than 1.5mmt.

In the coming years two markets are of critical importance. These are the two historical buyers of Cuban sugar: the CIS republics and the United States.

A.   The Commonwealth of Independent States

The CIS republics, as a group, are net importers of sugar, but the single largest potential customer is the Russian Federation. Although Cuba has lost the strategic political relationship it

---

[5]In Cuba prior to the Castro regime, the state exercised control of certain agricultural activities —sugar being one— in order to adjust the supply to the demand of foreign markets. All phases of the sugarcane agroindustry were basically governed by the "Ley de Coordinación Azucarera (Sugar Coordination Law) promulgated on 2 September 1937 and crop restrictions commenced the following year. This legislation was incorporated into the Cuban Constitution of 1940.

had in the context of the cold war, it is still of vital interest to Russia because that republic is the holder of Cuba's enormous debt that was contracted over 30 years with the Soviet Union.

Notimex, a Mexican news agency, on 28 July reported that the newspaper "Komsomolskaia Pravda" published an interview with a spokesman of the Russian Foreign Ministry, Piotr Aven, in which the Cuban debt was placed at an equivalent of US$75 billion. Other sources place the aggregate debt at a much lower level. The Deutsche Sudamerikanische Bank of Germany places the debt at US$22.4 billion. Also Cuba is heavily indebted to Western Banks for a further US$7 billion and has not serviced these obligations in many years.

Shipments of sugar from Cuba this year to Russia and the other CIS republics are about half of previous years tonnage. These countries are now buying through trade house or directly from a cross the border, Poland, or the East, Turkey and China. If Cuba cannot re-establish these transactions, it may very well be permanently displaced from those markets.

B.   Is there a place for Cuba in NAFTA?

In an expanded North American trading block[6] Canada is not likely to become self-sufficient in sugar and Cuba is a traditional supplier. In the case of Mexico the sugar situation is substantially more complicated and not clear at this time since the official text of the agreement has not been made public. Mexico is a net importer of sugar and has bought significant amounts from Cuba in the past. It is understood that Mexico —if the agreement is ratified— could be in a position to develop a HFCS industry based on imported U.S. yellow corn and/or HFCS. Mexico is a very large consumer of soft drinks and the bottling industry is currently using about 1.3 to 1.5mmt of sugar a year. This is a natural market for HFCS as it is in the U.S.

Expectations are that Mexico with HFCS in six or seven years time could become self-sufficient in sweeteners and thus a net exporter of sugar. Under NAFTA, if Mexico is considered a net exporter of sugar, those surplus amounts can then enter the U.S. without any restrictions after the seventh year of the agreement. If this should come about, it would have very serious repercussions for Cuba with regard to future sugar market opportunities. It would thus not only close the Mexican market, but more importantly eliminate any potential possibility of opening up of the U.S. market.

The sugar industry —if markets can be secured and production can be made competitive— will surely have an important role in the country and will contribute to economic growth. Just as the Cuban economy cannot depend only on sugar, it cannot rely on just the service sector —tourism, free zone or *maquiladoras*.

The most important consideration that can be made at this time is not to pre-judge the industry in light of past performance or to place sugar on a confrontational track —even before changes take place in Cuba— but rather to examine ways and means by which in the future, in a Democratic Cuba with a free market economy, the sugar industry can contribute to the countries growth.

---

[6]On August 13th, President Bush announced that an agreement had been reached by cabinet-level negotiators from Canada, Mexico and the United States on NAFTA. The text of this document has not been made public. It is to come into effect in 1994 but still has to be ratified by the legislative bodies of the three countries.

CUBA'S SUGAR INDUSTRY IN THE 1990s: POTENTIAL EXPORTS TO THE U.S. AND WORLD MARKETS[1]

José Alvarez

I. The Cuban Sugar Industry

A. Economic Importance[2]

There is an extensive literature on the Cuban sugar industry in the island and abroad. The reason is obvious: sugarcane has been, and continues to be, the dominant crop in Cuba's economy, and sugar the main source of foreign exchange. Data published by the Cuban government portray the sugar industry as the source of employment for almost 400,000 persons who, with their families, make up perhaps one-sixth of the Cuban population. It also accounts for about one-third of the total means of production used in Cuban industry. Sugar represents 80% of the value of Cuban exports and the industry as a whole contributes 10% to Cuba's Global Social Product (Feuer, 1987, p. 69, from *Comité Estatal de Estadísticas*).

B. The Production, Processing, and Marketing Sectors[3]

The production sector has been expanding in the last three decades. In the early 1960s, area harvested fluctuated around one million hectares and maximum total production reached 50 million metric tons of sugarcane. Today, production of sugarcane takes place on approximately 1.35 million hectares yielding about 53 metric tons of cane for a total production of over 70 million metric tons. Although state farms account for about 83% of the area harvested, their yields are slightly lower than those of private farms.

The trend toward mechanization started in the 1960s has continued. Almost all loading has been done with machines since 1970 and mechanical harvesting increased from 25% in 1975 to 45% in 1980 and to 67% in the 1988-89 season.

The processing sector of the sugar industry, despite an stable number of industrial facilities, has also experienced dramatic changes during the last 30 years. When the revolution took power on January 1959, the sugar industry consisted of 161 raw sugar factories, 16 refineries, over 20 distilleries producing alcohol and some press board and paper factories using bagasse as raw material (David, 1983, p. 100).

The entire sugar industry was expropriated in 1959-60. Today, all sugar mills and sugar refineries are owned by the State and managed by the Ministry of the Sugar Industry (MINAZ).

---

[1]This essay is an updated summary of preliminary work (Alvarez, 1992a; 1992b) conducted under a project coordinated by the International Agricultural Trade and Policy Center of the Food and Resource Economics Department at the University of Florida. The ultimate goal of that project is to estimate the economic impact (benefits and costs) of future trade between the United States and Cuba on Florida's agricultural economy. The author thanks José Alonso, Fernando Alvarez, Peter Buzzanell, Bill Messina and Jorge Pérez-López for their useful comments and suggestions on an earlier version. Special thanks to Bill for his extra support, and to Jorge for having written an extraordinary book on the economics of Cuban sugar. All the usual caveats apply.

[2]The first two sub-sections draw heavily from Alvarez and Alvarez (1991).

[3]When not specified otherwise, the statistics presented in this section appear in *Comité Estatal de Estadísticas* (various issues).

There are 156 raw sugar mills throughout the 14 provinces and 16 refineries in nine provinces.[4]

Cane milled per day has increased from around 489,000 metric tons in the 1960s (somewhat below the figures in the 1950s), to 529,000 metric tons in the 1970s, and to around 619,000 metric tons in the 1980s. The effective milling season, however, has lengthened by more than three weeks.

Statistics on raw sugar production, industrial yield (recovery rate), and polarization illustrate the industry's performance in the last four decades (Table 1).

Table 1. Selected Statistics for the Cuban Sugar Industry, by Decade, 1950s-1980s.

Decade	Production	Recovery Rate	Polarization
	million metric tons	Percent	Degrees
1950s	5.63	12.85	97.20
1960s	5.52	12.10	97.65
1970s	6.24	11.30	97.70
1980s	7.65	10.81	98.22

Source: Calculated from *Comité Estatal de Estadísticas* (various issues).

The average data per decade show a slight decline in total sugar production from the 1950s to the 1960s and an increase thereafter. The average recovery rate has decreased since the 1950s. Polarization, however, has been increasing in the last three decades.

Despite heavy capital investments made to renovate and modernize some industrial facilities, "the industry is still characterized by a significant number of small, inefficient operations. About two-thirds of the mills have a daily grinding capacity of 4,000 tons or less and over 85 percent were built prior to 1913" (Buzzanell and Alonso, 1989, p. 22).[5]

Sugar marketing is also under the control of the State. The domestic rationed quotas are distributed through the Ministry of Internal Trade (MINCIN), while CUBAZUCAR is the agency in charge of negotiating and marketing foreign sales.

C. U.S.-Cuba Sugar Relations Until 1960

Prior to the revolution of 1959, the United States and Cuba had been major trading partners and sugar was Cuba's most important export to the United States. Until 1960, Cuba provided over one-third of the total U.S. sugar requirements, playing the role of an "ever-normal granary" for U.S. sugar needs. One aspect of the preferential treatment it received in return is contained in the Sugar

---

[4]Appendices 1 and 2 in Alvarez (1992a) contain a list of Cuban raw sugar mills and refineries by province that include current name, former name and capacity.

[5]Of the 161 sugar mills operating in Cuba in 1958, 77 had been installed during the period 1796-1910, 73 during the period 1902-1920, and 11 during 1921-1927. No new sugar mills were built after 1927. The sugar mills were given a general overhaul every year and the equipment modernized, particularly during periods of sugar bonanza (Cuban Economic Research Project, 1965, p. 126). Since the 1959 revolution, 13 small sugar mills were dismantled and eight new ones have been built (see Appendix 1 in Alvarez, 1992a, pp. 32-36).

Act of 1948, which allocated to Cuba an import quota equivalent to 98.64% of the difference between U.S. consumption requirements and the sum of the fixed tonnage quotas for the domestic areas and the Philippines, with the remaining 1.36% going to other foreign countries. This arrangement allocated substantially all of the increases in U.S. consumption requirements to Cuba. The 1951 amendment to the Sugar Act set Cuba's share at 96%. The 1956 amendment enabled domestic producers to participate in the growth of the U.S. market; i.e., any growth in U.S. consumption beyond 8.35 million short tons was shared 55% by domestic areas and 45% by foreign areas. The July 1960 amendment provided for presidential actions under which sugar import quotas from Cuba were suspended.[6] Explicit in the legislation was the intention of restoring Cuba's quota at the time of its return to the free world. The Cuban sugar quota was allocated to domestic areas and foreign countries (Bates, 1968, p. 522).

The 1962 and 1965 amendments to the Sugar Act reallocated the Cuban sugar quota (Table 2). The 1965 amendment distributed the 50-percent Cuban share of the U.S. sugar requirements (remaining over the allocations to domestic sources, the Philippines, and other exceptions) on a pro-rata basis to other quota-holding countries. Not included in that quota, however, was Cuba's share arising from consumption requirements in excess of 10 million short tons, which would be prorated among members of the Organization of American States (Bates, 1968, p. 524).

D. Past and Emerging Trading Patterns of Cuban Sugar

Cuban exports of sugar to the United States amounted to 2.94 million tons in 1959. Until July 1960, when the Cuban quota was suspended, Cuba had exported 1.95 million tons of sugar to the United States.[7]

In July 1960, the Soviet Union rapidly announced its readiness to purchase the former U.S. Cuban sugar quota. Cuba, who had sold over 50% of its sugar exports to United States for many years, redirected its sugar exports to the Soviet Union, China, and Eastern European countries (Table 3). In 1959, only 5.5% of the 4.95 million tons exported went to the U.S.S.R., while the remaining 94.5% was exported to other countries, including the United States. Those figures changed dramatically in 1960 when Cuba sent 28.1% of its sugar exports to the U.S.S.R., 8.5% to China, 4.1% to Eastern Europe, and 59.3% to other countries. By 1965, the U.S.S.R. was purchasing 46.2% of Cuban sugar exports while other countries (not including China and Eastern Europe, with 7.5% and 12.7%, respectively) imported only 33.6% of the total.

That allocation, with some minor shifts, remained essentially unchanged until the late 1980s. The collapse of socialism in the countries of Eastern Europe, and the economic and social reforms that led to the demise of the Soviet Union at the end of 1991, initiated a new phase in the direction of Cuban sugar exports.

II. The Future of Cuban Sugar Exports

Forecasting the future direction of Cuban sugar exports is not an easy task. Politics played the major role in the redirection of Cuban sugar trade that took place in the early 1960s (Alvarez, 1978), and continued to do so afterwards. However, it is possible to describe potential scenarios for

---

[6]For a description of the political environment within which the embargo took place, and its effects on the United States and Cuba, the interested reader is referred to Alvarez (1978).

[7]On 13 October 1960 the United States declared a total embargo on Cuba.

the 1990s by looking at the current status of the Cuban sugar industry, the new trend of Cuban sugar exports developing since the late 1980s, and the legal and political environment of U.S.-Cuba future relations.

A. Status of the Cuban Sugar Industry Until the 1990-91 Crop

Before analyzing Cuba's sugar producing and exporting capabilities in the 1990s, one has to go beyond the summary provided at the beginning of this paper. Indicators of the industry from the last four decades provide the basis for a more thorough description (Table 4).

During the 1950s, Cuba milled an average of 43.9 million metric tons of sugarcane (not all the production was milled) at a rate of 507,000 metric tons per day to produce 5.63 million metric tons of sugar with a recovery rate of 12.85% and 97.2º polarization in 86.8 days. The precise role of sugar in the pre-revolutionary economy, according to Thomas (1971, p. 1152) is elusive. The sugar sector accounted for 28-29% of the national income figures during the period 1949-58, declining to about 25% in 1957-58 (Pérez-López, 1989, p. 1631). The national income figures, however, do not show the extent to which the whole economy depended on exports; and exports did depend on sugar. In the 40 years before Batista's overthrow in January 1959, sugar accounted for 82% of Cuban exports (Thomas, 1971, p. 1152). That figure did not change during the 1959-88 period (Pérez-López, 1989; 1991a, p. 32).

At the outset of the 1959 revolution, the Cuban leadership blamed the sugar industry as the major determinant of underdevelopment in the island. As the result of this campaign, the adequate care of sugarcane fields was abandoned and some fields were turned over to other agricultural production. The data in Table 4 reflect the consequences of that policy. In the 1960s, excluding the 1969-70 season, the average of all indicators dropped: sugarcane production fell to 42.31 million metric tons, cane milled per day decreased to 483,000 million metric tons, and sugar production averaged 5.19 million metric tons.

The 1969-70 sugar season was a turning point in Cuban sugar policy. After 10 years of neglect, Castro himself declared that sugar was the backbone of the economy and challenged his people to produce 10 million tons of sugar. Although a record crop of 8.54 million metric tons was produced, the harvest lasted 217 days (143 days of actual grinding), robbed sugarcane from upcoming crops, and inflicted staggering costs to the rest of the economy.[8]

Data from the 1970s and 1980s reflect the increased attention given to the sugar industry after the failure of the 1970 campaign. Average sugarcane production increased to 55.27 and 70.24 million metric tons in the 1970s and 1980s, respectively; milling rates increased to 530,000 in the 1970s and to 639,000 metric tons per day in the 1980s; and sugar production increased to 6.24 and 7.65 million metric tons in the 1970s and 1980s, respectively. Different trends are observed for recovery rate (decreasing) and polarization (increasing) in both decades. The average length of the season has also increased in both decades, to 103.7 days in the 1970s and to 110.2 days in the 1980s.

Before analyzing the new trends of Cuban sugar exports, it is important to evaluate the ability of the Cuban sugar industry to maintain production at the levels achieved during the 1980s. Recall

---

[8]This is just an example of the economic disruptions that have taken place in Cuba. For a full description of the different strategies followed while attempting to build a new society, and the results of 30 years of centralized economic planning in Cuba, the interested reader is referred to Alvarez (1990).

that the Cuban sugar industry is characterized by the lack of modern facilities and equipment which places some constraints at the processing level. Because hard currency shortages make it almost impossible to import parts, equipment, and additional oil, the total daily grinding capacity of 656,500 tons of the 1988-89 season will hardly be surpassed in the short-run. In the best possible scenario, Cuba could produce again the 8.12 million metric tons of sugar shown for the 1988-89 season. To maintain that level of output, the 75 million tons of sugarcane would have to show a recovery of 10.89% (average of the 1980s) with a mill efficiency of 85%. In the production sector, lack of hard currency to purchase fertilizer, oil and other inputs is impacting the industry's ability to maintain production at previous levels. Furthermore, the need to conduct business at world market prices has brought severe difficulties to Cuba. With respect to those difficulties, and referring to the 1990-91 Cuban sugar output, one publication stated:

> It is surprising that this has not already been reflected in production but assuredly as conditions deteriorate further as they must unless from some unlikely source there is a substantial injection of hard currency, it will become increasingly difficult for Cuba to maintain the current or recent level of output (Licht, July 1991, p. 342).

B. The 1991-92 Sugar Crop

Conditions did, in fact, deteriorate during the 1991-92 sugar campaign. Castro himself stated that, because of fertilizer shortages from the U.S.S.R., a large amount of the sugarcane for the 1991-92 season did not receive any fertilizer (*El Nuevo Herald*, Nov. 26, 1991, p. 3A). The 1991-92 harvest, normally underway by mid-November, did not start until mid-January amidst speculations about how much the current crop could drop below the 1990-91 output of 7.6 million metric tons.

No other official news concerning the 1991-92 crop was available until January 26, 1992. In an interview in the weekly *Juventud Rebelde*, Politburo member Carlos Lage acknowledged that it would be impossible to "even get close" to the 7.5 million metric tons they had hoped for. He also stated that, in addition to the late start and lack of adequate fertilization, the "material difficulties" from which the current crop would continue to suffer included: (a) poor maintenance and repairs of machinery during the off-season due to shortages of spare parts; (b) breakdown in the sugar transportation system; and (c) lack of fuel for field and mill operations.

Sugar traders and statisticians began lowering their projections about the volume of the 1991-92 Cuban crop. Despite the total blackout on news from the island, there seemed to be a consensus that even a 6.5 million metric tons might turn out to be substantially high and 5.0 million, although rather improbable, could no longer be dismissed out of hand (*Sociedad Económica*, 1992a, p. 1; Hagelberg, 1992; Rivero, 1992). The progressive downward adjustments continued in early April when the United States Department of Agriculture lowered its December forecast of 7.3 million metric tons to 6.0 million in its March release.

Also in April, two new pieces of information came out of Cuba. The first was given by Castro in his speech to the VI Congress of the League of Communist Youth on April 4. Breaking an unusual ten-weeks silence, Castro used the term "tense" to describe the current harvest, reiterated its delay, and blamed it on lack of fuel, fertilizer and spare parts. The second was contained in an interview to Juan Varela Pérez, *Granma*'s sugar correspondent, in *Radio Progreso* on April 14. He stated that the tense harvest was already suffering from unusual early heavy rains and that most of the standing canes were located in the key provinces of Ciego de Avila, Camagüey and Las Tunas, which had always performed well in previous seasons. These provinces, according to official 1988-89 figures, by volume of cane, were respectively the first, third and fifth largest producers of the 14-cane producing provinces in the country, accounting for 33% of total cane volume.

The official recognition that the harvest was not in full swing at the beginning of the month in which it was supposed to end revealed a state of affairs worse than anticipated. It appeared that a further downward adjustment in Cuba's total sugar output was in order. *La Sociedad Económica* (1992b) did that for the following reasons: (a) the time lost was longer than just the eight weeks from mid-November to mid-January reported before; (b) extending the harvest into the rainy months of May through July would exacerbate transportation difficulties; milling operations would consequently be affected by the sporadic flow of cane, and sugar yields would be reduced due to the deterioration of harvested, pre-milled cane; and (c) an extended harvest into the rainy season is also very energy-expensive. Although meeting this cost was possible in the recent past, present fuel shortages would work against the feasibility of an extended harvest in the current season.

The new projection by *Sociedad Económica* on April 20 was stated in the following way:

La Sociedad Económica estimates a final 1991/92 sugar crop of between 5 mmt and 5.55 mmt. By comparison, reported total output from 1989/90 and 1990/91 were 8.1 and 7.6 mmt, respectively. However, some members of La Sociedad Económica "Sugar Section" believe that even a final 1991/92 crop of 5 mmt is optimistic, and the possibility that Cuba will over-report its final crop cannot be ruled out (1992b, p. 2).

More information became available in early May. The first was made public at the end of an international conference of sugar specialists, to celebrate CUBAZUCAR's 30th anniversary and a meeting of GEPLACEA, held in Havana on May 5-7. When Juan Herrera Machado, Cuban Minister of the Sugar Industry, was asked at a press conference about the final output of the present Cuban sugar crop, he responded "we don't even know that yet." When pressed further he stated that, by placing it at between 5.5 and 7 million tons, he "wouldn't be in contradiction with any of the great estimators, those who compute, those who forecast" (*El Nuevo Herald*, May 9, 1992, p. 3A). The second news was provided by Sergei Barykin, president of PRODINTORG, when he announced in Havana that, as of June 1st., Russia would not need any more Cuban sugar for the remainder of 1992, and, consequently, would not ship any more oil to the island (El Nuevo Herald, May 8, 1992, pp. 1A, 4A). In addition to disruptions in the marketing of the current crop, that decision has important implications for the feasibility of this extended harvest. More drastic cuts in oil supplies will force the Cuban government to either use oil assigned to other purposes or minimize its efforts on sugarcane harvesting and processing during the final months of the 1991-92 sugar campaign.

The earthquakes felt in the eastern provinces during the month of June added more problems to the final phase of an already tense harvest. Although the official news contained no details of the damages to the sugar industry, it is not hard to believe that the industry suffered further disruptions on harvesting, loading, hauling and even milling operations as the result of damages to cane fields, roads, railroads, and mill equipment.

To complicate things further, heavy rains fell throughout the island during June 23-27. The harvest was temporarily suspended in the few eastern provinces that had not finished it. Politburo member Pedro Ross Leal used *Radio Rebelde* to request a final effort from Cubans working on the sugar campaign (Alfonso, 1992).

In mid-July, with some operations still underway, long and severe electricity blackouts were felt throughout the island. Again, no official news on damages or disruptions to the sugar campaign were made available although the breaking of a major power line that furnishes electricity to the central and eastern provinces must have disrupted milling operations.

On July 19, S. Diatchkov, associate director of the Latin American Division of the Russian Committee on Foreign Economic Relations, stated in Moscow that the last shipments of Russian oil and Cuban sugar for 1992 had reached their destinations. He went on to say that Russia does not have enough oil to export and is buying some sugar from Western Europe (Gluck, 1992).

When all the above factors are combined, the lowest end of the production range provided by Minister Herrera (5.5 million metric tons) has to become the highest end when forecasting Cuba's potential sugar production for the near future for two reasons. First, there seems to be no solution in sight for Cuba's current shortages of fuel, fertilizer, other inputs and spare parts. Second, the devastating effects of the 1991-92 season will impact on the performance of both fields and factories in future crops.

C. New Export Trends Since the Early 1990s[9]

For the reasons explained in a previous section of this paper, Cuban sugar exports began to experience a new reallocation in the early 1990s (Table 5). Since the early 1960s, the U.S.S.R. was the largest importer of Cuban sugar. In the 1980s, Cuban deliveries averaged below the four million tons specified in Cuba's contract with the former Soviet Union. The drastic changes in trade relations between Cuba and Russia during 1992 indicate that the 56.7% of Cuban sugar exports purchased by the former Soviet Union in 1991 has become history.[10]

Eastern Europe is a lost outlet for Cuban sugar. For political (more than economic) reasons, these countries imported substantial amounts of Cuban sugar for the past 30 years.[11] The amounts represented more than one million tons, or between 14.7 and 16.7% of total Cuban sugar exports until 1989. The figures fell to over 615,000 tons in 1990 and to 68,000 tons in 1991 when they represented only 1% of total Cuban sugar exports (Table 5).

Asia and Oceania, which include several socialist countries, have been purchasing over one million metric tons of Cuban sugar for the past several years. The countries in these areas accounted for 19% of Cuban sugar exports in 1991 (Table 5).

The Middle East and Africa show slight increases in Cuban sugar imports for 1990 and 1991

---

[9]The original version (Alvarez, 1992a) described the trends in Cuban sugar exports until 1990 and made predictions for 1991. The interested reader is referred to that source since it shows the rapid and drastic changes that Cuba is facing in sugar trading.

[10]The political environment within which Cuba-U.S.S.R. commercial relations took place changed rapidly. It began deteriorating at the outset of *glasnost* and *perestroika* and Castro's unwillingness to make changes in that direction. The Soviet Union began reducing her economic aid to Cuba. Cuba's implicit support of the aborted coup of August 1991 made things worse and could have been the reason behind Gorbachev's announcement (without previous consultations with the Cuban government) of the withdrawal of Soviet troops from the island. The previous five-year commercial agreements were replaced with one-year contracts, at world market prices and, when barter did not take place, goods and services were to be paid in convertible currencies, which Cuba lacks. The demise of the Soviet Union at the end of 1991 inflicted a severe blow on Cuba's trade prospects. However, most observers believed that it was in the best interest of those countries to continue their sugar trade with Cuba as the agreements with individual republics in early 1992 seemed to indicate. As stated in a previous section, that situation changed several months later.

[11]Pérez-López (1991b, pp. 14-15, 144) contains a description on how Cuba's agreements with the Council for Mutual Economic Assistance (CMEA) "consecrated Cuba's role as a purveyor of agricultural commodities within the socialist division of labor" (pp. 14-15).

when compared with the 1980s. These purchases now represent 11% of total Cuban sugar exports (Table 5).

Countries in the Western Hemisphere have also increased their purchases of Cuban sugar in the first two years of the 1990s. The main buyers include Canada, Venezuela and Mexico.[12]

Western Europe is not an important client of Cuban sugar. The 213,000 tons imported in 1991 have been the highest amount in many years but represented only 3% of total Cuban sugar exports (Table 5).

D. The 1992 Sugar Trade Agreements

Cuba's trade agreements for 1992 parallel the disastrous projections of sugar output in the current season. *La Sociedad Económica* (1992b, p. 2) assumes a maximum of 5.0 million metric tons. Other sugar analysts estimate Cuban sugar exports for 1992 at 4.5 million metric tons, compared with average annual worldwide exports of 7.1 million metric tons in 1988-90 (Hagelberg, 1992). The country breakdown, from early 1992 agreements with CIS and other countries and past sales, would be as follows:

CIS[13]..............	1,500,000
China.................	900,000
Other countries[14].....	1,600,000
Miscellaneous sales...	500,000
Total..............	4,500,000

The 4.5 or 5.0 million metric tons could very well represent maximum figures in the immediate future and are likely to decrease for three reasons. First, Cuba's Far Eastern markets are threatened by cheaper freight rates for sugar from Thailand and Australia. Second, the North African markets face competition from subsidized European exports of refined sugar (*La Sociedad Económica*, 1992a, p. 2). Finally, the current economic changes in the CIS countries will decrease the demand for Cuban sugar in the future. For example, Russia's decision to cancel the final phase of their 1992 sugar trade agreement with Cuba, which has reduced the CIS figure by 500,000 tons in 1992, was based on oil shortages and sugar purchases from the European Community.

E. U.S.-Cuba Future Relations

Future relations between Cuba and the United States will have a significant influence on Cuba's sugar industry and sugar exports. There are two possible scenarios: U.S. trade with Castro's

---

[12]The dramatic increases of Cuban sugar imports by Mexico may raise some questions regarding the pending North America Free Trade Agreement; i.e., Cuban sugar imports could be used to satisfy Mexican domestic consumption thus freeing Mexican sugar for exporting to the U.S. market (Polopolus and Alvarez, 1992). This behavior could be in line with the recent building of increased ties between Mexican businessmen and the Cuban government described by Bussey (1991). Those interested in the current situation and prospects of the Mexican sugar industry, including trade, are referred to Buzzanell (1991) and Rivero (1991).

[13]A total of 750,000 metric tons with options for additional deliveries of a similar amount later in the year. The republics include Russia, Ukraine, Kazakhstan, Kirghizia, Latvia, Lithuania, and Tadjikistan.

[14]Includes Canada, Japan, South Korea, Iran, Algeria, and Egypt.

Cuba and with a post-Castro Cuba.[15]

Based on the numerous statements made by President Bush against Castro and his regime,[16] the first scenario would seem unlikely (although not impossible) to occur under the current Administration. Smith and Morales (1988), however, have outlined major areas of disagreement between their two countries while advocating negotiations rather than continued confrontation.

Under the second scenario the United States would recognize a post-Castro government in a democratic Cuba and re-establish diplomatic and commercial relations with Cuba.

Although the two scenarios would bring about different trade relations between the two countries, there is no doubt that Cuban sugar would be a topic of major importance under both scenarios. The former Cuban sugar quota, although temporarily suspended in 1960, has disappeared as a result of decreasing imports brought about by expanded domestic production in the United States and shifts to less expensive substitutes caloric sweeteners like high fructose corn syrup. The three million tons average that Cuba exported to the United States in 1958 and 1959 represent twice the amount of total U.S. import requirements for 1991-92. Table 2 shows the reallocation of the Cuban quota in 1962 and 1965. Table 6 contains quota allocations for 1990-91 and 1991-92. The number of quota-holding countries, excluding Cuba, has increased from 21 in 1962 to 29 in 1965, and to 40 in 1991. Relative shares have also changed. However, it is interesting to note that, in previous cases similar to Cuba's, the U.S. Congress has reinstated sugar quotas withheld for political reasons. That was the case of Nicaragua, after the defeat of the Sandinista Government, and of South Africa as recent as 1991-92. Since sugar exports are the main source of Cuban foreign exchange, it is not unlikely that some type of provision may need to be made by the U.S. Congress for sugar imports from Cuba. Leaving the solution to politicians, let us take a look at the potential amounts of Cuban sugar that could become available for the U.S. and other markets.

F. Potential Surpluses of Cuban Sugar

The preceding analyses on Cuba's producing and exporting capabilities allow the projection of different levels of surpluses of Cuban sugar in the immediate future and the remainder of the decade (Table 7). As discussed above, current forecasts for the 1991-92 harvest fall between 5.0 and 5.5 million metric tons with the possibility of lower outputs in the current and following years.[17] For that reason, potential production ranges from a low 4.0 to a high 5.5 million metric tons. After deducting 900,000 tons for direct consumption and industrial use (allowing for a minor increase from the 810,000 tons average of the 1985-89 period computed from data shown in Pérez-López (1991a, p. 27)), potential amounts available for exporting range from 3.1 to 4.6 million metric tons. Finally, 1992 export projections amount to 4.5 or 5.0 million tons with potential decreases after 1992.

---

[15]For a description of the current debate on U.S.-Cuba relations, see Appendix 3 in Alvarez (1992a, pp. 38-42).

[16]The Cuban American National Foundation has compiled those statements in a 68-page monograph entitled *Bush on Cuba—Selected Statements by the President*, 1991.

[17]Pérez-López (1991a, pp. 38-40) contains a brief description of the potential disruptions that Cuba's former plans to expand production in the 10-12 million ton range by the late 1990s would create in the world sugar market (Table 8). However, the degree of deterioration of the Cuban economy has eliminated the possibility of those plans materializing under the current regime. On the other hand, even recognizing the physical possibility of achieving those targets under a system of private ownership, and based on current world demand conditions, he recommends the development of feasibility studies for restructuring (shrinking) the Cuban sugar industry while emphasizing the production of sugarcane derivatives (pp. 40-44).

The third row in Table 7 highlights the likely outcomes from different production levels in 1992 with exports assumed at 4.5 million tons. The figures do not take into account changes in stocks or increases in production and decreases in consumption in the importing countries.[18] If the most optimistic production figure of 5.5 million metric tons is achieved, Cuba will have a surplus of about 100,000 metric tons of sugar in 1992. In the following years, assuming additional losses in export markets and unless the crop reaches catastrophic proportions, higher surpluses are plausible. For example, Timm (1992) reported in late July 1992 that traditional buyers of Cuban sugar, from Japan to CIS countries, are turning to Thailand to solve their sugar needs. Uncertainty about future Cuban supplies are also forcing South Korea, Malaysia, and Iran to consider purchasing Thai sugar. These trade agreements will inflict severe damage to Cuba's future exporting capabilities.

There seem to be three courses of action for the Cuban government. First, Cuba could take away markets from other exporters by exercising the option of selling at a discount from world prices; but, as a sugar analyst has stated, "one difficulty is that in competing for significant Asian outlets against more closely located suppliers, Cuba operates under the disadvantage of higher transportation costs" (Hagelberg, 1992, p. 2). The second alternative would come about as the result of a successful agreement in the Uruguay Round of negotiations under GATT. This scenario, under which Cuban sugar would compete in a free world market, however, would take several years to materialize. The last alternative is access to the U.S. market. As discussed in the previous publication (Alvarez, 1992a; 1992b), and recognizing that some type of provision may need to be made by the U.S. Congress for sugar imports from a democratic Cuba, there is no reason to believe that the U.S. market can absorb Cuban sugar surpluses of around 1 million metric tons.

---

[18]They also exclude additional quantities of sugar that may not be available for other reasons. For example, "in 1987 and 1988, Cuba postponed several shipments to Japan, its most important non-socialist export market, and purchased a substantial amount of sugar in the open market. According to sugar trade experts and press reports, in 1988 and 1989 Cuba promised part of next year's crop as collateral to repay over 1 million tons of sugar borrowed from a major international trade house to fulfill its commitment to the Soviet Union under the current protocol" (Alonso and Buzzanell, 1991, p. 63). Paying back these and/or other borrowings would absorb some sugar supplies that would become available from lower exports to Eastern Europe and countries of the former Soviet Union.

Table 2. Reallocation of the Cuban Sugar Quota Among Foreign Countries
in the 1962 and 1965 Amendments to the Sugar Act of 1948[a]

Country	1962 Amendment	1965 Amendment With Cuban share	Cuban share reallocated[b]
		- - - - - - - -Percent- - - - - - - -	
In Western Hemisphere			
Cuba	57.77	50.00	--
Mexico	6.71	7.73	15.46
Dominican Republic	6.71	7.56	15.12
Brazil	6.37	7.56	15.12
Peru	6.71	6.03	12.06
British West Indies	3.19	3.02	6.04
Ecuador	0.88	1.10	2.20
French West Indies	1.06	0.95	1.90
Argentina	--	0.93	1.86
Costa Rica	0.88	0.89	1.78
Nicaragua	0.88	0.89	1.78
Colombia	--	0.80	1.60
Guatemala	0.71	0.75	1.50
Panama	0.53	0.56	1.12
El Salvador	0.36	0.55	1.10
Haiti	0.71	0.42	0.84
Venezuela	--	0.38	0.76
British Honduras	0.35	0.22	0.44
Bolivia	--	0.09	0.18
Honduras	--	0.09	0.18
Paraguay	0.35	--	--
Outside Western Hemisphere			
Australia	1.41	3.60	7.20
Republic of China	1.24	1.50	3.00
India	0.71	1.44	2.88
South Africa	0.71	1.06	2.12
Fiji	0.35	0.79	1.58
Thailand	--	0.33	0.66
Mauritius	--	0.33	0.66
Malagasy Republic	--	0.17	0.34
Swaziland	--	0.13	0.26
Southern Rhodesia	--	0.13	0.26
Netherlands	0.35	--	--

[a]Quotas represent relative shares of U.S. sugar requirements remaining over the allocations to domestic sources, the Philippines, and other exceptions as stated in each amendment.
[b]Assuming U.S. consumption requirements of not over 10 million short tons.

Sources: U.S. Congress and U.S. Senate Reports as they appear in Bates (1968, p. 525).

Table 3. Cuban Sugar Exports by Trading Partners, Selected Years, 1959-91

Year	Million metric tons, raw value					Percent of			
	USSR	China	Eastern Europe	Other countries	Total	USSR	China	Eastern Europe	Other countries
								Percent	
1959	0.27	0.00	0.00	4.68	4.95	5.5	0.0	0.0	94.5
1960	1.58	.48	.23	3.34	5.63	28.1	8.5	4.1	59.3
1965	2.46	.40	.67	1.79	5.32	46.2	7.5	12.7	33.6
1970	3.11	.53	.96	2.31	6.91	45.0	7.7	13.9	33.4
1975	3.19	.18	.58	1.79	5.74	55.6	3.1	10.1	31.2
1976	3.04	.25	.94	1.53	5.76	52.8	4.3	16.3	26.6
1977	3.79	.23	.64	1.58	6.24	60.7	3.7	10.3	25.3
1978	3.94	.53	.61	2.15	7.23	54.5	7.3	8.4	29.8
1979	3.84	.49	.74	2.20	7.27	52.8	6.7	10.2	30.3
1980	2.73	.51	.69	2.26	6.19	44.1	8.2	11.2	36.5
1981	3.20	.57	.91	2.39	7.07	45.3	8.0	12.9	33.8
1982	4.43	.92	.80	1.58	7.73	57.3	11.9	10.4	20.4
1983	3.31	.77	1.00	1.71	6.79	48.8	11.3	14.7	25.2
1984	3.65	.71	1.17	1.49	7.02	52.0	10.1	16.7	21.2
1985	3.71	.68	1.03	1.79	7.21	51.5	9.4	14.3	24.8
1986	4.02	.31	.86	1.51	6.70	60.0	4.6	12.9	22.5
1987	3.86	.61	1.02	.99	6.48	59.6	9.4	15.7	15.3
1988	3.31	1.40	1.04	1.22	6.97	47.5	20.1	14.9	17.5
1989	3.47	0.89	0.83	1.93	7.12	48.7	12.5	11.7	27.1
1990	3.58	0.89	0.52	2.18	7.17	49.9	12.4	7.3	30.4
1991	3.83	0.80	0.07	2.07	6.77	56.6	11.8	1.0	30.6

Sources: *International Sugar Organization*, various issues; Comité Estatal de Estadísticas, 1970-1986; and Licht (July 1991).

Table 4. Indicators of the Cuban Sugar Industry, 1950-51 through 1990-91

Crop year	Effective milling season	Cane milled for sugar	Cane mil. rate	Sugar product.	Recov. rate	Polarizat. (grade of sugar)
	Days	Million met.tons	1,000 m t/day	Mil.m t, raw val.	%	Degrees
1950-51	96	44.9	468	5.82	12.95	96.97
1951-52	120	59.5	496	7.30	12.26	97.03
1952-53	84	40.8	489	5.22	12.80	97.21
1953-54	79	39.3	495	4.96	12.62	97.23
1954-55	69	34.8	507	4.60	13.20	97.25
1955-56	72	37.0	514	4.81	13.00	97.27
1956-57	87	44.7	514	5.74	12.84	97.21
1957-58	84	45.7	544	5.86	12.82	97.29
1958-59	89	44.8	503	6.04	13.48	97.24
1959-60	88	47.5	540	5.94	12.51	97.32
1960-61	104	54.3	522	6.88	12.67	97.54
1961-62	76	36.7	483	4.88	13.30	97.32
1962-63	68	31.4	462	3.88	12.36	97.58
1963-64	82	37.2	454	4.47	12.02	97.70
1964-65	105	50.7	483	6.16	12.15	97.69
1965-66	76	36.8	484	4.54	12.34	97.83
1966-67	101	50.9	504	6.24	12.26	97.68
1967-68	87	42.3	486	5.16	12.20	97.75
1968-69	86	40.5	471	4.46	11.01	97.77
1969-70	143	79.8	558	8.54	10.70	97.66
1970-71	101	51.5	510	5.92	11.50	97.64
1971-72	91	43.5	478	4.32	9.93	97.69
1972-73	92	47.5	516	5.25	11.05	97.73
1973-74	95	49.6	517	5.93	11.96	97.88
1974-75	99	50.8	513	6.31	12.42	97.74
1975-76	99	52.0	525	6.16	11.85	97.75
1976-77	104	56.2	540	6.49	11.55	97.74
1977-78	119	67.0	563	7.35	10.97	97.78
1978-79	128	73.0	570	7.99	10.95	97.81
1979-80	109	61.6	565	6.67	10.83	98.18
1980-81	114	66.4	582	7.36	11.08	98.17
1981-82	124	73.5	593	8.21	11.17	98.14
1982-83	113	68.7	608	7.11	10.35	98.14
1983-84	126	78.4	622	8.21	10.47	98.15
1984-85	103	66.8	649	8.00	11.98	98.20
1985-86	104	68.3	657	7.26	10.63	98.26
1986-87	99	66.9	674	7.12	10.64	98.30
1987-88	100	68.4	680	7.42	10.85	98.31
1988-89	109	75.0	689	8.12	10.83	98.30
1989-90	NA	70.0	NA	8.00	11.40	NA
1990-91	NA	67.5	NA	7.62	11.30	NA

Source: Comité Estatal de Estadísticas (various issues); Buzzanell (1992).

Table 5. Cuba's Sugar Exports to Selected Countries and Regions,
Average 1984-88, 1989, 1990, and 1991

Region Country	Average 1984-88	Annual 1989	Annual 1990	Annual 1991
	- - - - - Metric tons, raw value - - - - -			
U.S.S.R.	3,710,000	3,469,000	3,576,000	3,835,000
Percent of total	53.4	48.7	49.9	56.7
Eastern Europe				
Albania	23,243	23,655	23,519	10,781
Bulgaria	332,566	308,382	145,874	42,631
Czechoslovakia	153,038	159,142	89,264	0
German Dem. Rep.	289,838	357,174	96,850	0
Hungary	0	0	0	0
Poland	58,633	58,384	0	0
Romania	163,882	266,368	259,720	14,670
Yugoslavia	4,176	18,104	0	0
Sub-total	1,025,376	1,191,209	615,227	68,082
Percent of total	14.7	16.7	8.6	1.0
Asia and Oceania				
Bangladesh	2,470	0	0	0
China	740,739	889,173	892,130	796,563
India	54,459	0	0	0
Indonesia	8,019	26,424	0	0
Japan	374,470	205,059	162,492	410,906
Kampuchea	1,193	0	2,165	0
Korea, Dem. P. Rep.	26,408	30,170	36,713	24,993
Malaysia	40,680	84,414	28,624	0
Mongolia	1,889	0	0	0
New Zealand	8,809	0	0	39,825
Pakistan	13,495	0	0	0
Sri Lanka	5,239	13,009	0	0
Viet Nam, Soc. Rep.	17,401	12,498	11,059	9,486
Sub-total	1,295,271	1,260,747	1,133,183	1,281,773
Percent of total	18.6	17.7	15.8	18.9
Middle East and Africa				
Algeria	83,301	190,314	195,326	199,912
Angola	46,215	9,659	13,815	0
Cape Verde	0	4,879	5,979	10,750
Egypt	177,091	38,518	278,874	141,653
Ethiopia	962	0	0	0
Ghana	8,631	12,939	15,040	33,560
Guinea-Bissau	217	0	0	0
Iran	0	0	0	0
Iraq	78,272	40,239	28,249	27,083
Jordan	0	0	13,017	14,753

Table 5. (continued)

Region Country	Average 1984-88	Annual 1989	Annual 1990	Annual 1991
	- - - - - Metric tons, raw value - - - - -			
Libya	50,217	44,369	86,677	89,178
Lebanon	0	0	0	15,782
Senegal	4,111	0	0	0
Syria	69,988	65,040	89,979	140,917
Tunisia	40,575	73,332	51,380	68,520
Turkey	0	0	13,017	0
Uganda	7,544	15,174	0	0
Yemen, Dem. Rep.	0	0	0	0
Sub-total	567,124	494,463	791,353	742,108
Percent of total	8.2	6.9	11.0	11.0
Western Hemisphere				
Brazil	0	149,144	163,046	0
Canada	152,055	179,758	290,725	332,407
Mexico	10,540	67,610	357,940	183,661
Nicaragua	4,344	10,699	0	0
Netherlands Antilles	411	0	0	1,084
Peru	21,525	29,379	0	0
Suriname	0	0	0	0
Venezuela	48,907	109,715	115,882	105,447
Sub-total	237,782	546,305	927,593	622,599
Percent of total	3.4	7.7	12.9	9.2
Western Europe				
European Community	34,130	68,025	41,106	93,224
Finland	49,162	74,750	51,643	93,622
Portugal	16,995	0	0	0
Sweden	12,604	11,473	31,383	25,193
Switzerland	3,040	3,205	1,505	1,141
Sub-total	115,931	157,453	125,637	213,182
Percent of total	1.7	2.2	1.8	3.2
Total exports	6,951,484	7,119,177	7,168,993	6,762,744

Source: International Sugar Organization, as it appears in Buzzanell (1992, p. 37).

Table 6. U.S. Sugar Tariff Rate Quota, 1990-91 and 1991-92

Country	1990-91 Quota Allocat.	1990-91 Actual imports	1991-92 Net diff.	1991-92 Quota allocat.
	- - - - - short tons, raw value - - - -			
Dominican Republic	394,638	392,158	2,480	256,348
Brazil	325,130	325,130	0	211,195
Philippines	354,280	351,637	2,642	196,630
Australia	186,109	186,109	0	120,892
Guatemala	107,630	107,533	97	69,913
Argentina	96,418	96,256	162	62,630
Peru	91,934	90,299	1,635	59,718
Panama	65,026	64,691	335	42,239
El Salvador	58,299	58,299	0	37,870
Colombia	53,883	53,492	391	34,956
South Africa	0	0	0	33,500
Nicaragua	47,087	46,344	743	30,587
Swaziland	35,877	35,877	0	23,304
Costa Rica	33,634	33,634	0	21,848
Thailand	31,392	31,287	105	20,392
Mozambique	29,150	28,242	907	18,934
Guyana	26,907	0	26,907	17,478
Mauritius	26,907	26,907	0	17,478
Taiwan	26,907	26,907	0	17,478
Zimbabwe	26,907	26,907	0	17,478
Belize	24,665	24,647	19	16,022
Ecuador	24,665	24,665	0	16,022
Jamaica	24,665	24,665	0	16,022
Honduras	22,423	21,929	494	14,565
Malawi	22,423	22,423	0	14,565
Fiji	20,180	20,180	0	13,109
Bolivia	17,938	17,619	319	11,653
India	17,938	17,794	144	11,653
Barbados	15,696	0	15,696	10,195
Trinidad-Tobago	15,696	15,536	160	10,195
Congo	8,852	0	8,852	8,001
Cote D'Ivoire	8,852	8,852	0	8,001
Gabon	8,852	8,852	0	8,001
Haiti	8,852	8,830	22	8,001
Madagascar	8,852	8,852	0	8,001
Mexico	8,852	8,727	125	8,001
Papua New Guinea	8,852	8,850	1	8,001
Paraguay	8,852	8,850	1	8,001
St. Kitts-Nevis	8,852	0	8,852	8,001
Uruguay	8,852	8,626	226	8,001
Subtotal	2,312,853	2,241,539	71,314	1,524,876
Specialty sugars	2,000	237	1,763	1,825
Total	2,314,853	2,241,776	73,077	1,526,701
Canada		27,127		17,000

Source: Economic Research Service, USDA (1991, p. 43).

Table 7. Potential Surpluses of Cuban Sugar in the Near Future at Different Levels of Production (minus consumption) and Exports

Exports	Production (million metric tons)						
	4.00	4.25	4.50	4.75	5.00	5.25	5.50
	Production minus consumption (million metric tons)						
	3.10	3.35	3.60	3.85	4.10	4.35	4.60
	Million metric tons						
5.00	-1.90	-1.65	-1.40	-1.15	-0.90	-0.65	-0.40
4.75	-1.65	-1.40	-1.15	-0.90	-0.65	-0.40	-0.15
4.50	-1.40	-1.15	-0.90	-0.65	-0.40	-0.15	0.10
4.25	-1.15	-0.90	-0.65	-0.40	-0.15	0.10	0.35
4.00	-0.90	-0.65	-0.40	-0.15	0.10	0.35	0.60
3.75	-0.65	-0.40	-0.15	0.10	0.35	0.60	0.85
3.50	-0.40	-0.15	0.10	0.35	0.60	0.85	1.10

References

Alfonso, Pablo. "Lluvias afectan viviendas y cosechas," *El Nuevo Herald*, Miami, Florida, June 25, 1992, p. 3A.

Alonso, José F. and Peter J. Buzzanell. "Cuba's Sugar Economy: Recent Performance and Challenges for the 1990s," in Scott B. MacDonald and Georges A. Fauriol (Eds.) *The Politics of the Caribbean Basin Sugar Trade*. New York, NY: Praeger, 1991, pp. 41-68.

Alvarez, Fernando and José Alvarez. "Commodity-Linked Transactions and Recapitalization Needs for Privatizing the Economy in a Democratic Cuba: The Case of Sugar," in *Cuba in Transition - Papers and Proceedings of the First Annual Meeting of the Asociation for the Study of the Cuban Economy (ASCE)*, Florida International University, Miami, FL, August 15-17, 1991, pp. 143-184.

Alvarez, José. "A Chronology of Three Decades of Centralised Economic Planning in Cuba," *Communist Economies* 2:1 (1990), pp. 101-125.

Alvarez, José. *Cuba's Sugar Industry in the 1990s: Potential Exports to the U.S. and World Markets*, International Working Paper IW92-2, Food and Resource Economics Department, University of Florida, Gainesville, Florida, February 1992a.

Alvarez, José. *Cuba's Sugar Industry in the 1990s: Potential Exports to the U.S. and World Markets*,

(Addendum to International Working Paper IW92-2), Food and Resource Economics Department, University of Florida, Gainesville, Florida, April 24, 1992b.

Alvarez, José. *Politics vs. Economics in International Trade: The Case of Cuba - U.S. Sugar Relations*. Staff Paper 73, Food and Resource Economics Department, Institute of Food and Agricultural Sciences, University of Florida, Gainesville, FL, February 1978, 14 pp.

Bates, Thomas H. "The Long-Run Efficiency of United States Sugar Policy," *Journal of Farm Economics* 50 (1968), pp. 521-535.

Bussey, Jane. "Mexico forging business-front ties with Cuba," *The Miami Herald*, October 13, 1991, pp. 1K, 3K.

Buzzanell, Peter J. "An Overview of Mexican Sugar," *Sugar y Azúcar* 86:12 (December 1991), pp. 27-34.

Buzzanell, Peter J. "Cuba's Sugar Industry - Facing a New World Order," *Sugar and Sweetener Situation and Outlook Report*, SSRV17N1, Economic Research Service, U.S. Department of Agriculture, Washington, DC, March 1992, pp. 24-41.

Buzzanell, Peter J. and José F. Alonso. "Cuba's Sugar Economy: Recent Performance and Challenges for the 1990s," *Sugar and Sweetener Situation and Outlook Report*, SSR14N2, Economic Research Service, U.S. Department of Agriculture, Washington, DC, June 1989, pp. 17-28.

Comité Estatal de Estadísticas, *Anuario Estadístico de Cuba*. La Habana: Editorial Estadística, various issues.

Cuban Economic Research Project. *Cuba: Agriculture and Planning, 1963-1964*. Coral Gables, FL: University of Miami, 1965.

David, Eduardo. "Sugar Production in Cuba," *Sugar y Azúcar* 78:2 (1983), pp. 100-108.

Economic Research Service. "Situation and Outlook Summary - Sugar & Sweeteners". Washington, DC: U.S. Department of Agriculture, September 30, 1991.

Economic Research Service. *Sugar and Sweetener Situation and Outlook Report*. Washington, DC: U.S. Department of Agriculture, December 1991.

El Nuevo Herald, Miami, Florida, November 26, 1991, p. 3A.

El Nuevo Herald, Miami, Florida, January 13, 1992, p. 4A.

El Nuevo Herald, Miami, Florida, May 8, 1992, pp. 1A, 4A.

El Nuevo Herald, Miami, Florida, May 9, 1992, p. 3A.

Feuer, Carl Henry. "The Performance of the Cuban Sugar Industry, 1981-85," in A. Zimbalist (Ed.) *Cuba's Socialist Economy Toward the 1990s*. Boulder, CO: Lynne Rienner Publishers, Inc. 1987, pp. 69-83.

Fundación Sociedad Económica de Amigos del País. "Cuba & Sugar: Looking to the Future," Bulletin 13, Report on the Seminar Sponsored by La Sociedad Económica, Dominican Republic, February 4-6, 1992a.

Fundación Sociedad Económica de Amigos del País. "Further Downward Adjustment of Cuba's 1991/92 Sugar Crop," (Press Release), London, UK, April 20, 1992b.

Gluck, Ken. "Cuba recibe última gota de crudo ruso, informan en Moscú," *El Nuevo Herald*, Miami, Florida, July 20, 1992, p. 1A.

Hagelberg, G.B. "Bleak Crop & Export Prospects," *Cuba Business*, London, February 1992, p. 2.

International Sugar Organization. *Yearbook*. London: International Sugar Organization, 1988.

Licht, F.O. "The Changing Sugar Pattern in East Europe," *International Sugar and Sweetener Report* 123:20 (June 1991), pp. 323-328.

Licht, F.O. "The Market for Cuban Sugar," *International Sugar and Sweetener Report* 123:21 (July 1991), pp. 339-342.

Pérez-López, Jorge F. "Sugar and Structural Change in the Cuban Economy," *World Development* 17:10 (1989), pp. 1627-1642.

Pérez-López, Jorge F. "Sugar and the Cuban Economy: Implications After Thirty Years," *Journal of International Food & Agribusiness Marketing* 3:2 (1991a), pp. 25-46.

Pérez-López, Jorge F. *The Economics of Cuban Sugar*. Pittsburgh, PA: University of Pittsburgh Press, 1991b.

Polopolus, Leo C. and José Alvarez. "Sugar and the North American Free Trade Agreement: Some Major Issues," *Food and Resource Economics Sugar Policy Series No. 7*, Institute of Food and Agricultural Sciences, University of Florida, Gainesville, Florida, July 1992.

Rivero, Nicolás. "Privatization of Mexico's Sugar," *Sugar y Azúcar* 86:12 (December 1991), pp. 35-40.

Rivero, Nicolás. "The Future for Cuban Sugar," *F.O. Licht's International Sugar and Sweetener Report*, Vol. 124, No. 10, March 20, 1992, pp. 157-165.

Smith, Wayne S. and Esteban Morales Domínguez. Eds. *Subject to Solution: Problems in Cuban-U.S. Relations*. Boulder, CO: Lynne Rienner Publishers, 1988.

Timm, Mark. "Compradores de azúcar descartan a Cuba," *El Nuevo Herald*, Miami, Florida, July 24, 1992, p. 5B.

SUGAR CONSUMPTION, SUGAR POLICY, AND THE FATE OF CARIBBEAN CANE GROWERS

Joseph M. Perry, Louis A. Woods, and Jeffrey W. Steagall

Sugar policies adopted by some developed countries since 1977 have caused measurable damage to the cane sugar industries of Caribbean Basin countries. The increasing use of high-fructose starch sweeteners (HFSS) and low-calorie sweeteners has also reduced the importance of cane sugar in overall consumption patterns. These problems have persisted over the past fifteen years, and will continue into the foreseeable future. Two potential changes in hemisphere trade configurations now pose another threat to Caribbean sugar producers.

The possibility that Cuba may again enter free-world sugar markets with its substantial productive capability suggests major policy decisions that must be made by the United States and other sugar importers. In addition, the burgeoning North American Free Trade Association may provide Mexico wider access to U. S. sugar markets. Both eventualities are viewed with concern.

This paper reviews the policies and patterns that have contributed to the world sugar market crisis, and suggests some questions that will have to be answered.

I.   Sugar Policies of Major Importers

The United States, the countries making up the European Community, and Japan, all offer large markets for imported sugar. Their governments also support sugar policies that maintain domestic sugar prices above prevailing world market prices, encourage overproduction by domestic cane and beet growers, and impose quotas on sugar-exporting countries that are often punitive.

United States Sugar Policy

The Jones-Costigan Act of 1934 set the tone for U. S. sugar policy until the early 1970's. It eliminated the tariff structure that had regulated trade since 1894, replacing it with a judgment call from a Federal administrator. The Secretary of Agriculture was required to project the sugar consumption level in the United States, and to allocate production among foreign and domestic producers to meet that need. Allocations to foreign producers were based upon their participation in the United States market between 1931 and 1933. A tax on sugar consumption was to be used to support sugar beet production.[1]

When the outbreak of the Second World War threatened the availability of sugar, measures were taken to ensure an adequate domestic supply. Production goals established in January, 1942, called for substantially more sugar output than in 1941. Both sugar beet and sugar cane plantings were encouraged.[2] Unfortunately, domestic plantings fell short of the established goals. The

---

[1]See Morris E. Morkre and David G. Tarr, *The Effects of Restrictions on United States Imports: Five Case Studies and Theory* (Washington, D. C.: U. S. Government Printing Office, June, 1980), pp. 89-90; and Jorge F. Pérez-López, *The Economics of Cuban Sugar* (Pittsburgh: University of Pittsburgh Press, 1991), pp. 132-133.

[2]Revised goals were published on January 16, 1942, accompanying a reorganization of the Department of Agriculture. The War Production Board was established at the same time, by Executive Order 9024. Murray Benedict, *Farm Policies of the United States, 1790-1950: A Study of their Origins and Development* (New York: The Twentieth Century Fund, 1953), pp. 432-433.

government's index of sugar crop output dropped from 105 in 1939 to 98 in 1941. It rose to 110 in 1942, then plateaued at 80 to 81 for 1943-44. By 1945, it was back up to only 94.[3] In order to meet domestic needs, the United States purchased the entire Cuban export sugar crop each year from 1942 to 1947.[4]

Postwar agricultural policy was initially codified in the Agricultural Acts of 1948 and 1949, which continued wartime levels of support for many basic crops, nominally until midyear 1950, but effectively through 1953. Subsequent confrontations between supporters of high support prices and proponents of a freer market resulted in the compromise Agricultural Act of 1954. This act continued supports for most commodities, but contemplated both a modernized parity formula and the disposal of many stocks held by the Commodity Credit Corporation, to relieve market pressure.[5]

Specific policies regarding imported sugar and sugar products, as a subdivision of broader agricultural policies, are reflected in a series of Sugar Acts and amendments, beginning in 1934, and extending initially to 1974. Although individual acts exhibited different details, according to Ralph Ives and John Hurley they all had the following common elements:

(1) a requirement for USDA to determine domestic consumption and to divide this market for sugar among domestic producers and foreign countries by assigning each a quota; (2) benefit payments to growers; (3) acreage restrictions; (4) an excise tax on sugar; (5) minimum wage rates for field workers; and (6) child labor provisions.[6]

Rising sugar prices caused new sugar legislation to fail in 1974. The Sugar Act expired on December 31, 1974. No support program was in place during 1975 and 1976.

Low world sugar prices prompted a renewed sugar support program in the Food and Agriculture Act of 1977, and again in the Agriculture and Food Act of 1981. Under the latter legislation, the President established country import quotas, based upon the participation of sugar-producing countries in U. S. imports from 1975 to 1981. The loan rate on sugar also rose from 17 to 18 cents per pound. The Food Security Act of 1985 continued these policies, and further required that the sugar program be maintained at no cost to the Federal government. All costs were to be borne by consumers.[7]

Title IX of the Food, Agriculture, Conservation and Trade Act of 1990 (P. L. 101-624) continues the U. S. government's price support and allocation program for sugarcane and sugar beets. If imports fall below 1.25 million short tons, raw value, the title imposes domestic marketing controls for sugarcane, sugar beets, and crystalline fructose. The provisions of the act are in force

---

[3]*Loc. cit.*, p. 441.

[4]Pérez-López, *The Economics of Cuban Sugar*, pp. 134-135.

[5]Murray R. Benedict, *Can We Solve the Farm Problem? An Analysis of Federal Aid to Agriculture* (New York: The Twentieth Century Fund, 1955), pp. 264-276.

[6]Ralph Ives and John Hurley, *United States Sugar Policy: An Analysis* (Washington, D. C.: USGPO, April, 1988), p. 1. This study was published under the aegis of the International Trade Administration, U. S. Department of Commerce. It focuses primarily on sugar policy between 1975 and 1985, and is clearly critical of policy impacts.

[7]Ives and Hurley, *op. cit.*, pp. 1-3.

until 1995.[8]

Mechanically, the operation of the act has changed very little. At the beginning of each fiscal year, and quarterly thereafter, the Secretary of Agriculture estimates annual sugar consumption in the United States, the level of domestic production, and the level of imports. If estimated imports fall below the 1.25 million short ton threshold, marketing allotments are then imposed on domestic producers to induce an increase in imports to the desired level. The allotments extend to domestic producers of crystalline fructose made from corn, in that fructose marketed may not exceed the equivalent of 200,000 short tons of sugar, raw value. The loan rate on sugar is set at 18 cents per pound until 1995.[9]

Although the latest sugar legislation establishes a 1.25 million ton threshold, reducing lower-end uncertainty for foreign sugar producers, it in no way liberalizes the market. The import minimum may also effectively be an import maximum. The support price mechanism also guarantees a domestic U. S. price for sugar that will exceed the world market price.

European Community Sugar Policy

The European Community protects sugar under its Common Agricultural Policy. Its "sugar regime" uses a rather complex combination of support prices and production quotas to provide protection for domestic sugar producers and processors. The policy also controls the flow of sweeteners such as molasses and high-fructose starch sweeteners (HFSS), and permits a "pass-through" of sugar purchased from some 19 less-developed countries under the provisions of the Lomé Convention.[10] Much of the sugar purchased under Lomé provisions comes from Western Hemisphere countries that cannot sell adequate amounts to the United States under current U. S. quota provisions. About 98 percent of all EC sugar comes from beets. Some French territories provide the remaining 2 percent of cane sugar.[11]

Sugar policies and preferential trade arrangements established by the European Community have resulted in an increase of approximately 30 percent in domestic sugar production (in the 12 EC countries) between 1975 and 1985. In the early 1970's, the EC was an importer of sugar. By 1985, it produced almost 15 percent of the world's sugar supply, and had become the world's largest exporter. It is estimated that this aggressive policy has added approximately three million tons of sugar to the world market supply.[12]

Japanese Sugar Policy

Japan established its Sugar Price Stabilization Law in 1965, in an effort to protect its domestic market and domestic producers from international market fluctuations. The law is adminis-

---

[8]U. S. Department of Agriculture, Economic Research Service, *Provisions of the Food, Agriculture, Conservation and Trade Act of 1990*, Agricultural Information Bulletin 624 (Washington, D. C.: USGPO, June, 1991), p. 29.

[9]*Ibid.*, pp. 29-30.

[10]Ives and Hurley, *loc. cit.*, pp. 86-87. See also Ron Lord and Robert D. Barry, *The World Sugar Market--Government Intervention and Multilateral Policy Reform* (Washington, D. C.: U. S. Government Printing Office, September, 1990), pp. 35-38 for a more detailed description.

[11]Ives and Hurley, *op. cit.*, pp. 89-93.

[12]Ives and Hurley, *op. cit.*, p. 96; Lord and Barry, *op. cit.*, pp. 12-14.

tered by the Japan Sugar Price Stabilization Agency (JSPSA). The initial impact of the program was felt primarily in domestic markets. Between 1975 and 1981, sugar prices rose, and competition from high-fructose corn sweeteners increased dramatically. The Japanese government reacted by altering its sugar policy to favor domestic producers.[13]

The program that was established in 1982 continues, with little change, to the present time. It is designed to stabilize the price of imported sugar within a pre-determined band, and to establish a minimum support price for domestically-produced sugar. Imported sugar is sold by business firms to the JSPSA, which sells the sugar back to those firms at a price that is adjusted for world sugar market conditions. In addition, all HFCS processors must sell their output to the JSPSA at a determined price.

The net effect of this market control has been an increase in domestic sugar production in Japan, from half a million tons per year in 1975 to about a million tons in 1985. Since domestic consumption of sugar has remained stable, imports of sugar have dropped dramatically. It is estimated that the Japanese sugar policy adds approximately 700,000 tons of sugar to the world market per year, as compared with market equilibrium levels in the absence of the policy.[14]

II.   The Economic Impact of Sugar Policies

Interestingly, U. S. government control of sugar markets through the mid-1950's appears to have exerted a positive net financial impact on the economy. The U. S. Department of Agriculture in 1954 estimated the total realized cost of crop programs aimed at price and income stabilization, over the period from 1932-1953, to be $7,510.4 million. Of all the major commodity programs covered under this rubric, only the Sugar Act showed a credit, amounting to $296.1 million.[15]

This positive policy impact on the economy was mirrored by productivity changes in the sugar industry. According to studies completed by John W. Kendrick, between 1899 and 1954, the average annual rate of change in output per manhour was 4.1 percent for beet sugar processing (2063), 2.8 percent for raw cane sugar processing (2061), and 1.8 percent for cane sugar refining (2062). The average for all manufacturing industries over this period was 2.2 percent.[16]

Any positive impact from sugar policies was lost in the following years. Mintz estimated the deadweight losses from U. S. sugar policies in 1970 to be $112 million. Morkre and Tarr assessed the sugar program as of 1978. They concluded that the present value of net welfare costs to the national economy could reach $658.1 million, reflecting both deadweight losses and labor market adjustment costs, if policies then in effect were maintained in the future.[17]

Ives and Hurley provide the latest estimates of the overall impact of sugar policies

---

[13]Ives and Hurley, *op. cit.*, p. 103-104.

[14]*Ibid.*

[15]U. S. Department of Agriculture, *Realized Cost of Agricultural and Related Programs, by Function or Purpose, Fiscal Years 1932-1953*, February, 1954, as reported in Benedict, *op. cit.*, pp. 472-480, 560-571.

[16]John W. Kendrick, *Productivity Trends in the United States* (Princeton: Princeton University Press, 1961), pp. 161-162, 476.

[17]Ilse Mintz, *U. S. Import Quotas: Costs and Consequences* (Washington, D. C.: American Enterprise Institute, 1973), passim; Morkre and Tarr, *op. cit.*, pp. 93-103, 190-192. See also D. Gale Johnson, *The Sugar Program: Large Costs and Small Benefits* (Washington, D. C.: American Enterprise Institute, 1974).

in developed countries. Japan's sugar policy cannot be easily assessed, except to say that domestic sugar prices exceed world prices, and that domestic overproduction results. In the European Community, similar impacts are observed. EC consumers paid an extra $1.3 billion per year for sugar between 1975 and 1985 because of the community's sugar policy. Without the "sugar regime", EC consumers would have consumed another 500,000 tons of sugar annually.[18]

The World Bank has computed "nominal protection coefficients" for the three areas. The NPC is the domestic price of sugar divided by the world price of sugar. In 1986, the United States showed an NPC of 1.40, while the EC had an NPC of 1.50. Data problems limit computation of the Japanese NPC to the 1980-1982 period, when it was believed to be 3.00.[19] In each instance, the coefficients reflect strong protectionist policies in favor of domestic sugar producers.

Concerning the United States, Ives and Hurley offer this sobering conclusion:

The sugar program has had the following major detrimental effects . . . (1) maintained the domestic price of sugar at several times the free-market level; (2) cost consumers over $3 billion annually; (3) encouraged a 40 percent per year increase in imports of some sugar-containing products competing against domestic goods; (4) caused a 40 percent reduction of the U. S. sugar refining industry; and (5) displaced about 12,000 jobs because imports of products containing world-priced sugar captured U. S. markets and encouraged offshore investment, and because of the job loss in the refining industry.[20]

It is worth noting that sugar policies adopted by major developed countries imply a move toward sugar production self-sufficiency. Lord and Barry point out that the European Community enjoyed a sugar self-sufficiency ratio (production divided by consumption) of 1.23 in 1986-1988. Brazil and Mexico also showed ratios greater than unity for the same period of time. The United States, while not completely self-sufficient, has raised its ratio from 0.40 in 1965-1967 to 0.85 in 1986-1988.[21]

III.   The Critical Position of Caribbean Sugar Producers

The countries that have suffered most over time from shifts in United States sugar policy are apparently the Philippines and the sugar-exporting Caribbean Basin nations. The latter group includes the Dominican Republic, Guatemala, El Salvador, Honduras, Costa Rica, Jamaica, Panama, Belize, Barbados, Trinidad and Tobago, Haiti, and St. Kitts-Nevis. The sugar industry is the Caribbean region's largest employer. Sugar is normally one of the top three or four exports in value for the region.[22]

For example, Ives and Hurley estimate that unemployment resulting from mid-1980's sugar

---

[18]*Ibid.*, pp. 86-96. The additional cost to consumers in the EC is based upon an assumed price elasticity of demand of -0.1, and a market price premium of 6 cents per pound.

[19]*Ibid.*, p. 104.

[20]Ives and Hurley, *op. cit.*, p. v.

[21]Lord and Barry, *op. cit.*, pp. 32-33.

[22]See U. S. Department of Commerce, *1991 Guidebook:Caribbean Basin Initiative* (Washington, D. C.: U. S. Government Printing Office, November, 1990); also Ives and Hurley, *op. cit.*, p. 41.

policies reached 100,000 persons in the Philippines and 20,000 persons in the Dominican Republic. Half the sugar workers in St. Kitts-Nevis were laid off. Similar proportionate impacts were felt in other supplying countries. It is also worth noting that the negative impacts of sugar policy often totally sterilize the financial aid that the United States provides the countries through other programs--the left hand giving and the right hand taking away, so to speak.[23]

Belize as a Case Study

The Central American nation of Belize may be advanced as a case study of the effects of U. S. sugar policy. Sugar is the most important Belizean crop, accounting for a third of export earnings. A statutory Sugar Board regulates production. Growers are represented by a Cane Farmers' Association, formed in 1959. The industry is located in the northern districts of Corozal and Orange Walk, where climate and land quality encourage cane growth.[24]

The commercial sugar industry is of relatively recent vintage in Belize, although records show almost continuous cane cultivation and sugar product exports since the seventeenth century. Some 30 to 50 small sugar mills operated at the time of the First World War. Their output satisfied local demand. Although the need for a central processing plant was evident, no move to establish one was made before 1935.[25]

In 1935, the Corozal Sugar Factory, Limited, was established, supported by a combination of Government loans and private investment. The company acquired second-hand equipment from the Bacardi Company, in Cuba, and began production in 1937, primarily for the local market. This situation remained static until 1955, with about 2,000 acres of cane under cultivation, and maximum annual sugar output of 2,120 tons.[26]

Hurricane Janet hit Belize in September, 1955, damaging both cane fields and the factory. Supporting legislation from government then encouraged reorganization of the growers along more efficient lines, and the renovation of the factory to a higher capacity level. Cane growing spread, processing activity rose, and output reached about 23,000 tons in 1963. Further expansion proved to be impossible without additional capital. Major shareholders therefore approached Tate and Lyle, a British firm, which acquired the Corozal Sugar Factory, Limited, in 1963. The company was renamed Belize Sugar Industries, Limited.

The acquisition seemed advantageous to Tate and Lyle. The company's access to sugar beets for processing had been limited by actions of the British Government, and its sugar operations in Jamaica and Trinidad had reached peak levels. The availability of suitable sugar cane land, cultivated by experienced growers, made the Belizean operation an attractive addition. It also appeared that the nearby U. S. market was a ready outlet for the country's sugar.

---

[23]Ives and Hurley, *op. cit.*, pp. vi, 72-75.

[24]See Government Information Service, *Belize in Figures:1992* (Belmopan: Government Printery, 1992); and <u>Fact Sheet: Belize</u> (Belmopan: Government Printery, 1992). During the nineteenth century, sugar was also cultivated in Toledo District, near Punta Gorda, by Confederate expatriates from the United States. This enclave gradually dwindled and died out.

[25]Belize Sugar Industries, *Belize Sugar Industries: A Brief History of Sugar in Belize and the Contribution Made by Belize Sugar Industries Ltd and Tate and Lyle PLC to the Development of the Industry from 1964 to 1989*. Belize City: Belize Sugar Industries Limited, 1989), p. 3. For a fuller description of early sugar industry growth, see Louis a. Woods, Jeffrey W. Steagall, and Joseph M. Perry, "Agroindustries in Belize: Their Role in the Economic Development Process," *passim*.

[26]The remainder of this historical section is based primarily upon Belize Sugar Industries, *op. cit.*, pp. 6-10.

More expansion followed, its pace dictated by a changing world sugar market. A new factory at Tower Hill was opened in January, 1967, just as world sugar prices hit new lows, and the United States reduced its quota of imported sugar from Belize. Company lands were widely sold to cane growers in 1972 to accommodate to financial troubles felt by the company. Rising sugar prices and a worldwide sugar shortage after 1974 permitted further expansion in the capacity of the Tower Hill factory. By 1978, that facility could produce 65,000 tons of sugar annually, giving the two-factory complex a combined annual capacity of 110,000 tons. Further expansion at Tower Hill brought its capacity to a peak level of 75,000 tons per year in 1980. Improvements were also made at the Corozal (Libertad) factory.

Market conditions worsened rapidly from that point. Sugar prices dropped, United States quotas were reduced, and exchange rates moved unfavorably. Tate and Lyle undertook a major restructuring in 1985, beginning a planned transfer of company assets to private Belizean owners that should culminate in 1994. The Corozal factory was also closed at that time, and was subsequently sold to Jamaican interests (Petrojam). By 1989, Tate and Lyle held only 10 percent of company shares. The remainder was held by BSI employees, the Government of Belize, and the Development Finance Corporation of Belize.

The impact of the industry is still substantial. There are 4,875 registered cane farmers, as of 1989. The industry is still the largest private-sector employer. BSI estimates that, if cane farmers and dependents are included in the calculation, between 15 and 20 percent of the 1989 Belizean population is directly dependent upon the sugar industry.[27]

The dramatic impact of unanticipated changes in U. S. import quotas on Tate & Lyle is shown by the figures. Raw sugar imports into the United States from Belize over the 1975-1981 period averaged 37,500 short tons per year. Raw sugar quotas for Belize reported by the United States government through 1988 were as follows:

1982/1983	19,600 short tons
1983/1984	21,294 short tons
1984/1985	17,780 short tons
1985/1986	12,500 short tons
1987	7,500 short tons
1988	5,770 short tons[28]

Note that the combined capacities of the two BSI factories before the crisis exceeded 100,000 tons per year.

Sugar industry leaders reacted rationally, trying to shift output to alternative markets as cultivation shrank. Great Britain was able to absorb much of the excess supply, under the Lomé Agreement, passing it through to world markets as described above. Cane farmers in northern Belize also reacted rationally. Many of them shifted to the illegal cultivation of marijuana, adding to the problems of drug regulation facing the national government. Even with some improvement in sugar markets recently, marijuana is still widely grown as a readily salable cash crop.

---

[27]*Loc. cit.*, p. 17.

[28]Ives and Hurley, *loc. cit.*, p. 74.

Sugar production has gradually risen since the mid 1980's, reaching 90,900 tons in 1990 and 100,300 tons in 1991. Exports of raw sugar from Belize during recent years have also risen, at least partly because of more favorable quotas from the United States. Its 1991/1992 allocation was 14,000 long tons, down from the 1990/1991 quota of 21,350 tons. Great Britain absorbed a large percentage of each year's crop, following the European Community sugar regime. The figures are as follows:

Table 1. Belize: Exports of Raw Sugar, 1980-1991

Year	Amount of Exports (long tons)	Amount of Exports (Bz$ mill)
1991	92,087	$84.5
1990	93,116	$85.7
1989	78,750	$66.1
1988	79,740	$70.0
1987	78,981	$62.6
1986	98,480	$62.9
1985	89,147	$45.9
1984	93,877	$65.1
1983	109,117	$70.9
1982	98,151	$66.7
1981	90,424	$85.3
1980	97,152	$95.4

Source: Central Bank of Belize, Quarterly Reports; Central Statistical Office; External Trade Bulletin.

Petrojam refurbished the Libertad factory, intending to produce wet ethanol. Since 1989, the plant has been absorbing some part of the annual cane crop for the production of molasses. During the first quarter of 1992 (January-March), for example, Petrojam processed 6,126 long tons of molasses, as compared with the BSI output of 12,521 long tons for the same time period.[29]

In short, the Belizean sugar industry has adjusted as rationally as it could to the uncertainties of the world market, shifting land to alternative production where possible, and finding alternative markets where possible. Even given the more favorable United States import quotas of 1989-1992, the industry is operating with excess capacity.

The experience of Belize is not unique, but rather representative of the damage done to smaller trading partners by the import policies of giant nations. Although Belize is now singled out for special treatment under the latest revision of the Caribbean Basin Initiative, much uncertainty still exists concerning future sugar sales to the United States. The uncertain future of the European Community reforms of 1992 suggests similar caution regarding the sugar market in Great Britain.

---

[29]See Woods, Steagall, and Perry, *op. cit.*, and Central Bank of Belize, *Quarterly Review*, Vol 16, No. 1 (March, 1992), pp. 5-7.

Two other potential trouble sources are found in an ongoing treaty negotiation process, for the North American Free Trade Association and the Enterprise for the Americas Initiative, and in an anticipated institutional breakdown in Cuba. Both create uncertainty about sugar markets in the Western Hemisphere.

IV.   Possible Impacts From NAFTA

President George Bush promulgated the Enterprise for the Americas Initiative (EAI) on June 27, 1990. The EAI envisions a hemispheric free trade system, beginning with the North American Free Trade Agreement (NAFTA) among Canada, Mexico, and the United States, and gradually expanding to include all of Central and South America. As enunciated by President Bush, EAI should ultimately bring a free trade area that stretches from Alaska to Tierra del Fuego. The initiative focusses on the three critical policy areas of trade, investment, and debt, offering substantial aid to hemispheric countries.[30]

Negotiations have already been extensive. Framework agreements on trade and investment are now in place with all Latin American countries except Cuba, Haiti, and Suriname. Typically, the framework agreements establish Trade and Investment Councils with oversight and counsel capabilities. Investment opportunities are being supported by a new sector lending program of the Inter-American Development Bank (IDB), with prospects of a $1.5 billion multi-country Multilateral Investment Fund being set up in the near future, including contributions from Europe and Japan. Debt restructuring and reduction are being addressed through a complex of support procedures for internal economic reform.[31]

In February, 1991, the United States, Mexico, and Canada agreed to begin formal negotiations to establish a three-country free-trade area. Formal meetings began in June, 1991. Since then, negotiations with Mexico regarding NAFTA have been frequent and visible, especially during the first half of 1992. Despite significant opposition from U. S. manufacturing and agricultural interest groups, an initial version of the treaty was signed by U. S. and Mexican representatives on August 12, 1992. Predictions are that the treaty will add as many as 600,000 jobs to the Mexican economy. It is estimated that 538,000 jobs in the United States were already supported by U. S. exports to Mexico in 1990.[32]

Since Mexico is one of the major producers of sugar in this hemisphere, and eighth in world production, recording a total output of 3.6 million tons in 1991, the possibility now exists that more of its modest sugar exports may find their way into the United States. Under the provisions of the signed agreement, Mexican sugar exports to the United States may increase by a small amount through the year 2000, but by a much larger amount thereafter. These exports would clearly be in competition with sugar from Caribbean producers and with sugar from Cuba, assuming the

---

[30]See U. S. Department of Commerce, *Business America* 112:14 (July 1, 1991), p. 10. A less official view, is given by "Turning the Hemisphere into a Free Trade Bloc," *Business Week*, December 24, 1990, p. 37, and "Mexico: A New Economic Era," Business Week, November 12, 1990, pp. 102-110.

[31] *Business America*, 112:15/16 (1991), inside front cover.

[32]"Building Free Trade Bloc by Bloc," *Business Week*, May 25, 1992, pp. 26-27; Linda Aguilar, "The North American Free Trade Agreement: the ties that bind," *Chicago Fed Letter*, No. 61 (September, 1992), pp. 1-2.

reestablishment of north-south trade with that country.[33]

V.   The Uncertain Future of Cuba

Cuba, conveniently located and blessed with climate and land resources suited to cane cultivation, actively pursued the U. S. market during the late nineteenth century. In doing so, it not only sold more sugar to North Americans, but encouraged the flow of investment dollars needed to expand its domestic industry. Galloway notes that, "by the end of the First World War, the Cuban sugar industry was preeminent in the world, producing annually about 4 million tons in 200 central large factories".[34]

Over the next half-century, Cuba occupied a special and privileged position as a trading partner to the United States. Although subject to import duties, like other foreign countries, it was awarded preferential rates and a virtually guaranteed market for its sugar. As Benedict and Stine point out, the Cuban supply provided a large part of sugar consumption in the United States, expanded quickly to take up deficits in production, and constituted "a strategic reserve of great importance to the United States".[35]

The details of the 1960 fracture in Cuban-United States relations, and a search for Eastern Hemisphere markets, are well known. Equally evident are the institutional and political changes in Europe and Asia that are robbing Cuba of her once-guaranteed markets.

Cuba's current critical position in the world sugar market is reflected in a specific provision of Title IX of the Food, Agriculture, Conservation and Trade Act of 1990. It requires the Secretary of Agriculture to determine the extent to which countries exporting sugar to the United States are concomitantly importing sugar from Cuba. Countries may certify that they do not import Cuban sugar for re-export, and are subject to presidential sanctions if they violate the limitation.[36] While the provision reflects political realities, it also reflects the impressive productive capacity of the Cuban sugar industry, even under present economic conditions.

Pérez-López points out that the pre-USSR-breakup plans laid by the Cuban government for sugar production were very ambitious. A combination of new and renovated mills, expanded cultivation, and rationalized production processes was intended to bring 1990 production levels to 11 or 12 million tons per annum. By the year 2000, output was to reach 13 to 14 million tons per annum. The breakup of the USSR and the Communist Bloc negated any plans for expansion. Output apparently reached 7.6 million tons in 1991, a still impressive figure, but dropped to about 5.5 million tons in 1992.[37]

---

[33]Bob Davis, "Free Trade Pact's Details are Sparking Squabbles as Congress Takes Up Review," *The Wall Street Journal*, September 8, 1992, p. A4.

[34]J. H. Galloway, *The Sugar Cane Industry: An Historical Geography from Its Origins to 1914* (Cambridge: Cambridge University Press, 1989), pp. 167-168.

[35]Murray R. Benedict and Oscar C. Stine, *The Agricultural Commodity Programs: Two Decades of Experience.* (New York: The Twentieth Century Fund, 1956), pp. 280-286.

[36]U. S. Department of Agriculture, *loc. cit.*, p. 32.

[37]Pérez-López, *op. cit.*, pp. 14-16; José Alvarez, "Cuba's Sugar Industry in the 1990's: Potential Exports to the U. S. and World Markets," paper presented at the Second Annual Meeting of the Association for the Study of the Cuban Economy, Miami, Florida, August 13-15, 1992, *passim.*

When trade relations open up between Cuba and the United States again, even in a limited fashion, it seems unlikely that sugar exports from that nation will be rejected. Pre-1960 relations are probably out of the question, but some major accommodation to Cuban agricultural production will clearly take place. Its likelihood and timing are other uncertainties that sugar-producing countries around the Caribbean are now facing. A Cuban sugar industry that occupied the same niche it held in 1959 would deal a severe blow to competing industries, assuming that protective policies in developed nations do not change.

VI. Sweetener Consumption Patterns

A related problem lies in consumer decisions. Consumers in developed countries crave sweeteners. On a per capita basis, use and consumption of sweeteners is still rising. Table 2 presents recent data for the United States, showing per capita use of all sweeteners increasing from 132.7 pounds in 1980 to 153 pounds in 1988, a 15.3 percent increase in only eight years. On the surface, this trend appears favorable toward cane sugar producers. The composition of sweetener consumption has changed radically in recent years, however. As the remaining data in Table 2 show, per capita consumption of cane and beet sugar in the United States has dropped by 20 pounds since 1980, while per capita use of corn sweeteners rose by over 29 pounds. Most corn sweeteners are found in prepared or processed foods and beverages. Equally noteworthy is the strong increase in the use of low-calorie sweeteners, such as saccharin and aspartame. These preparations now account for 13 percent of per capita sweetener use.

Table 2. Per Capita Consumption of Sweeteners in the U.S., 1980-1988
(In pounds, retail weight)

Year	Total Sweeteners, Dry Weight	Refined Sugar, Cane/Beet	Corn Sweeteners, Dry Weight	Non-Caloric Sweeteners
1988	153.0	62.0	69.6	20.0
1987	151.4	62.2	68.8	19.0
1986	147.2	60.2	67.1	18.5
1985	148.9	63.0	66.5	18.0
1984	142.4	67.3	57.8	15.8
1983	137.5	70.9	52.1	13.0
1982	132.5	73.6	48.1	9.4
1981	133.3	79.3	44.5	8.2
1980	132.7	83.6	40.1	7.7

Source: USDOC, *Statistical Abstract of the United States*, 1991, 1990, 1987, and 1981.

Since there is no reason to believe that these consumption trends will reverse themselves, it becomes clear that overall economic and population growth in the United States is less favorable to cane sugar producers than might be supposed. As the big, northern neighbor of the CBI nations gets bigger, its appetite for cane sugar will not necessarily grow at a commensurate rate.

VII.   Conclusions

The U. S. quota system acts as a two-edged sword toward cane sugar producers: it offers sugar prices that are above the world market level, but it restricts purchases to the extent that the exporting countries have to dump large quantities of sugar on the free market, or find alternative preferential treatment. Excess capacity and market uncertainty are constant problems under this system. Similar policies in other developed nations, including the European Community and Japan worsen the market situation.

Access to other, preferred markets, by less-developed countries may actually exacerbate the problem. The 19 sugar-producing countries operating under the provisions of the Lomé Convention countries may sell excess sugar to European Community buyers, which then pass the product through to world markets, depressing the price there. High domestic support prices clearly encourage domestic overproduction of sugar in the United States, the European Community, and Japan, as compared with free market conditions. Even with major political restructuring under way in Europe and elsewhere in the world, there appears to be no immediate hope that existing sugar policies will change.

Sweetener consumption patterns in developed countries are also threatening cane sugar producers. Increasing amounts of corn sweeteners and low-calorie sweeteners are being used by both processors and consumers. These trends appear to be well-established.

Finally, the negotiation of the North American Free Trade Association opens the door for increasing sugar exports from Mexico to the United States. The imminent downfall of the restrictive system in Cuba promises additional sugar supplies for Western Hemisphere importers. Post-Castro refurbishing of the Cuban sugar industry may well bring it to the level of efficiency envisaged by that regime.

For the cane sugar producing nations in and around the Caribbean, these trends suggest a problem that will not disappear, but will instead worsen. Countries such as the Dominican Republic and Belize and Guyana must find other uses for cane lands, other markets for cane products, and other means of acquiring needed foreign exchange. Diversification must take place. It seems clear that, in the immediate future, a strongly expanding world market for cane sugar is impossible. Expanding market shares for small western nations seem equally unlikely.

Short-term accommodation to long-term structural changes may be painful. Small countries may seek shelter under the CBI and Lomé umbrellas until they are able to reallocate resources. In any event, their major trading partners, primarily the United States and Great Britain, must be aware of and responsive to these problems, particularly if Cuban sugar once again dominates this hemisphere.

Comments

Jorge F. Pérez-López

Sugar has the dubious distinction of being the commodity with the longest history of international agreements to regulate production or prices. The first such agreement goes back to 1864 —four years before the start of the *Guerra de los Diez Años* in Cuba and nearly 40 years before the establishment of the Cuban Republic— when Belgium, France, the Netherlands, and the United Kingdom negotiated an agreement to phase out subsidies on domestic production and exports of sugar.

Cuba began to play a role in international sugar negotiations and agreements after 1926, when the government unilaterally cut production and exports to try to stabilize world prices. Cuba was a key participant in the 1929 Brussels Convention, the first international sugar agreement including both beet and sugarcane producers, and of each of the subsequent international agreements —at least five plus extensions— that have been negotiated since.

Despite international efforts to stabilize the international sugar market, the problems have not gone away: too much production, too many suppliers, production in both moderate (beet) and warm (sugarcane) climates, short-term inelastic supply, wildly-fluctuating prices, leaky cartels, declining per capita world demand.

In a sense, Cuba's isolation from the U.S. and Western markets in the last 30 years has been a blessing in disguise for other sugar producers. It now seems certain that this will change in the relatively short term. The situation of world sugar markets and prospects are sobering. To illustrate, Table 7 in Pepín Alvarez's paper shows that **total** U.S. sugar imports in 1990-91 were 2.2 million tons, while the 1991-92 sugar quota (distributed across some 40 countries) is just over 1.5 million tons. Compare these statistics with the nearly 3.0 million tons of sugar that Cuba <u>alone</u> exported to the United States in 1959 and the very share of U.S. imports allocated to Cuba.

The reintegration of Cuba into the international economy has already begun, as the Eastern European nations and the former Soviet Union have discontinued preferential trading and barter. It will accelerate when a new, market-oriented government takes over in Cuba. The sugar industry, whether one likes or not, is the one industry that has the potential for leading the way to Cuba's return to international markets —it produces a quality product at competitive prices— and must be part of an economic strategy for Cuba. But the challenges are immense.

The three papers in this session complement each other very well and are extremely useful in helping us think through the economic implications of the sugar industry in a market-oriented Cuban economy. The paper by Rivero (presented orally at the conference) emphasizes supply conditions in Cuba, while the paper by Perry, Woods, and Steagall focuses on demand-related issues, and paper by Alvarez looks at both issues and broadens the panorama to look at alternative markets for Cuban sugar.

Turning to the papers, I found Alvarez's contribution to be extremely valuable. It packs a tremendous amount of basic data that is essential to do a basic, cold analysis of the prospects of the Cuban sugar industry. It is extremely instructive to analyze in detail the changes over the last decades in the Cuban sugar industry and in world markets documented by Alvarez, particularly for those who believe that the *status quo ante* —Cuba recovering its pre-Castro share of the U.S. sugar market— can be accomplished.

The Perry/Woods/Steagall paper reviews very competently the largest traditional sugar consuming areas —the United States, the EC, and Japan— and how the sugar markets in these areas have changed over time. I agree with them that 1992 is not 1959. The sugar markets have changed tremendously. Advanced countries have held on to sugar production and, in the case of the EC, that group of countries is now the world's largest sugar exporter. Whether such allocation of resources is optimal or not is besides the point —it's a reality. As they continue to work on this topic, I would like for the authors to expand their work to look at other sugar markets as well, such as China and North Africa.

The brief case study of Belize illustrates the concern in the Caribbean from the anticipated competition of Cuban sugar in the U.S. market. It would seem to me that other Caribbean nations that **do not** have the cushion of preferential access to European markets through the Lome Convention (for example the Dominican Republic) could potentially be more adversely affected by the return of Cuban sugar to the U.S. market.

Overall, I found that the three papers are very sound and useful. They contribute to a better understanding of the Cuban sugar industry and its future.

THE FREE FARMERS MARKET:
A REJECTED APPROACH BUT A POSSIBLE SOLUTION

José F. Alonso[1]

I.   Introduction

In Cuba, the non-sugar agricultural sector produces significant amounts of food staples essential to the people's consumption and contributes handsomely to the international trade accounts of the nation. This is the only sector of the Cuban economy that operates with a significant number of private entrepreneurs (farmers and small parcel owners or *parceleros*). In 1989, over 35

Table 1
Private Sector Production of Selected Commodities
(in thousand tons)

Items	1970	1975	1980	1981	1986	1989
Roots & Tubers						
Total Production	122.8	302.5	736.8	728.9	674.9	681.2
Non-State Sector	40.8	91.7	225.6	190.0	186.6	188.4
%. Non-State	33.2	30.3	30.6	26.1	27.7	27.7
Vegetables						
Total Production	130.4	401.7	445.9	625.8	554.9	671.0
Non-State Sector	43.2	194.4	293.2	357.6	356.1	459.1
%. Non-State	33.1	48.4	65.8	57.1	64.2	68.4
Rice						
Total Production	374.5	446.7	477.8	460.9	575.7	550.0
Non-State Sector	8.7	24.5	35.0	37.3	84.9	83.2
%. Non-State	2.3	5.5	7.3	8.1	14.8	15.1
Beans						
Total Production	4.4	4.0	9.4	8.2	13.2	14.1
Non-State Sector	2.6	1.8	2.7	2.1	3.4	3.3
%. Non-State	59.1	45.0	28.7	25.6	25.8	23.4
Plantains						
Total Production	73.5	162.8	233.4	260.7	317.2	368.0
Non-State Sector	5.5	24.1	81.4	87.9	136.5	178.3
%. Non-State	7.5	14.8	34.9	33.7	43.0	48.5

Source: *Anuario Estadístico de Cuba*, 1989.

---

[1]No discussion, interpretation, results or comments contain herein can be attributed to any of the United States Government agencies, including the United States Information Agency, Voice of America, Bureau of Broadcasting, Radio Martí Program. All errors of omission or commission are only mine. The author wishes to express his appreciation to Nicolás Rivero, Jorge F. Pérez-López, and José D. Acosta for their helpful and insightful comments on this manuscript. This manuscript would have not been possible without the cooperation, review and patience of my wife Cindy and daughter Patti to whom I am grateful for all they have done to make this work possible.

percent of vegetables, tubers and fruits harvested and sold to the state were produced by the private sector. Table 1 shows the private sector's share of output for selected commodities.

In May 1992 Fidel Castro explained the importance of this sector during the VIII Congress of the National Association of Small Farmers (ANAP) as follows:

> If private farmers reduce their production or if there is no growth, the Food Program will be affected. This is due to the importance of their production. In some provinces, private farmers' output is more important than in others and for many crops, such as tobacco, their production is extremely important. Between the Agricultural Production Cooperatives (CPAs) and the private farmers, their output importance is tremendous (Castro, 19 May 1992. pp. 4-7).

The area dedicated to farming by the private sector diminished over time. In 1963 total arable land in the private sector was 36.5 percent while in 1981 it accounted for 15.3 percent. At the end of the collectivization drive of the eighties the private acreage further declined to 9.8 percent of the available agricultural land. Figure 1 reflects the agricultural sector land distribution by its principal tenants.

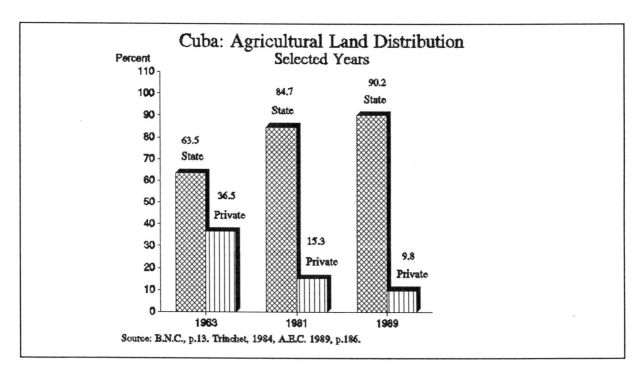

Although private farmers retain ownership of the land and are not allowed to contract labor, production is performed with minimal state guidance. However, inputs and output are under government control. Organizations such as ANAP channel equipment, seeds, fertilizers, financial resources, machinery and other essential inputs for production. Other government agencies such as *Ministerio del Azúcar* (MINAZ), *Ministerio de Agricultura* (MINAGRI) and the *Banco Nacional de Cuba* (BNC) also play a major role in agriculture.

Agricultural production is planned and controlled by the State through MINAGRI and

ANAP. Purchasing, consolidating, and distribution of agricultural products to retail is performed by a national system known as *acopio*. Once private sector production quotas are met and the state procurement agency purchases its share, the state allows farmers to keep the remainder for self-consumption or for other uses. On many occasions, the quantities not consumed directly by the private farmers become the supply source of a well-developed black market for agricultural products.

Production targets set by the state for the private sector have very seldom been met. Among the factors contributing to low output are the failure of the government to recognize the credit needs of private farmers and parceleros, while at the same time giving priority to the state sector (CPA's and State Farms) engaged in similar non-sugar production (Burnhill, p. 32). Equipment rental priority has been accorded to the CPAs and only equipment not needed is rented to private farmers.

In reality the effect of state policies has been to severely limit expansion of the agricultural sector in relation to domestic demand. The results of these policies has been to spend substantial sums of Soviet foreign economic assistance and hard currency in food imports to meet consumer needs. As far back as 1962, the government introduced rationing of food products to meet the country's demand. The rationing book included different food products as well as consumer goods. In relation to dietary needs, the concept of a minimum food basket was implemented through the rationing mechanism to achieve fair distribution of available products.

While rationing attempted to provide the minimum dietary requirements of every household since the 1960's, overall demand was not satisfied. Consequently, there was popular clamor for increases in the availability of durable and non-durable goods from the government. The poor availability of all types of goods and limited services resulted in an accumulation of cash in consumers' hands. In the late 1970's and early 1980's, the population felt that they deserved better living conditions. Furthermore, this desire for better living conditions was exacerbated by two factors: (a) the visits of Cuban friends and families living abroad, which provided a good example of consumerism (demonstration effect); and (b) wage increases and economic incentive policies implemented by the government during the early eighties.

To meet consumer demands and to curtail excess liquidity, the government introduced several measures considered non-conventional in Cuba's planned economy. Basically, these were to liberate a series of durable and non-durable products from the rationing book and to create several markets using the principles of supply and demand to determine prices. Among the markets created to supplement the official Rationed Market and reduce black market operations were the Parallel Market, the Free Farmers Markets (FFM), the Artisan Market and others. In addition, the government allowed carpenters, plumbers, electricians, and others to offer their services on a private remuneration basis.

While these markets successfully met consumer demands, the government's expectations were not fulfilled. In fact, the government became frustrated by the rise of consumerism, trading and wealth accumulation that took place during these years. After attempting to regulate them but continuing to observe and receive very negative reports and complaints from different segments of society, the FFM and artisan markets were abolished in May 1986.

The objective of this paper is to review the economic events and experiences of markets that functioned during the late seventies and eighties in Cuba. The scope of this paper is limited to the marketing of fresh produce (vegetables and tubers) and fruits. The food processing industry is state-owned and buys directly from official sources. The focus will be on the FFM, since it has the potential for providing short-term relief to the food shortages currently affecting the country. Some conclusions and recommendations for future use are also made based on experiences on the functioning of these markets.

II.   Overview of Food Markets in Cuba

Since the early 1960's, food distribution in Cuba was carried out through an official market system that consumers accessed through ration books and a black market. In order to

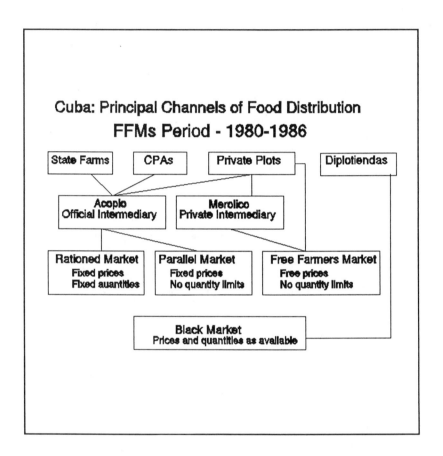

supplement deficiencies of produce and provide production incentives, the government during the eighties authorized a government-controlled Parallel Market and the use of the FFM.

To better conceptualize the economic and social implications of the FFM, a brief description and analysis of the functions and operations of the various market outlets is depicted graphically in the chart above.

III.   Market Channels of Distribution

Rationed Market. This market is supplied by the government distribution system *acopio* that purchases foods from state farms, CPAs and private farmers. Sales are made through established government retail outlets. Prices and quantities are fixed by the government and sales are conducted at designated government establishments through the ration book (*la libreta*). This marketing system has been in existence since 1962 until today.

Black Market. Since the beginning of the revolution, a lively black market has existed in Cuba as a direct result of food shortages. This illicit market serves as a clearinghouse for illicit operations. Its supplies are obtained from all domestic sources of production, and an additional important source is the *Diplotienda*. The *Diplotienda* is a supply outlet payable in U.S. currency, available to all foreigners registered in the country (diplomats, foreign students, etc.) that resells some merchandise to Cuban nationals.

Free Sales. Since the early seventies free sales of products were allowed in order to meet consumer demand for certain items. These products were sold in the official retail establishments but were not subject to quantity limitations. Prices were established by the government and resembled supply and demand conditions.

Parallel Markets. These were established in the late seventies to further supplement consumer demand and to introduce a certain degree of flexibility in meeting needs. These special stores did not require the use of the ration book. Almost any kind of consumer goods were available, including durable and non-durable products. It was also used as a vehicle to curtail black market operations and to reduce consumer excess liquidity. Sales took place in specified established government stores. Prices were not subsidized and were fixed by the government. Customer purchases were not limited, but subject only to availability.

Free Farmers Markets. The principal objective of these markets was to address consumer dissatisfaction with the quantity and quality of fresh vegetables, tubers, and fruits. It was conceived to provide additional incentives to those in the private agricultural sector by providing a legalized marketplace without government intervention. Prices were determined by supply and demand. These markets began to operate in 1981.

IV.   Economic Conditions Leading to the Enactment of the FFM

As Cuba entered the seventies, the economy and the agricultural sector were stagnant and needed a boost. Policy decisions made during the second half of the sixties concentrated on sugar production and resulted in the ten million-ton sugar campaign fiasco. Investment allocations for non-sugar agriculture were very small. As shown in Table 2 below, production of principal agricultural non-sugar commodities in which the private sector specialized —tobacco, coffee, vegetables and tubers— fell to their lowest levels since 1965. It was not until the late seventies, when the government began to pay adequate attention, that production of some commodities recovered.

In Table 2 we can see that tobacco production, a hard currency export-earning crop and a mainstay of the private agricultural sector, declined 31.6 percent over the period 1965-70. Production of other commodities such as coffee, yucca (cassava) and malanga (taro root), fell even more sharply, and consistently throughout the seventies. In general, recovery of production levels of these commodities occurred at a very slow pace.

In the 1970's, the low output of the non-sugar agricultural sector, combined with other political-economic events, began to put pressure on the government for an improvement in living conditions. In 1972, the political leadership decided that Cuba should enter the Council for Mutual Economic Assistance (CMEA) as a tropical agricultural product supplier. CMEA provided a guaranteed market for Cuban sugar and access to Soviet oil. Also, the country acquired on favorable terms additional quantities of agricultural inputs and commodities that were needed to supplement domestic production shortages. Domestically, the leadership implemented a series of policy changes during the early seventies that brought about a period known as the "institutionalization of the revolution." These policies attempted to introduce a more credible and sensible economic structure in the country. The new economic system was patterned after the Liberman Soviet model known as "*Cálculo Económico*" (Mesa-Lago, p. 29).

Table 2
Cuba: Selected Agricultural Production
(in thousand metric tons)

Commodity	1965	1970	1976	Percent Change	
				1965-70	1965-76
Tobacco	43,000	32,000	51,000	-0.26	0.19
Coffee	24,000	20,000	19,000	-0.17	-0.21
Malanga	47,000	12,000	45,000	-0.74	-0.04
Tomatoes	120,000	62,000	194,000	-0.48	0.62
Beans	11,000	5,000	3,000	-0.55	-0.73
Pork	48,000	15,000	52,000	-0.69	0.08
Yucca	62,000	22,000	84,000	-0.65	0.35

Source: Carmelo Mesa-Lago, *The Economy of Socialist Cuba: A Two Decade Appraisal* (Albuquerque: University of New Mexico Press, 1981), p. 37.

In 1973, *JUCEPLAN* (Central Planning Board), began to implement the *Cálculo Económico*. In 1975, the *Sistema de Dirección y Planificación de la Economía* (SDPE) was formally adopted and introduced a series of reforms that led to a greater workers participation in running the enterprises. Many of these measures and reforms were introduced in response to unacceptably low productivity and production levels (Mesa-Lago, p. 151).

While the SDPE was being implemented, consumers began to criticize the extensive rationing system and the lack of availability of good quality fruits, vegetables, and tubers. The government, while cognizant of the need for more quality consumer products, was also aware of the extensive black market in food products supported by private farmer sales. As a response, *JUCEPLAN's* junior economists, with the leadership's consent, decided to implement principles of market economics to obtain a more smoothly functioning economy. Several experiments were tried from 1973 to 1980. For example, a group of products were removed from the rationed list and allowed to be freely sold in unlimited quantities (*Ventas por la Libre*) to the public. Such sales reduced excess cash in the hands of consumers, the level of subsidies and, in some cases, forced consumers to pay scarcity prices for some items. Consumers began to receive the first round of liberalization measures with certain joy by consumers because they began to have access to many desirable products that had not been available for years. In addition, the general standard of living improved due to some general wage increases.

V. Creation and Initial Results of the CPAs

In addition to the free sale of items and other measures undertaken to upgrade the standard of living, the First Congress of the Cuban Communist Party held in late 1975 decided to transform the private agricultural sector. To accomplish this transformation, the Party authorized the creation of a new form of non-state-operated agricultural organization: the Agricultural Production Cooperatives-CPAs. ANAP was in charge of managing the organization, including recruiting members, organizing cooperatives, and providing material inputs and services. The justification was that the private sector needed to increase output and CPAs offered the most efficient form of organization. Incentives were offered to private farmers who pledged their land to form CPAs. The material incentives offered were as follows: preferential access to machinery, inputs, cheaper credit, lower taxes, housing, and electricity (Burnhill, p. 32-34). Cooperative managers were elected by CPA members. Output belonged to the state, with the *acopio* in charge of collecting and distributing products.

Initially, collectivization did not produce satisfactory results, although it was thought to be an effective method to improve production in a short period of time. The acceptance of the concept of collectivization by private landholders was slow (Deere, Meurs and Pérez, p. 9-11). Moreover, increments in production had a marginal effect on population consumption because the CPA's major output was in cash crops for export.

CPAs are dominated by the production of export crops, principally: sugarcane (43% of CPA land and CPA members); tobacco (10% of CPA land and 15% of CPA workers); and coffee (15% of CPA land 13% of CPA workers) (La Sociedad Económica, p. 3).

In addition, the CPA movement experienced serious organizational and managerial difficulties that inhibited its development. Among the difficulties were unprofitable enterprises, lack of adequate personnel in management, and shortage of labor to work in the fields (Deere, Meurs and Pérez, p. 13-18).

VI. The Parallel Market and General Price Increase of 1981

The Parallel Market, as previously mentioned, was a network of government retail outlets where customers could purchase unregulated scarce goods, in addition to agricultural products.[2] The experiment coincided with the time when the leadership believed it had regained control of the economy and signs pointed towards an economic recovery. Plans were to eventually free all products through the parallel market.

Serious challenges were posed to the leadership by this experiment as an economic and political agent. As a result of having to increase foreign currency expenditures, the state had to keep the market stocked and import durable and non-durable consumer goods as well as food products not available domestically. An example of this type of market were two stores located in downtown Havana —*Mercado Unico* and *El Centro*. Access to these "super" markets was allowed to Cuban expatriates with dollars who were visiting relatives. Consumers eagerly accepted the parallel market despite high prices. Prices were substantially higher and the leadership wanted them to reflect free

---

[2] That is, consumers could buy a TV, radio, tape deck, corn flakes, oatmeal, cocoa powder, cakes, luncheon meats, specialized meat cuts such as filet mignon, swordfish, coffee, tires, batteries, clothing, shoes, and also fruits, vegetables and tubers, etc.

market conditions (Deere and Meurs, p. 14). Through the parallel market the government expected to achieve the following:

1.   to increase availability and choices of consumer products.
2.   to sell surpluses of manufactured goods and other items not considered essential.
3.   to introduce prices based on supply and demand.
4.   to curtail black market operations and reduce consumer liquidity.

Agricultural production did not increase significantly with the creation of this market because it was essentially an outlet for state surpluses and imported goods. The newly-created CPAs were in no position to compete with the farmers supplying the black market because most of the CPAs were not engaged in the production of specialized crops (fruits, vegetables and tubers).

Concurrent with the establishment of the parallel market, several economic measures were enacted during the First Party Congress leading to major salary and wage reforms and the introduction of worker's incentives. These measures were the result of serious production problems resulting from poor work quality and absenteeism, and their expected results were increased productivity and output (Mesa-Lago, p. 146-150). Bonuses, overtime and production quotas began to function in state enterprises with the introduction of the SDPE, and with it came higher wages. Despite a general price increase in 1981, excess liquidity continued to be a concern:

> The 1981 price rises increased average family expenditures by an estimated 8 pesos per month and contributed to a significant reduction in the food subsidy. Wage increases, however, had provided the average family with an extra 36 pesos a month. To deal with the problem of excess demand the government also announced measures to encourage savings. More important, however, were measures designed to increase the supply of consumer goods and services (Utting, p. 128).

VII.   The Free Farmers Markets (FFM)

According to Figueroa and García, the FFM were a response to "the low efficiency of agriculture during the 70's, which was not capable of fulfilling consumer demand. The farmers also needed economic incentives to increase production." In 1976, non-sugar agricultural sector problems were taken up during the First Communist Party Congress. The focus of the debate was aimed at "the objective need of the agrarian economy of Cuba and the creation of a non-state market to commercialize a portion of the agricultural production" (Figueroa and García, p. 46-51). In addition, there were other considerations that affected the creation of the FFM, such as the continuation of black market operations despite the parallel market and free sales (*ventas libres*).

The FFM were sanctioned by Law-Decree 66 published in *Granma* on April 5, 1980. In addition to the primary purposes of the FFM, the government had plans to utilize them to:

> a) divert consumer complaints about the poor quantity and quality of produce and fruits in the regularly operated rationed market;
>
> b) create incentives, using the free pricing system, to stimulate production and better utilization of private farms and CPAs that produced specialized crops. This made it acceptable that prices would remain high for a while, close to those of the parallel

market and/or the black market for some goods. Increases in production from state farms and CPAs would stimulate the FFM and eventually eliminate the black market;

c) reduce consumer liquidity by forcing the consumers to pay higher prices; and

d) eliminate the apparent thefts of products from government organizations and enterprises, etc. (Figueroa and García, p.45-46).

Some of the principal dispositions and regulations were:

1. Authorized sellers in the FFM were: private farmers (CCS's-Credit and Service Cooperatives and Parcel Owners), areas of state farms set aside for self-consumption, and CPAs.
2. Participants were authorized to sell the portion of production not requisitioned by the state *acopio*.
3. Products which the state was not interested in acquiring through *acopio* could be sold at the market.
4. Sales would be made directly to the population at specified market locations.
5. Prices would be determined by supply and demand without government interference.
6. Intermediaries were strictly prohibited from participating in the market place.
7. Farmers in geographically disadvantaged areas were not required to meet their quota to *acopio*, and thus their entire production could be sold at the FFM.
8. A tax on gross income was imposed on independent farmers, parcel owners, and others.
9. Sales of produce were restricted to local nearby markets. Written permission was required to sell anywhere else in the country and direct sales to households and to private individuals at the farm were prohibited.
10. The only products excluded from the FFM were beef, tobacco, coffee and cocoa. (The state kept control over these commodities because their exports provided substantial convertible currency.)
11. The local Peoples Power authorities were in charge of market stall rentals and sales of packaging materials. Tax collection was supervised and under the control of the State Finance Committee (*Comité Estatal de Finanzas*).

An important consideration in the regulation of the FFM was the preference granted to CPAs, which were permitted to sell their output. Furthermore, special consideration was granted in obtaining prime location, logistical support and tax exemptions. CPAs were authorized to contract with the state transportation system to ship goods to market, thus receiving the benefit of low state shipping rates. This was a considerable advantage over private farmers.

Many government agencies intervened directly in the regulation, operation, and supervision of the FFM and at times created difficulties in their regular operations. The FFM began to operate in April 1980 and the initial reaction was very favorable. The consumer finally had the possibility of acquiring unlimited produce and other high quality agricultural products. The press gave positive accounts of the FFM.

After one year of operations, problems arose concerning high prices, dishonesty of some stall operators and other difficulties. Consumers reacted negatively to price fluctuations, price differentials due to location and transportation expenses, and questioned the origin of the merchandise. Despite these problems, consumers began to depend on the FFM for certain products. While prices were high, there was plenty of money in circulation and the government's newly-enacted wage policies injected more liquidity. Further incentives to agricultural producers were introduced in 1981, when agricultural prices were increased by an average factor of 1.6 to 1.7 (Utting, p. 130).

However, the government began to perceive that it was not receiving the expected benefits of the FFM. In effect, the government had lost control of the FFM —they had developed their own set of rules and the farmers were learning to operate at the fringes of socialist legality.

The national leadership and that of ANAP, who earlier praised the FFM, began to criticize its *modus operandi* (Ramírez, p. 15). Although during his initial speech announcing the creation of the FFM, Fidel Castro led consumers to believe that prices would be high for a while, but soon after would be reasonable, this never occurred. Both groups observed that prices were not decreasing, some consumers were complaining of limited access, black market operations had continued and farmers receiving higher income were competing for scarce government resources by following unorthodox business practices. Worse still, some farmers were getting rich, as were the intermediaries. The necessary middle-men, the "evil-like" *merolicos*, who made market operations possible, were a new class of entrepreneurs in a socialist country. One description went as follows:

> One semi-retired small farmer, who had sold off most of his land to the government in the late 1960's, proudly showed us the onions he had stored up for the farmers' market. While government farms produced only one variety, he could plant several varieties and staggered portions of the harvest as well as set aside some varieties that stored well. After the May 1981 harvest, government produce stores sold onions for 8 to 18 cents a pound. By October, when the government had no onions to sell, one could find them easily in the farmers' markets in Habana for 2.40-3.00 pesos a pound (Benjamin, et al. p. 62-63).

The government reacted strongly against intermediaries —*merolicos* and other market participants— by setting up several police intelligence operations which, according to press accounts, identified "criminal and felonious activities, wrongdoing and illegalities" (Barredo Medina, p. 6). The police operations discouraged many farmers temporarily from further participation in the market.

Opponents of the concept of FFM, including the leadership, warned against the potential development of an intermediary class and took to criticizing farmers who had gotten rich. This group was also very concerned about the theft of government property from state farms and cooperatives and the negative impact that the FFM were having on collectivization. On two occasions Fidel Castro declared his opposition to the free FFM. In May 1982, he stated: "But what happened? The go-betweens took over the markets and inflated the prices. Some of them would have been brilliant on the New York Stock Exchange." And, "people do not want to be robbed." But the thought of some people getting rich bothered him greatly. "You know there are millionaire farmers earning 10 times as much as an outstanding medical specialist" (*New York Times*, June 14, 1982, p. D1-D2). The government sought a mid-course review, devising a mechanism to control prices and profits without discouraging production (*Granma*, May 17, 1982, pp. 4-5). Private farmers and artisans reacted by not bringing their goods to market.

VIII. Mid-Course Review

Soon after the government concluded that the FFM had become troublesome, the press no longer gave the experiment positive reviews. An article by Barredo Medina appearing in *Granma* on May 27, 1982, criticized *acopio* officials for violations of contracts. In the article, he stated that it was evident that farmers and operators were finding "friends to do business with." The government was now on a collision course with the intermediaries, the farmers, the cooperatives, *acopio* personnel and others. In 1983, the government promulgated a new set of regulations affecting the FFM (Burnhill, p. 23). Among those implemented were:

a. Limit the access to the FFM to ANAP members only and to those who owned and tilled the land for their personal benefit. This excluded cooperatives from FFM.

b. Increase the sales tax from 3.0 percent to 20.0 percent, on a graduated scale.

c. Require the show of documentary proof that *acopio* quota had been met by the farmer.

The government's objective was to continue offering a variety of produce to the consumer through the FFM while protecting the goals of its collectivization program and limiting the access of intermediaries or middlemen to the market. Henceforth, cooperative production surpluses would be channeled through the government-operated parallel markets. The state was, therefore, challenging the FFM with the parallel market. Goods sold in the parallel market would command higher prices than in the rationed market, but profits generated would go to the state's coffers. As a result of the new regulations and police monitoring, the volume of sales in the FFM fell from 140 millon pesos in 1981 to 81 million pesos in 1984. A further drop occurred in 1985 when sales of 70 million pesos were recorded (Burnhill, p. 38).

New government regulations essentially curtailed access to some producers and discouraged consumers from using the markets for a while, but could not end major consumer complaints. Production continued to move from farmers' markets via intermediaries into the black market where prices were substantially higher. Farmers and operators, including *merolicos*, were getting richer and the newly-developed class of entrepreneurs was acquiring wealth and assets. Collectivization, a major goal of the government and of the ANAP leadership, was stagnant. This was essentially the result of the higher incomes realized by the private farmers and operators who stayed on their land. The government underestimated the power of the FFM to harm the state cooperative system.

IX. End of the Free Farmers Markets

Between 1983 and 1986, the FFM operated under a set of constraints and rules that reduced their scope and access for some of the previous participants (CPAs). However, there were still opportunities for participants and consumers. Consumers were reaping the benefits of new sources of products to supplement their basic food needs. The expanded parallel market "produced steady increases in private sector sales to the state, while private non-cane agricultural sales to the state grew only by 2.9 percent annually between 1975-80. Over the next five years, private sector sales averaged an annual increase of 4.9 percent" (Deere and Meurs, p. 25). Cooperatives were also pulling their weight in terms of marketable surpluses, "contributing 46 percent of private sector sales" despite opposition by the government (*Revista ANAP*, May 1986, pp. 6-7).

Complaints were raised by many ordinary consumers because their access to the FFM was becoming limited; many products were carrying very high prices in some locations, while in others they carried lower prices; lines were longer in the lower-priced locations. Produce prices in the parallel market were even higher than those in rationed markets and, on occasion, even in the black market. This resulted from state price rigidities and regulations that did not allow for prices to fluctuate freely in markets other than the FFM. After several rounds of discussions, in a very terse speech during the Second Meeting of the Agricultural Production Cooperatives, held in May 1986, Fidel Castro announced the end of the FFM experiment.

Several reasons were provided by Castro and others for the closing of the FFM (Figueroa and García, p. 55-60). Some were related to problems that had already been discussed, while others reflected new concerns. Among the problems raised by Castro during his speech were:

1. high income by farmers, middlemen (*merolicos*) and others participating in the market who were labeled as profiteers.

2. high prices because of limited production by the state system and the inability to compete with private farmers.

3. continuation of the black market, fueled by excessive liquidity.

4. difficulties in the *acopio* system, whose services were deficient and could not be improved due to transportation difficulties and poor administration.

5. purchase of assets by the private farmers and wealth effects felt throughout the entire economy as indicated by Fidel Castro during the mid-course review and as observed by the increasing level of savings.

6. state fear of losing control of the economy. If not checked, economic power of the farmers translated into potential political power.

7. fear of losing ground on collectivization efforts.

8. land and resources were sometimes diverted away from sugar and into productions of fruits, vegetables, and tubers where farmers could make a profit.

9. farmers had contracted labor to increase and diversify production within the plots, including private sharecropping.

Farmers became overnight entrepreneurs and the wealth effects began to be felt in other sectors of the economy. In a *Granma* article on 19 May 1986, it was reported that "the estimated income derived by the farmers from the FFM was in the order of 100 million pesos in profits while the state collected approximately one million pesos in tax revenues." Housing was attractive to the wealthy farmers as a way to spend their income. Again, according to *Granma*, in Cabaiguán a landlord reportedly built a house worth over 25,000 pesos (Deere and Meurs, p. 27).

Several positive aspects of the FFM were mentioned by other sources despite the virulent attack by the leadership. Among the positive results of the FFM that were mentioned were:

a.   a substantial increase in agricultural production and *acopio* operations due to the new material incentives provided to the private farmers.

b.   a better and more comprehensive use of the land in small parcels.

c.   an increase in the quantity and quality of the supply of fruits, vegetables, and tubers, especially supplies destined for the big cities and for the surrounding areas.

d.   a considerable increase in income of farmers and small parcel operators (Figueroa and García, p. 59).

In reality, very little of the market experience and outcome could have been positive for the leadership. Most of the benefits were received by consumers and by farmers. The latter received their due. They were finally paid for their production efforts and were able to reap the benefits of having higher incomes.

X.   State Distribution Difficulties After the End of the FFM

After the demise of the FFM, the government accepted that food distribution problems were more serious than originally suspected. *Acopio* operations were notorious for their failure to pick up produce from the farmer and its subsequent waste. The successor system, *Frutas Selectas,* and its marketing outlets, *Placitas,* were only an extension of parallel market operations. Experience with the *acopio* substitute revealed that it did not perform any better. According to a *Radio Rebelde* broadcast on October 23, 1989:

> Strolling through the agro-markets of the capital, there is ample evidence that there are not enough supplies of products in the units of *Frutas Selectas*. Why is it that fruits, vegetables and tubers do not arrive more regularly at this market, which functions similarly to the parallel market?

The FFM and the transportation and distribution difficulties exhibited by the performance of *acopio and Frutas Selectas* amply justified the role of the intermediary. The aftermath of the FFM demonstrated that the state was not interested in changing its predominant role in the economic endeavors of the country (*Cuba Annual Report*, 1987, p. 380-383).

XI.   An Encore for the FFM

Speculation centered around the Fourth Congress of the Cuban Communist Party held in October 1991, that the FFM would be reinstated. In fact, during the Congress, Manuel Alvarez, a delegate from Pinar del Rio Province, proposed the idea as a possible solution to "an uncontrollable black market" (Castro on Farmers' Markets, p. 45). This proposal prompted very negative responses by several delegates. For example, one delegate said: "I am terribly ashamed to be talking about this again, since we, as farmers, told Fidel that the free farmers market will never return." Fidel Castro reacted to the proposal by explaining at length why the free farmers market must no be reinstated. His remarks recognized the failure of *acopio* and the need to improve the situation. He said, "the free farmers market was an error that affected the cooperative movement and state production" (Radical Econ. Changes, p. 46). He also stated that

However, I feel that the way we are working is correct for solving the supply problems.

Another way would complicate things a great deal. What we are doing would become disorganized. It would sow corruption and cause a loss of morale. I am completely convinced of that. If things get worse, what would happen? Imagine if part of the population had to move to rural areas. Just imagine! (Castro on Farmers' Markets, pp. 45-46).

XII. Future of the FFM

It very difficult to predict the end of the present course of Cuba. The future will depend greatly on when and how the changes will occur and if these will result in destruction of assets and especially those related to agricultural activities. One of the lessons from the FFM experience was that given the price incentives of a free market, production could respond in a short period of time, usually the time between planting and harvesting (a crop cycle).

While the FFM do not provide a permanent solution to the problems of the agricultural sector, they will be an excellent source of fruits, vegetables, and tubers and could be expanded to include some meat products, pork, and poultry. A reasonable beginning will be to combine market forces with access to agricultural inputs, supplies, credit and machineries for all producers during the transition period to a market economy. Further support should be in the form of transportation, logistics, and storage facilities from government sources. Allocation of resources is a function of the markets and not of the government. Producers know best when to expand or reduce operations.

A future Cuban government could stimulate the expansion of agricultural production quickly during the transition to a market economy if the government and agricultural authorities begin without delay convert the state-controlled agriculture into a private economic activity. The following ideas and suggestions could facilitate the conversion process:

a. Convert the CPAs into market-oriented businesses (agribusiness) in which the cooperative system retains the property of the land but would join production and operate as a modern agricultural enterprise.

b. Facilitate the procurement of all agricultural inputs and credit to producers.

c. Ascertain that during the initial period, farmers have access to the market. Transportation, logistics and supplies, if available, should be facilitated to farmers at cost by the state. A poor distribution and marketing system contributes only to higher prices and inadequate resource allocation.

d. Disseminate price information to avoid imperfections and lack of transparency in the FFM. This objective could be achieved through clearly displayed posted prices which could serve as references. Information prices could be disseminated through farmers and consumers organizations and the media.

e. Educational support to farmers in agricultural practices and marketing techniques. Both areas will be essential in developing a reliable domestic source of food. This could be facilitated by MINAGRI with the support of international agencies, both private and public.

f. MINAGRI and monetary authorities, from the beginning, should formulate sound and clear lending policies, to have adequate financial resources and easy access to financial facilities without discrimination of any components of the agricultural sector. Financial assistance should be based on proven qualifications and repayment ability with minimal red tape.

g.   Provide investment incentives for agricultural and other related sectors.

h.   Obtain economic and technical assistance from by international agencies. Perhaps some contributing agencies such as USDA, UNDP, FAO and IICA could assist in agricultural sector expansion and in reordering of priorities.

i.   Establish an effective national **tropical agriculture extension program**. This should be a priority program of MINAGRI in cooperation with international agencies and universities throughout the world.

The goal during the transition period with regard to agriculture should be to smooth out difficulties created by production shortages which foster scarcity prices. As production increases and availability of products improves, excess liquidity will diminish and prices will tend toward equilibrium. Reaching an optimal solution for the future of Cuba's agricultural development will be complex and will require a combination of sound agricultural policies, with appropriate fiscal and monetary ones. In the longer term, agricultural expansion will depend on a legal framework that recognizes and protects private property. The government role will be vital but it should result in minimal interference in the production process and establish the basis for the creation of modern agribusinesses.

XIII. Conclusions

For the years that the FFM operated, they achieved the expected results with respect to consumer expectations. Some of the government's goals were also attained: consumers were able to purchase a better quality and a larger mix of vegetables and tubers. Scarcity prices resulted from insufficient production and higher demand.

The creation of the FFM was a political decision that took a number of years to implement (Rosenberg, p. 53 and 59). It appears that a compromise was made to promote collectivization of the private sector (create the CPAs) at the same time that the FFM were authorized to operate. The benefits gained by private farmers began to erode the collectivization drive because the profit motive was very strong. If left unchecked, the results could have been the creation of a powerful class of entrepreneurs competing with the cooperative system.

Intermediaries or *merolicos* provided an important link between producers and consumers through the FFM. These entrepreneurs contributed to the functioning of these markets. *Acopio* and its successor, *Frutas Selectas*, failed to operate an efficient distribution system that would meet the consumer's need. Rather than blame the farmer for his lack of market knowledge and marketing skills, the government could have done better by providing him with transportation equipment and facilitating his access to commercial centers.

The resource allocation function of the market could not occur since the state did not want to relinquish its prerogatives. The government prohibited the farmers from allocating production inputs and output independently. That is, the farmer could not optimize his production function with respect to cost, as well as maximize his income with respect to prices. The government sought to continue its control over the economy.

Planned distribution totally conflicted with the goal of the FFM. Socialist planners do not receive the benefits of price signals to adjust inputs or output. The centralized economic model is only optimized with respect to quantity because prices are rigid and subsidies distort the outcome. In the case of the FFM, the political premises and plans of the leadership were totally frustrated. If anything, the FFM created serious conflicts within the leadership. The attempt to use market tools to solve problems of self-generated distortions by the socialist economic model applied in Cuba was a failure. Ultimately, the leadership decided to finish the FFM due to its political control being challenged from within.

Attempts to reinstate the FFM during the Fourth Party Congress in 1991 resulted in a resounding veto by the leadership, who considered the idea quasi-counterrevolutionary. The FFM became a *de-facto* symbol among the population of the free enterprise system.

References

Acosta, José. "La revolución agraria en Cuba y el desarrollo económico." *Economía y Desarrollo*, No. 17, May-June 1973, pp. 137-163.

Aguero Gómez, Frank. "Minister Discusses Crackdown on Crime in Commerce." Interview with Minister of Domestic Trade, Manuel Vila Sosa, *Verde Olivo*, 1 April 1982, pp. 8-11.

Alonso, José F. "Se elimina el Mercado Libre Campesino en Cuba; posibles causas y efectos." Unpublished background paper, USIA, V.O.A., Office of Research, Economics, 24 May 1986. pp. 1-4.

Barredo Medina, Lázaro. "Matilda va, Matilda viene, pero al mercachifle lo detienen." *Granma*, 21 April 1982, p. 3.

Benjamin, Medea, Collins, Joseph and Scott, Michael. *NO FREE LUNCH: Food & Revolution in Cuba Today*. San Francisco, CA: Institute for Food and Development Policy, 1984.

Burnhill, Lauren A. "The Private Sector in Cuban Agriculture 1959-1985." Occasional Paper No. 8, Washington, D.C.: Central American and Caribbean Program, School of Advanced International Studies, 1985.

Castro Ruz, Fidel. "En el II Encuentro Nacional de Cooperativas de Producción Agropecuaria." *Cuba Socialista*, No. 23, Sep-Oct 86, pp. 49-76. Conclusiones de Fidel Castro Ruz en el II Encuentro, La Habana, 18 May 1986, *Granma*, 20 May 1986.

Castro Ruz, Fidel. Texto del Discurso del Comandante en Jefe Fidel Castro Ruz, en la clausura del VIII Congreso Campesino. Palacio de las Convenciones, La Habana, Cuba, May 17, 1992.

Comité Estatal de Estadísticas. *Anuario Estadístico de Cuba*. Various Issues, 1978-1989.

Comité Estatal de Estadísticas. "Balances de ingresos y egresos monetarios de la población." La

Habana: Dirección de Balances, Enero-Junio 1989 and Enero-Marzo 1989.

Deere, Carmen Diana and Meurs Mieke. "Markets, Markets Everywhere? Understanding the Cuban Anomaly," Working Paper Series, Working Paper No. 1990-6, Department of Economics, University of Massachussets, Amherst, MA 01003.

Deere, Carmen Diana, Meurs, Mieke and Pérez, Niurka. "Toward a Periodization of the Cuban Collectivization Process: Changing Incentives and Peasant Response." Paper prepared for the panel on "Politics in Contemporary Cuba," XVI International Congress, Latin American Studies Association, Washington, D.C. 4-8 April 1991.

Figueroa, Víctor and García, Luis A. "Apuntes sobre la comercialización agrícola no estatal." *Economía y Desarrollo*, No. 83, 1984, pp. 34-61.

Forster, Nancy. "Cuban Agricultural Productivity: A Comparison of State and Private Farm Sector," *Cuban Studies* 11:2/12:1, July 1981-January 1982.

Ghai, D, Kay, C and Peek, P. *Labour and Development in Rural Cuba*. London: The Macmillan Press for the International Labour Organisation, 1988.

Gómez, Orlando. "Positiva respuesta del campesinado habanero para abastecer a los mercados agrícolas estatales." *Granma*, 28 May 1986, p.3.

Hernández, Miguel. "Sustituidos ya los mercados libres campesinos." *Granma*, 21 May 1986, p.5.

Lezcano, Fernando. "El primer fin de semana." *Granma*, 26 May 1986, p.3.

Martínez Fagundo, Carlos. "Presencia e influencia de los factores de desiquilibrio en las finanzas internas en Cuba." *Economía y Desarrollo*, No.5, 1989, pp.166-190.

Mesa-Lago, Carmelo. *The Economy of Socialist Cuba: A Two-Decade Appraisal*. Albuquerque: University of New Mexico Press, 1981.

Pagés, Raisa. "Mejorar la organización y la gestion de venta." *Granma*, 30 May 1986, p. 6.

Pérez, Humberto. "Lo que el pueblo debe saber sobre el mercado paralelo." *Trabajadores*, 17 February 1979, p. 2.

Ramírez Cruz, José. El sector cooperativa en la agricultura cubana. *Cuba Socialista*, No.11, Junio-Agosto 1984, pp. 1-24.

Riding, Alan. "Effects of Incentives Are Troubling Cuba." *The New York Times*, 14 June 1982, pp. D1-D2.

Rodríguez, Raimundo. Farm Taxes Take Effect in July. *ANAP*, June 1982, p. 27 as found in FBIS, *Latin American Report*, June 1983, pp. 68-69.

Rojas, Bienvenido. "Drive Against Crime." *Havana Domestic Service*, 22 March 1982 as found in FBIS, *Latin American Report*, No. 2474, JPRS 80466, 1 April 1982, pp. 15-16.

Romero, Perfecto. "EL MERCADO LIBRE CAMPESINO." *Verde Olivo*, No. 22, 1980.

Rosenberg, Jonathan. "CUBA'S FREE MARKET EXPERIMENT: Los Mercados Libres Campesinos, 1980-1986." *Latin American Research Review*, 1992 (forthcoming).

United States Information Agency, Voice of America, Radio Martí Program, Office of Research & Policy. *Cuba Annual Report: 1986*. New Brunswick: Transactions Publishers, 1986.

United States Information Agency, Voice of America, Radio Martí Program, Office of Research & Policy. *Cuba Annual Report: 1987*. New Brunswick: Transactions Publishers, 1987.

Utting, Peter. *Economic Reform and Third-World Socialism A Political Economy of Food Policy in Post-Revolutionary Societies*. Houndmills, Basingstokem, Hampshire RG21 2XS and London: The Macmillan Press Ltd., 1992, pp. 117-305.

Unsigned articles and other sources

_____. "Illegalities Discovered in Free Farmers' Market." *Granma*, 17 March 1982, pp. 2-6.

_____. "PRIVATE PROPERTY RIGHTS IN CUBA (1992) : FARMLAND." La Sociedad Económica, Bulletin No.6, P.O. Box 927, London SW1P 2ND, UK, 8 April 1992, pp. 1-5.

_____. "REPORTAGE ON ENDING PROBLEMS IN FARMERS MARKETS." *Havana Domestic Service*, 20 March, 1982 in FBIS *Latin American Report*, No. 2474, JPRS 80466, 1 April 1982, pp. 15-16.

Decreto-Ley No. 66 del Comité Ejecutivo del Consejo de Ministros. "Reglamento del Mercado Libre Campesino." *Granma*, 5 Abril 1980, p. 5.

Decree Regulating Farmers Free Markets. [Council of Ministers Decree 106 issued 30 September 1982], *Gaceta Oficial*, No.48, 22 October 1982, pp. 223-226, in JPRS, *Latin American Report*, No. 2670, 26 April 1983, pp. 66-71.

"Establecido el mercado libre campesino." *Legalidad Socialista*. Editado por la Fiscalía General de la República de Cuba, La Habana, Cuba, Boletín No. 8, 1990. pp. 1-4.

"El principio del fin de la mala yerba." *Bohemia*, Año 78, No. 21, 23 May 1986. pp. 4-9. Comentarios y entrevistas sobre la II Reunión Nacional de Cooperativas de Producción Agropecuaria.

"Resultados de Terminar el MLC." *Bohemia*, Año 78, No. 24, 13 June 1986. p. 14.

"Castro Raps Corruption at Cooperatives Meeting." *EFE*, in Spanish, 19 May 1986, in FBIS, *Latin American Report*, Annex, 19 May 1986, pp. 2-3.

"Castro on Farmers' Market." *Habana Tele Rebelde and Cuba Vision Networks,* 14 October 1991, as in FBIS-LAT-91-199-S, 15 October 1991, pp. 45-46.

"Informe del Comité Central del Partido Comunista de Cuba al Primer Congreso." Documentos y Discursos: Habana: Editorial Ciencias Sociales, 1978.

"Radical Economic Changes Discussed." *Havana Tele Rebelde Network,* 14 October 1991, as in FBIS-LAT-91-199-S, 15 October 1991, p. 46.

THE CUBAN SECOND ECONOMY: METHODOLOGICAL AND PRACTICAL ISSUES RELATED TO QUANTIFICATION

Jorge F. Pérez-López

The "second economy" in Cuba comprises the set of activities outside of the centrally-planned economy (the "first economy") on which Cuban citizens rely to make ends meet and to *resolver* their day-to-day economic needs. Some of these activities (e.g., stealing goods from a government workplace and selling them) may be illegal and transgressors are subject to severe punishment if caught, while others (e.g., the direct sale of agricultural products by small farmers to consumers, as occurred in the late 1970s and early 1980s) are permitted forms of activity for private gain that nevertheless are discouraged by the government.

For obvious reasons, studying Cuba's second economy is a challenging task. Most economic agents involved in the second economy attempt to keep their activities hidden from the authorities lest they be punished by the government for committing economic crimes. Even where they are not illegal, there is very little systematic information on these activities, since they are not the government's preferred form of operation and participation is openly discouraged.

Nevertheless, the study of the Cuban second economy is important because of the generalized perception that it is large and dynamic. In some sense, the second economy complements the official, centrally-planned economy and corrects some of its failures. Moreover, the second economy is the only segment of the economy that responds to market signals and that seems to work. It is useful, then, to have some estimates, or at least some notions, of the dimension of the Cuban second economy either in absolute terms or relative to the official economy.

This paper is a first attempt at exploring the dimension of Cuba's second economy. It concentrates on conceptual and practical estimation problems rather than on making actual estimates. The first part defines the second economy and discusses a number of characteristics of centrally planned economies that encourage second economy behavior. The second part surveys methods that have been used to estimate the magnitude of second economy-like activities in market and non-market countries. The third part examines a number of quantitative indicators associated with second economy activity in Cuba.

1.   The Second Economy

Entrepreneurial economic activities outside of the scope of public regulation have been found to be present in all societies, albeit in different forms and to different degrees, regardless of level of development or form of economic organization. The variety and complexity of these phenomena is evident from the many names that have been used to describe them: "subterranean," "submerged," "parallel," "hidden," "occult," "informal," "unofficial," "underground," "irregular," "black," "unobserved," "unmeasured," "unrecorded," "shadow," "illegal," "criminal," "second," "clandestine."[1] Centrally planned economies (CPEs), characterized by direct public ownership of resources and highly regimented relationships among economic actors, are fertile ground for entrepreneurial activities outside of the public regulatory framework.

---

[1]Bruno Dallago, *The Irregular Economy* (Aldershot, England: Dartmouth Publishing Company, 1990), p. xv.

The Second Economy: Control v. Legality

In a seminal article, Grossman examined economic activities in the Soviet Union "where production and exchange often take place for direct private gain and just as often violate state law in some non-trivial respect."[2] He referred to this set of economic activities as constituting a "second economy." More formally, he defined the second economy (of the Soviet Union) as comprising all production and exchange activity that fulfills at least **one** of the following tests:

(a)   being directly for private gain; or

(b)   being in some significant respect in contravention of existing laws.

As is discussed below, this concept is particularly fitting for analyzing activities outside of the scope of public regulation in CPEs, including Cuba.

Grossman's definition of the second economy has been criticized (e.g., by Holzman[3]) as being too expansive because it lumps together private economic activities that are legal (e.g., private farming, repair work) with those that are illegal. Grossman[4] justifies the inclusion of legal activities for private gain as part of the second economy on the grounds that the latter is intended to capture all forms of deviations from the model of a socialist command economy. Along these lines, Feldebrugge[5] has defined the second economy of the Soviet Union as "those economic activities which for some reason escape control by the state," emphasizing that the cardinal criterion in the definition is "control" rather than "legality."

Diagram 1 illustrates the relationship between state control and legality of activities as it relates to the definition of the second economy. The vertical axis ranks activities with regard to whether they are under public or private control and therefore whether the income they produce is for public or private gain. The horizontal axis does the same with regard to whether the activities are legal or illegal. The lower left quadrant represents the ideal situation for a socialist, centrally planned economy: the gain from all activities accrues to the public and all activities fall within the legal framework. Movement out of that quadrant in any direction denotes motion into the second economy, as defined by Grossman; the farther into the other quadrants, the clearer it is that the activity belongs to the second economy.

Two important caveats regarding Diagram 1 are in order: 1) that three out of the four quadrants correspond to the second economy does not imply that the second economy is three times the size of the first economy; and 2) the diagram describes a continuum of activity in all directions; the exact position of the quadrants is not well defined. Moreover, the boundaries of the quadrants are not static, since they are a function of institutional considerations, especially the legal framework, which changes over time. For example, Galasi and Kertesi[6] have noted that in the 1970s and 1980s,

---

[2]Gregory Grossman, "The 'Second Economy' of the USSR," *Problems of Communism* 26 (September-October 1977), p. 25.

[3]Franklyn Holzman, "The Second Economy in CMEA: A Terminological Note," *The ACES Bulletin* 23 (Spring 1981), pp. 111-113.

[4]Gregory Grossman, "Comment on 'The Second Economy in CMEA: A Terminological Note' by Franklyn Holzman," *The ACES Bulletin* 24 (Spring 1982), p. 111.

[5]F.J. M. Feldebrugge, "Government and the Shadow Economy in the Soviet Union," *Soviet Studies* 36 (October 1984), p. 529.

[6]P. Galasi and G. Kertesi, "Second Economy, Competition, Inflation," *Acta Oeconomica* 35 (1985), pp. 269-293.

Diagram 1

**Interactions between First and Second Economies:
Control v. Legality**

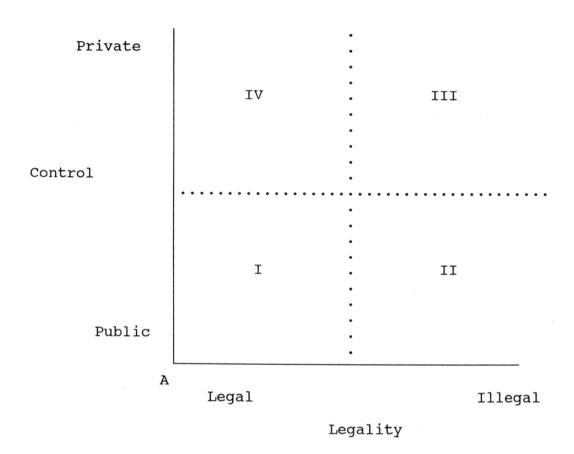

Hungary enlarged the legal framework of the second economy, thereby increasing significantly the number of economic activities that could be performed legally.

Systemic Reasons for the Second Economy

Some characteristics of CPEs account for the pervasiveness and dynamism of their second economies. They include: 1) government ownership of the means of production; 2) tautness and rigidity of central plans; and 3) suppressed inflation.[7] These characteristics are discussed very briefly below; selected examples of second economy behavior associated with each, drawn from the extensive literature on the second economy in the Soviet Union and Eastern Europe, are also presented.

---

[7]Peter Wiles, "What We Still Don't Know About the Soviet Economy," in NATO Economics Directorate, *The CMEA Five-Year Plans (1981-1985) in a New Perspective* (Brussels, 1982).

a)   **State Ownership**

In the idealized socialist CPE, the totality of productive facilities would be under state ownership. In practice, the degree of state ownership across CPEs has varied, but a common feature of each has been state control over the preponderance of productive facilities, with the exception of agriculture.

Public ownership of productive facilities results in lack of identifiable ownership and widespread misuse and theft of state resources. The following assessment of the situation in the Soviet Union is probably applicable to other CPEs as well: "Most reliable sources agree that theft of socialist (state) property is as widespread as state property itself."[8] Individuals in these societies have tended to treat state property as their own, with very little stigma attached to diversion of resources for their own use (i.e., to theft):

> Doubtless, the most common economic crime in the USSR is stealing from the state, under which we subsume stealing from all official organizations, including collective farms. All sources agree that it is practiced by virtually everyone, takes all possible forms, and varies in scale from the trivial to the regal. All also agree that the public takes it for granted, attaches almost no opprobrium to it--and on the contrary, disapproves of those who do not engage in it--and sharply distinguishes between stealing from the state and stealing from private individuals. The latter is generally condemned. With some liberty, one might perhaps assert that the right to steal on the job, within certain conventional limits, is an implicit but integral part of the conditions of employment in the Soviet Union.[9]

The high degree of state ownership also means that relatively little private activity has been allowed. CPEs have myriad state regulations waiting to be broken by enterprising individuals. In these societies "an ordinary economic impulse quickly shades over into a criminal act."[10] Thus, the combination of the sheer size of the public sector, and the web of regulations that circumscribe private activity, create opportunities for illegal behavior and for the use of state property for private gain. Examples abound:

- moonlighting workers repair dwellings and appliances of private citizens, often using tools and materials stolen from the official job or purchased in the black market.[11]

- a "system of relations," such as barter, tips, and bribes, the utilization of privileges, and speculation, related to the distribution of a number of consumer goods and services.[12]

- practicing an illegal trade or profession (e.g., private practice of physicians, dentists,

[8]F.J.M. Feldebrugge, "The Soviet Second Economy in a Political and Legal Perspective," in Edgar L. Feige, editor, *The Underground Economies* (Cambridge: Cambridge University Press, 1989), p. 318.

[9]Grossman, "The 'Second Economy,'" *op. cit.*, p. 29.

[10]Gregory Grossman, "Notes on the Illegal Private Economy and Corruption," in Joint Economic Committee, *Soviet Economy in a Time of Change* (Washington: U.S. Government Printing Office, 1979), p. 844.

[11]Grossman, "Notes on the Illegal Private Economy," op. cit., p. 837.

[12]Gunther Mans, "The Shadow Economy in the GDR," *Eastern European Economics* 29 (Spring 1991), p. 76.

dental technicians, teachers, and tutors) or producing a good for sale (e.g., *samovar* in the Soviet Union).[13]

Finally, the very personal power in the hands of bureaucratic officials and of agents of the official economy creates the conditions for taking bribes, getting cuts or kickbacks, and extorting graft. Exploitation of the power of an office for personal gain is enhanced by the dictatorial and secretive nature of the regime, and mutual solidarity of members of the political elite.[14]

b)   Tautness and Rigidity of Plans

CPEs tend to rely on taut, or overfull employment, planning. This form of planning is characterized by setting output targets for enterprises which are unrealistic in terms of available resources and possible rates of productivity growth. Simultaneous achievement of price stability (see below) and of the overambitious targets set by taut planning is illusory. The overcommitment of resources results in excess demand and inflationary pressures.

Another feature of central planning, as practiced by CPEs, is its rigidity. The central plan—with quantitative targets for production, delivery times, etc., for every good or service produced by the economy—is extremely complex and there is very little room for adjustment if events do not turn out as anticipated. There is a great deal of pressure on economic units within the state sector to meet, and exceed, production goals. However, inputs and other resources are often not available to do so.

Taut planning and the imperative to meet production goals often lead to informal, second economy arrangements. One such arrangement, apparently quite common in the Soviet Union, is the *tolkach*. *Tolkachi* are hired by firms to "push" for their interests and obtain supplies from other enterprises.[15] Another example, also drawn from the Soviet experience, is networks of supply relationships among enterprises, along the lines of mutual aid associations, where materials urgently needed by one enterprise and in surplus in another are bartered in circumvention of the central plan.[16]

Taut planning also results in excess demand for labor. In CPEs, full employment prevails although there is a great deal of padding of payrolls and underemployment. Salaries tend to be low and so is productivity. The old adage about workers in socialist economies has a great deal of explanatory power: "the Government pretends to pay us and we pretend to be working."[17] Many workers hold second jobs (moonlighting) or perform odd jobs after (or during) work hours. As noted above, this secondary (black) labor market is very important in CPEs, particularly in Hungary and in the Soviet Union with regard to construction and repair services.

---

[13]Grossman, "Notes on the Illegal Private Economy," *op. cit.*, p. 837.

[14]Grossman, "Notes on the Illegal Private Economy," *op. cit.*, p. 845.

[15]See, e.g., Joseph Berliner, "The Informal Organization of the Soviet Firm," *Quarterly Journal of Economics* 66 (August 1952), p. 358, and Abram Bergson, *The Economics of Soviet Planning* (New Haven: Yale University Press, 1964), pp. 152-154).

[16]Alec Nove, *The Soviet Economic System*, Second Edition (London: George Allen and Unwin, 1980), pp. 114-115.

[17]Andrezj Korbonski, "The 'Second Economy' in Poland," *Journal of International Affairs* 35 (Spring/Summer 1981), p. 9.

c)   **Repressed Inflation**

Another characteristic of CPEs is price stability, achieved by maintained prices fixed over extended periods of time. Prices in CPEs tend to be irrational, in the sense that they do not reflect demand and supply. Moreover, they are normally set administratively and bear no relationship to costs. The result is chronic scarcity of certain goods and services for which demand is high coexisting with excess stocks of goods or services that are unattractive or undesirable.

One of the ways in which CPEs have dealt with scarcity of consumer goods and services is through physical rationing schemes. These schemes tend to be quite inefficient and create specific groups of winners and losers.[18] As a logical response to physical rationing, a whole range of informal markets, some of them manifestly illegal, have spawned in CPEs.[19]

2.   Estimating the Dimension of the Second Economy

Traditional methods for measuring economic activity fail in the case of the second economy for three principal reasons: 1) economic agents involved in second economy activities have a strong incentive for remaining anonymous; 2) these agents often hold a job in the first economy which allows them to report some income while hiding the income derived from second-economy activities; and 3) a large portion of second economy activities are conducted in cash and not recorded in the national income and product accounts.

Although there are no systematic statistics on the dimension of the second economy for any nation, there are numerous estimates made by individual researchers and institutions. Comparison of these estimates is very difficult because typically they use different definitions of which activities correspond to the second economy. Moreover, even where differences in definition is not an issue, there is no consensus on the best method for estimating the dimension of underground activities.

Methods Applied to Western Countries[20]

In the 1970s and 1980s, there was a great deal of interest in industrialized countries in the study of a phenomenon referred to in the literature as the "underground" economy. This interest came about primarily because of the perception in Western market economies that a very active unrecorded economy was bypassing fiscal authorities with a consequent loss of substantial government revenue. Analysts have used direct and indirect methods to estimate the magnitude of the underground economy in Western countries.

a)   **Direct Methods**

Direct methods depend on contact with, or observation of, persons possibly involved in the underground economy. They tend to be based on national survey data and yield estimates of the magnitude of the underground economy overall, or of sub-sectors within it, at specific points in time.

---

[18]George Borjas, "The Economics of Non-Price Rationing." Mimeographed, 1986.

[19]Aron Katsenelinboigen, "Coloured Markets in the Soviet Union," *Soviet Studies* 29 (January 1977), pp. 62-85 and Aron Katsenelinboigen and Herbert S. Levine, "Market and Plan; Plan and Market: The Soviet Case," *American Economic Review* 67 (May 1977), pp. 61-70.

[20]This section of the paper relies heavily on Carol S. Carson, "The Underground Economy: An Introduction," *Survey of Current Business* 64:5 (May 1984), pp. 21-37.

Examples of the application of these methods for the United States are the surveys of household purchases from underground vendors conducted by the Survey Research Center at the University of Michigan[21] and income tax evasion studies.[22]

b) Indirect Methods

Indirect measures rely on indicators of underground activity. They tend to be macro in approach and yield both point ant time series estimates. Examples of the application of these methods for the United States include studies that rely on monetary aggregates[23] or on demographic variables.[24]

Estimates of the magnitude of the underground economy in the United States around 1980 obtained from the studies mentioned above ranged from under 2 percent of gross national product (GNP) based on household surveys to over 40 percent of GNP based on monetary aggregates. Even within the family of methods that rely on monetary aggregates, estimates of the size of the U.S. underground economy in 1980 ranged from 6.1 percent to 41.6 percent of GNP, depending on certain key assumptions.[25]

Methods Applied to CPEs[26]

It has been noted above that there are a number of caveats that apply to estimation of the dimension of the second economy in market economies. These also apply, probably to a higher degree, to the second economies of CPEs. An additional consideration is that estimation methods based on money demand are ruled out for CPEs because of the largely passive role of money in these economies.

Most available information on the dimension of the second economy of CPEs consists of very subjective estimates or is of an anecdotal nature.

- For example, a Western journalist who lived in the Soviet Union in the early 1970s estimated that the "unofficial" economy of the Soviet Union "may amount to 20

---

[21]E.g., James D. Smith, "Measuring the Informal Economy," *The Annals of the American Academy of Political and Social Sciences* 493 (September 1987), pp. 83-97.

[22]E.g., Internal Revenue Service, *Income Tax Compliance Research: Gross Tax Gap Estimates and Projections for 1973-1992*, Publication 7285 (Washington, 1988) and Berdj Kenajdian, "The Direct Approach to Measuring the Underground Economy in the United States: IRS Estimates of Unreported Income," in Vito Tanzi, editor, *The Underground Economy in the United States and Abroad* (Lexington: Lexington Books, 1982), pp. 93-101.

[23]E.g., Peter M. Gutmann, "The Subterranean Economy," *Financial Analysts Journal* 33 (November-December 1977), pp. 26-27, 34; Edgar L. Feige, "How Big is the Irregular Economy?," *Challenge* 22 (November-December 1979), pp. 5-13; and Vito Tanzi, "The Underground Economy in the United States: Estimates and Implications," *Banca Nazionale del Lavoro Quarterly Review* 135 (December 1980), pp. 427-453.

[24]E.g., David M. O'Neill, *Growth of the Underground Economy, 1950-81: Some Evidence from the Current Population Survey* (Washington: U.S. Government Printing Office, 1983).

[25]Richard D. Porter and Amanda S. Bayer, "A Monetary Perspective on Underground Activity in the United States," *Federal Reserve Bulletin* 70 (March 1984), p. 178.

[26]This section of the paper relies heavily on Dallago, *The Irregular Economy, op. cit.*, pp. 29-33 and Dallago, "Second and Irregular Economy in Eastern Europe: Its Consequences for Economic Transition," mimeographed (November 1990).

percent or more of the official one."[27]

- Soviet emigres interviewed by Katz in the early 1970s in Europe, Israel, and the United States estimated that the "unofficial" economy in the Soviet Union amounted to one-half of the official economy or more; others said that it amounted to between 10-25 percent.[28]

There are only a handful of studies that have attempted to estimate the size of the second economy of CPEs. Three methods have been used: a) information on criminal activities; b) the macroeconomic disequilibrium method; and c) the "building blocks" or combination method.

a)   Information on Criminal Activities

The press in CPEs often printed stories and letters concerning "anti-social" behavior: corruption, scandals, trials, protests, economic crimes, etc. Drawing on this information, as well as on work by criminologists,[29] official statistics, and other materials, economists have analyzed the characteristics and role of the second economy in CPEs.[30] These studies tend to be sectoral; moreover, because they rely on second-hand information whose publication was authorized by the government, the reliability of the information base is questionable.

b)   Macroeconomic Disequilibrium

Building on work by Brus and Laski,[31] Wisniewski[32] and Colijn[33] developed a method for measuring income earned in the second economy of CPEs arising from the existence of macroeconomic disequilibrium in the first economy. The method relates the second economy to the inability of the first economy of CPEs to supply sufficient goods and services to meet the consumption needs of the population. Unsatisfied demand creates an "inflationary gap," which can be measured as the difference between the flow of personal incomes and the flow of goods and services during a certain time period. The second economy is financed by the inflationary gap and therefore its size can be estimated from the size of the former and certain other parameters.

---

[27]E.g., Robert G. Kaiser, *Russia: The People and the Power* (New York: Pocketbooks Inc., 1976), p. 370. See also Hedrick Smith, *The Russians* (New York: Ballantine Books, 1976).

[28]Zev Katz, "Insights from Emigrés and Sociological Studies on the Soviet Economy," in Joint Economic Committee, *Soviet Economic Prospects for the Seventies* (Washington: U.S. Government Printing Office, 1973), p. 90. The most ambitious effort to obtain information about the second economy from Soviet emigres is a survey developed by Grossman and Treml. For a description of the survey see Gregory Grossman and Vladimir G. Treml, "Measuring Hidden Personal Incomes in the USSR," in Sergio Alessandrini and Bruno Dallago, editor, *The Unofficial Economy* (Aldershot, England: Gower, 1987), pp. 285-296. The results of the survey have appeared in papers published as part of the series *Berkeley-Duke Occasional Papers on the Second Economy in the USSR*.

[29]E.g., F.J.M. Feldebrugge, "The Soviet Second Economy in a Political and Legal Perspective," *op. cit.*

[30]E.g., Grossman, "The Second Economy of the USSR," *op. cit.*; Grossman, "Notes on the Illegal Private Economy and Corruption," *op. cit.*; Grossman, "The 'Shadow Economy' in the Socialist Sector of the USSR," in NATO Economics Directorate, *Soviet Economic Reforms: Implementation Under Way* (Brussels, 1982), pp. 99-115; and Gertrude E. Schroeder and Rush V. Greenslade, "On the Measurement of the Second Economy in the USSR," *The ACES Bulletin* 21 (Spring 1979), pp. 3-21.

[31]Wlodzimierz Brus and Kazimierz Laski, "Repressed Inflation and Second Economy Under Central Planning," in Wulf Gaertner and Alois Wenig, editors, *The Economics of the Shadow Economy* (Berlin: Springer-Verlag, 1985), pp. 377-388.

[32]Marian Wisniewski, "The Economy and Its Shadow," *Eastern European Economics* 24 (Summer 1986), pp. 29-39 and Wisniewski, "The Sources and Dimensions of the Second Economy in Poland," *Oeconomica Polona* 13 (1986), pp. 247-276.

[33]Leendert Colijn, "Some Proposed Methodologies to Quantify the Influence of Macroeconomic Disequilibrium on the Size of the Second Economy in Poland," in Alessandrini and Dallago, editors, *The Unofficial Economy, op. cit.*, pp. 337-345.

c)   **Building Blocks**

This method basically estimates the magnitude of specific components of the second economy using different techniques, or adopts estimates of components of the second economy made by others, and sums them up to arrive at an estimate of the overall magnitude of the second economy. It has the advantage of allowing for the tracing of the behavior of specific components of the second economy but has the disadvantage that it is affected by estimation errors for each of the components. Examples are the work by Dallago on Hungary[34] and by several Soviet researchers and institutions on the Soviet Union.[35]

The table below presents selected estimates of the magnitude of the second economy as a percentage of national income in Eastern European countries and in the Soviet Union in the 1970s and 1980s. The two sets of estimates for Poland rely on the macroeconomic disequilibrium approach, while those for Hungary and the Soviet Union were derived through variations of the building block approach.

Although the estimates are not comparable (e.g., those for Poland refer only to the portion of the second economy associated with unsatisfied consumer demand, while the estimate for the Soviet Union appears to include legal private activities and a range of illegal activities), they suggest that in each case the second economy is sizable, equivalent to more than one-tenth of first-economy national income. In the case of the Soviet Union, the second economy was largest, representing one-fifth to one-quarter of national income.

3.   **Estimating the Dimension of Cuba's Second Economy**

That Cuba's second economy has been severely understudied is not surprising considering the difficulties and challenges posed by study of the island's **first** economy: availability, timeliness, and reliability of information, ability to do field work, access to policymakers, etc.[36] To my knowledge, there is only one published paper that has examined specifically Cuba's second economy and has begun to focus attention on this complex phenomenon.[37]

There is, however, as is the case with other CPEs, a body of information that can be used to glean information about the island's second economy. Although this information does not permit estimates of the size of Cuba's second economy *per se*, it illustrates the pervasiveness of the second economy and allows some inferences regarding its dimension.

---

[34]Bruno Dallago, "The Non-Socialized Sector in Hungary: An Attempt at Estimation of Its Importance," *Yearbook of East-European Economics* 13 (1989), pp. 67-92.

[35]Particularly notable is the work by Tatyana Koryagina and others at the Economic Institute at the USSR Planning Committee (Gosplan). An excellent survey of the subject matter is Valeriy M. Rutzgaizer, "The Shadow Economy in the USSR," *Berkeley-Duke Occasional Papers on the Second Economy in the USSR* 34 (February 1992).

[36]On some of these issues see, e.g., Jorge F. Pérez-López, "Bringing the Cuban Economy into Focus: Conceptual and Empirical Challenges," *Latin American Research Review* 26 (1991): 7-53.

[37]Raymond J. Michalowski and Marjory S. Zatz, "The Cuban Second Economy in Perspective," in Maria Los, editor, *The Second Economy in Marxist States* (London: Macmillan, 1990), pp. 101-121.

Estimates of the Second Economy in CPEs
(percent of national income)

	Poland(a)	Poland(b)	Hungary	Soviet Union
1970	3.8			
1978		10.5		
1979		11.0		
1980	7.1	10.5		
1981	10.9	18.0		
1982		15.0		
1983	9.6	12.5		
1984		10.5		
1986			14.8	20-26

Source: Adapted from Dallago, *The Irregular Economy*, op. cit., p. 30.

Private Economic Activities

The state's degree of control over productive resources is probably higher in Cuba than in any other CPE, with the possible exception of North Korea. Agriculture is the only sector of the Cuban economy where private economic activity has a role of any significance, and even here it is very small (about 8 percent in 1988[38]) compared with the larger private agricultural sectors in Poland, Hungary, and the Soviet Union.

Table 1 presents official Cuban statistics on overall agricultural output and also on output produced by the state and non-state sectors (including production cooperatives). Thus, private sector production represented about one-fifth of total agricultural output over the 1970s and 1980s. Interestingly, however, the private sector's share of agricultural output is much higher (more than twice as high) than the share of resources in the hands of the private sector, suggesting that private agriculture has higher productivity than state-sector agriculture.[39] In particular, the private sector contributed more than one-quarter of non-sugar agricultural output; it was the output of these private farmers that was marketed through the short-lived, but very successful, *mercados libres campesinos* (farmer free markets).

---

[38]José Luis Rodríguez, *Estrategia del desarrollo económico en Cuba* (La Habana: Editorial de Ciencias Sociales, 1990), p. 61. He also estimates that in 1988, the Cuban state controlled 100 percent of the industrial, transportation, retail, wholesale, and foreign trade, banking, and education sectors.

[39]On the higher productivity of the non-state agricultural sector see Nancy Forster, "Cuban Agricultural Production: A Comparison of State and Private Farm Sectors," *Cuban Studies/ Estudios Cubanos* 11-12 (July 1981-January 1982), pp. 105-125.

Another way to infer the magnitude of private economic activity in Cuba is through the structure of employment (Table 2). In 1989, 94.1 percent of Cuba's civilian workers were employed by the state, 1.6 percent were cooperative members, and the remaining 4.3 percent were engaged in private activities: small farmers (3.2 percent), workers in private activities drawing a salary (0.4 percent), and the self-employed (0.7 percent). In that year, about 160,000 civilian workers were engaged in private economic activities; of these, about 41,000 workers, or slightly over 1 percent of total civilian employment, were engaged in private employment outside of agriculture.

Table 3 presents official Cuban data on the structure of population income.[40] Over the period 1975-89, the state sector generated 77-80 percent of population income, while the private sector, including cooperatives, generated 5-6 percent, and other sources (presumably pensions, transfer payments, etc.) about 15-17 percent. The share of population income generated by the private sector approximates the relative importance of private sector workers within the labor force in Table 2.

Based on the above official statistics, some very rough estimates of the magnitude of private economic activity in Cuba around 1988-89 can be made. Agriculture contributed about 14 percent of global social product (GSP) in those years.[41] Thus, the one-fifth share of agricultural production accounted for by the private sector translates into about 3 percent of GSP. Moreover, assuming that the average output per worker is the same across all sectors of the economy, it can be estimated that cooperative members generated 1-2 percent of national output in 1988-89, while private non-state workers generated about 4 percent; of the latter, about 3 percent originated from agricultural activities and the remaining 1 percent from non-agricultural activities (primarily self-employed workers in service sectors). From the income side, private sector activities generated about 5-6 percent of population income.

Illegal Economic Activities

There is a great deal of fragmentary information from the official press and from foreign sources on so-called economic crimes in Cuba. In addition, anecdotal information on a range of illegal economic activities is also available from interviews with emigres regarding their own experiences as consumers or producers in the island.[42] Despite the abundance of fragmentary information and anecdotes, there are no estimates of the dimension of illegal economic activities in the island.

The picture of generalized illegal economic activities that emerges from this literature is

---

[40]*Anuario estadístico de Cuba 1989, op. cit.*, p. 79, defines population income as "all monetary payments received by the population stemming from direct transactions with the state; excluded are monetary transactions among members of the population and payments in kind and in the form of services provided for free."

[41]GSP and value of agricultural output figures are from *Anuario estadístico de Cuba 1989*, p. 88. The GSP is the most aggregated measure of output made public by Cuba; it differs from GNP in two main ways: 1) GSP is affected by double counting; and 2) GSP does not reflect the value of some non-productive services (such as education, housing). On these differences see, e.g., Carmelo Mesa-Lago and Jorge Pérez-López, *A Study of Cuba's Material Product System, Its Conversion to the System of National Accounts, and Estimation of Gross Domestic Product per Capita and Growth Rates*, Staff Working Paper 770 (Washington: World Bank, 1985).

[42]E.g., Juan M. Clark, *Cuba: Mito y realidad* (Miami: Saeta Ediciones, 1990); Sergio Roca, "Management of State Enterprises in Cuba: Some Preliminary Findings," in Jack W. Hopkins, editor, *Latin American and Caribbean Contemporary Record*, vol. 3 (New York: Holmes and Meier, 1984), pp. 219-232; Roca, "Management of State Enterprises in Cuba: A Comparison of the Soviet Union and Cuba," mimeographed (1985); and Roca, "State Enterprises in Cuba Under the New System of Management and Planning," *Cuban Studies* 16 (1986), pp. 153-179.

consistent with the experiences of other CPEs and with expected behavior in an economy that is subject to an extremely high level of regulation. The most common illegal economic activities appear to be those associated with violations of the commodity rationing system that has been in place since 1962,[43] particularly the rationing system for food items.[44] These violations might range from the fairly benign *trueque* (barter) of commodities among households, to the more malevolent sale or purchase of commodities or services in the illegal black market. Sources of black market products include production by private farmers, cooperative members, or artisans, as well as illegal means such as misappropriation of government property, short-changing of customers, and corruption (*sociolismo*).

Illegal production and sale of goods does not appear to be as significant a component of Cuba's second economy as in other CPEs, e.g., the production and sale of *samovon* (home-brewed alcohol) in the Soviet Union. However, there are reported incidents in Cuba of illegal construction and repair of homes and other structures often using materials and equipment that have been diverted from the state, and of production of certain consumer goods (e.g., footwear, garments) and of operation of repair businesses often using raw materials stolen from the state.

Two foreign journalists have given the following description of the breadth and depth of illegal economic activities in contemporary Cuba:

> Every day, almost every Cuban I know does something illegal just to get by. They may buy black market coffee or shoes for their kids, call in sick at work so they can have time to shop for food, swipe supplies from the office to use at home, or get their toilet fixed by a plumber working illegally. They might be members of the Communist Party or staunch supporters of the revolution, but they break the law as a matter of course. And since everyone sees everyone doing it, it becomes part of the game. But deep down it creates a kind of double standard that flies in the face of the mores this revolutions stands for. In some ways, Cuba has created a nation of hypocrites and liars.[45]

> There was hardly a Cuban in military or civilian life who didn't resort regularly to the black market. It was an unavoidable —and until then [1989] widely tolerated— part of daily life. If your house's water pipes sprung a leak, you had no other recourse but to call an illegal plumber —the state provided no such service. If you needed a gate to protect your home, you had to call an illegal handyman —there were no government-licensed workers doing that job. If your roof was falling down, you spread the word among your friends that you needed a roofer, and somebody would soon come up with an unlicensed worker to do the job. There was no such thing as a government-run service for roof repairs. Roofers, plumbers and handymen in

---

[43]On the commodity rationing system see, e.g., Carmelo Mesa-Lago, *The Economy of Socialist Cuba* (Albuquerque: University of New Mexico Press, 1981); Eugenio R. Balari, *Cuba-USA: Palabras cruzadas* (La Habana: Editorial de Ciencias Sociales, 1985); Ela J. García de Frances, "La economía diaria: Posibilidades de mercados y consumos de los trabajadores y el pueblo cubano," mimeographed (1988); Rodríguez, *Estrategia del desarrollo económico en Cuba, op. cit.*; and José Luis Rodríguez and George Carriazo Moreno, *La erradicación de la pobreza en Cuba* (La Habana: Editorial de Ciencias Sociales, 1987).

[44]On rationing of food products see, e.g., Medea Benjamin, Michael Collins, and Michael Scott, *No Free Lunch* (San Francisco: Institute for Food and Development Policy, 1984); Collins and Benjamin, "Cuba's Food Distribution System," in Sandor Halebsky and John M. Kirk, editors, *Cuba: Twenty Five Years of Revolution, 1959-1984* (New York: Praeger, 1985), pp. 62-78.

[45]Medea Benjamin, "Things Fall Apart," *NACLA Report on the Americas* 19 (August 1990), pp. 20-21. The quote is attributed to a foreigner who resides in Cuba.

general were a black hole in Cuba's Socialist system.[46]

Excess Liquidity

Since 1960, demand for consumer goods has exceeded supply and an active black market has been in operation. The government has attempted to deal with the excess demand for consumer goods in several ways.

- First, as noted above, by instituting in 1962 a physical rationing scheme. While the rationing scheme has undergone some changes during the 30 years that it has been in effect, it still remains as an important mechanism to distribute basic goods to Cuban households.

- Second, in the 1970s and 1980s, the Cuban government permitted individual producers of agricultural and artisan products to sell their output directly to consumers at whatever price consumers were willing to pay. These so-called *mercados libres campesinos* (farmer free markets) and *mercados artesanales* (artisan markets) were eliminated in 1986.

- Third, to compete with the black market, a government-run parallel market has been established. Parallel markets allow consumers to purchase amounts of goods beyond those allotted by the rationing system at higher prices. The parallel market also gives consumers the opportunity to purchase other goods not subject to the rationing scheme but whose supply is limited (e.g., electro-domestic appliances) at higher-than-market prices.

Table 4 presents official data on population income and on population expenditures for the period 1975-89. The difference between the two is the inflationary gap, a rough indicator of unsatisfied consumer demand. Population income exceeded expenditures in all but three years (1975, 1980, and 1987). In some instances, the inflationary gap was quite significant, e.g., 4.0 and 4.5 percent, respectively, of population income in 1988 and 1989.

Accumulated cash balances that cannot be translated into consumption in the first economy create "excess liquidity"[47] or a "monetary surplus."[48] According to estimates (Table 4), excess liquidity was equivalent to 35-36 percent of population income in the mid-1970s, declined to about 29-30 percent by the mid-1980s, and rose sharply to over 35 percent in 1989.

Consumers may elect to hold on to cash balances that cannot be used to purchase goods and services in the first economy or to channel those balances into savings. An important reason for holding on to cash is the ability to purchase goods and services in the second economy. Estimates in Table 4 suggest that, in the late 1970s, Cuban consumers held on to 63-65 percent of unspendable income in the form of cash holdings, while the remaining 35-37 percent was channeled into savings. In the 1980s, in part as a result of a government campaign to reduce the amount of money in

---

[46]Andrés Oppenheimer, *Castro's Final Hour* (New York: Simon & Schuster, 1992), p. 139.

[47]This is the term used, e.g., by Carlos Martínez Fagundo, "Presencia e influencia de los factores de desequilibrio en las finanzas internas de Cuba," *Economía y Desarrollo*, no. 5 (September-October 1989), pp. 166-190 and Osvaldo Alpizar, "La liquidez monetaria en la economía cubana: Reseña estadística," *Boletín de Información sobre la Economía Cubana*, no. 4 (April 1992), pp. 19-23.

[48]This is the term used by Mesa-Lago, *The Economy of Socialist Cuba, op. cit.*, pp. 47-49.

circulation, personal savings rose faster than excess liquidity so that by 1987, unspendable income was divided almost evenly between cash holdings and savings. Nevertheless, in 1988-89, Cuban consumers held nearly 2 billion pesos in the form of cash, roughly 17 percent of population income. A similar amount was available in the form of demand deposits (savings).

4. Concluding Observations

Quantifying the broad range of economic activities that occur outside of the public regulatory framework is difficult in any society. There is no consensus among experts on a strict definition of such activities or on a methodology to quantify them. The strong desire on the part of economic actors to remain anonymous prevents the use of traditional measurement techniques. To get around this latter problem, indirect estimation methods have been developed. However, the application of these methods to market economies has yielded estimates of the magnitude of underground economic activities that vary very widely.

Centrally planned economies, characterized by direct public ownership of resources and highly regimented relationships among economic actors, are fertile ground for entrepreneurial activities outside of the public regulatory framework. Cuba is not exception. There is a great deal of descriptive information and anecdotal material on second economy activities in Cuba, but no quantitative estimates of their dimension.

Cuban official statistics suggest that around 1988-89, private economic activities not inconsistent with the legal system accounted for at least 6 percent of GSP and employed about 230,000 workers, or about 6 percent of total civilian employment. From the income side, private sector activities accounted for 5-6 percent of population income.

There is reason to believe that private economic activity in Cuba is substantially higher than suggested by the official data. According to a high-level government official, in early 1991 there were 200,000 self-employed workers authorized by the State Committee on Labor and Social Security--compared to the 25,200 self-employed workers reported in official statistics for 1989. Moreover, this same official estimated that "for each registered [self-employed] individual, there are three other Cubans engaged in private enterprise."[49] In the midst of employment dislocations associated with the special period, the IV Congress of the Cuban Communist Party (held in October 1991) recognized the importance of self-employment and promised to issue regulations that would ease its expansion in a manner consistent with other national objectives.[50]

There is a great deal of fragmentary information on illegal economic activities in Cuba. The available information suggests that the bulk of illegal activities are associated with the unauthorized sale and purchase of goods and services (black market activities); such transactions often involve an additional element of illegality, as the goods that are exchanged are themselves stolen from the state. Illegal production and sale of goods does not appear to be as significant a component of Cuba's second economy as in other former socialist countries. Services such as plumbing, appliance and automobile repair, and hair grooming are routinely performed by artisans and technicians outside of official channels. Announced policies that would broaden authorized self-employment seem to

[49]"Official Discusses Private Enterprise Restrictions," Notimex News Service (8 April 1991), as reproduced in *FBIS-LAT-91-076-A* (19 April 1991), p. 2. The quoted official is Eugenio R. Balari, Director of the Institute for Research and Orientation of Internal Demand.

[50]"Resolución sobre el desarrollo económico del país," reproduced in Pablo Alfonso, *Los fieles de Castro* (Miami: Ediciones Cambio, 1991), pp. 217-218.

be aimed at regularizing these now-illegal activities.

Illegal economic activities are normally conducted in cash. Black market participants anywhere abhor financial records and put a high premium on the anonymity associated with cash transactions. Official Cuban statistics on population income and expenditures suggest that Cuban consumers have large amounts of cash that cannot be used to purchase goods and services in the first economy. It has been estimated that in 1989, excess liquidity amounted to about 35 percent of total population income; excess liquidity was almost equally divided between cash holdings and savings. Given information that suggests that black market participation in Cuba is generalized, it is not unreasonable to assume that second economy transactions might account for roughly the amount of consumer cash holdings (i.e., about 17 percent of personal income) or even for a higher amount.

Table 1

Structure of Agricultural Output

(percentages; at constant prices of 1981)

	1970	Average 1971-75	1980	1981	1982	1983	1984	1985	1986	1987	1988
Agriculture	100.0	100.0	100.0	100.0	100.0	100.0	100.0	100.0	100.0	100.0	100.0
State	73.5	75.5	80.6	79.4	79.4	78.8	79.4	79.4	79.4	78.9	78.8
Non-state	26.5	24.5	19.4	20.6	20.6	21.2	20.6	20.6	20.6	21.1	21.2
Sugar Cane	100.0	100.0	100.0	100.0	100.0	100.0	100.0	100.0	100.0	100.0	100.0
State	77.0	82.5	84.0	83.0	82.8	80.1	82.2	82.3	82.7	83.0	81.2
Non-state	33.0	17.5	16.0	17.0	17.2	19.9	17.8	17.7	17.3	17.0	18.8
Non-Sugar Agriculture	100.0	100.0	100.0	100.0	100.0	100.0	100.0	100.0	100.0	100.0	100.0
State	72.7	71.4	75.6	71.2	72.0	72.5	71.8	71.9	72.4	71.1	73.1
Non-state	27.3	28.6	24.4	28.8	18.0	27.5	28.2	28.1	27.6	28.9	26.9
Livestock	100.0	100.0	100.0	100.0	100.0	100.0	100.0	100.0	100.0	100.0	100.0
State	68.4	71.3	81.1	83.3	82.8	82.4	82.9	82.6	82.5	82.0	80.9
Non-state	31.6	28.7	18.9	16.7	17.2	17.6	17.1	17.4	17.5	18.0	19.1

Source: *Anuario Estadístico de Cuba 1988*, p. 301.

Table 2

Structure of Civilian Employment, 1953-89

(in thousands and percentages)

	1953	1970		1989	
	Percent	Number	Percent	Number	Percent
Total civilian employment	100.0	2408.9	100.0	3870.2	100.0
State workers	12.7a	2078.8	86.3	3641.1	94.1
Non-state agricultural workers		264.9	11.0	187.6	4.8
Small farmers		264.9	11.0	123.1	3.2
Cooperative members				64.5	1.6
Private, salaried workers	63.3	35.2	1.5	16.3	0.4
Self-employed	24.0	30.0	1.2	25.2	0.7

a—Sum of categories labelled "State Workers" and "Other State Workers."

Sources: 1953—Mayra Espina Prieto and Lilia Núñez Moreno, "The Changing Class Structure in the Development of Socialism in Cuba," in Sandor Halebsky and John M. Kirk, *Transformation and Struggle: Cuba Faces the 1990s* (New York: Praeger, 1990), p. 211.
1970, 1989—*Anuario Estadístico de Cuba 1989*, p. 111.

Table 3

Structure of Population Income

(In million pesos and percentages)

	Total	State Sector		Private Sector		Other*	
	Value	Value	%	Value	%	Value	%
1975	5489	4240	77.3	349	6.4	900	16.4
1976	5813	4537	78.0	350	6.0	927	16.0
1977	6060	4774	78.8	318	5.3	969	16.0
1978	6464	5133	79.4	334	5.2	997	15.4
1979	6644	5284	79.5	343	5.2	1018	15.3
1980	6766	5404	79.9	339	5.0	1023	15.1
1981	8053	6392	79.4	517	6.4	1145	14.2
1982	8583	6842	79.7	518	6.0	1223	14.3
1983	9155	7330	80.0	539	5.9	1286	14.1
1984	9927	7928	79.9	574	5.8	1425	14.3
1985	10315	8122	78.7	598	5.8	1595	15.5
1986	10761	8404	78.1	651	6.1	1706	15.8
1987	10654	8350	78.4	592	5.6	1712	16.0
1988	11389	8924	78.4	610	5.4	1855	16.2
1989	11825	9223	78.0	632	5.3	1971	16.7

*   Presumably pensions and other transfer payments.

Source: *Anuario estadístico de Cuba 1989*, p. 104.

Table 4

Population Income, Expenditures, and Excess Liquidity

(In million pesos)

	Population Income	Population Expenditures	Excess Liquidity	Cash Holdings	Savings
1975	5489	5564	2012	1267	745
1976	5813	5772	2052	1307	745
1977	6060	5990	2122	1362	760
1978	6464	6415	2172	1394	778
1979	6644	6634	2181	1399	782
1980	6766	6855	2093	1344	749
1981	8053	7606	2541	1653	888
1982	8583	8466	2658	1573	1085
1983	9155	9086	2727	1567	1160
1984	9927	9722	2931	1655	1276
1985	10315	10149	3097	1701	1396
1986	10761	10671	3187	1529	1658
1987	10654	10657	3184	1521	1663
1988	11389	10937	3635	1816	1819
1989	11825	11296	4164	2103	2061

Source: Osvaldo Alpizar, "La liquidez monetaria en la economía cubana: Reseña estadística," *Boletín de Información sobre Economía Cubana*, no. 4 (April 1992), p. 23. Population income and expenditures are from *Anuario estadístico de Cuba 1989*, p. 104; monetary surplus, cash holdings, and savings are estimates by Alpizar.

THE DISTRIBUTION SECTOR IN A CPE: CUBA

Roger R. Betancourt[1]

Introduction

In most advanced economies the distribution sector accounts for 10 percent or more of GDP and a substantially higher percentage of employment. For example, in the U.S. it is second only to manufacturing in terms of contribution to GDP and it is first in terms of providing employment. Despite its quantitative importance, the study of this sector has been somewhat neglected by economists until very recently. At the conceptual level interest has been reawakened due to developments in the industrial organization literature, in particular modern analyses of the effects of vertical restraints on distribution, for example Rey and Tirole (1986) and Mathewson and Winter (1986), and recent conceptualizations of the role of retail firms in the economic system, for example Betancourt and Gautschi (1988, 1993) and Bliss (1988). At the practical level interest has been reawakened due to the realization that the role of this sector matters for important policy issues: Macroeconomic policy failure in Chile during the "tablita" period, for example Morande (1986), and the role of the distribution sector in preventing or facilitating trade associated with the Structural Impediments Initiative between the U.S. and Japan.

Neglect of this topic is even more pronounced in developing countries where attention has focused on the role of agriculture and the need to create a manufacturing sector. Nonetheless, very recent theoretical literature is seeking to explain how the division of labor or specialization actually arises and its implications for growth and its measurement, e.g., Borland and Young (1992) and Devereux and Locay (1992). Since part of the specialization process is the development of institutions specialized in wholesaling and retailing, the main components of the distribution sector, a greater understanding of the role of this sector in the economic system of a less developed country facilitates the integration of this topic in a growing body of literature. Finally, the rapid expansion and dynamism of this sector in the emerging market economies of Central and Eastern Europe, for example Gadjka (1992), suggests it may be of interest to study the distribution sector in a CPE prior to a transition and Cuba offers one of the few remaining examples.

Section I contains a brief conceptualization of the role of the distribution sector in the economic system. Section II discusses the considerations that are relevant in adapting this framework to a centrally planned setting such as the one existing in Cuba. Section III presents available information on the size and structure of this sector. Section IV highlights several aspects important for the functioning of that sector in the Cuban setting. By the way of a conclusion we discuss briefly factors leading to changes in this sector within and without the current system.

I. Conceptual Framework

The economic function of the distribution sector is to transfer goods and services from producers to consumers. In the performance of this function different institutional forms arise in order to increase the gains from exchange between producers and consumers. In some instances,

[1] I would like to thank J. Pérez-López and S. Roca for providing unpublished or difficult to obtain material for this paper and F. Alvarez for his comments at the second ASCE meetings where the paper was first presented. Part of the research for this paper was undertaken while the author was an IRIS Fellow. Errors, omissions and interpretations are the sole responsibility of the author.

for example, producers distribute products directly to consumers; in other cases, wholesaling or retailing institutions emerge. These different forms do not arise by accident. On the contrary, they are due to the existence of transaction costs in general and distribution costs in particular. These distribution costs will exist regardless of the nature of the economic system.

As long as producers and consumers are separate in the spatial domain, either the producer, the consumer and/or some institution specializing in the distribution function must bear this cost of exchange. The nature of the costs associated with this spatial separation will, of course, depend on the economic system, including the range of products generated by the production sector. Similarly as long as production and consumption are separated in the time domain, the producer, the consumer and/or some institution specializing in the distribution function must bear this cost of exchange. Once again the nature of this cost will depend on the economic system, including whether or not it is explicitly recognized. Its existence, however, will be independent of the economic system as long as there is non-simultaneous production and consumption.

These two as well as other features of the distribution process have led to the development of the following characterization of distribution systems which can be illustrated in simple schematic form as follows.

Fig. 1. The Role of Cost Shifting in the Performance of the Distribution Function

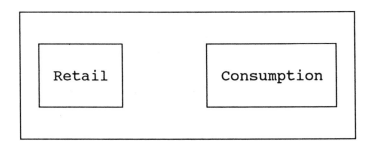

For simplicity Figure 1 represents the interactions between the retail sector and the consumption sector in the performance of the distribution function. Similar figures can be constructed to represent direct interactions between the production and the consumption sector, the production and the wholesale sector, etc. The existence of simultaneous arrows linking the sectors represents a set of distribution services that must be provided in any exchange between sectors. In systems other than self-sufficient households, a set of five broad categories of distribution services have been identified: accessibility of location, assortment, information, assurance of product delivery in the desired form and at the desired time, ambiance. These are five different aspects of bearing and allocating the distribution costs of exchange, Betancourt and Gautschi (1988). The drawing of arrows of different lengths emanating from the two different sectors purports to indicate the possibilities for shifting costs in the provision of distribution services between these sectors or agents.

From the economic point of view distribution services are outputs of an economic agent that must be provided at some level in order to bear the distribution costs associated with the exchange of goods and services between any two sectors. A methodological advantage of this formulation is the ability to characterize the economic behavior of the producing agent in terms of a joint cost function. On the demand side these distribution services can be viewed as fixed inputs into the production functions of the recipients of the explicit goods and services that are transferred in an exchange. In the case of the consumption sector, these distribution services can be viewed as fixed inputs into household production functions of consumers. The implications for demand analysis have been developed by Betancourt and Gautschi (1992). In the case of other economic agents similar implications follow, Betancourt (1992a). This conceptualization allows one to capture relevant economic features of two essential characteristics of the role of distribution costs in any exchange. First, the distribution services provided by economic agents in any exchange are not explicitly priced; secondly, the bearing of the costs of providing these distribution services can be allocated differently among any two agents participating in an exchange. Furthermore, associated with every exchange there is an allocation of these costs. Most of the time this allocation is implicitly done, sometimes it becomes explicit. For instance, the allocation of part of the cost of providing accessibility of location becomes explicit in an exchange between a retailer and a consumer when the latter charges an explicit fee to the former for home delivery.

In capitalist economies, these characteristics of distribution systems provide the basis for the existence of price dispersion in monopolistically competitive market structures, product choice in distribution services and the operation of multi-product, multi-market firms in the distribution sector. Distribution services provide instruments for non-price competition, affect the pricing policies of firms and the welfare evaluation of policies, for example Betancourt and Gautschi (1993).

Distribution systems will differ across economic systems because the main internal components (production, wholesale, retail and consumption) differ in their characteristics or because the external environment in which they operate differs across economic systems, i.e., differences in the legal framework, available infrastructure and institutional characteristics. Nevertheless, the basic function to be performed by the distribution sector remains the same across economic systems, namely bearing and allocating the distribution costs associated with exchange through the provision of distribution services.

II. Implications for a CPE

An issue that comes to the surface immediately is whether or not the characterization of agents behavior in terms of optimizing models is appropriate in a CPE. Standard practice by Western economists is to assume that it is appropriate to do so and to exert some effort in characterizing the environmental constraints faced by the agents. An excellent example of this argument in the case of labor supply is provided by Sanguinetty (1992). We shall adopt this procedure. Indeed, the discussion of the economic function of the distribution system in the previous section already points in this direction. A general discussion of the applicability of the new institutional economics to the Cuban economy is available in Betancourt (1992b).

CPEs are frequently characterized as shortage economies where rationing or unavailability of goods and services are pervasive features of economic activity. Three important factors in the operation of the distribution sector arise from this characteristic. First, since the distribution sector is normally responsible for carrying out the rationing procedure, the rationing scheme, including re-trading opportunities, and the extent of the shortages would be important determinants in the functioning of this sector and require special attention. Secondly, the extent of competition in distribution would also be an important factor in the functioning of the system. In some CPEs alternative markets[2] are allowed and the benefits generated by the distribution sector will depend on this characteristic. In a monopolistically competitive market if prices are fixed increased competition increases welfare by generating increases in the levels of distribution services provided to consumers, Betancourt and Gautschi (1993). Thus, parallel markets even with price ceilings can be welfare enhancing. Finally, monitoring in state owned enterprises creates a principal agent problem between the state and its employees that generates a sizable number of transactions of an informal nature. The small bulk of the commodities exchanged at the retail level provide a particular auspicious setting for the proliferation of these informal transactions in the distribution sector. Hence, the role of informality, defined as illegal transactions, in this sector is worthy of special attention. Incidentally, an insightful account of how the view of legality in the Soviet system leads to informal transactions is available in Litwack (1991).

One last feature of CPEs that has a special bearing in an analysis of the distribution sector is the nature of their accounting and organizational systems. As pointed out by Nove (1977), trade is basically divided into external and internal trade and the organizations that operate in the two sectors as well as the statistical information associated with their operations are separate from each other. When one looks at the distribution sector one usually focuses on the data for the internal trade sector. The main consequence of this is an underestimation of the role of the distribution sector in the economic system when compared with capitalist economies. For instance, in the U.S. Census of Wholesale Trade the activities of wholesalers dedicated exclusively to the import or export function would be counted as part of the distribution sector.

To conclude this discussion, it is worth noting that many of the same concerns about the operation of the distribution system would arise from a socialist perspective. In a recent article on the role of the distribution sector under socialism F. Gómez (1989, pp. 44-45) argues that commercial organization is somewhat backward under socialism relative to advanced capitalist countries and that some capitalist practices, purged of their objectionable features, should be considered for adoption because of their efficiency and time saving aspects. Since time saving is a common feature of almost all of the distribution services emphasized in the previous sections, it may be useful to adopt the framework of the previous section even from a socialist perspective. More generally, there seems to be an increasing preoccupation with the satisfaction of consumer wants in Cuba. This is manifested in appeals for scientific analyses of supply and demand for consumer products and the benefits they may bring, for example, Suárez-Lugo (1990), as well as in attempts to reduce waiting time at stores during the "special period."[3]

III. The Distribution Sector in Cuba: An Overview

The distribution sector in Cuba is broken up into five broad categories: supply of technical and material products; procurement of agricultural products (*acopios*); procurement of recycled products; wholesale trade; and retail trade. Most of the statistics available in the *Anuario Estadístico*, however, cover only the last two categories. One exception is information on the number of warehouses available. In the Appendix, Table A1 reproduces the information available on this topic in the 1988 statistical yearbook. As can be seen from the table, there was a considerable reduction in the number of warehouses between 1982 and 1983, the only two years available, at the same time that the area available for storage in the remaining warehouses increased. A similar process has

---

[2]Alternative markets can take the form of farmers markets, relatively free of government control, or parallel markets run by the government.

[3]Personal communication to the author by Pedro Monreal, April 1992.

taken place in warehouses with refrigeration. Two other pieces of information from this table are worth noting: First, the number of warehouses devoted to technical and material supplies takes up over 70 percent of the available storage area and over 50 percent of the available refrigerated storage volume; second, the refrigerated storage volume for food products decreased between 1982 and 1983.

A recent article by J. Neyra Saiz (1989) provides some insight into this process. It looks in detail at the wholesaling of non-food products and it explains several characteristics of the system. There are two wholesale networks for non-food products: a national one under the Ministry of Internal Trade, consisting of 7 enterprises located in Havana City, and a territorial (regional) one, consisting of 14 enterprises controlled by the *Poder Popular* in each of the provinces. The process of closing down old warehouses and building new ones with better equipment and larger storage areas has been taking place during the 1980s but at a much faster place in the warehouses controlled by the national network than in those controlled by the territorial network. This process is viewed by Neyra Saiz as following the economic rationalization of the wholesale system. He goes on to argue that the form of organization provided by the territorial network prevents specialization in wholesaling thus lowering efficiency. Finally, it is also suggested that going back to an administrative system with 6 provinces rather than the current 14 would improve the functioning of the distribution system.

In Table 1 we present information on the value of wholesale sales during the 1980s. We present data for 1980, 1982, 1985 and 1988. The choice of years was determined by the following factors: the introduction of a new accounting system in 1977, a price reform in 1981, the demise of the agricultural markets after 1985 and the last year in which a complete statistical yearbook was published (1988).[4]

Table 1. Wholesale Sales
(In millions of pesos)

	1980	1982	1985	1988	82/80	85/82	88/85
Total	7,290.9	9,527.7	11,612.6	11,716.8	1.307	1.219	1.009
Food	2,411.2	2,907.0	3,729.3	3,905.6	1.206	1.283	1.047
Beverages	940.2	1,451.4	1,456.8	1,794.8	1.544	1.004	0.957
Non-food	3,192.8	4,249.8	5,235.6	5,260.2	1.339	1.232	1.005
Durables	498.0	541.8	731.3	689.3	1.088	1.350	0.943

Source: Table X.2, *Anuario Estadístico*, CEE, 1988.

Several aspects of the table stand out. First, in every category of products the ratio of wholesale sales decreases between 85/82 and 88/85. This reflects the general slowdown of economic activity since 1985. Secondly, sales of durables are between 5 and 10 percent of total wholesale sales in every year. This reflects the developing country nature of the Cuban economy. In the U.S., for example, durables make up about 50 percent of wholesale sales. Of course, this difference is overstated because durables sold as part of the branch of supplies of technical and material products

---

[4] A much smaller yearbook is available for 1989.

are not included in the Cuban statistics. Finally, food sales account for more than 25 percent of the sales of the wholesale sector, which contrasts with about 15 percent for U.S. merchant wholesalers in 1987.

In the Appendix (Table A2), we provide information on the value of wholesale sales going to the retail sector for completeness. Two facts about the distribution system emerge from this table: First, over 50 percent of total sales of the wholesale sector go to the retail sector; the remainder goes to enterprises classified in other branches of economic activity. This is true for every category except beverages where the proportion going to the retail sector is much lower than 50 percent every year. A second fact emerges from comparing Table A2 in the Appendix with Table 2 below, which provides information on retail sales for the same years. Namely, the retail sector obtains between 50 and 60 percent of its products from the wholesale branch; the remainder comes from other branches, in particular agricultural procurement centers (*acopios*).

Table 2. Retail Sales
(In millions of pesos)

	1980	1982	1985	1988	82/80	85/82	88/85
Total	6,055.3	7,738.9	9,119.5	9,500.3	1.278	1.178	1.042
Retail Network	4,235.0	5,459.6	6,445.3	6,672.6	1.289	1.181	1.035
Eating & Drinking Establishments	1,820.3	2,279.3	2,674.2	2,827.7	1.252	1.173	1.057
Restricted Access	156.7	192.6	229.1	222.3	1.229	1.190	0.097

Source: Tables X.9-X.11, *Anuario Estadístico*, CEE, 1988.

Table 2 yields the same pattern of decline in economic activity as Table 1. That is, in every category there is a decrease in the ratio of retail sales between 85/82 and 88/85. The retail sector is decomposed into two broad categories: the retail network and eating and drinking establishments. The latter category contains sales through cafeterias at the work place or in schools, which are the main component in the restricted access entry. For completeness, Table A3 in the Appendix presents the distribution of sales in the retail network by type of stores. The most striking pattern that emerges is the high and increasing percentage of sales made up by food stores, i.e., from 48.2 percent in 1982 to 52.5 percent in 1988. The corresponding percentage in the U.S. was about 25 percent in 1987.

An important phenomenon in the development of the distribution system in the 1980s was the growth of parallel markets. Table 3 presents the available statistics. Its sales increased rapidly between 1983 and 1985 but slowed down considerably between 1985 and 1988, making up 16 percent of total retail sales in 1988. The slowdown is consistent with the general slow growth of economic activity during 1985-1988. Nevertheless, it is noteworthy that during the 1982-85 period the parallel markets had to compete with farmers markets and crafts markets whereas during the 1985-88 period it had much less competition.

Table 3. Retail Sales Through the Parallel Market
(In millions of pesos and percentages)

	1983	1985	1988
Total	565.0	925.3	1,018.1
Percent of Retail Sales	10.3	15.2	16.0
Food	414.1	555.3	613.9
Percent of Food Retail Sales	14.5	17.7	17.8
Non-food	150.9	370.0	404.2
Percent of Non-food Retail Sales	8.0	17.1	19.4

Source: Tables X.18-X.20, *Anuario Estadístico*, CEE, 1988.

Table 4. Employment in Distribution
(Thousands of workers)

	1980	1982	1985	1988
Total	297.7	318.4	360.4	381.0
Wholesale Network	37.7	43.6	48.6	51.3
Retail Network	122.2	140.7	152.8	155.6
Eating & Drinking Establishments	66.3	60.5	77.2	82.9
Technical & Material Supplies	51.0	52.3	52.4	53.4
Agricultural Procurement	18.1	18.8	25.3	37.8
Recycling	2.4	2.5	4.1	n.a.

Source: Table X.26, *Anuario Estadístico*, CEE, 1988.

Table 4 provides information on the employment generated by all branches of the distribution sector. Total employment growth during the period follows the pattern evidenced by the growth of sales, namely a slowdown between 1985 and 1988. The categories, however, yield two exceptions -- employment in agricultural procurement and in the supplies of technical and material products grew more rapidly during 85-88 than during 82-85. The percentage of the civilian labor force employed in the distribution sector is slightly over 10 percent in each of these years, e.g., 11.1 in 1988; in Japan and the U.S. it is about 17 percent for example. Finally, since 14 percent of the labor force is employed in the branch of supplies of technical and material products and this branch controls over 70 percent of the storage area, this data suggest a higher level of efficiency in this branch than in the wholesale or agricultural procurement branches.

One interesting piece of information in a retail setting is the number of establishments. Table 5 presents this information for various categories and subcategories of the retail sector. There is an increase for all entries, except non-food stores, between 1982 and 1985. Other things equal such increases are welfare improving since they lower purchasing costs to consumers. The number of employees per establishment in the retail sector rose from 5.18 to 5.34 between 1982 and 1985. In Japan, on the other hand, the number of persons engaged per outlet was 3.9 in 1985, Maruyama (1992). Finally, the number of establishments in the retail network per thousand members of the population was 2.81 in 1985 in Cuba; in Japan this density was 13.5 in 1985. Japan is notorious for its abundance of small outlets and this is also argued with respect to the Cuban retail sector, Clark (1990);[5] incidentally, assortments are much deeper and perhaps broader in Japan. In the U.S. this density was 2.71. Hence, with assortments much closer to the Japanese in terms of breadth, the accessibility of location of the stores is much closer to the U.S. This indicates that the retail sector provides very low levels of these two distribution services to consumers.

Table 5. Number of Retail Establishments

	1980	1982	1985
Retail Stores	28,719	27,153	28,593
Food Stores	17,001	16,406	17,317
Non-food Stores	2,680	3,770	3,498
Eating & Drinking Establishments	22,461	25,382	28,323
Limited Access	13,608	16,979	17,950

Source: Table X.28, *Anuario Estadístico*, CEE, 1988.

To conclude this overview, we note that the statistical yearbook also provides information on personal and repair services as part of internal trade statistics. The information is summarized in Table A4 of the Appendix. Total expenditures follow a similar pattern to those for retail and wholesale sales over the 1980s. Expenditures in these categories are equivalent to 19 percent of wholesale sales. They are of interest primarily because the trades that were liberalized during the IV Communist Party Congress in 1991 fall in these categories.

IV. Important Factors in the Functioning of the Distribution System in Cuba

In Cuba there are three interrelated factors that play a key role in the functioning of the distribution system: the rationing system, alternative markets and informal exchanges. The role of these three factors, however, varies over time depending on general economic conditions and ideological initiatives of the political leadership. We will discuss how these factors have evolved from 1980 to the current "special period in peacetime."

A sympathetic and engagingly written account of the distribution system in Cuba up to the

---

[5]The numbers contradict the perception in the case of Cuba and this perception may be due to the absence of large stores.

early 1980s is available in Benjamin, Collins and Scott (1984). Several characteristics of the system are important for our purposes. A ration book per household is distributed each year.[6] The households register with the National Rationing Board, indicating the neighborhood stores where they are to acquire the rationed items. Besides the grocery store this may include a butcher's shop, a vegetable stand, and a dairy shop. Prices of the rationed items were fixed from 1962 to 1981, quantities can vary with availability. The same stores may also sell products that are not rationed or in excess of the ration at higher prices. Lines are frequent at all the stores and alternative queuing schemes have been implemented to allow shorter lines for households where every adult is employed.

Such a system provides a fertile ground for the development of barter trade and informal transactions. For instance, butchers in Cuba have been frequently accused of shortchanging customers with the proportions and weights of the rationed items. In general those employed in the distribution sector are in a favored position to engage in informal transactions, for additional examples see Pérez-López (1992). One of the most important functions of this sector in any economic system is to provide assurance of product delivery in the desired form, which entails breaking the bulk of items into smaller sizes. In a heavily controlled CPE, private economic incentives to take advantage of this favored position to participate in the informal economy are powerful and the probability of detection tends to be low in settings associated with small items.

The extent of the informal economy, especially that generated by the nature of the rationing system, will be affected by the existence of alternative markets. Insofar as alternative markets exist, for example farmers' markets or parallel markets, the incentives for barter exchanges and informal transactions will be reduced. Basically the competition from these alternative supply sources lowers the gains from barter exchanges or informal transactions. In the case of Cuba farmers' markets were encouraged, somewhat grudgingly, during the 1980 to 1985 period. As we saw in the previous section, the parallel market also grew at a rapid rate in terms of sales between 1982 and 1985; separate locations for those markets were also built during this period. Benjamin, Collins and Scott (1984) report a tendency for higher quality and shorter waiting lines in the farmers' markets than in the parallel markets. Indeed, the same authors report internal discussions on the merits and demerits of the rationing system at this time. Of course, generally favorable economic conditions facilitated these developments.

Since 1986 this system was modified by the elimination of the farmers' markets. Political directives under the so-called rectification process played an important role in this change. Rodriguez (1990) provides a justification of this process from a Cuban perspective. One feature of the modified system is the creation of a State Agricultural Board, reported by Balari (1990). Another one is the slower growth of the parallel markets singled out in the previous section. A critical, compelling account of consumption and distribution activities covering this more recent period is available in Clark (1990). At this point, however, it is useful to note two general features of this system in the second half of the 1980s. Deterioration in general economic conditions enhance the importance of a rationing system and the gains from informal sector activities. The elimination of farmers' markets operates in the same direction by eliminating competition for the parallel market; namely, it enhances the scarcity value of informal sector provision of quality, assortments and shorter waiting times.

Clark provides information on the quantities available of rationed products for selected

---

[6]There is one for food and one for non-food items.

articles in several years. Comparisons of availability are difficult because the ration supplies a much different proportion of the diet depending on the period. Since 1983 was a relatively good year compared with 1989, we will compare these two years to get an indication of the tightening or loosening of the rationing system. The 1983 information comes from Benjamin, Collins and Scott (1984, p. 35); the 1989 information comes from Clark (1990, p. 279). Out of 12 categories in which a comparison is possible the amount available under the ration was the same in 8; it went down in two of them, beef and beans, and it went up in two, chicken and bread. One difference, however, is that in 1983 additional purchases could be made in the farmers' market or in the parallel markets whereas in 1989 they could only be made in the parallel market or in the black market. Thus, the elimination of the farmers' markets with a given level of rationing can be presumed to have fostered the development of the informal economy in the second half of the 1980s.

The process of relying on the rationing system cum the black market or informal economy has been accentuated by the vicissitudes of the economic system since the demise of Eastern European socialism in 1989 and the August coup in the Soviet Union in 1991. In a recent paper Roca (1992) describes some of the changes in the distribution system as a result of the "special period." Products are not to be placed in the parallel markets if they are scarce in the rationing network. Hence, 28 items available in the parallel market have been placed under the rationing network since 1990. In one of the parallel markets sites, for example, there were in 1990 115 fewer items than before. Among industrial products 181 were placed into the rationing system. Thus, the advent of the "special period in peacetime" has resulted in an increase in the importance of the rationing system in the distribution sector, at the expense of the parallel market. Of course, private economic incentives for informal sector activities have increased as a result.

One of the major changes affecting the distribution system, and the economy as a whole, in the recent period is the Food Program or *Programa Alimentario*. Mesa-Lago (1992) provides a thorough description of the program. Here, we will summarize the main features that impact the distribution system. The essence of the program is to use the excess labor released by the shortages, generated through the loss of traditional trading partners, in newly created state farms, especially near the cities of Havana and Santiago, in order to increase agricultural output and makeup for reduced imports. As a rationalization of the distribution system through generating shorter supply lines for major population centers, these changes could be beneficial. The problem, of course, lies in the opportunity cost of the resources (especially land) used for these purposes and in the feasibility of the scheme. With most agricultural activities weather patterns are critical in determining outcomes and some of the internal discussions reported by Mesa-Lago suggest that Cuban technicians expect the weather to be a critical factor in determining outcomes in this case. In addition, some problems are reported with regard to the efficiency of the agricultural procurement centers in delivering output to retail outlets. Such problems would be consistent with the information on the relative productivity of this branch reported in the discussion of Table 4.

Concluding Observations

Given the present circumstances of the Cuban economy the opportunities for change within the system are limited, but there are internal pressures for change. These vary from technical discussions to improve the functioning of the distribution system to the high level of private economic incentives for informal sector activities. The latter can only be countered by increasing the costs of informal sector participation, presumably through a higher level of repression or moral suasion. The regime's position on the Ochoa trial, as reported by Oppenheimer (1992) for example, illustrates both mechanisms.

Two elements are critical in evaluating substantial changes in the current distribution system. Given the importance of food products in the distribution sector and limited import capacity in the foreseeable future, substantial increases in agricultural output will be required for major changes in the distribution system to be worthwhile. Fuel shortages and inadequate transportation, the prevalence of multiple earner households and the low density of outlets create a high level of repressed demand for several distribution services, in particular the provision of accessibility of location by both wholesalers and retailers. Hence, expansion in the number of outlets and warehouses and/or of their assortments will have to be major features of any substantial changes that improve the economic efficiency of the distribution system.

Table A1: Network of Warehouses

ALMACENES

Concepts	Total				De ellos con refrigeración			
	Cantidad (u)		Area (m2)		Cantidad (u)		Capacidad (m3)	
	1982	1983	1982	1983	1982	1983	1982	1983
Total	3618	3342	4590020	5998143	325	240	240168	332930
Productos alimenticios	506	461	515129	512497	157	153	106346	87443
Productos no alimenticios	608	692	619427	636919	2	3	225	339
Productos farmacéuticos y medicos	72	90	70656	85869	42	41	22500	32970
Libros y revistas	53	45	33601	31171	3	1	627	-
Frigoríficos	18	18	2931	2931	18	18	35637	35637
Abastecimiento técnico material	1412	1278	3158560	4443982	94	18	73985	175694
Centros de acopio	207	183	135001	232529	9	6	848	847
Sub-centros de acopio	90	90	16727	16781	-	-	-	-
Puntos de acopio	652	485	37988	35464	-	-	-	-

Source: Table X.27, *Anuario Estadístico*, CEE, 1988.

Table A2. Flow of Wholesale Sales to the Retail Sector

	1980	1982	1985	1988
Total	4,173.3	5,067.6	6,046.5	6,178.6
Food	1,357.3	1,699.3	2,054.0	2,212.2
Beverages	274.4	258.3	363.3	429.2
Non-food	2,137.6	2,654.0	3,057.7	2,970.2
Durables	398.4	447.5	595.8	584.5

Source: Table X.4, *Anuario Estadístico*, CEE, 1988.

Table A3. Distribution of Sales by Type of Retail Establishments

	1980	1982	1985	1988
Food Stores	1,998.6	2,687.1	3,196.2	3,501.3
Non-food Stores	1,543.6	1,779.0	2,188.3	2,100.8
Pharmacies & Optical Products	238.8	262.5	302.3	320.7
"Rastros"	56.0	92.7	95.3	72.3
"Servicentros"	175.9	278.5	271.3	269.8
Other	222.1	359.8	391.4	407.7
Total	4,235.0	5,459.6	6,445.3	6,672.6

Source: Table X.16, *Anuario Estadístico*, CEE, 1988.

Table A4. Personal and Repair Services
(In millions of pesos)

	1980	1982	1985	1988
Repair	120.3	140.2	170.0	165.1
Personal	46.0	54.6	51.5	65.2
Total	166.3	194.8	231.5	230.3

Source: Table X.38, *Anuario Estadístico*, CEE, 1988.

References

Balari, E., "The Supply of Consumer Goods in Cuba" in Halebsky, S. and Kirk, J. (with R. Hernández), eds., *Transformation and Struggle: Cuba Faces the 1990s*. New York: Praeger Pub., 1990.

Benjamin, M., Collins, J. and Scott, M., *No Free Lunches*, San Francisco: Institute for Food and Development Policy, 1984.

Betancourt, R., "An Analysis of the U.S. Distribution System," OECD Report and Maryland Working Paper 92-6, 1992.

_____, "The New Institutional Economics and the Study of the Cuban Economy" in Montalván, G.P. and Pujol, J., *Cuba in Transition: Papers and Proceedings of the First Meeting of the Association for the Study of the Cuban Economy*, Miami: FIU Press, 1992.

Betancourt, R. and Gautschi, D., "The Economics of Retail Firms," *Managerial and Decision Economics*, June 1988, 9, 133-142.

_____, "The Demand for Retail Products: New Views on Substitutability and Complementarity," *Journal of Economic Behavior and Organization*, March 1992, 17, 257-275.

_____, "Two Essential Characteristics of Retail Markets and Their Economic Consequences," forthcoming, *JEBO*, 1993.

Bliss, Christopher, "A Theory of Retail Pricing," *Journal of Industrial Economics*, June 1988, 36, 372-391.

Borland, J. and Yang, X., "Specialization and a New Approach to Economic Organization and Growth," *American Economic Review*, May 1992, 82, 386-791.

Clark, J., *Cuba: Mito y Realidad*, Miami: Saeta Ediciones, 1990.

Comité Estatal de Estadísticas, *Anuario Estadístico de Cuba*, 1988, 1989.

Devereux, J. and Locay, L., "Specialization, Household Production, and the Measurement of Growth," *American Economic Review*, May 1992, 82, 399-403.

Gadjka, J., "Privatization in Poland," CIBER Occasional Paper #19, University of Maryland, May 1992.

Gómez Rodríguez, F., "Reflexiones sobre la circulación mercantil en el socialismo," *Economía y Desarrollo*, Nov-Dec 1989, 19, 40-50.

Litwack, J., "Legality and Market Reform in Soviet-Type Economies," *Journal of Economic Perspectives*, Fall 1991, 5, 77-90.

Maruyama, M., "A Country Study on the Distribution System in Japan," OECD Report, 1992.

Mathewson, G. and Winter, R., "The Economics of Vertical Restraints in Distribution" in Stiglitz, J. and Mathewson, G. (eds.), *New Developments in the Analysis of Market Structure*, Cambridge, Mass.: The MIT Press, 1986.

Mesa-Lago, C., "Cuba's Domestic Capacity to Confront the Crisis," paper presented at the Conference *Cuba in the Post Cold War Era*, University of Pittsburgh, April 1992.

Morande, F., "Domestic Prices of Importable Goods in Chile and the Law of One Price," *Journal of Development Economics*, April 1986, 21, 131-148.

Neyra Saiz, J., "El comercio mayorista en el sistema de comercio interior en Cuba," *Economía y Desarollo*, Mayo-Junio 1989, 19, 46-53.

Nove, A., *The Soviet Economic System*, London: George Allen, Ltd., 1977.

Oppenheimer, J., *Castro's Final Hour*, New York: Simon & Schuster, 1992.

Pérez-López, J., "Informality," paper presented at the Second ASCE Meetings, Miami, Fla., August 1992.

Rey, P. and Tirole, J., "The Logic of Vertical Restraints," *American Economic Review*, December 1986, 76, 921-39.

Roca, S., "El Programa Alimentario de Cuba: Reflejo y Proyección," paper presented at the meetings of the IEC in Orlando, June 1992.

Rodríguez, J.L., "The Cuban Economy: An Assessment" in Halebsky, S. and Kirk, J. (with R. Hernández), eds., *Transformation and Struggle: Cuba Faces the 1990s*, New York: Praeger Publishers, 1990.

Sanguinetty, J., "Non-Walrasian Properties of the Cuban Economy: Rationing, Labor Supply, and Output," paper presented at the Second ASCE Meetings, Miami, Florida, August 1992.

Suárez-Lugo, N., "Dirección científica e investigación de la demanda," *Economía y Desarrollo*, Marzo-Abril 1990, 20, 158-163.

Comments

Fernando Alvarez

Roger Betancourt and Jorge Pérez-López make the role of a discussant very difficult. Their topics are interesting and well-defined, and their exposition is clear and to the point. Therefore, the usual trick of summarizing in two pages their combined sixty pages does not work. After all, if I could do that, maybe they are in the wrong business! What I will do is outline what I learned from reading their papers and to offer some reflections of my own.

Both papers address topics ignored by economists who theorize about socialist economies. A recent survey article (van Brabant, *Journal of Economic Perspectives*, 1990) outlines the major differences between the two leading schools of thought about CPE; the Disequilibrium School and the Shortage Economy, whose main exponents are Richard Portes and Janos Kornay, respectively. It is almost beyond belief that theories that purport to explain the workings of a CPE do not have room for the re-trading of goods and services so central to the workings of the second economy investigated by Pérez-López, and the role of the distribution sector that Betancourt addresses. To me, it is like doing Hamlet without the prince.

A. The Second Economy

The main reservation I have about Jorge's paper is how he chose to motivate it; namely, "...that it is important because of the generalized perception that it is large and dynamic" (p. 1). Instead, I think we should be interested in measuring "private economic activities" because it gives us an estimate of the size of the entrepreneurial class in Cuba, a subject addressed by Sanguinetty in last year's conference. For example, Pérez-López reports that there are "three Cubans engaged in private enterprise for each registered self-employed individual" (p. 27), and this documents his statement that "[c]entrally planned economies, characterized by direct ownership of resources and highly regimented relationships among economic actors are fertile ground for entrepreneurial activities outside of the public regulatory framework" (p. 26). So, given that it is important that we measure the second economy in Cuba, can we do it? I'm afraid not. "There is no consensus among experts on a strict definition of such activities or on a methodology to quantify them" (p. 26). Furthermore, the best estimates of the US underground economy are in the ranges of 2% to 40% and from 6% to 42% of the total economy (p. 13). In other words, who knows?

This is the second time I've been called on to be a discussant for a Pérez-López paper. I find his work thorough, his documentation complete, and his analysis exhaustive. If Jorge can not find a way to do it, it just cannot be done. Therefore, I suggest we direct our attention to other projects that, although not as interesting or important as the measurement of the second economy, they are attainable and will contribute to our understanding of the issues we will face in the transition to a democratic Cuba.

B. Distribution Systems

Roger's introduction shows that the analysis of distribution systems in a CPE is an important issue. I prefer to think of Cuba as a PCPE (Previously CPE); therefore, my comments will look at the distribution system from the public policy perspective of a transition from a CPE to a PCPE. In a market economy, unlike in a socialist economy, firms expect to get paid for their goods and services; also, inventories and the opportunity cost of holding them are an important part of the distribution system. The implementation of Electronic Data Interchange (EDI) reduces the level of inventories needed to support a given level of sales, and facilitates payment and collection procedures. For the USA economy, the cost savings of implementing EDI are staggering. For example: in the automotive industry, EDI could save $200 to $1000 per car; the grocery industry could save $300 million per year if only 50% of its transactions were done by EDI.

One of the main obstacles to implementing EDI in the USA is a system of arcane rules and regulations exemplified by the McFadden Act of 1927 and rules of the Interstate Commerce Commission (ICC). The McFadden Act prohibits interstate banking. A result of this legislation is the proliferation of small banks, each with a separate way of handling accounts, and a strong incentive to keep things as they are to make it more difficult for customers to shop around for banking services. But this multitude of ways of doing the same thing makes it very hard to implement EDI, a system that thrives on standards. The ICC requires that detailed records must be maintained of all shipping documents. These records must be maintained for seven years in some physical form. Lawyers are still arguing whether a computer diskette is "physical." In the meantime the paper records of growing companies increase exponentially.

The lesson here for Cuba's transition to a PCPE is simple. Let's look at how laws and legislation affect the distribution system before we pass them.

UNA POLÍTICA O UN SISTEMA MONETARIO ÓPTIMO

Juan Luis Moreno Villalaz[1]

I.   Introducción

Después de su liberación e instauración de un gobierno democrático, Cuba tendrá que escoger su política monetaria. Existen dos alternativas para llegar a la mejor decisión. Una es la opción de una política monetaria de transición, de un sistema socialista planificado a una economía de mercado; la otra es tomar la decisión de un sistema monetario óptimo en forma permanente. La primera opción sería un sistema de emisión, con moneda propia. En este caso habría que diseñar una política monetaria adecuada, particularmente para el período de transformación. En la segunda alternativa se establecería un sistema donde la política monetaria sea automática, un sistema endógeno. Este es el caso del sistema monetario de Panamá, en el cual el dólar de Estados Unidos es la moneda de curso corriente y sólo se realizan emisiones fraccionarias de moneda local.

En este trabajo estudiamos, principalmente, lo que podemos aprender de las ventajas y conveniencias del sistema monetario panameño: cómo opera, cuáles son sus ventajas, qué flexibilidad tiene, cuál ha sido la experiencia con desequilibrio externos menores y mayores. También analizamos aspectos teóricos que validan la conclusión de que el sistema es óptimo. Por último se discuten temas relacionados a la ejecución de un sistema similar en Cuba.

II.   Cómo opera el sistema panameño

Cantidad de dinero

En el sistema monetario panameño, al igual que en uno de patrón oro o de tipo de cambio fijo, la cantidad de dinero y el crédito en la economía son endógenos y son determinados por los agentes económicos, a través del saldo en la balanza de pagos. Existen dos mecanismos para resolver desequilibrios por exceso de liquidez o falta de la misma. Uno es la oferta/demanda de crédito bancario o el nivel del gasto privado; en este caso el sistema se resuelve vía la actividad económica. Otro es mediante aumento/reducción de la posición internacional neta de la banca comercial, invirtiendo en instrumentos financieros externos o endeudándose. Este último le da gran flexibilidad al sistema.

Equilibrio de la Balanza de Pagos

El sistema contiene un mecanismo de ajuste automático de las crisis de balanza de pagos. Así, por ejemplo, una disminución transitoria en el precio de las exportaciones, reduce el flujo de oferta monetaria (ceteris paribus); debido a ello se produce un exceso de demanda dinero (flujos). En el proceso de ajuste esto se traduce —por Ley de Walras— en un exceso de oferta en el resto de los mercados financieros. Entonces las corporaciones, los individuos y el gobierno se deshacen de su excedente de activos no monetarios, lo que se traduce en un superávit en balanza de pagos, lo cual compensa el desequilibrio inicial en el mercado monetario. Este tipo de análisis es bien

---

[1]Este trabajo se hizo con la colaboración de Pedro Videla, de la Universidad Carlos III de Madrid. Agradezco los comentarios de mi hermano Gustavo Luis Moreno Villalaz, de Jorge Sanguinetty y la ayuda editorial de Gustavo A. Villa Jr. y Hernán Arboleda.

conocido en la literatura de la teoría monetaria de la balanza de pagos.

Si la disminución en el precio internacional del bien importable es percibida como permanente, el ajuste vendrá por una disminución en la demanda por dinero, como consecuencia de que la riqueza del país ha disminuido. Nótese que el ajuste es simétrico para el caso de superávit en la balanza de pagos y opera independiente del tipo de perturbaciones.

Otro mecanismo de ajuste, que le da flexibilidad al sistema y opera como un shock absorber, es mediante ajustes en la posición neta de activos internacionales del sistema. Cuando existe exceso de flujo de fondos, como en el presente, los bancos reducen su endeudamiento en el exterior y aumentan sus inversiones en el mercado internacional. El crédito comercial de importadores y la posición de empresas multinacionales también contribuyen a este proceso.

Inflación

La determinación endógena de la cantidad de dinero y el equilibrio automático de la Balanza de Pagos hace que la tasa de inflación interna converja con el nivel de inflación internacional. Esto impide que la autoridad fiscal local pueda recaudar el impuesto inflación y a la vez, se establece un mecanismo automático de control del gasto fiscal; las políticas expansivas del Gobierno no podrán sobrepasar los mecanismos tradicionales de recaudación impositiva.

La inflación en Panamá, es muy similar a la de los Estados Unidos. Hay diferencias menores en algunos períodos, como a principios de los años 70, debido a los aumentos de impuestos y costos laborales en Panamá. También durante la crisis de finales de los años 80, cuando los precios de los factores disminuyen y la inflación en Panamá fue menor que el nivel internacional. La inflación internacional, en particular la de los Estados Unidos, se transfiere a Panamá directamente por el aumento de precios de los productos de importación; pero esto también es el caso para los demás países.

La experiencia de los países latinoamericanos es que se utiliza el sistema monetario como un instrumento de poder político. Primero para establecer un impuesto sin representación, el impuesto inflacionario. Segundo para evadir, en situaciones de crisis, la decisión de quién y cómo se paga el costo de la misma. La inflación puede transferir el costo a ciertos sectores y agentes económicos, sin que estos lo perciban como una decisión gubernamental. El gobierno resuelve el problema inmediato, emitiendo. Se evade la decisión de quién o cómo se paga el costo de la misma. Posteriormente, se llama al FMI para que este "imponga" medidas de restricción fiscal-monetaria. Los gobiernos no se responsabilizan de las decisiones y de esta forma reducen su costo político de las crisis.

Tasa de interés

La tasa de interés en el sistema panameño converge a la tasa de interés internacional, con un diferencial que refleje el riesgo-país. El hecho que el sector privado determine la cantidad de crédito disponible en la economía, a través de los saldos en la balanza de pagos, garantiza el arbitraje de las tasas de interés.

Esta convergencia de tipos de interés establece un marco propicio para la inversión extranjera mediante la eliminación del riesgo cambiario y el establecimiento de reglas claras y estables. En segundo lugar, el arbitraje de tipos de interés elimina la posibilidad de triangulación financiera que conlleva a la fuga de capitales. Esto es así, ya que al eliminar la línea de demarcación entre el mercado financiero doméstico y el internacional, los incentivos para la fuga de capitales se eliminan.

Al abrirse el mercado de capitales (como pasó en Panamá y en Chile) se hace atractivo invertir en el país y los bancos piden prestado en el exterior para financiar proyectos locales. Los panameños no tienen fondos líquidos en el exterior[2], o sólo los tienen por razones de diversificación de portafolio.

La tasa de interés real positiva es considerada uno de los componentes más importantes para una política de desarrollo. Hay que indicar, también, que el sistema incluye libre movilidad de capitales. Esto es un elemento importante para atraer inversión extranjera. No es solamente que no hay riesgo cambiario, sino que no existe restricciones al retiro de utilidades o movimientos de capital. Esta es una de las características más destacadas y beneficiosas del sistema monetario panameño.

III. Los beneficios del sistema panameño

Los beneficios del sistema se miden a través de las decisiones que el mismo induce o los errores que no se realizan. Decir, únicamente, que el sistema monetario panameño logra estabilidad monetaria y no hay riesgo cambiario, no aclara el significado, alcance y las implicaciones de su operación.

Autoregulación de las finanzas y decisiones del gobierno

Uno de los principales beneficios del sistema monetario panameño es su efecto en las decisiones del sector público. El Gobierno sabe que la limitación de ingresos (budget constraint) es efectiva. Si no hay dinero no se puede gastar. El gasto público es igual a los ingresos fiscales más los créditos adquiridos. No se puede resolver el déficit fiscal mediante mayor gasto financiado con emisión monetaria. En años anteriores, en menor escala, el Gobierno financió inversiones en construcciones con bonos a contratistas. Pero la experiencia indicaba que eso era muy costoso.

La costumbre en Panamá es no subsidiar directamente. Aún en un Gobierno populista, como fue en el caso de Torrijos, se subsidiaba la electricidad y el agua de las poblaciones de menor ingreso mediante el sistema de "subsidios cruzados". Esto es, al precio de la energía y del agua potable se adicionaba un sobrecosto para compensar el subsidio a barriadas marginadas. Esto también se hizo manifiesto en la estructura de precios de los productos derivados del petróleo, donde se "subsidia" al diesel (con un impuesto muy bajo), se subsidia al transporte público y se subsidia al gas licuado esto se financia con recargos a los otros productos. En el caso del sistema telefónico se recargan las llamadas al exterior y al interior y se subsidia la tarifa básica y los teléfonos públicos. Otro ejemplo reciente son los subsidios a los jubilados, que se han hecho con recargos a las empresas privadas mediante una ley que determina descuentos en servicios cargados al sector privado y con nuevos impuestos que financian un fondo especial. Se han dado subsidios en la tasa de interés al sector agropecuario, pero compensados con recargos a los intereses en los préstamos comerciales.

En Panamá, no se han dado subsidios directos a precios de productos. En otras palabras, los subsidios existen pero son autofinanciables, de forma que no producen desequilibrios financieros,

---

[2]La información estadística sobre depósitos de panameños en el exterior incluye también los fondos de empresas extranjeras registradas en Panamá.

lo que es común cuando se puede emitir para financiar subsidios.

Las empresas estatales tienden a ser autofinanciables, con altos precios si es necesario. El precio del agua, del cemento, de la electricidad es alto, muy superior a los precios de la región. Cuando se registró un proceso inflacionario no existió dificultad política para aumentar el precio de la electricidad automáticamente. El público se acostumbró a la idea, de que no puede haber gastos si no existen los recursos con que pagarlos.

Cabe recordar la experiencia de países de la región, donde hubo subsidios a productos: la harina en Chile, el maíz en México, alimentos en Perú, el subsidio a los ferrocarriles en Argentina. Todo esto produjo substanciales déficits públicos, lo que a su vez incide en desequilibrios monetarios. En Panamá la existencia de un sistema monetario endógeno conduce a una forma de comportamiento que implica una racionalidad de mercado, lo que se convierte en "lo normal", aún en gobiernos poco conservadores financieramente.

Durante mucho años los gobiernos en Panamá confeccionaban un presupuesto donde los ingresos corrientes se utilizaban para cubrir los gastos de operaciones de las entidades públicas. La mayor proporción del programa de inversiones se financiaba con fondos de las instituciones financieras internacionales y la contrapartida con préstamos de la banca privada internacional.

Cuando existe una caída de ingresos o los mismos son menores que lo estimado en el presupuesto, inmediatamente se toman previsiones para corregir el déficit potencial. Lo que es imposible en otras partes, incluso en los Estados Unidos, es fácil en Panamá. Como asesor de varios gobiernos tengo la experiencia de saber que cuando no existían recursos, se realizaban los correctivos sin mayores traumas políticos. Proyectos o empresas deficitarias son detectados y corregidos de inmediato, como pasó con la extralimitación de fondos en el proyecto de construcción de viviendas, la Caja de Seguro Social en 1982. Las restricciones financieras incluso coadyuvan a correcciones estructurales, como la reciente reforma al sistema de seguridad social.

Cuando hay que recortar el gasto esto generalmente significa una drástica reducción en los gastos discrecionales, que en la práctica son los gastos de inversión. También se congelaban gastos de viajes, los nombramientos, no se realizan ascensos o aumentos de salarios (excepto los decretados por ley). Pero también se han hecho correcciones mayores, por ejemplo, cuando las empresas tienen déficit imprevistos, o cuando se cerró un ingenio o se reduce la zafra azucarera.

En esencia el sistema monetario panameño impone al gobierno una racionalidad de mercado versus la racionalidad de los políticos, en sus decisiones de política monetaria. La constricción presupuestaria (*hard budget constraint*) se hace real.

El costo de operar el sistema

¿Cuál es el costo real del sistema? ¿Cómo se compara con el costo de un sistema de emisión? El costo principal del sistema panameño es el costo del señoreaje pagado a los E. U. y la pérdida de ingreso de intereses por el uso de dólares como circulante. Comparativamente, el costo de un sistema con emisión es el diferencial de interés recibido por la reservas internacionales (que puede ser cero) y el que se tendría si se invirtieran estos recursos.

Una comparación de ambas situaciones para Panamá, asumiendo que el rendimiento de las inversiones es 10%, y el rendimiento de las reservas internacionales es 4%, es la siguiente:

Costo de un sistema de emisión fiduciaria

Valor de las Importaciones(en dólares E.U)	1650.0	
Reservas Internacionales (10 meses)	1375.0	
Rendimiento Promedio Normal de las mismas 4%:		
Costo (10% - 4%) x Cantidad de Reservas		82.5

Costo Estimado del sistema actual:

Estimación de Cantidad de Circulante en dólares[3]	400.0	
-(Con un PIB de $5.0 billones)		
-Aumento anual del mismo 5%		
Costo del sistema:		60.0
10% del Circulante	40.0	
Señoreaje	20.0	

Diferencial de Costo Directo[4]

	22.5

Se hace notar que la cantidad de reservas internacionales que Panamá tendría en un sistema de emisión es muy superior a la cantidad estimada de dinero efectivo circulante. Algo que no es comúnmente reconocido en Panamá.

Existen otros componentes de costos directos del sistema. Las pérdidas por destrucción de billetes, costos de tramitación por la substitución de los billetes. En un sistema de emisión hay costos de impresión de los billetes y existe el costo de operación del Banco Central. Estos costos extras hacen el costo directo de un sistema con emisión mayor que el de un sistema endógeno.

Por otra parte, el sistema panameño tiene beneficios adicionales. Existen servicios financieros, desde atraer depósitos de particulares de países con alta inflación, hasta el manejo de fondos de mercados negros. Estos servicios generan ingresos adicionales para el país.

La falta de comprensión del sistema monetario panameño se manifestó en el estudio de la CEPAL sobre la economía panameña en los años cincuenta. En dicho estudio se propuso que se emitiera dinero y que el ahorro de divisas (usadas como circulante) financiara un programa de inversiones. La realidad es todo lo contrario; el establecimiento de emisión requiere mantener más reservas de divisas, no menos.

Excedentes de recursos

Durante la segunda guerra mundial Panamá, como otros países latinoamericanos, acumuló un exceso de reservas internacionales. Las exportaciones de servicios al Ejército Sur de Estados Unidos fueron enormes, se estableció una multiplicidad de bases, a esto se agregaba el efecto del cruce del Canal por la flota americana hacia y desde el Pacífico. Las dificultades de gasto en

---

[3]Un 8% del PIB, el límite superior del estimado de Harberger (1970).

[4]La estimación es conservadora; no se toma en cuenta el comercio de la Zona Libre con el exterior, ni se deduce del circulante la moneda de plata.

productos importados resultó en acumulación de depósitos y riqueza, lo que también pasó en los otros países de la región.

Pero aquí existe una diferencia importante; esta acumulación estaba en manos privadas en forma de depósitos en la banca local, y en el sector financiero privado en forma de exceso de liquidez. En este sentido se puede decir que el sistema está privatizado. En cambio en los otros países de la región, esta riqueza se convirtió en propiedad del Gobierno, en forma de exceso de reservas internacionales del Banco Central.

Durante la crisis de 1987-89 se retiraron depósitos locales del sistema bancario de Panamá. Al reabrirse el sistema bancario estos fondos regresaron. Esto contrasta con la situación de otros países de la región, como México y Argentina, donde se mantuvieron cifras enormes depositadas en el exterior y posteriormente, pese a mayor estabilidad e incluso la introducción de depósitos en moneda extranjera, no han regresado sino una porción de estos activos.

El sistema frente a crisis menores

En varias ocasiones el sistema se ha enfrentado a crisis menores. Cabe preguntarse qué mecanismos de ajuste existen en dichos casos. ¿Reducción súbita de exportaciones se transfiere a reducción de la cantidad de dinero, generando fluctuaciones mayores en la economía? ¿Tiene el sistema algún mecanismo de ajuste?

Podemos investigar la experiencia de 1964, donde debido a un conflicto en la Zona del Canal existió una crisis política seria, que culminó con la ruptura de relaciones diplomáticas con Estados Unidos, y se registró una reducción temporal de ingresos de exportación. Los depósitos en el sistema disminuyeron de $136.3 millones en Diciembre de 1963 a $114.1 millones en Marzo de 1964.[5]

Pero el sistema monetario reaccionó financiando la salida de fondos locales con préstamos del exterior. Así, a pesar que depositantes extranjeros redujeron en B/12 millones su nivel de depósitos durante el año de 1964, el sistema aumentó su flujo interno disminuyendo sus activos externos en B/16 millones y aumentando sus pasivos internacionales (depósitos de bancos extranjeros y otros) en $18 millones. Como resultado de ello, a pesar de la crisis, la economía creció en 4.4% y no se agravó la inestabilidad interna.

En este proceso de intermediación financiera se nota la importancia de bancos internacionales, que tienen acceso inmediato a fondos de financiamiento de corto plazo. La existencia de una banca internacional perfecciona la operación del sistema y le da más competencia al mercado bancario interno.

Una segunda circunstancia, con resultados similares fue en 1973-74 con la fuerte alza en el precio del petróleo. De no existir un ajuste inmediato para pagar este gasto se hubiese tenido que reducir el gasto interno fuertemente. Los individuos y/o empresas reaccionaron al problema inmediato, bajando su liquidez y endeudándose, la banca acomodó esto, a su vez, financiando en el corto plazo con fondos externos. En 1973 la banca aumento su financiamiento a la economía panameña en $427 millones, pero no hubo nuevos financiamientos después.

Se puede decir que el mecanismo de mercado resolvió adecuadamente el primer problema

---

[5] Incluye reducción en depósitos internacionales, que en ese entonces financiaban el sistema local.

de la crisis del petróleo: no producir un shock inmediato por falta de liquidez. A su vez se empezó un mecanismo de ajuste automático. El Gobierno transfirió el aumento internacional del petróleo a los precios internos. Esto no fue un problema político, como en otras partes, porque era claro que no había alternativas. De esta forma se introdujo un efecto precios ("price effect"), pero sólo al petróleo y derivados, que fueron los productos que subieron de precios relativos. La inflación en Panamá fue similar a la de los Estados Unidos, de 1972 a 1975 el índice de precios en Panamá subió en 31.6% y en Estados Unidos en 28.5%.

En otros países las políticas de ajuste de precios no fueron necesariamente las más adecuadas. Algunos pospusieron el ajuste, o incluso subsidiaron el precio del petróleo. En muchos casos hubo devaluaciones nominales y reales, creando distorsiones en precios relativos de los bienes transables. Es decir políticas cambiarias y macroeconómicas introdujeron distorsiones de precios relativos a una clase de productos, cuando esto no estaba pasando a nivel internacional. Además la inflación interna fue muy superior a la inflación mundial.

El otro factor fue el ajuste monetario. Por un lado el sistema proveyó recursos financieros a corto plazo, pero temporales. Por lo tanto, automáticamente se inició un proceso de ajustes paulatino del nivel de gasto privado y público. El ajuste era inevitable, el mecanismo se ejecuta sin la intervención de las autoridades monetarias. Esto se hizo sin inflación adicional, sin una crisis interna. El proceso es óptimo.

En ambos casos la experiencia indica que no se necesitan reservas internacionales, o la intervención del gobierno, o la intermediación del FMI para resolver problemas temporales de Balanza de Pagos. La disponibilidad de crédito de la banca, en particular de bancos con casas matrices internacionales, y de los empresarios, crean mecanismos de ajuste de mercado. Hay una reserva potencial, una fuerza cinética disponible, un mecanismo de absorción de los choques (*shock absorber*).

El ajuste se hace en la dirección correcta y probablemente en la velocidad adecuada, es un proceso óptimo. En todo caso un proceso mucho más eficiente que la alternativa: la política macroeconómica, monetaria y de cambio de los gobiernos de la región frente a crisis externa.

El sistema frente a crisis mayores

Durante 1987-1989 Panamá experimentó una crisis política y económica sin precedentes. El proceso empezó con revelaciones sobre crímenes perpetrados por la dictadura militar contra dirigentes políticos. Con anterioridad habían protestas y se acentuaron los conflictos con el gobierno de Estados Unidos y grupos del sector privado.

Durante 1987 sucede la primera crisis y se retiran $185 millones de depósitos privados internos.[6] Respecto al manejo de la deuda, el gobierno acuerda con los bancos internacionales pagar su servicio en forma retrasada, se suspendió el pago de la deuda con la banca oficial internacional y se paralizó el programa de inversiones.

La banca privada panameña mantenía altos niveles de reservas líquidas, cercanas al 30 al 40% de sus activos. Estas reservas se depositaban en bancos extranjeros en Panamá. Como en ocasiones

---

[6]Excluye depósitos interbancarios.

anteriores la banca trajo dinero a Panamá[7] y no se produce un colapso del sistema bancario, a pesar de condiciones políticas, de la crisis fiscal y de las perspectivas muy desfavorables.

La contracción financiera paralizó la actividad de la construcción, un importante sector empresarial de la economía panameña. Por falta de demanda bajan las ventas y se reducen los inventarios y las importaciones. La economía empieza a sentir el efecto de una crisis. Dado el crecimiento que existía hasta mediados de año, los efectos de la crisis no se registran en su verdadera magnitud en las cifras anuales.

La segunda etapa de la crisis sucede a principios de marzo de 1988. El Gobierno de los Estados Unidos aplica sanciones económicas contra el gobierno de Panamá. Esto incluye restricciones a las empresas americanas para el pago de impuestos, suspensión de los pagos al gobierno por la operación del Canal, poner a la ciudad de Panamá fuera de límites para los soldados, retiro de americanos residentes, amenazas de fuerza militar.

Ante presiones de retiro de dinero en la Banca se cerró el sistema bancario por mes y medio. Cuando se reanudaron sus operaciones se trabajó en forma condicionada, con la suspensión de la obligatoriedad de pagar los depósitos locales. El gobierno autorizó a los bancos, en forma voluntaria, la emisión de certificados de depósitos e inversión (CEDIS) contra los depósitos restringidos; algunos bancos aceptaban los mismos como amortización de deuda.

El efecto en la economía fue inmediato. Por un mes no operaron los bancos. No había crédito, todas las actividades ligadas al mismo prácticamente se suspendieron: venta de autos, muebles, bienes duraderos. La industria de la construcción se paralizó. La industria de materiales de construcción quedó operando a un nivel mínimo. La economía decreció en un 16% en 1988.

El sistema y el mecanismo de ajuste en estas circunstancias extremas fueron:[8]

i)   Al momento de la crisis no existía una bolsa de valores en Panamá. De todas formas se transaban documentos financieros y había un mercado de propiedades y tierra. La crisis afectó los precios de dichos bienes y documentos reflejando las expectativas y los desajustes sectoriales.

Los CEDIS de los bancos americanos se vendían con 5-8% de descuento, el de los bancos nacionales entre el 15 al 20% de descuento. Una excepción fue el de un banco local importante pero identificado con la oposición al gobierno, el descuento en este caso llegó al 30%.

Los bonos del gobierno, que se vendían al 80% se descontaron al 50% durante la crisis. Los pagarés (a 6 meses un año) se descontaban al 15% de su valor.

Los agentes de propiedades y firmas de avalúos acordaron, lo que fue aceptado por la banca, un "factor de descuento por crisis". Esto descontó el valor de los edificios en los barrios de lujo entre un 25 al 33%, las propiedades de clase media alta entre un 15 al 20% y las de nivel medio entre un 10 al 15%.

El valor de las tierras, en muchos casos disminuyó en 30-40%. La baja en el precio de venta

---

[7]Hubo mayores retiros de depósitos internacionales, pero como éstos estaban respaldados con activos internacionales su ajuste no ocasionó dificultades.

[8]La información sobre valores financieros provino de los Srs. Mariana y Pedro Detresno.

de las tierras en Panamá no fue una baja del precio de la tierra, sino el efecto de liquidación de propiedades pignoradas, cuando no había compradores. Inversionistas con proyectos de vivienda en vías de desarrollo, que tenían deudas con los bancos por la construcción de infraestructura y la compra de la tierra para sus proyectos, tuvieron que liquidar para pagar intereses o mantenerse el resto de la propiedad. Como, temporalmente, no había demanda el precio de liquidación fue bajo. En una crisis existen actores particulares que tienen dificultad para ajustarse, principalmente por su endeudamiento.

De esta información y de conversaciones durante y después de la crisis, podemos colegir que no hubo pánico, que las expectativas de pérdida de riqueza por la crisis eran entre el 15-20% en términos reales. En algunos casos, dado que se estaba en medio de un "boom" de construcción, los precios pre-crisis eran algo especulativos y se ajustaron mas fuertemente. A pesar de lo que estaba pasando no hubo crisis de expectativa. El sistema monetario evitó inestabilidad en las expectativas, en este sentido sirvió de mecanismo estabilizador.

Un elemento importante en el problema de la crisis es la situación de actividades con alto grado de exposición (exposure): construcciones en proceso, desarrollistas, etc., que tienen fuertes compromisos financieros y pocas alternativas. Estos incurren en pérdidas mayores. Aún para estos grupos la pérdida de riqueza "en dólares" y las pérdidas de capital resultado de la crisis fueron menores que las que crea una devaluación cuando se tienen compromisos en moneda extranjera. Nuevamente el sistema monetario panameño evitó pérdidas mayores debido al efecto de la devaluación en el valor de los pasivos en dólares.

ii)   El sistema ajustó el nivel de gasto, principalmente por la reducción de ingresos, pero también ajustó más el gasto en importaciones. Las importaciones bajaron de $1,637 millones en 1987 a $1082 millones en 1988 aunque sin una devaluación que cambiara fuertemente los precios relativos.

El ajuste en el gasto de consumo se hizo mediante la reducción del gasto en los bienes duraderos, que se compraban al crédito (autos, aparatos domésticos) y el gasto en artículos no indispensables y de lujo, en ambos casos con un alto contenido importado. Además la baja general de inventarios redujo la demanda por importaciones y se registró una importante reducción del gasto en inversión.

Gran cantidad de empresas y personas quedaron en quiebra virtual, una especie de *Chapter 11* masivo. Los bancos liquidaron a ciertos negocios pero se abstuvieron de provocar quiebras masivas. Los banco americanos, quizás presionados por su gobierno, fueron mas estrictos.

iii)   El sistema demostró capacidad de ajuste en precios. El mercado de viviendas de alquiler sufrió una caída con la retirada de los americanos y extranjeros. Pero cambios en precios hicieron que estos apartamentos se alquilaran y se eliminara el excedente de apartamentos que se creó al iniciarse la crisis.

Los edificios de alquiler de lujo se ajustaron al mercado. Hubo una gran salida de americanos, algo mas de 3500 personas, además de japoneses y otros extranjeros. Quedó un excedente de apartamentos de lujo, lugares que se alquilaban a $1,200 antes de la crisis se alquilaron a $700-800 durante la crisis. Pero esto logró crear suficiente demanda como para absorber el excedente disponible. El nuevo alquiler, me informan, era cercano a lo que el dueño le pagaba al banco entre amortización e intereses.

Los sindicatos negociaron reducción de salario (incluso modificaciones de convenciones colectivas), se aceptaron reducciones en el número de horas de trabajo e incluso reducción de la fuerza laboral. También hubo reducción de salarios de empleados públicos, aunque en menor escala. Durante la crisis el nivel de salario real bajó como puede verse en el Cuadro 1 por la reducción de la mediana de salario en distintos sectores.

Cuadro 1. Panamá: Mediana de salario semanal, hombres, area metropolitana
(Dólares)

Rama de Actividad	1987	1988
Industria Manufacturera	72.4	69.2
Construcción	72.4	66.7
Comercio y Restaurantes	62.9	56.8
Establecimientos Financieros	86.6	80.7
Servicios Sociales	106.9	99.9
Servicios de Diversión	75.6	67.3
Servicios de Reparación	62.1	49.9
Servicios Domésticos (Mujeres)	23.8	22.8

Fuente: Dirección de Estadística y Censos, *Encuesta de Hogares.*

Durante los ochenta se registró una "devaluación real" en Panamá, como puede verse de la comparación de la evolución de los índices de precios al consumidor que aparecen en el Cuadro 2. Los precios en Estados Unidos crecen más que en Panamá. Esto se manifiesta en forma más acentuada durante el período de la crisis.

iv)   Se tomaron medidas para proteger a los depositantes extranjeros ya que las restricciones no se aplicaron a las operaciones *off-shore*. Se permitió que bancos regionales cambiaran su licencia para convertirse en bancos de licencia internacional y, entonces, pagar a sus depositantes.

Los fondos que se retiraron de Panamá, en gran parte porque no se podía usar el sistema bancario para hacer transacciones, se utilizaban cuentas en el exterior. Al restablecerse la apertura del sistema regresaron estos fondos, aumentando los depósitos de particulares locales en $700 millones. La economía se empezó a recuperar, a pesar de que se agravaba el conflicto político interno y externo. El producto bruto no creció en 1989, pero esto debido a las pérdidas por vandalismo durante la invasión.

Crisis mayor en una economía con moneda fiduciaria

En el caso de una economía con moneda, como Chile, la crisis se acentúa. La devaluación se hace imprescindible porque frente a la crisis se crea la certeza de que la moneda no puede resistir. Las personas empiezan a retirar fondos en moneda local y se especula en el cambio en la paridad.

Una primera devaluación no es suficiente, se crea un pesimismo de expectativas, como en los casos de una burbuja (*bubble*). Esto produce una inestabilidad mayor. El sistema monetario contribuye a desestabilizar la economía vía expectativas negativas creando una especie de "*black noise*". Hay una distorsión en las decisiones que resultan en retiro de fondos de la economía local, lo que intensifica la crisis económica. Esto crea un efecto similar a una reorientación en la demanda (*demand shift*) y revierte con creces el efecto-precio de la devaluación.

Cuadro 2. Panamá y EE.UU.: Indice de precios al consumidor, 1980-1990

Año	Panamá	Crecimiento	EE.UU.	Crecimiento	Diferencia
1980	100.0	---	100.0	---	---
1981	107.3	7.3	110.3	10.3	3.0
1982	111.9	4.2	117.1	6.2	2.0
1983	114.2	2.1	120.9	3.3	1.1
1984	116.0	1.6	126.1	4.3	2.7
1985	117.2	1.1	130.6	3.6	2.5
1986	117.2	-0.1	133.0	1.8	1.9
1987	118.3	1.0	136.8	2.9	1.9
1988	118.8	0.4	143.5	4.9	4.5
1989	118.6	-0.1	150.4	4.8	4.9
1990	119.3	0.6	158.5	5.4	4.8

Fuente: IMF, *International Financial Statistics*.

Otro fenómeno importante es el efecto de la crisis-devaluación en los mercados de capitales y riqueza. Para quienes tienen pasivos en otras monedas se produce una pérdida de riqueza, o de valorización de sus activos medidos en dólares. Esto lleva a problemas de solvencia que pueden producir quiebras de empresas. Como mínimo aumenta el riesgo existente. Para evitar peores males el gobierno, tanto en Chile como en Argentina, absorbió la deuda en dólares. Esto redujo en gran parte el problema de inestabilidad e incertidumbre. Pero lo hizo a un alto costo social, la población en su conjunto termina subsidiando a grupos de propietarios, grupos de mayor ingreso. El sistema no es honesto, las ganancias se retienen, los riesgos son transferidos, los depositantes y ahorristas pierden. La solución correcta es reducir la pérdida financiera, lo que sucede en el caso del sistema monetario panameño.

En estos casos la política de devaluación puede acentuar la crisis en vez de corregirla, y se convierte en un mecanismo de desajuste en lugar de un mecanismo de ajuste. Los argumentos macroeconómicos de la devaluación como mecanismo de ajuste toman en cuenta principalmente el efecto en el mercado de bienes y servicios. No se estudian los fenómenos de fuga de capitales y sesgo en las expectativas. Los modelos de expectativas racionales introducen expectativas "neutras" (con *white noise*).

El gobierno, por su naturaleza, introduce un elemento de inestabilidad e incertidumbre en el sistema económico. Esto es particularmente cierto en períodos de crisis. El gobierno no opera en forma "óptima"; en muchas ocasiones prefiere resolver sus problemas aún cuando eso desestabilice más la economía. En la práctica no existe el "planificador ilustrado" o el "gobierno tecnócrata". La experiencia panameña, debemos enfatizar, es que el mercado se ajusta mejor frente a una crisis.

IV.   Un modelo teórico sobre el sistema monetario o la política monetaria óptima

Como hemos visto en la experiencia panameña los beneficios del sistema también se manifiestan en el corto plazo, al establecer mecanismos automáticos de ajuste ante distintas perturbaciones que afecten a la economía.

Esta característica del sistema es puesta en duda por los proponentes de políticas monetarias activas como mecanismo de estabilización económica (Turvnosky 1980, entre otros). Ellos plantean que el establecimiento de sistema de moneda endógena (o sistema de cambio fijo con un gobierno pasivo) implica el sacrificio de una de las herramientas más importante para el manejo de política económica en el corto plazo. Este también pareciera ser el paradigma existente en los organismos multilaterales (i.e., Banco Mundial, BID y, principalmente, FMI) a juzgar por sus recomendaciones de política a sus países miembros.

Estos argumentos en pro y contra de las bondades del sistema de moneda unificada en el corto plazo son analizados en el modelo que presentamos en el apéndice. En él se comparan las desviaciones del producto (respecto de su tendencia), ante distintos sistemas cambiarios, cuando la economía se ve afectada por distintas perturbaciones domésticas y foráneas.

Del análisis se desprende que, primero, si la autoridad monetaria sigue una política discrecional y no una regla de creación de dinero (supuesto sustentado por múltiples experiencias en los países en desarrollo), es preferible un sistema como el panameño porque el mismo elimina las perturbaciones monetarias y los cambios en las expectativas de devaluación. Esto corrobora la experiencia de Panamá, el sistema monetario endógeno, en particular en momentos de crisis, es un factor estabilizador del sistema.

En segundo lugar, el modelo deja en claro que si la autoridad renuncia a la discrecionalidad y sigue una regla monetaria que minimice las fluctuaciones del producto en el corto plazo, entonces ella debe comportarse como si tuviera un sistema de moneda unificada. Sólo en este caso, la cantidad de dinero interna responderá a los ajustes de portafolio dictados por la demanda. Es decir, que la política monetaria óptima es operar como si no existiera una moneda propia, lo que por definición se garantiza en el sistema panameño.

Un sistema monetario alterno, pero similar, es el que se usa en Hong Kong y en Argentina. La Junta Monetaria o el Banco Central, por ley, emiten billetes y monedas convertibles en una cantidad igual a la cantidad de reserva externa, a un tipo de cambio fijo. Este sistema es un sistema endógeno y un sustituto cercano al uso directo del dólar. Tendría las mismas propiedades del sistema panameño, aunque con ciertas limitaciones en cuanto a la confiabilidad para atraer depósitos externos. Por otro lado, tendría la ventaja de que se tendría una unidad monetaria propia, lo que es más aceptable políticamente por razones de soberanía.

V. Conclusiones sobre el modelo panameño

El sistema monetario "a la panameña" es un sistema eficiente y óptimo. Garantiza estabilidad, promueve la inversión extranjera, crea su propia exportación de servicios financieros, tiene bajo costo de operación, elimina el riesgo cambiario. Una ventaja importante del sistema es que se establece una economía de "precios reales".

El sistema también tiene sus propios mecanismos de ajuste que lo hacen flexible y óptimo. Choques externos se resuelven mediante mecanismos de mercado. Un primer mecanismos, un *shock-absorber*, es mediante fluctuaciones en la posición neta de activos internacionales de los bancos. Un segundo mecanismo es la transmisión, mediante cambios en oferta/demanda de inversiones/gastos o de la cantidad de dinero, al nivel de actividad económica. Un tercer mecanismo es cambios en precios relativos, aunque dentro de tasa de cambio fijo, en donde estas fluctuaciones son pequeñas.

El sistema monetario contribuye a que el Gobierno tome decisiones racionales, a que existe una verdadero "*budget constraint*". En este sentido podemos decir que introduce una "racionalidad de mercado" a las decisiones, incluso las del gobierno. Por último el sistema es eficiente en términos de formación de expectativas.

VI. El sistema endógeno y el proceso de transformación

Los problemas durante la transición

En los trabajos de Felipe Pazos "Problemas económicos de Cuba en el período de transición" y de Ernesto Hernández-Catá, "Long-Term Objectives and Transitional Policies: A Reflection on Pazos' Economic Problems of Cuba", presentados a conferencias previas de esta organización se discuten los problemas monetarios del período de transición.

En dichos trabajos de discute el problema de un proceso inflacionario, Los déficit fiscales, la devaluación del peso, los ajustes de precios, la dificultad que la inexistencia de independencia del Banco Central pueda promover exceso de emisión monetaria con la resultante inflación. La experiencia de transformación de varios países socialistas es una advertencia al respecto.

Otro problema es cómo absorber la moneda existente y eliminar la existencia de un exceso de dinero en circulación (*monetary overhang*). Aquí la experiencia de Rusia nos indica la tentación, incluso justificada por los temores inflacionarios o de liquidar el exceso de circulante mediante una expropiación. El Brazil, recientemente, expropió las tenencias de dinero en forma de depósito. Esto fue una violación de los derechos de propiedad. Además, junto con la inflación, es una forma de imponer un impuesto a los sectores informales y los mercados negros, que son mecanismos importantes en el proceso de transformación.

Un tercer problema es el sistema y la tasa de cambio. Se menciona la posibilidad de una "sobre-devaluación" del peso. ¿Cuál es la tasa de cambio "correcta"? Hernández-Catá propone, inicialmente, un sistema flexible. En Rusia hubo dificultades, se impusieron tasas diferenciales para los inversionistas extranjeros, no hay garantías de retiro de las ganancias. Esto reduce el flujo de inversión privada externa cuando más se necesita y puede, en efecto, provocar una sobre-devaluación.

Por otra parte, un flujo de capital considerable, como ha pasado en España, sobrevalúa la moneda, con perjuicios a la competitividad de la economía. Esto no pasa en un sistema monetario como el panameño. Exceso de flujos de capital se invierten en moneda extranjera.

Un problema importante es cómo corregir el sistema artificial de precios. Hay tres sistema de precios, el del mercado de bienes y servicios, incluyendo impuestos, precios de productos de las empresas estatales; el de los macro precios; el nivel de precios, el precio de los factores, la tasa de interés y el tipo de cambio; por último, el precio de los bienes-riqueza, el capital existente, las instalaciones, las empresas, las tierras y la vivienda. Hay que llegar a un sistema de precios reales, en una economía de mercado. Algunos de estos problemas están interrelacionados, o influyen o están influidos por el sistema monetario, pero estrictamente son problemas diferentes.

Felipe Pazos introduce el principio de separación entre las políticas durante el período de transición y las políticas óptimas de largo plazo. Hernández-Catá recomienda que las políticas deben ser diseñadas de manera que eviten desviaciones permanentes con los objetivos de largo plazo. La experiencia de países en vías de desarrollo indica cómo medidas temporales, muchas veces distorsiones, permanecen por largo plazo.

Las discusiones sobre política monetaria llevan a "compromisos" entre lo óptimo y lo inmediato. En el documento de Hernández-Catá se discuten varios casos en donde se aceptan, temporalmente, políticas de control de precios para productos esenciales, intervención en los tipos de cambio. El manejo de la política monetaria introduce el peligro de tener una economía "administrada", con decisiones influidas por objetivos políticos, con alto riesgo de equivocaciones o que retrasen el proceso de transformación.

Por último, cabe mencionar lo que podríamos llamar "el principio de la ignorancia". Hay muchas cosas que no sabemos cómo van a suceder, qué problemas se van a encontrar. Tampoco tenemos soluciones "a priori", teóricas o prácticas. La necesidad de resolver simultáneamente distintos problemas monetarios cuando a su vez se están haciendo otras transformaciones deja áreas grises. En la práctica hay problemas por resolver en cualquier sistema que se adopte. Usar el dólar es tener fe en la operación del mercado para resolver dichos problemas, versus tener fe en la discrecionalidad del gobierno para implementar las mejores decisiones.

Para todos los problemas macro-monetarios mencionados está claro que el sistema en dólares es la solución óptima, incluso durante el proceso de transición. No existe un problema de inflación, o cuál es el tipo de cambio correcto, o expropiación de los activos en moneda. La introducción del dólar puede acelerar la transformación del sistema de precios. Es claro que el objetivo de la política monetaria es lograr un clima de estabilidad y confianza, para lo cual se necesita mantener la inflación bajo control, y fomentar el ahorro y la inversión local e internacional. Todo esto esta garantizado con el sistema monetario propuesto.

La introducción del dólar como moneda

La primera medida es autorizar la circulación del dólar y depósitos en dólares. Se libera cualquiera restricción de cambio o de pagos, se permite, sin restricciones, el uso del dólar para cualquier transacción. Se declara cómo va a ser el sistema en el futuro.

Inmediatamente el turismo, los cubanos que regresan, la inversión extranjera, las exportaciones, le inyectan dólares al sistema y van estableciendo la base monetaria. El sistema de precios en dólares se produce primero por los precios de los productos importados. Segundo por la demanda y oferta en dólares para la compra-venta de bienes y servicios en sectores donde se transa en dólares, como servicios turísticos. Productores privados empezaran a pedir precios en dólares y precios en pesos.

Se debe autorizar la operación de un mercado privado de cambios. Esto puede ser un mercado formal o con la operación de bancos internacionales, a los que se les daría licencia temporal de operaciones. Se permiten la transacciones de divisas sin intervención del gobierno.[9]

El estado recibirá dólares y/o pesos como pago por la venta de sus activos. La moneda local desaparece al ser recibida por el gobierno en pago de activos. De esta forma la moneda local se irá absorbiendo y desapareciendo, sin que los tenedores sufran una pérdida por ello. Los tipos de cambio del peso serían establecidos por el mercado.

Por un tiempo el gobierno puede seguir pagando salarios y jubilaciones en pesos. Posteriormente se introducen el pago de salarios y jubilaciones parcialmente en dólares. Aproximándose al precio en dólares de la mano de obra en el mercado. Recursos de ayuda internacional podrán ser usados para balancear temporalmente el presupuesto en dólares. Persiste el problema de que los salarios reales pueden ser muy bajos. Para evitar la emisión excesiva se debe establecer una fecha de 6 a 9 meses para la terminación de la moneda local, mientras tanto se deberá reducir la emisión.

Aquí el gobierno se enfrenta a la obligación de ser transparente. ¿Qué precio en dólares tendrán las jubilaciones, o el gasto en el ejército? En otros países la inflación hace recargar el costo de la crisis en sectores particulares. Una decisión política que se hace sin decir, minimizando los costos políticos. En el sistema en dólares el gobierno tiene que enfrentarse a estos problemas y proclamar su decisión como suya.

En Panamá, en 1904, la transición al dólar no tuvo dificultades aparentes. Pero esto se debía a que ya existía un sistema de precios reales y una economía privada. Es la conversión del sistema de precios artificiales al sistema de precios reales lo que da problemas. En algunos casos los precios en dólares (de ciertos salarios, por ejemplo) pueden ser muy bajos o habrá la necesidad de una reforma de precios. Pero esto también está pasando en Rusia.

El uso del dólar acelera la reconversión del sistema de precios artificales a uno de precios reales, porque existirán incentivos para utilizar el sistema de precios en dólares. Durante el período de transición hay falta de confianza en la moneda local. La instalación del nuevo sistema monetario elimina este problema y además sería una señal importante de que se va en camino del establecimiento de una economía de mercado.

En resumen recomendamos la creación de un sistema monetario como el sistema panameño. Sabemos que es óptimo a largo plazo. Creemos que también lo es durante el período de transición. Esta propuesta parece original y novedosa, pero para los economistas que conocemos el sistema monetario panameño, es simple y obvia. De no hacerse se estaría perdiendo la oportunidad de orientar la economía hacia un camino de progreso.

---

[9]Queda por resolver el precio de los bienes-riqueza. Se puede emitir un documento especial que será usado para comprar propiedades estatales. Estos documentos, como se ha hecho en algunos países, se distribuyen a los habitantes como su participación en la riqueza nacional (tierras, viviendas, establecimiento), pero puede venderse. Este documento también podrá ser usado para saldar reclamos sobre propiedades expropiadas.

Anexo: El Modelo

Supóngase una economía pequeña y abierta que enfrenta perturbaciones de origen interno y externo. Ella produce un vector de bienes comerciables (agregados a la Hicks) cuyo precio esta exógenamente dado por la paridad del poder de compra. De forma análoga, el mercado financiero esta perfectamente integrado al resto del mundo, de tal manera que la paridad (no cubierta) de tipo de interés se cumple.

Todas las variables del modelo (excepto el tipo de interés) están expresadas en forma de logaritmo natural y representan desviaciones respecto a un nivel no estocástico o de largo plazo. En otras palabras, ellas representan desviaciones respecto de la tendencia.

Primero consideraremos una economía con una autoridad monetaria que acuña moneda local e impone que las transacciones domésticas se realicen haciendo uso de ella. La estructura de esta economía puede ser representada por las siguientes ecuaciones:

$$y = \Theta \ (P - P_0) \tag{1}$$

$$P = P^* + e \tag{2}$$

$$i = i^* + e_{+1} - e \tag{3}$$

$$m^d - P = y - \alpha i \tag{4}$$

$$m^s = \chi \tag{5}$$

La ecuación (1) es la oferta de Lucas [Lucas (1972)] que indica que en el corto plazo las desviaciones del producto real dependen de los errores que los agentes económicos incurren al predecir el nivel de precios de la economía. La ecuación (2) indica que el nivel de precios esta determinado por la paridad del poder de compra. La ecuación (3) especifica la paridad no cubierta de tipos de interés reflejo que los activos financieros domésticos son sustitutos perfectos de los extranjeros. La ecuación (4) indica que la demanda real de dinero local depende positivamente del nivel de actividad económica y negativamente del tipo de interés doméstico. Finalmente, la ecuación (5) indica que las desviaciones de la oferta de dinero es igual a una variable estocastica, χ, que no es observable por los distintos agentes de la economía.

Las expectativas se suponen racionales o endógenas, es decir:

$$Z_t = E_{t-1}(Z_t)$$

donde E_{t-1} es el operador de valor esperado condicional a toda la información disponible en el período t-1. Así, por ejemplo, P_0 indica la expectativa del nivel de precio de hoy formada ayer. Que los agentes económicos tengan expectativas endógenas significa que ellos consideran la estructura del modelo (i.e., los supuestos de formación de los precios, tipo de cambio y comportamiento del gobierno) en la formación de sus expectativas.

El modelo contiene tres fuentes de perturbaciones: χ de origen doméstico y P^* e i^* de origen externo. Normalmente la literatura de modelos macroeconómicos estocásticos supone que las perturbaciones son variables aleatorias que se distribuyen independientemente a través del tiempo. Es decir, que ellas son no anticipadas y percibidas como transitorias. Nosotros no las restringiremos de esa manera, lo único que supondremos es que las perturbaciones externas son exógenas al país pequeño en cuestión.

La expresión para la expectativas del tipo de cambio se obtiene a partir del equilibrio del mercado monetario. Tomando la esperanza condicional a la información disponible en el período t-1 obtenemos una ecuación en diferencia homogénea de primer orden del tipo de cambio, ésta es:

$$e - \lambda e_{+1} = [-\alpha i^* - P^* + \chi]/1+\alpha \tag{6}$$

Donde:

$$\lambda \equiv \frac{\alpha}{1+\alpha}$$

cuya solución estable[10] es "*forward looking*", indicando que el valor esperado del tipo de cambio es el valor presente de una suma infinita de perturbaciones presentes y futuras que afecten a esta economía:

$$e_{1+J} = \frac{1}{1+\alpha} \sum_{j=0}^{\infty} \lambda^j \Omega_{1+J} \tag{7}$$

Donde: $\Omega_{1+J} \equiv \chi_{1+J} - \alpha i^*_{1+J} - P^*_{1+J}$

Cualquier perturbación que cree un exceso de demanda flujo de dinero presente o futuro, creará expectativas de depreciación de la moneda local respecto a la moneda extranjera. Por tanto, la política monetaria y la percepción que tengan los agentes económicos de ella, juega un papel fundamental en la determinación de las expectativas de tipo de cambio.

Esta expectativa también determinará el comportamiento del producto y el empleo de corto plazo. La solución de las variables endógenas y y e es igual a:

$$y = \left[\frac{\theta}{\Delta} \alpha P^* - (1+\alpha) P_0 + \chi - \alpha(i^* + e_{+1}) \right] \tag{8}$$

Donde: $\Delta \equiv 1+\alpha+\theta$

$$e = \left[\frac{1}{\Delta} \chi - (1+\theta) P^* + \alpha (i^* + e_{+1}) + \theta P_0 \right] \tag{9}$$

---

[10] La solucion estable se obtiene suponiendo que todos los términos transientes de la forma $C\lambda^j$ son iguales a cero para cualquier constante arbitraria C, i.e., suponiendo la no existencia de burbujas explosivas (Sargent, (1981).

La ecuación (8) indica que el producto de corto plazo depende de la política monetaria, y de las perturbaciones de carácter doméstico y foráneo que enfrente esta economía. Esta ecuación, en conjunto con la ecuación (7), deja en claro que, en la eventualidad de que el gobierno tenga un comportamiento errático en la conducción de su política monetaria (i.e., χ distinto de cero) la variabilidad del producto y empleo se incrementará.

Por su parte la ecuación (9) indica que el tipo de cambio que regirá en la economía depende positivamente de la política monetaria, ya sea directamente a través de x o indirectamente a través de sus expectativas. Nuevamente, si la autoridad monetaria no es disciplinada, introducirá ruido en el sistema que afectara negativamente al funcionamiento de la economía.

Estos efectos negativos potenciales de la política gubernamental se eliminan si se deja que las fuerzas del mercado determinen la cantidad de dinero y crédito. Una alternativa para endogeneizar la cantidad de dinero es la introducción de competencia en la acuñación e intercambio de dinero. Esto elimina el monopolio del gobierno al existir diversas monedas, tanto nacionales como extranjeras, en circulación. Si algunas de las firmas de la industria del dinero desvaloriza su producto mediante una emisión por sobre de lo deseado por los agentes, ellos dejarán de aceptar esa moneda como medio de cambio y reserva de valor, desplazándola fuera del mercado [Hayek (1976)].

Una alternativa más sencilla de implementar y empíricamente probada en el caso Panameño (al igual que en Hong-Kong) es eliminar el proceso de acuñación de moneda local y aceptar libremente la circulación de moneda estable extranjera (dólar en Panamá, libra esterlina en Hong-Kong). En este caso podemos replantear el modelo presentado arriba mediante: primero, igualar el tipo de cambio a 1 (por tanto, e=ln(E)= 0 cuando E=1), indicando que la moneda usada en las transacciones domésticas será la internacional; segundo, y tal como el enfoque monetario de la balanza de pagos lo indica, explicitando que la cantidad de dinero es igual al saldo de la balanza de pagos (i.e., cambio en la posición neta de las reservas internacionales del país) que designaremos con la letra R.

La cantidad nominal de dinero (saldo de balanza de pagos), conjuntamente con el producto, son las dos variables endógenas a determinar en una economía con estas características que representaremos con las siguientes ecuaciones:

$$Y = \theta(P^* - P^*_0) \tag{10}$$

$$P = P^* \tag{11}$$

$$i = i^* \tag{12}$$

$$m^d - P^* = y - \alpha i^* + v \tag{13}$$

$$m^s = R \tag{14}$$

Además de los cambios al modelo descritos más arriba, hemos incluido un componente estocástico en la demanda por dinero (análogo a χ del modelo anterior) el cual designamos con la letra v (ecuación 13). El explicitará el mecanismo de ajuste de la oferta de dinero ante variaciones de corto plazo en la demanda.

Al ser la cantidad de dinero endógena, el mercado monetario estará siempre en equilibrio. Un corolario de esto es la neutralidad de las variables nominales. Como vemos en la ecuación (10), el dinero no afecta la determinación del empleo y producto, sino que éste último determina la cantidad de dinero a través de la demanda del mismo (ecuación (13)).

El saldo en balanza de pagos, la otra variable endógena del sistema, esta dado por:

$$R = (1 + \theta) P^* - \theta P^*_0 - \alpha i^* + v, \tag{15}$$

es decir, por las perturbaciones externas e internas (cambios autónomos en la demanda por dinero v). El mecanismo de ajuste es sencillo: un exceso demanda (oferta) flujo de dinero, crea un exceso de oferta (demanda) de bienes y bonos. Dado que el país toma precios y tipos de interés, este exceso de oferta se manifiesta en superávit (déficit) en BOP que automáticamente equilibra el desequilibrio inicial en el mercado monetario.

Este mecanismo automático permite que la economía se ajuste a las perturbaciones que la afectan minimizando los costos en desempleo y variabilidad del producto. Esto puede ser fácilmente comprobado si volvemos al primer modelo y nos preguntamos cual es la regla de política monetaria que minimiza la varianza del producto. Para esto, reemplazamos la oferta discrecional de dinero representada por la ecuación (5), por una regla que liga la oferta de dinero al conjunto de variables que la autoridad observa contemporáneamente, esto es:

$$m^s \gamma_0 P^* + \gamma_1 i + \gamma_2 e \tag{16}$$

Es decir, hemos supuesto que la autoridad observa contemporáneamente el precio externo, el tipo de interés y el tipo de cambio del mercado. Con respecto a la disponibilidad de la información sobre el producto, se ha supuesto que ella se obtiene con cierto rezago y por tanto no la incluimos en la regla monetaria.

Haciendo uso de la paridad de tipo de interés (ecuación (3)), la regla de oferta monetaria se puede reescribir como:

$$m^s = \mu_1 e + \mu_2 P^* + \mu_0 (i^* + e_{+1}) \tag{17}$$

la cual utilizamos para obtener el nivel de producto que regirá en esta economía, esto es:

$$y = \left[\frac{1}{\Delta} (1+\alpha-\mu_1) \theta (P^*-P_0) \theta (1-\mu_2) P^* + (\alpha+\mu_0)(i^*+e_{+1}) \right] \tag{18}$$

lo que deja en claro que la regla de política monetaria puede estabilizar el producto en el corto plazo. Suponiendo que el objetivo de política monetaria es minimizar las desviaciones con respecto al nivel de largo plazo, es decir:

$$\text{Var}(y) = E \left\{ \left[\frac{1}{\Delta} (1+\alpha-\mu_1)\theta(P^*-P_{-1}) - \theta(1-\mu_2)P^* + (\alpha+\mu_0)(i^*+e_{+1}) \right] \right\}^2 \tag{19}$$

La función objetivo (19) se minimiza cuando las siguientes condiciones se satisfacen:

$$\mu_0 = -\alpha \tag{20}$$

$$\mu_1 = 1 + \alpha \tag{21}$$

$$\mu_2 = 1, \tag{22}$$

las cuales al ser reemplazadas en la regla de oferta monetaria (17) implican:

$$m - p = -\alpha i \tag{23}$$

La ecuación (23) indica que la óptima regla monetaria es aquella que ajusta la cantidad de dinero real de manera tal que compense los cambios provocados por los ajustes de portafolio en la demanda por dinero. Por ejemplo, si la demanda por dinero cae como consecuencia de un incremento en el tipo de interés, la óptima política monetaria disminuirá los saldos reales para equilibrar el mercado. Esto es exactamente el mecanismo automático existente en el caso de moneda endógena a través de los saldos en BOP. El análisis indica entonces, que la óptima política monetaria es comportarse como si la cantidad de dinero fuera endógena respondiendo a los requerimientos de saldos reales que el mercado dictamine.

La existencia de un sistema como el panameño nos asegura que la oferta monetaria es siempre optima. Desafortunadamente, no hay nada en el sistema con moneda local que nos asegure que este sea el caso. Aún más, la historia esta llena de evidencia de comportamiento no óptimo de la autoridad monetaria, haciendo a muchos creer que la existencia de un banco central no es condición necesaria sino que suficiente para la existencia de crisis de balanza de pagos.

Bibliografía

Comisión Económica para América Latina, "Análisis y Proyecciones del Desarrollo Económico, VII: El Desarrollo Económico de Panamá", Naciones Unidas, 1959.

Harberger, Arnold C., "Reflexiones sobre el sistema monetario panameño", en *Estudios sobre el sistema monetario y bancario de Panamá*, Dirección General de Planificación, Panamá, 1970.

Hayek, Freidrich von, *Denationalization of Money*, London: Institute of Economic Affairs, 1976.

Lucas, R.E, Jr., "Expectations and the Neutrality of Money", *Journal of Economic Theory*, 4:103-124, 1972.

Sargent, T., *Macroeconomics*, Cambridge: Harvard University Press, 1981.

Turnovsky, S. J., "The Effectiveness of Monetary and Fiscal Policy Rules in an Open Economy under Rational Expectations," *Manchester School*, 48:39-62, 1980.

ENDOGENOUS POLITICAL STRUCTURES

Luis Locay and Carlos Seiglie

Eastern Europe and the former Soviet Union have recently experienced political transformations that have resulted in a reduction, often very substantial, in the power of the ruling communists parties and other groups in their ruling coalitions. The political transformations have been accompanied by economic transformations, of varying intensity across countries, away from socialism and toward a market economy. Some countries, such as Hungary, are well on the road to a market economy, while others have made little progress in that direction.

Communist countries outside the region have not experienced the type of political transformations underway in Eastern Europe and the former Soviet Union, but in some cases there has been considerable economic change. China, for example, has been increasing its reliance on markets for over a decade, although its communist leadership appears to remain firmly in control. Cuba, on other hand, has reversed market experiments of the 1980's, and currently is as centralized as ever.

In view of its gross inefficiency, why did so many countries end up with socialism - meaning here central planning plus direct government control of most productive activity - as their economic system? While it seems clear to us that socialism redistributes income in favor of certain groups in society, it is not so clear why socialism would be the best way carry out such redistribution. Would it not be better, for example, to organize production through a market system and use appropriate taxes and subsidies to achieve the desired redistribution? We offer two reasons why socialism may be preferred by the ruling group.

First of all, socialism may lower the cost of maintaining control over other groups.[1] A second reason is that the policy instruments and information available to governments may be so imperfect, that achieving extensive redistribution in a market economy severely distorts markets and creates large dead weight losses. Substitution is possible at so many margins in a market economy, that redistributive government policy can be substantially undone. The cost of redistribution is therefore lower in a socialist economy.

In the next section we develop a one period model of political and economic change in a socialist economy. The model formalizes the considerations discussed above. In section 2 we perform various comparative static exercises, emphasizing the Cuban situation. We close in section 3 with a brief discussion of future change in Cuba and extensions of the model.

I. The Model

Suppose that a society's economic system can be centrally planned or market oriented. We denote variables under each system by the superscript "c" for centrally planned, and by the superscript "m" for market economy. The choice of economic system is up to whatever group in society is in power. We assume that society is composed of two groups. One group, which we designate by the subscript "B", is in power, and the other group, designated by the subscript "A", is

---

[1] Lott and Reiffen (1986) attribute this notion to Hayek (1944) and Friedman (1962).

not.

The group in power can choose not only the economic system, but also the distribution of income between groups A and B within the system. Group incomes will be denoted by y_A^c, y_B^c, y_A^m, y_B^m. Each economic system has a possibility frontier between the incomes of groups A and B defined by the following:

$$y_A^c + \theta^c y_B^c = y^c \qquad \text{(Centrally Planned),} \quad (1)$$

$$y_A^m + \theta^m y_B^m = y^m \qquad \text{(Market Economy),} \quad (2)$$

and $y_A^c, y_A^m \geq z_A$, and $y_B^c, y_B^m \geq z_B$. Income levels y^c and y^m are measures of the potential output of each system. Following our previous discussion, we assume that $y^c < y^m$. The parameters θ^c and θ^m are the "prices" of redistributing income toward group B under each economic system. It is the rate at which income can be transferred from group A to group B. Since we expect such redistribution to involve deadweight losses, we assume that $\theta^c, \theta^m > 1$. We also assume that it is less costly to redistribute income to group B under central planning than under a market economy, that is, $\theta^c < \theta^m$. Finally, we have placed lower bounds on the incomes of each group under both systems, so redistribution can never drive the income of one group to zero without also driving the economy's output to zero. Figure 1 shows the two constraints.

If group B loses political power to group A, that group will maximize its income by choosing a market economy and driving group B's income to its lowest level, z_B. The resulting income for group A, call it w, is given by $w = y^m - \theta^m z_B$. In order to remain in power, group B must pay some cost. This cost will be an increasing function of the difference between group A's current income, and its income if group B loses power, w. Formally, we assume that group B's costs of staying in power are given by:

$$C^c(w - y_A^c) , \ C^{c\prime} > 0, \ C^{c\prime\prime} > 0 \ \text{(Central Planning),}$$

$$C^m(w - y_A^m) , \ C^{m\prime} > 0, \ C^{m\prime\prime} > 0 \ \text{(Market Economy).}$$

As we mentioned in the introduction, we expect that the cost to group B of staying in power will be lower with central planning than with a market economy. Formally this means that for any income differential, x, we have that $C^c(x) < C^m(x)$. Figure 2 shows the cost functions for each economic system.

If group B remains in power, its net income, conditional on each of the two economic systems, is given by:

$$U^c(y_A^c, y_B^c) = y_B^c - C^c(w - y_A^c), \qquad \text{(Central Planning)} \quad (3)$$

$$U^m(y_A^m, y_B^m) = y_B^m - C^m(w - y_A^m), \qquad \text{(Market Economy)} \quad (4)$$

Group B's decision problem can be divided into two stages. In the first stage, group B maximizes (3) and (4) subject to constraints (1) and (2), respectively.[2] The solutions are shown graphically in figure 3. In that figure we have superimposed the optimal iso-income curves on the constraints of

---

[2] The net income functions used here are similar to the political support functions in Peltzman (1976).

figure 1. Points C and M are the income combinations chosen by group B conditional on its staying in power and choosing, respectively, central planning or a market economy. In the third alternative where group B loses power, group A chooses a market economy, and group B gets z_B (group A gets w). That point is labeled L in figure 3.

The second stage of group B's decision problem consists in choosing from among points C, M, and L, and their corresponding economic/political systems, the one that provides them with the highest net income. Unfortunately we cannot tell from figure 3 which point that will be, since that figure shows only gross incomes.

II. The Transition to Market Economies

A. The Problem of Calculation Under Socialism

In his classic paper, "The Use of Knowledge in Society," Hayek (1945) points out the problem of allocating resources in socialist economies in the absence of market determined prices. Central planners can use historical prices and prices in similar, but market oriented economies, as guides. With the passage of time, however, these guides should become less relevant. We would expect, therefore, that allocative inefficiency would increase over time in a centrally planned economy. In our model this can be viewed as a decline in y^c.

Figure 4 illustrates how the solution changes as y^c falls. Initially group B attains a net income of U^{c1} with central planning, which we assume is the best they can do ($U^{c1} > U^m, z_B$). The fall in y^c lowers net income under central planning to U^{c2}, so a transition to a market economy becomes more likely. If group B remains with central planning they must absorb the full decline in y^c.[3]

The problems of economic calculation under central planning should also increase with the complexity of the economy. Furthermore, such complexity should increase over time as an economy develops and increases in size.[4] Complexity of the economy may also increase the drift from efficiency that occurs as the available pricing guides become less relevant.

Table 1 provides approximate dates of the ascension to power of communist parties in various socialist or previously socialist societies. Two measures of the complexity of the economy - percent of commodity exports accounted for by top five commodities (three digit SITC code) and the total size of the economy - are also provided. As can be seen, Cuba ranks low in complexity and communist control is relatively recent. Both argue for Cuba being slow to make a transformation to a market economy.

B. The Role of Human Capital

Improvement in education, a point of pride among many socialist societies, can also contribute to bringing about a transition to a market economy. The reasons are several. First of all, increases in human capital make the problems facing central planners more difficult. The assignment problem of who should study what, and what jobs they should be assigned to, becomes more complex with increasing education. Furthermore, the social loss from mistakes in assignments

---

[3] Group B's relative income will fall, which may be associated with some degree of liberalization within the framework of central planning.

[4] See Locay (1990) and Yang and Borland (1991) for models where economic development is positively related to an economy's complexity.

should also increase. The implication is not that the central planning constraint necessarily shifts in with increases in human capital, but rather that it shifts out less than the market economy constraint. In our model the effect can be captured by an increase in y^m.

Figure 5 shows the changes in the constraints and in group B's choices, resulting from an increase in y^m. Initially group B is in power with central planning and net income of U^{c1}. The corresponding net income with a market economy and group B in power is U^{m1}. It must be the case that $U^{c1} > U^{m1}$. The increase in y^m shifts not only the market economy constraint out, but also changes the entire map of iso-income curves. The reason for the latter effect is that the higher value of y^m increases the income group A can attain if it obtains power, w. The cost to group B of maintaining power therefore rises, changing the iso-income curves.

U^{c2} and U^{m2} are the levels of net income attainable by group B if it retains power after the increase in y^m, under central planning and a market economy. Interestingly, under both systems the income of group A will rise by the increase in y^m. With the market economy this means that the increase in y^m is passed on to group A (this is what group B pays to stay in power). Group B's net income remains unchanged, so it must be the case that $U^{m1} = U^{m2}$. With central planning, however, no increase in the constraint is experienced, so the rise in group A's income comes from a reduction in group B's income. It follows that $U^{c1} > U^{c2}$, so a transition to a market economy will occur if the increase in y^m is sufficiently large. Even if the economy remains centralized, however, we should see a rise in the relative income of group A, which we believe could correspond to some degree of liberalization.

The above discussion about the effects of an increase in human capital suggests that the price of redistribution, at least in the market oriented economy, should also increase. If both y^m and θ^m increase, the market economy constraint not only shifts out, but also becomes steeper. In this case group B's net income declines in both a centrally planned and a market economy, but it falls less in the latter. Once again a transition to a market economy will occur, with or without group B remaining in power, if the increase in y^m is sufficiently large.

One final effect of an increase in human capital is that it may alter the composition of the two groups. Suppose that low education, low income individuals are part of group B. An increase in education will shift some persons to group A.[5] In our framework this can be modelled by assuming that the cost of remaining in power curves shift against group B. The increase in costs should be greater under central planning, since with a market economy group A gets to keep more of its income. This effect, therefore, should also make it more likely that a transition to a market economy will take place.

Table 2 shows school enrollment ratios for secondary schooling and higher for most of the countries in table 1.[6] The secondary school enrollment ratio has been used as a proxy for future human capital in recent empirical work on growth. For changes occurring in 1990, the ratios of 1975 are probably more relevant than the ratios of 1989. We report both. As can be seen from the 1975 figures, Cuba's educational level is between the low levels of China and Viet Nam, where political

---

[5] Some of the newly educated group B members can be absorbed by the ruling and bureaucratic apparatus, but probably not all.

[6] The ratios are gross enrollment ratios which means total enrollments are divided by all person in the corresponding age group. A better measure would be net enrollment ratios, which use only the enrollments of persons in the corresponding age group. The difference between net and gross ratios are particularly large for Cuba. In 1989, for example, the net secondary enrollment ratio is 69%, compared to a gross ratio of 89% in table 2.

transitions have not occurred, and the higher levels of Eastern Europe, Mongolia, the Soviet Union, where it has.

C.   The Original Revolutionary Leadership

Casual empiricism suggests that the presence of the original revolutionary leadership (or of those responsible for the major changes toward communism) is associated with a lower likelihood of political change. Cuba and North Korea, the two countries where the least political and economic liberalization has occurred, are still ruled by their original Revolutionary leader. There are ways to model this effect in our framework.

The simplest way is to assume that in the event that group B loses power, there is a penalty, P, to B's income, which increases the greater the presence of the original leadership. The reason for this penalty is that when group A takes power, it may be less likely to let bygones be bygones, if the original leaders who were responsible for their oppression are still around. If group B loses power, its income would now be $(z_B - P)$. The implication of such a penalty is straightforward. It is less likely that group B will give up power the greater is P. The choice of economic system, conditional on B remaining in power, is not affected.[7]

An alternative way to model this effect is to assume that the original leadership commands greater loyalty or is more charismatic than subsequent leaders. If that is the case, then the more of the original leadership that is present, the lower the cost of remaining in power. The presence of the original leadership would then make it less likely that a political transition would take place. The implication for an economic transition under group B's control would depend on what is assumed about the relative reduction in the cost of remaining in power from more of the original leadership being present, under each of the economic systems.

A related concept which is probably related to the presence of the original revolutionary leadership, is that of encompassing interests, developed by Mancur Olson. Olson (1992; 56) provides a simple statement of the principle:

> If an individual, or an organization with enough coherence and discipline to act with rational self-interest, obtains a substantial portion of any increase in the output of a society and bears a large portion of any drop in this social output, then that individual or organization has an encompassing interest in that society. This encompassing interest gives the actor in question an incentive to care about the productivity of the society and to attempt to increase it.

To the extent that such encompassing interests are associated with the original leaders, such as Castro in Cuba, the presence of the original leadership will reduce the likelihood of a political transition. If over time, as Olson (1992) argues, an encompassing interest tends to disappear, this would be an additional reason why over time a transition would become likely.

---

[7] In a more general model with uncertainty, where the probability of losing power is greater under a market system than under central planning, it would be less likely that group B would choose a market economy as P increased.

D.   The Decline of the Soviet Union

In our modeling of political and economic change we have so far ignored external affects across countries. Such effects are clearly present, and they probably are more important for the smaller socialist countries.

The primary external effect we have in mind is the decline in the power of the old Soviet Union, and of its communist party. A small ally of the Soviet Union would be affected in several ways. The most direct and easily observed way is a loss in Soviet subsidies, if those were present, as happened in Cuba. To the extent that such subsidies were conditional on the economy being centrally planned, their loss would be a reduction in y^c, thus increasing the likelihood of a transition to a market economy.[8]

A very different effect would arise from the loss of political and military protection. With the Soviet Union unable or unwilling to defend the communist regimes of its allies, the regimes in those countries are more vulnerable to external political and economic pressures. In 1956 in Hungary and in 1968 in Czechoslovakia, it was direct Soviet military intervention that saved the communist regimes in those countries. In our framework the decline of Soviet willingness or capacity to support other communist regimes would translate into an increase in the cost of remaining in power curves, especially under a market economy. The implication is that the ruling group would be more likely to give up (or lose) power as has happened in much of Eastern Europe. But in countries where the ruling group did not give up power, such as in Cuba, central planning would become even more entrenched.[9] We believe this dependence on the old Soviet Union is important in understanding the very different behavior of the Cuban and Chinese regimes in the 1980's and 1990's. Being a large country which was not dependent on the Soviet Union for protection, China was not affected to a great extent by the political transition in the Soviet Union. The costs of remaining in power of its ruling group were not sharply increased, and it could proceed to move toward a market economy without greater fear of losing political control than before the Soviet collapse. The crushing of the revolt at Tianamen Square and the subsequent feeble international reaction would prove them correct. Such a favorable outcome for the ruling group in Cuba were a similar revolt to take place there would appear to be unlikely.

III.   Conclusion

We have constructed a simple but formal model of political and economic change in socialist societies. We view this as the first step in the development of a model with uncertainty and true strategic behavior.

Our model can explain the political transition in the old Soviet Union as the result of an increasing gap between the opportunities available under a market system and under central planning.[10] The disparity between the two systems could have increased because of increasing difficulty of coordinating an increasingly complex economy, increasing levels of human capital, a

---

[8] Subsidies could be conditional on having a centrally planned economy not because the old Soviet Union cared about how market oriented its ally was, but because there would be less need for such subsidies if its ally had a market economy.

[9] It is interesting to note that some economic and political liberalization took place in Hungary after the revolt was crushed by the Soviet Union.

[10] Not all the old Soviet republics have made a political and economic transition.

decline in an "encompassing interest," and the disappearance of the revolutionary and Stalinist leadership. Military competition with the United States may have also precipitated the transition. We believe that several of the Eastern European countries would have abandoned socialism much earlier if it had not been for Soviet support of the ruling groups. The situation in Cuba, however, is different. Its original revolutionary leader is still in power, its economy is small and comparatively simple, and it has lower levels of human capital and income. Declining Soviet support for its regime has led Cuba away from economic and political liberalization out of fear, our model would imply, that down that road lies the loss of political control.

Our model also suggests, that actions by other countries or external groups whose results are to shift up the constraints facing Cuba, would not precipitate political change. Other countries can offer economic aid or improved trade in exchange for economic and political liberalization, but our model implies that the ruling group will accept such offers only if their own position is improved. If liberalization runs a serious risk of loss of political control it will not be implemented.

The model does suggest two other types of policies that may speed up political change. One is to increase z_B-P, the income the ruling group receives if it looses power. The problem here is being able to make a credible offer. The second type of policies are those aimed at increasing the costs of remaining in power. The drawback here is that repression will probably increase before a transition is achieved.

Table 1

Country	Approximate Date of Communist Takeover	Top Five Exports 1989 Percent of Total Exports	GNP 1989 US$ (Billions)
Albania	1944		
Bulgaria	1944		24.6
China	1949	13.2	225.3
Cuba	1959	85.5	15.5
Czechoslovakia	1949	25.3[a]	53.3
GDR	1945		110.7
Hungary	1949	9.7[a]	23.8
Poland	1947	29.0	61.1
Romania	1948		27.9
Soviet Union	1917-21	14.5	812.6
Viet Nam	1954		
Yugoslavia	1945	26.3	61.7

Sources: *1989 International Trade Statistics Yearbook*, United Nations, 1991; *Social Statistics Yearbook*, UNESCO.
a - 1987.

Table 2

School Enrollment Ratios

Country	1975 2nd Level	1975 3rd Level	1989 2nd Level	1989 3rd Level
Albania	48	<5.4	80	8.5
Bulgaria	89	19.2	75	26.2
China	46	0.6	44	1.7
Cuba	49	10.9	87	20.7
Czechoslovakia	72	12.1	85	17.6
GDR	81	29.5	79[a]	33.5[a]
Hungary	63	11.7	76	28.0[b]
Mongolia	79	7.8	92[c]	21.8[c]
Poland	72	16.8	81	20.3
Romania	65	9.2	88	8.6
Soviet Union	94	21.9	96	25.1
Viet Nam	39	2.1	42[d]	2.3[e]
Yugoslavia	76	20.0	88	19.0

Source: *Statistical Yearbook 1991*, UNESCO.
a - 1988, b - 1987, c - 1986, d - 1985, e - 1980.

Figure 1

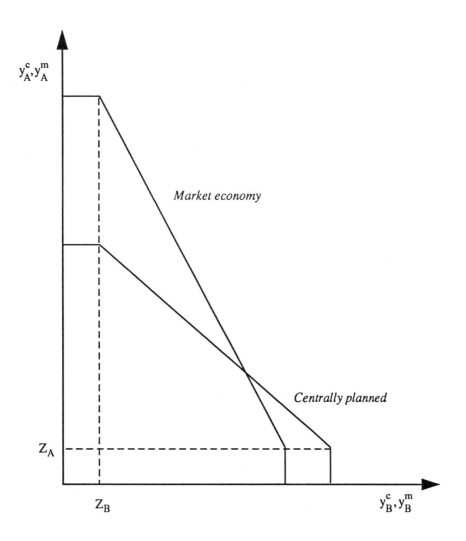

Figure 2

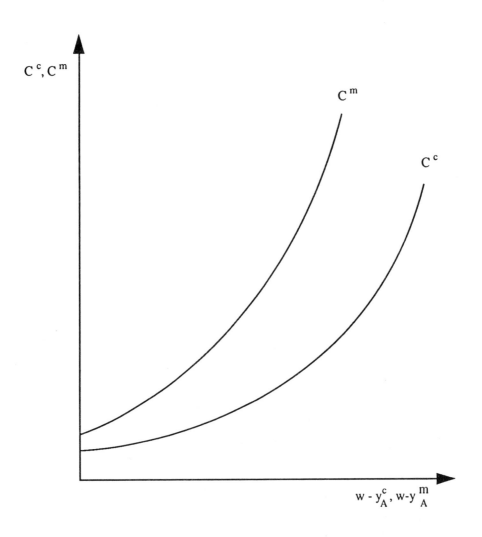

Figure 3

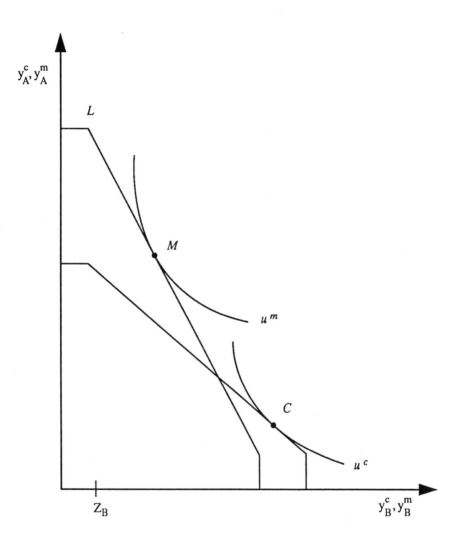

Figure 4

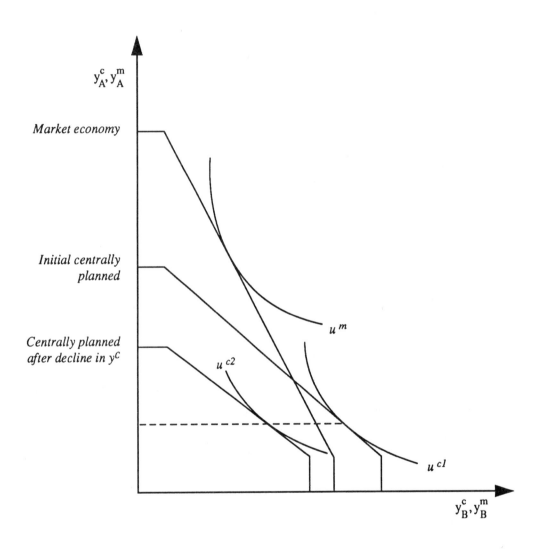

Figure 5

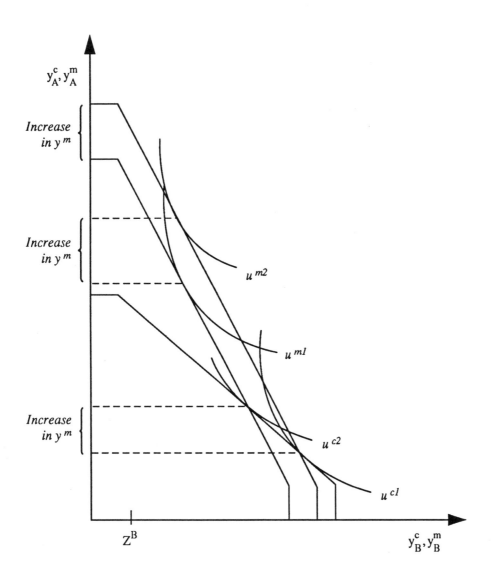

References

Friedman, Milton. *Capitalism and Freedom*. Chicago: Chicago University Press, 1962.

Hayek, F. A. "The Use of Knowledge in Society." *American Economic Review* (Sept 1945).

Hayek, F. A. *The Road to Serfdom*. London: George Routledge and Sons, 1944.

Locay, Luis. "Economic Development and the Division of Production between Households and Firms." *Journal of Political Economy*, 98 (Oct 1990): 965-982.

Lott, John R., and Reiffen, David. "On Nationalizing Private Property and the Present Value of Dictators." *Public Choice*, 48 (1986): 81-87.

Olson, Mancur. "The Hidden Path to a Successful Economy," in *The Emergence of Market Economies in Eastern Europe*, Christopher Clague and Gordon C. Rausser, eds.. Blackwell: Cambridge, MA, 1992.

Peltzman, Sam. "Towards a More General Theory of Regulation." *Journal of Law and Economics* 19 (1976): 211-240.

Yang, Xiaokai and Borland, Jeff. "A Microeconomic Mechanism for Economic Growth." *Journal of Political Economy*, 99 (June 1990): 460-482.

Comments

Lorenzo L. Pérez[1]

Professors Locay and Seiglie have developed a model of political and economic change to explain the endogenous forces that might generate the transformation of a socialist economy into a market economy. The model assumes that there are two groups in the economy: the one that holds the political power and the rest. An important assumption of their model is that it is less costly to the group in power to distribute income in their favor under a socialist economy. Under a market economy, the original group in power might experience a drastic reduction in their income. The authors note that as the economy becomes more complex it is more difficult to have a central planning system and that a transition to a market economy becomes more likely. In these circumstances to avoid a drastic decline in its income as a result of growing allocable inefficiencies the group in power makes some concessions, while still maintaining the main elements of a socialist economy.

Professors Locay and Seiglie also identified other factors that would affect the possibility of a transformation from a socialist to a market economy and explain how some of them can be taken into account in their model. Specifically they discuss the timing of the ascension to power of communist parties (the more recent is the installation of the regime the less likely is change); whether the original leadership is still in command (the original leadership would resist changes); and human capital (negatively correlated with change because it makes central planning more difficult and increases the opportunity cost of having a centralized economy). The authors conclude that these factors suggest that change is not likely to come soon in Cuba. On the other hand, they believe that a reduction of subsidies from the ex-Soviet Union or loss of trade preferences from the Eastern European countries would encourage change in Cuba.

This paper obviously attempts to model a very complex situation. The authors are the first ones to recognize that this is a first step in the development of a model with uncertainty and strategic behavior. The model would indeed need to be expanded to better describe reality and improve its predictive power. For example, the model could include more than two groups (e.g. top leadership, managerial class, and workers). These distinctions would enrich the model and might permit to better highlight the differences between the interest of the top leadership and the rest of the population. Some work also needs to be done of the dynamics of change by considering more than one period. In this respect the initial conditions, and the speed of change might have important implications. In addition the impact of the characteristics of the economy need to be explored more than has been done in this paper, although it might not be possible to model them formally. A more thorough analysis of how complex the economy in question is, the implications of different types of educational achievements and the linkages with the rest of the world should make the model more useful.

However, even if the model is expanded along these lines, one is still left with the question whether the type of model proposed by Professors Locay and Seiglie would be able to take into account nonmonetary considerations in a satisfactory way. The utility function of a totalitarian political leader might have important non-economic arguments that might lead him to resist change at all cost. If this is the case the model might not be able to reflect well a situation where change

---

[1]The views expressed here are those of the discussant and in no way represent the official views of the International Monetary Fund.

does not take place because non-economic considerations prevail. This could occur even if a socialist economy is so distorted that the gains from eliminating the distortions are large enough to make all members of society better off (economically speaking) after the transformation to a market economy.

In his paper, Dr. Moreno considers as an optimum monetary system the one prevailing in Panama where a convertible currency (the U.S. dollar) is used as the means of payments. Given that the demand for money is endogenously determined by economic agents. Under this system the economy adjusts to liquidity disequilibrium through the credit market or changes in private sector expenditure (i.e. through changes in economic activity). The economy can also adjust through changes in the net international reserve position of the banking system. There is full convertibility of the currency in circulation and since the government cannot impose an inflation tax, inflation and interest rates converge to international levels.

Dr. Moreno believes that a U.S. dollar-based monetary system with its automatic adjustment mechanism can facilitate the process of transition from a socialist to a market economy. The first step would be to authorize the circulation of the U.S. dollar in the economy as well as the creation of a private foreign exchange market. The domestic currency could be taken out of circulation as the Government sells private assets and a deadline could be established for its abolition. In this way the author believes that the confidence problem on the currency of a country that is in transition can be avoided.

The proposal of Dr. Moreno has to be given serious consideration in light of the experience of many Latin American countries that have tried to finance the activities of the public sector through monetary expansion. These experiences have inevitably finished in balance of payments crises and in an acceleration of price pressures. However, it should be highlighted (as the author admits) that the same beneficial results of this monetary system could be obtained with a fixed exchange rate system that is supported with appropriate fiscal and monetary policies. In effect it should be clear that regardless of the monetary system that is adopted, there is no escape from the need to implement a sound fiscal policy and a prudent external borrowing policy for the public sector. Measures to promote the international competitiveness of the economy (including incomes policy) and savings and investment are also crucial for the attainment of a sustainable growth path.

Countries like Panama which used the U.S. dollar as currency also can run into difficulties if the above mentioned policies are not followed. During the 1970s and early 1980s Panama implemented a relatively expansionary fiscal policy with the government financing its operations to a large extent through borrowing from foreign commercial creditors that were in retrospect too eager to lend to the country. This eventually forced the country to negotiate a concerted refinancing of its commercial debt and later, with the advent of the political crisis in late 1987, to start running arrears in the servicing of its commercial debt which to this date have not been settled yet.

In considering the adoption of a monetary system based on a convertible currency, two other considerations should be kept in mind. First, that the country in doing so is giving up the option to implement a relatively active monetary policy that might be appropriate to facilitate an economic recovery when price pressures are under control and the external sector is strong. Second, the adoption of a foreign convertible currency as a country's currency makes that country particularly vulnerable to pressures from the country issuing the convertible currency.

REFLECTIONS ON SYSTEMIC ECONOMIC POLICY REFORM: LESSONS, EVALUATION, AND SOCIAL COSTS

Juan J. Buttari

I will offer reflections on three different but related issues bearing on structural economic reform:[1]

(1) lessons learned from the process of economic liberalization of, approximately, the last ten years in the developing world and in Central and Eastern Europe;

(2) why don't we know more?

(3) impact of the reform process on the poor and the record of compensatory social programs.

The first area, lessons learned, is of direct relevance to anyone interested in shedding light on the economic reform path best suitable to post-socialist Cuba —or any other country making the transition from centralized to open-market-based economies. The second —why is our knowledge so limited— is relevant because there is need for analysis that improves our understanding of how the impact of broad and deep reform processes take place.[2] As will be argued below, the methodological difficulties involved are a barrier to achieving this objective. Lastly, attention on the impact of reforms on the poor and the record of social compensatory programs is called for, as a post-Castro government will have to come to grips with this issue.

I.   Lessons Learned[3]

1. The process has to be undertaken with a long term focus. This means that policy makers and the public must be prepared to face a process that will raise standards of living to the level enjoyed by, say, the high tier of the lower-middle-income countries in a matter of no less than five to ten years. This does not mean that beneficial impacts cannot be felt sooner; some effects such as the resurgence of entrepreneurship and small enterprises should be visible during the first year depending on the pace of the reforms. But it does mean that the full positive impact of the reforms is likely to take much more time. An implication is that statements which convey that most of the benefits of the systemic reforms can be achieved in a short period of time (one or two years) are

---

[1]A few words on definitions are in order. In the literature the terms "structural reform", "stabilization", and "economic adjustment" have often been used in loose and even inconsistent ways. From this paper's perspective, "economic stabilization" refers to efforts to restore price stability and balance of payments viability to a country. In the same perspective, stabilization is intimately linked to the "structural reform" process in that it helps create the foundations for sustained growth without resource to prolonged extraordinary official foreign assistance. The term "structural reform" relates to policy and institutional reform efforts to enhance the supply capacity of the country by setting the conditions for static and dynamic allocational efficiency. "Economic adjustment" refers to the process that encompasses both economic stabilization and structural reform. To make for a less dull prose, in the paper, references to structural reform processes implicitly involve prior or concomitant stabilization. Analogously, the term "systemic economic" reform involves both stabilization and structural reform but also conveys the sense the one is dealing with a radical reorientation of the economic system -- as in the transition from socialism to market economies.

[2]It was interest in this aspect, with the view of the potential applications in post-socialist Cuba, that stimulated the creation of the Association for the Study of the Cuban Economy.

[3]In preparing this section the author benefited from a presentation by Sebastian Edwards at a Institute for Policy Reform seminar.

risky and probably counterproductive because they are likely to give rise to excessively optimistic expectations (more on this below in this section).

2. On the broad sequencing of macroeconomic stabilization and structural reforms. While both have to start immediately after the instauration of the reformist government, until adequate internal fiscal and monetary controls are in place and working, some direct state intervention in the economy is likely to be unavoidable (see McKinnon, 1991, p 2). This is the story in Eastern Europe. The challenge is to make the transition as fast as possible.

3. Progress of the overall reform process will be conditioned by how fast the institutions for an open market economy are put in place. As has been pointed out elsewhere, the quality of a country's institutions is a principal determinant of its economic performance. Economic policy reform must include the conventions that govern the way people deal with each other -- property rights, contracts, conflict resolution, etc.[4] Moreover, it is not only those conventions that have an obvious and direct link to economic activity that are of relevance. Also basic political and civil rights are essential. Jointly, by reducing uncertainty and risk, such institutions create the setting where entrepreneurship and allocational efficiency can prosper. (See comments below on governance.)

4. Gradualism or shock therapy?[5] Two extreme currents of thought were evident among economists working on the transition from socialist to market economies. One, the shock-therapy school, favored quick, sweeping changes toward a market economy; the other, the gradualist school, favored step-by-step, relatively slow, changes. While the shock therapy approach prevailed at first, recently among specialists and in the reforming countries themselves, gradualism has received increasing support.[6]

On this one may observe that the dichotomy shock-therapy versus gradualism may have been artificially simple. Even in the context of shock therapy there are critical issues of timing and sequence —initial emphasis on stabilization and, especially, on greater control of the fiscal deficit as a precondition for success of structural reforms; need for a basic legal, judicial, and regulatory setting for the flourishing of market transactions; etc. Likewise, even gradualists acknowledged that fast movement on some fronts was necessary —the institutional setting.

Nonetheless, the issue of an overall fast or relatively slow reform pace persists. The case for gradualism has been buttressed, at least until recently, by the relative paralysis of the reform process in Poland, as well as by the economic recession that has afflicted Eastern Europe.

However, such events do not negate the case for a fast reform pace. Although a shock-therapy transition to a market economy does mean doing away with significant sectors of industry that are not viable, gradualism is riskier. The modernization of vast numbers of firms while under state control is impractical for both fiscal and political reasons. Foreign investment cannot be counted upon to come to the rescue. Even in Hungary, the country which has received most private foreign capital inflows, the flow has been modest.

---

[4]Several authors have recently made these points. Mancur Olson has repeatedly emphasized these aspects during his writings and presentations, and a recent book edited by Clague and Rausser relates these issues directly to the experience in Eastern Europe (Clague and Rausser 1992). For an overview of modern currents of thought in institutional economics one may refer to Betancourt (1991).

[5]On this issue see a recent article of The Economist reproduced in The World Bank, Transition, Volume 3 No. 5, May 1992.

[6]See, for example, McKinnon (1992).

5. Pay attention to the basic principles of economics.[7] Excessive expansion of the money supply causes inflation; people respond to economic incentives —witness the vast literature on the response by farmers to economic incentives and the substantial response of LDC's exports to the elimination of trade barriers and the realignment of exchange rates; the overwhelming record with foreign exchange, trade, and price controls is one of corruption, shortages, and lack of economic viability.[8]

6. Beware of basing important policies on concepts whose relevance for specific situations has not been tested. An example of what I mean was the use of the "infant industry" concept to structure protectionist regimes. Such concepts were traditionally intertwined with the valid notion of externalities to justify government intervention and control. All that without any attempt at providing any but vague support to these concepts. How important are the externalities? How does one distinguish and infant from a noninfant industry? I have seen many times these concepts used in an extremely cavalier way to justify the allocation of resources and policy. Generally these efforts have led to waste and policy failure.[9]

7. Do not give in to populist and nationalist pressures. The former has generally led to artificially protecting urban workers and punishing other segments of the society -- mainly agricultural workers. Generally, the mechanisms have been deficit-financed subsidies to consumers, impeding the shedding and reallocation of excess labor, and penalizing competitive industries and sectors through artificial controls. The latter has discouraged the free flow of foreign investment and skills, as well as the misallocation of international capital flows that do come in.

8. Import substitution industries tend to be significantly more capital intensive than export industries. Accordingly, the empirical record has shown that such industries constrain the potential for productive employment creation and foster more unequal distributions of incomes.[10]

9. Regimes that promote lobbying and rent-seeking in lieu of directly productive activities have a high economic and developmental cost.[11] Probably this is were most of the costs of economic protection and broad state intervention in productive activities lie. While relevant, deadweight welfare losses associated with discretionary interventions (e.g., taxes and tariffs) are much smaller. Lobbying and rent-seeking activities, along with their close relative, generalized corruption, thrive under import-substitution and strong state control. Their impact goes beyond pure economic constructs. They are a root cause behind the alienation of a people with the political system, and a key cause of political instability. In such contexts, economic development and sustained growth becomes almost impossible. People must perceive that the overall political and economic systems meet minimum standards of fairness.

10. Governance matters. Until very recently, many development economists were skeptical about the capacity of democratic systems to undertake difficult systemic reforms. The rationale was

---

[7]This and the following point are based on the excerpts of a speech by Larry Summers to the Hudson Institute Conference on Baltic Economic Reform. See World Bank, *Transition*, (1991).

[8]On some of these issues see Edwards (1992).

[9]Anne O. Krueger has addressed these issues on several of her works. See her comments on Harberger, Krueger, Fox, and Edwards (1992).

[10]See Krueger (1978, 1983).

[11]On these points see Edwards (1992).

that economic adjustment —i.e. stabilization and structural change— involved hurting established interests and adding short-term penury, and that only authoritarian regimes could cope with that. Mounting empirical evidence is challenging that view. While the political difficulties of systemic reforms cannot be underestimated, neither can the proposition that governments must be accountable to their citizens. This leads back to the need for the institutions of democracy.[12]

11. The importance of conveying to the public the rationale, nature, objectives, difficulties, conditions for success, and timetable involved cannot be exaggerated. Explanations must be transparent and devoid of technical jargon. The reasons for the failure of the previous economic system and policies must be understood by the public. In the case of authoritarian regimes which have attempted to disguise their failures by shifting the blame to external enemies (e.g., Castro's Cuba by blaming U.S. policies), detailed and clear explanations of why Marxist regimes have failed is essential. Likewise, the reasons for the generalized emphasis on economic liberalization throughout the developing world is also of the utmost importance.

Once the new economic policy course has been explained, the government should move decisively leaving no doubt about the irreversibility of the policy orientation. The government must seek at all costs to maintain the trust and respect of the majority of the population. The recent record offers grounds for optimism. In time of crisis people are willing to try radical alternatives. In the case of Cuba where economic and political crisis has been a way of life for many years, most people are likely to be willing to go along with a clear alternative course of action provided they understand the rationale, the policies that will be employed, and the benefits that will be reaped.

II.   Need for Expanding Our Capacity to Learn From the Ongoing Structural Reform Process

The economic policy and institutional reforms in the developing world and in countries of the former socialist bloc present economists with immense possibilities for learning about interrelations among economic variables, and among economic, political, and social factors. While valuable lessons have been learned, still the gap in knowledge surrounding key issues is great. Why don't we know more? How does one evaluate the success or failure of systemic economic reform?

The short answer to the question of why don't we know more is that it is relatively soon, it is difficult, and evaluation tools are still grossly imperfect. The next sections expand on this short answer by reviewing why evaluating the success or failure of broad structural reforms is particularly difficult, and make considerations about the instruments that must be brought to bear to increase our scope of knowledge. A historical introduction on how only recently systemic economic policy reform came to occupy the center stage in development economics, and the implications for evaluation, is helpful background.

A Historical Perspective to Economic Policy Reform

The emphasis on economic policy and related institutional settings consistent with liberal economic frameworks is relatively recent in the developing world and among international development agencies.

The focus of development action shifted several times during the last four to five decades.

---

[12]See World Bank (1991).

The initial emphases were inspired by the impressive reconstruction of Europe after World War II and the influence of Harrod-Domar type growth models. Such models highlighted physical capital accumulation as the strategic factor for development. Accordingly, international development efforts focused on infrastructure capital projects.

Other factors influenced concurrent or ensuing emphases. Those factors were the key role of governments in the victorious World War II campaigns of the Allies, the perception that the socialist economies were succeeding, and the influence of some academic and international centers which stressed planning and government control. As a result, international agencies concentrated many of their efforts in helping government develop more effective planning and control tools.[13]

In spite of the substantial, but at the time not well documented, improvements in worldwide living conditions that took place during the 1950s through the early 1970s, a new strain of thought and development influence took hold. Such line of thinking held that living conditions in developing countries were not only experiencing little progress, but in fact, actually deteriorating. Such propositions found a conceptual basis on what may be loosely called dependency theories —whose common link is the hypothesis that the international economic order prevented the development of low income countries. Intertwined with such vision of the world and poor societies' prospects was the argument that conventional economic theory —frequently pejoratively referred to as orthodox or neoclassical— was little else but an ideological rationalization that favored the wealthy and the centers of power in the world economy.[14]

Such perceptions eventually translated into a shift in the orientation of international development agencies. Vaguely referred to as "basic needs", the new conventional wisdom emphasized that development resources had to be allocated directly to the poor and also favored redistributive interventions. Alternative courses of action were deemed as ineffective and derogatorily and hazily branded as "trickle down." This was the current of thought which inspired international donors' actions during the seventies and early 1980s.[15]

The oil crises of the mid-seventies and early 1980s, the inability to meet debt service obligations by many oil importing and even some oil rich countries, the successful performance of a set of East Asian economies, and a more careful review of the empirical record of recent decades, forced a reassessment of development strategies and a shift in the emphases of the international agencies. Economic policy reform, and related institutional change, gained the center stage. Economic liberalization became the objective, mainstream economics once again guided economic international action.

Nonetheless, because a focus on broad, fast, and deep economic liberalization is relatively

---

[13]See Little (1982) and Krueger (1991).

[14]For literature presenting the views of dependency theorists see Meier (1989), pages 105-110.

[15]On the initial formulation of a "basic needs" approach during the seventies, see International Labour Office (1976). For an analysis of "trickle down" see Arndt (1983). It is to be noted that, while human capital theorists had demonstrated the high economic returns attaching to investment in human beings, under "basic needs" resource allocations to education and health were frequently justified primarily under redistribution or "equity" considerations. Nonetheless, "basic needs" also inspired efforts to raise the productivity of selected population groups —small farmers, for instance— through technological innovation.
The comments in the text on the impact of the "basic needs" approach relates essentially to the type of projects often promoted under the basic needs rubric. Moreover, while "basic needs" need not be inconsistent with "neoclassical" economics (see Harberger 1984), much of the literature inspired by "basic needs" rejected neoclassicism.

recent in the history of development analysis and assistance, there is a still very limited understanding of the complexities of the transition from highly regimented to liberal economies. A result is that development and international funding agencies, or governments, have not adequately developed the tools for evaluating related policy reform processes —neither has academia.

Evaluation Implications of the Change in the Focus of Development Action (or why is evaluating economic policy reform efforts hard?)

Real evaluation is never easy because to answer the fundamental question that evaluations should address —was the program worth it?— causality has to be established. In all contexts, be it project or program evaluation, this involves establishing a without project scenario (the "counterfactual" case), contrasting such scenario with the with-project situation, and inferring program impact from the difference.[16] This approach is specially difficult when the program relates to transforming the economic policy setting and related institutions for a whole country, or for broad sectors of the economy.

As elaborated below, one difficulty relates to the quantification of policy reform impact. Such difficulty is particularly troublesome because many of the variables or conditions the reforms aim to influence are, in principle, quantifiable —e.g. poverty, growth in real income per capita, inflation, productivity. Accordingly, it would seem reasonable to expect quantitative estimates of impact.

A related difficulty refers to the complexity of developing adequate without-reform scenarios. The causation channels through which policy operates are not always clear —theories are continuously challenged and the empirical record is often inconclusive.

Furthermore, the impact of new policies may be felt only after significant time lags, and exogenous factors distort outcomes.[17] This means that it is difficult to isolate the impact of specific policy changes from changes in other variables.[18] Such other variables include changes in other policies and short-term and secular variations in nonpolicy factors —domestic and external. For example, the impact on foreign capital inflows of a change in interest rate policy might be offset by changes in the exchange rate or international transactions regime. Likewise, the potentially beneficial impacts of exchange rate adjustment might be negated by fiscal policy, an adverse change in terms of trade, a recession in the country's trade partners, or domestic politics. Moreover, conditions in the country such as labor force growth and productivity levels, while partially affected by economic policy variables, are influenced by secular trends that also reflect the impact of other

---

[16]The distinction between projects and programs can be fuzzy. As used in this paper, the term "program" refers to a coordinated set of long-term multi-activity endeavors directed toward specific goals and implemented by various institutions (see Brinkerhoff 1991). Programs may not have clear ending points and, usually, have strong policy contents. Projects relate to a narrower and discrete set of activities with clear starting and ending points and which may, or may not, form part of a program. Projects may or may not involve policy changes.

Regarding policy reforms, the perspective adopted in this paper is that program efforts relate to "macro" or economy-wide reforms, as well as to sector-wide reforms. (A sector or subsector relates to basic categories into which economic transactions are grouped.) In contrast, the policy reforms that may go with projects are linked to specific project goals and usually do not form part of a broader policy reform scheme.

Unless otherwise indicated, statements in this paper referring to programs apply to projects as well.

[17]In this paper, exogenous variables refer to those variables whose values are determined by factors other than the policy changes under analysis. By contrast, endogenous variables are those whose values are influenced by the policies analyzed.

[18]See on these points Berg and Hunter (1992).

variables.

The lagged effects of policy changes means two things. One, by their nature, the impact of some policies require time to work themselves out —for example, the impact of real interest rate changes on investment, or of exchange rate variations on exports may not be immediate— and the duration of lags is not well known. Second, the supply response to policy changes is dependent on production structures and on the initial institutional and economic setting. Say, given favorable changes in prices, the supply response in services may be faster than in agricultural production. Likewise, the velocity of the supply response is likely to be influenced by habits and practices developed under previous regulatory regimes. Moreover, the phased impact of trade and exchange rate reforms on imports, for instance, will depend on the original availability of international reserves.

There also is the complication that it is very difficult to standardize for degree of policy change. For example, measuring the degree of openness of a trade regime is very difficult and, consequently, the same amount of tariff reduction in two countries might involve very different degrees of trade opening.[19] Likewise, the nature of the reform process itself —shock or gradual, broad or limited— has to be taken into account.

The implications of all this is that while all these factors must be taken into account as rigorously as possible, the methodological approach to do it will be complex and, necessarily, will have to incorporate a significant element of conjecture.

On top of it, there are complicating social and political dimensions. Who gains and who loses from the reforms depends on the time horizon considered and, for a given point in time, may be not totally clear. Moreover, by definition, broad and deep policy reforms change the fundamental context in which economic activities take place.

Accordingly, all economic agents are touched. This last factor gives rise to social reactions that depend on perceptions of how narrow interests are to be affected and the degree to which the future is discounted. Such reactions affect policy reform implementation and sustainability, economic thinking that influences public opinion, and ultimately, the build-up of the conterfactual case embodied in the without-reforms scenario. Thus, even more than in evaluating nonpolicy interventions, the analyst must take into account socio-political dynamics.

Attribution, Impact Evaluation, and Project Rationale

The challenge boils down to a single question: can one measure causality? The point is that, to derive lessons learned that can serve as a basis for future policies, one is interested in assessing the impact that policy reform interventions have had in LDCs. The central issue is establishing causality. This means identifying and, to the extent possible, quantifying the impact of the reforms.

For the analysis of the impact of the reforms, traditionally the most common approach taken is to rely on a blend of judgments and rather loose before-and-after correlations. The latter concept relates to:

(1) reviewing existing conditions before and after the reforms —this review generally

---

[19]See Dornbusch (1992).

focuses on performance indicators;

(2) in some studies, but not always, making a judgment regarding what proportion of the difference in before and after conditions can be attributed to exogenous (i.e. nonpolicy reform) factors;

(3) to the extent that such conclusion is consistent with economic principles, inferring that the residual reflects the impact of the reforms —it is to be noted that frequently this approach does not take into account alternative policy measures a government might have taken in face of deteriorating economic conditions.

In conclusion, there is a need to develop a feasible yet more rigorous approach that builds on the advantages of the traditionally used methods. Such approach would formally and explicitly establish cause and effect channels, take into account the complexity of interactions among different economic variables and sectors, and provide reasonable quantification of impact.

What Approaches Should Be Explored?

Economic policy reform evaluations will always have to blend judgment, economic theory, and quantification.[20] To such end, one needs an approach that rests on qualitative and quantitative information. The following paragraphs review the elements of basic procedures.

Using Qualitative Information

As used in this paper, qualitative information consists of empirical data which are not intrinsically measurable in a cardinal sense.[21] In economic policy reform evaluations, qualitative information will relate to such aspects as timing, the role of international agencies, degree of influence (were minds changed?), perceptions regarding how implementation could have been more effective, opinions regarding whether technical advice was sound and timely, whether it was conveyed through effective channels, whether either key officials in government or in the private sector were adequately consulted, and perceptions regarding what would have taken place in the absence of international assistance and the government's chosen reform path.

One use of qualitative information would be in the assessment of the soundness of quantitative estimates (see below) and thus, in a complementary way, helping to assess impact. Qualitative information may be obtained from documents and key informants.

---

[20]The evaluations will also build on the stock of existing studies of policy reform impacts. Two types of approaches have frequently been used: multi-country assessments and case studies.

In multi-country assessments, typically, countries are grouped into categories that reflect whether they have carried out significant structural reforms or not, and, when applicable, the pace at which the reforms were undertaken. After controlling for various factors, the difference in economic performance among the groups is used as a basis for inferring policy reform impact. The World Bank, for example, has applied this methodology in three reports on adjustment lending (see World Bank, 1992).

In case studies, the analysis focuses on single-country experiences. These studies frequently pay detailed attention to the country's institutions and political setting. An example of this approach is A.I.D.'s evaluation series on economic policy reform in Africa (see Agency for International Development, 1991).

[21]For example: being in the labor force or not; extent to which a donor agency influenced host government actions. Such data could be quantified, however, by representing different categories or degrees with numbers. For instance, individuals in the labor force could be represented by a one, those not in the labor force by a zero.

Using Quantitative Information

Quantitative information consists of (1) descriptive statistics, (2) values, parameters, and relationships estimated using probabilistic methods, and (3) values, parameters, and relationships estimated using non-probabilistic methods. As further elaborated below, quantitative information can be used to:

> describe before-and-after policy reform situations

> account for the influence of exogenous variables

> develop models that describe interrelations
> among variables

In all instances the key objective in using quantitative information will be to measure program effectiveness. Such effectiveness is defined as the difference between economic performance once policy reforms have taken place, and economic performance without the reforms (i.e. the counterfactual scenario). The simple description of before-and-after situations may be considered just a crude approximation to the counterfactual case and, in most cases, should be taken only as useful background. However, before-and-after situations can be significant because they shed light on the political sustainability of the reforms.

A different but complementary approach —measuring performance under the reforms against performance objectives— is to be used in assessing how well original program objectives were attained, and the intervening factors. However, such approach is not equivalent to measuring program impact and thus should be only an element in policy reform evaluations.[22]

Descriptive statistics are used to analyze before-and-after policy reform scenarios. They will relate to strategic variables and are taken from official publications or estimates. They have been amply used for these purposes by A.I.D. and international funding agencies in their policy reform evaluations.[23] Descriptive statistics are to be used also to establish and monitor what may be called intermediate indicators of progress (say, reduction in effective trade barriers by a given amount within a given time period) as opposed to ultimate program impact.

However, before-and-after comparisons are inadequate to measure the impact of a program. Not all the difference between the before-and-after reform situations can be attributed to policy reforms. As mentioned in a previous section, exogenous factors (terms of trade shifts, international recession, droughts, etc) might have influenced economic performance. Moreover, negative shocks prior to the implementation of reforms under a program would have made a favorable performance more likely. Besides, one has to take into account how government policy would have reacted even in the absence of intervention by international donors.[24]

For such reasons, before-and-after comparisons will have to be adjusted to take into account

---

[22]Moreover, concentrating only on how well were objectives achieved begs the question of whether the objectives were adequate in the first place. For discussion of how the International Monetary Fund has approached these same issues see Guitian (1981) and Goldstein and Montiel (1986).

[23]See for example, A.I.D.'s Impact Evaluation Reports and World Bank (1990).

[24]On these issues see World Bank (1990).

the impact of exogenous factors and likely host government reactions in the absence of international donors' programs. This will require the application of quantitative techniques to disentangle the impact of the exogenous factors.

A related point refers to the use of modeling to isolate the impact of policy changes on economic performance. In essence, as used here, the term "model" refers to a set of equations that describe how the economy, or parts of it, work.[25] For the purposes of this paper, and from the perspective of model breadth, models can be of three types: (a) models that focus on single variables of interest (e.g. exports, savings, real income growth) and explain changes in a variable as a function of policy and non-policy variables —in technical jargon this approach is frequently referred to as "partial equilibrium" analysis; (b) sector-wide models, i.e. models that relate policy reforms to fundamental changes in a sector (e.g. models that explain events in the external, financial, or labor sectors of an economy); and (c) economy-wide models that describe interrelations among different sectors of an economy. In all cases, the models would be applied to develop the counterfactual scenario.

The advantages of economy and sector wide models is at least four-fold:

(1) They enable the analyst or evaluator to isolate the impact of actions in one sector or subsector (say, monetary or interest rate policy) on variables in other sectors or subsectors (e.g. international capital flows or housing investment). Accordingly, they could be used to disentangle the impact of simultaneous policy actions. For example, a policy advisor might have simultaneously promoted interest rate liberalization and reforms in property rights legislation as a means to promote productive investment. In assessing impact, what weight can one attach to each reform?

(2) They force the analyst to trace the causation flows and interactions throughout the economy and, therefore, are valuable tools for learning how an economy operates. Accordingly, they can be used to evaluate the quality of policy reform programs and their design.

(3) They lead to mutually consistent results.

(4) They force the analyst to make explicit what often are implicit, often unnoticed, assumptions.

Two main difficulties can be raised in connection with models. First, a model might require more information than is available in a specific developing country where time series data, in particular, might be of short duration, of dubious quality, and non-comparable over time. Secondly, models are sensitive to the assumptions and theoretical propositions on which they are built. The first difficulty implies that (a) model design has to take into account data availability for specific countries (as well as specific country characteristics), and (b) many of the model parameters may have to be estimated using non-probabilistic approaches and be based on simpler methods or, alternatively, explore the appropriateness of using parameter estimates from available systematic

---

[25]This definition is taken from Almon (1990), page 1.

studies in other countries.[26] The second difficulty implies that the theoretical foundations of models must be consistent with mainstream economics and with the lessons of development of the last thirty years.

Simulation models should be used to complement, not substitute for, the insights on impact gained with other tools. Interestingly, while simulation models have been used by economists in almost all international funding institutions and in many developing country governments, they have not been used for impact evaluation. Something similar happens in the World Bank and the International Monetary Fund where intensive use of economic simulation models takes place, but where models have not been used for impact evaluation.[27]

III. Does Structural Reform Hurt the Poor, and What Is the Record of Social Compensatory Programs?

The issue of how adjustment affects the poor has attracted considerable attention. To a large extent, this is the result of literature that has argued that the social costs of adjustment are substantial and that they fall mainly on the poor.[28]

The case that the cost of adjustment falls principally on the poor has been widely contested, and in this author's opinion, is on shaky grounds. Nonetheless, the topic is of great interest in its own right because, in principle, adjustment **may** have significant short term adverse impacts on some of the poor.[29] I will largely base the comments below on two sets of ongoing studies carried out under A.I.D. auspices.

In Latin America the issue of whether the situation of the poor deteriorated during the 1980s is controversial.[30]   On the one hand, on the basis of what Berg and Hunter refer to as input indicators, income and expenditure data support the proposition that the incidence of poverty has spread. The strongest evidence is from per capita private consumption which is reported to have fallen in 13 out of 20 countries. Likewise, real government per capita expenditures in education and, especially, health fell throughout the decade. Nonetheless, even income and expenditure indicators show, for some countries, a stable or even improving situation.

On the other hand, the picture portrayed by outcome or direct indicators of welfare —are the people in worse or better health? eating better or not? with more or less access to educational opportunities?— suggest clear trends of improvement.[31] Calorie availability improved or remained

---

[26]In any case, models would be tested for tracking performance -- that is, how well simulated values match historical values. Testing is of course harder when one is dealing with broad and deep structural reforms. In such case, sensitivity analysis should help in establishing reasonable value ranges. On these issues see Khayum (1991), Almon (1990) and Khan, Montiel, and Haque (1991).

[27]This might change soon at the World Bank where the use of models by the Operations Evaluation Department is under consideration. The International Monetary Fund is moving toward the establishment for the first time a formal evaluation unit.

[28]Much of this literature has originated in the United Nations Children's Fund organization (UNICEF). The best known of this work, and the one that has had most impact, is the 1987 UNICEF-sponsored volume *Adjustment with a Human Face.*

[29]This has led to considerable World Bank interest on the subject (World Bank 1990). Likewise, the Inter-American Development Bank funded a set of studies focusing on Latin American presented at a conference on policies of adjustment and poverty in February 1992.

[30]Unless other wise indicated, references to Latin America are based on Berg and Hunter (1992).

[31]Data on direct outcomes for the poor do not exist. Accordingly, Berg and Hunter had to work with national averages with the implicit assumption that marginal changes in outcomes will generally reflect changes in the status of the most vulnerable groups.

stable in 14 out of 21 countries. Data from national surveys of nutritional status reported by PAHO for nine countries show unambiguous improvement over time. Child mortality rates continued to decrease between 1980 and 1985. Likewise, data on infant mortality rates and life expectancy indicate improvement. Analogously, progress in vaccination coverage was prevalent (only in 2 out of 20 countries that was not the case). Finally, net primary enrollments increased for most countries for which data was available to the analysts.

What are the reasons for the apparent inconsistencies between input and output data? There is no clear answer, but Berg and Hunter mention some of the possible explanations.

One potential explanation relates to the weakness of the data base. Indeed, much of the social indicators or welfare data, the indicators of output, are weak. Yet these are the data on which analysts and governments use, and on the basis of which decisions are made. Moreover, the quality of some of it has been improving and others have been refined to weed out the most unreliable (infant and mortality, for example). Finally, it is doubtful that the errors are so big that they can explain the difference between input and output measures.

Another potential explanation is that the outcome measures are correct but that the social costs of decreased expenditures in the social sectors have been deferred to the 1990s and that social conditions have continued to improve because of past investments.

A third explanation relating to health is that low-cost interventions have had quick and substantial impacts on health —e.g., oral rehydration therapy and vaccinations.

Finally, a fourth explanation for the inconsistency between input and output data is that the fall in social expenditures by central governments may have been partially offset by other sources -- for example, state and local governments, non-government nonprofit organizations, and through the private sector provision of services largely on a fee-for-service basis.

Mainly in connection with Africa, the conclusion of analysts under the Cornell Food and Nutrition Program has largely been that the proposition that economic adjustment —stabilization and structural reform— hurts the poor has by and large been based on anecdotal and casual information, as well as built on pre-existing views that economic liberalization was not helpful and, even counterproductive.[32] The following paragraphs highlight some of the main points made after applying diverse methodologies to the issue at hand.

There has been confusion between poverty resulting from, or aggravated by, conditions existing before or independently of the reforms. Moreover, the correct comparison is not between before and after the reforms, but what would the conditions of the poor be under alternative policy scenarios. The continuation of the pre-existing economic policy orientation —and delaying structural reforms— may have meant worsening the conditions of the poor. In any case, given that adjustment became inevitable for many LDCs (the Central American countries are a good example), postponing the structural economic policy reforms would have meant a rougher adjustment process.

Likewise, references to purported adverse effects of adjustment on the poor do not adequately take into account that adjustment mainly hurts the beneficiaries of the *status quo ante*. These were rent-seekers who became influential through access to government officers and the

---

[32]The next seven paragraphs build on Sahn (1992). This work contains a good bibliography on the subject.

persons linked to protected activities. Such state of affairs hurted the poor.

In fact, the poor are more likely to suffer from failures to launch serious economic liberalization efforts, as well as when there are policy reform reversals, or undue delays in the reform process. Are there doubts that the poor did not benefit from negative real interest rates, cheap food, subsidized fertilizers, government marketing boards of agricultural products, general prices controls, and overvalued local currencies?

Nonetheless the poor may suffer some short-term adverse impacts. Reductions in the fiscal deficit that involve cuts in government expenditures may be translated, for example, into reductions in subsidized health activities and education that do reach at least some of the poor. (However, one cannot just assume that cuts in social sector expenditures will necessarily hurt the poor. The reason is that the intrasectoral allocation of resources is frequently skewed toward uses —secondary and higher education, hospital-based care, for example— of which the poor are not the main beneficiaries. For example, in the early 1980s, Malawi allocated only around 7 percent of health spending to preventive services, most of Ghana's health budget was for curative services in urban areas, and Tanzania, which supposedly emphasized social policies, allocated only some 6 percent of its health budget to prevention, while 68 percent went for hospital services.)

So where are we? In spite of the mounting evidence that the poor are not the ones that primarily suffer from adjustment, almost every adjustment program supported by development agencies has called for a compensatory social program. The reasons for this are several: (1) by arguing that adjustment hurts the poor and therefore they should be protected, advocates for social programs are able to attract more resources for such programs; (2) compensatory programs fulfil a political role by helping sell the reform program; (3) compensatory programs are often off-budget which may mean that they are less subject to scrutiny and, therefore, coveted by governments.

On principles on which the programs may be founded, growth-oriented programs based on raising the returns to factors owned by the poor seem preferable to direct transfer programs (Sahn 1992). Second, the opportunity costs of the programs must be taken into account —this is particularly valid of closely related alternatives such as direct food transfers to selected groups versus food distribution through the market. Third, transfers must be transparent and should not foster the distortions that gave rise to the reform process in the first place —for example, subsidized interest rates for certain groups are generally a bad idea.

On the issue of how have compensatory programs worked, the basic answer is ... not well.[33] First, more often than not, so-called special social safety net or social compensatory programs do not meet "truth in labelling" standards. They frequently have just been a repackaging of pre-existing "anti-poverty" programs, or new ill-conceived efforts which take into account neither opportunity nor recurrent costs. Moreover, there has been little by way of attempting to find areas of complementarity between adjustment with growth and long-term poverty alleviation.

The above does not mean that all attempts have totally failed. For example, a severance payment scheme included in Mali's Voluntary Departure Program of the 1980s was deemed as more successful in generating new business than a complicated training and studies loan program. Likewise, although with several controversial aspects, the Bolivian Emergency Social Fund of 1986, designed to fund small projects, create infrastructure, and generate employment is regarded as having

---

[33]On these points see Kingsbury (1992).

had positive impacts. Analogously, the post-1973 Chilean Emergency Employment Programs seems to have been relatively effective in targeting beneficiaries (by setting wages at 25 percent of the legal minimum and requiring that participants be unemployed), and for providing employment for women who had difficulty in accessing formal labor markets.

Yet even these "success" stories are controversial, and probably involved substantial allocations of resources to activities which could not be justified on the basis of economic returns.

In sum, more analysis is required on the central issue of whether and how adjustment does really hurt the poor, and, in any case, on the relative merits of alternative mechanisms for compensating the poor for potentially adverse effects.

Conclusions

The lessons of the last decade of development experience are very relevant for moving to a market economy in a post-Castro Cuba. It would be a pity to ignore them and proceed to use the policy making misconceptions that prevailed in the developing world until not long ago.

Unfortunately, during the last two years, some of what I have heard in connection with post-Castro Cuba —use of subsidized and directed credit, selecting sectors for priority treatment, concern about "selling the country to foreign investors", convoluted planning schemes, etc.— makes me fear that the risk of such mistakes is high. There is much in this respect that can be learned from ongoing experiences in Africa, South-Asia and the Far East, Eastern and Central Europe, and Latin America. However, extracting such knowledge will require not only more analysis, but a refinement of our analytical approaches in ways that integrate economic and socio-political considerations.

Finally, the analysis of how the poorest Cubans are likely to fare under systemic reform, and the mechanisms to alleviate their lot during the transition as necessary, is a relatively virgin area for research. The payoff of analytic work on the topic will be high.

References

Almon, C., *The Craft of Economic Modeling* (Needham Heights, Ma: Ginn Press, 1990).

Arndt, H.W., "The Trickle-Down Myth" *Economic Development and Cultural Change*, Vol 32 No 1, October 1983, pages 1-10.

Berg, E. and G. Hunter, *Social Costs of Adjustment: The Case of Latin America and the Caribbean* (Bethesda, Maryland: DAI for U.S. Agency for International Development, 1992).

Betancourt R., "The New Institutional Economics and the Study of the Cuban Economy" in *Cuba in Transition*, Papers and Proceedings of the First Annual Meeting of the Association for the Study of the Cuban Economy, ASCE 1992.

Brinkerhoff, D.W., *Improving Development Program Performance* (Boulder, Colorado: Lynne Rienner Publishers Inc., 1991).

Clague C. and Rausser G.C. (editors), *The Emergence of Market Economies in Eastern Europe*, Basil Blackwell 1992.

Dornbusch, R., "The Case for Trade Liberalization in Developing Countries" *The Journal of Economic Perspectives*, Vol 6 No 1, Winter 1992, pages 69-85.

Edwards S., *Trade Reforms, Liberalization and Exchange Rate Policy*, draft, Institute for Policy Reforms, June 1992.

Goldstein, M. and P. Montiel, "Evaluating Fund Stabilization Programs with Multicountry Data" *International Monetary Fund Staff Papers*, Vol 33, 1986, pages 304-344.

Guitian, M., *Fund Conditionality:Evolution of Principles and Practices*, Pamphlet Series No. 38 (Washington D.C.: International Monetary Fund, 1981).

Harberger A., Krueger A.O., Fox J.W., and Edwards S., "Interface between Economic Techniques and Economic Policy" *Contemporary Policy Issues*, volume X, no 3, July 1992, pages 1-3.

Harberger, A.C., "Basic Needs versus Distributional Weights in Social Cost Benefit Analysis" *Economic Development and Cultural Change*, Vol 32 No 3, April 1984, pages 455-474.

Kingsbury D.S., *Compensatory Social Programs and Structural Adjustment: A Review of Experience*, DAI for the U.S. Agency for International Development, April 1992.

International Labour Office, *Employment, Growth, and Basic Needs : A One-World Problem* (Geneva: ILO, 1976).

Khan, M.S., P.J. Montiel, and N.U. Haque, *Macroeconomic Models for Adjustment in Developing Countries* (Washington D.C.: International Monetary Fund, 1991).

Khayum, M.F., *Macroeconomic Modeling and Policy Analysis for Less Developing Countries* (Boulder, Colorado: Westview Press, Inc.,1991).

Krueger, A.O., *Ideas Underlying Development Policy In the 1950s*, draft (Washington D.C.: Institute for Policy Reform, 1991).

Krueger, A.O., *Trade and Employment in Developing Countries*, Vol 3, *Synthesis and Conclusions* (Chicago, Ill. University of Chicago Press, 1983).

Krueger A.O., *Foreign Trade Regimes and Economic Development: Liberalization Attempts and Consequences* (Cambridge, Mass.: Ballinger Press for the National Bureau of Economic Research, 1978).

Lieberson, J.M., *A.I.D. Economic Policy Reform Programs in Africa: A Synthesis of Findings from Six Evaluations* (Washington D.C.: Agency for International Development, Center for Development Information and Evaluation, 1991).

Little, I.M., *Economic Development Theory, Policy, and International Relations* (New York: Basic Books, Inc., Publishers, 1982).

Meier, G.M., *Leading Issues in Economic Development* (New York: Oxford University Press, 5th ed, 1989).

Sahn D.E., *Has Policy Reform Hurt the Poor in Africa?*, paper prepared for the U.S. Agency for International Development, Cornell University, September 1991.

World Bank, *The Third Report on Adjustment Lending: Private and Public Resources for Growth* (Washington D.C. : Country Economics Department, 1992)

World Bank, *Report on Adjustment Lending II: Policies for Recovery and Growth* (Washington D.C.: Country Economics Department, 1990).

World Bank, *Transition*, Volume 2 No 10, November 1991.

World Bank, *Transition*, Volume 3 No 5, May 1992.

World Bank, *World Development Report 1991: The Challenge of Development*, International Bank for Reconstruction and Development, 1991, chapter 7.

CUBA: FUNDAMENTOS DE UNA PROPUESTA PARA EL ESTABLECIMIENTO Y DESARROLLO DE UNA ECONOMÍA SOCIAL DE MERCADO[1]

Rolando H. Castañeda[2]

I. Introducción

A.   Propósito

El colapso del régimen socialista de Cuba es inevitable, inminente y necesario, debido a la profunda e irreversible crisis sistémica económica y financiera que padece. Pronto el país será libre con un sistema político democrático y multipartidista y con una economía de mercado. Ello implica una magna, compleja y ardua transformación por las secuelas de una cultura totalitaria, el atraso de la economía, las formas de propiedad socialistas extremas y generalizadas, la estructura de precios muy distorsionada, la ausencia de instituciones y mecanismos de mercado, la regulación inflexible, la centralización burocrática inoperante y los planes inadecuados para realizar los cambios requeridos. Por eso es conveniente considerar, cuanto antes, cómo realizar esta transformación en la forma más sencilla, completa, viable y rápida posible.

Este ensayo se propone contribuir a la transformación con una propuesta, en respuesta al Debate Nacional solicitado por la Declaración de los Intelectuales Cubanos el 20 de mayo de 1991. Espero que a su vez aliente otras propuestas alternativas globales, o sobre algunos de los tópicos cubiertos en este ensayo u otros iguales o más importantes que aquí no se hayan cubierto. Es imprescindible que los cubanos superemos las lentas experiencias de transformación de otros países latinoamericanos y de Europa Oriental, y para ello deberíamos prepararnos y estar decididos a realizar los cambios necesarios. Pensemos en Cuba en grande. Cuba tiene que plantearse una nueva manera de organizarse. Hay que mirar a Cuba a principios del siglo XXI.

Terminemos nuestra tragedia. La magnitud y gravedad de la crisis que atravesamos, es tan dramática, evidente e insostenible, que no es difícil coincidir en que hay que superarla. Mientras el cambio se prolongue más, más abrupto y costoso será iniciarlo. Promulguemos una economía en la que casi todos, o al menos una mayoría, coincidamos, y que sea consistente con el entorno internacional, es decir, una **economía de mercado, basada en la propiedad privada y la iniciativa individual, con intervención limitada del estado, con un compromiso decidido hacia los grupos más vulnerables de la sociedad y que proteja nuestros recursos naturales.** Aquí ya tenemos una plataforma básica, capaz de revitalizar nuevamente a Cuba con progreso y paz social. Esta propuesta se basa en dicho consenso.

La propuesta tiene sus raíces en el lema **libertad y vida,** consigna del movimiento de derechos humanos de Cuba, la cual se contrapone al anacrónico, apocalíptico y cada vez más

[1]Este trabajo fundamenta y amplia los principales planteamientos económicos de "Una Opción por la Libertad, el Desarrollo y la Paz Social", ensayo presentado en la reunión de The Association for the Study of the Cuban Economy el 29 de enero de 1992 y que después fuera publicado como parte de *Cuba in Transition* (Papers and Proceedings of the First Annual Meeting of the Association for the Study of the Cuban Economy), Miami: Florida International University, 1992, pp 257-308. El autor agradece los comentarios y las recomendaciones de Alicia R. Castañeda, José A. Herrero, Ricardo Puerta y Manuel Lasaga.

[2]Economista del Departamento de Operaciones del Banco Interamericano de Desarrollo. Las opiniones sobre todos los temas tratados en este ensayo son estrictamente personales.

desacreditado lema de **socialismo o muerte** todavía propuesto por el gobierno totalitario.[3]

B. Resumen y Conclusiones

Cuba se sostuvo artificialmente por la masiva ayuda soviética y del bloque socialista desde 1960 a 1991. La ayuda era a través de transferencias en forma de petróleo barato, precios altos y artificiales para el azúcar y el níquel; préstamos externos, con un elevado componente concesional; y una cobertura amplia de los déficits comerciales. La ineficiencia ha estado expresada por la sobrevaluación del peso, el lento crecimiento de la productividad, la limitada utilización de nuestros valiosos recursos humanos, el deterioro de los recursos renovables, la limitada capacidad de exportar y las dramáticas caídas de la producción, del empleo productivo y del ingreso medio efectivo. Cuba socialista no es viable. Cuba, con una economía de mercado, sí lo es, según ya ha sido probado por la corta experiencia liberalizadora del socialismo cubano (1980-1985) que reactivó moderadamente su economía y el perfil relativamente avanzado de la era anterior a 1959.

La propuesta es concreta, coherente y pragmática para transformar la economía socialista a una economía social de mercado en Cuba en 6 años. Responde al reto de democratización y desarrollo sostenible del país, con equidad social. Integrándola principalmente al bloque económico de Norte América en las áreas comercial, de servicios y financiera y conduciría a Cuba al siglo XXI. Técnicamente, la propuesta tiene los elementos básicos de un plan económico, con el señalamiento de ciertas condicionantes y efectos tanto en lo político, como en lo social. No es un programa general de gobierno, pues le faltan otros componentes difíciles de precisar, bien porque habría que elaborarlos *in situ*, después de oír opiniones autorizadas, o porque escapan al alcance de este estudio.

La propuesta parte de un gobierno civil o militar, que tiene suficiente legitimidad y decisión política para emprender los cambios necesarios. Las transformaciones requeridas incluyen pasar de una estructura y cultura totalitarias a otras democráticas. Los cambios se efectuarían a través de medidas de política macroeconómica y de reformas estructurales coherentes, interrelacionadas y apoyadas entre sí, dentro de un marco general orientado **al objetivo final: establecer una economía social de mercado (ESM) muy competitiva y abierta, basada en la propiedad privada y en la libertad e iniciativa individuales, con un papel limitado y subsidiario, pero fuerte del estado.** La ESM a través del funcionamiento del mercado, la apertura al comercio exterior y el establecimiento de políticas globales de ordenamiento de la economía hará posibles un alto crecimiento y gran dinamismo de la economía. La ESM es la alternativa al socialismo de mercado, al dirigismo estatal y al liberalismo a ultranza. Por sus efectos, la propuesta permitiría la modernización del país y crearía bases sólidas para el desarrollo de una sociedad libre y democrática, con efectiva participación ciudadana y en paz social.

La propuesta recomienda realizar los cambios institucionales y económicos orientados a la estabilización y la apertura económica **en forma secuencial y ordenada, pero progresiva, sistemática,**

---

[3]En Cuba se anticipa como chiste popular que en la próxima edición del diccionario de la lengua castellana, los vocablos de socialismo y muerte aparecerán como sinónimos, utilizando como justificación el trágico caso cubano.

integral y con una dinámica propia.[4] Como lo han hecho Chile, la antigua Checoslovaquia y Hungría, en vez de lo realizado en Perú, Polonia y la antigua URSS. En tal sentido, es imprescindible complementar las medidas de estabilización de tipo macroeconómico con profundas reformas estructurales, a fin de asentar bases microeconómicas firmes, alentando el aumento de la oferta agregada desde un principio y que faciliten después el proceso de liberalización; algunas de estas medidas requieren tiempo. Dentro de lo propuesto, la protección de los derechos de propiedad, la desregulación de la actividad económica, el desmantelamiento de los monopolios y oligopolios artificiales y la privatización de los medios de producción, deberían iniciarse pronto y ser realizados de manera decidida para mejorar las condiciones de la oferta, haciéndola ágil, flexible, tecnológicamente avanzada y abierta a la competencia internacional, asegurando así una respuesta productiva en un plazo razonablemente rápido.

La aplicación de medidas correctivas exclusivamente macroeconómicas resulta insuficiente a menos que se atienda en sincronía el aspecto institucional y microeconómico. Los cambios propuestos buscan soluciones permanentes que aseguren la sostenibilidad del crecimiento social y políticamente, no soluciones cortoplacistas que son no viables porque crean serios problemas de mediano y largo plazo. Los objetivos de mediano y largo plazo sirven de guía para el manejo de la política económica de corto plazo y para efectuar los cambios en secuencia, con el debido contenido y la correcta interacción. Teniendo en cuenta la experiencia de Japón y Alemania después de la Segunda Guerra Mundial, no es necesario que un programa de estabilización tenga necesariamente fuertes efectos recesivos en Cuba, en parte también, porque su economía ya se ha vuelto tan regresiva, que anda por niveles de ingreso muy similares a los de finales de los años 1960. Además, una recesión extrema forzaría a una discontinuidad de las reformas, ante el excesivo descontento social y político.

C. Organización

El Capítulo II considera las condiciones políticas para efectuar los cambios en la Sección A, las ventajas comparativas de la economía cubana en la Sección B, descarta por insuficiente el regreso al marco institucional y jurídico pre-socialista en la Sección C, y, finalmente, desarrolla la conceptualización y los detalles de la propuesta en la Sección D.

II. Propuesta para reconstruir y modernizar la economía cubana y sus instituciones en el período de la transformación

Esta propuesta presenta la conceptualización de un programa para lograr en Cuba una economía social de mercado, muy competitiva y orientada al exterior. Incluye sus principales políticas macroeconómicas y reformas estructurales. Los lineamentos contenidos en esta propuesta tienen un alcance político porque, de seguirse, incidirían en la conducción del gobierno. Pretenden recuperar el *ethos* en la vida nacional, es decir, el poder ético que desde el gobierno apela a la conciencia activa del ciudadano.

---

[4]La secuencialidad equivale a no hacer todos los cambios y reformas estructurales a la vez en los sectores reales, financiero, fiscal, externo e institucional. Sin embargo, se recomienda un ajuste fiscal, de precios y de tasa de cambio inicialmente; es decir, un especie de "shock" drástico, pero parcial, un "little bang" para eliminar la hiperinflación y estabilizar la tasa de cambio. La secuencialidad evitaría repetir las experiencias negativas ocurridas ya en varios países, debido a la intensidad de las medidas de estabilización, a conflictos entre las medidas de estabilización de corto plazo y las reformas estructurales de mediano y largo plazo. La secuencialidad permitiría también lograr efectos que compensen, al menos en parte, los grandes costos de las medidas de estabilización y reformas. Si los problemas de corto plazo fueran muy severos, sería imposible continuar con las reformas.

La propuesta se recomienda en consonancia con el entorno internacional muy competitivo y dinámico; la difícil situación económica e institucional del país;[5] y sus ventajas comparativas. Propone un ajuste secuencial, pero progresivo y completo, a la McKinnon (1991).[6] También utiliza como paradigma la integralidad de las reformas de Chile, las cuales son ajustadas en sus aspectos sociales y ambientales desde las primeras etapas.[7]

A.   Condiciones políticas para su implantación

Ante la continuidad del régimen cubano, la propuesta podría parecer ingenua; sin embargo, hay varios escenarios políticos donde podría implantarse, o al menos, ser útil. [8] Es posible que la dirigencia del gobierno socialista: (1) se retire voluntariamente del país debido a la cada vez más deteriorada y incorregible situación económica y política; (2) haga elecciones libres ante la creciente presión de los gobernantes hispanoamericanos,[9] bajo el decidido liderato del Presidente Carlos Menem de Argentina y de los intelectuales cubanos y latinoamericanos,[10] a fin de extender a Cuba la democracia de casi todo el continente; (3) determine comenzar un proceso imprescindible de reformas; y (4) continúe el deterioro y la represión hasta llegar al extremo del colapso, cuando el aparato represivo decida o no pueda reprimir más. También Fidel Castro podría desaparecer por muerte natural, accidental o de otra forma.[11]

Los militares podrían tomar el poder para restablecer el orden para evitar el inminente caos o frenarlo, después de algunas manifestaciones espontáneas reprimidas a la rumana, y decidan sentar nuevas bases para la institucionalización del país, impulsando un cambio estructural radical, a la Chile.[12] Como muy acertadamente señala Aguilar-León (1992) con respecto a las fuerzas armadas, el régimen socialista no tiene salida, pero los militares sí la tienen.[13]

---

[5]Castañeda (1992, p 260-269) resume esta situación, la cual se ha venido empeorando progresivamente por la disminución del comercio y la cancelación de la ayuda externa. No obstante, no hay datos macroeconómicos oficiales recientes; los últimos corresponden a 1989.

[6]Castañeda (1992, Anexo 1, p 288-293) resume los principales planteamientos de McKinnon sobre las etapas en la transformación del socialismo a la economía de mercado.

[7]Castañeda, 1992 (Anexo 2, p 296-302) resume la experiencia chilena en 1973-1992.

[8]   Ernesto Betancourt (1988) presenta un marco general y algunas alternativas de transición política para Cuba, que deberían desembocar en una apertura económica y en el cambio del sistema socialista. Aguilar-León (1992) ofrece reflexiones históricas y políticas sobre la inminente caída del régimen socialista, probablemente por la intervención de las Fuerzas Armadas.

[9]Declaración de los 13 Presidentes de los Países del Grupo de Rio de Cartagena de Indias del 2 de diciembre de 1991.

[10]Entre los que se destaca la valerosa poetisa y escritora María Elena Cruz Varela del Grupo Criterio Alternativo, quién fuera sentenciada a dos años de prisión el 27 de noviembre de 1991, por los delitos de asociación e impresión ilícitos y por desacreditar las instituciones del estado socialista, aunque en realidad fue por pensar, soñar y anhelar.

[11]La salida de Fidel Castro del poder sigue siendo el eslabón perdido en la cadena de hechos de quienes buscan un desenlace político e incruento del régimen actual cubano. A pesar de esto, el castrismo está más preparado para sobrevivir en una política de agresión que una de diálogo y oposición pacífica.

[12]Cabe señalar que los cambios socioeconómicos de Chile tuvieron lugar en un período que no se entendieron bien debido al régimen militar y autoritario que las implantó y a las ideas intervencionistas y socialistas que prevalecían en el continente. Además, se cometieron algunos errores socioeconómicos y políticos innecesarios.

[13]Las Fuerzas Armadas cubanas muestran un cambio cualitativo por la experiencia africana, principalmente la angoleña. Vuelven de Africa a Cuba como una clase social, con conciencia y privilegios propios, distinta a la generación histórica del ejército o los comandantes de la Sierra Maestra y asaltantes del Cuartel Moncada. Fue la primera gran fisura, de este tipo, entre los militares cubanos. El General Arnaldo Ochoa Sánchez es el símbolo de estos internacionalistas, quienes en las Fuerzas Armadas constituyen el grupo de los "generales profesionales" frente a los "comandantes guerrilleros". En sus concepciones políticas, la mayoría de los generales son perestroikos y muchos sobreviven en Cuba bajo retiro forzoso.

En el menor de los usos, la propuesta es útil para las corrientes democráticas —liberal, democristiana y socialdemócrata— que se oponen dentro y fuera de Cuba al socialismo cubano y puedan elaborar con más referencias técnicas un plan de gobierno, o revisen el que ya tienen, al menos para la etapa transitoria. A pesar de las diferencias entre esas corrientes, lo coincidente supera a lo diverso, sabiendo al mismo tiempo que cualquier plan tendrá que ser corregido en su marcha.

La posible convergencia en esas corrientes no es un mero deseo. La Declaración de los Intelectuales Cubanos del 20 de mayo de 1991, el Programa Socialista Democrático de diciembre 1991/enero 1992 y el reciente circulado Programa Transitorio del Movimiento Cristiano Liberación de julio de 1992, coinciden en muchos puntos, entre ellos: la necesidad de moverse hacia una economía de mercado; una sociedad libre, abierta y pluralista; un gobierno, que en vez de coartar, garantice libertades individuales y sociales; y el logro del progreso y la justicia social.[14]

En cualquier caso, es necesario que comience un debate nacional más sistemático sobre el futuro del país. Que los cubanos de la isla y de fuera tengamos propuestas, lo más completas y coherentes posibles, para sacar a Cuba de la mediocridad y la declinación. La necesidad se vuelve imperiosa ante la insistencia del régimen, fuera de todo criterio realista, de convertir a Cuba en el último bastión del socialismo totalitario y de economía centralizada del mundo, aún cuando ya no existe la ayuda masiva, ni el comercio del bloque soviético, los pilares **artificiales** del régimen por más de tres décadas. Irónicamente, esta posición extrema facilitará todo lo contrario en el futuro: el establecimiento de una economía social de mercado con el apoyo de la inmensa mayoría de la población. Los cubanos de la isla ya están hartos de no poder expresar su capacidad creativa e iniciativas, salvo en forma clandestina o en instituciones reprimidas.

B. Las ventajas comparativas de Cuba

Las principales ventajas de la economía cubana consisten en:

(1) Los recursos naturales para la agricultura, el turismo y la pesca. Cuba sigue siendo un país de múltiples productos agrícolas. Muchos productos cubanos, frescos o procesados, tienen un mercado permanente en países desarrollados. Algunas cosechas se obtienen en épocas de demanda insatisfecha en mercados internacionales, permitiendo aprovecharse de estas "ventanillas". Cuba, desde tiempos coloniales, es una atracción turística por sus bellezas naturales, clima, condición de isla grande, cultura, población, etc. Cuba tiene plataformas apropiadas para la pesca.

La población de origen latino en los EUA es un mercado de gran potencial como posible consumidor de productos y servicios originados en Cuba. Se estima en más de 20 millones de habitantes, 5 millones ubicados en la costa oriental norteamericana o lugares aledaños, la región más accesible de EUA a Cuba.

(2) Posición geográfica cercana a los EUA, el mayor mercado del mundo, ahora en proceso de integración con Canadá y México y eventualmente con todo el Hemisferio Occidental, **y como punto de escala estratégica entre América y Europa, así como entre Norte América y Sur América.**

(3) Lo excepcional de su clase empresarial, profesional, administradora y trabajadora, la que

---

[14]Las medidas inmediatas incluyen: libertad para los presos políticos, legalización de los grupos de oposición (políticos, intelectuales y sindicales), retorno de los exilados, reunificación familiar, promesa de elecciones libres y multipartidistas, y desestatizar la economía.

parcialmente se radicó con éxito y ha ganado extraordinarias experiencias en los EUA, América Latina y Europa, aumentando así su capital humano y su cosmopolitanismo.

(4) Otra ventaja de Cuba es llegar de última a la apertura económica, ya que no tendrá que experimentar en muchos áreas y podrá adoptar fórmulas que ya resultaron útiles.

Uno de los grandes errores del gobierno socialista desde el punto de vista económico, ha sido propiciar oleadas de emigración, principalmente en 1960-1961, 1965-1971 (Camarioca y los vuelos de la libertad) y 1980 (Mariel) porque produjo el drenaje de cerebros del país, principalmente del capital humano no conformista. El gobierno socialista permitió la salida de cubanos de la isla, por medios legales e ilegales, una constante de los últimos 33 años, para debilitar la oposición interna, real y potencial, frente al gobierno y aumentar la movilidad social en la población que no emigra, por ésta quedarse con bienes confiscados y con servicios públicos y empleos abandonados.

El régimen, sin embargo, ha realizado un esfuerzo en aumentar la cobertura educacional y de salud, que se refleja en el número y distribución geográfica de sectores medios en la población actual. En consecuencia, el país dispone de una fuerza laboral más educada y sana que en la mayoría de los países latinoamericanos.[15] Estos recursos necesitan ser actualizados en técnicas modernas, sobre todo de administración y gerencia, aplicables a una economía de mercado. Es necesario también ampliar los horizontes empresariales en los técnicos y profesionales para que puedan operar con más diversidad y eficiencia productiva en un sistema que ya no sería centralizado, ni estatista. Esta población podría mejorar su productividad y competir ventajosamente en la producción de bienes y servicios con otros países de la región, una vez fijada una tasa de cambio realista y efectuados los ajustes requeridos en la organización productiva.

Aunque la reconstrucción de Cuba dependerá, en definitiva, del papel efectivo que asuma, después del socialismo, la población cubana que nunca emigró, Cuba debería crear las condiciones propicias para recuperar la población radicada en el exterior y aplicarla a los problemas del desarrollo nacional en la reconstrucción del país, por sus conocimientos, destrezas y experiencias empresariales, profesionales, gerenciales y administrativas; sus recursos financieros y tecnológicos; y sus contactos, los que facilitarían el acceso a los mercados externos. La transferencia de estos recursos a toda la población tendría un impacto positivo en el país.[16] En tal sentido, se puede anticipar que los empresarios cubanos del exilio no dominarán la futura economía cubana, aunque sí tendrán una participación mayoritaria en el sector de la economía que esté orientada hacia el exterior. Aún la población que permanezca en el exterior puede aportar su valiosa experiencia y sus conexiones para el establecimiento o ampliación de empresas cubanas que tengan sucursales y subsidiarias en el exterior, colocándolas en un plano de mayor competitividad con las empresas multinacionales.

Dada la situación y las expectativas del mercado mundial del azúcar,[17] Cuba no deberá especializarse artificialmente para un mercado externo protegido, con las distorsiones que ello

---

[15]Además de ser más educada, sana y de poseer sectores medios más amplios y distribuidos geográficamente, la población cubana de hoy es también más joven, más negra, más mulata, más urbana, y más intolerante y frustrada políticamente, que la de 1958.

[16]Después de quedar desolada por la cruenta Guerra de Independencia en 1895-1898, Cuba creció extraordinariamente a principios del siglo XX, gracias, entre otros factores, a la inmigración española y la inversión de EUA en una época cuando prevaleció un marco institucional y jurídico similar al que se propone en este ensayo.

[17]Actualmente prevalecen precios por debajo de los costos de producción debido al creciente desarrollo de sustitutos en la Comunidad Económica Europea y los EUA. Es de esperar que este tipo de desarrollo continué en los próximos años.

conllevaría en los sectores internos y externos del país. Asimismo, debe alentar la diversificación de productos vinculados con el azúcar de mayor valor agregado, tales como: alcoholes, papel, ron, bagazo, furfural, etc. Cuba debería orientar su economía a actividades que utilicen intensivamente sus recursos de mano de obra, conocimientos tecnológicos, capacidad empresarial y recursos naturales. El país podría competir con rapidez en cuatro sectores: la agricultura y el procesamiento de su producción (la agroindustria), el turismo, la pesca y los servicios de tránsito internacional. La rapidez equivale a una reducida inversión inicial por lo excepcional de sus recursos naturales, su posición geográfica y por las inversiones realizadas en esas ramas económicas por el gobierno socialista. Estas recomendaciones muestran que el país debería esforzarse, especialmente, en el manejo, la conservación y el uso racional de sus recursos naturales, para asegurar, entre otros efectos, un medio ambiente puro.

En síntesis, se destaca el gran potencial de crecimiento del sector agropecuario y de la agroindustria, por la fertilidad de sus suelos —reforzada por obras de irrigación y drenaje— el fácil acceso al mercado cubano-americano y latino en los EUA, y la complementariedad con los climas de Canadá y los EUA. El turismo debido a que Cuba es una isla tropical con excelente clima, bellas y extensas playas y paisajes naturales; sus reliquias coloniales; la diversidad de sus aves, variedades marinas y su flora tropical; las inversiones que se están realizando y la posibilidad que la agricultura nacional genere la mayoría de los alimentos que requerirán los visitantes. Sólo los ingresos generados por los cubanos radicados en el exterior que decidan visitar la isla podrían volverse significativos en el turismo.[18] Igualmente se debería aprovechar el turismo ecológico y al país, como punto de escala para los viajeros entre Europa y América, entre Norte América y Sur América y para los cruceros del Caribe. La pesca, por las importantes inversiones realizadas en el sector y por las plataformas apropiadas. Eventualmente, Cuba podría también desarrollar actividades de alta tecnología para aprovechar más la educación de su fuerza laboral y la capacidad empresarial de su población del exterior.

C. ¿Es suficiente el regreso al marco institucional presocialista?

No es suficiente. Si bien dicho marco permitió que el país alcanzara niveles de vida elevados en América Latina, había elementos que se establecieron y desarrollaron que no se adaptan a la situación y problemas actuales del país, ni al dinámico entorno internacional. Además, Cuba experimentó un estancamiento del PIB por habitante a precios constantes durante la década de los años 50, tal vez porque los niveles del PIB de principio de esa década se debieron a los precios muy favorables del azúcar por la Guerra de Corea, los cuales no se pudieron superar con la política expansionista compensatoria, seguida por la el gobierno de Batista en 1952-1958.

Entre los problemas del marco institucional presocialista, cabe destacar la legislación laboral con base en los Artículos del Título VI de la Constitución de 1940 que protegía la inamovilidad del empleado y los beneficios del trabajador ocupado, pero que era un verdadero desincentivo para contratar nuevos trabajadores y por ello favorecía tecnologías intensivas en capital, en una situación que había altas tasas de desempleo abierto y empleo de baja productividad. Otra era la legislación de la industria azucarera de 1937, que tenía sus orígenes en la gran depresión de los años 30. Esta legislación distribuía equitativamente los ingresos del azúcar entre los obreros agrícolas e industriales, los colonos, los hacendados, etc. Sin embargo, limitaba la capacidad de acumulación de capital, restringía los incentivos para la modernización de la industria y frenaba la expansión de otras actividades agrícolas rentables, debido a que creaba una clase rentista, preocupada más por

---

[18]El turismo ha jugado un papel muy importante en el desarrollo de varios países del mediterráneo europeo: España, Italia y Grecia.

proteger sus privilegios que por promover el crecimiento de la economía nacional. El historiador Aguilar-León (1992) y la socióloga Pérez-Stable (1992) han comentado, de manera similar, dicho marco institucional.

La Cuba postsocialista necesita un marco institucional y jurídico que promueva una economía competitiva y dinámica, con libertad y en democracia. Cuba tiene la oportunidad, sin precedentes en su historia, de comenzar, desde sus inicios, una economía de mercado y, para ello, debería optar por una moderna base institucional y legal, propia del siglo XXI.

D. La propuesta

Para superar la situación de caos económico que caracteriza a Cuba es imprescindible diseñar un plan apropiado y aplicarlo adecuadamente. Algunos cambios recomendados, en especial las políticas macroeconómicas, son inevitables aún para la estrategia de desarrollo emprendida por el régimen socialista basada en el turismo, las empresas mixtas, las exportaciones de biotecnología y el plan alimentario. En el caso de Cuba hay problemas especiales que hay atender, tanto por el lado de exceso de la demanda, como por el lado de capacidad inutilizada por el lado de la oferta.

1. Objetivos y estrategia fundamental de cambios (Secuencialidad y transparencia)

Los objetivos principales de la transformación compartidos por la mayoría de los cubanos son: obtener el pleno ejercicio de las libertades y los derechos individuales; lograr la reconciliación nacional y la reunificación familiar; impulsar el crecimiento, desarrollo y modernización de la economía; promover la paz social; y reinsertar a Cuba en la comunidad internacional. El Cuadro 1 presenta mayores detalles sobre los objetivos y las políticas y reformas para alcanzarlos.

Uno de los instrumentos principales para lograr dichos objetivos sería establecer y desarrollar una economía social de mercado, competitiva y muy abierta, con base en la propiedad privada y la libertad e iniciativa individuales, alentadoras del esfuerzo, el ingenio, la energía, la espontaneidad, la creatividad, el espíritu crítico y la imaginación de los cubanos, dejando un papel limitado y subsidiario al estado. El mercado de libre competencia será el mecanismo de asignación de recursos, mediante el cual, el sector privado cumpliría su papel de agente y protagonista del crecimiento, y dinamizador principal de la economía. El estado realizaría actividades que le son inherentes, y que el sector privado no puede desarrollar, buscando los equilibrios macroeconómicos; estableciendo y asegurando la aplicación de un marco institucional y jurídico estable, sencillo, claro y no discrecional para el desarrollo del sector privado y de la sociedad civil; corrigiendo distorsiones o imperfecciones del mercado;[19] asegurando una mayor igualdad de oportunidades, atendiendo a los grupos más vulnerables y prestando los servicios públicos en forma eficiente, tales como: la preservación del orden y la administración de la justicia.

La acción del estado sería fuerte, decidida y activa en la etapa de la transformación, precisamente para reducir su exagerado ámbito y realizar reformas institucionales y jurídicas para la modernización, es decir, para desarrollar una economía de mercado estable, y dinámica en la cual todos seamos propietarios e inversionistas, manteniendo al mismo tiempo un compromiso con la población más vulnerable; sin embargo, no es estatizante en sus fines, ni en sus medios. El estado desmantelaría el régimen de propiedad socialista, las empresas monopólicas y oligopólicas, la centralización y el intervencionismo autoritarios, burocráticos e inefectivos, o sea, las estructuras del

---

[19]En las actividades donde la rentabilidad privada es significativamente menor que la rentabilidad social.

Cuadro 1
Objetivos, Metas, Políticas y Reformas Económicos Fundamentales
de la Propuesta

Objetivos	Metas	Políticas Macroeconómicas y Reformas Institucionales
Establecer y consolidar el pleno ejercicio de las libertades y derechos individuales, promoviendo una auténtica participación ciudadana en un estado de derecho.	Establecer y desarrollar una economía social de mercado descentralizada y una sociedad civil.	Dictar leyes sobre libertades y derechos económicos básicos. Libre entrada a las actividades económicas, servicios públicos y sociales, profesiones y oficios. Eliminar los controles de precios y de salarios a las empresas privadas, así como trabas y regulaciones a los mercados. Promover la rápida formación de los mercados agrícolas. Privatizar los medios de producción. Alentar a las entidades privadas sin fines de lucro.
	El estado tendría un rol limitado y subsidiario y sería descentralizado y participativo.	Reformar integralmente y reducir el ámbito, funciones, atribuciones y discrecionalidad del estado. Privatizar parcialmente los servicios públicos y los sociales. Expandir el papel de las provincias, los municipios y las comunidades en la ejecución y fiscalización de los programas del gobierno.
Lograr el reencuentro y la reconciliación nacional, así como la reunificación familiar.	Sustituir la confrontación por la cooperación y la solidaridad ciudadanas.	Eliminar los órganos del partido comunista y seguridad interna, las milicias, los comités de barrios y las brigadas de respuesta rápida. Reducir el tamaño del ejército. Atraer y reintegrar a los cubanos radicados en el exterior.

Objetivos	Metas	Políticas Macroeconómicas y Reformas Institucionales
Impulsar el crecimiento, desarrollo y modernización del país y encaminarlo adecuadamente al siglo XXI y a la integración al mercado de Norte América.	Desarrollar una economía muy competitiva.	Desregular actividades económicas. Desmantelar los monopolios y oligopolios estatales artificiales. Cada planta una empresa. El estado no otorgará concesiones económicas especiales, ni exclusivas. Privatizar por ventas o por arrendamientos de largo plazo. Prohibir monopolios laborales.
	Desarrollar una economía muy abierta.	Establecer un régimen arancelario ajustable y decreciente. Alentar la inversión privada extranjera en todos los sectores.
	Establecer y desarrollar una economía estable, moderna y dinámica.	Banco Central será autónomo. Regular y supervisar el crédito bancario. Establecer balance en las finanzas públicas. Reformar integralmente el alcance del estado para reducir su tamaño y aumentar su eficiencia. Reformas se harán secuencial, pero progresiva e integralmente.
Promover la paz social.	Establecer una Red de Solidaridad e Inversión Social.	Otorgar asistencia temporal a los desempleados. Asegurar necesidades básicas a la población de bajos ingresos. Fomentar el ahorro mediante apoyo inicial a soluciones habitacionales.
Reinsertar a Cuba económica y financieramente en la comunidad internacional.	Restablecer relaciones con la comunidad internacional.	Alentar la inversión privada extranjera. Entrar a organismos financieros internacionales. Renegociar la deuda externa. Alentar operaciones de reconversión.

atraso y la crisis sistémica. Igualmente, descentralizaría la acción del gobierno a las provincias, los municipios y las comunidades; fomentaría una auténtica participación ciudadana, aproximando la fiscalización de los servicios a los usuarios y estimulando la creación de corporaciones comunales privadas, sin fines de lucro, para el desarrollo local. Comprometería constructivamente mediante el diálogo y la concertación a los sectores sociales y políticos en la construcción y modernización del país.

A tal efecto el estado transformaría la economía socialista existente en Cuba a una de mercado, dentro de un marco general y consistente de políticas macroeconómicas y reformas institucionales **secuenciales** definidas a priori. Los cambios se aplicarían **progresiva, sistemática e integralmente** en la estabilización, liberalización, privatización y desburocratización del país, a fin de asegurar su efectividad y hacerlos sostenibles política y socialmente. Habría flexibilidad en la aplicación de las medidas a adoptar en cada etapa, pero **hay interrelaciones, interacciones, causalidades y secuencias necesarias** que hay que observar, que no se pueden violentar y que por no respetarlas, han sido el fallo del enfoque de gran explosión o de cambio total y simultáneo. La liberalización sólo se debe realizar cuando se haya logrado la estabilización o ciertos equilibrios macroeconómicos fundamentales. La secuencialidad pretende desarrollar la capacidad de respuesta a las medidas y reformas que requieren tiempo, mientras se eliminan rigidices y fricciones, para evitar que se desaten espirales inflacionarias, los cuales una vez aparezcan, desarrollan una inercia muy difícil de controlar, la concentración de la propiedad en unas pocas manos y el mantenimiento de estructuras monopólicas; todos costos sociales innecesarios. Las experiencias de ajuste de América Latina muestran que se requieren alrededor de 4 años para estabilizar la economía y alrededor de 6 años para crecer, pero no hacer nada sería mucho peor.

Se seguiría el esquema completo de McKinnon (1991), con algunas desviaciones y ampliaciones para realizar un proceso de privatización más rápido e intenso y adoptar medidas institucionales de desregulación de la producción y de desmantelamiento de los monopolios y oligopolios artificiales (conglomerados). Con estas medidas se buscan resultados catalíticos e influencias sinérgicas sobre el aumento de la producción. La propuesta es congruente con el conjunto de medidas que Williamson (1990) definió como consenso básico sobre los procesos de ajustes y de reformas recomendados por las instituciones financieras de Washington.

En el enfoque de McKinnon es imprescindible que cada fase se complete antes de comenzar la siguiente. No obstante, estas son condiciones necesarias, pero no suficientes. En atención a ello, las finanzas públicas deben balancearse antes de emprender la apertura financiera interna, de lo contrario dicha apertura quedaría distorsionada por las presiones inflacionarias creadas por el déficit del sector público y habría una demanda monetario-crediticia sobredimensionada, la cual impediría el adecuado acceso del sector privado al crédito por los requerimientos de crédito del sector público. La desregulación de la producción no respondería correctamente a las señales de precios en un ambiente de fuertes presiones inflacionarias; por ello, la desregulación de la producción no comenzaría hasta completar la racionalización financiera. La apertura comercial externa no comenzará hasta que se realicen ciertos ajustes fundamentales y el aprendizaje tecnológico necesario en la producción interna, ya que la producción nacional es de baja calidad y requiere más insumos y empleo que los necesarios; de lo contrario, se estaría sujeto a quiebras y desempleo innecesarios. Por último, la apertura financiera externa, si se hace prematuramente, podría atraer una entrada de capitales que paralizaría la apertura comercial, al perjudicar a las exportaciones.

Con base al análisis de McKinnon y el similar hecho por Fischer y Gelb (1991), así como lo aprendido en la experiencia gradual chilena (Muñoz, 1992), se recomienda cinco etapas, de un año (la emergencia y el comienzo de la estabilización) y dos años (la consolidación de la estabilización) las dos primeras, respectivamente, o sea, para las dos etapas de estabilización; y de un año cada una para las tres restantes, o sea, las tres etapas de la liberalización (véase cuadro 3 para mayores detalles). Haciendo un total de 6 años, término mínimo para asegurar que las reformas requeridas e insoslayables tengan resultados sostenibles y sinérgicos. No obstante, la situación internacional, hoy caracterizada por la recesión, así como la situación particular del país en ese momento, determinarán los plazos relevantes.

Las reformas devolverían a los individuos atribuciones, funciones y actividades que les fueron conculcadas por el estado, incluyendo derechos básicos (tales como: de asociación, de reunión, de entrar y salir del país, de libre expresión, de información, de trabajo, etc.) que les permitiría responder a las señales del mercado. Igualmente, se propone que las reformas incluyan privatizar servicios públicos y sociales, o al menos, permitir la acción privada en ellos, servicios que antes eran del dominio exclusivo del estado, aún antes del gobierno socialista. De esta manera, la economía sería más eficiente y competitiva, lo cual es imprescindible no sólo por razones del entorno internacional, sino por el atraso y la situación de inferioridad de los cuales Cuba partirá para su reconstrucción. En un mundo tan dinámico y competitivo como el actual, el estancamiento o lentitud significa retroceso.

La propuesta apoya la privatización por razones de eficiencia y para promover una sociedad más competitiva y dinámica. No como medio para financiar el estado. La privatización, en sentido amplio, incluye: la libertad de entrada del sector privado a todas las actividades, la eliminación de monopolios y oligopolios estatales, la eliminación de actividades estatales y la disposición de activos y de empresas estatales. Esta última sería por venta de las empresas, al contado o a plazos. Tales medidas se recomiendan por la situación de la producción, de las finanzas públicas y del exceso de dinero, así como para atender adecuadamente varias áreas críticas: la red de solidaridad e inversión social, las obligaciones financieras con los obreros de pagos por cese laboral y jubilación, la deuda externa y las compensaciones para pagar las confiscaciones efectuadas. Sin embargo, se incluirían también privatizaciones por contratos de arrendamiento a largo plazo ("leasings") y por contratos de administración para toda o parte de una misma empresa. Se estimularía a los fondos de pensión, a empleados, obreros y ciudadanos en general, para que adquieran acciones en las empresas privatizadas. La meta es difundir y descentralizar la propiedad para evitar la concentración como pasó en la primera etapa de la privatización en Chile.

La propuesta considera atender y amortiguar los elevados costos sociales, expresados en el sufrimiento real y concreto de las personas afectadas por el desempleo y la reducción de su ingreso real, que este proceso de reformas conllevará inevitablemente al principio de la transformación. Además, las medidas sociales se consideran parte integral del plan económico, especialmente en un país que ha expandido significativamente la cobertura de los servicios sociales (educación, salud y seguridad social). En tal sentido, una red de solidaridad e inversión social es indispensable para que la transición sea sostenible, tanto política como socialmente. La red financiaría programas concentrados en unas pocas áreas para asegurar soluciones a las necesidades básicas de la población más vulnerable, a fin de impedir serios e irreversibles deterioros físicos en su condición y para dar empleo **temporal** a los desempleados, adiestrarlos para que aumenten sus potencialidades de establecer una empresa o conseguir un empleo fijo y remunerable y puedan integrarse, lo antes posible y en forma efectiva, a la economía de mercado. También ayudaría a la población más pobre, si ésta decide ahorrar para obtener una solución habitacional propia. Igualmente, le ofrecería apoyo técnico y financiero para el mantenimiento y mejoramiento de las viviendas existentes, preferiblemente por medio de entes privados.

La propuesta no supone un programa masivo de ayuda externa. Pero sí pretende alentar decididamente el retorno, la inversión, las visitas y la ayuda de los cubanos radicados en el exterior; así como abrir el país a la inversión privada extranjera, estimulada, en parte, con operaciones de reconversión de deuda externa. No se darían concesiones especiales a la inversión privada extranjera; ésta recibiría igual trato que el capital privado nacional. Cuba entraría, cuanto antes mejor, a los organismos financieros internacionales para recabar colaboración técnica y financiera de ellos.

Con base a la experiencia de los países europeos ex-socialistas y a que las antiguas propiedades cubanas han sido, en general, transformadas sustancialmente en los últimos 33 años,[20] se les daría a los residentes en el país primera opción para reclamar sus propiedades, o continuar con la compensación establecida por el gobierno socialista. A los cubanos radicados en el exterior que tuvieron que abandonar su patria y que sufrieron confiscaciones, se les compensaría, después de cumplir con el debido procedimiento legal, con títulos para compra de viviendas, empresas, activos o acciones de empresas estatales. Estos criterios se refieren a las tierras agropecuarias, bienes, bienes raíces incluyendo viviendas, empresas pequeñas, medianas y grandes.

Las reformas y políticas económicas durante toda la transformación y en cada una de sus etapas deben hacerse de la forma más simple y transparente posible y ser debidamente explicadas, para que la población comprenda con claridad y a cabalidad de los planes y acciones del gobierno, y se solidarice con ellos, apoyando los objetivos y metas propuestos, con entusiasmo o apoyo crítico, y no sólo por resignación y oposición reprimida. Los objetivos bien definidos, y aceptados en un consenso nacional, facilitarían el período de transformación y de reformas y ayudarían a conseguir credibilidad y confianza. Se comienza desde una situación muy desfavorable, debido a la reiterada incapacidad, por más de tres décadas, del gobierno socialista para cumplir sus promesas de mejorar el nivel de vida la población. El pueblo está anímicamente agotado ante tantos paraísos prometidos, inexistentes o perdidos, y se ha vuelto muy incrédulo. La poetisa Cruz Varela nos lo recuerda: "No se puede exigir mayores sacrificios sin dar nada a cambio" (Declaración de Principios, 15 de noviembre de 1990).

2. Fundamentos de la estabilización y el saneamiento

La magnitud de los desbalances internos y externos de la economía cubana y los principales factores de la crisis sistémica hacen muy difíciles el proceso de estabilización. La (capacidad de) respuesta de los agentes económicos a las medidas macroeconómicas no es igual en una economía socialista extrema, por ello la importancia de emprender las reformas estructurales para establecer un marco favorable a la economía de mercado y sanear el funcionamiento de la economía.

La propuesta busca una consistencia entre las medidas de tipo macroeconómico y la creciente capacidad de respuesta a las mismas por los agentes económicos, mediante indispensables reformas estructurales, tales como: desregulación, desmonopolización y privatización. Esto posibilitaría que tanto las metas de estabilización como las de liberalización se alcancen a plenitud.

Los objetivos básicos de la estabilización son eliminar el caos financiero actual, el racionamiento y las escaseces, así como restaurar el equilibrio de precios y de la tasa de cambio.

---

[20]Por ejemplo en el caso de las tierras agrícolas, mediante nuevos caminos, canales, instalaciones de riego, terraplenes, embalses de agua, naves para la cría de aves y cerdos, vaquerías, talleres de maquinaria, almacenes, viviendas, bateyes, pequeñas poblaciones, etc. En el caso de la industria por el canibalismo de piezas y equipos y por la integración artificial de las empresas.

La estabilización es un requisito indispensable para el crecimiento sustentable a largo plazo. La estabilización no es un fin en si mismo, su razón es el establecimiento de condiciones adecuadas que faciliten un crecimiento sostenido, con equidad social, capaz de garantizar condiciones apropiadas de vida a la población más vulnerable, lo que conducirá a una sociedad más integrada, a mediano y largo plazo. También daría un ambiente propicio para la reunificación de la nación cubana y el fortalecimiento de la democracia.

La estabilización supone un programa inicial de muy corto plazo, rápido y efectivo —de unos tres a seis meses— destinado a detener la inflación, ahora reprimida, una vez se liberen y ajusten los precios y se devalúe la tasa de cambio.

Las medidas iniciales de estabilización incluyen: una corrección fiscal, basada en el aumento o la liberalización de los precios de las empresas estatales, la reducción de los gastos (militares, políticos y subsidios) y en el establecimiento de impuestos; la devaluación y la unificación cambiaria; la reforma monetaria, el control monetario y crediticio y la fijación de tasas de interés reales positivas; y la liberalización de precios de las actividades privadas y de las pequeñas y medianas empresas estatales. Estas medidas serían simples y fáciles de implantar, y estarían complementadas por otras aplicadas al manejo de la política monetaria y fiscal, a efectuar reformas institucionales y jurídicas, y a atraer recursos del exterior que requieren más tiempo para ejecutarse (ver columna de la primera etapa en el Cuadro 3).

El incremento de precios de bienes y servicios y tarifas de servicios públicos, la devaluación de la moneda y la reforma monetaria contraerán el acervo real de dinero. Las políticas fiscal y monetario-crediticia asegurarán que el flujo de dinero, o incrementos de la oferta monetaria posteriormente, no aumente más allá del ritmo requerido por el aumento de las reservas internacionales, la producción y la monetización de la economía. El nivel cambiario se fijará para que las exportaciones se vuelvan competitivas y se irá ajustando paulatinamente después. No se permitirán la libertad de entrada y salida de capitales de corto plazo y la flotación cambiaria, lo que determinaría un bajo crecimiento con estabilidad, ya que la tasa de cambio quedaría fijada por debajo del nivel de competitividad externa, debido a que es imposible atender desde el inicio la elevada deuda externa y a que tasas de interés altas atraerían una gran entrada de capitales que tendería a sobrevaluar la moneda.

Los efectos de la política de estabilización (reducción de la demanda agregada, tasas de interés reales muy elevadas y crédito restrictivo) son recesivas y deben desalentar la inversión privada. Por eso es muy importante tomar medidas para contrarrestar dichas tendencias y alentar la inversión privada decididamente. Las medidas pueden incluir incentivos tributarios para ganancias reinvertidas, regímenes temporales de depreciación acelerada, subsidios implícitos para la inversión a través de la privatización de empresas vendidas por debajo de su valor real, etc.

Se utilizaría un enfoque heterodoxo con cinco anclas para romper con las expectativas inflacionarias, brindar credibilidad y lograr la estabilización: el balance fiscal, la tasa de cambio administrada, la restricción monetario-crediticia, la congelación de los salarios públicos y la congelación de los precios y tarifas de las empresas estatales grandes.

También la estabilización comprende una serie de políticas macroeconómicas y reformas institucionales, orientadas a continuar con el esfuerzo, lograr la estabilidad en forma permanente y sentar las bases para la etapa de la liberalización, metas que requieren un incremento de la productividad y de la capacidad productiva, frenadas en estos últimos años por la escasez de insumos importados. Especialmente incluye una política dirigida a aumentar las exportaciones de bienes y servicios, y atraer la inversión y las transferencias del exterior, permitiendo una mayor capacidad de importaciones y un mayor nivel de actividad económica. Hay que superar el cuello de botella que enfrenta Cuba actualmente y recuperar el nivel de la producción, lo que disminuiría los costos de la estabilización. Esto se lograría en unos tres años.

El Cuadro 2 resume el efecto de las medidas macroeconómicas y de las reformas institucionales sobre las presiones inflacionarias, la recuperación de la producción y la mejoría de la balanza de pagos en la etapa de estabilización.

Si bien la búsqueda de crecimiento durante la etapa de estabilización puede reducir su efectividad, el caso de Cuba envuelve la reconstrucción necesaria y la recuperación imprescindible de la oferta agregada, disminuida por las ineficiencias actuales del sistema y la crisis imperante en el sector externo. Cuba tiene un amplio potencial de recuperación por los recursos no utilizados y los utilizados ineficientemente, además de su potencial para lograr incrementos en productividad con tecnologías fácilmente disponibles. La promoción de un sólido crecimiento de las exportaciones es básico en cualquier estrategia de recuperación y desarrollo. También es posible lograr un aumento de la inversión, que sea compatible con la reducción del gasto global y la expansión de la producción. Seguir con una subutilización innecesaria de la capacidad productiva y con la caída de la producción, podrían aumentar los costos sociales a niveles explosivos.

Es imprescindible consolidar el proceso de estabilización antes de emprender el proceso de liberalización, ya que muchas de las reformas requieren un marco favorable. La estabilización es una condición necesaria, pero no suficiente para el crecimiento. Igualmente, el crecimiento es indispensable para mantener la estabilización.

3. Fundamentos de la liberalización (o reformas de ajuste estructural)

La amplitud y profundidad de la propiedad socialista, la centralización y complejidad burocrática en las decisiones económicas, la organización monopólica y oligopólica de la producción, y la estructura de precios muy distorsionada, dificultan los procesos de privatización, desregulación y apertura, propios de una auténtica y radical solución, como lo están haciendo muchos países latinoamericanos, desde México hasta Chile.

La liberalización tiene como objetivo establecer y lograr el funcionamiento apropiado de mercados libres y competitivos, utilizados como los mecanismos principales en la asignación de recursos, ayudados a su vez por la reducción y eliminación de obstáculos indebidos al sector privado, tales como: prohibiciones, controles y restricciones. En esta etapa, embarcarse en esfuerzos sustanciales, o aún marginales, por seguir reduciendo la inflación, serían muy costosos en términos de crecimiento, empleo y equidad social, y por lo tanto, no se justifican. Un crecimiento alto y sostenido es la condición indispensable para que el conjunto de la población cubana alcance, paulatinamente, mayores niveles de ingreso, empleo y bienestar.

La liberalización no sólo pretende la profundización de las aperturas financiera y externa, sino también de los principales mercados de bienes y servicios y de los factores de producción (tierra, trabajo, capital, etc.). Estas aperturas fomentarían la existencia de un aparato productivo eficiente y viable, en consonancia con el entorno internacional altamente competitivo que prevalece hoy día. La liberalización deberá ir acompañada de un trabajo decidido de organización y desarrollo de mercados, sobre todo en la agricultura, para que el productor se beneficie directamente de la

CUADRO 2
Efectos a Mediano Plazo de las Principales Medidas Económicas Propuestas

	Presiones infla-cionarias	Expansión de la producción	Mejora de la balanza de pagos
Reformas institucio-nales y jurídicas a/	-	+	+
Ajuste de precios y salarios b/	+	+	+
Política monetaria y crediticia restrictiva c/	?	-	+
Austeridad fiscal c/	?	-	+
Privatización y rees-tructuración produc-tiva a/	-	+	+
Sobredevaluación d/	+	+	+
Inversión privada ex-tranjera a/	-	+	+
Retorno de ciudadanos del exterior a/ y e/	?	+	+
Transferencias unilate-rales e/	+	+	+
Cooperación financiera internacional a/	-	+	+

Efectos: - negativo, + positivo, ? indefinido

a/   Aumenta la oferta agregada.
b/   Debe mejorar la asignación de recursos en el país y la competitividad externa mediante ganancias en eficiencia, pero debe aumentar los precios.
c/   Disminuye la demanda agregada y es deflacionario; sin embargo, puede tener efectos inflacionarios vía costos (costos del capital de trabajo e impuestos al valor agregado y tarifas de servicios públicos).
d/   Aumenta los precios, mejora la balanza de pagos y, si las elasticidades de exportaciones e importaciones son apropiadas, aumenta la producción.
e/   Financia con divisas el aumento de la demanda agregada.

REFORMAS Y POLITICAS	ESTABILIZACION Y SANEAMIENTO (TRES AÑOS)		LIBERALIZACION O AJUSTE ESTRUCTURAL (TRES AÑOS)		
	ETAPA 1 o de EMERGENCIA (AJUSTE FISCAL, DE PRECIOS Y DE LA TASA DE CAMBIO)	ETAPA 2 (COMIENZO DE LA PRIVATIZACION Y AJUSTE MONETARIO-CREDITICIO)	ETAPA 3 (PROFUNDIZACION DE LA PRIVATIZACION Y APERTURA FINANCIERA INTERNA)	ETAPA 4 (APERTURA AL COMERCIO EXTERIOR)	ETAPA 5 (APERTURA FINANCIERA EXTERNA)
INSTITUCIONALES Y JURIDICAS	ESTABLECER, GARANTIZAR Y HACER CUMPLIR DERECHOS DE PROPIEDAD, LIBRE EJERCICIO DE PROFESIONES Y OFICIOS, LIBRE ENTRADA A NEGOCIOS. DEFINIR TRÁMITES SIMPLES Y EXPEDITOS PARA INSTALAR NEGOCIOS. DICTAR LEYES DE COMERCIO Y DE QUIEBRAS, NORMAS DE CONTABILIDAD. APOYAR SINDICALIZACION LIBRE Y DEMOCRÁTICA.	FORMULAR MODERNAS LEYES DE SOCIEDADES COMERCIALES Y DE CONTROL DE MONOPOLIOS, OLIGOPOLIOS Y CARTELES.	FORMULAR MODERNA LEY LABORAL CON DERECHO A HUELGAS, A CONTRATACION COLECTIVA Y ELIMINACIÓN DE RIGIDECES IMPIDEN UTILIZAR MANO DE OBRA TEMPORAL Y ESTACIONAL.		
PRECIOS Y SALARIOS	LIBERAR TOTALMENTE LOS PRECIOS Y SALARIOS DEL SECTOR PRIVADO Y LOS PRECIOS DE LAS PEQUEÑAS Y MEDIANAS EMPRESAS ESTATALES. AJUSTAR PRECIOS DE EMPRESAS ESTATALES GRANDES PARA REFLEJAR COSTOS Y ESCASECES INTERNACIONALES. LOS SALARIOS DE EMPRESAS ESTATALES PERMANECERIÁN CONGELADOS Y SE AJUSTARÍAN DESPUES POR AUMENTOS DE PRODUCTIVIDAD.	LOS AJUSTES SALARIALES DE LAS EMPRESAS ESTATALES ESTARIAN SUJETOS A AUMENTOS PRODUCTIVIDAD.	ELIMINAR CONTROLES DE PRECIOS, EXCEPTO A MONOPOLIOS NATURALES. LOS AJUSTES SALARIALES DE LAS EMPRESAS ESTATALES GRANDES ESTARIAN SUJETOS A AUMENTOS PRODUCTIVIDAD.		
FINANCIERAS	EFECTUAR REFORMA MONETARIA, EMITIR NUEVO PESO. CANCELAR ACTIVOS Y PASIVOS FINANCIEROS DE EMPRESAS ESTATALES Y DOTARLAS DE CAPITAL DE TRABAJO PARA OPERAR. MANTENER ESTRICTO CONTROL MONETARIO-CREDITICIO. ESTABLECER TASAS DE INTERÉS REALES POSITIVAS PARA DEPÓSITOS BANCARIOS PRIVADOS Y DE EMPRESAS LIBERALIZADAS Y PARA CRÉDITOS A EMPRESAS ESTATALES CONTROLADAS.	ESTABLECER BANCO CENTRAL AUTÓNOMO Y SUPERINTENDENCIA BANCARIA CON ESTRICTAS REGULACIONES Y SUPERVISIÓN DE LA SOLVENCIA Y CALIDAD DEL CRÉDITO BANCARIO. INICIAR DEPÓSITOS Y DEUDAS A MEDIANO Y LARGO PLAZO. ESTABLECER BOLSA DE VALORES.	PRIVATIZAR LA BANCA COMERCIAL ESTATAL. LIBERALIZAR TASAS DE INTERÉS. FORMULAR MODERNA LEY DE INSTITUCIONES FINANCIERAS, PERMITIR TODO TIPO DE INSTITUCIONES, SUJETAS A ESTRICTAS REGULACIONES Y SUPERVISIÓN SOBRE SOLVENCIA. LEGALIZAR LAS HIPOTECAS DE TIERRA.		
FISCALES	LOGRAR BALANCE FISCAL. REDUCIR GASTOS DE DEFENSA Y ELIMINAR SUBSIDIOS, GASTOS DE SEGURIDAD INTERNA Y POLITICOS. IMPULSAR REFORMA INTEGRAL DEL ESTADO. CREAR CONTRALORIA INDEPENDIENTE QUE VELE POR EL EMPLEO DE TÉCNICAS DE COSTO/BENEFICIO PARA SELECCIONAR INVERSIÓN PUBLICA Y DE LICITACIÓN PUBLICA O CONCURSO DE PRECIOS PARA ADQUISICIONES. ESTABLECER IMPUESTOS IVA, SOBRE INGRESOS NETOS DE LAS EMPRESAS Y DE LAS PERSONAS, AL CONSUMO DE BIENES SUNTUARIOS Y SOBRE BIENES RAÍCES.	EQUILIBRAR PRESUPUESTO CON BASE EN EL FLUJO DE CAJA. ELIMINAR TODOS LOS SUBSIDIOS. ESTABLECER MATRICULAS PARA LA EDUCACIÓN SUPERIOR.			ESTABLECER LEY DE PRESUPUESTO BALANCEADO. INSTITUIR ESTADO DESCENTRALIZADO Y EFICIENTE CON PAPEL LIMITADO Y SUBSIDIARIO. AUMENTAR LA COMPETENCIA Y AUTONOMÍA DE LAS AUTORIDADES PROVINCIALES, MUNICIPALES Y COMUNALES.
SECTOR EXTERNO	DEVALUAR EL PESO, UNIFICAR LA TASA CAMBIARIA, ELIMINAR CONTROLES CUANTITATIVOS Y FIJAR CONTROL DE CAMBIOS. FIJAR TARIFA DEL 100% PARA LOS BIENES DE CONSUMO FINAL Y DEL 20% PARA LOS BIENES DE CAPITAL E INTERMEDIOS. NEGOCIAR ACCESO AL MERCADO DE EUA.	REDUCIR AL 70% LA TARIFA PARA LOS BIENES DE CONSUMO FINAL. ESTABLECER LEY ANTIDUMPING CON SOBRETASAS PARA BIENES EXTERNOS SUBSIDIADOS.	REDUCIR AL 40% LA TARIFA PARA LOS BIENES DE CONSUMO FINAL.	FIJAR TARIFA UNIFORME DEL 15% PARA TODAS LAS IMPORTACIONES.	LIBRE CONVERTIBILIDAD PARA TODAS LAS TRANSACCIONES DE LA BALANZA DE PAGOS SUJETO A LA LEY DE INVERSIONES EXTRANJERAS. REDUCIR LA TARIFA UNIFORME AL 10%.

CUADRO 3. PRINCIPALES POLITICAS Y REFORMAS PROPUESTAS PARA LA RECONSTRUCCIÓN DE CUBA (CONTINUACIÓN)

REFORMAS Y POLITICAS	ESTABILIZACIÓN Y SANEAMIENTO (TRES AÑOS)		LIBERALIZACIÓN O AJUSTE ESTRUCTURAL (TRES AÑOS)		
	ETAPA 1 (AJUSTE FISCAL, DE PRECIOS Y DE LA TASA DE CAMBIO)	ETAPA 2 (COMIENZO DE LA PRIVATIZACIÓN Y AJUSTE MONETARIO-CREDITICIO)	ETAPA 3 (PROFUNDIZACIÓN DE LA PRIVATIZACIÓN Y APERTURA FINANCIERA INTERNA)	ETAPA 4 (APERTURA AL COMERCIO EXTERNO)	ETAPA 5 (APERTURA FINANCIERA EXTERNA)
RESTRUCTURACION PRODUCTIVA Y PRIVATIZACION GENERALIZADA	INCENTIVAR SEGUNDO EMPLEO PARA EMPLEADOS PÚBLICOS Y PARCELAS AGRÍCOLAS INDIVIDUALES. DESCENTRALIZAR DECISIONES A EMPRESAS ESTATALES PEQUEÑAS Y MEDIANAS. IMPONER SEVERAS MULTAS A EMPLEADOS Y ADMINISTRADORES DESHONESTOS. FIJAR CRITERIOS PARA RACIONALIZAR Y SEGMENTAR COMPLEJOS MONOPOLICOS Y PARA DETERMINAR QUIEBRAS. CREAR COMISIÓN RECTORA DE LA PRIVATIZACION.	PRIVATIZAR POR VENTA AL CONTADO/CRÉDITO O POR LEASING LAS EMPRESAS ESTATALES PEQUEÑAS Y MEDIANAS Y LAS VIVIENDAS ARRENDADAS. SEGMENTAR Y COMENZAR A VENDER LAS ACCIONES DE LAS EMPRESAS ESTATALES GRANDES.	PRIVATIZAR LA PREVISION SOCIAL, LAS EMPRESAS DE ELECTRICIDAD, TELECOMUNICACIONES, COMBUSTIBLES, TRANSPORTE AEREO Y MARITIMO, LA CONSTRUCCIÓN Y MANTENIMIENTO DE CARRETERAS, AEROPUERTOS Y PUERTOS, LOS SISTEMAS DE ACUEDUCTOS Y ALCANTARILLADOS.	DESCENTRALIZAR Y PRIVATIZAR PARCIALMENTE LA EDUCACIÓN PRIMARIA Y SECUNDARIA, LA SALUD PUBLICA Y OTROS SERVICIOS PÚBLICOS. EL ESTADO SEGUIRÍA FINANCIANDO LOS SERVICIOS, PERO EL SECTOR PRIVADO LOS BRINDARÍA EN LA MEDIDA DE LO POSIBLE.	
RETORNO DE CIUDADANOS	PERMITIR ENTRADA DE MENAJES DOMÉSTICOS, RECIBO DE PENSIONES Y DE CAPITALES LIBRES DE IMPUESTOS. EL LIBRE EJERCICIO PROFESIONAL Y DE OFICIOS.	ENTRADA DE MENAJES DOMÉSTICOS SUJETOS A TARIFAS EXISTENTES.			
TRANSFERENCIAS UNILATERALES	LIBRE ENTRADA DE TRANSFERENCIAS MONETARIAS A LA TASA DE CAMBIO OFICIAL. LAS ORGANIZACIONES PRIVADAS DE DESARROLLO Y HUMANITARIAS DE INTERÉS SOCIAL Y SIN FINES DE LUCRO PODRÁN ABRIR OPERACIONES LIBRE DE IMPUESTOS.				
INVERSIÓN PRIVADA EXTRANJERA	LIMITADA A NUEVAS INVERSIONES EN PLANTA Y EQUIPOS O FINANCIERAS DE MAS DE UN AÑO. SE PODRÍAN REPATRIAR GANANCIAS SIN LIMITES DESDE EL INICIO. SEVERA RESTRICCIÓN PARA LA INVERSIÓN EN EMPRESAS ESTATALES. SE SOLICITARA A LA OPIC QUE COMIENCE ACTIVIDADES DE FINANCIAMIENTOS Y SEGUROS.	FORMULAR MODERNA LEY CON IGUAL TRATO A LAS EMPRESAS NACIONALES Y EXTRANJERAS.			
COOPERACION FINANCIERA Y TÉCNICA INTERNACIONAL	SOLICITAR MEMBRESIA COMO ASOCIADO A LAS INSTITUCIONES FINANCIERAS INTERNACIONALES PARA TENER ACCESO A COOPERACIÓN TÉCNICA Y COMENZAR A PREPARAR PROPUESTAS DE PRESTAMOS. SOLICITAR ASISTENCIA TÉCNICA AL GOBIERNO DE CHILE EN LA IMPLANTACIÓN DE LAS REFORMAS ECONÓMICAS PROPUESTAS.	LOGRAR COMPLETA MEMBRESIA Y ACCESO A LA COOPERACIÓN ECONÓMICA Y TÉCNICA DE LAS INSTITUCIONES FINANCIERAS INTERNACIONALES.			
DEUDA EXTERNA	DISEÑAR UNA ESTRATEGIA CON UN GRUPO DE APOYO PARA RENEGOCIAR Y REDUCIR LA DEUDA EXTERNA CON EL CLUB DE PARÍS QUE INCLUYA OPERACIONES DE RECONVERSIÓN.	ALENTAR LAS OPERACIONES DE RECONVERSIÓN Y COMENZAR EL SERVICIO DE LA DEUDA EXTERNA.			
SECTORES PRIORITARIOS	LA AGRICULTURA, LA AGROINDUSTRIA, EL TURISMO, LA PESCA Y LOS SERVICIOS DE ESCALA INTERNACIONAL.		MANUFACTURA DE ENSAMBLAJE Y SERVICIOS CONEXOS PARA EXPORTACIÓN.		INDUSTRIAS DE ALTA TECNOLOGÍA.

producción. La liberalización requiere una normatividad apropiada y transparente, mejor que la prevaleciente antes del gobierno socialista, la cual mostraba una serie de sesgos de distinto tipo: monopólicos, laborales y a favor de la industria del azúcar (ver la Sección C de este Capítulo II).

4. Detalles de las políticas y reformas propuestas[21]

En el Cuadro 3 se presenta un resumen de las principales políticas macroeconómicas y reformas institucionales que se propone realizar en cada una de las cinco etapas durante los procesos de estabilización y liberalización.

El objetivo principal inmediato del estado sería que la sociedad y la economía se estabilicen, se estructuren a través de mercados eficientes y funcionen en forma ordenada, pero cambiante al garantizar las libertades y derechos básicos establecidos en la Declaración Universal de Derechos Humanos, el cumplimiento de leyes simples y generales y la protección de la propiedad, impidiendo específicamente la ocupación ilegal de empresas y activos estatales. Se aseguraría la integridad y autoridad de las instituciones de servicio público que definan, ejecuten y hagan cumplir las orientaciones, políticas y reformas.

a. Reformas institucionales y jurídicas

Las reformas institucionales y jurídicas deben ser comenzadas de inmediato para acabar con la crisis sistémica. La situación de Cuba es privilegiada para establecer, en el dinámico entorno mundial existente, el marco institucional y el ordenamiento jurídico más adecuado para el funcionamiento transparente, efectivo y eficiente de una economía social de mercado que incluyan tres elementos básicos: definir derechos de propiedad, las normas para entrar y salir de actividades productivas en el mercado y las normas para hacer transacciones en el mercado. Este marco es imprescindible para una apropiada y completa reacción a las políticas macroeconómicas propuestas. A tal efecto, el gobierno establecería, garantizaría y haría cumplir el ordenamiento jurídico y las instituciones de una economía de mercado competitiva, tales como:

— un sistema judicial con un Tribunal Supremo, independiente de los otros poderes, confiable, probo, asequible y capaz de representar y proteger los intereses básicos de los ciudadanos, en el cual todos tengan la confianza y la expectativa de que su causa o derecho vulnerado será rápida y debidamente atendido;[22]

— los derechos de propiedad, incluyendo titulación, patentes, transferencias y venta de bienes;

— se establecería la libre entrada de empresas privadas a las actividades económicas, servicios públicos y sociales, incluso a algunos que antes del gobierno socialista se consideraban ámbito exclusivo del sector público o monopolios estatales;

— se definirían trámites simples y expeditos para instalar, excepto algunas limitaciones por razones de seguridad o sanidad, y cerrar negocios, a fin de facilitar la energía, la creatividad y la iniciativa, frenadas por más de tres décadas de incompetencia y controles burocráticos, a fin de introducir nuevos productos, mercados y modernizar las técnicas de gerencia,

---

[21]A menos que se indique lo contrario, las medidas se adoptarían en la primera etapa.

[22]La administración de la justicia no deberá ser onerosa, lenta, burocrática, formalista, corrupta, ni procesalmente complicada.

administración, producción y distribución;

— el libre ejercicio de las profesiones, los oficios y los trabajos, especialmente los vinculados con la prensa;

— ley de cooperativas y de empresas autogestionarias;

— ley de entidades no lucrativas con fines humanitarios y de desarrollo;

— ley de quiebra y liquidación de las empresas;

— libre contratación de bienes y servicios, incluyendo procedimientos simples para la contratación, movilidad y despido de la fuerza laboral,[23] y para establecer contratos a largo plazo;

— leyes comerciales y de control de prácticas desleales de comercio;

— normas y procedimientos de contabilidad y auditoría generalmente aceptados;

— se permitiría plena libertad, democracia y autonomía sindical, incluyendo el derecho de los trabajadores a organizarse, afiliarse o desafiliarse a los sindicatos y a elegir libremente sus propios dirigentes.[24] Sin embargo, no se permitirían huelgas hasta la tercera etapa (por los primeros tres años), debido a la crítica situación de la producción, pero habría arbitrios de aceptación obligatoria por las partes con base a lo propuesto por ellas;

— se prohibirían los trabajos y movilizaciones "voluntarios" promovidos por el estado, o sea, el eufemismo para el trabajo forzado; las vacaciones y el trabajo en horas extras no remunerados,[25] así como el despido por razones políticas; y

— se haría un programa de adiestramiento para jueces, abogados, contadores, auditores, administradores y economistas sobre las instituciones básicas y operación de una economía de mercado.

Estas medidas y otras destinadas a facilitar el acceso de los agentes económicos a los mercados sin exclusividades y discriminaciones, y a eliminar segmentaciones de los mercados, restricciones y regulaciones estatistas inhibidoras de la iniciativa privada, de la movilidad de los factores y del funcionamiento ágil de los mercados, sentarían las bases para el estado de derecho y los procesos de privatización, de desregulación y de liberalización de la economía.

En la segunda etapa, se formularían modernas leyes de sociedades comerciales y de control de monopolios y oligopolios, prohibiendo la exclusividad o limitación artificial en la producción y comercialización de bienes y la prestación de servicios, se prohibirían carteles o acuerdos orientados a reducir la competencia entre las empresas que producen los mismos bienes o servicios.

---

[23]Se permitirían contratos estacionales y temporales de trabajo, lo cual es muy importante para actividades tales como: caña, frutas cítricas, café, la pesca y el turismo.

[24]Por votación directa, secreta y universal.

[25]En Cuba el tiempo dedicado a estudios militares para las Milicias de Tropas Territoriales se considera "vacaciones". Véase Informe de la AFL-CIO del Estado de los Derechos de los Trabajadores en Cuba (AFL-CIO, 1991).

En la tercera etapa, se aprobaría una moderna legislación laboral que establezca el derecho a huelga, la negociación colectiva por empresa, que el mercado determina los salarios y que elimine las rigideces que impiden utilizar mano de obra temporal o estacional.

b. Política de precios y salarios

Se liberarían completamente los precios y salarios del sector privado y los precios de los bienes y servicios de las pequeñas y medianas empresas estatales, o sea, aquellas actividades en que pueda haber competencia interna. La liberalización de precios traería una importante ganancia de bienestar como consecuencia de la eliminación del racionamiento, las escaseces y del tiempo derrochado en buscar la subsistencia diaria. El propósito es corregir las enormes distorsiones en los precios relativos, lograr un ordenamiento de mercados con competencia y libre determinación de precios, obtener una mejor asignación de recursos escasos y estimular una mayor participación del sector privado en las actividades económicas. Sólo en mercados competitivos coinciden la rentabilidad, la eficiencia económica y la eficiencia productiva. Como principio indicativo inicial, las empresas estatales fijarían sus precios para autofinanciarse y sanear sus finanzas, es decir, cubrir sus costos, incluso depreciación e impuestos, y para lograr un excedente para pagar un retorno al capital productivo.

Los precios de los bienes y servicios de las empresas estatales grandes, incluyendo las tarifas de los servicios públicos (teléfono, electricidad, gasolina y otros combustibles, transporte, correos, agua, alcantarillado, etc), se ajustarían para reflejar sus costos y escaseces relativas en la economía mundial más que en la distorsionada economía nacional, con una corrección para los servicios no transables en el exterior, debido al elevado desempleo abierto y encubierto existente.[26] De esta forma, los precios de los monopolios de bienes no transables en el exterior se mantendrían controlados hasta el desmantelamiento del monopolio o hasta la tercera etapa. La liberalización de estos precios desde el inicio podría perjudicar la competitividad de toda la actividad económica del país, debido a su poder monopólico.

Los salarios del sector público (empresas estatales y gobierno) permanecerían congelados. El propósito es ajustar los salarios o ingresos reales teóricos de los empleados de las empresas estatales y del gobierno a los ingresos reales efectivos debido a la deteriorada situación de la producción, la cual se refleja en el racionamiento y las escaseces.[27] También deberían ajustarse los salarios monetarios de forma que incluyan todos los beneficios no monetarios de las empresas, los cuales deberán ser pagados directamente por el empleado a partir de ese ajuste. Una alternativa a la congelación de salarios sería efectuar parte de las remuneraciones en dinero y parte en certificados que sirvan para comprar las empresas estatales que se privatizarían o acciones de las mismas. Se sentaría el principio que una vez hecho este ajuste inicial por una concertación social, los salarios reales de las empresas estatales se ajustarían tomando en consideración los aumentos de la productividad o se complementarían por participación en las ganancias de las empresas hasta que éstas se privaticen, lo cual tendería a mejorar la eficiencia productiva. Se establecerían mecanismos para que los trabajadores presenten propuestas sobre las decisiones de las empresas a sus directivos.

La formación de fondos de pensiones y el reconocimiento de garantizar un retiro razonable a la fuerza trabajadora serían elementos fundamentales del reajuste y reorganización del mercado

---

[26]Es necesario que eventualmente las tarifas de los servicios públicos se fijen a su costo marginal de producción a largo plazo.

[27]Es decir, este ajuste tendría como propósito que la práctica muestre la realidad tal cual es. Además, la población recuperaría el tiempo que derrocha en "colas" y para adquirir los bienes que necesita para subsistir en el mercado negro.

de trabajo.

En la segunda etapa, se autorizarían ajustes de salarios en las empresas estatales relacionados con los aumentos de productividad.

En la tercera etapa, se eliminarían todos los controles de precios y salarios, excepto los de los monopolios naturales. Los salarios de las empresas monopólicas estarían sujetos a los aumentos de productividad.

c. Política monetario-crediticia y desarrollo del mercado de capitales

Se realizaría una reforma monetaria con la emisión de un nuevo peso para determinar la legitimidad de la liquidez existente y reducir el acervo de dinero. Se eliminarían todos los activos y pasivos financieros (depósitos y deudas financieros) de las empresas estatales, pero se les dotaría del circulante necesario para realizar las transacciones (capital de trabajo) y para reponer los repuestos y otros bienes esenciales. La reforma precedería la descentralización de las decisiones a las pequeñas y medianas empresas estatales y pretende evitar beneficios indebidos a la *nomenklatura*, la mafia y los narcotraficantes, que han hecho acumulaciones ilegítimas de dinero. Otro objetivo de la reforma es evitar que la economía se continúe dolarizando, lo cual junto con las llamadas tiendas diplomáticas, ha creado una presión permanente sobre los precios. En síntesis, la reforma facilitaría la monetización de la riqueza existente y la esterilización de la riqueza espuria.

Se fijarían tasas de interés reales positivas altas, mayores que las tasas mundiales debido a la escasez de ahorros y al escepticismo inicial respecto al proceso de estabilización, pero no se permitirían tasas libres para evitar el proceso de selección adversa por el cual las empresas en dificultades están dispuestas a endeudarse a cualquier costo para subsistir, mientras las empresas sanas no lo están. Además, tasas de interés reales muy elevadas, se podrían interpretar como indicio de una elevada inflación futura o de una inminente devaluación.

Se separaría el banco central (el Banco Nacional de Cuba) de la banca comercial estatal (sucursales del Banco Nacional de Cuba). El crédito de la banca estatal, incluyendo sobregiros, se limitaría a préstamos a corto plazo a las grandes empresas estatales controladas y no tendría subsidios, ni controles cuantitativos sectoriales. La banca estatal no otorgaría créditos a las personas, las empresas privadas y las pequeñas y medianas empresas estatales liberalizadas, pero otorgaría intereses por sus depósitos en instrumentos reajustables para captar el exceso de liquidez existente. Asimismo, dichas unidades podrían concederse créditos entre sí o a través de cooperativas de ahorro y crédito, que se estimularían. Esta restricción equivale a bancos comerciales con 100% de reserva. De mantenerse esta política se reforzarían los procesos de remonetización y desdolarización. La expansión de la base monetaria en esta primera etapa resultaría del incremento en las reservas internacionales.

Se autorizaría el establecimiento de bancos comerciales privados que operen de manera temporal exclusivamente con empresas extranjeras y empresas exportadoras.

En la segunda etapa, se establecería la autonomía del Banco Nacional con normas estrictas para el control monetario y una fuerte superintendencia bancaria y de instituciones financieras. La superintendencia tendría normas estrictas para la regulación y supervisión de la solvencia y de la calidad del crédito bancario, incluyendo colaterales, garantías e hipotecas para el funcionamiento más transparente y fluido del mercado financiero. En general, no se podría prestar a empresas que estén incurriendo en pérdidas, las empresas estatales en esta situación se reorganizarían o liquidarían. Se establecería una bolsa de valores. En esta etapa el Banco Nacional expandiría el crédito con base en el incremento en las reservas internacionales, la expansión de la producción real y los procesos de remonetización y desdolarización.

En la tercera etapa, se crearía un mercado de capitales eficiente, que promueva el ahorro y lo canalice a las inversiones productivas. Se liberalizarían los mercados financieros y las tasas de interés activas y pasivas. Se ampliaría y fomentaría la variedad de instrumentos disponibles de depósitos y créditos a mediano y largo plazo, incluyendo instrumentos reajustables por la inflación, a fin de fomentar la competencia para reducir los costos de intermediación financiera y reducir la brecha entre tasas de interés de depósitos y de préstamos. Al respecto, se aprobarían modernas leyes de instrumentos negociables y de instituciones financieras, permitiendo todo tipo de instituciones financieras sujetas a estrictas regulaciones y supervisión para asegurar su solvencia y la calidad de sus instrumentos activos y pasivos. Se permitiría la enajenación e hipotecas de las tierras agrícolas.

d. Política de balance fiscal

Es imprescindible superar la insostenible situación de déficits del sector público, a tal efecto, las finanzas públicas se balancearían drásticamente con el aumento de los precios y las tarifas de las empresas públicas, la reducción de los gastos y los subsidios, y el establecimiento de impuestos. La austera política fiscal pretende reducir el exceso de demanda agregada y que el sector público tenga fuentes propias de financiamiento (presupuesto balanceado incluyendo gastos corrientes y de capital), con lo cual se eliminaría la causa principal de los desbalances internos y una de las causas más importantes de los desbalances externos. Así las funciones que el estado seguiría financiando o brindando, facilitarían los procesos de expansión de las empresas privadas y la privatización de las empresas públicas. Si no se controla el déficit fiscal se podría desatar una espiral inflacionaria de precios/salarios/precios, una vez se liberen los precios.

i. Gastos públicos (redefinición y restructuración del estado)

Los gastos de defensa, de seguridad interna y de la burocracia del Partido Comunista se reducirían marcadamente,[28] y, en general, se eliminarían los subsidios. Los gastos públicos se racionalizarían y deberían financiarse completamente con impuestos. Las funciones principales que el estado seguiría brindando o financiando serían los servicios de educación, salud, saneamiento, previsión social, justicia, defensa, seguridad pública, una red de solidaridad e inversión social y la infraestructura física básica.

La red de solidaridad social ofrecería empleo y entrenamiento **temporales** a los desempleados y garantizaría las necesidades básicas de nutrición, solución habitacional y salud a la población más vulnerable de la sociedad, especialmente a los niños menores de seis años, madres embarazadas y lactantes, ancianos e impedidos. Estudios y encuestas precisarían estos grupos y que los beneficios llegaran efectivamente a ellos. Se preferiría a los organismos no-gubernamentales u organismos privados voluntarios para canalizar los servicios, bienes y transferencias a los beneficiarios conjuntamente con los gobiernos municipales en vez de que el gobierno central los brinde directamente. Debe quedar establecido que la capacidad de actuar en el orden social dependería

---

[28]Eliminándose de inmediato los pioneros, las milicias, los comités de barrios, las brigadas de respuesta rápida y el Ministerio del Interior. El ejército estaría a cargo de la inmediata disolución de estos grupos.

de la situación de producción. Sólo se puede distribuir aquello generado antes; o sea, la capacidad productiva de la economía es la condición necesaria para una política social eficiente. A los que queden desempleados por despido de las instituciones o empresas estatales se les daría la opción de un empleo temporal hasta por el máximo de un año o un pago mayor por terminación de servicios por una sola vez, que se podría utilizar para comprar acciones o empresas o para instalar nuevas empresas. Cualquier compensación por desempleo temporal exigiría la contribución del beneficiario a un programa de obras públicas municipales, *lotes con servicios o solución habitacional mínima* (basado en el esfuerzo propio y la ayuda mutua) o de servicios de apoyo al sector agropecuario, así como el reentrenamiento técnico del beneficiario para incorporarlo efectivamente a una economía de mercado.

Se comenzaría una reforma administrativa integral del estado a fin de redefinir y limitar la organización, las funciones y el personal de las instituciones públicas. Se reduciría el tamaño y las funciones y se eliminarían instituciones y actividades duplicativas o innecesarias, incluso ministerios y otras agencias estatales, inadecuados a un modelo de libertad de mercados y de protagonismo del sector privado, tales como ministerios de producción. Los servicios del estado se sistematizarían, consolidarían, simplificarían, se definirían la competencia de las agencias públicas y del sector privado, se seguirían procedimientos simples y ágiles, y serían de alta calidad y oportunidad. Se definirían mecanismos de articulación de las funciones centrales y de las provinciales y municipales. Temporalmente se apoyaría el desarrollo de las instituciones de mercado, que promuevan la competencia y la organización de productores que aceleren la respuesta de éstos a los incentivos de mercado.

Se fortalecerían las funciones del estado en materia normativa, de formulación y seguimiento de políticas generales y sectoriales y de asignación y seguimiento de recursos presupuestarios y de inversión en el marco macroeconómico e institucional propuesto. Se fortalecerían las funciones e instituciones estatales que permanezcan para prestar servicios eficientes y efectivos a la sociedad y a los sectores productivos, tanto a nivel nacional como regional. Se sentaría el principio que el estado cobraría por los servicios prestados a los sectores productivos. En los sectores sociales, en los cuales hay tanta capacidad instalada y un nivel de servicios que supera la capacidad económica del país, se pondría énfasis en la racionalización de los gastos corrientes para prestar servicios de mayor calidad y más adecuados en vez de efectuar nuevas inversiones en ellos, en seguir una decidida política de mantenimiento, y en subsidiar a las más necesitados y no al servicio en general. La educación técnica se podría completar con cursos de capacitación diseñados con participación de la empresa privada, adecuados a las necesidades y requerimientos del sistema productivo.

Las técnicas de costo beneficio se utilizarían para determinar la prioridad de las inversiones públicas y del gasto público. Se crearía una Contraloría independiente que velaría porque las adquisiciones y las contrataciones del estado estén sujetas a concurso de precios o licitación pública, que asegure la transparencia y honestidad administrativa de los funcionarios e instituciones del estado, así como establezca los mecanismos de control y evaluación de su ejecución, incluyendo el seguimiento de denuncias públicas.

En la segunda etapa, se eliminarían todos los subsidios y se equilibraría el presupuesto público total con base al flujo de caja. A fin de modernizar, descentralizar y desarrollar verdaderos centros de excelencia con total libertad académica y continuar con la reforma fiscal, se establecerían matrículas y altos requisitos de entrada a las universidades y otros centros de educación superior, para financiar los costos de esas instituciones. La educación superior representará un beneficio directo y notorio para los que la obtienen en una sociedad en expansión, de modo que no se justifica en absoluto su gratuidad. El estado otorgaría préstamos a los estudiantes de familias de escasos recursos. Se alentaría que las universidades y otros centros de educación superior prestaran servicios de capacitación, especialmente a los administradores, e investigación al sector privado.

En la quinta etapa, se establecería una ley de presupuesto balanceado, que contemple que las funciones del estado serían descentralizadas y eficientes, con un papel limitado y subsidiario, y con un compromiso cada vez mayor con los grupos más vulnerables de la sociedad en términos de la capacidad económica del país. Se aumentaría la autonomía y competencia de las autoridades provinciales y municipales, así como de las comunidades rurales y urbanas en la aplicación y la ejecución de los programas públicos, especialmente en servicios sociales y asistenciales. La política de descentralización diseminaría el poder político, abriría caminos a una efectiva participación de la comunidad, contribuiría a igualar las oportunidades de acceso de los ciudadanos a las diversas actividades públicas (sociales, culturales y asistenciales) y haría menos conflictiva la función orientadora del estado.

ii. Ingresos públicos[29]

Se establecería un sistema tributario sencillo, neutral para la asignación de recursos y de fácil administración basado en unos pocos impuestos que genere ingresos suficientes. El sistema constaría de un impuesto uniforme al valor agregado (IVA) del 20% a todas las empresas; un impuesto uniforme a los ingresos netos de las empresas y de las personas del 30% retenibles en la fuente,[30] con unas pocas excepciones entre ellos los ahorros personales; impuestos al consumo de bienes suntuarios, no necesarios y generadores de externalidades negativas;[31] y un impuesto elevado a los bienes raíces.[32] Se eximirían del impuesto a los ingresos, las ganancias reinvertidas hasta por un período máximo de 4 años, o sea, hasta completar la tercera etapa, inclusive a las empresas privadas extranjeras, para elevar rápida y sustancialmente los niveles de ahorro e inversión. También habría un régimen acelerado y flexible para las depreciaciones de las nuevas construcciones e inversiones. Los impuestos se cobrarían cada mes y los pagados con rezago se indexarán por la inflación para evitar el efecto Olivera-Tanzi.

El gobierno encautaría y pondría a venta pública, a través de las municipalidades y con ayuda del ejército, las edificaciones, terrenos, viviendas, equipos, vehículos y otros activos, asignados al Partido Comunista, el Ministerio del Interior, los pioneros, las milicias, los comités de barrios y las brigadas de respuesta rápida.

e. Política sobre el sector externo (tasa de cambio y niveles arancelarios)

Después de una sobredevaluación para corregir la marcada sobrevalorización del peso y para fijar una tasa competitiva, se unificaría la tasa de cambio para todas las transacciones externas. Se eliminarían todas las barreras no arancelarias (excepto las fitosanitarias y zoosanitarias) y el

---

[29]Esta sección plantea un sistema tributario orientado a imponer los flujos y acervos ("stocks"). J.A. Herrero sugiere un sistema tributario orientado a imponer sólo los acervos a fin de reducir las distorsiones del sistema tributario sobre los flujos.

[30]El impuesto a la renta no debería ser progresivo, ni admitir exenciones personales elevadas. Su propósito sería alentar la igualdad de oportunidades, no buscar la igualdad de resultados, lo cual atenta contra la naturaleza misma de la economía de mercado. El impuesto a la renta para las empresas mixtas del 30% es muy razonable (Artículo 26 del Decreto -Ley 50 del 15 de febrero de 1982).

[31]Vehículos de lujo, casas de lujo, yates, joyas, bebidas alcohólicas, cigarrillos, armas de fuego, etc. En general se desalentaría el consumo prescindible.

[32]Para así evitar el aumento innecesario de la tierra urbana cuyo efecto inmediato es el encarecimiento del precio de la vivienda.

monopolio estatal de las actividades de exportación e importación, pero se mantendrían controles de las transacciones de capital de corto plazo hasta la quinta fase. La devaluación tiene por objeto estimular la producción de exportaciones y de bienes competitivos con las importaciones (bienes transables) y desalentar las importaciones.

Una entrada de capitales de corto plazo podría apreciar el peso por encima de la tasa real de equilibrio y alentar la inestabilidad cambiaria por razones coyunturales externas. Asimismo, una fuga de capitales, por temores o falta de confianza, podría crear presiones indebidas en la tasa de cambio, dada la dolarización que se ha venido observando en la economía. No se permitiría a los residentes cubanos tener grandes cantidades de moneda extranjera, ni activos en el exterior. Como al principio no se podría pagar la deuda externa, la tasa de cambio se administraría manteniendo una subvalorización del peso, favoreciendo la capacidad exportadora del país para integrarlo adecuadamente a la economía mundial y la acumulación de reservas internacionales, así como aislándolo de las fluctuaciones externas en los términos de intercambio que podrían ser muy marcadas debido a la dependencia del país de los precios del azúcar, permitiendo una política monetario-crediticia consistente con las metas de reconstrucción. Por años, Cuba tendrá que experimentar un superávit en la balanza de pagos, y tal vez en la balanza comercial, para enfrentar el servicio de la deuda externa. Las divisas disponibles se venderían entre los importadores y otros interesados a las tasas de mercado.

Las medidas anteriores eliminarían la restricción externa de la economía, reintroducirían la competencia externa y tenderían a cambiar la estructura de precios. Por ello habría una protección transitoria alta (tarifas arancelarias del 100%) para las importaciones de bienes de consumo, a fin de facilitar que las empresas hagan los ajustes y eliminen las rigideces en la capacidad gerencial, la gestión, tecnologías y equipos de producción y en la utilización de insumos y el empleo, así como ajustarse a las normas de los mercados occidentales, en línea con las recomendaciones de McKinnon (1991) y Williamson (1991). Una vez se cierre una empresa es muy difícil abrirla de nuevo. Las materias primas y los bienes de capital tendrían tarifas arancelarias bajas del 20%, excepto las utilizadas por las exportaciones que estarían exentas y se reintegrarían al momento de la exportación. Se eliminaría el IVA a los bienes utilizados en la producción de las exportaciones.

Se definiría que las tarifas se reducirían automáticamente, en fechas predefinidas y preanunciadas públicamente, hasta llegar a una tarifa uniforme del 10% en la quinta etapa. La protección temporal alta tiene por objeto reducir los costos de producción y de empleo del proceso de ajuste, especialmente en la etapa inicial de estabilización y requeriría de una buena administración de aduanas. Asimismo, contribuiría a desalentar de manera temporal el consumo de bienes importados por años reprimido y con una gran acumulación de bienes insatisfechos, y a canalizar las escasas divisas a aumentar la disponibilidad de materias primas y de bienes de capital importados.

Con base en las políticas anteriores, el gobierno de Cuba solicitaría ser reincorporada al Acuerdo General de Comercio y Tarifas (GATT). El gobierno de Cuba entraría en negociaciones inmediatas para tener un amplio acceso sin barreras al mercado de bienes agropecuarios, servicios turísticos y de capitales de EUA. Cuba necesita buenos mercados para sus exportaciones y acceso adecuado a los mercados de capital, a fin de participar lo antes posible en el sistema comercial internacional. En caso de que el país no progrese, habría una **fortísima presión** de la población para emigrar a los EUA, lo cual podría realizarse sin mayores dificultades utilizando los vínculos familiares de los cubano-americanos. Se ha estimado que un millón de cubanos desean emigrar a los EUA (Bergner, 1992). A corto plazo, esa emigración sería una solución para el gobierno de Cuba, pero un problema para el gobierno de EUA. A largo plazo sería otra pérdida para Cuba y su capacidad de desarrollo.

Se harían colocaciones de valores denominados en dólares a más de un año con tasas de interés reajustables entre los cubanos residentes en el exterior para captación con propósitos de desarrollo.

En la segunda etapa para proseguir con la apertura comercial, se reducirían sin excepciones las tarifas arancelarias a los bienes de consumo final al 80%. Se establecería una moderna ley "antidumping" y se permitirían sobretasas y derechos especiales para compensar la competencia de aquellos bienes internacionales vendidos a precios subsidiados, pudiendo ocasionar con ello perjuicio a la producción nacional.

En la tercera etapa para proseguir con la apertura comercial, se continuaría con la reducción, sin excepciones, de las tarifas arancelarias a los bienes de consumo final al 40%.

En la cuarta etapa, se abriría aún más el sector real al rigor y las oportunidades del mercado internacional, mediante la fijación de una tarifa arancelaria uniforme del 15% para todas las importaciones. Con ello se generaría competencia y mejoraría la asignación de recursos, aún para las empresas estatales que todavía quedaran. El crecimiento económico sostenido de Cuba sólo será factible mediante el aumento y la diversificación de exportaciones hacia todo el mundo debido a su reducido mercado interno.

En la quinta etapa, se fijaría una tarifa arancelaria uniforme del 10% para todas las importaciones y se permitirían todas las transacciones externas, incluso las de la cuenta de capital de la balanza de pagos, mediante la libre convertibilidad de la moneda nacional conforme a lo dispuesto por la ley de inversión extranjera.

f. Restructuración productiva (desregulación y desmonopolización)

Se autorizaría e incentivaría a los empleados del gobierno y de empresas estatales para que tomen un segundo trabajo privado, o sea, se alentaría intencionalmente la informalidad o la segunda economía. A aquellos que ulteriormente decidan quedarse en ese segundo trabajo a tiempo completo, se les daría un pago por terminación de empleo en efectivo o en certificados, que podría utilizarse para la compra de empresas y activos estatales. Todos los empleados podrían optar por un pago en certificados por el tiempo de servicio que podría utilizar para la compra de activos o acciones de las empresas. También se alentaría que los agricultores se dividieran de común acuerdo y en partes iguales las tierras que cultivan colectivamente, que sean divisibles, pertenecientes a las empresas agrícolas estatales y a cooperativas de producción y a que comiencen a trabajar en forma individual las parcelas divididas o se les darían pequeñas parcelas individuales de las empresas agrícolas en aquellos casos que sería conveniente mantenerlas integralmente desde el punto de vista productivo. En cualquier caso hay que garantizar al ocupante de las tierras que tendrá permanente uso de las mismas, a fin de alentar que la ponga a producir de inmediato. La asignación de las parcelas individuales sería por sorteo. Se reinstalarían los mercados de tierras agrícolas y de viviendas.

Se daría autonomía a las empresas estatales para decisiones de producción, financiamiento y empleo y se alentaría la competencia para mejorar los productos y reducir los costos, incluyendo fórmulas que estimulen el retiro voluntario del personal excedente. Esta práctica de hacer a las empresas unidades independientes, autofinanciables y maximizadoras de ganancias, estaría orientada a evitar el despilfarro y el robo, y aumentar la productividad y la disciplina. Las pequeñas y medianas empresas estatales podrían determinar a través de la libre competencia sus precios, cómo utilizar sus recursos y sus ganancias (qué, cuánto, cómo y para quién producir, cómo comercializar, en qué y cuándo invertir, sus niveles de empleo, etc.). En general, sólo las empresas con ganancias podrían invertir, excepto las empresas estatales reguladas, cuyos proyectos competirían para inversiones con el resto del sector público. Además, los administradores y trabajadores tendrían una participación en las ganancias o recibirían aumentos de salarios por incrementos en la productividad. En la primera etapa, los administradores de empresas estatales no estarían autorizados para vender activos principales de las empresas o realizar contratos de largo plazo. Se establecerían severas multas y penalidades, pagaderos con sus liquidaciones por terminación de empleo, para los administradores y trabajadores que se apropien de una parte del capital social de las empresas, mediante decisiones empresariales depredadoras, evidentes conflictos de interés u obteniendo aumentos salariales o beneficios sociales especiales subsidiados por las empresas. En todo este proceso de reajuste de la organización de la empresa productiva, la revisión de ingresos y la redistribución de la riqueza deben orientarse a facilitar el financiamiento y robustecimiento de los planes de pensiones que jugarían un papel muy importante en el mercado de capitales.

Se determinarían criterios para sanear y racionalizar, administrativa y financieramente, así como reestructurar y segmentar en empresas más pequeñas, los complejos industriales o conglomerados organizados en forma artificial vertical y horizontalmente, a fin de asegurar un precio más justo por las empresas y de propiciar una economía competitiva, ágil, de mayor empleo y menos capital, de acuerdo con la actual dotación de recursos de Cuba y el entorno internacional. Se sentaría el principio de que cada planta diferente es una empresa diferente. Las empresas estatales grandes estarían sujetas a presentar estados financieros dictaminados por auditores externos independientes. Se establecería un tribunal de tierras y propiedades para procesar todas las reclamaciones.

Quedaría establecido que la intervención del estado, cuando se justifique, no se realizará mediante autorizaciones discrecionales, sino a través de normas claras, conocidas y de aplicabilidad general. No se privatizarán monopolios de servicios públicos a menos que existan instrumentos y entidades reguladoras que aseguren que la producción de servicios que ellos generan crecerá adecuadamente. Los intereses de los consumidores deberán ser escuchados por dichas entidades.

g. Proceso secuencial de privatización generalizada

Se definiría que la privatización se orientaría a que el sector privado adquiera la posesión y ejerza la libre y legal disposición de las empresas y los activos, de la mayoría de las empresas estatales. A fin de operar las empresas estatales más eficientemente, aún las que se mantengan como tales y las que no se puedan vender, tendrían contratos de administración con empresas privadas que estén dispuestas a comprar parte de las acciones.

Se establecería una comisión rectora temporal, que oriente, regule y controle el proceso de privatización, integrada por técnicos y profesionales reconocidos y apolíticos. La comisión designaría a los nuevos administradores de las empresas estatales, que serían personal técnico capacitado. Aclararía que el objetivo no es desarrollar un sistema de propiedad y producción socialista de mercado, ni un sistema de cooperativas de producción. Definiría criterios para las condiciones en las cuales las empresas estatales quebrarían automáticamente y tendrían que liquidarse o reestructurarse, deshaciéndose de componentes no rentables, por su situación financiera de deudas con el sistema bancario, por la no entrega de impuestos o sobrantes al gobierno. Estas operaciones, y transacciones se realizarían de manera que la documentación necesaria sea, sin excepciones, de dominio público.

El tipo de privatización propuesta permitiría a los trabajadores participar activamente en la propiedad y gestión de las empresas. Sería sana financieramente en el sentido que las empresas privadas pagarían el IVA y los impuestos sobre las ganancias y se daría total preferencia a la venta, "leasing" o contratos de administración de empresas sobre su transferencia gratuita. La privatización sería rápida y generalizada.

En la segunda etapa, las pequeñas y medianas empresas estatales, incluyendo el comercio al detalle y al por mayor, las empresas y tierras estatales agrícolas, los servicios y la flota de transporte terrestre (incluyendo parte del equipo militar) serían privatizados, mediante venta en oferta pública abierta a los trabajadores y administradores o al mejor postor, o mediante devolución a los antiguos propietarios. Los trabajadores y administradores podrían utilizar como pago parcial por los activos o empresas estatales las obligaciones que el estado tiene con ellos en forma de pagos por terminación y derechos de jubilación. También se venderían las viviendas, excepto las de lujo, a los arrendatarios. Las ventas a los trabajadores, administradores y a otros individuos o familias, podrían realizarse parcialmente a crédito, pero sujetas a colateral, garantías o hipotecas de los propios bienes vendidos y serían realizadas a través de los gobiernos provinciales y municipales, que conservarían parte de los ingresos de las privatizaciones y enviarían el resto al gobierno central. Igualmente habría las opciones de alquileres a largo plazo ("leasings") y de contratos de administración.

Una vez completado el esfuerzo de segmentar, reorganizar, racionalizar y sanear los complejos industriales artificialmente grandes, se harían sociedades anónimas accionarias de las grandes empresas estatales y se venderían hasta el 51% de las acciones a los fondos de pensión, empresas, individuos, suplidores o clientes, nacionales o extranjeros, que quieran encargarse de la administración de las empresas, dando preferencia a los antiguos propietarios. El resto de las acciones de las grandes empresas se distribuirían entre aquellas instituciones afectadas en forma directa por las mismas (fondos de pensión de las empresas, los cuales tomarían acciones por un valor similar a las obligaciones del estado de los pagos por jubilación de los empleados; gobiernos provinciales y municipales) y se les vendería a los trabajadores hasta un 20% de las acciones a un descuento del 50%, el cual podría pagarse con las primas por antigüedad, lo cual equivaldría a capitalizar un pasivo. Una forma legítima de privatización sería la de suplidores internacionales que estuvieran dispuestos a comprar a crédito y administrar una empresa, ofrezcan como garantía y aporte su propia inversión y pagaran con sus propias ganancias ulteriormente. Al representante de los sindicatos libres, se le daría un asiento en la junta directiva de las empresas. Los grupos con mayoría en las empresas podrían comprar el resto de las mismas.

En la tercera etapa, se privatizarían, al menos parcialmente, mediante venta pública abierta, incluyendo a empresas extranjeras,[33] la banca comercial, las empresas de electricidad, de teléfonos y otras telecomunicaciones, combustibles, transporte aéreo y marítimo, la construcción y mantenimiento de carreteras mediante concesiones de derechos de peaje, la construcción y la operación de puertos y aeropuertos, los sistemas de acueductos y alcantarillados, así como el sistema de seguridad social. Los monopolios naturales quedarían regulados por ley con base en normas objetivas para evitar corrupción administrativa.

En la cuarta etapa, se descentralizarían y privatizarían parcialmente la educación primaria

---

[33]Dependiendo de la naturaleza de la empresa, podría ser por licitación o por negociación directa con empresas precalificadas.

y secundaria, la salud pública, así como otros servicios públicos, tales como: aseo de ciudades (recogida de basura y limpieza). El estado seguiría financiando estos servicios, pero se contratarían preferentemente con el sector privado. Se subvencionaría al beneficiario y no el servicio, dándole opciones, de elegir entre unidades que brindan el servicio. Se descentralizaría la administración de los servicios a las unidades operativas (escuelas, centros de salud, etc.) de manera que sean controlados y operados por sus usuarios y empleados.

Los recursos de la privatización se utilizarían para financiar un programa de inversiones públicas. En última instancia la privatización subsidiaría la difusión de la propiedad y la inversión pública, ya que la propiedad pública posiblemente se venda por debajo de su valor debido a la situación del mercado de capitales. No obstante, fortalecería los fondos de pensión, y con ello la seguridad de los empleados, el mercado de capitales, los gobiernos provinciales y municipales.

h. Retorno de ciudadanos

A todos los nacidos o antiguos residentes en el país y sus descendientes, que deseen radicarse permanentemente en el mismo, se les permitiría la entrada de menajes domésticos incluyendo un automóvil, el recibo de pagos de jubilación del exterior, la entrada de capitales libres de impuestos, así como el libre ejercicio profesional y de oficios. En etapas posteriores, la entrada de menajes domésticos incluyendo un automóvil, se haría a la tarifa vigente para los bienes de consumo.

i. Transferencias unilaterales

La entrada de transferencias unilaterales o remesas personales del exterior en efectivo, se permitiría libre de impuestos a la tasa de cambio oficial. El envío de bienes estaría sujeto a las tarifas arancelarias vigentes. Las organizaciones privadas, humanitarias y de desarrollo, de interés social y sin fines de lucro, aunque sean extranjeras o mixtas, podrían abrir operaciones libres de impuestos en Cuba y hacer operaciones de reconversión de la deuda externa.

j. Inversión privada extranjera

A fin de lograr el acceso a nuevas tecnologías del exterior y captar recursos para financiar la reconstrucción y el crecimiento económico, se dictaría una ley parcial que permitiría la inversión privada extranjera. Esta sería mediante recursos financieros, nuevos equipos y plantas en todos los sectores productivos, pero habría una severa restricción para la adquisición de las empresas estatales existentes hasta la segunda etapa cuando comience el proceso de privatización. Se garantizaría la libertad de exportación, importación, comercio, industria y propiedad privada a las empresas extranjeras, así como la libre repatriación de ganancias. No se alentarían movimientos de capital de corto plazo. Todas las inversiones financieras deberían ser por el mínimo de un año.

Cuba solicitaría formalmente a la Overseas Private Investment Corporation (OPIC) y a otras instituciones similares de Europa que comiencen sus operaciones de financiamiento y seguros en el país con el fin de reducir los riesgos no comerciales del inversionista extranjero. Además, debería comenzar discusiones inmediatas para lograr acuerdos bilaterales sobre doble tributación de manera que los inversionistas puedan descontar los impuestos que pagan en Cuba en sus países de origen.

En la segunda etapa, se dictaría una ley de inversión privada extranjera mediante la cual se le permita invertir en todos los sectores de la economía, salvo aquellos considerados como que no convienen a la seguridad del país, y se daría a las empresas extranjeras igual trato que a las nacionales. Esto podría considerarse una extensión de la Doctrina Calvo que establece la igualdad ante la Ley de los nacionales y los extranjeros radicados en el país, lo cual sería contrario a lo que ha hecho el gobierno socialista que ha dado trato preferencial a los extranjeros. No se contemplarían incentivos, ni subsidios especiales, ni concesiones monopólicas. Se permitiría la repatriación de ganancias desde un inicio, pero no del capital invertido que no se podría repatriar por tres años.

k. Cooperación financiera y técnica internacional

Cuba solicitaría ser miembro asociado en los organismos financieros internacionales de desarrollo (BID, BIRF y FMI) con objeto de recibir cooperación y asesoría técnica para preparar planes detallados de las reformas y propuestas de préstamos para etapas posteriores, mientras se determina su cuota de entrada en ellos. La cooperación financiera de los organismos internacionales facilitaría alcanzar los resultados necesarios y eliminaría la necesidad de imponer medidas más drásticas. Cuba solicitaría asistencia técnica al Gobierno de Chile para la implantación de las reformas propuestas al sistema económico. La asistencia técnica podría ayudar en el adiestramiento rápido de gerentes, administradores, contadores, auditores, economistas y abogados. En la medida que el gobierno socialista permanezca en el poder después de 1992, sería necesario un programa inicial de emergencia alimentaria para atender una hambruna, que superaría tan pronto se ponga a producir el agro adecuadamente.

En la segunda etapa, Cuba solicitaría ser miembro regular en los organismos financieros internacionales de desarrollo (BID, BIRF y FMI) con objeto de recibir cooperación financiera y técnica. Cuba podría obtener significativos flujos positivos con propósitos de desarrollo, ya que no tiene ninguna deuda pendiente con los organismos internacionales. Un programa de ajuste estructural apoyado por las instituciones financieras de desarrollo sería muy útil para negociar la deuda externa con el Club de París y tener nuevamente acceso al crédito comercial y bancario internacional. La ayuda externa que se recibiera daría preferencia a apoyar directamente la reconversión productiva de las pequeñas y medianas empresas privadas, para que se capitalicen adecuadamente; financiar los programas de solidaridad e inversión social orientados a asegurar una calidad de vida mínima en la etapa de transición; obtener asistencia técnica temporal de los cubanos del exterior que decidan permanecer fuera del país; expandir la infraestructura económica y renegociar y reducir la deuda externa.

l. Manejo de la deuda externa

El alto nivel de la deuda externa desalentará las inversiones, ya que significa transferencias en términos de impuestos y devaluación esperada. Se diseñaría una estrategia para reunir un grupo de países de apoyo a fin de renegociar, reduciendo el monto y los términos, y postergando el vencimiento de la deuda externa con el Club de París. Dicha estrategia consideraría que es imposible que el país pague la deuda a la vez que estabiliza y reestructura la economía y que es necesario apoyarlo en términos de líneas de crédito de corto plazo. Se permitirían operaciones de reconversión, dando preferencia a proyectos ecológicos, asistenciales y de desarrollo local dirigidos a poblaciones de bajos ingresos, pero se incluirían todo tipo de operaciones en nuevos proyectos de infraestructura o en la adquisición de las empresas estatales existentes que se expandan.

Hay que afrontar el problema del nivel y la carga de la deuda externa que no sólo es responsabilidad del gobierno socialista de Cuba sino de aquellos que le prestaron. El gobierno no adoptaría ninguna medida especial para pagar una deuda externa desproporcionada a la capacidad de pagos del país e impondría **severas** sanciones a las empresas que hayan participado en el establecimiento y desarrollo del sistema de "apartheid" económico en Cuba, u obteniendo beneficios no previstos en el Decreto-Ley 50 del 15 de Febrero de 1982, o utilizando activos confiscados previamente a empresas o individuos nacionales o extranjeros.

En la segunda etapa, se alentarían operaciones de reconversión de la deuda externa en capital de inversión, fijándose un monto mínimo por transacción. Una alternativa sería porque el estado diera recursos en moneda nacional equivalentes a más del 100% del valor de la deuda en los mercados internacionales. Los términos y condiciones de la deuda externa se renegociarían y se haría un esfuerzo para comenzar su servicio a fin de reinsertar a Cuba en los mercados internacionales.

m. Sectores prioritarios

Cuba necesita insertarse activamente en la economía mundial. Requiere un esfuerzo sistemático de expansión de sus exportaciones que logre penetrar los mercados externos con precios remunerativos y que promueva el desarrollo productivo nacional. A tal efecto debe desarrollar una infraestructura científica y tecnológica con las universidades y centros superiores de estudios e investigación aplicada, así como una política al respecto.

Los sectores que se comentan a continuación tiene ventajas comparativas, evidentes economías de escala, aprendizaje, especialización y externalidades dinámicas. Pueden impulsar actividades que tengan un efecto de arrastre mediante eslabonamientos, tienen especial importancia para concentrar los esfuerzos de desarrollo institucional, la infraestructura de apoyo y las negociaciones de acceso a los mercados externos.

La producción agropecuaria y agroindustrial, el turismo, la pesca y los servicios de escala internacional (marítimos y aéreos), se establecerían como actividades prioritarias para el crédito a proyectos rentables de las empresas estatales grandes y los gastos y servicios públicos. El país tiene ventajas comparativas en estos sectores que son claves para la reactivación de la economía y la elevación del nivel de vida de la población. El estado sería responsable de fijar metas sectoriales, determinar el marco institucional, coordinar recursos, controlar por vía de excepción y asegurar servicios básicos adecuados a estos sectores, pero muchos de ellos se brindarían directamente por el sector privado. Habría consistencia entre los marcos de políticas sectoriales y del programa global.

El gobierno establecería la legislación forestal, pesquera y de aguas para dar al sector privado una mayor participación en su asignación y aprovechamiento y a su vez evitar la sobrepesca, la acidez, la salinización, la erosión y la desforestación. Se involucrarían los usuarios, a través de asociaciones, en su manejo y financiamiento para promover una explotación racional de los recursos naturales renovables. Se eliminaría el monopolio estatal de mercadeo agrícola y se fomentaría el de pequeñas empresas y cooperativas. Se mantendría un fuerte papel del sector público en extensión, investigación, y controles de calidad, fitosanitarios y zoosanitarios a fin de elevar la competitividad en los mercados internos y externos. Se difundiría información sobre métodos y procesos de producción agropecuaria, semillas, mantenimiento de plantas y equipos, envases, precios nacionales e internacionales, normas de calidad, mejoramiento de suelos y protección de cuencas, directrices de protección ambiental, gerencia, administración y contabilidad de empresas, etc. Se informaría sobre grupos asociativos que han sido exitosos en otros países.

En la tercera etapa se determinaría que la manufactura de ensamblaje para la exportación y sus servicios de apoyo son sectores prioritarios para el gasto y la inversión pública. Cuba tiene un alto porcentaje de mano de obra estacional debido a los ciclos productivos de varios bienes agrícolas y del turismo que se podría utilizar en las actividades manufactureras.

En la quinta etapa se determinaría que la industria de alta tecnología es un sector prioritario para el gasto y la inversión pública. Cuba tiene una población joven con grandes destrezas técnicas y una población en el exterior con grandes destrezas empresariales y administrativas que se utilizaría en esa industria.

Bibliografía

American Federation of Labor and Congress of Industrial Organizations (AFL-CIO, 1991), *Estado de los Derechos de los Trabajadores en Cuba*, Washington, D.C.

Luis Aguilar-León (1992), *Cuba y su futuro*, Miami: Ediciones Universal.

Ernesto Betancourt (1988), *Cuban Leadership after Castro*, Coral Gables, Florida: Research Institute for Cuban Studies.

Jeff Bergner (3 de enero de 1992), "Let's Stop Isolating Cuba", *The Washington Post*, Washington.

Rolando Castañeda (1992), "Opción por la Libertad, el Desarrollo y la Paz Social " *Cuba in Transition* (Papers and Proceedings of the First Annual Meeting of the Association for the Study of the Cuban Economy), Miami: Florida International University, pp 257-308.

Comisión Económica para América Latina y el Caribe, Naciones Unidas (CEPAL, 1990), *Estudio Económico de América Latina y el Caribe 1989*, Santiago de Chile, diciembre.

Stanley Fischer y Alen Gelb (1990), *Issues in Socialist Economic Reform*, Washington, D.C.: World Bank Working Papers, No. 565.

Ronald McKinnon (1991), *The Order of Economic Liberalization*, Baltimore: The Johns Hopkins University Press.

Oscar Muñoz, editor, (1992), *Reformas Económicas en Chile*, Washington: Banco Interamericano de Desarrollo, Serie de Monografías, No 7.

Marifeli Pérez-Stable (1992), "Towards a Maket Economy in Cuba? Social and Political Considerations" en *Cuba in Transition* (Papers and Proceedings of the First Annual Meeting of the Association for the Study of the Cuban Economy), Miami: Florida International University, pp 27-34.

Lance Taylor (1983), *Structuralist Macroeconomics*, New York: Basic Books.

John Williamson (1990), "What Washington Means by Policy Reform" en John Williamson editor, *Latin America How Much Has Happened?*, Washington: Institute of International Economics.

John Williamson (1991), *The Economic Opening of Eastern Europe*, Washington: Institute of International Economics.

Abstract

SOME ANALYTICAL AND PRACTICAL RECOMMENDATIONS FOR THE ECONOMIC RECONSTRUCTION OF CUBA

José Antonio Herrero

This paper is based on the methodology developed by Lance Taylor,[1] with modifications applied to the Cuban case, and includes the real and monetary sectors as well as basic structural relationships. It tries to determine the likely effects of the main instruments of monetary policy, several tax alternatives, devaluation, export promotion and some major institutional reforms on production, the external accounts, inflation, and income distribution.

Some of the structural implications of adjustment examined in the model include: the interrelationships among investment, productivity, real wages and employment; the importance of income or value-added taxes in the absence of other fiscal revenues —in this connection, the higher level of unemployment can only be addressed through a direct unemployment subsidy financed by the tax revenues; the type of tax and policies with respect to agricultural land —if land is leased and rents are collected, it would not be necessary to establish a significant tax system, and the importance of monetization of lease payments is shown in the model for the monetary sector; and the importance of establishing a tariff structure that will promote backward linkages —therefore a uniform level of tariffs should not be instituted, but rather one that decreases as backward linkages are established.

One interesting aspect of the model is to show that a value-added tax and restrictive monetary policies could create important inflationary pressures through higher prices and interest rates. Another feature of the model is to show the strategic importance of an export promotion policy to counteract the recessionary effects of fiscal and monetary policies and the initial effects of a major devaluation.

---

[1]Lance Taylor, *Structuralist Macroeconomics*, New York: Basic Books, 1983.

Comments

Manuel Lasaga

One of the buzzwords associated with the period after the LDC debt crisis has been structural reforms. At one time, most external sector problems were viewed by agencies such as the IMF as liquidity problems caused by bad management of the central bank's balance sheet. However, the change in policymakers' approach towards growth-oriented structural changes has contributed in large part to the success of the LDC loan crisis workout. Recently these theories have been put to the test with the collapse of the communist system and introduction of market reforms in eastern Europe. While it is too early to draw definitive conclusions, as J. Buttari explains in his paper "Reflections on Systemic Economic Policy Reform," structural reforms have become the creed for reform minded governments throughout Latin America and the former communist countries.

The paper is divided into two parts: the first reviews some of the lessons from the experience; and the second discusses why we don't know more about the effects of structural reforms. The author offers some insightful comments on the experiences with structural reforms. Among the economic aspects, I think the following two deserve special mention: (i) structural reforms require a long-term focus and not the quest for a short-term payout; and (ii) a successful outcome will depend on how fast institutions for a market economy are put in place. His sensitivity to the political environment is particularly important. Buttari concludes that democracy and economic adjustment can mix, but warns against giving in to populist or nationalist pressures in setting reform policies.

Buttari reviews the debate over gradualism versus shock therapy and seems to conclude that the gradualism approach is getting more support, particularly in view of the experiences in eastern Europe. I think the issue is not which of the methods is right, but when should each method be applied. Because of the nature of the problem and the complexity of the economic structures, systemic reforms are going to call for the application of gradualism in some areas, and shock therapy in others. Price liberalization may be necessary during the initial stage, but the government may have to exercise some control over price increases during a subsequent phase to allow time for the materialization of supply responses. Initially a government may have to announce a maxi-devaluation but subsequently control the exchange rate until the foreign exchange market can regain stability. In the area of privatization, the first step may be a gradual sell-off of state entities to allow the market to digest the new offerings, followed by a much more aggressive privatization campaign later on.

The second part of the paper concludes that the lessons from the experience are so far limited to anecdotal evidence. I agree with this assessment. On the one hand, it is too early to make any definitive evaluations on structural reforms that may take more than ten years before they produce tangible results. On the other hand, structural reforms involve complex issues which defy the use of existing analytical tools and for which we lack quantifiable information to measure their impact. Even after structural reforms have had a chance to work, by then it may be next to impossible to separate the growth factor attributed to one set of reform policies from a myriad of other events and polices mixed together which over the years have also contributed to the economy's development. As the author persuasively states: "Economic policy reform evaluations will always have to blend judgment, economic theory, and quantification."

Buttari recommends the use of economic models to analyze structural changes. However, I think this might be a perilous approach in view of the limited scope of existing economic/econometric models. Most models are constructed under the aegis of comparative static analysis in which the structure of the economy is assumed to remain intact. The proper analysis of structural changes will necessitate the development of new models that are capable of endogenously altering parameters in response to structural adjustments.

Perhaps one of the more intriguing arguments in the paper is the one which challenges existing views on the social cost of economic adjustment. Buttari doubts that economic reform programs entail a net loss to the less privileged people. He questions the conclusions of analysts who use the decline in income per capita data to demonstrate the social cost of adjustment. Buttari points to the increased caloric intake as well as decline in infant mortality to support his view that there has been a welfare gain despite the austerity programs implemented in Latin America after the debt crisis. I strongly depart from this view. First, the welfare function is a complex of many variables whose weight in the final result depends on non-quantifiable factors. In other words, income per capita may have grater weight than infant mortality; or the change in income per capita could more than offset the effects of the change in infant mortality. Second, if the delivery of health care in countries subjected to economic austerity programs has improved, the price of that increase in health care services needs to be incorporated in the analysis of the net welfare gain/loss. For example, the US spends more than any other industrial country in health care per person, yet it has one of the highest infant mortality rates. And third, there are cases in which austerity programs have resulted in riots and loss of human life which add significantly to the social cost of adjustment. A massive devaluation can inflict severe hardship on the less privileged people. I support the notion that there is a net cost to adjustment programs, but these can be ameliorated through the application of transfer payments to cushion the pain.

The task of reconstructing a post-Castro Cuba is bound to challenge most *a-priori* plans and to put in question some of the established views on the path to market-based economics. Castañeda's "A Plan for a Social Market Economy" will no doubt be subjected to sizeable revisions once the flow of events take their unpredictable course. Nevertheless, his paper represents an exhaustive and thought-provoking analysis that helps to focus attention on the critical issues associated with the rebuilding of the economy. From the start, he proposes a plan that is simple, complete, orderly, sequential and which involves a rapid process. His prescription calls for shock followed by orderly adjustment. While I think this is a laudable objective, the authors should warn the reader that in most instances the logical and the orderly never occur. His choice of a social market economy is confusing and needs to be explained. The terms *social* and *market* economy, appear contradictory in that a market economy with social considerations would imply government interference in the normal workings of the market place.

It is impossible to define a logical process for reconstruction if there are no structures with which to work. In Cuba, markets have not functioned for more than thirty years. Because of this, the initial phase of reconstruction is more likely to call for dismantling of existing structures and then to create some order out of the ensuing chaos. The rebuilding of the country may thus require an eclectic yet comprehensive approach in dealing with the economic problems. This would involve the development of a menu of options, such as the ones outlined in the paper, but without a predetermined structure. In other words, the initial strategy may involve operating in a reactive mode by responding spontaneously to events until a clear pattern emerges. This could lead to seemingly contradictory policies such as price liberalization and controlled exchange rates. Once the problems have been adequately identified and their solutions agreed upon, then one could argue more persuasively for an orderly plan. The success of the economic reconstruction will nonetheless hinge on the viability of the political process. Without a stable political environment, economic reforms will never work.

The basic model developed by the author is based on the notion of comparative advantage in agriculture and tourism, Cuba's location next to the US market, and the strong availability of human capital in the exile community. The key industries identified by the author for rapid development are agriculture and agro-industries, fishing, tourism, and international trade services. I would add to this list assembly industries, which are ideal for countries with ample supply of low-cost labor. The success of the so-called *maquiladoras* could be replicated in Cuba, particularly in the areas of textiles, electronics and pharmaceuticals. Like Mexico, Cuba has the advantage of close proximity to the US market.

While the design of the transition from a centrally-planned to a market-based economy will benefit from the experiences of Eastern Europe and the ex-Soviet republics, the process in Cuba is likely to be more akin to the experience of Latin America. Cuba's transition is likely to begin at the stage Latin America went through starting in the 1950's. The transformation will take it from a centrally planned economy to a mixed and then to a market economy. However, in this case the transition will have to be accomplished in a much shorter period of time. In this regard, the author maps out a five-step plan for Cuba which he predicts will take six years. I think this may be too ambitious; however, I am sure the aim of his paper is not to predict how long it will take, but rather how best to implement a successful transition.

Castañeda presents a detailed action plan for the rebuilding and restructuring of the Cuban economy. The following comments refer to some of the issues contained in his proposals.

Privatization: The process of privatization is going to be more complex than the recent experience of mixed economies in Latin America. The critical issue is to determine what can be privatized. The answer to this question will depend on how far the government wants to go in privatization, and on which of the existing entities are worth privatizing. The companies slated for privatization may not elicit sufficient response from investors. Worker participation in privatized companies should also be considered.

Stabilization: Unfortunately there is no quick fix for an economy that has been dysfunctional for more than 30 years. The author's proposal of an initial shock treatment of three months that would set the stage for structural reforms may prove to be overly optimistic. The experience of Latin America and Eastern Europe has demonstrated that it takes numerous shocks to the system before the economy begins to respond. Only after repeated trials and many errors will prices settle at realistic levels, fiscal imbalances diminish to manageable proportions, and exchange rates unify at competitive values. In the meantime, these shocks can inflict unnecessarily severe hardship on the people.

Liberalization: Under suitable conditions structural changes can provoke a notable supply response. However, price changes and other structural adjustments can trigger a supply response only if there is sufficient idle capacity or resources to invest in creating that additional capacity. Cuba's current production infrastructure may be quite limited. The design of liberalization programs should be based on a careful analysis of Cuba's capital and labor constraints. A good part of the existing plant and equipment may be obsolete. The labor force may require extensive training in new production techniques.

Legal framework: The need for a legal framework that guarantees basic rights is imperative. This is probably one of the areas where immediate action will be required. The issue of confiscated properties and compensation will have to be at the top of any government's agenda. However more thought needs to be given to a proper regulatory structure. Establishing the rules of the game in a new market-oriented economy is not sufficient; these have to be supported by strong supervisory institutions such as the superintendency of banks and companies which would play a critical role in ensuring the integrity of any new economic system.

Monetary and credit policies: More attention needs to be paid to the reconstruction of Cuba's financial system. Credit allocation decisions should be quickly transferred from the monetary authorities to the banking system. Credit policies should be determined by financial institutions which are freed from political considerations.

Fiscal reforms: The overhaul of the public sector and the return of public companies to the private sector should be the overriding objective. Nevertheless, this task cannot be accomplished without a comprehensive program of technical assistance in all areas of public administration and project evaluation. Significant resources will be needed to develop a comprehensive base of economic information. Investors need information in order to make investment decisions. At present, Cuba is deficient in most areas of economic, financial, demographic, and sociological information. The evaluation of any privatization strategies should clearly indicate how the government intends to use the resources from the sale of public entities.

External sector: The external sector will play a crucial role in the reconstruction of the Cuban economy. Foreign exchange will be the principal resource in the rebuilding efforts since almost everything needed to get the economy moving again will have to be imported. I think the external reform polices need to support the objective of maximizing foreign exchange inflows using shock treatment as well as the gradualism approach. Unfortunately, a maxi-devaluation followed by currency unification as recommended by Castañeda has not worked well in countries with similar experiences in Latin America. It may be necessary to maintain several exchange rates until Cuba's international reserves are sufficient to assure the stability of the currency. At the same time, free capital repatriation could encourage foreign investors to make only short-term investments that would maximize their payout, instead of longer-term projects that would be driven by market fundamentals. The author's suggestion of imposing a 100 percent tariff on imports of consumer goods could have the undesirable effect of creating inefficient industries under the protection of the tariffs which could later on convince the government to retain the tariffs in order to protect employment. Clearly external sector issues are quite complex, but the success of reforms in this area will be the determining factor in Cuba's recovery.

NON-WALRASIAN PROPERTIES OF THE CUBAN ECONOMY: RATIONING, LABOR SUPPLY, AND OUTPUT

Jorge A. Sanguinetty

I. Introduction

The range of opportunities to carry out empirical research on the Cuban economy is generally limited by the lack of data or by the nagging suspicion that the available data do not tell all there is to know, especially during the last thirty three years of government control of the sources of information. Economic theory, however, can be applied to understand many problems, including those associated with important policy implications that often require a qualified opinion even when they cannot be thoroughly investigated for lack of data. In this paper, economic theory is applied to explain how individual preferences are still able to play a fundamental role in the Cuban economy, despite the lack of opportunities to exercise free choice.

Though individual choice is oppressively constrained in Cuba and free markets are virtually non existent (with the possible and highly qualified exception of black markets), Cubans have found ways to accommodate their preferences in terms of their own orderings or priorities, not the government's. The Cuban Government has been able to apply its power by imposing constraints, but this power does not appear to be capable of changing the ordering of individual preferences within constrained choice sets.

Despite massive ideological indoctrination and political intimidation to change values (preferences) in Cuba, there is no evidence that general patterns of individual behavior (consumers' and workers') depart from the neoclassical tenet of utility maximization. The Cuban Government's apparent inability to recognize or understand this principle has caused grave damage to the productive capacity of the country. Yet, the notion that utility maximization is still an important principle to explain consumer and worker behavior in Cuba serves to provide some explanations for the performance of the national economy during the last three decades.

From the outset, government policy in Cuba was against the market system, blaming it for most of the country's economic and social problems. Instead of correcting market imperfections and distortions, the government decided to install a command economy under a central planning system. The notion of general equilibrium was implicit in central planning, but the real challenge was, at least from an economic point of view, how to achieve equilibrium while administering prices and quantities of a number of goods and services. The introduction of rationing consolidated the notion that if equilibrium was feasible, it would not be Walrasian since rationing would prevent the clearance of at least some markets. As rationing was extended to almost all kinds of markets, however, it became apparent that equilibrium may not be attainable based on three critical conditions: a) market inflexibility, b) the elimination of signals to guide resource allocation processes towards their most efficient uses, and c) the concomitant elimination of incentives to work. All this contributed to create an economic system incapable of achieving equilibrium, let alone the grandiose targets fixed by the government at different times. The magnitude of the ensuing economic crisis makes one wonder about whether its main cause is an outstanding incompetence on the part of the Cuban leadership or whether there is a different public policy agenda.

This paper consists of an analysis of the effects of rationing on the labor supply in Cuba, and its subsequent impact on the national levels of output. The paper applies Becker's (1965) theory of the allocation of time to build a model linking the effects of rationing of goods with the supply of labor. The paper also provides the analytical groundwork to explain the current policy to attract foreign investments and to anticipate some of the effects of a process of price liberalization, when such opportunity arises.

II.   Theoretical Background

There is relatively little research about the relationship between rationing of goods and the supply of labor. A serious political issue in Great Britain during the Battle of England (there was constant war propaganda appealing to workers' patriotism to work beyond material incentives constrained by rationing of goods), rationing was sparsely investigated in the fifties and sixties and more intensely afterwards.

Among the earliest work is Samuelson's (1947) who identified the Le Chatelier principle to characterize the reduction in price elasticities of non-rationed goods when rationing is introduced. Later, Henderson (1952) developed a model of consumer choice under multiple constraints that opened the way to the application of constraints other than income. Tobin and Houthakker (1950-1951) concentrated exclusively on forms of demand elasticities under rationing, McManus (1956) formulated rationing theory based on revealed-preference theory, and Shinkai (1966) compared the advantages of straight rationing (quotas), point rationing (coupons), and consumption taxes. The only study that included some considerations about income and leisure was Tobin's (1952).

More recently, Hirshleifer (1980) discusses the basics of rationing and of time as a constraint, but without going into the effects on the supply of labor. Kooreman and Kapteyn (1985) employed a model by Deaton and Muellbauer (1981) that jointly determines family income and male and female labor supply of individual households in the Netherlands, but the concept of rationing is applied to the supply of labor. Neary (1987) briefly reviews rationing theory without going into the area of interest of this paper. Benassy (1987a), on the other hand, presents a treatment of rationed equilibria that opens a promising methodological avenue to investigate the Cuban economy in terms of non-Walrasian general equilibrium. In this context, it is worth mentioning Benassy (1987b) again and his work in the analysis of disequilibrium.

Walrasian equilibrium is achieved when all markets (consumer and factor goods and services) clear under conditions of free choice by supply and demand agents. The equalization of supply and demand is possible when prices are flexible. Price inflexibility, on the other hand, will lead to disequilibria, either as excess supply or excess demand in certain markets. As soon as inequality constraints or ceilings are imposed on prices, rationing usually follows in the form of queues as excess demands persist. A rationing regime may be implemented as an attempt to organize the distribution of the affected goods or services and reduce the uncertainty and inconvenience of waiting lines. Though there are several rationing regimes, the quota system is the only one examined in this paper, since it is the predominant form of rationing instituted in Cuba. This system consists of imposing a maximum amount allowed to be purchased by each buyer at the official (fixed) price per period.

When well calculated, the quota should be able to "clear" the market in the sense that no queues are necessary. The presence of queues is a signal that official quotas are not always fulfilled by the suppliers, and that buyers do not trust that a given shipment has enough quantity of the rationed good to satisfy all the quotas at a given distribution point. Chronic inability by the government to keep the promised quotas in Cuba explains why waiting lines have become a permanent feature of life in the country. Thus, in rigor, queues cum rationing mean a rationing regime within another.

Regardless of the reliability of the rationing quotas, there are at least two ways in which a non-Walrasian equilibrium can be achieved. One is allowing sufficient free market transactions in which individuals can exchange rationed goods at prices different than those officially established. Therefore, free markets can help achieve balance between demand and supply under a system of partial price flexibility.[1] The other form of non-Walrasian equilibrium could be achieved with a very competent, precise and disciplined bureaucracy that would calculate prices an ration quotas consistently according with demand and supply conditions. This of course would never be as efficient as a totally free market system, but it would have a better chance of achieving equilibrium under strict a socialist or communist administration.

A necessary condition to achieve equilibrium in such circumstances is to avoid that the rationing system provoke a reduction in the supply of factors of production, especially labor, to the point of forcing a reduction in the levels of output that support the established rationing quotas. Despite imperfections, and price rigidities and distortions, there are factor markets in Cuba. In the case of labor markets, it is important to keep in mind that the supply is private, while the demand is mainly public. Thus, the former is more likely to react to price and market signals more quickly than the latter.

Yet, contrary to basic principles of efficient resource utilization and to its own economic interests, the Cuban Government adopted a combination of rationing regimes and sets of prices that deepened the inefficiency of the intrinsically inefficient socialist economy. Such a combination of variables seems to have thrown the Cuban economy into a state of monotonic (non-oscillatory) dynamic disequilibria. Market inflexibility combined with a rationing regime of arbitrary quotas and caused a contraction in the supply of labor, followed by a contraction in the levels of output that fed back into the reduction of the rationing quotas.[2] This positive (reinforcing) feedback system created an output deflation spiral that can be singled out as the pivotal cause of disequilibria of the Cuban economy. It is also the cardinal cause of the country's inability to be economically viable, leading to its chronic dependence on external subsidies. The demise of the Soviet Union and the Socialist block has forced a drastic reduction of the subsidies, and a major adjustment of the Cuban economy, throwing the country into what may be the worst economic crisis of its history.

III. The Functional Relationship Between Rationing and the Supply of Labor

The traditional approach to consumer behavior is based on the principle of utility maximization in the presence of an income constraint and a given set of prices. Consistent with this approach, preferences between income and leisure were defined to explain individual labor force participation. This theoretical construct could be used to establish the functional linkage between rationing and the supply of labor. This model, however, focuses on the structure of preferences between income and leisure and does not lend itself to the analytical objectives of this paper. Becker's theory of allocation of time is preferred in this paper because it is more adaptable to

---

[1]This means that the consumers' budget constraints are "kinked" at the point where the quota inequality is intersected.

[2]In many cases the reductions were not made official but materialized in form of delays in the delivery periods. For instance, quotas that were supposed to be deliver every week would take eight or more days. If the situation persisted for a long time, the quota could be officially reduced.

empirical investigation and suitable for explaining labor phenomena in terms of changes in relative prices and levels of income, rather than in terms of changes in consumer-worker preferences or tastes.

Another reason to apply Becker's model is that, in focusing on the allocation of time, it provides a powerful methodological opportunity to study individual behavior in Cuba, since time is virtually the only resource over which Cubans can still exercise a certain degree of control. Becker's model introduces the time factor as a second constraint, especially focusing on the amount of time available for consumption activities. This constraint is partially convertible in income through the labor market.

The traditional individual income constraint requires little explanation and is given by the following equation:

$$\sum p_i x_i \le w T_w + I_0 \qquad (1)$$

where p_i is the nominal price of good or service i (for i= 1,...,n in an n-dimensional choice set or, simply, in a world of n goods and services) and x_i its quantity, while w is the wage rate by unit of time, T_w the amount of time dedicated to income generating activities, and I_0 income endowments.[3]

The consumer will also face a time constraint for consumption activities and leisure. The corresponding equation, however, requires some explanation for those not familiar with Becker's theory of allocation of time. This theory is based in the Lancasterean notion that commodities purchased by consumers do not directly produce utility. Rather, they are inputs in household production functions that actually generate the utility-bearing goods. In such household production functions, time itself is an input, and w its price.

Therefore, if a consumer buys x units of a good i, he must pay a price in money p_i and dedicate a certain amount of time (a price in terms of time) to elaborate it in the household.[4] Thus, utility is not directly generated by the amount x_i but derived from the final household consumption good produced with x_i as an input. For mathematical simplification, the household production function is obviated here, and fixed coefficients of household production are assumed. This yields the following equation:

$$\sum t_i x_i \le T_c = T - T_w \qquad (2)$$

where t_i is the "price" in time needed to process and consume a unit of x_i, and T_c is the total time

---

[3]This is the income received in the form of pensions, bank account proceeds or regular government payments, if any, to former owners of confiscated property that may still reside in Cuba.

[4]Even pure leisure usually needs complementing with money. See Juster and Stafford (1991) for an empirical study on this subject.

dedicated to consumption activities (sometimes called leisure time). As total available time T in a given time aggregation horizon is equal to $T_c + T_w$, we have the following result:

$$\sum (p_i + wt_i)x_i \leq wT \qquad (3)$$

This represents the actual constraint against which consumers may maximize utility. It can be called the full-income constraint and provides a richer conception of price, given by $(p_i + wt_i)$. The second term of the sum represents the opportunity cost of that particular consumption activity, or another reminder of the notion that time is money.

The utility-maximizing consumer[5] with a utility function $U = U(x_i)$ will choose the values of x_i such that each binary set of relative prices $(p_i + wt_i)/(p_j + wt_j)$ (for each $i,j = 1,...,n$ with $i \neq j$) to be equal to the corresponding marginal rate of substitution $-\delta x_j/\delta x_i$. If at least one of the prices p_i is fixed below the equilibrium level that clears that particular market, some form of rationing will appear, preventing those consumers that can afford buying more than the corresponding quota from achieving maximum satisfaction with their levels of income.

The introduction of additional constraints in the form of straight rationing quotas will be analyzed by means of a graphical representation. A two-good world without savings is postulated by aggregating the n goods into two major groups 1 and 2, x_1 representing quantities of the aggregate commodity that is relatively less expensive in terms of money but relatively more time consuming or time intensive. This means that x_1 has low p_1 in relation to p_2, while t_1 is high relative to t_2. Consistently, x_2 represents quantities of the more expensive commodity aggregate in terms of money, but less time consuming relative to good 1.[6]

This is better understood by means of examples of close substitutes. For instance, raw food to be prepared at home costs less money and more time than pre-cooked food or preserves. Old clothing mended at home is more money saving and time using than new clothes. Watching a baseball game on television is more money using and time saving than watching the same game at the stadium, because of transportation costs and the exceedingly inexpensive tickets that the Cuban Government has made available to the population. Laundry sent to a shop is also relatively more money using and time saving than laundry done at home. Finally, repairing the old car or TV set is generally not only less expensive in money and more time using than buying a new one, but the

---

[5] I avoid the term *rational* to leave room for those who, following the communist creed, may behave unselfishly or with opportunism but still rationally without satisfying these optimality conditions.

[6] We assume that the following condition is verified:

$$\frac{p_2}{p_1} < \frac{p_2 + wt_2}{p_1 + wt_1} < \frac{t_2}{t_1}$$

only option available in Cuba.[7]

Figure 1 represents a worker-consumer for whom ration quotas are effective, i.e., are placed below his equilibrium position under free choice. The figure depicts several equilibrium positions, starting with the one consistent with Walrasian equilibrium and moving towards other equilibria as different policy measures are implemented. Line II' represents the two-dimensional version of equation (1), i.e., the traditional budget constraint. Line TT' represents the time constraint generalized in equation (2). The convertibility between the time dedicated to consumption T_c and the time dedicated to generate income T_w determines that shifts of both constraints are always in opposite directions. An upward (downward) shift of TT' that augments (diminishes) the availability of consumption time is simultaneous to a downward (upward) shift of the income constraint II' diminishing (augmenting) earned income. The reader should notice that lines II' and TT' move as a pair of scissors, since the full-income constraint FF', or dotted line, is the locus of all possible intersections of II' and TT'.

The full-income constraint equation is not shown to avoid overloading the graphic, but is the two-good version of equation (3). FF' only changes its position when the wage rate changes and/or the relative prices in money and time terms change. At this point there is no need to be concerned with different levels and slopes of FF'. The important point is that it is under this constraint where the consumer maximizes utility by selecting a bundle of goods that determines simultaneously its allocation of time between the labor market and household activities, including pure leisure.[8]

In Figure 1, the worker-consumer maximizes satisfaction at point A under conditions of free choice, i.e., before any extraneous constraint like rationing is introduced. Point A represents a specific bundle of goods in quantities x_1 and x_2 and a level of satisfaction depicted by indifference curve U_1. Discarding any changes in prices, he could only improve his standard of living (level of utility) if the wage rate w rises. Likewise, his level of welfare would be reduced if the wage rate is lowered.

Though the early signs of rationing appeared in Cuba in 1960 and became more apparent in 1961, in the form of waiting lines, a formal regime was not implemented until March 1962 in Havana and other urban centers of the country. The first goods to suffer severe scarcities, and even total disappearance from the market, were generally imported. Many of these goods were time saving but relatively expensive in terms of money, like consumer durable goods, canned food, all kinds of spare parts, apparel, etc. In general it can be said that rationing was more severe in relation to time-saving, money-using goods than in time-using, money-saving goods. This is depicted in Figure 1 by the vertical line representing the constraint (or aggregate quota) $x_2 \leq Q_2$.

The first result of this new situation is that the consumer will suffer a welfare loss since the optimum position A is no longer attainable. As the maximum quantity the consumer can buy

---

[7]In Cuba, rationing is not universal. We should recognize an upper class of Cuban officials and party leaders who enjoy more freedom of choice as consumers. As they are mostly bureaucrats, it is reasonable to assume that their implicit salaries are above the value of their marginal productivities, therefore, their net contribution to the national economy as workers must be negative. In the strictest Marxist analysis based on the labor theory of value, they are net consumers of surplus value and, by definition, exploiters. The essential difference between this type of exploiter and the capitalist stereotype is that the latter contributes to the equilibrium of the economy while the former contributes to deepen its disequilibrium.

[8]Pure leisure could be defined in several ways, but none of them would be significant enough to alter the results of the ongoing analysis. Nevertheless, it is suitable to recognize the possibility of extreme idleness or non-utility producing time in some extreme circumstances where severe insufficiencies of goods (or money) appear.

Figure 1

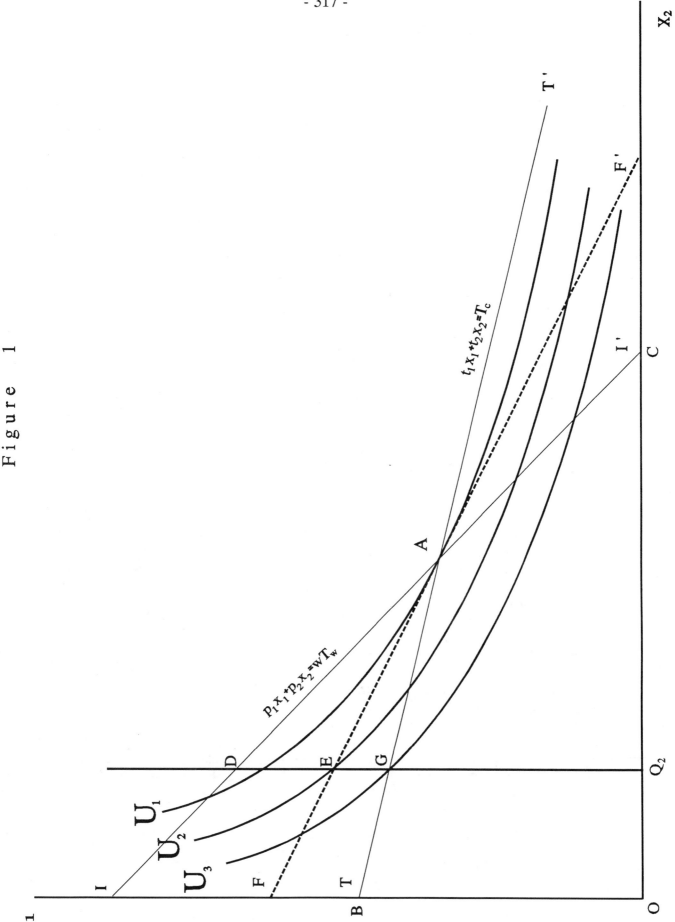

(legally) is $x_2=Q_2$, he will also be confronted with an excess of money and a shortage of time at the suboptimal position A. In order to achieve this constrained maximum, however, he would have to retire time from the labor market to have more time for consumption.

Under these circumstances, the new equilibrium is at point E, where level of utility U_2 is attained, but it does not satisfy the first-order optimality condition of equalization between relative prices (in terms of full income) and the marginal rate of substitution between aggregate goods 1 and 2. This condition would be consistent with non-Walrasian equilibrium if the level of output for the entire economy could sustain the quotas. As we proceed, we will notice that equilibrium has not been attained and it may not be attainable until the system reaches an extreme point.

But before we proceed, let us finalize this section by pointing out that as ration quotas tend to be uniform for the entire population, at least in principle, workers with higher wage levels will have a stronger incentive to transfer time from the labor market to the household than workers with lower wages. The same can be said for individuals with non-wage income. This implies that this system of rationing generates a backward-bending supply curve of labor when rationing is severe enough and is biassed against time-saving goods, since it reduces and even eliminates incentives to work for income.

This condition becomes more detrimental to the Cuban economy as there are little or no incentives to save either. If the Cuban economy were more flexible, intertemporal transfers of resources could be channeled through savings. If there were a well-founded rationale for current sacrifices, individuals would nurture rational expectations for a higher level of utility tomorrow at today's expense.

IV.   From Utility Maximization to Mandatory Altruism

A market exists as long as there is the possibility of a transaction or trade. Although extremely imperfect and even hard to observe, labor markets exist in Cuba since there are many forms of supply of labor as well as many forms of demand. True, there is very little, virtually no mobility in such markets, no equilibrium possibilities, let alone a mechanism for wage determination, beyond bureaucratic formulas. Nevertheless, workers have shown and continue to show reactions to the lack of incentives to work. As soon as rationing appeared in the early sixties, a frequent complaint by the government was about the pervasiveness of absenteeism. Such a phenomenon appears to have been most frequent in industries with flexible hiring regimes and shifts such as agriculture, construction, transportation, and longshoremen, rather than being subject to fixed office hours or shift indivisibilities.

Thus, absenteeism in Cuba appears to be the most expedite vehicle for individual workers to affect the supply of labor in the short-run. Possibly the second most important vehicle (or perhaps the most important one, though not as obvious) is by reducing the intensity, efficiency or level of dedication to their individual jobs (shirking). This in fact, reduces the supply of labor in efficiency units but it would be more easily observable in terms of labor productivity decreases. Mesa-Lago (1981, pages 132-139) provides an excellent review of this chronic condition of the Cuban economy under socialism.

Though there is no solid quantitative evidence about the level of absenteeism, the continuing public complaints uttered by government spokesmen provided the most significant evidence that the phenomenon reached alarming proportions. To combat absenteeism, the government adopted a two-pronged approach. On the one hand, repeated appeals were made to patriotic values and revolutionary fervor by the media and all instruments of mass control available to the government, including meetings at the work place, etc. On the other hand, the government adopted measures that were tantamount to attempts to ration leisure or consumption time. During certain periods, police forces would comb beaches asking bathers for identification cards and proof of being on vacation. Another attempt was the recruitment of volunteers (in many cases under a certain amount of pressure) to work in agriculture, mostly during harvest times.

All this implies that as many worker-consumers were adjusting their new equilibrium positions after rationing was imposed, from point A to point E (Figure 1), the government was pushing in the direction of point G, an even inferior alternative from the point of view of the utility mapping (U_3). A consumer would be at point G by conviction (altruism) or by compulsion. Without compulsion, the segment EG represents the spectrum of possible attitudes with respect to the stated ideological goals of the revolution; the building of a new man devoid of greed. The closer consumers are to E, the less realistic the official policy would be in terms of depending on moral incentives-- rather than on material incentives--to develop the economy. On the other hand, the closer they are to point G the greater the success of the government in forcing individuals to behave as if they were real socialists, or in convincing that they in fact are socialists.

It is important to notice that at point E, lines II' and TT' could intersect, which means that individuals would spend all their earnings and all their consumption time, but they would be maximizing their utility at the second best level U_2. At point G, however, lines II' and TT' continue to intersect at A. All the time available for consumption would be spent, but not all the money. Consumers would find that at the end of the period, after having conducted their purchases in legal markets only (this assumption is lifted below), they would have excess earnings measured by DG/p_1, their contribution to the monetary overhang. The standard of living given by U_3 is inferior to second best U_2.

In the aggregate, the reality would probably be somewhere between points E and G, possibly more as a result of indivisibilities of work shifts than of altruistic (true or dictated) consumer behavior. Wherever the equilibrium position is, it does not appear to have stability conditions, i.e., it could fluctuate up and down, adding uncertainty to the Cuban economy's production capabilities. The closer that equilibrium point is to E, the more severe is the contraction of the supply of labor and its deleterious impact on Cuba's output capacity and vice versa.

Notice that if the government had opted for price flexibility to take care of any shortages, they would have left the work incentive system intact. The shortage of time-saving goods would have caused a raise in prices. This would be represented in Figure 1 as a reduction of the slope of line II' and a corresponding reduction in the slope of the full-income constraint FF'. It can de demonstrated that the new equilibrium position is inferior to the one corresponding to point A, but superior to E.

This point is made to establish the differences between the Walrasian and the non-Walrasian forms of equilibrium. In the former case, without rationing, there would be a less egalitarian distribution of the rationed goods, but no loss of the incentive to work. In the latter case, the distribution would be more egalitarian, but there would be a loss of the incentive to work. In this case, the poor will not suffer the consequences of the scarcity in the short run, but will do it in the long run as the contraction in the supply of labor reduces the level of output affecting the entire economy. Despite the illusion of a trade off, there is none. The poor will be worse off in the long run if the attempt to achieve equilibrium in a non-Walrasian system fails.

V.   Extending Rationing to Money-Saving, Time-Using Goods

Thus far, the analysis focused on the rationing of the most relatively time-saving goods. In practice, rationing was imposed simultaneously to time-intensive, money-saving goods. The difference is that in the former group, shortages were so severe, that entire categories of goods and services disappeared from the markets for years (some forever) and were never really subject to a formal rationing system. During the seventies, some consumer durable goods started to reappear, but were distributed through trade unions and other organizations as prizes (in recognition for some socialist deed, including labor-related issues) or on the basis of need. Despite this primitive allocation system, the buyer still had to pay with money for the purchase.

Figure 2 depicts an additional rationing constraint represented by the inequality $x_1 \leq Q_1$. Now the consumer choice set is further reduced to the rectangle OQ_1HQ_2, with the corresponding level of utility U_4, representing an additional welfare loss.[9] Notice that without the quota Q_2, the worker-consumer in this situation would find himself with an insufficiency of money and an excess of time to be able to maximize utility at point M (the corresponding indifference curve is not shown for clarity but it corresponds to a level of utility between U_1 and U_2). Point M represents an incentive to exchange time for a little more money in the labor market. In fact, this would have been an attractive option if the Cuban government's policy intended to stimulate the supply of labor in behalf of the economic development of the country. The government, on the contrary, maintained a much more severe constraint on time-savings goods and workers did not have any incentive to save the unspent income. Many seemed to have reasoned that it was not worth the effort to put the unspent money in the bank for a rainy day because there were no guarantees that the government would not confiscate it. Besides, the official propaganda was categorical in dismissing the value of money following Marxist dogma and the communist utopia of its eventual disappearance.

The black market, on the other hand, represented an incentive to earn a certain amount of income, but it would be very difficult, perhaps impossible, to determine whether such an incentive was strong enough. It seems that black market transactions were never as widespread and intense as to represent a major factor in the allocation of time by individuals, especially because black market transactions were almost exclusively limited to foodstuffs and were always severely persecuted by the government. Though a certain level of black market activity would place the consumer somewhere, but not too far, Northeast of point H (Figure 2), we can take H as a point of departure to approximate a measure of the loss of resources that rationing came to represent. Assuming that the worker-consumer remains at point A in terms of his allocation of time between work and consumption and leisure, his idle income (or contribution to the monetary overhang) has now increased to HD/p_1 (minus any possible black market expense), while HN/t_2 is the time "overhang" or total waste, which would include the time of searching for black market opportunities or, most importantly, the time waiting in lines.

Figure 2 shows the two major dimensions of waste imposed on the Cuban economy for thirty years of rationing. The first is that time wasted can be measured in terms of foregone earnings, in terms of foregone human capital investment opportunities, or foregone consumption and leisurely activities. The second dimension, money, measures the amount of resources presumably produced but dedicated to activities over which the consumer had no control or even knowledge, a great

---

[9]The metric equivalences conveyed by the graphic are not realistic. Any lack of proportion was necessary for clarity.

Figure 2

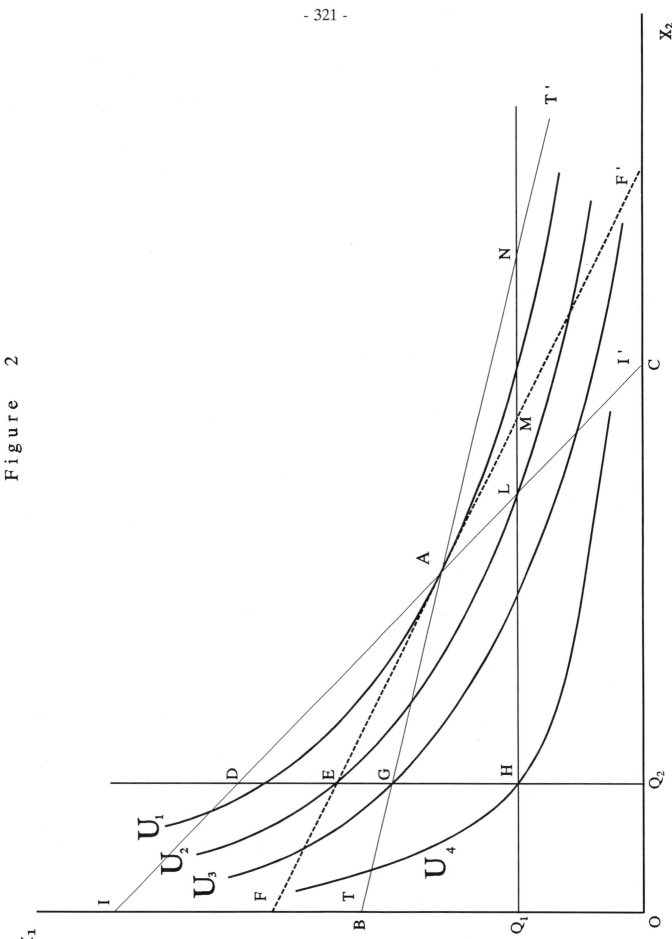

difference from explicit taxation. Even if the loss of income to the worker-consumer under this model was well-spent in infrastructure, public education, and health, the result seems to have been a contraction of the supply of labor of such magnitude that the negative impact on the levels of output affected the economy's capacity to fulfill the quotas of rationing.

Until recently, this mechanism was not easy to observe since Cuba enjoyed significant subsidies from the Soviet Union. Those subsidies were in fact necessary to maintain the Cuban economy afloat and save her from her chronic disequilibrium. With the demise of the Soviet Union and the gradual but fast disappearance of the subsidies, the nakedness of the Cuban economic system has become increasingly visible.

Now the government is trying a bizarre strategy, not only from an orthodox Marxist point of view but from many others: the importation of foreign capital in a desperate attempt to stop its continuing decline. Although the initiative to attract foreign investors started in the mid eighties, the efforts have been intensified in the last few years for the reasons just mentioned. Interestingly, capital is not the only thing that the government wants, but also managerial capabilities that the central planning system and the government enterprises have failed to provide. To achieve this, labor practices have been radically changed for those working in foreign enterprises, mainly dedicated to international tourism. Whether this policy will be able to take the Cuban economy out of its current predicament is also an open question. In the meantime, the rest of the economy appears to continue a slow process of deterioration, now with increasing unemployment, physical decay of infrastructure, and increasing signals of labor dissatisfaction.

VI. The Path Toward Recovery

As the productive capacity shrinks on all fronts, one wonders about how fast the Cuban economy can recover from the current quagmire. It seems that Cuba's economy has suffered losses on a number of areas, for instance, physical assets and general infrastructure, markets, know-how, workers' attitudes, international credit, etc. But the most difficult aspect of its recovery will be changing the organization of the economic system, and with that, the development of a new legal system, the emergence of competitive entrepreneurs, and the formulation and implementation of an economic recovery program. The challenge goes well beyond that of simple policy definitions. Among the most critical problems will be how to move from the current system of rationing, fixed prices, bureaucratic enterprises, and central planning, to a system of price flexibility and private initiatives.

Figure 3 may help visualize the magnitude of this problem. The figure is a simplified version of Figure 2 with some minor but critical changes. The rationing constraints at Q_1 and Q_2 are kept and in fact divide the graphic in a special way. The areas to the West of Q_2 and to the South of Q_1 represent the past of frozen nominal prices. Once rationing is eliminated, the reality will look as the quadrant North East of H. As the economy deteriorated, both internally and in its ability to attract foreign currency, prices increased pari passu in real terms and the income budget constraint collapsed accordingly. This is not evident to the general public until they are allowed to operate again without the rationing restrictions, i.e., to the East of Q_2 and North of Q_1.

The old constraint II' is missing its center D'D", and it shows a different slope as relative prices are expected to change with a negative bias against imported goods that tend to be more time saving than domestic ones. Concomitantly, the full-income constraint also collapses in the middle, represented by the segment E'E". The time constraint could be assumed to remain intact if the

Figure 3

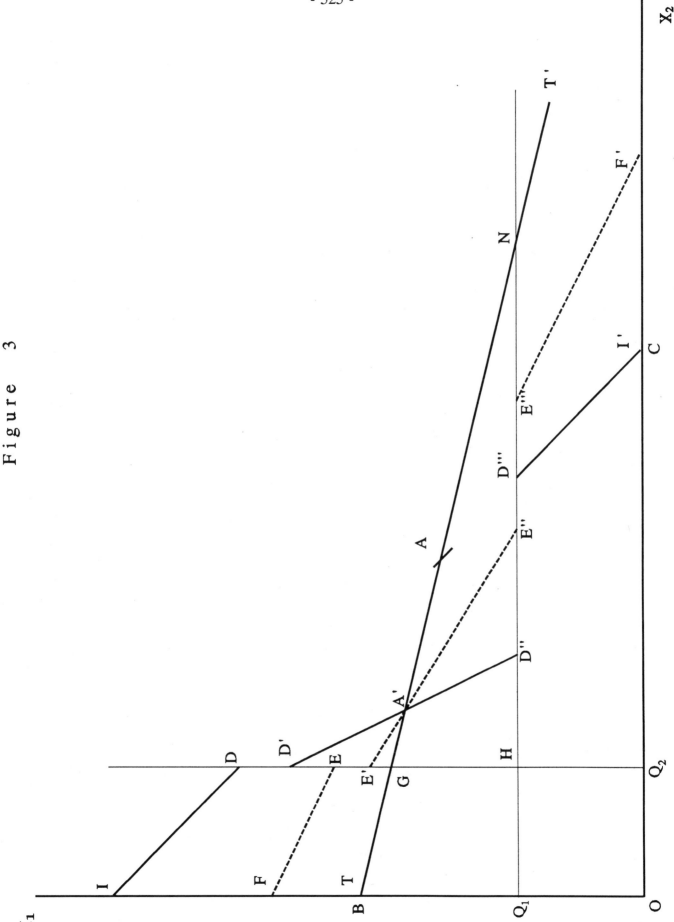

values of the t_is do not change in relative or absolute terms. Nevertheless, there is room for conjecture in this regard, since the regression of the Cuban economy may have affected the levels of efficiency of the uses of time. In other words, if there have been fundamental changes in the "technologies" of household production functions, then the North East segment of the time constraint TT' also collapses.

The figure shows that the old equilibrium position at A is not attainable, but there is an improvement in moving from H to A' (or its equivalent for a lower TT'). Under these conditions, a radical price liberalization seems the most natural measure to adopt since it would improve consumers' welfare allowing them to buy beyond their old rations, and also would stimulate the labor supply. Then, why is price liberalization so much feared in societies that became liberated recently from central planning? One answer depends on the pattern of distribution of income in combination with the sources of income. Those living on fixed incomes would definitely suffer, since many of those who have more income than the necessary to purchase the old rationing quotas can afford the new prices and buy greater quantities than before. Also, those making a living in activities that do not produce the goods in high demand (government servants, military) will fear the movement, because their salaries cannot be liberalized consistently with the rest of the economy. Another answer is based on the expectation that price increases will be abusive, well beyond competitive equilibrium levels. The reason for this is that if price liberalization takes place before government enterprises are privatized or forced to behave competitively, they will abuse their monopolistic or quasi-monopolistic positions.

None of the arguments are compelling enough to impede the liberalization of prices at one point in time, the sooner the better. Nevertheless, the process should be engineered in a way that takes care of all the necessary adjustment at the same time. The problem cannot be solved by the stroke of a pen; it also requires designing and implementing a complex program to dismantle the system without generating unnecessary suffering to the population.

VII.   Conclusion

One of the main conclusions of this paper is that Cubans appear to behave as utility maximizers. This is despite government efforts to make them work without material incentives but on ideological motivation alone. Utility-maximizing behavior is revealed as Cubans continue excercising free choice about the only resource they still own: time. By allocating their time consistently with their own interests, Cuban workers have contributed to the economic stagnation, and even regression of the country. This is the result of the government failure to create an economic system capable of making individual interests compatible with the common good. This demonstrates that an economic system that systematically ignores the fundamentals of human behavior is doomed to fail.

Another fundamental conclusion of the paper is that Cuban worker-consumers may be ready to react to a new and more liberal price mechanism. As consumers, no one doubts that they would know how to allocate their time and money budgets to obtain the most satisfying combination of goods. As workers, they can be expected to be equally sensitive to the signals of free labor markets. Nevertheless, when the transition to a market economy becomes a possibility in Cuba, not all economic agents will be as well prepared to respond to market signals as consumers and workers. The latter are already in control of their preferences, their labor services, their time, and their human capital. That part of the economy is already private. But the enterprises that must continue producing the goods the consumers purchase, and hiring the workers who produce them will not be prepared to react efficiently to market signals until some profound changes are introduced. This fundamental asymmetry about price responsiveness by different economic agents in a transitional economy must be recognized and dealt with before any price liberalization plan is implemented.

The Cuban economy is a study in anomalies and disequilibria. As in other branches of science, these extreme phenomena offer fresh opportunities for theoretical research and better understanding of all the elements that make an economic system work, especially market economies. Too often, we take for granted many of those elements as we get used to study well-structured economic systems in the Western tradition. Alternatively, we become too involved with aggregate economic analysis and its corresponding functional relationships, or simply too focused in some narrow areas of interest. As we study the Cuban economy, it is almost impossible not to feel the obligation to adopt a systemic approach, i.e., everything matters. This happens as soon as one becomes interested in how a transition from central planning to a market economy should be designed and implemented.

To prepare for the transition to a market economy, the importance of understanding the workings of the centrally planned system cannot be exaggerated. A new economic system cannot be changed by policy declarations or by decree. There is the need to design and build new institutions and develop new mentalities. The effort goes well beyond the typical design and implementation of economic policies. In the socialist revolution, the process consisted of a reduction of the institutional complexity of the economy. Enterprises were concentrated into monopolies as they were confiscated. Entire sectors and activities disappeared, like banking, insurance, advertising and free markets. Property rights were either eliminated or severely limited; the legal system was radically transformed. Whole generations have been educated in the new system, with little or no knowledge of alternative economic regimes and opportunities. Their understanding of market economics is flawed by preconceptions about the role of interest rates, all forms of intermediation, property rights, risk, and the role of the government in economies.

The process from central planning to free markets proceeds inversely; from a state of low institutional complexity to one of higher complexity. It is one characterized by hysteresis, which implies that a much more sophisticated strategy is required. The socialist destruction of property rights and financial intermediation requires building these institutions anew, as well as a legal system and even a constitutional framework. Perceptions or mentalities that make people willing to accept or oppose fundamental changes in their societies is also a dimension of the transition that must be dealt with from the beginning of the process. If the future builders of the transition in Cuba understand all these factors, they would be avoiding the simplemindedness of adopting extreme positions like "shock therapy" or "gradualism". The fact is that some public policy measures will require quick, even drastic decisions. Many others will require more than just decisions. The real challenge is to gather the wisdom to design new institutions and the patience to construct them and make them work.

References

Becker, Gary S. (1965), A theory of the allocation of time, *The Economic Journal*, September.

Benassy, Jean-Pascal (1987a), Rationed equilibria, *The New Palgrave*, Vol. 4, The Macmillan Press Ltd.

Benassy, Jean-Pascal (1987b), Disequilibrium analysis, *The New Palgrave*, Vol. 1, The Macmillan Press Ltd.

Deaton, A. and Muellbauer, J. (1981), Functional forms for labor supply and commodity demands with and without quantitative constraints, *Econometrica*, 49.

Henderson, John S. (1952), *Production and Consumption*, University of Alabama Studies, No. 7.

Hirshleifer, Jack (1980), *Price Theory and Applications*, Second Edition, Prentice-Hall.

Juster, F. Thomas, and Stafford, Frank P. (1991), The allocation of time: Empirical findings, behavioral models, and problems of measurement, *Journal of Economic Literature*, Vol. XXIX, No. 2.

Kooreman, Peter and Kapteyn, Arie (1985), The systems approach to household labor supply in the Netherlands, *De Economist*, Vol. 3, No. 1.

McManus, Leeds (1956), Points rationing and the consumer, *Metroeconomica*, August.

Mesa-Lago, Carmelo (1981), *The Economy of Socialist Cuba: A Two-Decade Appraisal*, University of New Mexico Press.

Neary, J.P., (1987), Rationing, *The New Palgrave*, Vol.4, The Macmillan Press Ltd.

Samuelson, Paul A. (1947), *Foundations of Economic Analysis*, Harvard University Press.

Shinkai, Yoichi (1966), A comparison of quota spending tax and points rationing, *Oxford Economic Papers*, July.

Tobin, James (1952), A survey of the theory of rationing, *Econometrica*, October.

Tobin, James and Houthakker, H. S. (1950-1951), The effects of rationing on demand elasticities, *Review of Economic Studies*.

ENVIRONMENTAL DETERIORATION AND PROTECTION IN SOCIALIST CUBA

María Dolores Espino

I.   Introduction

The extent of the ecological damage that has recently been brought to light in the former socialist bloc has given rise to serious concerns about the state of the Cuban environment. However, Cuba's report to the United Nations Conference on the Environment and Development held in Rio de Janeiro, Brazil in the summer of 1992, though admitting to some ecological problems, makes a case for the harmonious interaction between the environment and economic development in the island (Comisión Nacional de Protección del Medio Ambiente y el Uso Racional de los Recursos Naturales —COMARNA— 1991). Fidel Castro made the point explicitly (Castro 1992, p. 46) as follows:

> The radical changes generated by the Cuban Revolution have had direct benefits for the environment, by transforming living conditions and in this way creating the prerequisites so that people are not forced to act against the environment.

This paper is a preliminary attempt to assess environmental degradation in Cuba, and is divided into four parts. In the first section, the factors affecting environmental deterioration in Cuba are discussed. The second portion presents a snapshot of the present state of the Cuban environment. In the third section environmental legislation and regulation in Cuba are discussed. Finally, the last section offers some concluding remarks.

II.   Reasons for Environmental Deterioration in Cuba

No modern society has escaped environmental disruption. In socialist as well as capitalist societies, environmental deterioration occurs due two primary reasons: (1) population growth, urbanization and industrialization place increasing pressure on the environment and natural resources; and (2) society fails to incorporate the true cost of environmental resources in its production and consumption decisions.

Through time, demand for environmental resources increases, while at the same time the public good nature of these resources hinders their efficient allocation. It is not the "evil of profit motivation" that creates environmental disruption in capitalist economies, but rather the divergence between the private and the social good. In spite of the rhetoric, when dealing with environmental resources (and other public goods) the same divergences appear in socialist economies.

There are, however, some special characteristics of socialist societies that create added incentives and tendencies towards environmental deterioration (Goldman 1970). Some of these factors include:

- an emphasis on production maximization nationwide and in meeting production norms at the firm level without any consideration of cost involved;

- the non-specific nature of laws regulating the environment and the inability to create clear lines of authority and responsibilities for enforcement of these laws; and

- the absence of a free press and independent environmental groups which can bring pressure to bear on public officials.

These factors have contributed to environmental degradation in Cuba, which has been a socialist society for the past 30-some years. Cuba, however, is also a developing country and is afflicted by many of the same problems other developing nations have. Some of these factors also adversely affect the environment (World Commission on the Environment and Development 1987). They include:

- economic dependency on agricultural exports and monoculture;

- chronic external imbalances and increasing debt burden;

- the use of inefficient, inappropriate and/or obsolete technology in production and waste treatment; and

- lack of funds to implement waste treatment and for social infrastructure projects.

Additionally, in Cuba years of economic dependence and subsidies, both pre- and post-1959, have led to price distortions and the irrational utilization of resources. It is thus not surprising to find that Cuba, a poor socialist island in the Caribbean, has more than its share of environmental problems.

III. State of the Cuban Environment

Due to the lack of independent studies on Cuban ecology and natural resources, reliable data on pollution and environmental degradation is not readily available. In this section I present data available from different sources in order to get a better picture of the present state of Cuba's environment.

A. Land Resources and Use

The Cuban archipelago consists of 110,992 km² of surface area. Plains and lowlands cover about 75 percent of the surface area. Mountains extend over 21 percent of the surface, and wetlands and marshes make up the remaining 4 percent (COMARNA 1991, p. 1).

In Table 1, estimates of surface land by type of use are provided. For 1989, according to the Cuban Statistical Yearbook, 40 percent of surface land was under cultivation, 17.2 percent was utilized as pasture, and 23.7 percent was covered by forests of some type.

In the official report submitted to the United Nations Earth Summit in Brazil this past summer, Cuba admitted to some serious problems of land and soil degradation (see Table 2). It is estimated that 70 percent of all land surface, or about 7.7 miles hectares (ha.), suffered from some degree of erosion. About 1.0 million ha., or 15 percent of all agricultural land, has been affected by salinity. Acidity is also recognized as a growing concern but no estimate of area affected has been provided. The report also estimates that 2.7 million ha. of surface land suffers from inadequate drainage. To alleviate this problem Cuba has invested in the construction of 1000 Km.

Table 1. Cuba: Distribution of Surface Land by Use, 1946-1989
(In thousands of hectares)

	1946[a]	1957[b]	1957[c]	1967[d]	1970[d]	1975[d]	1980[d]	1985[d]	1989[d]
Total Area	9080.2	9054.6	9058.4	5541.4	6610.9	7908.9	8450.6	8589.2	11016.4
Cultivated	1970.4	2335.2	2036.8	2826.6	3059.9	3153.0	3399.9	3125.9	4410.4
Pastures	3897.2	3702.4	3993.2	1338.0	1320.9	1722.7	1309.6	1360.3	1889.2
Forest	1265.7	1206.0	1112.2	383.6	789.9	1731.1	2493.4	2688.5	2608.3

Sources:

a. From the 1947 Census of Agriculture.
b. From estimates made by the Consejo Nacional de Economistas 1957; cited by Arredondo, A. in *Reforma Agraria: La Experiencia Cubana.*
c. From estimates by INRA in 1963; cited by Arredondo, *op. cit.*
d. CEE, *Anuario Estadístico de Cuba*, various issues.

of drainage ditches that provides partial drainage for 32.5 thousand ha. of affected land.

Table 2. Cuba: Land and Soil Degradation

	Thousands of Hectares	% of total Land Area
Total Surface Area	11016.4	100.0
Affected by:		
Erosion	7711.5	70.0
Salinity	1000.0	0.1
Acidity	N/A	25.0
Inadequate Drainage	2700.0	N/A
Strip-Mining	11.0	--

Source: COMARNA 1991, p. 11-12.

Soil degradation in Cuba has been accelerated by the large expansion of land area under cultivation and the excessive use of fertilizers, pesticides, and irrigation. Land under cultivation has almost doubled since 1957, from 2,335.2 thousand ha. that year, to 4,410.4 thousand ha. in 1989 (see Table 1). From 1960 to 1985 there was a ten-fold increase in the application of fertilizer and a four-fold increase in the application of pesticides (Rodríguez 1987). In 1959 only 15 percent of cultivated land was under irrigation; at present, over 25 percent of all cultivated land, excluding rice, are irrigated.

Table 3. Cuba: Cultivated Land Under Irrigation, By Crop

	Under Irrigation %
Rice	95
Tobacco	62
Citrus	61
Vegetables, Tubers and Roots	43
Sugar Cane	23

Source: COMARNA 1991, p. 19.

Excessive irrigation depletes water resources faster than they can be replenished. This increases the natural salt content of water and permits salt water intrusion in areas near the coast. Irrigating with salty water is one of the main causes of soil salinity. Since 1960, the Cuban government has undertaken massive investments in irrigation systems. There are currently 200 dams and 800 micro dams in the island. Reservoir capacity stands at 9,000 million cubic meters. Around 70 percent of reservoir water use is for agricultural irrigation (COMARNA 1991, p. 9). The construction of dams undoubtedly entailed the loss of valuable agricultural land flooded by reservoirs. There is, however, no estimate of the number of hectares affected.

Finally, another economic activity that creates an adverse effect on land and soil quality is open-face or strip mining. The areas most affected by strip-mining in Cuba are Moa and Nicaro, two localities in the Eastern region of the island with substantial nickel deposits. It is estimated that 11.0 thousand ha. of surface area have been affected by strip-mining in Cuba (COMARNA 1991, p. 12).

B. Forest Resources

The 1989 Cuban Statistical Yearbook reports that forests cover 2,608.3 thousand ha. of land, or 23.7 percent of total surface area. If correct, this figure would reflect that forested areas have more than doubled since 1957. However, it is unlikely that the 1989 figures are accurate. More reasonable statistics are cited in the report presented to the Earth Summit (see Table 4). These figures indicate an increase of 4.0 percent in natural forest coverage over that existing in 1957. There is, however, reason to be concerned about Cuba's forest coverage.

Table 4. Cuba: Forest Resources

	thousand ha.	% of total land surface
Forest area	2,021.2	18.2
Natural forests	1,688.4	15.2
Plantations	332.7	3.0

Source: COMARNA 1991, p. 20.

First, a large portion of Cuban forest is very young and its survival to maturity is not yet guaranteed. Evidence suggests that Cuba experienced a significant amount of deforestation in the 1960s (see Table 1). In the first decade of the revolution, about half of Cuba's forests were destroyed. Recovery of forest coverage has been accomplished due to an aggressive reforestation effort started in the late 1970s. Presently, 110.0 thousand hectares are being replanted annually (COMARNA 1991, p. 20).

Secondly, a significant portion of one of Cuba's most valuable forest resources, the mangroves, has been damaged or lost, due to over-exploitation. Mangroves cover over 4.8 of total surface area in the island and make up 26 percent of total forest resources (COMARNA 1991, p. 9).

Finally, the current energy crisis has created an immediate demand for firewood, that is seriously threatening Cuba's forests.

C. Fresh Water Resources

Estimates of Cuba's renewable fresh water resources range between 23.9 and 34.5 km^3. Fresh water withdrawals in the island, for 1975 and the 1990s, are shown in Table 5.

Table 5. Cuba: Fresh Water Withdrawals, 1975 and 1990

	1 9 7 5	1 9 9 0
Total Withdrawal	8.10km^3	12.7km^3
Per Capita Withdrawal	868m^3	1200m^3
Withdrawal by Sector:		
Agricultural	89%	74%
Domestic	9%	12%
Industry	2%	14%

Sources: WRI 1992, p. 328; COMARNA 1991, p. 9.

In spite of high per capita water use, Cuba does not experience an over-all deficit in water due to its vast water resources. Cuba's per capita water use has been estimated as the highest in the Caribbean and Central America.

Although, at present, water availability does not constitute a serious problem in Cuba, water quality has deteriorated significantly since the 1950s. A number of failures have contributed to water degradation, with population growth and the island's rapid urbanization among the major contributors.

Although Cuba has one of the lowest rates of population growth among developing nations, population has almost doubled since 1958, from 6.5 million to 10.6 million in 1989. The 1953 census showed the Cuban population as 57 percent urban and 43 percent rural. By 1989 the urban population accounted for 72.8 percent, or 7.8 million people (CCE 1989, p. 52).

The increase in urban population has placed a strain on public services and has outstripped the ability to handle sewage and domestic waste. Only 38.7 percent of Cuba's urban population is hooked up to sewage systems (COMARNA 1991, p. 11). In the largest cities, the sewage system dates back to the 1940s and 1950s, and are in serious need of repair. In Cuba, as in much of Latin America, it is common practice to dump untreated municipal water into the nearest body of water.

Another factor contributing to water quality deterioration in the island is the increase in industrial output and the accompanied increase in industrial or hazardous waste. Although Cuba remains primarily an agricultural economy, industrial output has increased. Average annual growth rates of real industrial output for the period 1975-1981 have been estimated as low as 1.5 percent and as high as 5.3 percent (Pérez-López 1991, p. 22).

At present there is no way to estimate independently neither the total number of contaminating sources nor the type and volume of waste these sources generate. Official sources, however, acknowledge 355 point-sources of contamination in three industries: sugar, food production and basic goods (COMARNA, 1991, p. 5). The same source indicates that by 1990, some preventive measures had been implemented in 65 percent of the 355 contamination sources. From this we can conclude than in at least 124 cases, waste is still being discharged into the environment without any previous treatment.

The practice of dumping untreated industrial waste into rivers, lakes, and streams has been documented by the official Cuban press. For example, press reports on the contamination of the Almendares River in Havana cite 67 contaminating sources discharging untreated waste directly into the river or into canals, streams and drains that feed into the river (Dávalos 1985a). The waste that is discharged into the Almendares River include (Dávalos 1985a; 1985b; 1985c):

- organic waste discharge by several beer breweries, food processing plants and a poultry slaughterhouse;

- particles and solids from saw mills, an asbestos-cement plant, and marble-granite plants; and

- toxic and hazardous waste-discharges by a medical lab, textile and apparel mills, a perfume factory, a shoe polish factory, paper mills, a gas plant, and a paint factory.

In another of the capital city's rivers, the Luyanó, 41 contaminating sources have been identified (Gómez 1985b). The majority of these were identified as originating from the food processing or the sugar industry.

The excessive use of fertilizers, pesticides and herbicides in Cuban agriculture has probably also contributed to fresh water contamination in the island. The chemicals used in these products often intrude into the water supply through agriculture run or groundwater seepages.

The Cuban economy's dependency on sugar production has also proven detrimental to fresh water resources across the island. The sugar industry is a heavy user and polluter of fresh water. In an attempt to diversify industrial production, Cuba has invested in the development of industries that use sugar by-products, including alcohol distilleries, plants that produce paper, newsprint, cardboard, and particle board from bagasse, and plants that manufacture torula yeast from sugar and urea (Feuer 1987, p. 80). Over 40 by-products are currently being commercially produced in Cuba (Zimbalist and Brundenius 1989, p. 105-106). The majority of these industries have proven themselves to be polluters.

The contamination of Cuba's rivers has been aggravated by the numerous irrigation projects throughout the country. Due to the island's geography, Cuban rivers are of low flow and volume and ill-suited to carry even a small amount of waste streams. Dams, reservoirs and other irrigation works have further reduced the rivers' capacity to handle waste. In some areas, during dry season, rivers have turned into waste pools and insect breeding grounds, raising serious health concerns (Dávalos 1985a; Gómez 1985a).

D. Marine and Coastal Resources

Cuba, the largest island in the Caribbean, has about 3,755 km of coastline and claims over 362.8 thousand km^2 of sea as exclusive economic zone (WRI 1992, p. 336). Cuba's coastal waters, coral reefs, bays and estuaries are breeding grounds for a wide variety of marine life. A number of species are exploited both commercially and recreationally, including conch, oysters, lobsters, shrimp, other shellfish, and a variety of fish. Though reductions in fish catch in Cuba's coastal waters have been reported due to over-exploitation, the most serious damage to Cuba's marine resources can be attributed to contamination and destruction of habitats.

Contamination of coastal waters can be traced to urban run-off, municipal and industrial effluent discharges, agricultural run-off, and commercial shipping traffic. Sixty-two percent of Cuba's population, or over 6.6 million people, live in coastal urban agglomerations (WRI 1992, p. 336). The largest coastal urban agglomeration in Cuba is the Havana metropolitan area, which is home to 20 percent of the island's population. Coastal waters around Havana are so contaminated that swimming or other recreational activities have been prohibited or limited due to possible health hazards (Hernández 1983b; Rassi 1983; *The Miami Herald* 1992).

Rain water run-off, domestic waste and other urban run-off have been cited as major contributors to the contamination of Havana's coastal areas (Hernández 1983, Rodríguez 1991). Other major contaminating sources are untreated urban sewage and municipal waste discharges directly into the coastal waters and the industrial and agricultural wastes which reach the coast through the capital's contaminated rivers.

Similar patterns of contamination have been reported for other coastal areas of the country (Dávalos 1984a; 1984b). Additionally, in some areas, sedimentation from soil erosion, agricultural run-off and mining waste is also a major source of contamination.

Most of the country's bays are suffering from a serious degree of contamination. The majority of Cuba's bays are enclosed, with limited water flow to help in self-purification. Havana Bay and Nipe Bay in Eastern Cuba are reported eutrophic, and others are on the way to eutrophication (Hernández 1983a; Dávalos 1985d). A similar fate is feared for Cuba's enclosed estuaries and intercoastal waters.

Cuba's bays are also affected by hydrocarbon contamination, traceable to commercial shipping traffic and spills from petroleum refineries. In the late 1980s, an annual average of 6.0 million metric tons of crude petroleum, 4.3 million metric tons of petroleum products and 15.0 metric tons of dry cargo were loaded and unloaded through Cuba's ports (WRI 1992, p 336). A larger source of hydrocarbon contamination is the oil refineries currently operating in Cuba. These oil refineries are located in Havana, Santiago de Cuba, Cabaiguán and Cienfuegos (Oro 1992, p. 58). In Havana Bay during 1981-1985, 33 tons of hydrocarbons per day were discharged into the bay, with the oil refinery being the principal contaminating source (Rodríguez 1991). Other sources of hydrocarbon contamination in Havana Bay are a natural gas plant and run-off from gasoline stations located near the bay. Through the use of more modern equipment at the refinery and a more efficient treatment system in the gas plant, hydrocarbon discharges into the bay have reportedly been reduced by 60 percent (Rodríguez 1991).

Aside from contamination, Cuba's marine resources have also been damaged by outright destruction of habitats. Mangroves, sand-dunes, sea-marshes, and coral reefs form important habitats that serve as breeding grounds for the island's marine life. Though little documentation is available about damage to marine habitats in Cuba, some current practices and economic trends point to serious problems in this area.

Mangrove swamps, one of Cuba's most important coastal resources, have been disappearing at an alarming rate (Dávalos 1984b, COMARNA 1991, Peláez 1992). Contamination has damaged some areas, but most destruction is attributable to the clearing of coastal areas for building projects and the cutting down of mangroves for lumber and firewood.

The mangrove swamps, estuaries and sea marshes have also been harmed by the extensive damming of Cuba's rivers. Dams are known to have an adverse effect on the ecology of marine habitats. They reduce the release of sediment and nutrients into productive estuaries, altering the ecological system and jeopardizing marine life (Dixon et. al. 1989). Dams and other irrigation projects also reduce the flow of fresh water into estuaries. Reductions in fresh water flows in tropical regions are known to raise salinity level in mangroves and marshes, damaging these resources and reducing their productivity (IUCN, 1983). Reduced fish catch due to contamination and ecological damage have been reported in the Cuban press (Hernández 1983; Dávalos 1984d; 1985a; 1985b.)

Another possible danger to coastal habitats is the increasing practice of aquaculture. The annual average aquaculture production in Cuba during 1987-1989 was about 17.5 thousand metric tons (WRI 1992, p. 340). Aquaculture ponds intrude and destroy natural habitats, reducing biodiversity.

The preservation and protection of marine and coastal resources took a new economic urgency in the 1980s as Cuba started promoting international tourism. In 1991, 424,000 foreigners vacationed on the island. International tourists are attracted to Cuba by its beaches and other coastal amenities. The industry, however, places added stress on the island's coastal ecology.

To accommodate the increasing number of tourists, Cuba has embarked on an ambitious plan of hotel and resort development. Many of these developments are taking place in sensitive coastal areas, including barrier islands and keys (Espino 1992, p. 208-209). Though government regulation restricts new construction of tourist facilities to a distance of 80 to 120 meters beyond sand-dunes, added density and human activity will undoubtedly take their toll on the fragile ecological systems.

One special concern is the ecological impact of "*pedraplenes*" or causeways, which are being built to bridge the barrier islands to the mainland and to one another. The building of these causeways will further reduce water flow in the intracoastal waters, exacerbating contamination and destroying coastal and marine habitats.

E. Air Resources

Cuba's carbon dioxide (CO_2) emissions from industrial processes in 1989 stood at 3.44 million metric tons per capita. This is one of the highest per capita emission levels among developing nations. In the Caribbean, only Barbados and Trinidad-Tobago, an oil producing and refining state, have emission levels higher than Cuba's. Among Latin American countries, only Mexico, Venezuela and Argentina have per capita levels close to Cuba's (WRI 1992, p. 346).

In spite high per capita (CO_2) emissions from industrial processes, Cuba does not have a serious air pollution problem. Low per capita use of automobiles and the island's geography —long and narrow— keeps overall air pollution levels low. Some localized problems, however, are evident. One of Cuba's largest and dirtiest air polluting industries is cement manufacturing. Cement manufacturing has also been one of Cuba's fastest growing industries. In 1989, Cuba produced 3.8 million tons of cement, up from the 742,000 tons produced in 1958 (COMARNA 1992, p. 10). During 1989, the cement manufacturing industry emitted 1.8 million metric tons of CO_2 into the atmosphere (WRI 1992, p. 346).

A number of other industries also contribute to air quality deterioration in Cuba. Among these are the chemical industry, the metal processing industry and other metal smelting industries (Oro 1992).

Other harmful emissions come from land clearing. These emissions are estimated at 890,000 metric tons annually. Methane emissions from a number of sources are estimated at about 310,000 metric tons annually (WRI 1992, p. 348).

F. Wildlife and Habitats

Cuba has greater biodiversity in plant and animal life than any other island in the Caribbean. Currently, there exist in Cuba 39 species of mammals, 286 of birds, 100 of reptiles, and 40 of amphibians. Seven thousand flora taxa also exist on the island. The number of threatened animal species, and the percentage of species which are endemic, are shown in Table 6 below.

Table 6. Cuba: Wildlife, Threatened and Endemic Species

	# of Species	# of Threatened Species	% Endemics
Mammals	39	2	36
Birds	286	15	22
Reptiles	100	4	82
Amphibians	40	N/A	N/A

Source: WRI 1992, p. 304.

As expected, due to Cuba's insular nature, invertebrates represent the largest number of animal species and are almost entirely endemic. The number of insect species is not shown, but insects in Cuba are reported to be up to 90 percent endemic (COMARNA 1991, p. 9).

On the other hand, less than half of Cuba's flora taxa are endemic. Some exotic flora in Cuba have presented historical ecological problems. Especially troublesome has been the proliferation on the island of *marabú*, a thorny exotic, first introduced to control cattle grazing. The 1945 agricultural census reported that 3.0 percent of the island's terrain was covered by *marabú*. By 1957, *marabú* coverage had resided to .8 percent of total terrain (Arredondo 1969, p. 49). Though in the more recent land surveys no data is given on marabú coverage, this exotic continues to proliferate.

Cuba has a number of important ecological systems and habitats such as wetlands, mangroves, rain forests and coral reefs. Law No. 33 passed in 1981, provided for the establishment of a national system of protected areas (*Gaceta Oficial* 1983). Currently 29 sites, covering 714,000 hectares of land, are protected under this national system and meet specifications set forth by the International Union for the Conservation of Nature and Natural Resources (IUCN). Eighteen of these sites fall under the IUCN category of totally protected areas, while 11 are only partially protected. Totally protected areas are maintained in a natural state. Although no extractive activity is permitted in totally protected areas educational and recreational use is allowed. In partially productive areas, restricted mining and other commercial activity is allowed (WRI 1992, p. 310).

The percentage of Cuba's land protected under IUCN specifications is 6.4 percent. In the Central America and the Caribbean region, only Costa Rica and Panamá protect a greater percentage of land area.

Other protected areas in Cuba include 227,000 hectares of marine and coastal habitats in 6 different sites and 4 internationally-protected biosphere reserves which encompass 324,000 hectares (WRI 1992). Additionally, the Cuban national system of protected areas includes 35 protected sites which do not meet IUCN specifications (COMARNA 1991, p. 20; WRI 1992, p. 298).

G. Energy Resources

Cuba's primary energy resources are very limited. There are no significant coal reserves; small amounts of oil are produced, but although exploration has intensified in recent years, current reserves remain small. Cuba's rivers are not well-suited for hydroelectric production, and only small amounts of hydroelectric energy is generated. The only source of primary energy produced in Cuba in significant quantities is baggase, a by-product of the sugar industry, which is consumed almost entirely by the same industry. Data on total production and consumption of commercial energy in Cuba is shown in Table 7 below.

Table 7. Cuba: Production and Consumption of Commercial Energy, 1987 and 1989

	Production	Consumption	Per Capita Consumption	% of Consumption
	In thousand barrels of oil equivalent	in thousand barrels of oil equivalent	in barrels of oil equivalent	From imports
1987	6,372.6	69,608.4	6.86	91.0
1989	5,228.8	76,961.4	7.35	93.0

Sources: WRI 1990, p. 316; WRI 1992, p. 314-316.

Consumption of commercial energy in Cuba greatly outstrips production. In 1987, 91 percent of all commercial energy consumed came from imported sources. In 1989, the dependence on imported energy sources increased to 93 percent.

Consumption of energy in Cuba has been stimulated by low oil prices subsidized by the Soviets. Over 74 percent of all energy consumption in Cuba comes from hydrocarbons, primarily imported oil. The existence of cheap Soviet oil promoted investment in energy-intensive industries and the construction of low energy-efficient plants. Over 41 percent of total energy consumption in Cuba in 1989 was by the industrial sector; the transportation sector accounted for 23 percent of energy consumption, the residential sector for 14 percent, and the agricultural sector for 4 percent (COMARNA 1991, p. 10, Pérez-López 1992, p. 233-34; WRI 1992, p. 316).

Although since the mid-1980s Cuba has promoted a national energy conservation plan, until 1988 increases in energy consumption were outstripping increases in national income (Pérez-López, 1992, p. 235). Sharp reductions in oil imports and the elimination of oil price subsidies has forced Cuba to conserve energy. In the last couple of years, energy consumption rates have fallen more sharply than national income (COMARNA 1991, p. 10).

An important aspect of the Cuban energy program involves the promotion of alternative energy sources. Although most of these are environmentally sound renewable energy sources, a number of projects bring with them added environmental risk. Some of the riskier projects include:

- promotion of peat burning for fuel and fire wood, which threaten the ecosystem of Cuba's wetlands.

- the projected construction of a hydroelectric complex on the Toa river in Eastern Cuba, one of the island's most pristine areas.

- the Cuban nuclear program, especially the Jaraguá nuclear complex near Cienfuegos.

IV. Environmental Regulation in Cuba

The principle of environmental protection in socialist Cuba is established in Article 27 of the Cuban Constitution adopted in 1976. Article 27 reads (de la Cuesta 1976):

> To ensure the well-being of citizens, the state and society are the protectors of nature. It falls within the jurisdiction of the legally qualified agencies, and of each and every citizen, to watch over the cleanliness of the water and of the air and to protect the soil, the flora and the fauna.

In 1981, the National Assembly enacted Law No. 33, titled "On the Protection of the Environment and the Rational Use of Natural Resources" (*Gaceta Oficial*, 1981). Law No. 33, which is broad and general in nature, constitutes the basis for all environmental regulation in Cuba today. It consists of four chapters. In the first chapter, general principles are set forth, and include:

- the protection of the environment is the responsibility of the state, society and individuals;

- the environment and natural resources are the common property of society;

- relationships with the environment are based on the principle of social ownership of the means of production and on the principle of planning of social and economic development; and

- all funds and financial resources for environmental protection are to be assigned through the State's Plan for Economic and Social Development.

The second chapter addresses the different spheres of the environment. The spheres identified are water, land, mineral resources, marine resources, flora and fauna, air, food resources, solid waste, and tourism resources. In this chapter, most forms of environmental degradation are prohibited outright and the enhancement of natural resources is mandated. The law also authorizes the Council of Ministers to establish a system of protected areas and calls for the implementation of the best available technology for pollution control in all future investment projects.

In the third chapter, Law No. 33 establishes the formation of the "National System for the Protection of the Environment and the Rational Use of Natural Resources" and calls for the harmonious participation in this system of governmental agencies and entities, their dependencies and corporations, political organizations, mass organizations and citizens in general. The Council of Ministers is assigned the task of formulating norms to regulate environmental protection.

Finally, in the fourth chapter, the Council of Ministers is given authority to enforce environmental laws and norms. The law also sets broad guidelines for the administration of environmental regulations and how fees for violations should levied and collected.

The agency responsible for coordinating regulations and enforcement of environmental protection is the Comisión Nacional de Protección del Medio Ambiente y el Uso Racional de los Recursos Naturales. (COMARNA). Founded in 1977, COMARNA consists of representatives of 21 of the State's central administrative agencies, the Presidents of the fourteen provincial environmental commissions and representatives of mass organizations. The state agencies represented are those with jurisdiction over the different environmental spheres and contaminating sources. (COMARNA 1991, p. 14). COMARNA, which reports to the Council of Ministers, has the following tasks: (1) to propose environmental policy and coordinate environmental policy; (2) to serve as a watchdog over the national environment; (3) to promote environmental education; and (4) to conduct scientific studies and act as technical advisor in environmental matters.

The fourteen provincial commissions, along with a number of municipal commissions, have been functioning since 1980. These commissions are presided over by a member of the executive of the local People's Power (*Poder Popular*) and also include representatives from governmental agencies and mass organizations. The responsibility of enforcing environmental regulations falls mainly on these local commissions.

Although the principle of environmental protection is rooted in the Cuban Constitution, the non-specific nature of Cuba's environmental laws make them hard to enforce. The problem is aggravated by unclear lines of authority, and the uncertainty of who is to be held responsible for environmental damage. The quantitative production incentives in Cuba's economic system, the lack of financial resources and the absence of an independent regulation and enforcement agency, add to the problem. Conflicts of interests often arise, with those responsible for overseeing and enforcing environmental regulations also being responsible for the production goals to be met.

Examples of the inadequacy of environmental enforcement in Cuba are given by the official Cuban press (Dávalos 1984a, 1984b, 1985a, 1985b; Gómez 1985a, 1985b). In the early 1980s, with the help of the United Nations' Environment Program (UNEP), plans for the decontamination and restoration of Havana Bay were developed. The plan called for a reduction of waste discharges into the bay both from direct and indirect sources. The Cuban entity responsible for the implementation of the plan was the provincial COMARNA in the City of Havana. The local COMARNA was presided by Oscar Fernández Mell, then president of Havana's *Poder Popular*. Other members of the Commission were representatives of various industrial ministries, the very same ministries which were responsible for industrial production of the contaminating firms.

In a series of meetings widely covered in the Cuban press, Fernández Mell met with representatives of the polluting firms. His primary resource seems to have been persuasion. He stressed the gravity of the problem, challenging the firms to think in terms of the well-being of the nation, making the point that what constitutes a saving for the firm might turn into a social cost somewhere else along the line. Fernández Mell, however, also recognized the lack of resources and the need to continue production, but exhorted firm officials to use low-cost solutions whenever possible. He pointed to the fact that there were cases where treatment facilities existed since before the revolution and were not being utilized.

It is not surprising that the plan to decontaminate Havana Bay failed. Recent reports conclude that there has been no significant reduction in the amount of domestic and industrial waste discharge into Havana Bay (Rodríguez, 1991).

V.   Concluding Remarks

The dissolution of the socialist bloc and the disappearance of Soviet subsidies has forced Cuba to face some long-ignored economic realities. It has been forced to implement a harsh economic adjustment plan and to move toward are more mixed economy. Both of these actions have had, and will continue to have, an environmental impact on the island.

The Cuban economic adjustment plan, the "Special Period in Time of Peace," has had both positive and negative impacts on the environment. On the positive side, there has been a drastic reduction in the import and use of chemical fertilizers, pesticides, and herbicides. Agricultural production in Cuba has had to rely more on natural and labor resources.

The reduction in imported intermediate inputs has also cause decreased industrial production which, though devastating for the economy, has reduced industrial waste and pollution. All sectors of the economy have been impacted by the reduction in oil and forced energy conservation. Finally, the generalized scarcity prevailing in the economy has promoted greater recycling and reuse of goods and commodities.

On the other hand, the current economic crisis has also created new incentives for environmental disruption. Short-run economic performance is being given highest priority, even if at times it conflicts with environmental goals. Potentially risky for the environment are tourism development, the accelerated development of the biotechnology industry, and the increase in sugar production, which are being promoted to ease the hard currency crunch.

Other adverse consequences of the Special Period are the increasing demand for firewood brought about by the energy crisis, which seriously threatens Cuba's forests. Fish and wildlife are also being affected by over-exploitation, both sanctioned and unsanctioned by the authorities. Finally, a number of environmental investment projects have fallen victim to economic austerity and lack of funds. Among these is the much-needed new sewage system for the City of Havana.

The transition toward a market economy will not by itself bring environmental relief to Cuba. Market economies have not prevented environmental disruption and the state of the environment in some developing nations following market principles is arguably as bad or worse than that of Cuba.

As sectors of the Cuban economy open up to market forces, a number of concerns arise. First, in the absence of a strong legal system, specific legislation and an independent environmental regulatory system, there will be no incentives for environmental costs to be taken into consideration in production and consumption decisions. Second, in the absence of a comprehensive tax structure, the privatization of Cuba's most productive and lucrative industries will mean less resources for government and less funds for environmental protection. This much is evident from the current experience in the former Soviet Union and Eastern Europe (French 1990, Pryde 1991).

The road to environmental recovery in Cuba is long and costly. In the foreseeable future, with or without a market economy, Cuba will remain a poor country. This will make the choice between short-run economic gains and environmental preservation an especially painful one.

Bibliography

Arredondo, Alberto. *Reforma agraria: la experiencia cubana.* Puerto Rico: Editorial San Juan, 1969.

Castro, Fidel. *Tomorrow is Too Late.* Melbourne, Australia: Ocean Press, 1992.

Comité Estatal de Estadísticas (CEE). *Anuario estadístico.* Various issues.

COMARNA. *Informe Nacional a la Conferencia de Naciones Unidas Sobre Medio Ambiente y Desarrollo, Brasil 1992: Resumen Ejecutivo.* Habana, Cuba: 1991.

Dávalos, Fernando. "En tres años la Bahía de Nipe será esteril, si no se detiene la contaminación." *Granma*, November 9, 1984a.

_____. "Ostión Cero", Parts I-VI. *Granma*, December 13-20, 1984b.

_____. "Emprende Ciudad de la Habana el saneamiento del Rio Almendares." *Granma*, April 5, 1985a.

_____. "Urge resolver los vertimientos nocivos de fabricas de la industrial básica al Almendares." *Granma*, May 16, 1985b.

_____. "Comprométense centros de la industria ligera y la salud a resolver de inmediato problemas que dañan al Río Almendares." *Granma*, May 22, 1985c.

_____. "Grave peligro amenaza la vida marina en la Bahía de Nipe, Holguín." *Granma*, July 4, 1985d.

Dixon, John A., Lee M. Talbot, and Guy J.M. LeMorge. *Dams and the Environment: Considerations in World Bank Projects.* Washington, D.C.: The World Bank, 1989.

Espino, María Dolores, "International Tourism in Cuba: An Economic Development Strategy? in *Cuba in Transition.* Association for the Study of the Cuban Economy Conference Proceedings. Miami: Florida International University, 1992.

Feuer, Carl Henry. "The Cuban Sugar Industry, 1981-85." A. Zimbalist, ed. *Cuba's Economy Towards The 1990s.* Boulder, Colorado: Lynne Rienner Publishers, 1987.

French, Hilary F. *Green Revolutions: Environmental Reconstruction in Eastern Europe and the Soviet Union.* Worldwatch Paper 99. Washington: World Watch Institute, 1990.

Gaceta Oficial de la República de Cuba. *Ley No. 33: De protección del medio ambiente y del uso racional de los recursos naturales.* February 12, 1981.

Goldman, Marshall I. "The Convergence of Environmental Disruption," *Science* Vol. 170, 1970.

Gómez, Orlando. "No se percibe todavía el inicio de la descontaminación del Río Almendares." *Granma*, June 3, 1985a.

_____. "Se inició la batalla por la descontaminación del Rio Luyanó; mejora la situación del Almendares." *Granma*, December 17, 1985b.

Hernández, Gregorio. "Visita de trabajo: Descontaminación." *Bohemia*, August 8, 1983a.

_____. "Contaminación marina: Afectaciones y soluciones en el litoral habanero." *Bohemia*, August 25, 1983b.

International Union for the Conservation of Nature and Natural Resources (IUCN). "Global Status of Mangrove Ecosystems." *The Environmentalist*, Vol 3, Supplement 3, 1983.

Peláez, Orfilio. "Mangroves SOS." *Granma International*, September 13, 1992.

Pérez-López, Jorge F. "Bringing the Cuban Economy into Focus: Conceptual and Empirical Challenges." *Latin American Research Review*, Vol. 26 No. 3, 1991.

_____. "Cuba's Transition to Market-Based Energy Prices." *Cuba in Transition*. Association for the Study of the Cuban Economy Conference Proceedings. Miami: Florida International University, 1992.

Pryde, Philip R. *Environmental Management in the Soviet Union*. Cambridge: Cambridge University Press, 1991.

Oro, José R. *The Poisoning of Paradise: Environmental Pollution in the Republic of Cuba*. Miami: Open Road Press, 1992.

Rassi, Reynold. "Alerta sobre el uso indebido del área total del Malecón por parte de los bañistas." *Granma*, July 7, 1983.

Rodríguez, José Luis. "Agricultural Policy and Development in Cuba." A. Zimbalist, ed. *Cuba's Economy Towards the 1990s*. Boulder, Colorado: Lynne Rienner Publishers, 1987.

Rodríguez, Raimundo. "Bahía de la Habana: La batalla contra la contaminación." *Granma International*, June 30, 1991.

The Miami Herald. "In the Americas: Cuba." August 4, 1992, p. 12A.

World Commission on Environment and Development. *Our Common Future*. Oxford: Oxford University Press, 1987.

World Resources Institute. *World Resources: 1990-91*. Oxford: Oxford University Press, 1990.

_____. *World Resources: 1992-93*. Oxford: Oxford University Press, 1992.

Zimbalist, Andrew and Claus Brundenius. *The Cuban Economy: Measurement and Analysis of Socialist Performance*. Baltimore: The Johns Hopkins University Press, 1989.

POLÍTICA AGRÍCOLA A MEDIANO Y LARGO PLAZOS PARA CUBA

PRINCIPALES OBJETIVOS

Raúl Fernández

En la reunión anual de la Association for the Study of the Cuban Economy celebrada en agosto de 1991, tuvimos el privilegio de presentarles unas "Notas sobre una Estrategia Agropecuaria para Cuba", las cuales, por limitaciones de tiempo, quedaron circunscritas al corto plazo. Hoy, una nueva invitación que mucho agradezco a nuestro presidente, Roger R. Betancourt, me da la oportunidad de completar esa tarea, extendiendo aquellas Notas al mediano y largo plazos. Para empezar, hagamos un brevísimo recuento de los aspectos más importantes de lo dicho hace un año.

Entonces sugerimos que entre las principales responsabilidades inmediatas del Gobierno que suceda al actual régimen, destacarían el mantenimiento de la paz y el orden y la reactivación de la economía. Dentro de ese contexto señalamos la importancia, así como los medios de incrementar rápidamente la producción de alimentos. Para ello propusimos la privatización inmediata de las actividades de provisión de insumos agrícolas y de la comercialización de la producción y el establecimiento de mecanismos de crédito. Indicamos que el destino de la tierra en las grandes fincas estatales correspondería resolverlo al pueblo de Cuba, oportunamente, mediante la celebración de una asamblea constituyente. En ese período de transición el pequeño agricultor que aún se mantiene independiente, recibiría un decidido apoyo del Estado....Hasta aquí una apretada síntesis de lo dicho el año pasado. Ahora, pasemos a la parte substantiva de nuestro trabajo de hoy.

Cuba se asomará a un renacer democrático en un escenario de cambios de gran significación. La industria azucarera, que origina alrededor del 75% de los ingresos por exportaciones[1] y que por siglos fue la columna vertebral de la economía isleña, hoy afronta una demanda contraída y una oferta donde compiten los más variados productores. El tabaco, pierde batalla tras batalla en la preferencia de los consumidores y parece estar condenado a una reducción progresiva de su importancia económica. Aún la carne de res muestra reducciones significativas en el consumo per cápita en los principales mercados. Todos esos factores se acumulan negativamente en la balanza comercial. En el lado positivo se confirma el potencial turístico de Cuba, que ya sostenía una industria prometedora en 1959. Además, la capacidad de Cuba de producir vegetales de invierno para los mercados del norte, permite alentar esperanzas de que estos podrían constituir un renglón más importante en el futuro de lo que ya fueron en el pasado. También, la exportación de cítricos y la pesca parecen ser prometedoras. Pero Cuba tendrá que innovar si quiere alcanzar niveles de vida satisfactorios. Al descenso de algunos de los renglones tradicionales como el azúcar y el tabaco, deberemos responder con creatividad.

Una de las más importantes tareas que habrá de afrontar una Cuba democrática es el ordenamiento de la propiedad rural. Con la excepción de alrededor del 16% de la tierra arable, que había permanecido en el sector privado por lo menos hasta 1987, el resto es estatal y comprende unos 417 latifundios con un promedio de 14,260 ha cada uno, los que ocupan un total de 5,946,420 ha; además se encuentran las "cooperativas de producción" con 1,019,200 ha.[2] Cada una de estas

---

[1]"International Sugar and Sweetener Report", *F. O. Lichts*, Vol. 123 No. 20, 21 June 1991, Ratzeburger, Germany, p. 56.

Andrew Zimbalist and Claus Brundenius, *The Cuban Economy* (Baltimore: The Johns Hopkins University Press, 1989), p. 113.

categorías debería recibir un tratamiento diferente. A la parte de las tierras en manos privadas que no estén sujetas a conflictos debería dársele todo el reconocimiento y apoyo posibles a fin de estimular la producción y simplificar el proceso de saneamiento de la propiedad. Las cooperativas estarían sujetas al examen de las condiciones particulares de cada una. De no haber serios conflictos por la posesión y la propiedad de los bienes, se adelantaría en todo lo posible la privatización de las cooperativas. Las decisiones sobre las fincas estatales, que ocupan más de la mitad del territorio nacional, deberían ser adoptadas por el pueblo de Cuba mediante los mecanismos apropiados, como por ejemplo una asamblea constituyente. Lo que a nuestro juicio se plantea como cuestión fundamental con respecto a las tierras confiscadas por el régimen comunista es si es posible y deseable reconstituir la situación de tenencia de la tierra que existía en 1959. Para evaluar esta situación, basémosnos en los datos del Censo Agrícola de 1946, los únicos disponibles al respecto. De acuerdo con dicho Censo, las fincas mayores de 100 ha (equivalentes a 7.45 caballerías) constituían el 8% del número total de fincas pero ocupaban el 71% del área. En el otro extremo, las fincas pequeñas, de hasta 99.9 ha representaban el 92 % del número de fincas pero ocupaban sólo el 29 % del área. Dicho de otra manera, la finca promedio de los pequeños agricultores ocupaba 18 ha mientras la finca promedio de los grandes productores ocupaba 505 ha, o sea, era 28 veces más grande.

Aún cuando sea posible, ¿conviene al futuro de la democracia cubana, restablecer el estado de la tenencia de la tierra que describe el Censo Agrícola? ¿No sería más conveniente devolver a los dueños parte de las propiedades y compensar el resto con bonos emitidos al efecto, mientras la parte no devuelta se destina a una distribución más equitativa entre campesinos que califiquen? ¿Tendría facultades un gobierno provisional para disponer de la inmensa riqueza agrícola en poder del Estado, o debería reservarse tal cosa a lo que dictamine una asamblea constituyente y un gobierno elegido por el pueblo? ¿Es posible arribar a decisiones jurídicamente bien fundadas, con la celeridad que se requiere para que la producción agrícola no descienda aún más, considerando que han transcurrido más de tres décadas de las confiscaciones y se ha producido toda clase de situaciones con respecto a los dueños originales y sus herederos? Sabiendo que las empresas inactivas se deterioran rápidamente, ¿es razonable crear situaciones inciertas en cuanto al control de las fincas en litigio y provocar así su parálisis? ¿Sería aceptable ver al pueblo careciendo de alimentos al lado de grandes fincas improductivas o con baja producción, en espera de que se resuelvan en los tribunales pleitos interminables entre los que se atribuyen el derecho de propiedad? En el caso de devolver la totalidad de la tierra confiscada a sus dueños ¿debe exigírseles que pongan en producción inmediata sus fincas? ¿Debería el Estado prestarles recursos para esos fines? ¿Debe quedar condicionada la propiedad de la tierra al uso racional del suelo y del agua?

Nosotros no quisiéramos improvisar respuestas a esas preguntas. Creemos, eso sí, que sólo el pueblo de Cuba, por procedimientos aceptables, es quien tiene la autoridad para tomar las decisiones que esas preguntas sugieren. Cuba ha vivido una penosa tragedia durante más de tres décadas, las consecuencias de la cual podrían afectar por muchos años el futuro de la nación. Se han perdido vidas que jamás se recuperarán. Años han pasado en cárceles abominables, años que nadie podrá devolver. Ante ese cuadro complejo pensamos que las mejores credenciales que nuestra generación puede mostrar a quienes nos sucedan, es que de la inmensa tragedia de la nación y de las limitadas ventajas que el destino puso a nuestro alcance, supimos sacar para Cuba el mejor provecho. Dejemos aquí la cuestión de la tenencia de la tierra y pasemos a otros asuntos también importantes.

La producción agrícola requerirá el apoyo del crédito. Independientemente de los arreglos provisionales que se hagan para solventar las necesidades financieras inmediatas de la agricultura cubana, el sistema de crédito que en definitiva se establezca, debería satisfacer determinados requisitos. Permítaseme enumerar los requisitos que recomendamos, los que son el producto de observaciones personales y de consultas hechas, durante un período prolongado, con diversos expertos en varios países, y que fueron validados, directa o indirectamente, por estudios específicos. Nótese que sus alcances van más allá del crédito, para adentrarse en aspectos de economía agrícola y sociología rural. Esto nos parece apropiado porque el crédito agrícola no es una actividad independiente, sino por lo contrario depende de múltiples factores. Por ello recomendamos que lo que sigue se tenga en cuenta como parte de nuestras sugerencias, aplicables, en lo pertinente, tanto al crédito como a los objetivos que deben tratar de lograrse en el sector agrícola. Por supuesto, la legislación que en 1950 creó al Banco de Fomento Agrícola e Industrial de Cuba (BANFAIC), contiene numerosas disposiciones que podrían servir de orientación a los nuevos legisladores de mañana. Sin más preámbulo, el sistema de crédito agrícola debería:

(a) Trabajar dentro del marco del plan nacional de desarrollo y ayudar eficazmente a alcanzar las metas nacionales.

(b) Conducir sus operaciones con pleno reconocimiento de la necesidad de promover el uso racional de los recursos naturales.

(c) Adaptar sus operaciones a las necesidades y características de los agricultores, en la medida en que éstos lleven a cabo actividades sanas desde los puntos de vista económico y ambiental, especialmente considerando la aptitud de los suelos para el tipo de producción propuesta.

(d) Tener la capacidad de atraer ahorros, con especial énfasis en aquellos generados en el medio rural.

(e) Poder satisfacer completamente toda la demanda sana de crédito generada por agricultores bien establecidos, así como tener la capacidad de ayudar, a los agricultores economicamente marginales, a desarrollar plenamente su potencial.

(f) Recibir los recursos necesarios para desempeñar sus funciones sin interrupción.

(g) Mantener costos operativos (incluyendo las pérdidas normales debidas a créditos malos), en un nivel comparable con los ingresos ordinarios del sistema. Dentro de este principio general, es aceptable la posibilidad de operar programas con pérdidas temporales debidas a gastos iniciales, extraordinarios o de emergencia.

(h) Situar las instalaciones donde se toman las decisiones tan cerca como sea posible de los deudores, y promover la participación de éstos en el proceso de adopción de dichas decisiones.

(i) Aprovechar todos los conocimientos, equipos y tecnologías disponibles para proveer un servicio sencillo, rápido, accesible y eficiente, con los costos operativos más bajos posibles. A este fin, se deben explorar diferentes formas de organización de los agricultores, así como su clasificación con vista a reducir al mínimo la supervisión de los buenos clientes y estimular a otros a mejorar el cumplimiento de sus obligaciones con el incentivo de disfrutar un tratamiento preferencial.

(j) Establecer tasas de interés realistas, para las operaciones activas y para las pasivas. Al respecto, se debe evitar tanto el subsidio de los intereses como cargar tasas excesivas para cubrir indebidamente altos costos operativos o mala administración. Como regla general, las tasas de interés deberían poder cubrir los gastos de operación normales y la inflación, si existe, y además proveer recursos para acumular reservas razonables y pagar una compensación adecuada por el uso del capital.

(k) Estar protegido contra influencias malsanas de grupos políticos o de intereses especiales. Al respecto, el sistema de crédito agrícola debería establecerse en un marco legal, institucional y financiero compatible con el mantenimiento de una alta administración y personal que sean honestos, capaces, estables, independientes, bien seleccionados, dedicados y competitivamente remunerados. Las políticas administrativas deben promover el elevamiento permanente de la capacidad del personal.

(l) Tener una organización con funciones y responsabilidades bien definidas y con reglamentaciones claras y simples.

(m) Estar sujeto a frecuentes y periódicas inspecciones de auditores independientes, además de las inspecciones que realicen sus propios auditores internos.

Debemos ahora referirnos a otra cuestión que aunque no es de naturaleza agrícola, influye en la agricultura y en toda la economía cubana. Se trata del hecho de que Cuba ha sido y es dependiente, en gran medida, del petróleo importado como fuente de energía. En 1988 y 1989 Cuba importó de la ex-URSS petróleo y sus productos por valor de 1054.6 y 970.3 millones de rublos respectivamente, los que calculados a una tasa no comercial de 0.612 y 0.633 rublos por dólar arrojan importaciones por valor de 1723 y 1533 millones de dólares respectivamente.[3] Hoy, los estragos producidos por la reducción reciente de los suministros de Rusia, han puesto en evidencia, cuan vulnerable es la economía cubana a la disponibilidad del llamado oro negro. Creemos, sin embargo, que si bien es difícil encontrar una solución total a este problema, ya existen posibilidades de atenuarlo significativamente como veremos enseguida.

Cuando señalamos las posibles restricciones a las exportaciones de azúcar y tabaco y sus efectos en la balanza comercial, no debemos olvidar que ésta tiene dos platillos: uno correspondiente a las exportaciones y otro a las importaciones. La sustitución parcial del petróleo por otro tipo de energía podría reducir el peso en el platillo de las importaciones. Ello permitiría mejorar la balanza comercial. Ahora bien, en relación con la situación del petróleo debemos registrar el hecho de que al menos una compañía francesa y otra canadiense se encuentran en el proceso de realizar exploraciones en Cuba[4]. No obstante esa información, cuyos resultados finales no podemos predecir, parecería prudente enfocar el problema del abastecimiento de petróleo a Cuba en base a los datos conocidos.

El medio rural podría ser el escenario de un esfuerzo destinado a reducir nuestra dependencia del petróleo, y mejorar la calidad de vida en los campos, mediante el aprovechamiento de la energía del sol, de la energía del viento y de la biomasa, especialmente del alcohol. ¿Cuánto bienestar y economía podrían disfrutar nuestros agricultores y campesinos del uso de refrigeradores, ventiladores e iluminación alimentados por la electricidad fotovoltaica derivada de la energía solar?

---

[3]"Cuba, Dominican Republic, Haiti, Puerto Rico", *The Economist Inteligence Unit*, Country Report No. 4, 1991, October 29, 1991, London, Appendix 3.

[4]"Cuba, Dominican Republic, Haiti, Puerto Rico", *The Economist Intelligence Unit*, Country Report No. 2 1992, June 8, 1992, London, p. 17.

El rápido descenso del costo de la electricidad fotovoltaica de $60 por kilowatt-hora en 1970 a $1 en 1980 y a entre 20 y 30 centavos en 1990[5], permite abrigar esperanzas de que se acerca el momento en que este tipo de electricidad sea ampliamente competitivo. Numerosos países alrededor del mundo, adelantan programas para sacar provecho de esta fuente inagotable de energía. Cuba no debe quedarse detrás en esta carrera.

Vivimos en una época donde los inventos y las innovaciones se suceden con tal rapidez que tanto las personas como las instituciones y las propias naciones se ven constantemente sometidas al reto de actualizarse o quedar rezagadas. Los países que generan las tecnologías innovadoras son usualmente los que cuentan con más recursos y poseen mas rica tradición científica. Cuba no podría competir extensamente en ese campo en un futuro predecible, pero sí puede y debe organizarse para aprovechar, mediante la debida adaptación, muchos de los nuevos descubrimientos científicos e innovaciones tecnológicas. Prestigiosos centros internacionales y nacionales de investigación agrícola, así como departamentos agropecuarios de poderosas empresas privadas, deberían ser objeto de consulta sistemática a fin de desarrollar, en beneficio de Cuba, los mecanismos adecuados de cooperación técnica. Cuba, por su parte, deberá adiestrar y preparar a sus agricultores y a sus técnicos para la gran tarea nacional de adaptar y trasplantar a la Isla lo mejor de la tecnología mundial. A esos fines deberá crear y mantener los mecanismos institucionales apropiados. Esta idea no constituye novedad alguna. Entre las naciones más avanzadas hoy, se encuentran algunas que dieron sus primeros pasos apoyándose en los éxitos de otras más adelantadas.

¿Cuales deberían ser las prioridades de un programa de tecnificación de la agricultura? Lo primero, valga la redundancia, debe ser lo primero. En agricultura lo primero es la tierra y es el agua. Desde países hermanos del Caribe en la actualidad, hasta los sumerios en la Mesopotamia hace más de 4000 años, la erosión del suelo y la salinización de éste y de las aguas de riego, han destruído civilizaciones y empobrecido, hasta los límites de la miseria, a pueblos enteros. ¿Cual es la situación de Cuba al respecto? Quisiera contestar esa pregunta sin apoyarme en fuente alguna que ofrezca sospecha política. Tomo por tanto como base un informe que, como resultado de una visita a Cuba a invitación del Director del INRA señor Carlos Rafael Rodríguez, preparó en 1963 el líder socialista francés agrónomo René Dumont, quien previamente había visitado la Isla en 1960. Dice así Dumont: "La erosión: amenaza de catástrofe nacional. Con el Ingeniero Alonso Olivé (continúa Dumont) hemos señalado su suma gravedad desde 1960 y subrayado algunas de las principales precauciones a tomar para evitarla. A través de la Isla esta erosión asume ahora a consecuencia de los desmontes y de la ausencia total de precauciones, proporciones a veces temibles. Las granjas responsables del patrimonio nacional no tienen generalmente ningún cuidado de respetarlo y protegerlo. Es preciso que la Revolución no sea algún día acusada de haber dilapidado la propiedad de todo el pueblo".[6] Hasta aquí la cita. Añadimos nosotros que el Ingeniero Raúl Alonso Olivé ha disfrutado siempre de gran prestigio profesional.

El manejo adecuado del suelo, la administración racional de las aguas y en general del hábitat, deberá constituirse en una prioridad permanente del gobierno que suceda a la actual tiranía. A esos fines podría hacerse necesario, una vez que se conozca la situación sobre el terreno, revisar la actual infraestructura de riego. Además, el uso de pesticidas debe ser manejado con extremo cuidado y, en la medida de lo posible, sustituído por métodos de control biológico. Como una

---

[5]Carl J. Weinberg and Robert H. Williams, "Energy from the Sun", *Scientific American*, Special Issue, Scientific American Inc.,New York, NY,September 1990, 101.

[6]René Dumont, "Los principales obstáculos para una expansión más rápida de la agricultura cubana: estructurales, técnicos y económicos", *Seminario de Asuntos Cubanos*, 1964, p. 39.

cuestión de política agrícola mencionamos antes y reiteramos ahora la sugerencia de que en cualquier legislación destinada a reordenar la propiedad rural en Cuba, se establezca la obligación de quien resulte dueño de la tierra, de realizar el aprovechamiento de ésta de acuerdo con normas que tiendan a preservar su capacidad agrícola productiva. Otras cuestiones que podrían incluirse en la legislación agraria, son disposiciones que favorezcan la introducción de innovaciones e inversiones que promuevan el aumento de la productividad. Si el patrimonio natural de Cuba de más valor es su potencial agrícola, resulta obvio que la preservación o recuperación, en su caso, de ese potencial debe constituir una preocupación permanente de las autoridades y la ciudadanía cubanas.

Al hablar de planes a mediano y largo plazos, una de las variables cuya mención no debe omitirse es el crecimiento de la población cubana. Cuba contaba en 1990 con 10,603,000 habitantes (cifra que no incluye más de 1,200,000 exilados), comparados con 5,850,000 en 1950.[7] En otras palabras, la población prácticamente se ha duplicado en 40 años. La actual poblacion residente en la Isla representa una densidad de 95.6 personas por kilómetro cuadrado. Para fines de comparación cabe citar a México con 41.8 , o sea menos de la mitad.[8] Cuando se menciona la planificación del sector agropecuario no es excusable omitir la variable poblacional, aunque obviamente, su complejidad reclama un tratamiento no sólo multidisciplinario, sino la participación explícita de demógrafos, líderes cívicos y religiosos, políticos, médicos, sociólogos, psicólogos, economistas, etc. Quede anotada esta preocupación y no olvidemos que mientras el tiempo pasa, como se diría en inglés: *"the population bomb is ticking"*.

Podemos ahora concretar nuestras ideas sobre los principales objetivos de una política agrícola a mediano y largo plazos para Cuba, los que deberían ser:

• Reordenar oportunamente la propiedad rural siguiendo los lineamientos que, por los procedimientos apropiados, disponga el pueblo de Cuba. Se considera deseable que tal reordenamiento favorezca el desarrollo de empresas privadas, medianas, productivas, que usen racionalmente los recursos naturales.

• Evaluar alternativas tecnológicas y de mercado de la industria azucarera y sus subproductos y derivados, y ajustarla a un dimensionamiento óptimo.

• Enfatizar la producción de alimentos para la población y las industrias, incluyendo la industria turística.

• Estimular la producción de energía aprovechando las fuentes que derivan del sol, de la biomasa y del viento, con el fin de reducir la dependencia del petróleo, mejorar la balanza de pagos y elevar el nivel de vida de la población. Al alcohol, como fuente de energía, se le dará especial atención por su vinculación a la industria azucarera.

• Promover el uso racional de los recursos naturales en general.

• Organizar cuerpos técnicos y científicos que se dediquen a la captación de conocimientos

---

[7]The World Resources Institute, *World Resources 1992-93*, Oxford University Press, 1992, p. 246.

[8]"1992 Book of the Year", *Encyclopaedia Britannica*
, Encyclopaedia Britannica Inc., Chicago, 1992, p. 581 y 658.

y tecnologías de posible aplicación en Cuba. Dentro de este concepto, a la educación, capacitación y adiestramiento agrícolas se dará cuidadosa atención. Merecerán prioridad la investigación agrícola aplicada y la ingeniería genética.

• Hacer un esfuerzo sostenido para elevar la calidad comercial de las frutas y vegetales cubanos con vista al abastecimiento del mercado interno y a la exportación.

Dicho lo anterior, ¿qué faltaría para completar un cuadro de circunstancias que permitan el mejor desempeño posible del sector agropecuario cubano? A nuestro juicio faltaría lo siguiente:

• Condiciones del mercado que permitan la venta de la producción a precios que la estimulen. A esos fines Cuba deberá hacer un esfuerzo vigoroso por recuperar y ampliar sus mercados tradicionales.

• Políticas de precios, fiscales, de importación y de cambio que no discriminen injustamente contra la producción doméstica.

• Existencia de un sistema de crédito agrícola moderno, ágil, capaz, honesto e independiente de la política sectaria, sobre el que ya se expusieron diversas sugerencias.

• Disponibilidad, a precios razonables, de los insumos necesarios, los que deben satisfacer adecuados estándares de calidad.

• Servicios de investigación y extensión que provean conocimientos y asesoría para resolver los problemas de producción que experimenten los agricultores y que den a los productos de éstos una ventaja competitiva.

• Infraestructura física que permita que las operaciones de producción se realicen a tiempo y con eficiencia.

• Disponibilidad de seguros y otros servicios que protejan a los agricultores de riesgos indebidos.

• Ambiente sociopolítico donde la producción agrícola normal pueda florecer.

Resumiendo: los objetivos de la política agrícola cubana a mediano y largo plazos deberían ser la creación de un sector agropecuario eficiente y diversificado tanto en lo producido como en relación con los mercados. Estructuralmente el sector debe descansar en un régimen de tenencia de la tierra basado en fincas privadas de tamaño intermedio y debe estar apoyado por instituciones de crédito, seguros, etc., así como por un sistema educacional que promueva el conocimiento de las ciencias agropecuarias, y un servicio de investigación y extensión que labore dentro del país y que se mantenga en estrecha comunicación con centros dedicados a labores similares en otras partes del mundo. Este servicio estará al tanto de los progresos en las técnicas agropecuarias y adoptará aquellas que resulten apropiadas para Cuba. La política agrícola debe dar una clara prioridad al uso racional de los recursos naturales y al empleo de fuentes renovables de energía. En fin, la agricultura cubana debe crear empleos, generar divisas, producir alimentos y materias primas, y debe contribuir a dar estabilidad a la nación.

La tarea no parece fácil, pero ciertamente no es imposible. Cuba tiene tierras agrícolas de excelente calidad, un clima benigno subtropical con un régimen de lluvias bien definido y una posición geográfica envidiable. Lo que se requiere además, es la voluntad de todos de acometer la gran tarea, no de reconstruir a Cuba, sino de construirla. De construir de una vez la república que ha sido siempre la inspiración de los cubanos. La república que definió Martí con la sencillez característica de los genios verdaderos, la república sagaz y cordial, con todos y para todos.

Comments

Antonio Gayoso[1]

(A) "Rationing and Labor Supply in Cuba" by Jorge Sanguinetty

Behind the apparent diversity of this session's presentations, one common theme are the distortions introduced by, and the perverse results of misguided Cuban Government economic and investment policies of the last thirty years.

Mr. Sanguinetty's paper presents an interesting analysis of how Soviet style central planning, and a comprehensive rationing scheme, have introduced significant distortions in the economic system. These distortions have resulted in large changes in workers' behavior and decreases in the level of effort, i.e. decreases in labor supply. In turn, changes in workers' attitude towards work have led to decreased output. This result is not what planners expected, who believed that more egalitarian access to food and other supplies would stimulate workers' efforts and insure increased support for the regime.

I will not dwell on the geometrical characteristics of the model used in the paper. It is, nonetheless, an elegant approach consistent with my own observations of reality in Cuba. Rather, I would like to focus on some of the points Mr. Sanguinetty raises in his analysis. Of particular importance is the changed attitude towards work that rationing has introduced. Because of restricted supplies and lack of alternative legal markets to obtain needed goods, workers have decreased effort to that necessary to insure access to a minimum basket of rationed goods. This change had led to decreased output which has made the rationing system less effective, while, at the same time, making it even more necessary from a political point of view.

A secondary factor providing negative incentives for workers has been the well known existence of special markets where the ruling political and managerial classes have had access to goods of all kinds. The existence of these markets has created resentment among those who do not have access. The model developed for this presentation clearly shows the relationship between availability of commodities and level of effort.

Workers' behavior, evolved during the last thirty years, may result in significant impediments to a rapid transition to an open market system. During transition, commodity prices are likely to increase to their market clearance level. There may be, in the short run, actual shortages in key traditional staples, and a need to substitute cheaper alternative foods for the ones consumers would prefer. People may become disillusioned that the long awaited opening of the market and the political system is not leading to immediate increases in welfare and consumption. Under these circumstances, workers may continue to withhold their best effort, precisely the opposite of what the country would need as it emerges from three decades of inefficient centralized planning.

Mr. Sanguinetty's presentation warns us that there will be a need to develop entire institutional systems which are critical to the functioning of a market economy. The challenge, in his view, is how to turn around current attitudes so they do not undermine economic recovery

---

[1]The comments made by the discussant do not necessarily reflect the policy positions on these or any other issues by the US Agency for International Development.

programs. Current experience in Central and Eastern Europe validate this concern. Yet, experience with Cuban boatlift refugees suggests that, provided with the proper stimulus, people will rapidly change economic behavior. Most "Mariel" refugees have reacted very well to the incentives offered by the US market economy. The key may have been a combination of the material abundance found in the US, i.e. work is rewarded with increased capacity to consume, and the newly found realization that, to a large extent, they are the masters of their own destiny in a free society.

In my own view, these two threads must be present if any program designed for the transition period is to overcome the behavior identified by this paper. Somehow the supply of food and other essentials must be assured. International food aid may be a critical element at the beginning, though caution will be needed to minimize its negative stimulus to local production. As important will be to offer effective institutional means to facilitate popular participation in the political process. Goals and objectives should be clear, understood by all, and agreed by the majority. The population will need to know how fixing the distortions of the past will require massive restructuring and a lot of effort. Mr. Sanguinetty's paper is valuable for having identified the existence of this behavior and the need to change it in the future.

(B) "Environmental Deterioration and Protection in Socialist Cuba" by María Dolores Espino

This presentation is a valuable effort to in identify a framework to assess the impact of Cuban Government policies on the environment. Ms Espino submits that there has been grave environmental deterioration as a result of policies and programs implemented during the last thirty years. Her assertions are corroborated by a number of assessments, conducted by UN agencies who operate in Cuba, that document the biological death of river systems and harbors in Cuba.

In terms of the earlier presentation by Mr. Sanguinetty, it is useful to speculate that the incentive system put in place by the Socialist regime may have similar effects on the level of care for the environment in Cuba as it did on work effort. Social ownership of most assets makes them resemble common property, or, in other words, nobody's property. Under such a system, use can become abuse. Allocation of investments under political criteria, common to highly centralized regimes, is frequently not informed by assessments of environmental consequences or costs. Thus, project managers and users will ignore environmental consequences for which costs have not been identified.

Ms. Espino highlights that most irrigation projects in Cuba have been carried out without in depth assessments of environmental impact. During an official visit I made to Cuba in 1980, I was shown several irrigation systems and reservoirs. My escort, a Cuban PHD candidate in hydrology from the University of Vladivostok, had not been trained to look at sustainability or environmental issues and could not answer questions on these issues asked by the visiting technical team. He confided they were experiencing salinity and other contamination problems and expressed interest in learning more about what was being done outside of Cuba.

I was also able to observe and discuss the widespread waste of water in Havana as a result of poor maintenance practices. Rationing of water was the solution offered instead of more repairs and maintenance. As in the former Soviet Union and Central Europe, problems of contamination and environmental degradation will be major factors slowing down a recovery process. There are not enough data to assess the magnitude of the problem in Cuba, though Ms Espino offers indications sufficient to believe the problem is will remain a very serious one.

(C) "Cuban Agricultural Policy in the Medium and the Long Term" by Raúl Fernández

Mr. Fernández' paper is lucid and to the point. This presentation represents an expansion of that presented by the author at the first ASCE Conference in Miami, in 1991. The essay proposes a basic agenda that will guide additional though and research. I am pleased that it addresses, from inception, the need to clarify and decide property rights in agriculture. In my view, no system of economic incentives would stimulate investments, increased effort, and, consequently, increased production, unless the producer or investor feels there is a guarantee that benefits would accrue to him or her who makes the effort.

There are many studies and anecdotes that illustrate this point. For instance, three years ago, while on a business trip to the island of Lombock, Indonesia, I asked as young man about his origin. He said his parents had rented a small farm for more than thirty years. Asked what kind of fruit trees they had planted, or what king of physical structures they had built in those three decades, he quickly answered that none. He explained that, since they did not own the land, there was no pay off in planting trees or building anything. I felt that, given the apparent stability of the rental agreement, their decision was overcautious. Yet, on second thought, I concluded that such stability could have ended if the land owner had become interested in repossession had the renters invested in permanent improvements in the farm.

For rural people, ownership, or protected legally permanent use of the land, *is* the most critical element affecting investment decisions and supply response. Mr. Fernández' paper raises a number of key questions in this regard, but is shy of making specific recommendations regarding alternative approaches to property issues during transition from socialism, similar to those he makes concerning other institutional and policy elements of the rural development process.

In my view, no system of incentives will be effective until property rights are defined and legally established. Large investors and rural producers react exactly alike when land tenure rights are not well established. In Eastern Europe, failure to do so rapidly, after abandoning socialism has caused insecurity and a very low level of investment in the rural sector. In the case of Cuba, only the current private sector, with less than ten percent of the land under cultivation, would react to the incentive system proposed. The area they cover is, however, too small to close the food gap.

The option of returning to the land tenure structure which existed in 1959 would require a long time and much litigation. A thorough cadastral survey would be required. Second, the legal identity of former owners and the validity of their claim would need to be established. Third, valuation of land assets, after thirty years of numerous investment schemes would need to be decided and apportioned. Fourth, criteria would be needed to deal with assets which have disappeared, etc. These are but a few of the complex legal issues that would need decision if return of the land to the former owners is sought. It would probably take a decade before achieving what Mr. Fernandez calls "restructuring of rural property."

In order to get agriculture moving rapidly, one would need to privatize state-owned land much faster than that. The advice that many distinguished western agricultural economists are giving the former Soviet Union is roughly as follows:

Give property of state land, in fee simple, to current users, possibly excluding the managers. New owners can decide freely whether to farm as a group (a stock company) or to divide the land among themselves. Such land should be probably sold by the state to those receiving it.

Create private corporations or independent western style coops to handle input supply and marketing services formerly provided by the state coop.

Insure competition by creating multiple companies in the regions involved.

Organize efficient extension services to assure adequate access to technology. Extension can be both public and private.

In the case of Cuba, just compensation for past confiscations could be handled by special courts organized for this purpose, but independent from the process of establishing new property rights. Failure to de-link issues of compensation from those dealing with the need to rapidly reorganize and privatize the rural sector would lengthen the current food-agricultural crisis in Cuba.

In addition, one could stimulate joint endeavors between former owners and new owners, many of whom left Cuba, where each would contribute according to their comparative advantage, and derive benefits proportional to those contributions.

Returning to the core of Mr. Fernández's paper, I found his recommendations regarding the need to develop bio-mass based, alternative energy systems to be right on target. His concern for the need for environmental recovery in Cuba are amply supported by the third presentation in this session.

Agriculture and agro-industry will remain the basic core of the Cuban economy and its major source of employment for years to come. Cuban agriculture will need to become more energy efficient and more environmentally protected to assure resource sustainability. Mr. Fernandez's paper is a useful contribution in that direction.

APPENDIX A

ABSTRACTS OF PAPERS PRESENTED IN SPANISH

Business Ethics and the Integral Development of Cuba

Alberto Martínez Piedra

The fall of the Marxist-Leninist regime in Cuba will bring about substantial changes that will not be easy to implement. To carry out the recovery of Cuba at the least social cost possible, the following two variables will have to play a leading role during the transition period: 1) the need for a responsible and efficient entrepreneurial class; and 2) the recognition that the business firm consists of a community of persons within which the labor factor plays the preponderant role.

We have chosen these two variables not because there are no others of similar importance, but because the ones selected are intimately linked to the human person —whether entrepreneur or common laborer. They both enjoy the gift of freedom and are not exempt from value judgements. Thus, they are morally responsible for their freely-taken actions. It is precisely in this area of decisionmaking where economics, in spite of being an autonomous science, cannot divorce itself from ethics.

The businessman's legitimate desire for profits is a crucial factor that cannot be ignored if a healthy and sustained economic development is to take place. Without it the economy would stagnate and the creative subjectivity of man would tend to disappear. Man would have no incentive —if any— to invest and produce the goods and services that are necessary to satisfy consumer demand. The right of economic initiative cannot be denied to man unless society wants to put in jeopardy that very spirit of initiative which is the prime motor of all progress.

However, the firm must be considered as a community of persons within which both the entrepreneur and the worker cooperate in a joint productive effort. The worker cannot be considered as a mere input or tool of production that can be disposed of easily once he is no longer useful. He is above all a human being and not simply an object of production. That is why the production function must be "humanized." The entrepreneur, as the organizer of production, has the obligation to foster a spirit of cooperation among all the participants in the process of production.

The entrepreneur must not limit himself to the exercise of his "entrepreneurial function" or what some economists have called his creative function. He must also exercise a social function. This social function, which is normally geared toward improvements in the standard of living of the workers, cannot be ignored by the businessman if he really wants to enjoy more cordial and friendly relations with his employees and with labor in general. The social function of the entrepreneur flows directly from the concept that the firm is a community of persons joined together by links of genuine solidarity.

It is the task of the businessman, as a leader in society, to give examples of both creativity and solidarity within the firm itself. The businessman must become the soul of a new spirit of mutual trust and solidarity which will redound not only to his benefit but also to the benefit of all his employees, both at the level of the professionals and of the common laborers. This way, society and the business firm will be able to work in a more favorable productive environment and, as a result, the levels of efficiency and productivity would increase. The falsehood of the doctrine of Marx and his followers, proclaiming the inevitability of the class struggle, would be proven true once again.

In the new era that is approaching, the entrepreneur's contribution to the economic development of Cuba and, consequently, to man's integral development will become more necessary than ever. There lies his strength and at the same time his enormous responsibility. But, the failure of Castro's collectivist policies should not open the doors to a capitalism *a outrance*. The profit motive and the mere accumulation of wealth should not be the main motivations of the Cuban entrepreneurial class who will have to play such an important and crucial role in the recovery of Cuba's economy. They should always keep in mind that a disproportionate accumulation of temporal goods can lead to avarice and to a not very recommendable search for power which would be nefarious for the future well-being of Cuba.

Fortunately, Cuba does not lack a competent and experienced entrepreneurial class. We are convinced that the same way Cubans have demonstrated their entrepreneurial abilities in Miami and other areas of the world during their years of exile, they will also be able to combine that same entrepreneurial spirit with a genuine spirit of solidarity once they return to Cuba. It is our hope that Cuban entrepreneurs, both in Cuba and outside of Cuba, will join forces and exercise their entrepreneurial and social functions in a spirit of true justice and in such a way that all Cubans will be able to benefit from the political and economic freedoms that they have lacked for over thirty years. Otherwise, the sufferings of the Cuban people during the tragic years of the Castro-led Marxist revolution would have been to no avail.

The Legal-Juridical Framework for a
Provisional Government of National Unity in Cuba

José D. Acosta

After a summary of the background behind my current concerns on the future of Cuba, a brief description is given of the paper's underlying assumption: that there is a possibility that Cuba will return to the rule of law and a democratic system in the foreseeable future. Independently of the successive line of events that might lead to such an outcome, the paper's central hypothesis is formulated: that the starting point on the road to democratic rule of law is the formation of a *de facto* government which must be provisional in nature (e.g. one year duration), which will function within a certain juridical-institutional framework. The purpose of this Provisional Government of National Unity (PGNU) will be to take care of day-to-day government while two basic successive undertakings are conducted: convocation of a Constitutional Assembly and, once the resulting Constitution is approved, the convocation of General Elections under a free system of political pluralism. Neither convocation poses substantial legal problems: the legal instruments whereby the 1940 Constitutional Assembly was convoked and the General Elections that were to be held in 1952, shortly after Batista's *coup de état*, might be used for this purpose. The caretaker functions are also briefly described, including the liberalization of agricultural production and distribution through the return to the free farmers' markets of the 1980s.

Using a juridical technique consistent with the Cuban legal system, the purpose of the paper is to set the juridical foundation for **a legal opinion which concludes that the 1940 Constitution**

remains in full legal force because it has never been properly reformed under the constitutional amendment requirements provided therein, nor a Constitutional Assembly has ever been properly convoked to replace it, following the traditionally recognized pattern of those that resulted in constitutions that have been generally accepted and recognized as valid, such as the 1902 and the 1940 constitutions. On the contrary, all attempts to amend, partially or totally, the 1940 Constitution have been made either by the Council of Ministers or by the so-called National Assembly of People's Power, which having been elected under a system of absolute control of the electoral process by a single party —the Communist Party of Cuba— cannot claim legitimate popular representation.

On the other hand, it is also shown that the current regime's purported legitimacy may be traced to a Cuban Supreme Court Resolution dated January 1, 1959 which, on the basis of the doctrine of the *fait accompli* typified by the abandonment of the government by the Batista regime, its *de facto* appropriation by the rebel forces, their support by most opposition groups, including the urban underground and a substantial majority of the Cuban people, found that such situation precluded the application of Article 149 of the 1940 Constitution on presidential succession, which provides that "in any case in which the presidential substitutes established by this constitution are lacking, the Presidency of the Republic shall be temporarily occupied by the oldest Justice of the Supreme Court, who shall call a national election to be held within a period of not more than 90 days." A request to that effect had been submitted by such person, Justice Dr. Carlos M. Piedra y Piedra. Notwithstanding this finding, the Resolution clearly assumes that although the Constitution remained in force, an exception to Article 149 had to be made. It also refers to the President appointed by the rebel forces and the opposition groups as an *ad interim* president, thus implying that he should call general elections within 90 days, pursuant to this very Article. Indeed, the revolution had attained its political support on the basis that the 1940 Constitution would be fully restored, not only on a *pro forma* basis as in the prior dictatorship, but also in substance and compliance. Thus, any confusion regarding any Constitutional Power having been delegated or received by the new regime is totally out of the question.

Instead, the rebel regime, which during 1958 had issued normative instruments in open conflict with the 1940 Constitution, such as subjecting civilians to the Rebel Army military jurisdiction, within 10 days of assuming power began to formally amend the Constitution, particularly certain important items such as criminal law, basic guarantees regarding submission to a law and court existing at the time of the imputed crime; the subversion of the independence of the Judicial Power; the creation of exceptions to the prohibition of property confiscation; the addition of exceptions to the application of the death penalty, etc., geared to grant all manner of political jurisdiction to the infamous Revolutionary Tribunals. Obviously, these attempts implicitly recognized that the 1940 Constitution was the basic law of the land.

Moreover, less than a month later, on February 7, 1959, the President and the Council of Ministers undertook a full reform of the 1940 Constitution, which was replaced by a Fundamental Law, including all the amendments that the regime saw fit at this time. Obviously, such action was taken without compliance with the provisions of Article 286 of the 1940 Constitution applicable to integral or complete constitutional amendments. This provision required that such a proposal be approved by a "plebiscitary assembly", to be convened within six months and which is empowered to approve or reject the integral or total amendment.

This situation lasted 16 years, with no constitutional amendment approval by a "plebiscitary assembly" under Article 286, nor a call to general elections within 90 days, pursuant to Article 149. In 1975, efforts were started towards a new constitution, but the first draft and successive revisions were made by joint commissions of the Communist Party of Cuba and the Council of Ministers. The final draft was then submitted to the First Party Congress and after approval, it was the subject of a lengthy popular "indoctrination—consultation" process conducted on the Cuban people by the infamous Committees for the Defense of the Revolution and other communist-controlled mass organizations. Finally, when the optimal saturation point was attained, a "plebiscite" was called, the terms and conditions of the convocation of which were not made public, with the convenient result that, pursuant to the "Maximum Leader's" statement, showed a 97.7% of popular approval! No information was offered on the percentages of those who voted against or abstained. Before closing this item, let it be known that this process has never been constitutionally nor legally legislated. It was **concocted along the way** during the approval process of the current 1976 constitution, Article 5 of which postulates that "The Communist Party of Cuba, the organized Marxist-Leninist vanguard of the working class, is the highest leading force of society and the State, which organizes and guides the common effort toward the goals of the construction of socialism and the progress toward a communist society". So much for democracy and the right to dissent.

Based on these reasons and also on others explained in the paper, my conclusion is that **the 1940 Constitution is still fully and legally in force in Cuba**, and that any **PGNU must obtain its legitimacy out of submitting to it**. This legal opinion results in a highly effective and efficient way of legally disposing of all constitutional intents which have taken place in Cuba since March 10, 1952, when the last democratic government of Cuba was overthrown.

This legal opinion also facilitates the approach regarding the complete replacement undertaken by the regime of the basic laws which properly fit into the 1940 constitutional framework, with "laws" designed to complement and consolidate the communist constitutional conception. For instance, the Organic Law of the Judicial Power was replaced in 1977 by a Law on Organization of the Judicial System, which provides (Article 122) that the tribunals are subservient to the National Assembly and the State Council, thus wiping out any vestige of independence of the Judicial Power from the other two powers; the 1902 Civil Code was fully replaced in 1987 by a new one in which Article 2 states that its provisions "shall be interpreted and applied in conformity with the political, social and economic principles expressed in the constitution"; the 1936 Social Defense Code was totally replaced in 1979 by a new Penal Code that converts political crimes, as defined by it, into common crimes that enable the regime to state that there are no political prisoners in Cuba and brings into the political sphere what is called a "dangerous-tendency state" (*estado de peligrosidad*) which may include any discrepancy or dissention from communism or the regime and its leaders, and the 1934 labor regulations were fully replaced in 1984 by a Labor Code that contains such new institutions as the personal work record, kept by the work center management, which has evolved into a tremendous instrument of control and coercion of individual workers, because its entries are required and taken into consideration in all governmental decisions that might affect the worker and his welfare.

Finally, the paper advances some recommendations on how to speedily restore the rule of law in Cuba, in the event that a PGNU is established and on how to cope with other sensitive issues such as maintaining order, reorganizing an independent Judicial Power, disarming the existing repression force and replacing it with a professional police force with international multinational technical support. Obviously, the paper assumes that all political decisions on economic reorganization based on private enterprise and free markets, with due regard for social justice, should be of the exclusive competence of the Constitutional Assembly and the Democratic Government elected in a pluralist General Election, particularly those decisions on the disposition of confiscated and nationalized properties and instruments of production including land, dwellings, and commercial and industrial plants.

Considerations Regarding a Proposed Bill
on Urban and Rural Dwellings in Cuba

Julio Romañach, Jr.

The article is a commentary on the author's proposed bill on urban and rural dwellings in Cuba. The proposed legislation is intended to take effect after the termination of Fidel Castro's government.

The goals of the proposed legislation are three-fold: 1) avoidance of forced eviction or ejection of persons presently residing in the dwellings affected by the statute; 2) establishment of a methodology for ranking claims to real property involving dwellings; and 3) the establishment of a right of first refusal in the State concerning any transfer of possessory rights to real property containing dwellings, as well as a regulatory scheme governing this right.

The proposed legislation distinguishes between "existing" (*i.e.*, dwellings constructed or in the process of construction when Castro's government terminates) and "new" dwellings. The argument is made that the shortage of housing, combined with the bankrupt state of the Cuban economy and the indigent status of the average Cuban, amply justify the moratorium on evictions or ejectments, as well as other measures set forth in the proposed legislation. Based primarily on the provisions of Article 87 of the Cuban Constitution of 1940, the opinion is advanced that the proposed legislation is firmly rooted in Cuban constitutional law.

In part one of the article the proposed statute's moratorium on evictions and ejectment is explained. The statute's moratorium scheme revolves around the concept of "legitimate occupant" (*ocupante legítimo*), who is basically defined as a person in peaceful possession of a dwelling at the termination of Castro's government. Such a person is deemed to be a good faith possessor of the dwelling at issue and to have a right to remain residing therein (*derecho de permanencia*). The statute excludes, from the protective ambit of the moratorium, the citizens of other countries with non-democratic regimes residing in Cuba.

Part two of the article deals with the ranking of property rights to dwellings and unimproved lots in Cuba. In this part, the compensatory scheme provided in the statute for dispossessed owners of real property is explained.

Finally, part three of the article focuses on the section of the proposed dwelling law regulating the State's right of first refusal concerning transfers of possessory rights to real property. The importance of granting the State a right of first refusal as to transfers involving existing dwellings is explained. The observation is made that the proposed legislation purports to prevent speculation on existing dwellings at the termination of the Castro regime, noting the probable very low prices for which the owners will, in all likelihood, be prepared to sell their houses.

An Optimal Monetary Policy or an Optimal Monetary System

Juan Luis Moreno Villalaz

This paper proposes the use of the dollar as currency in Cuba, as in the case of Panama. This is considered to be the optimal system. The principal operational characteristics of the Panamanian system, or any system with endogenous money supply, are related to the concepts developed in the "Monetary Theory of the Balance of Payments". The interest rate is the world market rate, plus an addition for country risk. The inflation rate is the world's rate which makes Panama a very stable country. The amount of money is demand determined. There is an automatic equilibrium of the Balance of Payments, via changes in the available amount of dollars and their effect on the level of expenditures.

The paper describes in detail how the system forces a "hard budget constraint" in government financial decisions. Because the government cannot spend more than what is available, nor does it have any influence on money supply, the monetary system imposes an economic rationality to politicians. It is noted that the system, in spite of using dollars as currency, needs relatively less foreign exchange than other countries.

The system has advantages for economic growth due to its stability, the lack of devaluation risk and additional finances. Additionally, open capital markets are very attractive to foreign investors. It also produces its own "service exports", and produces more local savings as residents do not deposit abroad.

The paper discusses the experience of Panama when a minor and major crisis, or external shock, occurs. Several political crises and the oil crisis are discussed. It is found that in both cases, the initial effect was absorbed by foreign finances coming from the banking system. These give the economy an important shock absorption mechanism and more flexibility, thus avoiding macro fluctuations. Afterward, there is an adjustment process.

In the major crisis (1988-1990) the process of adjustment includes a capital market adjustment, an expenditure adjustment and a price adjustment, including a change in the "real exchange rate". The lack of destabilizing expectations about devaluation, as in the case of Chile in 1982, makes the adjustment process more efficient and stable.

A theoretical model is presented in which the "endogenous monetary system" (as in Panama) is compared with a system with its own currency. An analysis is made under the condition that the variance of economic activity is minimized, given certain external shocks. If the monetary authorities act with an independent rule, the optimal solution is to behave as if the money supply were endogenous, as in the case of Panama. On the other hand, if the monetary authorities use all the information available, the optimal solution is to let the amount of money be demand determined, because in that way no disturbance is introduced by the monetary policy; again the Panamanian system.

In the last part of the paper, the author discusses the monetary issues related to the conversion of a centralized socialist economy, such as Cuba's, to a market economy. It is argued that the endogenous monetary system, in addition to its advantages in the long run, has important advantages in the transition period as well, and can even help in the conversion process of the price system.

The overall conclusion is that the Panamanian monetary system is optimal in terms of stability, growth, adjustment to external shocks, and in implementing a market economy. This has been shown in both theory and practice.

Economic Rationale and Justification
for a Proposal to Develop a Social Market Economy in Cuba

Rolando H. Castañeda

The main topic of this paper is to present the economic rationale and justification behind a proposal for quick, deep, and lasting reforms in the Cuban institutions and policies to completely transform the socialist economy into a very competitive and open market economy. The aims of the structural reforms are to establish and consolidate an efficient and externally-oriented economy with stability, growth, and social justice. Failure to implement the proper transition could lead to a huge emigration to the United States based on the Cuban American family tie connections.

In a world of increasing commercial and financial integration, the economic and political trends are both towards democracy and open market economies. However, Cuba confronts severe repression, internal and external economic imbalances as a result of systemic institutional problems. These imbalances are further accentuated due to the cessation of massive subsidies and trade from the former USSR and Eastern European countries. There has been a drastic decrease in the gross social product that started with a recession during the period 1986-1989, associated with the elimination of all liberalization measures of the early 1980's, and that has become a profound depression since 1990. The Cuban economy is characterized by high disguised and open unemployment, enormous repressed inflationary pressures, extreme fiscal and balance of payment disequilibria, and an unmanageable external debt.

The implementation of sound and rigorous policies, and sustainable and coherent reforms, based on a radical, but sequential and gradual approach, is recommended for the stabilization and liberalization of the economy. Simultaneously, with a swift process of enacting institutional and legal reforms for the deregulation of the economy, for the privatization of state enterprises, and for dismantling the artificial monopolies and oligopolies to facilitate the proper transition.

The sequential approach, as opposed to the "big bang" approach, is recommended to avoid any further deterioration of the already precarious Cuban economy while other conditions are established or developed to insure the appropriate response to the structural reforms. This sequential approach will assure internal consistency, coherency, and it will limit political and social resistance. The proposal is based on Ronald McKinnon's book "The Proper Order of Liberalization" (1991); the Chilean successful transformation from a situation of complete chaos in 1973 to a solid and dynamic economy; and, finally, the arduous transitions associated with the "big-bang" approach both in Poland and in Russia.

TABLE A

MAIN POLICIES AND REFORMS PROPOSED FOR THE RECONSTRUCTION OF THE CUBAN ECONOMY

REFORMS AND POLICIES	STABILIZATION (THREE YEARS)		LIBERALIZATION OR STRUCTURAL ADJUSTMENT (THREE YEARS)		
	FIRST STAGE (FISCAL AND PRICE ADJUSTMENTS)	SECOND STAGE (BEGINNING OF THE PRIVATIZATION AND MONETARY AND CREDIT ADJUSTMENTS)	THIRD STAGE (PRIVATIZATION DEEPENING AND INTERNAL FINANCIAL LIBERALIZATION)	FOURTH STAGE (FOREIGN TRADE LIBERALIZATION)	FIFTH STAGE (EXTERNAL FINANCIAL LIBERALIZATION)
TIME DURATION	ONE YEAR	TWO YEARS	ONE YEAR	ONE YEAR	ONE YEAR
INSTITUTIONAL AND LEGAL (development of a competitive private sector)	ENACT, GUARANTEE AND ENFORCE PROPERTY RIGHTS, FREE ENTRY TO MARKETS, PROFESSIONS AND TRADES, SIMPLE AND SWIFT PROCEDURES TO INITIATE BUSINESS ACTIVITIES. ESTABLISH NORMS FOR PRIVATE CONTRACTS, TRADE AND BANKRUPTCY LAWS, ACCOUNTING AND AUDITING STANDARDS, SUPPORT FREE AND DEMOCRATIC LABOR UNIONS.	ESTABLISH ANTIMONOPOLY, ANTIOLIGOPOLY AND MODERN BUSINESS LAWS.	ENACT MODERN LABOR LAW WITH RIGHT TO STRIKES AND COLLECTIVE BARGAINING. ALLOW MARKETS TO DETERMINE WAGES.		
PRICES AND SALARIES	FULL LIBERALIZATION OF PRICES FOR PRIVATE, SMALL AND MEDIUM STATE ENTERPRISES. PRICE ADJUSTMENTS FOR LARGE STATE ENTERPRISES TO REFLECT INTERNATIONAL COSTS. STATE ENTERPRISES SALARIES SHOULD REMAINED FROZEN. LIBERALIZE PRIVATE SECTOR SALARIES.	STATE ENTERPRISES SALARIES SHOULD BE ADJUSTED BY PRODUCTIVITY GAINS.	ELIMINATE ALL PRICE AND SALARY CONTROLS, EXCEPT FOR NATURAL MONOPOLIES. SALARY ADJUSTMENTS OF LARGE STATE ENTERPRISES SHOULD BE BASED ON PRODUCTIVITY GAINS.		
FINANCIAL	ENACT A MONETARY REFORM ISSUING A NEW PESO. ELIMINATE ALL FINANCIAL ASSETS AND LIABILITIES FOR STATE ENTERPRISES, PROVIDE THEM WITH WORKING CAPITAL. ENFORCE TIGHT MONETARY AND CREDIT POLICIES. ESTABLISH POSITIVE REAL INTEREST RATES FOR PRIVATE SECTOR DEPOSITS AND FOR LIBERALIZED STATE ENTERPRISES.	ESTABLISH A STOCK EXCHANGE, AN AUTONOMOUS CENTRAL BANK AND A BANKING INSTITUTION TO REGULATE COMMERCIAL BANKING CREDIT. DEVELOP FINANCIAL INSTRUMENTS FOR MEDIUM AND LONG-TERM DEPOSITS AND DEBTS.	LIBERALIZE INTEREST RATES. ENACT MODERN FINANCIAL INSTITUTIONS LAW. ALLOW ALL TYPES OF FINANCIAL INSTITUTIONS, BUT SUBJECT TO STRICT REGULATIONS AND SUPERVISION.		
FISCAL	ESTABLISH FISCAL BALANCE. REDUCE DEFENSE AND INTERNAL SECURITY EXPENSES. ELIMINATE SUBSIDIES. DESIGN A COMPREHENSIVE REFORM OF THE STATE ROLE. USE COST AND BENEFIT ANALYSIS TO SELECT PUBLIC INVESTMENT AND ESTABLISH PUBLIC BIDDING FOR PUBLIC ACQUISITIONS. ESTABLISH VAT, INCOME TAX FOR ENTERPRISES AND INDIVIDUALS, EXCISE TAXES ON LUXURY GOODS, AND REAL ESTATE TAXES.	KEEP BALANCE BUDGET BASED ON CASH FLOWS. ELIMINATE ALL SUBSIDIES. CHARGE TUITION AND FEES FOR COLLEGE EDUCATION.			APPROVE BALANCE BUDGET LAW. ESTABLISH A DECENTRALIZE AND EFFICIENT STATE WITH A VERY LIMITED AND SUBSIDIARY ROLE. IN-CREASE THE AUTONOMY AND AUTHORITY OF PROVINCES, MUNICIPALITIES AND COMMUNITIES.
EXTERNAL SECTOR	DEVALUATE AND UNIFICATE THE EXCHANGE RATE. ESTABLISH TEMPORARY EXCHANGE CONTROLS. ELIMINATE ALMOST ALL QUANTITATIVE CONTROLS AND BARRIERS. ESTABLISH UNIFORM TARIFF OF 100% FOR CONSUMER GOODS, AND 20% FOR CAPITAL AND INTERMEDIATE GOODS. NEGOTIATE ACCESS TO THE USA MARKET AND TO GATT.	REDUCE TARIFF FOR FINAL CONSUMER GOODS TO 70%. ENACT ANTI-DUMPING LAW.	REDUCE TARIFF FOR FINAL CONSUMER GOODS TO 40%.	ESTABLISH 15% UNIFORM TARIFF FOR ALL GOODS. FREE CONVERTIBILITY FOR ALL TRANSACTIONS IN THE CURRENT ACCOUNT OF THE BALANCE OF PAYMENTS.	REDUCE UNIFORM TARIFF FOR ALL GOODS TO 10%. FREE CONVERTIBILITY FOR ALL TRANSACTIONS OF THE BALANCE OF PAYMENTS SUBJECT TO FOREIGN INVESTMENT LAW.

TABLE A

MAIN POLICIES AND REFORMS PROPOSED FOR THE RECONSTRUCTION OF THE CUBAN ECONOMY

(CONTINUED)

REFORMS AND POLICIES	STABILIZATION (THREE YEARS)		LIBERALIZATION OR STRUCTURAL ADJUSTMENT (THREE YEARS)		
	FIRST STAGE (FISCAL AND PRICE ADJUSTMENTS)	SECOND STAGE (BEGINNING OF THE PRIVATIZATION AND MONETARY AND CREDIT ADJUSTMENT)	THIRD STAGE (PRIVATIZATION DEEPENING AND INTERNAL FINANCIAL LIBERALIZATION)	FOURTH STAGE (FOREIGN TRADE LIBERALIZATION)	FIFTH STAGE (EXTERNAL FINANCIAL LIBERALIZATION)
TIME DURATION	ONE YEAR	TWO YEARS	ONE YEAR	ONE YEAR	ONE YEAR
PRODUCTIVE RESTRUCTURING AND GENERALIZED PRIVATIZATION	PROVIDE INCENTIVES TO PUBLIC EMPLOYEES FOR A SECOND JOB AND FOR THE PARTITION OF STATE FARMS INTO INDIVIDUAL LOTS. DECENTRALIZE DECISIONS TO SMALL AND MEDIUM STATE ENTERPRISES. ENABLE SEVERE PENALTIES TO MANAGERS AND WORKERS WHO STEAL FROM STATE PROPERTIES. ESTABLISH CRITERIA FOR THE BANKRUPTCY OF STATE ENTERPRISES AND TO DISMANTLE MONOPOLISTIC STATE ENTERPRISES. ESTABLISH A PRIVATIZATION COMMISSION.	PRIVATIZE PUBLIC HOUSING, SMALL AND MEDIUM STATE ENTERPRISES BY CASH/CREDIT SALES OR BY LEASING. DISMANTLE AND INITIATE THE STOCK SALE OF LARGE STATE ENTERPRISES.	PRIVATIZE PENSION PLANS, STATE COMMERCIAL BANKING, TELECOMMUNICATIONS, ELECTRICITY, OIL AND TRANSPORTATION ENTERPRISES, HIGHWAY CONSTRUCTION AND MAINTENANCE, AIRPORTS AND PORTS OPERATIONS, WATER AND SEWAGE SYSTEMS.	PARTIAL DECENTRALIZATION AND PRIVATIZATION OF PRIMARY AND INTERMEDIATE EDUCATION, PUBLIC HEALTH AND CITY SERVICES. THE STATE WOULD FINANCE THE SERVICES BUT THE PRIVATE SECTOR WILL PROVIDE THEM.	
CITIZENS AND FORMER RESIDENTS RETURN	ALLOW TAX FREE IMPORTATION OF HOUSEHOLD ITEMS, PENSION PAYMENTS, CAPITAL INVESTMENTS. FREEDOM OF PROFESSIONAL AND TRADE PRACTICES.	ALLOW IMPORTATION OF PERSONAL HOUSEHOLD ITEMS SUBJECT TO EXISTING TARIFFS.			
UNREQUITED TRANSFERS	FREE MONETARY TRANSFERS AT THE OFFICIAL EXCHANGE RATE. FOREIGN NON-PROFIT PRIVATE ORGANIZATIONS ARE ALLOWED TO OPEN ACTIVITIES FREE OF TAXES.				
FOREIGN INVESTMENT	LIMIT TO NEW ENTERPRISES. NO TIME OR AMOUNT LIMITS FOR PROFIT REMITTANCES. SEVERE RESTRICTION TO INVEST IN STATE ENTERPRISES.	ENACT MODERN FOREIGN INVESTMENT LAW WITH EQUAL TREATMENT FOR NATIONAL AND FOREIGN FIRMS.			
EXTERNAL FINANCIAL AND TECHNICAL COOPERATION	REQUEST ASSOCIATE MEMBERSHIP TO THE INTERNATIONAL FINANCIAL INSTITUTIONS FOR ACCESS TO TECHNICAL COOPERATION AND ORIENTATION AND ADVICE FOR FUTURE LOAN APPLICATIONS. SEEK TECHNICAL ASSISTANCE FROM THE CHILEAN GOVERNMENT FOR THE IMPLEMENTATION OF THE STRUCTURAL REFORMS AND TRAINING.	REQUEST FULL MEMBERSHIP TO THE INTERNATIONAL FINANCIAL INSTITUTIONS FOR ACCESS TO ECONOMIC AND TECHNICAL COOPERATION.			
FOREIGN DEBT	OUTLINE STRATEGIES TO RENEGOTIATE AND REDUCE EXTERNAL DEBT INCLUDING RECONVERSION SCHEMES.	START FOREIGN DEBT SERVICE AND INITIATE RECONVERSION OPERATIONS.			
PRIORITY SECTORS	AGRICULTURE, AGROINDUSTRY, FISHERIES, TOURISM AND SERVICES RELATED TO INTERNATIONAL STOPOVERS.		EXPORT MANUFACTURING ASSEMBLY ACTIVITIES AND SUPPORTING SERVICES.		HIGH TECHNOLOGY ACTIVITIES.

Medium-Term Effects of the Main Economic Measures

	Inflationary pressures	Production expansion	Balance of payments improvement
Institutional and legal reforms a/	-	+	+
Price and salary adjustment b/	+	+	+
Tight monetary and credit policy c/	?	-	+
Fiscal austerity c/	?	-	+
Privatization and productive restructuring a/	-	+	+
Overdevaluation d/	+	+	+
Foreign investment a/	-	+	+
Citizens and former residents return a/, e/	?	+	+
Unrequited external transfers e/	+	+	+
External financial and technical assistance a/	-	+	+

Effects: - negative, + positive, ? indefinite

a/   It increases aggregate supply.

b/   It should improve resource allocation in the country, and external competitiveness through increases in efficiency, but should increase prices.

c/   It reduces aggregate demand and it is deflationary; however, it could have inflationary effects through cost increases (working capital costs, value-added taxes and tariff adjustments).

d/   It increases prices, improves balance of payments, and, if the elasticities are the proper ones, increases production.

e/   It finances increases in aggregate demand with foreign exchange.

At the outset of the transition, legal and institutional reforms must be enacted to enable individuals to establish and develop new enterprises and activities. Fiscal and price adjustments will aim to reduce the level of excessive expenditures, which is generating both inflationary pressures and balance of payment difficulties; to stop the expansion of the money supply; to set the basis for a stable process of privatization in future years; and last, but not least, to initiate the implementation of a solidarity and investment social safety net for the low income people without sacrificing fiscal discipline. Subsidies should be eliminated. Defense, communist party, and internal security expenditures must be drastically reduced or eliminated, and a comprehensive and simple tax system should be put in place. A full price liberalization for private, small and medium-size state enterprises will foster a competitive climate. A drastic overdevaluation of the Cuban peso, the elimination of all quantitative barriers to trade, and the establishment of two uniform tariff levels will be needed to restore external equilibrium, competitiveness, and export diversification. A monetary reform, tight monetary and credit policies should be pursued to eliminate inflationary pressures.

At the second stage of the transition, the encouragement of foreign investment; financial assistance from the international financial agencies and from the foreign-based Cuban community; and the privatization of small and medium size state enterprises through cash or credit open sales are also necessary and desirable to expand the minuscule private sector and to improve the fiscal situation. Further details on the recommended reforms and policies, and their effects on production, inflation pressures, and balance of payments are summarized in attached tables A and B.

Main Objectives of a Long and Medium Term
Agricultural Policy for Cuba

Raúl Fernández

As a follow-up to the short-term strategy paper presented at the 1991 ASCE meeting, this paper considers the medium and long term goals of an agricultural policy for Cuba. Such a policy must deal with problems such as: 1) providing the Cuban population with satisfactory food supplies; 2) settling the ownership conflicts derived from the massive confiscation of rural properties after 1959; 3) reviewing the sugar industry and deciding its optimal size in the present circumstances; and 4) finding innovative technologies to substitute oil with cheaper sources of energy.

The rural property problem, due to its massive size and that more than 30 years have elapsed since the confiscations, should be addressed by the Cuban people through a constitutional assembly. Only this procedure appears to present a fair chance that the best Cuban interests would be served. In the meantime, agricultural production should continue without being impaired by endless litigations. Basically, a moratorium should be established freezing the status quo of the large state farms until a constitutional solution is achieved. Small private farmers, still in possession of their farms, should be recognized and encouraged.

The Cuban sugar industry and its by-products should be subjected to an evaluation of its technological and market alternatives with the aim of adjusting it to an optimum size.

The need for energy sources other than oil is explored. Emphasis is given to the falling cost of photovoltaic electricity. Normally, Cuban consumption of oil has fluctuated annually at approximately US$ 1.6 billion. This figure underlines the importance of developing other sources: sun, alcohol, wind, waste, etc.

Soil erosion and salinization are stressed as potential major problems. There are indications that substantial damage might have been inflicted to the soil by mismanagement and possible ignorance. A review of the irrigation infrastructure should be made as early as possible in order to correct deficiencies.

A healthy agricultural sector will require institutions specialized in agricultural credit, research, extension and others. Credit is examined from different angles.

As the paper is concerned with medium and long-term goals, population increase is reviewed. Even without counting the exiles, the Cuban population has almost doubled between 1950 and 1990. The paper recognizes the importance of this factor, which falls beyond its scope. Nevertheless, it is suggested that a multidisciplinary group of specialists should study the dynamics of population at due time.

In summary, the objectives of a medium and long-term Cuban agricultural policy should be the development of an efficient and diversified agricultural sector, made up of private medium-sized farms and should be supported by institutions such as research and extension, that should be aware of innovations developed around the world for possible introduction in Cuba. Finally, let us be reminded that Cuba has soils of excellent quality, a benign subtropical climate with well-defined rainy seasons and a good geographical position. This could be the springboard from which to launch, with the proper effort, a substantial and rapid recovery.

APPENDIX B

AUTHORS AND DISCUSSANTS

José D. Acosta had a long career at the OAS, where was both a tax policy economist and a lawyer. He retired in 1989 as Director of the Department of General Legal Services at the Secretariat of Legal Affairs, after serving as a Principal Economist in the Joint Tax Program OAS/IDB/ECLA. He has a Doctorate of Laws, Havana University, and Graduate Studies in economics at Universidad de Villanueva, Havana, at the PhD candidate level, and at George Washington University. He was a Senior Partner of Bufete de Machado, Havana, and a professor of Law and of Economics in the Schools of Law and of Economics at the Universidad de Villanueva, Havana.

Irma T. de Alonso is Associate Professor and Graduate Program Coordinator at the Department of Economics, Florida International University. Her latest contribution is *Trade Issues in the Caribbean*, published by Gordon and Breach Science Publishers, Inc., in 1992.

José F. Alonso is the Senior Economic Researcher of Radio Martí. He specialized in market studies and computer systems design, and over the past five years has been research economist for the U.S. Information Agency, where he has undertaken macroeconomic analyses of internal and external accounts and international trade studies. For 12 years he served as market economic analyst at the International Price Division, U.S. Bureau of Labor Statistics. He graduated in international economics and development from Catholic University of America.

Fernando Alvarez is an assistant professor of finance at Babson College, Massachussetts. He is a Ph.D. candidate at New York University. His teaching and research interests include agribusiness project finance in Latin America, short-term financial management, and the use of simulation technology in financial risk management.

José Alvarez is Professor of Food and Resource Economics at the University of Florida's Everglades Research and Education Center where his research and extension programs deal with farm management and production economics. He is currently a Principal Investigator in a research project intended to estimate the economic impact (benefits and costs) of future trade between the United States and Cuba on Florida's agricultural economy. He received his Ph.D. in Food and Resource Economics from the University of Florida.

Ernesto F. Betancourt is a consultant to the UNDP on institutional development and has done consulting work for the World Bank, IDB, AID and the OAS on that subject throughout Latin America. He also lectures on analysis of revolutionary propensity and is author of the recently-published Transaction book *Revolutionary Strategy: A Handbook for Practitioners*. He has an MPIA from the University of Pittsburgh, majoring in economic and social development. He has been Director of VOA's Radio Martí program directed at Cuba, Director of Organization Development and Director of Finance and Budget at the OAS, and Managing Director of the Cuban Bank of Foreign Trade. He was Castro's representative in Washington during the revolution against Batista.

Roger R. Betancourt is Professor of Economics at the University of Maryland-College Park. He received his Ph.D. from the University of Wisconsin-Madison. Many of his contributions to the analysis of capital utilization and shift-work systems are summarized in the entry on "Capital

Utilization" in J. Eatwell, M. Milgate, and P. Newman (eds.), *The New Palgrave Dictionary of Economics*, The Stockton Press, 1987. In recent years he has been a Visiting Professor and Scholar at INSEAD (Fontainebleau, France) where he developed his current research interest in the analysis of distribution systems.

Juan J. Buttari is Senior Economist with the Agency for International Development (A.I.D.) and a member of the United States Foreign Service. Prior to joining A.I.D. he held positions with the International Labour Organization, United Nations Development Programme, and the Brookings Institution. He has taught, written and published on development issues. He holds a Ph.D. in Economics from Georgetown University.

Rolando H. Castañeda is currently a Senior Operations Officer working with Chile and Peru at the Inter-American Development Bank (IDB), where he has held different positions since 1974. Before joining the IDB, he worked as an economist at the Organization of American States; the Rockefeller Foundation at the University of Cali, Colombia; the University of Puerto Rico at Río Piedras; and the Puerto Rican Planning Board. He has an M.A. and is a Ph.D. candidate at Yale University, majoring in monetary policy and econometrics.

Néstor Cruz, president of St. George's Associates, is an attorney in private practice in Washington, DC. He was Associate Legal Counsel (Director, Advice and Litigation), EEOC, Washington, DC; Director, Office of Review and Appeals, EEOC, Falls Church, VA; Assistant City Attorney, Miami, FL; Counsel to the Chairman, NLRB, Washington, DC; Director of Finance and Corporation Counsel, Rohm y Haas de Venezuela, S.A. He holds a B.A. in Science (Chemistry) from Villanova University (1966), an M.B.A. from the Cornell Graduate School of Management (1969), and a J.D. from Cornell University Law School (1970).

Sergio Díaz-Briquets is with Casals and Associates, a Washington, DC-area consulting firm. His previous appointments include Research Director of the U.S. Congressional Commission for the Study of International Migration and Cooperative Economic Development, Research Associate Professor at Duquesne University's Economic Sciences Department, and Program Officer at Canada's International Development Research Centre (IDRC). The author of a number of publications on Cuba, he received a Ph.D. in Demography from the University of Pennsylvania.

María Dolores Espino is currently Assistant Professor of Economics at Florida International University. She received her Ph.D. from Florida State University. She has conducted research on the tourism industry in Florida and in Cuba. Her current research interests focus primarily on the Cuban economy.

Raúl Fernández is an agronomist who has worked extensively in agricultural projects in Cuba and in most of Latin America and the Caribbean. From 1962 to 1964 he coordinated an IDB mission to the Dominican Republic and was Professor of Agricultural Economics at the University of Santo Domingo. In Costa Rica and Brazil he directed major studies on the agricultural credit situation in those countries, which were published by the Pan American Union and the Central Bank of Brazil respectively. His book, *Metodología de la Investigación*, based on those studies, was published in Mexico in 1977 and reprinted in 1981 and 1983.

Agustín de Goytisolo is a partner in the Miami-based law firm of Goytisolo, Martínez, de Córdoba & Gutiérrez. He received his Doctor of Laws degree *cum laude* from the University of Havana in 1947 and was *scholar juris* at the Georgetown University Law Center in 1968. Mr.

Goytisolo practiced law for 13 years with one of Havana's largest civil law firms, and is a member of the Florida Bar, the American and the Cuban American Bar Associations.

Antonio Gayoso is Agency Director of the Human Resources Directorate in the Bureau for Science and Technology at the Agency for International Development in Washington, D.C. He received a B.S. in Business Administration, an M.A. in international trade and finance, and is a Ph.D. candidate in Agricultural Economics at the University of Florida, and a Lic. in economics from the University of Villanova. He has held various other positions at A.I.D. and the U.S. Department of State and was previously Professor at American University, Assistant Professor in the Department of Agricultural Economics of the University of Florida, and Junior Economist in the Ministry of Finance of the government of Cuba.

José M. Hernández was Associate Dean, School of Languages and Linguistics, Georgetown University until his retirement in 1991. A lawyer and historian, he holds an LL.D. from the University of Havana, and an M.A. and Ph.D. in History from Georgetown University. He was a Senior Associate Attorney in the law firm of Gorrín, Mañas, Maciá & Alamilla in Havana, Cuba, and was a professor of civil law at the University of Villanueva, and of history at George Mason and Georgetown Universities. His most recent publication is *Cuba and the United States: Intervention and Militarism, 1868-1933*, University of Texas Press, forthcoming.

José Antonio Herrero is an international economic consultant who has been advisor to the governments of the Dominican Republic and Puerto Rico, and taught economics at the University of Puerto Rico. He received his university education at Villanueva University in Havana, the University of Puerto Rico, ESCOLATINA in Chile, and the Massachusetts Institute of Technology. His research interests include econometrics and macroeconomic theory and policy.

Armando M. Lago is President of Ecosometrics Inc., an economic consulting firm. He has a Ph.D. in economics from Harvard University. His specialties include demand analysis and pricing, models of urban growth and regional input-output analysis. He is co-author of *The Politics of Psychiatry in Revolutionary Cuba*, Transaction Books, 1991.

Manuel Lasaga, an international economics and finance consultant, is Managing Director of International Management Assistance Corporation (IMAC) in Miami, Florida. His professional experiences have been with Southeast Bank in Miami, Citicorp in New York City, and with Wharton Econometric Forecasting Associates in Philadelphia. He is on the Board of Governors of the Greater Miami Chamber of Commerce, President of the Economic Society of South Florida, member of the Board of Economists of *The Miami Herald* and a member of the District Export Council. He holds an M.A. and a Ph.D. degree in Economics from the University of Pennsylvania and is an Adjunct Professor of International Economics and Finance at Florida International University.

Luis Locay received his Ph.D. in Economics from the University of Chicago in 1983. He is currently Associate Professor in the Department of Economics at the University of Miami. He was previously Assistant Professor of Economics at the State University of New York at Stony Brook. His areas of specialization include development, economic demography, and applied microeconomics.

Alberto Martínez Piedra is professor of economics at the Catholic University of America. He received a degree in Political Economy at the Universidad Complutense de Madrid (1957) and a Ph.D. in Economics from Georgetown University (1962). He was Deputy U.S. Ambassador to the Organization of American States (1982-84), U.S. Ambassador to Guatemala (1984-87), and Special

Assistant to the U.S. Mission to the United Nations (1987-88). His research interests include economic development and business ethics.

Raúl Moncarz is Professor and Chair of the Department of Economics, Florida International University. He received a B.S. degree from Florida Atlantic University (1965), an M.B.A. (1966) and a Ph.D. in economics (1969) from Florida State University. His area of research interest is monetary economics, and he also has a strong interest in Central America, having been a visiting Fullbright professor in El Salvador in 1971.

George Plinio Montalván, currently an international economic consultant, was Chief Economist at the Organization of American States, where he was employed for almost 20 years. Prior to that, he did economic research at the Brookings Institution. His most recent publications include *Latin America: The Hardware and Software Markets,* and *Promoting Investment and Exports in the Caribbean Basin* (OAS, 1989). He has a B.A., an M.A., and is a Ph.D. candidate in Economics from the George Washington University, specializing in national income, business cycle and productivity analysis, and labor economics.

Juan Luis Moreno Villalaz is an economist with Development Technologies, Inc. He studied at universities in Panama and Chile, has a Ph.D. in Economics from the University of Missouri, and did post-doctoral work at the University of Chicago. He is an advisor to the government of Panama and is one of the leading advocates of market-oriented economic policies in that country.

Lorenzo Pérez has a Ph.D. from the University of Pennsylvania, and his areas of professional interest are macroeconomics, international economics and economic development. He has been with the International Monetary Fund since 1978, after working at the U.S. Department of the Treasury and the Agency for International Development. He is currently chief of the Maritime Division (Venezuela, Jamaica, Barbados and St. Lucia) of the Western Hemisphere Department of the IMF.

Jorge F. Pérez-López is an international economist with the Bureau of International Labor Affairs, U.S. Department of Labor. His writings on international economic issues —especially on the Cuban economy— have appeared in professional journals and several edited volumes. He is the author of *The Economics of Cuban Sugar*, University of Pittsburgh Press, 1991. He received his Ph.D. from the State University of New York at Albany.

Joseph M. Perry is Professor of Economics at the University of North Florida in Jacksonville. He holds a Ph. D. degree in Economics from Northwestern University. Dr. Perry's research interests include regional economic development and American economic history. His most recent research work has focussed on the problems of economic development in Belize.

Francisco Proenza is currently an economist with the Food and Agriculture Organization in Rome. He received his Ph.D. from the University of Florida in 1981. His main interest is in agricultural economics, and has worked in this area at the U.S. Department of Agriculture and the Organization of American States. He has also served as a consultant to the World Bank.

Joaquín P. Pujol is currently Assistant Director in the Exchange and Trade Relations Department of the International Monetary Fund, with responsibility for the evaluation and review of all macroeconomic programs supported by the IMF. He served previously in various capacities in the Western Hemisphere Department of the IMF, including as Chief of the Mexico Latin Caribbean Division. He is a graduate of the Wharton School and pursued post-graduate studies in economics and regional science at the University of Pennsylvania. Prior to joining the IMF he taught economics at the Wharton School and did research on economics and econometrics for the National Bureau of Economic Research, the Foreign Policy Research Institute, the Regional Science Institute and the Economic Unit of the University of Pennsylvania.

John Paul Rathbone is Research Secretary of *La Sociedad Económica* in London. He received his M.A. from Oxford University in 1984 and is a frequent contributor on international affairs for the Colombian newspaper *El Espectador* and the Times Literary Supplement.

Nicolás Rivero is the Managing Director of Rivero International. Specialized in international trade and U.S. legislation, he led for 28 years commercial policy and export promotion programs at the Organization of American States. Since 1989 he has continued his specialization in international trade —now in the private sector— with particular emphasis on inter-American trade and U.S. legislative affairs. He is Director for Latin America on the Advisory Board of Information Resources, Inc., a research firm dealing with petrochemical and oxygenated fuel industries. He is an international economics graduate of Georgetown University.

Julio Romañach, Jr. has been engaged in the practice of law in New Orleans and Baton Rouge since 1978 and is a partner of Romañach & Lawrence. He received his B.A. (1974) and J.D. (1978) from Louisiana State University and was admitted to the Louisiana State Bar Association in 1978. His professional affiliations include: attorney, Louisiana State Law Institute; consultant to the Director of the Center of Civil Law Studies, Louisiana State University; and member of the Louisiana, American, and Baton Rouge Bar Associations. He has authored legal publications in the United States, Spain, Costa Rica, Dominican Republic and Nicaragua and lectured in Latin America. His fields of expertise are Latin American law, Louisiana law, and civil law.

Jorge Salazar-Carrillo is Director of the Center of Economic Research and Professor of Economics at Florida International University. He has published many books and articles, his latest being *The Latin American Debt*, published by MacMillan of London in 1992 (distributed in the U.S. by St. Martin's Press).

Jorge A. Sanguinetty is President of Development Technologies, Inc., a Washington, D.C.-based international and domestic economic consulting firm. He received his Ph.D. in Economics from the City University of New York, and was Director of the Latin American Program in Applied Economics at The American University. He was head of National Investment Planning at the Central Planning Board in Cuba.

Carlos Seiglie is Assistant Professor at Rutgers University in Newark, New Jersey. A graduate of Rutgers, he received his Ph.D. in Economics from the University of Chicago. He previously worked as a consultant for Arthur Andersen & Co. and taught economics at Northwestern Illinois University. He has published a number of articles and participated in numerous conferences on defense economics. He is a Phi Beta Kappa, a Rutgers Scholar and an Eli Lilly Fellow in Economics. He is a member of the Economics Division of the National Science Foundation and a Journal Referee for *Conflict Management and Peace Science* and for *Defense Economics*.

Jeffrey W. Steagall is Assistant Professor of Economics at the University of North Florida in Jacksonville. He holds a Ph. D. degree in Economics from the University of Wisconsin at Madison. Dr. Steagall's research interests include the econometric analysis of regional growth, and the impacts of trade problems in Latin American countries.

Louis A. Woods is Associate Professor of Geography and Economics at the University of North Florida in Jacksonville. He holds a Ph. D. degree in Geography from the University of North Carolina at Chapel Hill, and has also done graduate work in economics.